Plato and the Older Academy

You are holding a reproduction of an original work that is in the public domain in the United States of America, and possibly other countries. You may freely copy and distribute this work as no entity (individual or corporate) has a copyright on the body of the work. This book may contain prior copyright references, and library stamps (as most of these works were scanned from library copies). These have been scanned and retained as part of the historical artifact.

This book may have occasional imperfections such as missing or blurred pages, poor pictures, errant marks, etc. that were either part of the original artifact, or were introduced by the scanning process. We believe this work is culturally important, and despite the imperfections, have elected to bring it back into print as part of our continuing commitment to the preservation of printed works worldwide. We appreciate your understanding of the imperfections in the preservation process, and hope you enjoy this valuable book.

Cornell University Library
B395 .Z51

Plato and the older academy / translated

3 1924 029 119 646

olin

WORKS
ON
SOCIAL & POLITICAL PHILOSOPHY.

THE STOICS, EPICUREANS, and SCEPTICS. Translated from the German of Dr. E. Zeller, by the Rev. O. F. Reichel, M.A. Crown 8vo. 14s.

SOCRATES and the SOCRATIC SCHOOLS. Translated from the German of Dr E. Zeller, by the Rev. O. F. Reichel, M.A. Crown 8vo. 8s. 6d.

ARTHUR SCHOPENHAUER, his Life and his Philosophy. By Helen Zimmern. Crown 8vo. Portrait, 7s. 6d.

The LIFE, WORKS, and OPINIONS of HEINRICH HEINE By William Stigand. 2 vols. 8vo. Portrait, 28s.

On the INFLUENCE of AUTHORITY in MATTERS of OPINION. By the late Sir George Cornewall Lewis, Bart. 8vo. 14s

CONSTITUTIONAL HISTORY of ENGLAND since the ACCESSION of GEORGE III. 1760–1870. By Sir Thomas Erskine May, K.C.B. D.C.L. 3 vols. crown 8vo. 18s.

DEMOCRACY in EUROPE. By Sir Thomas Erskine May, K.C.B. D.C.L. 2 vols. 8vo. [In the press.

DEMOCRACY in AMERICA. By Alexis de Tocqueville. Translated by Henry Reeve. 2 vols. crown 8vo. 16s.

INTRODUCTION to the SCIENCE of RELIGION, in Four Lectures delivered at the Royal Institution; with two Essays on False Analogies and the Philosophy of Mythology. By F. Max Müller, M.A. Crown 8vo. 10s. 6d.

PHILOSOPHY WITHOUT ASSUMPTIONS. By the Rev. T. P. Kirkman, M.A. F.R.S. &c. 8vo. 10s. 6d.

HISTORY of PHILOSOPHY from THALES to COMTE. By George Henry Lewes. Fourth Edition. 2 vols. 8vo 32s.

ESSAYS, POLITICAL, SOCIAL, and RELIGIOUS. By Richard Congreve, M.A. 8vo. 18s.

The NEW REFORMATION: A Narrative of the Old Catholic Movement, from 1870 to the Present Time. By THEODORUS. 8vo. 12s.

HISTORY of EUROPEAN MORALS from AUGUSTUS to CHARLEMAGNE. By W. E. H. LECKY, M.A. 2 vols. 8vo. 28s.

HISTORY of the RISE and INFLUENCE of the SPIRIT of RATIONALISM in EUROPE. By W. E. H. LECKY, M.A. 2 vols. crown 8vo. 16s

HISTORY of CIVILISATION in ENGLAND and FRANCE, SPAIN and SCOTLAND. By HENRY THOMAS BUCKLE. 3 vols. crown 8vo. 24s.

ORDER and PROGRESS, PART I. Thoughts on Government, Part II. Studies of Political Crisis. By FREDERIC HARRISON, M.A. of Lincoln's Inn. 8vo. 14s.

COMTE'S GENERAL VIEW of POSITIVISM and INTRODUCTORY PRINCIPLES. Translated by J. H. BRIDGES, M.B., formerly Fellow of Oriel College, Oxford. 8vo. 21s.

COMTE'S SOCIAL STATICS, or the ABSTRACT LAWS of HUMAN ORDER. Translated by FREDERIC HARRISON, M A. of Lincoln's Inn. 8vo. 14s.

COMTE'S SOCIAL DYNAMICS, or the GENERAL LAWS of HUMAN PROGRESS (the Philosophy of History). Translated by E. S BEESLY, M.A. Professor of History in University College, London. 8vo. [Ready.

COMTE'S SYNTHESIS of the FUTURE of MANKIND. Translated by RICHARD CONGREVE, M.A. M.R.C.P. formerly Fellow and Tutor of Wadham College, Oxford. With an Appendix, containing Comte's Minor Treatises, translated by HENRY DIX HUTTON, M.A., Barrister-at-Law. 8vo.
[In the press.

HUME'S TREATISE on HUMAN NATURE. Edited, with Notes, &c by T. H. GREEN, M.A. and the Rev. T. H. GROSE, M.A. 2 vols. 8vo. 28s.

HUME'S ESSAYS, MORAL, POLITICAL, and LITERARY. By the same editors. 2 vols. 8vo. 28s.

*** *The above Four Volumes form a complete and uniform Edition of* HUME's *Philosophical Works.*

London, LONGMANS & CO.

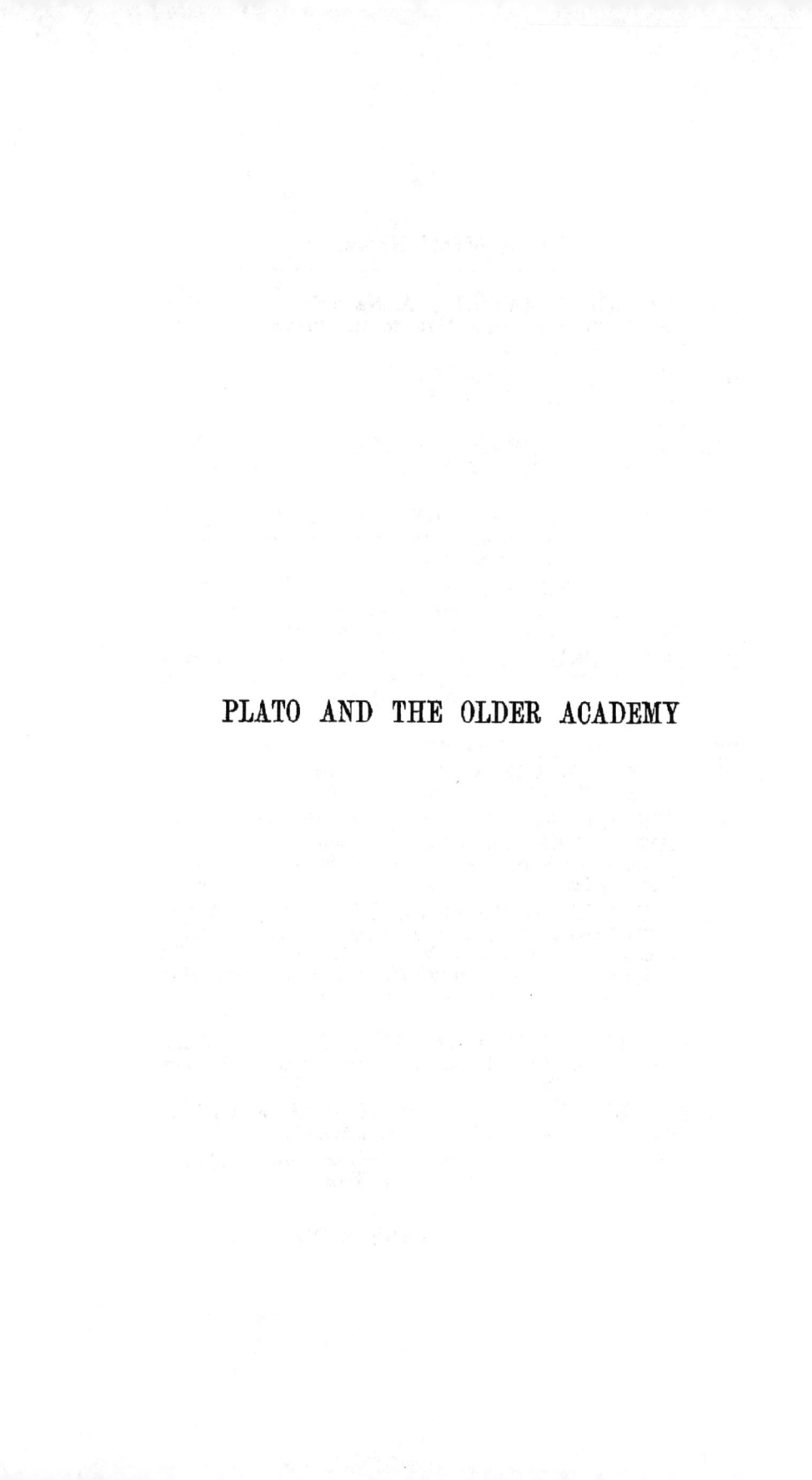

PLATO AND THE OLDER ACADEMY

LONDON : PRINTED BY
SPOTTISWOODE AND CO., NEW-STREET SQUARE
AND PARLIAMENT STREET

PLATO

AND

THE OLDER ACADEMY

*TRANSLATED WITH THE AUTHOR'S SANCTION
FROM THE GERMAN OF*

DR. EDUARD ZELLER

BY

SARAH FRANCES ALLEYNE

AND

ALFRED GOODWIN, M.A.

Fellow and Lecturer of Balliol College, Oxford

LONDON

LONGMANS, GREEN, AND CO.

1876

All rights reserved

p. 543

PREFACE.

THIS TRANSLATION of Dr. ZELLER's 'Plato und die ältere Akademie'—Section 2, Part 2, Vol. II. of his 'Philosophie der Griechen'—has been made from the third and enlarged edition of that work, an earlier portion of which ('Sokrates und die Sokratiker') has already appeared in English in the translation of Dr. REICHEL.

The text has been translated by Miss ALLEYNE, who desires to express her grateful acknowledgments to Dr. ZELLER for his courteous approval of the undertaking. For the notes, and for the revision of the whole, Mr. GOODWIN is responsible.

The references in the notes require some explanation: Simple figures, with or without *supra* or *infra*, indicate the pages and notes of the English translation. Vol. I. means the first (German) volume of the 'Philosophie der Griechen,' and Part I. the Erste Abtheilung of the second volume.

Of the value of Dr. ZELLER's work in the original, it

is unnecessary to speak. Professor JOWETT has recently borne ample and honourable testimony to it in the preface to the second edition of his Plato. It is hoped that the present translation may be of use to some students of Plato who are perhaps less familiar with German than Greek.

CONTENTS.

CHAPTER I.
PLATO'S LIFE.

	PAGE
Childhood and Youth	1
Relation to Socrates	9
Sojourn at Megara. Travels	14
Teaching in the Academy	25
Attitude to Politics. Second and third Sicilian journeys	29
Death	35
Character	36

CHAPTER II.
PLATO'S WRITINGS.

General Enquiry into the State of our Collection; its Completeness	45
Genuineness	49
External Evidence	50
References of Aristotle	54
Review of these	64
Value of their Testimony	72
Criterion of Authenticity in Platonic Writings	77
Particular Dialogues	81
Plato's Writings the Records of his Philosophy	87

CHAPTER III.
THE ORDER OF THE PLATONIC WORKS.

Scope and Design of the Enquiry	92
Early Attempts at an Arrangement of the Writings	97

	PAGE
Schleiermacher	99
Hermann	102
Their Followers	104
Standard of Criticism	109
Its application to our Collection	117
Early Works	119
Gorgias, Meno, Theætetus, Euthydemus, Phædrus	125
Sophist, Politicus, Parmenides, Philebus, Euthydemus, Cratylus, Symposium, Phædo	136
Republic, Timæus, Critias, Laws	139

CHAPTER IV.

CHARACTER, METHOD, AND DIVISION OF PLATO'S PHILOSOPHY — 144

Character in relation to Socrates	144
To the pre-Socratics	147
Dialectic Method	150
Form of Plato's Writings. Philosophic Dialogue	153
Connection with the Personality of Socrates	159
Myths	160
Division of the System	164

CHAPTER V.

PROPÆDEUTIC GROUNDWORK OF PLATO'S DOCTRINE — 170

1. Ordinary Consciousness. Its Theoretic Side	170
Its Practical Side	175
2. Sophistic Doctrine. Its Theory of Knowledge	183
Its Ethics	184
Sophistic as a Whole	189
Philosophy	190
The Philosophic Impulse, Eros	191
The Philosophic Method, Dialectic	196
Its Elements; Formation of Concepts	199
Classification	204
Logical Determinations	208
Language	210
Philosophy as a Whole; Stages of Philosophic Development	214

CONTENTS.

CHAPTER VI.

DIALECTIC, OR THE DOCTRINE OF IDEAS. . . 225

1. The Doctrine of Ideas founded upon that of Knowledge . 225
   And of Being 228
   Proofs as given by Aristotle 232
   Historic Origin of the Doctrine 233
2. Concept of Ideas 237
   Ideas as Universals or Genera 238
   As Substances 240
   As Concrete Unities 248
   Or Numbers 254
   As Living Powers 261
3. The World of Ideas 271
   Extent 271
   Subdivisions 276
   The most Universal Categories 277
   The Highest Idea, the Good, and God . . . 276

CHAPTER VII.

PHYSICS.

General Causes of the World of Phenomena . . . 293

1. Matter. Its Derivation 293
   Description of Matter 297
   Not a Primeval, Corporeal Substance . . . 300
   Not the Product of Envisagement or Opinion . 309
   But of Space 312
   Difficulties of this Theory 312
2. Relation of Sensible Objects to the Idea . . . 315
   Immanence of Things in Ideas 317
   No derivation of the World of Sense . . . 319
   Reasons against the Identification of Matter with the Un-
     limited in the Ideas 320
   Lacuna in the System at this point . . . 332
   Participation of things in Ideas 335
   Reason and Necessity, Physical and Final Causes . 337

CONTENTS.

	PAGE
3. The World-Soul	341
Connection of this Doctrine with Plato's whole System	343
Nature of the Soul	345
The Soul and the Mathematical Principle	351
The Soul as the Cause of Motion	356
And of Knowledge	356

CHAPTER VIII.

PHYSICS (CONTINUED).

The World-System and its Parts	361
How far these Discussions are valuable and important	361
1. The Origin of the World. Question of its beginning in Time	363
2. Formation of the Elements. Teleological Derivation.	368
Physical Derivation	371
Properties, Distribution, Admixture, Motion, Decomposition	375
3. The World-System; the Heavenly Bodies; Time; the Cosmical Year	379
The World as the Become (Gewordene) God	386

CHAPTER IX.

PHYSICS (CONTINUED).

Man	388
Nature of the Human Soul	389
Its Mythical History	390
Dogmatic Element in this mode of Representation	396
Immortality	397
Pre-existence	404
Recollection, Transmigration, and Future Retribution	406
Parts of the Soul	417
Freewill	419
Relation of the Soul to the Body	421
Physiological Theories	423
Plants and Animals	432
Difference of Sex	433
Diseases	433

CONTENTS.

CHAPTER X.

ETHICS 435

1. The Highest Good 436
    Withdrawal from the World of Sense . . . 438
    Relative Value ascribed to it 441
2. Virtue 444
    Virtue and Happiness 445
    Socratic and Platonic Doctrine of Virtue . . . 448
    Natural Disposition 449
    Customary and Philosophic Virtue 450
    Plurality of Virtues; Primary Virtues . . . 451
    The Distinctive Peculiarities of Plato's Ethics . . 454

CHAPTER XI.

ETHICS (CONTINUED).

The State 461
End and Problem of the State 461
Philosophy as the Condition of the true State . . . 466
The Constitution of the State 468
Importance of Public Institutions; aristocratic character of the
    Platonic Constitution 469
Separation and Relation of Classes 471
This Constitution based upon Plato's whole System . . 473
Social Regulations, Parentage 477
Education 478
Citizens' Manner of Life; Community of Goods, Wives, and Children 481
Significance of this Political Ideal from Plato's Point of View.
    Influences that led him to it 482
Its affinity with the Modern State 490
Defective States 492

CHAPTER XII.

PLATO'S VIEWS ON RELIGION AND ART . . 494

1. Religion. The Religion of the Philosopher; Purification of
    the Popular Faith 495
    Visible Gods 499
    Popular Religion 500
    General Result 503

		PAGE
2 Art	.	505
The Beautiful	.	506
Artistic Inspiration	.	508
Imitation	.	509
Supervision of Art	.	511
Particular Arts	.	513
Rhetoric	.	514

CHAPTER XIII.

THE LATER FORM OF PLATONIC DOCTRINE. THE LAWS . 517

The Platonic Doctrine according to Aristotle	517
The Laws. Point of View	522
Philosophy less prominent	523
Religious Character	525
Importance of Mathematics	527
Ethics	529
Particular Legislation	531
Politics	533
Constitution	533
Social Regulations	540
General Character of the Laws; Divergences from Plato's original Point of View—the Evil World-Soul	543
Authenticity	548

CHAPTER XIV.

THE OLDER ACADEMY. SPEUSIPPUS . . . 553

Platonic School. External History	553
Character of its Philosophy	565
Speusippus' Theory of Knowledge	566
First Principles; the Good and the Soul	568
Numbers	572
Magnitudes	575
Fragments of his Physics	576
Ethics	578

CHAPTER XV.

THE OLDER ACADEMY CONTINUED — XENOCRATES . . 581

	PAGE
Divisions of Philosophy	582
Kinds and Stages of Knowledge	583
First Principles	584
Number and Ideas	586
Spatial Magnitudes	587
The Soul	589
Cosmology	591
Gods and Dæmons	593
Elements. Formation of the World	595
Psychology	596
Ethics	597

CHAPTER XVI.

OTHER PHILOSOPHERS OF THE ACADEMY . . 604

Metaphysical Inquiries	604
Heraclides	606
Eudoxus	611
The Epinomis	612
Polemo	617
Crates, Crantor	618

PLATO AND THE OLDER ACADEMY.

CHAPTER I.

PLATO'S LIFE.

THERE is hardly another philosopher of antiquity with whose life we are so intimately acquainted as with Plato's; yet even in his case, tradition is often uncertain and still more often incomplete.[1] Born some years

[1] According to Simplicius, Phys. 268 a. m Schol. 427 a. 15. De Coelo, 8 b. 16 sq 41 b. 1 sq. Karst. (Schol. 470 a. 27, where, instead of Karsten's reading βίῳ, should be read βίου, 474 a. 12.) Xenocrates had already written περὶ τοῦ Πλάτωνος βίου. Whether this means a special work or merely an incidental notice in connection with some other disquisition must remain undecided. Steinhart, Plato's Leben, 8. 260 sq. adopts the latter supposition on account of Diogenes' silence as to any such work.) Speusippus apud Diogenem, iv. 5. Apuleius de Dogmate Platonis i. mentions an ἐγκώμιον Πλάτωνος (which must be identical with the περίδειπνον Πλάτωνος ap. Diog. iii. 2, unless we suppose with Hermann and Steinhart, that the titles of the writings of Speusippus and Clearchus are confused: see respectively Plat. 97, 45, loc. cit. 7, 260). Finally we know of a treatise of Plato's scholar Hermodorus, which gave information both about his life and his philosophy, and likewise of a work of Philippus of Opus περὶ Πλάτωνος (see Diog ii. 106, iii. 6. Dercyllides ap. Simpl. Phys. 54 b. 56 b. Vol. Hercul. Coll. Alt. i. 162 sqq. Col. 6; cf. my Diatribe de Hermodoro, Marb. 1859, p 18 sq. and for the latter Suidas s. v. Φιλόσοφος) But from these most ancient sources we have only a few notices preserved to us. Later writers, the greater part of whom are known to us only from Diogenes, are of very unequal value (a review of them is to be found in Steinhart, loc. cit. 13 sqq.); Diogenes himself is to be relied on only so far as he indicates his authorities, and this is equally true of the Προλεγόμενα (in Hermann's edition of Plato, vi. 196 sqq.) and of the short biographies of Olympiodorus and the anonymous writer who for the most part simply copies these. Of the Platonic letters the 7th is the

after the commencement of the Peloponnesian war,[2]

most important for the history of Plato's life; still, it cannot be accepted as genuine, nor does it merit the unlimited confidence placed in it by Grote (Plato, i 113 sqq), who is actuated not so much by the interest of a true historian as by that of an advocate. The remaining Platonic letters are quite worthless as historical evidence On the other hand, Plato's genuine writings give but very few points from which we can derive any knowledge of his life. The minor accredited accounts are false and not seldom self-contradictory. The more recent literature bearing on Plato's life is given by Ueberweg, Hist. of Phil. i. § 39. Steinhart, loc. cit. 28 sq.

[2] A tradition in Diogenes Laertius, iii. 3, says that he was born at Ægina, in which island his father had received an allotment on its occupation by an Athenian colony, about 430 B.C. This statement is doubtful in itself, and is rendered more so by the obvious falsity of the succeeding statement, that he only returned to Athens after the Spartan expulsion of the colonists, B.C. 404. The date of Plato's birth is uncertain Apollodorus, according to Diog. iii 2 sq., assigned it to the 88th Olympiad (i e. Olympiad 88, i.), B C. 427, on the 7th of Thargelion (May 21) (on the reduction to our months cf. Ueberweg, Exam. of the Platonic Writings—Steinhart, loc. cit. 284); and this, according to Plutarch, Quæstiones Convivales 8, 1, 1, 1, 2, 1, and Apuleius, De Dogm Plat. 1, was really kept as his birthday. With this Hermodorus (ap. Diog 6) agrees, when he says that Plato was 28 years old when he went to Megara, i.e. directly after Socrates' death, vide p. 14, 26, supra. On the other hand, Athenæus, v. 217 a. says that he was born in the archonship of Apollodorus, Ol. 87, 3 (B.C. 429), and with this we may connect Diogenes' statement, loc. cit, that the year of Plato's birth was that of Pericles' death, if (as Hermann, History and System of the Platonic Philosophy, i. 85, A 9, points out) we assume that Diogenes follows Roman reckoning. Pericles died two and a half years after the outbreak of the Peloponnesian war, in the autumn of B.C. 429 (Ol. 87, 4), in the archonship of Epameinon. The statement in the pseudo-Plutarch (Vita Isocratis 2, p. 836), that Isocrates was seven years older than Plato, points to the same date. Isocrates was born Ol. 86, 1 (436 B C.); vide loc. cit. and Diog. iii. 2 ; Dionysius, Judicium de Isocrate, init. Diogenes himself, in assigning Plato's birth to the archonship of Epameinon, and accordingly making him only six years younger than Isocrates, is going on a false reckoning, exclusive of the year of Pericles' death. It may be observed that Diogenes, or our present text of him, has ἐπ' 'Αμεινίον instead of ἐπ' 'Επαμείνωνος; and in connection with this is the assertion of the Προλεγόμενα τῆς Πλάτωνος φιλοσοφίας, C 2 (Plato, ed. Herm. vi. 197. Diog. Laert. ed. Cobet, appendix, p. 6), that Plato was born while Pericles was still alive, in the archonship of Ameinias, Ol. 88 This introduces mere confusion; and Eusebius, in his Chronicon, followed by the Paschal Chronicle, in dating his birth Ol.

the son of an ancient aristocratic house,[3] favoured

89 i, has only given an instance of his own carelessness

As to the year of Plato's death, tradition is more consistent. Apollodorus apud Diog. v. 9, Dionysius Halicarnassiensis Ad Ammæum, 5, and Athenæus v. 217 b, agree in assigning it to the archonship of Theophilus, Ol. 108, i. The accounts of his age, however, again present a great discrepancy. Hermippus apud Diog. iii. 2 (with whom are Lucian, Macrobii 20, Augustine, De Civitate Dei viii. 11, Censorinus, De Die Natali, 15, 1, and the Prolegomena C. 6) says he was 81. Seneca states even more definitely (epistle 58, 31), that he died on his 82nd birthday; and it seems only an inexact expression of Cicero's (De Senectute 5, 13) that he died writing in his 81st year, with which we may compare what Dionysius says (De Compositione Verborum, p. 208), that he had been constantly polishing his works up to his 80th year.

On the other hand, Athenæus loc. cit., and Valerius Maximus viii. 7, 3, make him 82; Neanthes apud Diog. loc. cit., 84. This statement is highly improbable, as it would compel us to put back the birth of the philosopher to 431 or 432 B C However, the statement which allows him to attain 81 years would very well agree with the supposition that he was born B.C 429, and died B C. 348. But even if he was born B C. 427 and died a short time after completing his 80th year, in one case his death falls under the archonship of Theophilus, in the other case in his 81st year. For this determination of the date we have the authority not only of the careful chronologist Apollodorus, but also that of Hermodorus, who, as a personal pupil of Plato, more than all other witnesses has the presumption on his side of being well informed on this point. (The opinions against his trustworthiness will be tested pp. 14, 26, note) He may therefore be depended upon for the chronology of his own times, (I here retract the opinion I formerly shared with earlier writers), and the most probable supposition is that Plato was born B C. 427, and died 347, B C., perhaps shortly before the middle of the year This conclusion is favoured, amongst others, by Grote, Plato i. 114; Ueberweg, Hist. of Phil. 1. § 39; Examination of Plato's writings 113; and Steinhart loc cit 37, without absolutely rejecting the date 428 B.C. for his birth. To the latter supposition is of course opposed the fact that Plato, if his birthday actually fell on the 7th of Thargelion and consequently earlier than Socrates' death, had already attained his 29th year at the time of the flight to Megara, and could not rightly be said by Hermodorus to have been only 28. That Plato's nominal birthday might very possibly belong to the mythic traits of his Apolline character (as O. Muller, The Dorians, 1. 330, conjectures: cf Leutsch ap. Hermann, Plato 85 A. 7; Steinhart loc. cit. 39 sq.) has been already remarked p. 43. The whole question is specially treated by Corsini De die Natali Platonis (in Gorius' Symbola Literaria vi. 97 sqq.) Cf. Fasti Attici in 229 sq.

[3] His father Aristo, according

also by wealth [4] no less than birth, he must have found in his education and surroundings abundant intellect-

to Plutarch, De Amore Prolis 4, p. 496, died before Plato reached manhood. Beyond this, we know nothing of him; and of the grandfather, Aristocles, we only know that Plato himself bore his name, until it was superseded by the nickname Πλάτων given him by his gymnastic master on account of his powerful build. Cf. Alexander and Neanthes apud Diog. iii. 4—transcribed by Olympiodorus, Vita Platonis 2, and the Prolegomena, c. 1—Seneca, ep. 58, 30; Sextus Empiricus adversus Mathematicos 1, 258; Apuleius, Dogm. Plat. 1, &c. Thrasylus, however, apud Diog. 1, and after him Apuleius, loc cit, notice his father as a descendant of Codrus: Olympiodorus, c. 1, says, of Solon; but this is obviously an oversight. His mother, Perictione, as she is called by the great majority of the biographers —while a few are said (Diog. 1) to have substituted Potone, the name of his sister, Speusippus' mother (vide Diog. iii. 4. iv. 1)— was a sister of Charmides (vide supra, p. 106, 1), and cousin of Critias, deriving her descent from Dropides, a friend and kinsman of Solon's, and through him from Neleus, the ancestor of the last kings of Attica, vide Diog. 1, who, however, wrongly makes Dropides Solon's brother. (In this he is followed by several writers, and is partly misunderstood by Olympiodorus, c. 1, and the Prolegomena, c. 1). See also Apuleius, Dogm. Plat., init; Plato, Charmides, 155 A, 157 E; Timæus 20 D, and Ast, Life and Writings of Plato, 16 sq., together with Hermann, Plato 23 sq., 93, and Martin, Études sur le Timée. 1, 246. On the further question as to Plato's brothers, and their relation to the Glaucon and Adeimantus of the Republic, and Parmenides, vide on one side Hermann, Allgemeine Schulzeitung for 1831, p. 653; his Plato, 24, 94; and his Disputatio de Reipublicæ Platonis tempore (Marburg, 1839), forming part of the Vindiciæ Platonicæ; and Steinhart, Works of Plato, 5, 48 sq. on the other, Böckh's Berlin Lectures for the summer of 1839; Munk, Die Naturliche Ordnung der Platonischen Schriften, page 63 seqq., 264 sq., (his arguments and conjectures are of very unequal merit). Susemihl, Genetische Entwicklung der Platonischen Philosophie 2, 76 sqq. The former authorities recognise, both in the Republic and the Parmenides, two older relations of Plato's, his mother's brothers, who are as little known to us as their father Aristo. The latter, following Plutarch and others, see in these characters Plato's own brothers. On the grounds given in the Abhandl. d. Berl. Akad. v. J. 1873, Hist. Phil. Kl. S. 86, the latter supposition alone seems to me to be tenable Whether in Repub. II, 368, A. Plato's father is mentioned as still living at the supposed time of this dialogus (40⅔ B.C.) cannot be made out with certainty; according to Apol. 34 A, 38 B, we must suppose that he did not live to see the trial of Socrates. Cf. Plut. de Amore Prolis 4, S. 496. Antiphon, a half-brother of Plato, and the son of

ual food; and even without the express testimony of history,[5] we might conclude that he profited by these

Pyrilampes, appears in the introduction of the Parmenides, and (128 B) appears to be younger than the sons of Aristo (that this Antiphon was Plato's half-brother, and not an older relation, has been shown by Bockh loc. cit.). However, the legends of Plato's Apolline descent cannot be appealed to as evidence that he was the first child of his mother (vide supra, pp. 44, 111: according to Plato's Apology 34 A. Adeimantus appears to be older.

[4] The later writers certainly represent Plato as a comparatively poor man: e g. Gellius, Noctes Atticæ iii. 17, 1 (according to tradition he was tenui admodum pecunia familiari); Damascius,Vita Isidori 158; πένης γὰρ ἦν ὁ Πλάτων; repeated by Suidas, voce Πλάτων, and Apuleius, Dogm. Plat. 4. The story in Plutarch, Solon c. 2 fin., of his getting the means to travel by selling oil in Egypt, points the same way. Ælian, Variæ Historiæ 3, 27, says that he had heard a tale (which he doubts, in this place, though in 5. 9 he repeats the like about Aristotle without hesitation) of Plato's having once been ready, under pressure of poverty, to serve as a mercenary soldier, when Socrates dissuaded him. Cf. Hermann, Plato 77 sq , 98, 122. All these accounts, however, were no doubt invented by ascetic admirers or opponents of the philosopher in later times. Plato's whole family belongs to the aristocratic party, who were generally the great land-holders; his uncle Charmides had been rich, and was only reduced to necessity by the Peloponnesian war (Xenophon, Symposium 4, 29 sqq.; Memorabilia iii. 6, 14), but that Plato's parents were not involved in this calamity, we may see from the Memorabilia, loc. cit, where Socrates advises Glaucon, before he aims at the care of the whole state, to undertake that of an individual; for instance, of his uncle, who really needed it Had his father and mother been poor, the example lay nearer to hand. Apart from this, none but the son of a rich family could have entertained the notion of pressing forward, before his twentieth year, to the leadership of public affairs. Again, Plato names himself (Apol. 38 B) as one of the four who offered to bail Socrates for 30 minæ; so that he must have been a solvent person, ἐγγυητὴς ἀξιόχρεως. His journeys, too, are evidence of his being well off; for the tale about the oil-selling does not look much like the philosopher who despised trade; if true at all, it can only mean that he took some of his own produce with him to Egypt instead of ready money. Finally, even though his choregia (Plutarch, Aristides 1, Dion 17; Diog. 3) as a freewill service, the cost of which was borne by Dion, be no proof of wealth, and the purchase of the writings of Philolaus (vide subter), involving great expense, be not quite well authenticated, or may have been effected with other people's money, we still have sufficient evidence of his having been a man of some means, not only in his will, (in Diogenes

advantages to the fullest expansion of his brilliant genius. Among the few further particulars that have descended to us respecting his earlier years,[6] our atten-

---

[4] 41 sq), but also in what is told of his way of life and domestic management; vide Diog. 6, 25 sq. Hieronymus adversus Jovinianum 2, 203, ed. Martianay, certainly establishes nothing.

[5] Apuleius, dogm. Plat. 2 : nam Speusippus domesticis instructus documentis pueri ejus acre in percipiendo ingenium et admirandæ verecundiæ indolem laudat: et pubescentis primitias labore atque amore studendi imbutas refert · et in viro harum incrementa virtutum et ceterarum testatur. Cf. Hermann, Plato 97.

[6] To these belong specially the tales about his early education and teachers. Reading and writing he is said to have learnt from the Dionysius who is immortalized in the Anterastæ, gymnastic from Aristo of Argos, who brought him on so well that he entered the Isthmian games as a wrestler. (For his gymnastic, cf. after Dicæarchus, Diogenes 4; Servius on Æneid 6, 668; Apul. c. 2 , Olympiod. c. 2; Prolegomena, c. 2. Apuleius and Porphyry apud Cyrillum contra Julianum, 208 D, make him enter at the Pythian games as well; the Prolegomena remove the victory to the Isthmian and Olympic contests). Music he learned under Draco, a pupil of Damon, and Metellus of Agrigentum (Plutarch, De Musica 17, 1; Olymp. and Proleg, loc. cit.; cf. Hermann, p. 99). How much of these accounts is historical cannot be determined, and is a matter of comparative indifference. That he repeatedly appeared and was victorious in public contests is certainly not true; whether he even entered at the Isthmia may be doubted, for after his acquaintance with Socrates had begun he hardly ever took part in athletic struggles, and previous to that he was too young. (Hermann, p. 100, conjectures that the origin of the story may be traced in the Crito, 52 B.) The name of his writing master is probably derived from the Anterastæ; and, similarly, the story in Diog. 5 (Apul. loc. cit.; Olymp. 2; Prolegg. 3), to the effect that he enjoyed instruction from artists, and thence acquired the knowledge of colour shown in the Timæus, may be merely an arbitrary assumption based on that dialogue. The strange assertion of Aristoxenus apud Diog. 8 (cf. Ælian V. H. 7. 14), that he took part in three campaigns, not only to Corinth (Olympiad 96), but to Delium (Ol. 89, 1), and Tanagra (Ol. 88, 3), and at Delium obtained the prize for valour, is doubtless modelled on the three campaigns of Socrates (vide supra, p. 50), whose words with reference to them (Apol. 28, D.) are put into Plato's mouth in Diogenes 24.

What we know of the state of Athens towards the end of the Peloponnesian war would certainly lead us to conclude that he must have seen some military service, and perhaps he also took part in that action at Megara (409 B.C., Diodorus xiii. 65), in which, according to his own statement in Rep. ii. 368 A., his brother distinguished himself.

tion is principally drawn to three points, important in their influence on his mental development.

Of these we may notice first the general condition of his country, and the political position of his family.

Plato's youth coincided with that unhappy period succeeding the Sicilian defeat when all the faults of the previous Athenian government were so terribly avenged, all the disadvantages of unlimited democracy so nakedly exposed, all the pernicious results of the self-seeking ethics and sophistical culture of the time so unreservedly displayed. He himself belonged to a social class and to a family which regarded the existing constitution with undisguised, and not always groundless discontent. Several of his nearest relations were among the spokesmen of the aristocratic party.[7] But when that party had itself been raised to power by the common enemy, on the ruins of Athenian greatness, it so misused its strength that the eyes of its blindest adherents were inevitably opened. It is easy to see how a noble, high-minded youth, in the midst of such experiences and influences, might be disgusted, not only with democracy, but with existing State systems in general, and take refuge in political Utopias, which would further tend to draw off his mind from the actual towards the ideal.

Again, there were other circumstances simultaneously working in the same direction. We know that Plato in his youth occupied himself with poetical

[7] Critias, as is well known; Memorab. 111, 7, 1, 3; Hellenica Charmides, according to Xenophen, 11. 4, 19.

attempts,[8] and the artistic ability already evinced by some of his earliest writings,[9] coupled with the poetical character of his whole system, would lead us to suppose that these studies went far beyond the superficiality of a fashionable pursuit.[10] There is, therefore, little reason to doubt (however untrustworthy may be our more precise information on the subject [11]) that he was intimate with the great poets of his country.

Lastly, he had, even before his acquaintance with

[8] Diog. 5. He is said to have practised composition in verse, at first dithyrambs, and then songs and tragedies; and even to have conceived the idea of becoming a competitor in the tragic contests, when he became acquainted with Socrates, and, following his example, burnt his poems. So Olymp. 3, Proleg. 3. Ælian, V. H. ii. 30, gives a somewhat different account. According to him, Plato's first essay was in epos; but seeing how far short his productions came of their Homeric model, he destroyed them (on this, however, cf. Hermann, Plato 100, 54), and next composed a tragic tetralogy, which was actually in the performers' hands, when his acquaintance with Socrates decided him to abandon poetry for ever. Of the epigrams ascribed to Plato (some ascribed as early as Aristippus, περὶ παλαίας τρυφῆς, apud Diog. 29; who is followed by Diogenes himself, loc. cit., Apuleius de Magia c. 10, Gellius xix 11; Athenæus xiii. 589 C.; and others: cf. Bergk, Lyrici Græci, 489 sq.), which are mostly amatory trifles, the great majority are evidently forgeries, or attributed to him by some confusion; the rest are at least quite uncertain, and so is the little epic fragment in the Anthologia Planudea, 210. Cf. Bergk, loc. cit., and Hermann, Plato, 101.

[9] Specially in the Protagoras; but in some of the minor dialogues too, e.g. the Lysis, Charmides, and Laches, the dramatic element is greatly in excess of the dialectic.

[10] That poetry in Athens at that time was largely of this character is shown, among other testimony, by the passages from Aristophanes quoted by Hermann on page 100; Frogs 88 sq.; Birds 1444 sq.

[11] Diog. iii. 8, says that he first brought Sophron's mimes to Athens (this, however, could only have been after his journey), and took such delight in them that he used to keep them under his pillow. The latter statement also occurs in Val Max. 8, 7, sectn. 3; Olymp. 3; and Proleg. 3 (with regard to Sophron and Aristophanes). Probably, however, these assertions only originate in the endeavour to find models for his dialogues. He is also said to have taken Epicharmus as a pattern, but not much reliance can be placed on this. Vide Part 1, p. 428 sq.

Socrates, turned his attention to philosophy, and through Cratylus the Heraclitean [12] had become acquainted with a doctrine which in combination with other elements essentially contributed to his later system.[13]

All these influences, however, appear as of little importance by the side of Plato's acquaintance with Socrates. We cannot, of course, say what direction his mind might have taken without this teacher, but the question may well remain unanswered. We know enough to prove from all historical traces that the deepest, most lasting, most decisive impression was produced by the philosophic reformer on his congenial disciple. Plato himself is said to have esteemed it as the highest of Fortune's favours, that he should have been born in the lifetime of Socrates,[14] and later tradition has adorned with a significant myth [15] the first

---

[12] Vide Part 1, p. 601 sq.

[13] Aristotle, Metaphysics 1, 6, init., ἐκ νέου τε γὰρ συνήθης γενόμενος πρῶτον Κρατύλῳ καὶ ταῖς Ἡρακλειτείοις δόξαις, ὡς ἁπάντων τῶν αἰσθητῶν ἀεὶ ῥεόντων, καὶ ἐπιστήμης περὶ αὐτῶν οὐκ οὔσης, ταῦτα μὲν καὶ ὕστερον οὕτως ὑπέλαβεν. Σωκράτους δὲ περὶ μὲν τὰ ἠθικὰ πραγματευομένου, &c.; ἐκεῖνον ἀποδεξάμενος, &c. Diog. 6, Olymp. 4, and Proleg. 4 date the acquaintance with Cratylus after Socrates' death; but, in face of Aristotle's express testimony, we can, of course, attach no weight to this. Diogenes also mentions, in connection with Cratylus, the Parmenidean Hermogenes (who appears in the Prolegomena as Hermippus), but this is merely an arbitrary inference from the dialogue Cratylus; the Hermogenes of which (vide Cratyl. 384 A, 391 C.) is certainly the well-known disciple of Socrates, (vide supra 166, note 1). Similarly from the Parmenides is derived the assertion (Anonymus apud Photium, Cod. 249, p. 439 a.), that Zeno and Parmenides instructed Plato in logic.

[14] Compare the expression in Plutarch, Marius 46, Lactantius, Institutiones Divinæ 3, 19; though its genuineness may be doubted, as we have the same put into the mouth of Socrates, or even Thales, ap. Diog. 1, 33.

[15] Pausanias, 1, 30, 3; Diog. 5; Olymp. 4; Proleg. 1; Apul. dogm. Plat. 1; Socrates is said to have dreamt that a swan, the bird of Apollo, flew towards him with a

meeting of the two men. But apart from this, the fact must always be regarded as one of those remarkable contingencies which are too important in their bearing on the course of history to be severed from it in our thought. During a long [16] and confidential intercourse,[17] Plato penetrated so deeply into the spirit of his distinguished friend that the portrait of that spirit which he was able to bequeath to us is at once the most faithful and the most ideal that we possess. Whether at that time he directed his attention to other teachers of philosophy, and if so, to what extent, we do not know; [18] but it is scarcely credible that a youth so

melodious song. Next morning Plato presented himself, and Socrates immediately recognised the meaning of the dream.

[16] According to Hermodorus apud Diog. 6, he was twenty years old when he became acquainted with Socrates, and twenty-eight when he went to Euclid, after Socrates' death. According to this, he would be born in Ol. 88, 1 (vide supra, 286, 1). Exact information, however, can hardly be got on this point. The absurd statements of Suidas, sub voce Πλάτων, and Eudocia in Villoison's Anecdota 1, 362, about a twenty years' intercourse with Socrates, are obviously wrong

[17] How close the two were to each other is shown by the whole attitude of the Platonic writings, and by the portraiture of Socrates in them, more completely even than by some single passages. We may, however, compare Xenophon, Mem. 3, 6, 1, Plato, Apology, 34 A, 38 B; Phædo, 59 B.

[18] That he was already acquainted with the Pythagorean philosophy might be inferred from the Phædrus, if it were certain that this dialogue was composed before Socrates' death. But the accounts which might warrant such a conclusion (e.g. the statement that the Phædrus was his earliest work, and that the subsequent Lysis had been read and disowned by Socrates, for which vide Diog 38, 35. Olymp. 3. Prolegg. 3) are not trustworthy enough, and the supposition itself is far too improbable. Still more dubious is the conjecture (Susemihl Genet. Entw. 1, 3, 444; Munk, Natur. Ordn. 497 sqq.; and cf. Herm. Plat. 528), that, in the Phædo, 95 E sqq., Plato puts the history of his own philosophic development in the mouth of Socrates. This assumption has given rise to a string of others equally untenable. The influence on the earlier formation of Plato's mind which can alone be certainly attested, that, namely, of the Heraclitean philosophy, is obviously not touched upon here Nor does

highly educated, and so eager for knowledge—whose first impulse, moreover, towards philosophy had not come from Socrates—should have made no attempt until his thirtieth year to inform himself as to the achievements of the earlier philosophers, should have learned nothing from his friend Euclid about the Eleatics, nor from Simmias and Cebes about Philolaus: that he should have enquired no further respecting the doctrines continually brought to the surface by the public lectures and disputations of the Sophists, and left unread the writings of Anaxagoras, so easily to be obtained in Athens.[19] It is nevertheless probable that the overpowering influence of the Socratic teaching may have temporarily weakened his interest in the earlier natural philosophies, and that close and repeated study may afterwards have given him a deeper insight into their doctrines. Similarly, his own imaginative nature, under the restraining influence of his master's dialectic, was probably habituated to severer thought and more cautious investigation; perhaps, indeed, his idealistic tendencies received at first an absolute check;

---

the passage in the Phædo, on the whole, convey the impression of a biographical account it is rather an exposition of the universal necessity of progress from the material to final causes, and thence to the Ideas. It takes the form of a personal confession; but 'Plato is not giving a historical narration of the philosophical development either of himself or Socrates, he is laying down in outline the principles which lead from the philosophy of nature to conceptual philosophy.' Brucke, Plat. Stud. iii. 427, with whom Steinhart agrees in the main, in spite of the admission that the development of Socrates is here described. Ueberweg, Exam. of Plat. Writings, 92 sq.

[19] Plato Apol., 26 D Phædo, 97 B. With regard, too, to the writings of Parmenides and Zeno, Schaarschmidt rightly observes that they were read quite as much in Athens as in Megara.

and conceptual science, together with the art of forming concepts, was only to be attained by him—a stranger like his contemporaries to all such things—through the dry prosaic method of the Socratic enquiry.[20] But Plato needed this schooling to give him the repose and certainty of the scientific method—to develope him from a poet into a philosopher; nor did he in the process permanently lose anything for which his natural temperament designed him. Socrates' conceptual philosophy had given him a glance into a new world, and he forthwith set out to explore it.

The tragic end of his aged master, a consummation which he seems at the outset to have thought wholly impossible,[21] must have been a fearful blow to Plato; and one consequence of this shock, which still seems long years afterwards to vibrate so sensibly in the thrilling description of the Phædo, may have been perhaps the illness which prevented the faithful disciple from attending his master at the last.[22] We are,

---

[20] As I have observed in the Zeitschrift fur Alterthumswissenschaft for 1851, page 254, this is rendered probable by the constitution of those minor Platonic dialogues which we are justified in dating before the death of Socrates. If in these dialogues the dry formality of the dialectic discussions is found to present a striking contrast to the completeness and vivacity of the dramatic investiture; if there is a remarkable absence in them of youthful fire; if, in later works, e.g. the Phædrus and Symposium, similar subjects are treated with much greater vigour and élan than in an early production like the Lysis; the most obvious explanation seems to lie in the influence of Socrates.

[21] Cf. p. 161, note 1.

[22] Phædo, 59 B. Cf. Herm. Plat. 34, 103; Plutarch, De Virtute Morali 10, p. 449, does not seem to warrant any conclusion. It is not impossible that his absence owing to ill-health is a mere fiction, by means of which he wished to secure greater freedom for himself in narrating the speeches which preceded the death of Socrates. His readiness to stand bail for Socrates has been already mentioned, p. 288 sq. The statement of Justus of Tiberias,

however, more immediately concerned with the enquiry as to the effect of the fate of Socrates on Plato's philosophic development and view of the world; and if for this enquiry we are thrown upon conjectures, these are not entirely devoid of probability. On the one hand, for example, we shall find no difficulty in understanding how his reverence for his departed teacher was immeasurably increased by the destiny which overtook him, and the magnanimity with which he yielded to it; how the martyr of philosophy, faithful unto death, became idealized in his heart and memory as the very type of the true philosopher; how principles tested by this fiery ordeal received in his eyes the consecration of a higher truth; how at once his judgment on the men and circumstances concerned in the sacrifice of Socrates grew harder,[23] and his hope as to any political efficiency in those circumstances fainter;[24] nay, how the general tendency was fostered in him to contemplate reality in a gloomy light, and to escape from the ills of the present life into a higher, supersensuous world. On the other hand, it may perhaps have been better for his scientific growth that his connection with Socrates

ap. Diog. 2, 41, Proleg. 3, that Plato wished to undertake Socrates' defence himself, but was prevented by the clamour of the judges, like everything else about Socrates' trial, is disputed. Cf. p. 161 sq.; and Herm. loc cit.

[23] Cf. specially the way in which he speaks of the great Athenian statesmen in the Gorgias, 515 C sq., and 521 C sq.; Theætetus, 173 C sq., on the condition of his native city and the relation of the philosopher to politics; besides later judgments, e.g. Politicus, 298 A sq.; Republic, vi. 488 A— 497 A; viii 557 A sq.; 562 A sq.

[24] According to the 7th Platonic letter, 324 B sq., Plato had intended to take an active part in politics, first under the Thirty Tyrants, and, after their expulsion, under the democracy; but was deterred both times by the state of affairs, and specially by the attack on Socrates. We cannot, of course, give much weight to this debateable testimony.

14   PLATO AND THE OLDER ACADEMY.

lasted no longer than it did. During the years of their intercourse he had made his teacher's spirit his own, in completer fulness than was possible to any of his fellow students; it was now for him to perfect the Socratic science by the addition of new elements, and to fit himself by the utmost expansion in many directions for erecting it on an independent basis: his apprenticeship (Lehrjahre) was over, his travelling time (Wanderjahre) was come.[25]

After the death of Socrates, Plato, with others of his pupils, first betook himself to Megara, where a circle of congenial minds had gathered round Euclid.[26]

[25] I borrow this denomination from Schwegler, Hist. of Phil. 41.

[26] Hermodor. ap Diog. ii. 106, iii 6. The migration took place according to this authority when Plato was twenty-eight, doubtless immediately after the execution of Socrates. He indicates its motive in the words—δείσαντας τὴν ὠμότητα τῶν τυράννων. Formerly by these τύραννοι were understood the so-called Thirty Tyrants, and little weight was therefore attributed to the evidence of Hermodorus. But this explanation can no longer be entertained, now that we know from Simplic. Phys. 54 b. 56 b. (supra 1, 1), that the Hermodorus whose statement is preserved for us in Diogenes, is no other than the well-known Platonist. How can it be supposed that a personal pupil of Plato, like Hermodorus, could have been so ignorant as to think that Socrates was executed under the tyranny of the Thirty? We need not understand the τύραννοι in this sense. Indeed, often as the Thirty are mentioned, the expression 'the Thirty Tyrants,' or simply 'the Tyrants' (without τριάκοντα), is not used as the ordinary appellation for 'the Thirty' in any writer of that period, or, in fact, in any writer preserved to us before the time of Cicero and Diodorus. The invariable title is οἱ τριάκοντα. A τύραννος, according to the Greek view, is a single chief who rules without laws; a rule like that of 'the Thirty' is not a tyranny. but, as it is often called, an oligarchy. The Thirty are only once called τύραννοι in oratorical exaggerations, e.g. by Polycrates in Arist Rhet. ii. 24, 1401, a. 33; but we cannot conclude from this that it was the usual appellation for them, and that every one who spoke of the τύραννοι must have meant the Thirty. Hermodorus' expression must be understood in a different way; the τύραννοι are the democrats who brought about the execution of Socrates, just as Xenophon, Hellen. iv. 4, 6, calls the democrats who held sway at

He afterwards undertook[27] journeys which led him to Egypt, Cyrene, Magna Græcia, and Sicily.[28] Owing to

Corinth τοὺς τυραννεύοντας on account of their reign of terror. Similarly the seventh Platonic letter, 325 B, calls the accusers of Socrates δυναστεύοντές τινες. (The distinction which Steinhart, Pl. L., 122 sq., draws between τύραννοι and τυραννεύοντες is, I think, too fine, and I see no reason why an adversary might not have applied the term τύραννοι to violent democrats just as much as to violent oligarchs. I will not, of course, dispute the possibility that this expression is not borrowed from Hermodorus himself. Stein (Sieben Bücher z. Gesch. d. Plat. ii. 66, 170 sq.), and after him Schaarschmidt (Sammlung d. plat. Schr. 65 sq), have been led into error through a false pre-supposition, in rejecting Hermodorus's date and his evidence for Plato's sojourn in Megara, on the ground that τύραννοι can only mean 'the τύραννοι so-called κατ' ἐξοχήν'—those who 'have always been understood as the Tyrants at Athens,' viz the Thirty only. Schaarschmidt has so far misconstrued the τύραννοι of Hermodorus as to identify, in a hasty reading of the seventh Platonic letter, the δυναστεύοντες who brought Socrates to trial with the 'τύραννοι' mentioned earlier (the quotation marks are Schaarschmidt's); but in the Platonic letter there is not a word about 'τύραννοι,' whereas the τριάκοντα are twice mentioned (324 C, 325 B). (According to Schaarschmidt's theory Hermodorus could not of course have been the immediate pupil of Plato, in spite of Dercyllides, who still possessed his work, and in spite of the other witnesses cited on p. 1, 1). Equally unjustifiable is the assertion of Stein against Hermodorus, with regard to some of the well-known Socratics, such as Xenophon, Antisthenes, Æschines, that it is highly improbable, if not quite impossible, that they were with Plato at Megara. Hermodorus does not state that *all* the Socratic students had gone there Diog. merely says, in 6, ἔπειτα . . . καθά φησιν Ἑρμόδωρος εἰς Μέγαρα πρὸς Εὐκλείδην σὺν καὶ ἄλλοις τισὶ Σωκρατικοῖς ὑπεχώρησεν [ὁ Πλάτων], and if we compare ii. 106: πρὸς τοῦτον (Euclid) φησὶν ὁ Ἑρμόδωρος ἀφίκεσθαι Πλάτωνα καὶ τοὺς λοιποὺς φιλοσόφους, the meaning is obviously not (as Steinhart, Pl. L. 121, understands) all the philosophers who were at that time in Athens, but the rest known to the reader (*i.e.* the reader of Hermodorus, or of the writer whose statement is here made use of) who had left Athens with Plato. We might be more ready to doubt, with Steinhart (Pl. L. 121) whether danger threatening one of their number afforded Plato and his friends any ground for apprehension. It is quite possible that Hermodorus attributed this motive to them from his own conjecture, in which he was really mistaken. However, the state of affairs after the death of Socrates is so little known to us that we cannot decide whether there was not some occasion, though perhaps unwarranted, for apprehension.

[27] On what follows cf. Herm. Plat 51 sq ; 109 sq.

[28] All testimony agrees that his travels extended at least thus far.

the meagreness, and sometimes the contradictoriness, of the traditions,[29] it is impossible to ascertain with cer-

For his travels in Egypt, we may quote his acquaintance with Egyptian institutions (vide page 358, note 2). The order of the journeys is variously given. According to Cicero, Republic, i. 10; De Finibus, v. 29, 87; Valerius Maximus, viii. 7, ext. 3; Augustine, De Civitate Dei, viii. 4, he went first to Egypt, and then to Italy and Sicily. It should be remarked, that Valerius, like the declamator he is, transfers the date of the travels to the period when Plato had become famous. On the other hand, Diogenes, iii. 6 (with whom is Quintilian, Institutes, i. 12, 15), makes him visit Cyrene first, then the Pythagoreans in Italy, then Egypt (accompanied by Euripides, who had died some time before, however), and thence return to Athens. According to Apuleius, Dogm. Plat. i. 3; and the Prolegomena, c. 4, he went first to Italy to visit the Pythagoreans, then to Cyrene and Egypt, and thence back again to Italy and Sicily. The most credible of these statements is the first. We can scarcely suppose that Plato visited Italy twice running (the 7th Platonic letter, 326 B, only knows of one Italo-Sicilian journey), while everything is in favour of Sicily's having been the end of his travels (vide subter). And the opposite account gives us an unhistoric motive in the assertion of Apuleius and the Prolegomena, that he visited Cyrene and Egypt to investigate the sources of Pythagoreanism. The conjecture of Stallbaum, Plat. Polit. 38; Plat. Opp. i. xix., that Apul. is following Speusippus, is quite indemonstrable. According to Diog. 7, he had intended to visit the Magi (and according to Apul. loc. cit., the Indians too), but was prevented by the wars in Asia. Lactantius, Institut 4, 2, actually makes him travel to the Magi and Persians; Clemens, Cohortationes 46, to the Babylonians, Assyrians, Hebrews, and Thracians. Cicero, Tusculans, 4, 19, 44, speaks of the ultimæ terræ which he had explored; according to Olymp. 4, Prolegg. 4, he had been initiated in the doctrines of Zoroaster by Persians in Phœnicia; Pausanias, iv. 32, 4, repeats this, and says that he was also acquainted with Chaldean lore; and according to Pliny, Natural History 30, 2, 9, he acquired the Persian magic while on his travels. These, however, are doubtless the inventions of later times, analogous to the tales about Pythagoras, and perhaps to some extent modelled on them. A still more palpable fiction is the alleged acquaintance with Jews and Jewish scriptures, on which cf. Brucker, i 635 sq. Hermann, p. 114 A, 125; with the writers he quotes, and the 3rd part of the present work, 221, 300, 2nd edit. Lactantius, loc. cit. wonders that Plato and Pythagoras had not visited the Jews.

[29] Diogenes 6 would lead us to suppose that he went from Megara straight to Cyrene, and from thence to Sicily. On the other hand, the 7th Platonic letter makes a long interval of active teaching elapse before his coming to Megara. Vide next note.

tainty how long he continued in Megara, when he commenced his travels, whether they immediately succeeded the Megaric sojourn, or a return to Athens intervened; whether his stay in Athens was long or short; and whether he had or had not become a teacher of philosophy before his departure. But if he really returned from Sicily only ten or twelve years after the death of Socrates,[30] there is great probability, and even some

[30] The only source for this is, of course, the 7th Platonic letter, 324 A; and that account becomes suspicious, because it is connected with the assertion in 325 C sq. that even before his journeys Plato had acquired and expressed the conviction, κακῶν οὐ λήξειν τὰ ἀνθρώπινα γένη, πρὶν ἂν ἢ τὸ τῶν φιλοσοφούντων ὀρθῶς γε καὶ ἀληθῶς γένος εἰς ἀρχὰς ἔλθῃ τὰς πολιτικὰς ἢ τὸ τῶν δυναστευόντων ἐν ταῖς πόλεσιν ἔκ τινος μοίρας θείας ὄντως φιλοσοφήσῃ. If with this we compare Rep. v. 473 C, we can hardly doubt that the above-quoted words are to be referred to this place in the Republic. Consequently, the composition of the Republic must be dated before Plato's first Sicilian journey. But this (vide subter) is in the highest degree improbable. At the same time, the statement of the letter as to Plato's age at the time of his journey receives a confirmation which has been noticed by Stallbaum, Plat. Polit p. 44, in correcting his earlier theory (De Argumento et Artificio Theæteti, 13) that Plato did not return till the year 386. The confirmation is this. On his way back from Sicily, Plato is said to have been sold for a slave at Dionysius' instigation, in Ægina, and, according to an apparently accurate account in Diog. iii. 19, his execution was actually debated on, as a plebiscite punished all Athenians who entered the island with death. Ægina, therefore, must at this time have been at open war with Athens. Now, according to Xenophon, Hellenica, v 1, 1, this state of things cannot be dated before the last years of the Corinthian war; up to that time, the intercourse between Athens and Ægina had received no check This would give us 389 or at most 390 B.C., and we may therefore accede to the views of Hermann (p. 63) and almost all the later writers, that it was about this time that Plato returned to Athens. Grote, Hist. of Greece, xi 52, would date his arrival at Syracuse not earlier than 387; on the ground that Dionysius would hardly have had leisure, before that time, during his war with Rhegium, to attend to the philosopher. We need not, however, attach much importance to this argument; and, according to Diodorus, xiv. 110 sq., the conquest of Rhegium dates later than the peace of Antalcidas, after which the treatment experienced by Plato in Ægina was impossible.

external evidence,[31] that long before this journey he had

Some time, too, must be allowed between Plato's arrival and his departure. Tennemann, Platon's Philosophie, i. 46, inclines to the belief that Plato's first appearance in the Academy was in Ol. 99. an opinion which needs no special refutation, in face of the previous remarks and the facts to be presently adduced.

[31] We may not be inclined to give much weight to the expressions of the 7th letter on this point (quoted on pp. 15, 28; 17, 30), or to Valerius Maximus, both being too little trustworthy. But the theory is undoubtedly favoured by the circumstance that we possess a series of important works of Plato's, composed in all probability before his return from Sicily, and at least some of them after his sojourn at Megara. The first of these is the Theætetus. The occasion of the dialogue is connected with a meeting with Theætetus, who is returning sick to Athens from the army at Corinth This can only refer to the Corinthian War, B C. 394–387. Munk (Nat Ordn. d. Pl. Schr. 391 sq) and Ueberweg (Exam. of Plat. writings, 227 sq.) make the reference to B.C. 368: cf. Diodor. 15, 68. At that date, however, Theætetus would have been no longer under any obligation to take part in a foreign campaign, and the dialogue would have to be dated later than various considerations, to be brought forward presently, will warrant. Between the two dates given there was no Athenian army at Corinth. In its later years the Corinthian war was carried on by Athens with mercenaries only (Xen. Hell. 4, 4, 1; 14: Diodor. 14, 86, 91 sq.), so the dialogue must refer to the first period. 39⅔. The date of its composition cannot be much later; the introduction—almost a dedication to Euclid—points to a time at which Plato had not so decidedly broken with the Megara School as he has in the Sophist, and gives us the impression that it relates to matters still fresh in the Greek reader's mind. (Ueberweg, p. 235, thinks such a dedication awkward; I only say that the frame in which the dialogue is set amounts to a dedication. Cicero has dedicated his 'Posterior Academics' to Varro in the same way.) Munk and Ueberweg object that if Plato wrote the Theætetus so early, he must have foreseen Theætetus' achievements in mathematics, attested by Proclus in Eucl p. 19, 25. But Socrates does not say (Theæt. 142 D) that Theætetus will live to be a distinguished mathematician, he only predicts that he will become an ἐλλόγιμος ἀνήρ; and there was no reason why he should not have said this at the date 392-388. If Theætetus is called (143 E sq.) μειράκιον in B.C. 399, it does not follow that he was no more than 16, as Munk thinks; in the Symposium 223 A, Agathon, at the time of his first victory, is called μειράκιον; and in Plutarch, Pericl. 36, Pericles' betrothed son is denoted by the same title: on the other hand, Theætetus is called ἀνήρ in page 144 D. Several other works (vide subter) seem to have preceded the Theætetus, and probably most of them were composed at Athens. Plato could not have given the requisite pains and concentration while on his travels; and to suppose them written at

settled in Athens,[32] and there worked as teacher and author; even granting that at this period his instructions were confined to a select few, and that the opening of his school in the Academy took place later on.[33] What, in this case, we are to think about the journey to Egypt and Cyrene—whether the visit to Sicily was immediately connected with it, or whether [34] Plato first returned to Athens from Egypt, and only undertook the Italian journey after an interval of some years, cannot be certainly determined, but there is a good deal in favour of the latter alternative.[35]

Megara would be to assume a longer residence there than our evidence warrants. (See following note.) Some trace of such a stay, beyond the notice in Hermodorus, would naturally have been preserved. The sharp polemic of the Theætetus, (which Hermann, 499, and Steinhart, Plat. Werk. iii. 81, 556, appear to be wrong in ignoring), and the probably contemporaneous Euthydemus against Antisthenes (vide supra, pp. 248, 1, 4; 252, 3; 254, 1; 255, 2; 256, 1,) might indeed warrant the conjecture, that at the time when he wrote these dialogues, Plato had already had some personal encounters with Euclid, and known him as his opponent in Athens. If at this period Plato had already passed some years of literary activity at Athens, we can hardly imagine that the philosopher who will only allow a written document as a reminder to oral delivery (Phædrus 276 D sq.) should have refrained from enunciating his views in personal intercourse with others.

[32] If fear for his personal safety was the reason of his retirement to Megara, he must soon have been enabled to return home without danger; and again, as the philosophic intercourse with Euclid, supposing this to be Plato's object, could just as well be enjoyed from the neighbouring Athens, it is impossible to see what could detain the philosopher a year at Megara.

[33] Grote agrees with the above, Plato i. 121. He rightly considers it highly improbable that Plato should have spent the 13 (strictly speaking 10-12) years before his return from Sicily in voluntary banishment.

[34] As Steinhart conjectures, Pl W. iii. 100; 213, 316, 473.

[35] Most of our authorities take it for granted that he came straight from Egypt to Italy. But the varying accounts of the order of his travels, noticed above, show the utter want of exact information on the point. The 7th letter is silent about the journey to Egypt; if we are to follow it, we must conclude that he went straight from home to Italy; and

If, indeed, Plato had already attained to manhood when he visited the countries of the south and west; had already, that is, before his personal acquaintance with the Italian Pythagoreans, found the scientific bases of his system, and laid them down in writings,[36] these journeys cannot have had the striking effect on his philosophical development which is often ascribed to them in ancient and modern days. Besides the general enlargement of his views and knowledge of human nature, his chief gain from them seems to have consisted in a closer acquaintance with the Pythagorean school[37] (whose principal written book he appears to have purchased),[38] and in a deeper study of mathe-

---

Plutarch's statement (Plut. de Genio Socratis 7, p. 579) which makes Plato visit Delos on his return from Egypt, perhaps goes on the presupposition that he was not on a voyage to Italy, but to Athens. The main point, however, is that this theory gives the easiest arrangement of his works with reference to his life. The Politicus shows traces of his acquaintance with Egypt (vide subter, p. 22, 41). But on these points conjecture is all that is possible.

[36] We shall see presently that the Theætetus and dialogues of the same date presuppose the doctrine of Ideas, and a certain acquaintance with Pythagorean tenets.

[37] The details on this point seem to rest on mere conjecture. Cicero, loc. cit, names Archytas, Echecrates, Timæus, and Acrion, or Arion (Valerius Maximus adds Cœtus), as Pythagoreans, whose acquaintance he had made at that time Olympiodorus gives Archytas, (the name of Timæus seems to have dropped out). Apuleius, loc. cit., Eurytus and Archytas; Diogenes, Eurytus and Philolaus (the latter can scarcely have been alive at the time). Cf. Bockh, Philol. 5 sq.; and Pt. 1, p. 287, of the present work.

[38] The first writer known to us who mentions the purchase of Philolaus' works by Plato is Timon the Sillographer, apud Gellium, iii. 17 He only says, however, that Plato bought a small book for a large price, and with its help wrote his Timæus. That the purchase was made on his travels, he does not say; nor does the price of the book—as given by Gellius, 10,000 denarii = 100 Attic minæ—seem to come from him. On the other hand, Hermippus, ap. Diog. viii. 85 (about B c. 230), says, on the authority of a writer not named, but doubtless an Alexandrian, that Plato, on his visit to Sicily, bought Philolaus' work from his relations for 40 Alexandrine minæ, and copied his Timæus

matics. To this study, Theodorus is said to have introduced him,[39] and we have at any rate no proof against the correctness of the statement.[40] He may have received further mathematical instruction from Archytas and other Pythagoreans, so that we can scarcely be wrong in connecting with this journey his predilection for the science,[41] and his remarkable knowledge of it: [42]

from it. Others (ibid.) say that the book was a present in acknowledgment of Plato's having obtained the freedom of one of Philolaus' scholars from Dionysius. Cicero, Rep. i. 10, says less definitely that Plato acquired it during his stay in Sicily. According to Satyrus ap. Diog. iii. 9, viii. 15 (followed by Iamblichus de vita Pythagorica, 199) it was not Plato himself, but Dion by his commission, who bought it for 100 minæ. This sum, adds Diogenes, he could easily afford; for he is said to have been well off, and, as Onetor tells, to have received from Dionysius more than eighty talents. (The latter statement is not merely exaggerated, but plainly fictitious; cf. also Diog. ii. 81, and page 312, 2). Tzetzes, Chiliades x. 790 sq., 999 sq., xi. 37, makes Dion buy it for him from Philolaus' heirs for 100 minæ We may probably agree with Bockh, Philologus 18 sq., Susemihl, Genet. Entwickl., 1, 2, sq., and Steinhart, Pl. C. 149, sq., in saying that Plato certainly was acquainted with the work of Philolaus, perhaps actually possessed it; but beyond this, when, where, and how he acquired it, cannot be determined, owing to the contradictory, ambiguous, and partially improbable nature of the accounts that have come down to us. *A priori*, it would be more likely that it came to him at Athens through the instrumentality of Simmias and Cebes. The Prolegomena, c. 5, transfer the myth of the world soul to the pseudo Timæus

[39] Diog. iii. 6; Apul. loc. cit. That Plato was acquainted with Theodorus seems probable from the Theætetus, 143 D sqq., and the opening of the Sophist and Politicus. The acquaintance had doubtless been made at Athens. Theodorus had visited Athens shortly before the death of Socrates. (Plato, loc cit.; and cf Xen. Memor. iv. 2, 10.)

[40] The possibility, of course, remains that the journey to Cyrene was a mere invention, in order to assign to Plato the mathematical teacher on whom he bestows the acknowledgment of mention.

[41] We shall see later on what significance Plato attached to mathematical relations, and how much he valued a scientific knowledge of them. They are to him the peculiar connecting link between Idea and Phenomenon; and thus the knowledge of them is the intermediate step, leading from sensuous envisagement to rational contemplation of the idea. Cf. Plut. Quæst. Conviv. viii. 2, init.; Philop. de An. D, 6, o. David Schol. in Arist.

while, on the contrary, the stories about the mathematical lore, priestly mysteries, and political ideas which he is stated to have acquired in Egypt,[43] are in the

26, a, 10; Tzetz. Chil., viii. 972 sq. ascribe to him, without sufficient authority, the inscription over his lecture-room, μηδεὶς ἀγεωμέτρητος εἰσίτω, which is generally stated to have been of Pythagorean origin.

[42] Vide Ciceron. de Oratore, i. 50, 217, and Proclus in Euclidem, ii. 19, who notices him as one of the most important contributors to the advance of mathematical science. Phavorinus apud Diog. iii. 24, and Proclus, loc cit. and p. 58, attribute the invention of analysis and the conic section to him. Both statements, however, are doubtful; Proclus himself, p. 31, gives Menæchmus as discoverer of the conic section. See, however, Ideler on Eudemus, Abh d. Berl. Ak. 1828, Hist. Phil. Kl. S. 207, for Phavorinus' statement. The tale of his solving the Delian problem —(how to double a cube), while at the same time he found fault with the usual mathematical processes, is widely spread. Plut. de Ei. 6, 386, De Genio Socratis 7, p. 519; Quæst. Conviv. viii. 2, 1, 7, p. 718, Marcellus, c. 14; Theo Smyrn. c 1. Still, the accounts are very mythical: he reduced the problem to the finding two mean proportionals between two given lines. This may be correct. Cf. Eutocius in Archim de Sph. et Cyl. Archim. ed. Torelli, p. 135. Philop. in An. Post. p. 24, 117. (Schol. in Ar. 209 a, 36 b, 21 sq.) Ideler, loc. cit. He is also said to have invented a time-piece, Athen. iv. 174 c. In the Theætetus, 147 D sqq., he puts several new arithmetical definitions in Theætetus's mouth, doubtless his own discoveries; as the idea of stereometry, in Republic vii. 528 A sq., is represented to be, with special reference to the αὔξη τῶν κύβων. For mathematical passages in his writings, the reader may be referred to Meno 82 A sq. 87 A; Rep. viii. 546 B; Timæus, 35 A sqq., 31 C sqq., 53 C sqq.

[43] According to Cicero de Finibus, v. 29, 87, he learned from the Priests numeros et cœlestia (so Val Max viii. 7, 3); according to Clemens, Cohort. 46 A (cf. Stromata, i. 303 C) he learned geometry from the Egyptians, astronomy from the Babylonians, magic from the Thracians (evidently a reminiscence of Charmides, 156 D), and the rest from the Assyrians and Jews. Strabo (xvii. 1, 29. p. 806) was actually shown the house in Heliopolis where Plato had stayed with Eudoxus for thirteen years! (For thirtsen, some MSS. of the Epitome read three, arbitrarily: vid. Strabo, ed. Kramer.) Against the whole statement, vid. Diog. viii. 86 sq. Ideler, loc. cit. 191 sq. Plato is said to have stayed at Heliopolis until he induced the priests to communicate some of their astronomical lore to him. At all events, they kept the greater part to themselves. Clemens (Strom. loc cit: cf. Diog. viii. 90) even knows the names of the priests who taught Plato and Eudoxus. He separates the two latter in time. Plut. Gen. Socr. c. 7, p. 518, gives him Simmias for a com-

PLATO'S LIFE.

highest degree improbable.[44] In Sicily, Plato visited

[43] panion. Apuleius, Dogm. Plat 3, and the Proleg. 4, make him learn sacred rites in Egypt, as well as geometry and astronomy. Vide Olymp. 5; Lucan, Pharsalia x. 181. Philostratus, Vita Apollonii 1, 4, only speaks of geometry and astronomy, which Plutarch de Iside, c. 10, p. 354, also mentions Quintilian, 1, 12, 15, speaks indefinitely of the secrets of the priests; Diodorus, 1, 98, mentions the laws which Plato, like Solon and Lycurgus, had borrowed from Egypt. He is here following Manetho or some other Egyptian authority.

[44] The external evidence has no authority per se. It belongs altogether to a time far removed from Plato's, and abounding in arbitrary fictions which derived all Greek wisdom from the East. Some of the oldest legends, as in Strabo and Diodorus, sound so incredible and point so plainly to dim Egyptian sources, that we cannot attach the slightest weight to them. There is no historic probability that Plato borrowed anything of importance from the Egyptians (vide pt. 1, p. 31 sqq.). And if we seek traces of the alleged Egyptian influence in Plato's doctrines and writings, we find pretty nearly the opposite of what, according to these later traditions, we might expect. He certainly shows some knowledge of Egypt (Polit. 264 C, Phædr 274 C); he makes use, perhaps, once of an Egyptian myth (Phædr. loc cit.); he derives another, really of his own invention, from Egypt, while he enlarges on the great antiquity of Egyptian legends (Timæ. 21 E sqq); he praises particular institutions (Laws ii. 656 D, vii. 799; the gravity and religious character of the music, ibid vii. 819 A; the regard paid to arithmetic in the popular education); while he blames others (loc. cit ii. 657 A, ἀλλ' ἕτερα φαῦλ' ἂν εὕροις αὐτόθι. Specially, in xii 953 E, if the remarkable words καθάπερ κ.τ.λ. are really Plato's, he censures the Egyptian cruelty towards strangers). On the whole, he is inclined to disparage the moral condition and mental capacity of the Egyptians, and ascribes to them not the scientific, but only the industrial character. (Rep iv 435 E; Laws, v. 747 C). This does not look as if he were sensible of any great philosophic debt to Egypt, and there is really nothing in his system to point to Egyptian sources. Throughout, his philosophic attitude appears independent of any but Greek influences: the mathematical element in him is most nearly connected with Pythagoreism; (cf. p. 301, and Arist. Metaphysics, 1. 6, init.); his religious references are confined to the Greek cultus; his politics find their illustration only in Greek types and Greek circumstances. Even the separation of classes in the Republic, as will be shown in its place, is not to be explained as an imitation of the Egyptian caste-system. Indeed, the most marked feature in the Egyptian constitution, the priestly rule, is altogether absent in Plato; and in the Politicus, 290 D sqq., with express reference to Egypt, he very decidedly disapproves of it. Cf. with the preceding Herm. p. 54 sqq, 112 sqq, where there are fuller quotations; and my Part i. p. 25 sq.

the court of Dionysius the elder.[45] But in spite of his close intimacy with Dion,[46] he gave great offence there by his plain speaking,[47] and the tyrant in wrath delivered up the troublesome moraliser to the Spartan ambassador Pollis, by whom he was exposed for sale in the slave-market of Ægina. Ransomed by Anniceris, a Cyrenian, he thence returned to his native city.[48]

[45] Of this there can really be no doubt. All our authorities are unanimous on the point, and Plato himself, in drawing the picture of the tyrant (Rep. viii. fin. ix init.) seems to be speaking from personal experience of what he describes. The circumstances of the visit are variously given. We find, in quite ancient times, a calumnious story to the effect that it was the Sicilian kitchen which attracted the philosopher to Syracuse. (Cf. Ep. Plat. vii. 326 B sq.; Apul. Dogm. Plat 4, Themistius, Orationes, 23, 285 c.; Aristidee, Orationes 46 de quatuor viris, T. 301, Dind.; Lucian, Parasite, 34, Olymp. 4; Diog. iii. 34, vi. 25, &c. We find a similar account in Philostr. v. Apoll 1, 35, ὑπὲρ πλούτου Σικελικοῦ.) The usual account is that he went to see the volcano (Diog. iii. 18, Apul. 4, Olymp. 4; Proleg. 4, Hegesander ap Athen. xi. 507 b; the seventh Platonic letter is less definite, 326 D; and Plut Dion. 4, follows it, in saying that chance or some Divine guidance brought him to Sicily). According to Diog., Dionysius obliged Plato to visit him; according to Plutarch, it was Dion who introduced Plato to his brother-in-law. Olymp. says that he sought out the tyrant uninvited, to induce him to lay down his power. Cornelius Nepos, x. 2 (with whom, in the main, Diodor xv 7 agrees), says that Dionysius invited Plato from Tarentum at Dion's request.

[46] Vide the places quoted, specially the 7th Platonic letter. This of course is as little trustworthy as any of the other letters; but it shows that Dion was generally assumed to have stood in close relations with Plato. For his alleged services to him, cf. Nepos, Plutarch, Cic. de or iii. 34, 139, and pp. 288 sq., 300, 3.

[47] Thus much is probably correct. The more detailed accounts in Plut., Diog, Olymp., loc. cit., appear to be mere arbitrary colourings of the main fact The anecdotes about Plato's meeting with Aristippus (referred by many to this period) are equally uncertain. Vide supra, 291, 2, 312, 2.

[48] Here too there is a great diversity in the accounts. According to Diodorus xv. 7, Dionysius sold the philosopher in the Syracusan slave market, for 20 minæ; his friends freed him, and sent him to a friendly country. Diogenes, 19 sq., on Phavorinus' authority, says that Dionysius was at first disposed to put Plato to death, but was dissuaded by Dion and Aristomenes, and only delivered him to Pollis to sell. Pollis took him to Ægina; and there, in accordance with a

Plato seems now to have made his first formal appearance as a teacher. Following the example of Socrates, who had sought out intelligent youths in the Gymnasia and other public places,—he, too, first chose as the scene of his labours a gymnasium, the Academy, whence, however, he subsequently withdrew into his own garden, which was adjacent.[49] Concerning his

decree of the people, Plato would have been executed, as being an Athenian, but was allowed, as a favour, to be sold instead. Diogenes adds, that Dion or other friends wished to repay Anniceris his expenses, 20 or 30 minæ; this he refused to take, but bought with it, for Plato's use, the garden in the Academy, the price of which is given in Plutarch (de exilio 10 S. 603) as 3000 drachmæ (30 minæ). So Heraclitus, Alleg. Homer C. 74, S. 150. Plutarch himself (Dion 5, cf. de tranquillitate animi 12, 471), and an account in Olympiodorus in Gorg. 164, says that when Plato had incurred Dionysius' enmity, his friends hurried him away on board the ship with which Pollis sailed to Greece (this is scarcely credible, if Sparta and Athens were then at war). Dionysius had given Pollis secret orders to kill Plato, or sell him, and to effect this Pollis brought him to Ægina. Tzetzes, Chil. x. 995 sq., has a wonderful version, Plato was bought by Archytas from Pollis, and then instructed in the Pythagorean philosophy. Seneca (ep. 47, 12, and apud Lactant. Inst. iii. 25, 15 sq.), mentions the transaction, while he blames Anniceris for only having paid 8000 sestertii – 20 minæ—for a Plato. Olympiodorus, 4, actually puts the whole occurrence in the second journey. Gottling, Geschichtlichen Abhandlungen 1, 369, endeavours to free Dionysius from the guilt of the sale; but his arguments, doubtful in themselves, are hardly in accord with Plutarch's statement. There is no real certainty in any of the various versions of the affair; cf. Steinhart's critique (Plato's Leben, 151 sqq.).

[49] Diog. iii. 5, 7, 41; cf Herm. 121 sq., who makes the necessary remarks on the statements of Olymp. c 6, and the Proleg. c. 4. According to Ælian, iii. 19, it was after his third Sicilian journey that he withdrew for some months into his garden, being dislodged by Aristotle; which is manifestly false. Ælian again, ix. 10, and Porphyry, De Abstinentia 1, 36, tell us that the Academy was reputed to be unhealthy, but that Plato refused to move from it for the sake of longer life. It could not, however, have been very bad; for Plato, Xenocrates, and Polemo lived to a good age in it. Hieron. adv Jovin. ii. 203, Mart., actually thinks that Plato betook himself to the unhealthy spot, ut cura et assiduitate morborum libidinis impetus frangeretur; judging the philosopher rather too much by his own experience. So too Æneas of Gaza, Theophr. ed. Barth, p. 25.

manner of instruction tradition tells us nothing;[50] but if we consider how decidedly he expresses himself against the rhetoricians who made long speeches, but knew neither how to ask questions nor how to answer them;[51] and how low, on the same ground, was his estimation of written exposition, open to every misunderstanding and abuse,—in comparison with the living personal agency of conversation,[52]—if we mark the fact, that in his own works, the development of thought by dialogue is a law, from which in his long literary career he allowed himself not a single noteworthy departure,—we can scarcely doubt that in his oral teaching he remained true to these main principles.

On the other hand, however, we hear of a discourse on the Good, published by Aristotle[53] and some of his fellow pupils, and belonging to Plato's later years. Aristotle himself mentions discourses on Philosophy;[54] and that these were not conversations, but in their general character at any rate continuous discourses, is witnessed partly by express testimony,[55] partly by their internal evidence, which can be taken in no other way.

[50] Olymp. 6 has not the value of a witness, and can lead us to no conclusion of any moment.

[51] Prot. 328 E sqq., 334 C sqq.; Gorgias 449 B.

[52] Phædr. 275 D sq.; 276 E.

[53] The references on this point, from Simplicius, Physica 32 b, 104, 117; Alexander on the Metaphysics 1, 6 (Schol. in Aristot. 551, b. 19), Philoponus De Anima C, 2, are given by Brandis, De perditis Aristotelis libris de ideis et de Bono, p. 3 sq., 23 sqq. To the same treatise may be referred the statement of Aristoxenus (on Aristotle's authority), Harmoniæ Elementa, ii. p. 30, and this work, Part ii. b. 48. 2, 771, d. 2.

[54] De Anima i 2, 204 b. 18; on the question whether the Aristotelian books (and consequently the Platonic discourses) on the Good were identical with those on philosophy, or not, vide Brandis loc. cit. 5 sq.; Gr. R. Phil. ii. b. 1, 84 sq.

[55] Aristot. loc. cit. calls them ἀκρόασις, Simpl. λόγοι and συνουσία.

Also, there are many portions of the Platonic system which from their nature could not well be imparted conversationally. It is most probable, therefore, that Plato, according to circumstances, made use of both forms; while the supposition must be admitted that as in his writings, so in his verbal instruction, question and answer gave place to unbroken exposition, in proportion, partly to the diminished vivacity of increasing years, partly to the necessary advance in his teaching, from preparatory enquiries to the dogmatic statement of his doctrine in detail.

That, side by side with the communications intended for the narrower circle of his friends, he should have given other discourses designed for the general public, is not likely.[56] It is more credible that he may have brought his writings into connection with his spoken instruction, and imparted them to his scholars by way of stimulus to their memories.[57] On this point, however, we are

---

[56] Diog. iii 37 (vide note 4) does not warrant such a conclusion, the reference there seems to be to a prelection in the school. On the other hand Themist., or. xxi. 295 D, tells us that Plato once delivered a discourse which a large audience flocked to hear from Athens and the country. When, however, he came to the doctrine of the Good, the whole assembly, down to Plato's usual hearers, dispersed. No doubt this is only an arbitrary expansion of what Aristox. loc cit. tells on Aristotle's authority, that the majority of Plato's disciples were greatly astonished, in the discourse on the Good, to hear, not of things usually considered good, but of mathematics, astronomy, and finally of the One Good. Plato certainly would not expound the most ideal part of his system to a miscellaneous concourse of hearers, as Themistius imagines; and, apart from that, with his views as to the conditions of any fruitful study of philosophy, and his low estimate of mere popular display speeches, he is hardly likely to have troubled himself with giving discourses to people who had not fulfilled his requirements.

[57] Cf. Phædr. 276 D. Instead of other amusement, a man might write books, ἑαυτῷ τε ὑπομνήματα θησαυριζόμενος, εἰς τὸ λήθης γῆρας ἐὰν ἵκηται, καὶ παντὶ τῷ ταὐτὸν ἴχνος μετιόντι.

entirely without information.[58] Plato doubtless combined with intellectual intercourse that friendly life-in-common to which he himself had been accustomed in the Socratic circle and the Pythagorean Society. With a philosopher so little able to separate philosophic from moral endeavour, it might be expected that community of knowledge would naturally grow into community of life. In this way he appears to have joined his scholars at stated intervals in social repasts.[59] There can be no doubt, from what we know of his sentiments on the subject,[60] that his instructions were altogether gratuitous; and if, on certain occasions, he accepted presents from some of his rich friends,[61] there is no reason

---

[58] The tale given by Diog. 37, from Phavorinus, that at the reading of the Phædo all present, except Aristotle, gradually withdrew, is highly improbable. Philosophic interest and respect for the master cannot have been so scanty, even in Plato's inferior scholars, as to allow of anything of the kind, least of all at the delivery of such a masterpiece. Besides, at the time when Aristotle was Plato's pupil, the Phædo must have been long published.

[59] Athenæus xii. 547, d sqq., quoting Antigonus Carystius, tells with some censure of the extravagance introduced by Lycon the Peripatetic at certain meals held on the first day of each month, to which the scholars contributed. They were connected with sacrifices to the Muses. Athen. continues, οὐ γὰρ ἵνα συρρυέντες ἐπὶ τὸ αὐτὸ τῆς ἕως τοῦ ὀρθρίου γενομένης τραπέζης ἀπολαύσωσιν, ἢ χάριν ἐξοιρίας ἐποιήσαντο τὰς συνόδους ταύτας οἱ περὶ Πλάτωνα καὶ Σπεύσιππον, ἀλλ' ἵνα φαίνωνται καὶ τὸ θεῖον τιμῶντες καὶ φυσικῶς ἀλλήλοις συμπεριφερόμενοι καὶ τὸ πλεῖστον ἕνεκεν ἀνέσεως καὶ φιλολογίας. It would appear from this that monthly banquets of the Muses were an institution of the Academy, and with them we may connect the well-known tale about the general Timotheus, who, after a meal with Plato, said, 'With such company one need fear no headaches to-morrow.' (Plat. de sanitate tuenda 9, p. 127; Quæst. Conv. vi. proem.; Athen. x. 419 c; Ælian, V. H. ii. 18, from the same source.) At all events, Athen. loc. cit. says, as of something well known, τὸ ἐν 'Ακαδημίᾳ συμπόσιον, and so again i. 4 E, ἐν τῷ Πλάτωνος συσσιτίῳ. To what new Pythagorean, however, he is indebted for the information in the second passage that the number of the guests used to be 28 (4 × 7) he has not informed us.

[60] On which compare Part I. 888.

[61] Anniceris is said to have

to conclude that such voluntary offerings were therefore customary among his disciples in the Academy.

Plato's sphere of work seemed to him to be limited to this intellectual and educational activity, more and more, as experience deepened his conviction that in the then state of Athens, no diplomatic career was compatible with the principles he held.[62] The desire, however, that it might be otherwise was none the less strong in him;[63] and that he had not abandoned the hope of somehow and somewhere gratifying this desire is proved by his two great political works, which are designed not merely to set forth theoretical ideals, but at the same time to exert a regulative influence on actual conditions. Consequently though he, as little as his great master, himself wished to be a statesman, both may

bought for him the garden in the Academy, Dion defrayed the expenses for the purchase of the writings of Philolaus and for equipping a chorus (supra 24, 48; 20, 38; 4, 5). Not one of these accounts is sufficiently established, the two first only on feeble evidence. The statement of the 13th Plat. Lst. 361 A sq. is quite worthless.

[62] Cf. p. 13. Of the illustrations given there, only the most apposite, Rep vi. 496 C, need be quoted here. In the present condition of society, says Plato, few ever succeed in devoting themselves to Philosophy and remaining true to her. Καὶ τούτων δὴ τῶν ὀλίγων οἱ γενόμενοι καὶ γευσάμενοι ὡς ἡδὺ καὶ μακάριον τὸ κτῆμα, καὶ τῶν πολλῶν αὖ ἱκανῶς ἰδόντες τὴν μανίαν, καὶ ὅτι οὐδεὶς οὐδὲν ὑγιὲς ὡς ἔπος εἰπεῖν περὶ τὰ τῶν πόλεων πράττει οὐδ' ἔστι ξύμμαχος μεθ' ὅτου τις ἰὼν ἐπὶ τὴν τῶν δικαίων βοήθειαν σώζοιτ' ἄν, ἀλλ' ὥσπερ εἰς θηρία ἄνθρωπος ἐμπεσών, οὔτε ξυναδικεῖν ἐθέλων οὔτε ἱκανὸς ὢν εἷς πᾶσιν ἀγρίοις ἀντέχειν, πρίν τι τὴν πόλιν ἢ φίλους ὀνῆσαι προαπολόμενος ἀνωφελὴς αὑτῷ τε καὶ τοῖς ἄλλοις ἂν γένοιτο, ταῦτα πάντα λογισμῷ λαβὼν, ἡσυχίαν ἔχων καὶ τὰ αὑτοῦ πράττων, οἷον ἐν χειμῶνι κονιορτοῦ καὶ ζάλης ὑπὸ πνεύματος φερομένου ὑπὸ τειχίον ἀποστάς, ὁρῶν τοὺς ἄλλους καταπιμπλαμένους ἀνομίας, ἀγαπᾷ, εἴ πῃ αὐτὸς καθαρὸς ἀδικίας τε καὶ ἀνοσίων ἔργων βιώσεται. κ.τ.λ.

[63] Ἀλλά τοι, is the rejoinder, loc. cit., οὐ τὰ ἐλάχιστα ἂν διαπραξάμενος ἀπαλλάττοιτο: to which Socrates replies, οὐδέ γε τὰ μέγιστα, μὴ τυχὼν πολιτείας προσηκούσης· ἐν γὰρ προσηκούσῃ αὐτός τε μᾶλλον αὐξήσεται καὶ μετὰ τῶν ἰδίων τὰ κοινὰ σώσει. Cf. ibid. v. 473 C sq.

certainly be credited with the aim of forming statesmen;[64] and if he repudiated political activity in cir-

[64] It has truly been said of a series of men who distinguished themselves by their political activity that they came out of the Platonic school. However, even in antiquity, the opinions as regards the political character of this school were very divided; and if the admirers of Plato like Plutarch adv. Col. 32, 6, sqq p. 1126, bring into connection with him as pupils as many as possible of the greatest statesmen of his time, not seldom exceeding the bounds of historical fact, it cannot be expected that adversaries like Athenæus xi. 508, d, sqq., and his predecessors, will be precise about their evidence for the statement that the majority of the Platonic pupils were τυραννικοί τινες καὶ διάβολοι. According to Plutarch. loc. cit. Dion (concerning whom vide pp. 24, 46, 32 sq.) belonged to Plato's pupils, together with Aristonymus, Phormio (Plutarch Præcepta. Reip. ger. 10, 15) and Menedemus, who respectively gave laws to the Arcadians, Eleans, and Pyrrhæans. (Menedemus is mentioned by the contemporary comedian Epicrates in Athenæus, 59, d in connection with Plato and Speusippus, in Plutarch Sto. Rep. 20, 6, p. 1043 in connection with Xenocrates); further Delius of Ephesus (called in Philostratus, Vit. Soph. 1, 3, p. 485 through a slip of the pen Δίας), who under Philip and Alexander was the active promoter of the expedition against Persia, together with Pytho and Heraclides of Ænos, the murderers of the Thracian king Cotys (Arist. Polit. v. 10, 1311 b. 20, mentions as such the brothers Parrhon and Heraclides, with whom Pytho appears to have connected himself), the first of whom is known as the speaker and agent of King Philip (cf. Steinhart, Life of Plato 195, 322, 16); both are cited as Platonists by Diogenes iii. 46. It must be from a confusion with the above-mentioned Heraclides, that Demetrius of Magnesia according to Diogenes v. 89 assigned the murder of a tyrant to Heraclides Ponticus, who bore the same name. Besides these we have Chio (the supposed writer of a letter in the Epist. Socrat.) and Leonides, who perished in the murder of the tyrant Clearchus of Heraclea (Justin xvi. 5, Suidas, Κλέαρχος, who adds to them as a third Antitheus; opposed to this Memnon ap. Phot. Cod. 224, p. 225, a. 10 sqq., says that Lysimachus killed him and his brother, because they had murdered their mother); Euphræus of Oreos (Suid. Εὐφρ.) about whose influence at the court of Perdiccas (to whom the Plat. epist. v. recommends him). Athenæus it is true (loc. cit. cf. 506, E), according to Antigonus of Karystus, expresses himself very unfavourably, but who we learn from Demosth. Philipp. iii. p. 126 sqq. (by which Athenæus' account of his death is set right) was a martyr to Grecian liberty; Leo, who as statesman and commander defended his mother-city Byzantium against Philip. (Plut. Phoc. 14, Philostr. Vit. Soph. 1, 2. Suidas Λέων); Hermias, prince of Atarneus, the well-known friend of Aristotle (Diog. v. 3, 5 sqq. Strabo xiii. 1, 59, p. 610. Diodor. xvi. 52,

cumstances which he considered hopeless,[65] there was, at the same time, nothing in his principles to keep him

Dionys. ep ad. Arrim. 1, 5. Suidas 'Ερμίας. Part ii b 16 sqq 2nd edit) Besides these Diog. iii. 46, mentions Euæon of Lampsacus and Timolaus of Cyzicus, both of whom according to Athenæ. 508 sqq. (who calls the one Euagon and the other Timæus) made unsuccessful attempts to usurp tyrannical power in their respective cities; Athenæus adds to them Charon of Pellene as one of the profligate tyrants who came out of the school of Plato and Xenocrates, with what justice we do not know. According to Athenæus loc. cit. Diog. iii. 46, Callippus, also, the murderer of Dion, was a scholar of Plato, which statement is opposed by the Plat. epist. vii. 333 C, Plut. Dion, 34. The Clearchus mentioned above, according to Suidas Κλέαρχ, attended the Academy only a short time. It is very improbable that Chabrias was a student of the Academy (Plut. adv. Col. 32, 6, cf. Pseudo-Ammon, vita Arist. p. 10, West., who makes him out a relation of Plato's). The account (λόγος in Diog. iii. 23 sq.) that Plato alone stood by him at his trial is worth little historically, as Arist. Rhetor. iii. 10, 1411, p 6, mentions another defender of Chabrias; and the defence which in Diog. is put in the mouth of Plato obviously originated from the Apology, 28 E. Timotheus (Ælian, Varia Hist ii. 10, supra 28, 59) it is true was proved to be a friend but by no means a pupil of Plato; his relation to him cannot at all have been so intimate as Ps.-Ammon loc. cit. would have it. Phocion in his younger days may have heard Plato, and later on Xenocrates (Plut. Phocion, 4, adv. Col. 32, 6); with regard to the latter, however, he must have confined himself to being present at isolated discourses. Though Chamæleon and Polemo in Diog. iii 46 represent the orators Hyperides and Lycurgus (of whom also the Pseudo-Plutarch vitæ decem Orat. vii. p. 841 makes the same assertion) as pupils of Plato, their speeches (as Steinhart remarks, Plato's Life, 174 sqq.) show no proofs of the influence of Platonic thought and expression. Still less can we claim Æschines for a pupil of Plato (with the scholiast on Æsch. de falsa legat. i, who appeals to Demetrius Phalereus, compare Apollon. Vit. Æsch. p 14); and though Demosthenes, his great adversary, is variously stated, sometimes with greater and sometimes with less precision, to have been a pupil of Plato, still, however, in his orations no influence of Platonic philosophy appears, significant as may have been Plato's influence on him as a stylist. (Plut. Demosth. 5, according to an anonymous writer in Hermippus, vitæ X orat. viii. 3, p. 844. Mnesistratus in Diog. iii. 47. Cic. de Orat. i. 20, 89. Brut 31, 121; Orat. iv. 15, Off. i. 4; Quintil. xii. 2, 22, 10, 24; Lucian, Encomium Demosthenis, 12, 47; Schol. in Demosth. contra Androt. 40; Olympiod. in Gorg. 166) The 5th letter attributed to him does not make Demosthenes to speak as a Platonist, but only to express his good opinion of the Platonic school, under which he

back from it, should there arise a favourable opportunity for the realization of his ideas.[66] Such an opportunity seemed to offer after the death of the elder Dionysius,[67] when Dion, and, at his instigation, Dionysius the younger, invited him pressingly to Syracuse.[68]

obviously does not include himself. Cf. Steinhart loc. cit. 175 sqq. Schäfer, Demosth. 1, 280 sqq ; and besides the authorities mentioned above, particularly Hermann, Plat. 74 sq, 119 sq. Steinhart, 171-189. With regard to the relations of Isocrates with Plato we shall speak later on (p 345, 2, 2nd edit). No one represents him as his pupil, as he was eight or nine years older than Plato, and their friendship asserted in Diog. iii. 8, is established only for the earlier years of their lives by the writings of both.

[65] According to Plutarch, Ad principem ineruditum, i. p. 779; Lucullus, C 2; Ælian, V. H. xii. 30, the people of Cyrene (beside whom Diog. iii. 23 and Æl. V. H. ii. 42, give the Arcadians and Thebans at the founding of Megalopolis) asked him for a scheme of laws; but he refused both, in the former case because Cyrene was too luxurious for him, in the latter because he perceived ἴσον ἔχειν οὐ θέλοντας, οὐ πείσειν αὐτοὺς τιμᾶν τὴν ἰσονομίαν. The last statement is very improbable, for Plato would without doubt have given them a constitution just as little democratic as they gave themselves; and moreover it is incredible that Epaminondas, who after the victory of Leuctra promoted the founding of Megalopolis for the protection of Arcadia against Sparta, should have invited an Athenian, and particularly so outspoken a friend of Sparta as Plato undoubtedly was, to lay down the new constitution. The absurd 11th Platonic letter cannot come under consideration as historical evidence.

[66] Plato himself lays it down as a necessary condition, that philosophers should not withdraw from politics. The corresponding duty is an immediate consequence. And that this duty should only be binding with regard to one's own state, would hardly be a maxim with one so fully possessed by his political ideal as Plato.

[67] This happened Ol. 103, 1, at the beginning of the winter, and therefore 368 B.C. Diodor. xv. 73 sq. Plato's journey must be assigned to the following year. Cic. de Sen. 12, 41 (with which cf. Part i. p. 244, 3) dates it, or at all events, according to Fin v. 29, 87. the first journey, 405 A.U.C., which needs no refutation.

[68] Ep. Plat. vii. 327 B sqq.; ii 311 E; iii. 316 C sq ; Plut. Dion, 10 sq. (cf. c. princ. Phil. 4, 6, p. 779), who adds that the Pythagoreans in Italy joined their entreaties to Dion's. Cf. Corn. Nep., Dion, C 3, &c The 7th Platonic letter is certainly not trustworthy, and all the following ones depend on it. What other sources of information Plutarch may have had we do not know. That Plato, however, did make a

PLATO'S LIFE.

Could this potentate indeed be won over to Philosophy and to Plato's political beliefs—(and of this Plato, or at any rate Dion, appears certainly to have indulged a hope),[69] the most important results might be expected to follow, not only in his own kingdom, but in all Sicily and Magna Græcia, indeed throughout the Hellenic states. Meanwhile the event proved, only too soon, how insufficiently this hope was founded. When Plato arrived in Syracuse, the young Prince received him most politely, and at first showed lively interest in the philosopher and his endeavours;[70] but he very shortly became weary of these serious conversations, and when his jealousy of Dion, which was not entirely groundless, had led to an open rupture with that statesman, and at length to the banishment of the latter, Plato must have been glad to escape from the painful position in which he found himself, by a second return home.[71] Nevertheless, after some years, at the renewed

---

second and a third journey to Sicily cannot be doubted. The testimony is unanimous; and if he had not taken the journey, the composer of the letter would have had no reason for defending him on that score. That his motives were actually those ascribed to him is probable in itself, and made more so by the whole political situation; and this is borne out by the passage in the Laws, iv. 709 E sqq., in which Hermann, p. 69, rightly recognises an expression of the hopes which led Plato to Syracuse. These hopes, he later on maintains, have not failed in regard to their universal foundation, even though they were not accomplished on that particular occasion.

[69] Diogenes' counter-statement, iii. 21, that he asked Dionysius for land and people towards the realization of his state, is certainly false. Apul dogm. Pl. 4 is a misunderstanding.

[70] More detailed information, but of doubtful worth, may be found in Plut. Dion 13; De Adulatione 7, p. 52, 26, p 67, Pliny, Natural History, vii. 30; Æl. V. H. iv. 18; Nepos, loc. cit. The alleged meeting of Plato and Aristippus at the Syracusan Court has been already discussed, Part i. pp. 291, 2; 312, 3.

[71] Ep. Plat. iii 220 B sqq., iii.

*D

solicitations of the tyrant and entreaties of his friends, he resolved upon yet another voyage to Sicily. His immediate aim was doubtless to attempt a reconciliation between Dion and Dionysius;[72] to this may have linked themselves more distantly, new political hopes: the undertaking, however, turned out so unfortunately that Plato was even in considerable danger from the mistrust of the passionate prince,[73] and only evaded it by the intervention of the Pythagoreans, who were then at the head of the Tarentine state. Whether, after his return,[74] he approved of Dion's hostile aggression on Dionysius, we do not know;[75] but for his own part, from

318 C, Plut. Dion 14, 16, Diog. iii. 21 sq. The latter assigns to this journey what, according to better authorities, happened in the third; and he therefore puts an incident in the first, which Plutarch relates of the second. Cf. also Stobæus, Florilegium, 13, 36, who, however, connects with it a circumstance generally told of Dionysius and Aristippus.

[72] Dion, who appears in the two previous journeys as Plato's enthusiastic admirer, had, according to Plutarch, Dion 17, become still more intimate with him during a long stay at Athens, in the course of which he also became a close friend of Speusippus.

[73] Ep. Plat. iii. 316 D sqq.; vii. 330 B; 33 D, 337 E sqq.; and from these sources Plutarch, Dion 18-20; Maximus Tyrius, Dissertationes xxi. 9; Diog. 23. The particulars are uncertain; the letter of Archytas ap. Diog 22 is certainly spurious. According to Plut c 22 (cf. Ep. Plat ii 314 D) Speusippus accompanied him to Syracuse; according to Diog., Xenocrates. He is said to have left the conduct of his school at Athens during his absence to Heraclides. (Suidas, voc. 'Ηρα-κλείδης.) The Epistolæ Heraclidis, quoted there by Ast, and even by Brandis—the former in Pl. Leben u. Schr p. 30, the latter Gk -Röm. Phil. ii. a. 145—do not exist. The quotation is due to a misunderstanding of Tennemann's words, Plat. Phil. i. 54, 'Suidas in Heraclides Epistol. (Platonicæ sc.) 11 p. 73' (Bipont.).

[74] According to Ep. vii 350 B (cf. p 345 D) this must be dated in the spring of 360 B.C., for he is said to have met Dion at the Olympic games (which can only be those of the year named) and informed him of events in Syracuse. His hither journey would then be 361. Cf. Herm. p. 66

[75] Plutarch. adv. Col. 32, 6, p. 1126. Cic. de Orat. iii. 34, 139, and Ælian, V. H. iii. 17, represent the impulse as coming from Plato. But this is an exaggerated infer-

this time, having now attained his seventieth year, he seems to have renounced all active interference with politics.[76] The activity of his intellect, however, continued amidst the reverence of countrymen and foreigners,[77] unabated till his death,[78] which, after a happy and peaceful old age,[79] is said to have overtaken him at a wedding feast.[80]

ence from Ep. Plat. vii. 326 E. Cf. Ep iv. Dioo found warm support from Speusippus and other Platonists, Plut Dio 22, 17. His companion and subsequent enemy, Callippus, is noticed as a scholar of Plato's (vide p. 31)

[76] Athenæus, xi. 506, indeed says that he was intimate with Archelaus of Macedonia, and later on, paved the way for Philip's supremacy so that we might infer his sympathies to have been in general with the Macedonian party. As regards Archelaus, however, the statement is refuted by chronology, and by the Gorgias, 470 D sq.; and the alleged support of Philip narrows itself down, even on Athenæus's own quotations, to the circumstance that Plato's scholar Euphræus had obtained for Philip a certain territory from Perdiccas, and this Philip used for the furtherance of greater designs. Any personal intercourse between Plato and Philip there does not seem to have been. Æl. V. H. iv. 19, certainly says that Philip paid honour to Plato, as to other learned men; but, according to Speusippus ap. Athen. loc. cit., and Diog. 40, he expressed himself unfavourably about him.

[77] Cf (besides what has been quoted, p 32, 65, and about his relation to Dion and Dionysius),

Diogenes, 25, and what will be presently remarked on the extension of the Platonic school.

[78] Of his literary works this is expressly witnessed (vid. supr. p. 3, and Diog 37, Dionys. comp. verb. p 208, Quint. viii. 6, 64, on which however cf. Susemihl, Gen. Ent. 11, 90 sq.). And we may safely conclude that it was the same with his activity as teacher. The alleged interruption of his work by Aristotle will be discussed later in the life of that philosopher.

[79] Cicero, de Senect. 5, 13.

[80] Hermippus ap. Diog. iii 2. Augustine, C. D. viii 2. Suid. voc. Πλάτ. Cicero's scribens est mortuus, loc. cit., is not at variance with this latter, if we remember that it need not be taken literally According to Diog. 40, a certain Philo had used the proverbial expression Πλάτωνος φθείρες, and Myronianus concluded from this that Plato died of φθειρίασις, as it is said Pherecydes and others did Of course this is false. Perhaps the expression comes originally from the place in the Sophist, 227 B, or the passage may at least have given a handle to the story. As to Plato's burial, monument, and will, vide Diog. iii 25, 41 sqq. Olymp. 6, Pausan. 1, 30, 3; Herm. p. 125, 197.

Even in antiquity, the character of Plato was the subject of many calumnies.[81] The jests of the comic poets which have come down to us [82] are indeed harmless enough, and concern the philosopher more than the man; but there are other reproaches, for the silencing of which Seneca's apology [83]—that the life of a philosopher can never entirely correspond with his doctrine,—is scarcely sufficient. On the one hand, he is accused of connections, which, if proved, would for ever throw a shadow on his memory;[84] on the other of unfriendly, and even of hostile behaviour towards several of his fellow disciples.[85] He has

[81] One of these critics of Plato was Timæus the Locrian, Plut. Nic. 1; two others we shall meet with in Aristoxenus and Theopompus, the pupils of Isocrates, who, in this way, retaliated for the attacks of Plato and the Platonists on Isocrates and Rhetoric: cf. Dion. Hal ep ad Pomp. p 757, De præc. Hist 782; Athen. xi. 508 c. Epict. Diss. 11, 17, 5.

[82] Ap. Diog iii. 26 sq.; Athen. ii. 59 c sq.; xi 509 c.

[83] Vita beata, 18, 1.

[84] Vide Diog 29; Ælian. V. H. iv. 21; Athen. xiii. 589 c., and supra, p. 8, 8 Even Dion is here called his favourite; and an epitaph is quoted, which Plato (at the age of seventy three) is said to have composed on his friend, who must have been sixty at least. That Antisthenes alluded to some amours of Plato's by the title of his Σάθων is a mere arbitrary conjecture. The censure of Dicæarchus ap Cic Tusc. iv. 34, 71, is levelled not at his character, but his philosophy. On the other hand, Suidas, p 3000, ed. Gaisford, affirms that he never entered into any sexual relations. But this, again, can only be a dogmatic invention, originating with the asceticism of later schools.

[85] The only hostility that can be demonstrated, however, is between Antisthenes and Plato; vide Part i. 255, and supra, p 18, 31. Antisthenes is allowed on all hands to have been the aggressor, and always to have displayed the greater vehemence and passion. The assertion that Plato behaved ill to Æschines has been discussed, Part i. p. 167, 6, 204, 3; and his alleged neglect of him in Sicily (Diog. ii. 61) is contradicted by Plut. de Adul. c 26, p 67. He certainly passed censure on Aristippus, vide Part i. p. 242, but it was well merited, and we may well believe there was no love lost between them, even though the anecdotes of their meeting in Syracuse (vide Part i p 291, 2) do not tell us much, and the accounts of a certain He esander ap. Athen. xi. 507 b. still less. At all events,

PLATO'S LIFE.

also been charged with censoriousness and self-love; [86] not to mention the seditious behaviour after the death of Socrates which scandal has laid to his account.[87] His relation with the Syracusan court was early [88] made the handle for divers accusations, such as love of pleasure,[89] avarice,[90] flattery of tyrants; [91] and his political character

what we do know cannot turn to Plato's disadvantage. We get repeated assertions of an enmity existing between Plato and Xenophon (Diog. iii 34, Gell. N. A. xiv. 3; Athen. xi. 504 e.). But Boekh has shown (de simultate quæ Platoni cum Xenophonte intercepisse fertur, Berlin, 1811) how little ground there is for such a belief in the writings of either; and the writings are the only real authority. Most likely the whole story is an invention Cf Steinhart, Pl. L. 93 sq.

[86] Dionysius ad Pompeium, p. 775 sq., Athen. xi. 506 a 'qq., Antisthenes and Diogenes ap Diog. vi. 7, 26, Aristides de quatuorviris The accusation is mainly grounded on Plato's writings, which cannot be said to justify it, however one-sided many of his judgments may be. The conscious superiority, to which he had a real right, may have been too prominent in particular cases; even disadvantageously so, sometimes, for others. Cf. the quotation from Aristotle, Part i. p. 289, 2. But this can hardly bear out such accusations as the above. Of the anecdotes given in Plutarch de adul. c. 32, p. 70; Ælian, V. H. xiv. 33 (Diog. vi 40), the first is irrelevant, the second certainly untrue, and what Hermippus ap. Athen. xi. 505 d., gives, looks unhistorical too. Aristoxenus apud Diog. ix. 40, taxes Plato with the childish design of buying up and destroying the writings of Democritus. But of this we may unhesitatingly acquit him Aristoxenus is too untrustworthy a witness; and we may at least credit Plato with the sense to see that a widely spread mode of thought could not be abolished by the burning of a few books. His own distaste for merely material science and his general disparagement of such studies may perhaps account for his never mentioning the physicist of Abdera

[87] Hegesander ap. Athen. xi. 507 a. sq, the falsehood of the statements need not be pointed out to any reader of the Phædo or the Symposium. The dream of Socrates related ibid. is a malicious parody of that mentioned above, p. 9, 15.

[88] The seventh Platonic letter is a refutation of such charges. According to Diog. iii 34; vi. 25, the charges were openly made even in Plato's lifetime.

[89] Vide p. 23, 45.

[90] Philostr. v. Apoll. 1, 35; Diog. iii 9. The anonymous assertion in Arsen. Violet. ed. Katz, 508, and the Florilegium Monacense (Stob. Flor. ed Meineke. T. iv. 285), No. 227, that in old age he became avaricious, is of the same kind. Seneca, v. 6, 27, 5, remarks that he was reproached

has especially suffered at the hands of those who were themselves unable to grasp his ideas.[92] Lastly, if we are to believe his accusers, he not only, as an author, allowed himself numerous false assertions [93] respecting his predecessors, but also such indiscriminate quotation from their works, that a considerable portion of his own writings can be nothing more than a robbery from them.[94] All these complaints, however, so far as we are

---

for taking money. Others say (v. supr. Part 1. p. 312, 3, and Diog. ii. 81) that he did not do so even at Syracuse. The seventh letter recognises no reason for defending him against the charge.

[91] Diog vi. 58. Against which it is unnecessary to refer to Plut Dion 13, 19, and the quotations on p. 24, 47

[92] The quotations given by Athenæus, xi. 506 e sqq., 508 d. sqq, have but little importance. Some are plainly untrue (vide supra, p. 34, 76), or misrepresentations, and the rest, even if true, would not have much reference to Plato himself. On the other hand, we may see from the places quoted, pp. 29, 62; 32, 68, that Plato had occasion to explain his political inactivity and his relation to the younger Dionysius. And we may expect to find that both were cast in his teeth, just as his political idealism and his preference for aristocratic government must necessarily have given offence. Cf. also Rep. v 472 A, 473 C, E

[93] Cf. the list of offences in Athen. v. c 55, 57–61, the correction of which we may spare ourselves, together with the absurd complaints about the fictitious speeches which he puts in the mouth of Socrates and others: xi. 505 e. 507 c : Diog 35.

[94] So he is said to have borrowed from Philolaus' writings for his Timæus (v supr. 20, 38), and from a work of Protagoras for the Republic (Aristox. and Phav. ap. Diog. iii. 37, 57). According to Porphyry ap. Euseb Præparatio Evangelica, x. 3, 24, he is indebted to the same source for his objections to the Eleatics Alcimus ap. Diog. iii. 9 sq., reproached him with having taken the foundations of his system from Epicharmus Theopompus, ap. Athen. xi. 508 c, said that he borrowed most of his dialogues from Aristippus, Antisthenes, and Bryso. With regard to Epicharmus, the assertion is groundless, as has been shown in Vol i. 428 sq. To the statements of Aristoxenus and Theopompus no one who knows the untrustworthiness of the writers will be inclined to give much weight The statement of the former (whom his assertions about Socrates already sufficiently characterise, supra, 51 sq., 48, 54, 6, 59, 5) is improbable on the face of it, if true at all, it can only have reference to some unimportant points. And the same applies to Theopompus's story (cf. supra, 36, 81), apart from

in a position to test them, appear so unfounded that scarcely a fraction of them will stand the process of investigation;[95] and the rest are supported by such weak evidence, that they ought not to affect that reverence for the character of the philosopher which is certain to ensue from the perusal of his works. So far as a man may be judged by what he has written, only the very highest opinion can be formed of the personality of Plato. To appreciate him correctly, however, he must be measured by a standard that takes account of his natural disposition and historical place. Plato was a Greek, and he was proud of being one. He belonged to a rank and to a family, the prejudices as well as the advantages of which he was content to share. He lived at a time when Greece had touched the highest point of her national life, and was steadily declining from political greatness. His nature was ideal, adapted rather to artistic creation and scientific research than to practical action; which tendency, nourished and confirmed by the whole course of his life, and the strong influence of the Socratic School, could not fail to be still further strengthened by his own political experiences. From such a temperament and such influences might be evolved all the virtues of

the common Socratic element, which Plato did not need to borrow of anyone Porphyry's assertion may possibly have some basis of truth; but it can hardly redound to Plato's discredit. Finally, if Plato was indebted to Philolaus for the construction of the elements and other details of physical science in the Timæus, and for the deductions as to the limit and the illimitable in the Philebus, we can find no fault with him for this in itself; and in both cases he has sufficiently pointed out his sources in making a general reference to the Pythagoreans, even if he has not named Philolaus.

[95] Vide preceding note.

a man and a philosopher, but nought of the grandeur of a politician. Plato might desire the very best for his country, and be ready to sacrifice for her sake everything except his convictions: but that he should have thrown himself into the turmoil of political life, for which he was quite unfitted,—that he should have lavished his soul's strength in propping up a constitution, the foundations of which he thought rotten,[96]— that he should have used means that he felt to be useless to stem the torrent of opposing fate,—that he, like Demosthenes, should have led the forlorn hope among the ruins of Grecian freedom,—would be too much to expect. His province was to examine into State problems and the conditions of their solution; their practical realization he abandoned to others. Thus inner disposition and outward circumstances alike designed him for philosophy rather than state-craft. But even his philosophy had to be pursued differently from that of Socrates, nor could his habits of life exactly resemble his master's. He desired to be true in the main to the Socratic pattern, and by no means to return to the mode of teaching adopted by the Sophists.[97] But aiming as he did at the formation and propagation of a comprehensive system,—aphoristic conversation, conditioned by a hundred accidental circumstances, was not enough for him; he wanted more extensive machinery,

[96] Vide supra; p. 29, 62; cf. Ritter ii. 171 sqq.

[97] He not only took no fees for his teaching (Diog. iv. 2, and Proleg. c. 5, cf. p. 314, 4), strongly disapproving of the Sophists' conduct in this respect (vide Vol. i. p. 888 sq), but he also censured the form in which the Sophistic doctrine was enunciated. (Protag. 328 E sqq; 334 C sq; Gorg. 449 B. sq.; Hipp. Min. 373 A. Cf. supra, p. 26, 51).

skilled labour, intellectual quiet; he wanted hearers who would follow his enquiries in their entire connection, and devote to them their whole time; his philosophy was forced to withdraw itself from street and market, within the precincts of a school.[98]

Here already were many deviations from the Socratic way of life; many more sprang from Plato's own habits and inclinations, which were generally opposed to it. Simplicity and temperance were indeed required by his principles,[99] and are expressly ascribed to him;[100] but the entire freedom from wants and possessions to which Socrates attained, would not have suited a man of his education and circumstances. Himself full of artistic taste, he could not deny all worth to life's external adornments;[101] extending his scientific research unreservedly to all reality, he could hardly, in ordinary life, be so indifferent to the outward, as they who, like Socrates, were satisfied with moral introspection. Socrates, in spite of his anti-democratic politics, was, by nature, a thorough man of the people : Plato's personality, like his philosophy, bears a more aristocratic

---

[98] Cf. Diog. 40: ἐξετόπιζε δὲ καὶ αὐτὸς τὰ πλεῖστα, καθά τινές φασι Olymp. c. 6.

[99] Cf specially Rep. iii. 403 E sq.; Gorg. 464 D.

[100] Vide the places quoted p. 28, 59; and Diog. 39. In the same connection we may notice the doubtful tale in Stobæus, Flor. 17 36 (attributed to Pythagoras by Flor. Monac. 231), of his pouring away the water with which he meant to quench his thirst, as an exercise of self-denial.

[101] Plato is indeed said not to have disdained a certain amount of luxury in domestic management (Diog. vi. 26); some of his pupils were ridiculed by contemporary comic writers on account of their fine clothes and their haughty behaviour. (Athenæ. xi. 509, xii. 544 sq.) On the other hand Seneca ad Helv. 12, 4, says that Plato only had three slaves; his Will in Diog. iii. 42 mentions five.

stamp. He loves to shut himself up in his own circle, to ward off what is vulgar and disturbing; his interest and solicitude are not for all without distinction, but only or chiefly for the elect who are capable of sharing his culture, his knowledge, his view of life. The aristocracy of intelligence on which his State rests has deep roots in the character of Plato. But precisely to this circumstance are owing the grandeur and completeness that make his character in its particular sphere unique. As Plato in his capacity of philosopher unites the boldest idealism with rare acuteness of thought, a disposition for abstract critical enquiry with the freshness of artistic creativeness;—so does he, as a man, combine severity of moral principles [102] with lively susceptibility for beauty, nobility and loftiness of mind with tenderness of feeling, passion with self-control,[103] enthusiasm for his purpose with philosophic calm, gravity with mildness,[104] magnanimity with human kindliness,[105] dignity [106] with gentleness. He is great because he knew how to blend these apparently conflicting traits

[102] An epitaph in Diog. 43 calls him σωφροσύνη προφέρων θνητῶν ἤθει τε δικαίῳ.

[103] To this belongs the well-known tale, that Plato asked a friend to chastise his slave because he himself was angry. Another version is, that he said to the slave himself, 'Luckily for you, I am angry; or you would get stripes.' Plut de educatione puerorum, 14, p. 10; de sera numinis vindicta 5, p. 551. Sen. de Ira iii. 12, 5; Diog. 38 sq.; Stob. Flor. 20, 43, 57, Flor Mon. 234. Perhaps it is with reference to this story that Themistius, Or. 2, 30 d., holds him up as a model of gentleness.

[104] Cf. the quotations in Part i. p. 286, 9.

[105] A beautiful instance is given by Ælian, V. H. iv. 9.

[106] Heraclides ap. Diog. 26 tells us, that in his youth he never allowed himself to laugh immoderately; and Ælian, V. H. iii. 35, says laughter was forbidden in the Old Academy We need not take either of these statements literally, but they show that Plato was regarded as a very serious character. Another instance is given by Seneca, de Ira ii. 21, 10.

PLATO'S LIFE. 43

into unity, to complement opposites by means of each other, to develope on all sides the exuberance of his powers and capabilities into a perfect harmony,[107] without losing himself in their multiplicity. That moral beauty and soundness of the whole life, which Plato, as a true Greek, requires before all things,[108] he has, if his nature be truly represented in his works, brought to typical perfection in his own personality.[109] Nor is the picture marred by incongruity of outward semblance with inward reality, for his bodily strength and beauty have been especially recorded.[110] But throughout, the most striking peculiarity of the philosopher is that close connection of his character with his scientific aims, which he owes to the Socratic school. The moral perfection of his life is rooted in the clearness of his understanding; it is the light of science which disperses the mists in his soul, and causes that Olympian serenity which breathes so refreshingly from his works. In a word, Plato's is an Apollo-like nature, and it is a fitting testimony to the impression produced by

[107] Olympiodorus says (C 6) of Plato and Homer, δύο γὰρ αὗται ψυχαὶ λέγονται γενέσθαι παναρμόνιοι.

[108] E g. Rep. iii. 401 B sq; 403 C. Phileb. 64 C sq.; 66 A.

[109] Cf. also Panætius ap Cic. Tusc. i. 32, 79, and the verses of Aristotle quoted, ii 9, 2, 2nd edit.

[110] Epict. Diss. i. 8, 13, καλὸς ἦν Πλάτων καὶ ἰσχυρός. Further cf Apul. dogm Plat. 1, and the quotations supra 339, 1, 242. 2, on Plato's build and gymnastic dexterity Among the portraits of Plato (on which see Visconti. Iconographie grecque, 1. 169 [228] sq), the statuette, a drawing of which Jahn after Braun, Mon. Ined. d. Instit. iii. 7, had prefixed to his edition of the Symposium (the original has vanished), is the only one which bears his name and displays any likeness. Other supposed busts of Plato represent Asclepios or the bearded Dionysos. Phavorinus in Diog. iii. 25 mentions a statue on his tomb by Silanion. According to Plut adul. et amor. c. 9, p. 53, Plato had high shoulders which his affected admirers tried to imitate, and according to Diog. 5, a thin clear voice.

himself on his contemporaries, and by his writings on after generations, that many myths should have placed him, like Pythagoras, in the closest union with the god who, in the bright clearness of his spirit, was to the Greeks the very type of moral beauty, proportion, and harmony.[111]

[111] This view had influence in the celebration of his birthday feast, and perhaps even in the particular date assigned for it: vide supr. 338, 1. We find from Diog. 2 (Olymp. 1 Prol. 1), Plut. Qu. Conv. viii. 1, 2, 4 · Apul. dogm Pl. 1, Æl. V. H x. 21, that even in Speusippus' time the tale went that Plato was a son of Apollo. As throwing light on the origin of these stories Steinhart (Pl. L. 8, 36, 282) refers to the Greek cultus of heroes, and particularly to the similar stories about Alexander; he indeed conjectures that it was owing to these same stories that people wished to place Plato as a spirit-hero beside the deified world-conqueror; for we cannot believe that this legend belongs to the time of Speusippus. I think we are not entitled to deny the possibility of this; especially as the stories about Pythagoras offer a still closer parallel than the stories about Alexander (cf. Vol. i. 265 sq.) However, it cannot be proved that the further amplification of the myth was already known to Speusippus, according to which a vision had forbidden Aristo to touch his wife before the birth of her first child. At the most important crisis of his life he is said to have been introduced to Socrates by a significant dream as the swan of Apollo, supra, p 9, 15. He himself dreamed, just before his death (according to Olymp. 6, Proleg. 2), that he had become a swan. We may recognise the theme of all these myths in 'the Phædo, 85 B. Later writers compare him as Physician of Souls, with Apollo's other son, Asclepius, the Physician of the Body. (Cf. Diog. 45; the idea can hardly be his own; out of his epigram Olymp. 6 makes an epitaph, and the Prol. 6, with some additions, an oracle) The pleasing story (given in Cic Div. i. 36, 78, Val Max. i. 6, ext. 3, Olymp. 1), of the bees on Hymettus feeding the child Plato with their honey, is brought by the Prol. C 2, into connection with a sacrifice to the shepherd god Apollo. Probably, however, it had an independent origin in the Apolline myth, as a natural symbol for one from whose lips, as from Nestor's, 'flowed forth speech, sweeter than honey.'

CHAPTER II.

PLATO'S WRITINGS. ENQUIRY AS TO THE COMPLETENESS AND GENUINENESS OF OUR COLLECTION.

THE most eloquent monument of the Platonic spirit, and the most important source for our knowledge of the Platonic doctrine, are in the writings of the philosopher himself.[1] His literary activity extends over the greater part of his life, a period of more than fifty years,[2]—and by a special favour of Fortune, it has so happened that not one of the works which he intended for publicity has been lost. This is at any rate a

---

[1] Schleiermacher, Platon's Werke, 6 Bde. 1804 (2nd edition 1816). Ast, Platon's Leben u. Schriften, 1816. Socher, Ueber Platon's Schriften, 1820. Hermann, Geschichte und System des Platonismus, 1830, p. 343 sqq. Ritter, Geschichte der Philosophie, vol ii. 181-211. Brandis, Griech-Rom. Phil ii a 151-182. Stallbaum, in his Introductions. Steinhart, in the Introductions to Plato's Works, translated by Muller, 1850 Suckow, Die Wissenschaftliche und Kunstlerische Form der Platonischen Schriften, 1855 Munk, Die Naturliche Ordnung der Plat Schriften, 1857. Susemihl, Die Genetische Entwickelung der Plat Phil., 1855. Ueberweg, Untersuchungen uber d. Echtheit und Zeitfolge der Plat Schrft., 1861. H v. Stein 7 Bucher z Gesch d. Plat. vol. 1, 2, 1862-1864. Schaarschmidt, die Sammlung d. plat. Schrift. 1866. Bonitz, Plat. Studien, 1858. Grote, Plato, 3 vols., 1865. Ribbing, Genet. Entw d. plat. Ideenlehre, Part ii

[2] We shall find that in all probability several of his dialogues were composed, partly after the death of Socrates, partly perhaps even before; ancient testimony abundantly proves his having continued his literary labours to the last (vide pp. 3; 35, 78). The Laws are said to have been found unfinished after his death (Diog. iii. 37), and there is also internal evidence that this work was his latest (vide subter).

reasonable inference from the fact that no reliable trace of the existence of any Platonic writing no longer in our possession has come down to us; for the spuriousness of the lost dialogues of which we do hear [3] is beyond question,[4] and some other writings which might be supposed to be Platonic,—the 'Divisions' ($\delta\iota\alpha\iota\rho\acute{\epsilon}\sigma\epsilon\iota\varsigma$),[5]

---

[3] Ap. Diog iii. 62: Μίδων, Φαίακες, Χελιδών, Ἑβδόμη, Ἐπιμενίδης, ap. Athen xi. 506, d., Κίμων, ap. Doxopat in Aphthon, Rhet. Graec. ed. Walz. II. 130, cf. Simpl. in Categ. 4 ζ, βas. Θεμιστόκλης (unless this is after all merely another title for the Cimon, in which, according to Athenæus, Themistocles was strongly criticised; we have no right with Hermann to conjecture 'Theætetus' instead of Themistocles, or to assume in the Cimon of Athenæus a confusion with the Gorgias) Other apocryphal writings are given by the Arabian in Casiri's Biblioth. Arab. 1 302, who professes to quote Theo.

[4] Diog loc. cit. introduces the list of the above mentioned and some other dialogues with the words νοθεύονται ὁμολογουμένως If we consider how ready the scholars of the Alexandrine period were to accept as Platonic a series of writings, the spuriousness of which we can scarcely doubt, we cannot avoid concluding that those writings which they unanimously rejected must have had very distinct signs of spuriousness, and must have appeared at a comparatively late period.

[5] Aristotle mentions repeatedly Platonic διαιρέσεις, Gen. et Corr ii. 3, 330, b. 15; those who presuppose only two original elements, represent the rest as a mixture of these; ὡσαύτως δὲ καὶ οἱ τρία λέγοντες, καθάπερ Πλάτων ἐν ταῖς διαιρέσεσιν · τὸ γὰρ μέσον (sc. στοιχεῖον) μῖγμα ποιεῖ. Part. Anim 1, 2, 642, b. 10, we must not form a classification of animals on different arrangements of the limbs, οἷον τοὺς ὄρνιθας τοὺς μὲν ἐν τῇδε τοὺς δὲ ἐν ἄλλῃ διαιρέσει, καθάπερ ἔχουσιν αἱ γεγραμμέναι διαιρέσεις· ἐκεῖ γὰρ τοὺς μὲν μετὰ τῶν ἐνύδρων συμβαίνει διῃρῆσθαι τοὺς δ' ἐν ἄλλῳ γένει. The first of these passages can refer neither to Philebus, 16 E, nor to Timæus, 27 D, 48 E sq, or 31 B sq 53 A sq.; for neither is the denotation διαιρέσεις appropriate to any of these passages, nor does any one of them contain the quotation here from the διαιρέσεις. The first four are not concerned with the corporeal elements, the ἁπλᾶ σώματα, to which the remark of Aristotle applies (though Ueberweg, Unters Plat Schrift disputes this); the Timæus 31 B sq. 53 A sq. certainly treats of these, but neither of the passages could well be denoted by διαιρέσεις, and both have four elements instead of the three which Aristotle found in the διαιρέσεις, and the two middle elements, so far from exhibiting a mixture of the two exterior, are rather (p. 53 B), according to their stereometric combination, related to only one of them, and with it stand in contrast to the other. We cannot, however, think of a refer-

Discourses about Philosophy, and about the Good,[6] the

ence to a merely orally delivered utterance of Plato's (Ueberweg, loc. cit. Susemihl, Genet. Entw. 11, 548), because in this case, according to Aristotle's invariable custom, instead of the present ποιεῖ a past tense must stand, and an oral exposition would without doubt have received some further notice. The διαιρέσεις here mentioned must therefore be a composition not included in our collection of Plato's works, either written by Plato himself, or else an exposition of Platonic doctrines In the second passage (Part. An.), Aristotle can only mean a written treatise by γεγραμμέναι διαιρέσεις ; and for this we must not think of any of the Platonic writings which have survived to us, because that denotation for any one of them or for any paragraph out of one of them would be very strange; and the quotation of Aristotle, about the birds being placed partly in the same class with the aquatic animals, partly in another class, is not to be found in the passages to which one would most readily turn in this case, Soph. 220 A sq ; Polit. 264 D (the former passage is referred to by Hermann, Plat. 594; Susemihl, loc. cit. Pilger uber die Athetese d. Plat. Soph. 6, the latter by Ueberweg, loc. cit. 153 sq.). On the contrary, the διαιρέσεις here are not referred to Plato, and so far the passage in Part. Anim. *taken by itself*, would not contradict the supposition of Suckow (Form d. Plat. Schr 97 sq.) that the γεγραμμέναι διαιρέσεις were neither a written treatise of Plato's, nor an exposition of Platonic doctrines (Suckow is entirely mistaken in saying that they could not be so because Plato is not here named; as we shall find, Aristotle very often refers to Plato without naming him) If, however, we are quite convinced from the passage De Gen. et Corr. that Aristotle actually had in his hands an exposition of Platonic Classifications, it is most natural to conclude that he is referring to the same book in De Part. Anim. It cannot however be supposed that this proceeded from Plato himself, or was at least given out as his work, because in that case Aristotle would have (Part. Anim 1, 2) expressed himself differently, and doubtless either this treatise itself or some more authentic trace of its existence would have been preserved than is found in its alleged transmission to Dionysius, Ep. Plat. xiii. 360 B. The latter passage seems rather to refer to the διαιρέσεις which Alexander apud Philoponum in Arist. De Gen. et Corr. 50 b., med. mentions among the spurious writings in circulation at his time under Plato's name, of which however Philoponus himself knew nothing. The διαιρέσεις referred to by Aristotle were a collection of classifications of mundane existences, used in the Academic school and based on Platonic enunciations. The existence of such a writing is shown by the fact that διαιρέσεις are attributed to Speusippus (Diog. iv. 5), Xenocrates (Ib. 13), and Aristotle (Diog. v. 23. Simpl. Categ. Schol. in Arist 47 b 40: the Arabian ap. Rose, Arist. Fragm. in 5th vol. Berl. Acad. Arist. 1471, 52); Hermodorus ap. Simpl. Phys 54 b. (transcribed in my Diatribe de Hermodoro, p. 20, and Susemihl's

'unwritten doctrines'[7]—originally never claimed to be the works of Plato at all.[8] There is no ground even for

Genet. Entw. ii. 522), seems to refer to Platonic discourses in which such classifications occurred. The assumption (Alberti Geist. und Ordn. d Plat. Schrf. 37, 64), that Aristotle was himself the composer of the διαιρέσεις which he refers to, is rendered highly improbable by the way in which they are cited and criticised; if the διαιρέσεις attributed to Aristotle by the later writers were the same as those from which Diog. iii. 80-109 borrowed what he tells us, with repeated reference to Aristotle, about the Platonic Classifications, they cannot be either (as Suckow thinks loc. cit. 96) a work of Aristotle, or one used by him, but merely a work of the later schools. Just as little can we look for the Διαιρέσεις referred to in Aristotle's exposition of the Platonic discourses on the Good (with Brandis, De perd Arist. libris 12). (On these discourses cf. Part ii. b 48, 2, 2nd edit) We should sooner look for the reference in the ἄγραφα δόγματα (vide p. 382, 2), Philop. loc. cit., Karsten de Plat epist. 218; Schaarschmidt, Samml. d. Plat. Schr. 104; still the different denotation makes us suppose different writings. But however that may be, in any case we cannot consider the Διαιρέσεις referred to by Aristotle to be either a Platonic or an Aristotelian writing. The Διαιρέσεις which were subsequently current under the name of one or the other of these two philosophers can only be considered as a post-Aristotelian interpolation or perhaps a recasting of the older work.

[6] Cf. p. 26, 53, 54, and Part ii. b.

48, 2, 2nd edit.

[7] Phys iv. 2, 209 b. 13. Aristotle says, after he has mentioned the determinations of the Timæus about space, ἄλλον δὲ τρόπον ἐκεῖ τε λέγων τὸ μεταληπτικὸν καὶ ἐν τοῖς λεγομένοις ἀγράφοις δόγμασιν, ὅμως τὸν τόπον καὶ τὴν χώραν τὸ αὐτὸ ἀπεφήνατο. It is manifest that no Platonic written treatise can be intended by these ἄγραφα δόγματα, yet on the other hand this name is not suited for a reference to an oral discourse as such; we can therefore only understand by it a collection of notes of such Platonic views as were still up to that time ἄγραφα, embodying the contents of Platonic discourses. The way, however, in which the allusion is made precludes the supposition that Aristotle himself was the author of this collection (as Philop. ib., Schol. in Ar. 371 b. 25, and Gen. et Corr. 50 b. thinks); and though Simplicius (Phys. 126 a. m. 127 a. o. Schol. in Ar. 371 b. 3, 372 a. 21) is right in referring the ἄγραφα δόγμ. to ἄγραφοι συνουσίαι of Plato, still he is hardly justified in understanding by them συνουσίαι specially on the Good Themist. on the passage (p. 259, Speng.), states on mere conjecture (his own or some one's else) that in the ἄγρ δόγμ. Plato represented matter as participating in the ideas not κατὰ μέθεξιν, as in the Timæus, but καθ' ὁμοίωσιν: Aristotle is speaking merely of a variation in the denotation of the participating matter itself.

[8] The expressions which Arist. Top vi. 2, 140 a. 3, cites as Platonic occurred not in lost

thinking that any Platonic writing was ever more complete than it is now.[9]

Fortune has indeed bestowed less care on the purity of the Platonic collection. Even the learned among the Greeks regarded as spurious several of the writings that bore Plato's name;[10] the critics of our own century,

---

writings, but in oral discourses; whatever in Timæus' Platonic Lexicon is alien to Plato's works as we have them, comes generally not from Plato, but from another writer; vide Hermann, Plato, 556. As regards the remarkable statement of an obscure myth-writer of the middle ages (in A. Mai's Auct. Class. 183) who appeals to an alleged 'Philosophus' of Plato in support of a very un-Platonic view of the origin of the belief in Gods, cf. Schaarschmidt, Samml. d. plat. Schr. 89.

[9] For, from Menander π. ἐπιδεικτ. p. 143 W. 337 Sp (ὁ γοῦν Πλάτων ὕμνον τοῦ παντὸς τὸν Τίμαιον καλεῖ ἐν τῷ Κριτίᾳ) we cannot conclude that this rhetorician had the Critias in a more complete form than we have. Had this been so, still further traces of it would have been preserved; whereas we see from Plut Solon, 32, that in Plutarch's time only the introduction and the beginning of the narrative remained; his words seem rather to be merely an inexact expression, meaning that the subject of the Timæus was treated in the beginning of the Critias as a hymn of praise to the Cosmos, because Timæus here prays to the God, whose origin he has described, that, in case he has uttered anything παρὰ μέλος, God would τὸν πλημμελοῦντα ἐμμελῆ ποιεῖν.

[10] All the lost dialogues (vide p. 46, 3) and those of the existing number marked in the editions as Dialogi nothi, except the Clitophon (vide Hermann, pp. 424, 594, 225, et cet). Even in ancient times the Epinomis (Diog. iii. 37, Suid. φιλόσοφος. Prolegg. in Plat. c. 25, following Proclus) was by many ascribed to Philippus of Opus, the second Alcibiades (Athen. xi. 506 c), to Xenophon (this cannot possibly be right), and the Anterastæ and Hipparchus were considered doubtful (Thrasylus, ap. Diog. ix. 37, and Æl. V. H. viii. 2 respectively). On the contrary, it is scarcely credible that Panætius actually condemned the Phædo as spurious, in order to deprive the belief in immortality of the authority of Plato (Asclepius, Schol. in Ar. 576 a. 39. Anthol. Græc. ix. 358; according to David, Schol. in Ar. 30 b. 8 Syrian, as our text stands, the latter Epigram was written on the Phædrus, for which, however, the Phædo is obviously to be read), this statement seems to have originated in a misunderstanding of the tradition of Panætius' doubts as to the genuineness of the Phædo, and of his opposition to the Platonic doctrine of immortality (Cic. Tusc i. 32, 79). Had he declared the Phædo spurious on the grounds stated, he would have spared himself this opposition.

sometimes unanimously, sometimes by an overwhelming majority, have rejected a still greater number; others are yet upon their trial, and among these, as formerly happened on the first appearance of Ast[11] and Socher,[12] is to be found more than one work the repudiation of which would considerably affect our apprehension of the Platonic philosophy. Though an exhaustive investigation of this subject would exceed the limits of the present treatise, we must to a certain extent examine it, and notice the points of view on which our judgment of it depends. With regard then first to the external evidence, from the consideration of which every such enquiry must start,—by far the most important is that of Aristotle. For setting this aside, very few remarks of ancient authors concerning the works of Plato have been handed down to us,[13] either from his own or

[11] Platon's Leben und Schriften, 1816.

[12] Ueber Platon's Schriften, 1820.

[13] Isocrates certainly seems to mean Plato's political writings by his mention (Philippic 13, written 346 B.C.) of νόμοις καὶ πολιτείαις ταῖς ὑπὸ τῶν σοφιστῶν γεγραμμέναις. Still this reference, if the passage be taken by itself, cannot prove that Plato was the only one or the first who had written on the formation of the state and on laws; we know of several similar works, besides those of Plato, in the period before Isocrates: the Πολιτεία of Protagoras, the work of Antisthenes π. νόμου ἢ π. πολιτείας (Diog. vi. 16), those of Phaleas and Hippodamus (Arist. Polit ii 7, 8, who also 1267 b. 37, 1268 a. 6, in reference to the latter of the two, expressly mentions his proposals as regards the νόμοι), and Polit. 1, 6, 1255 a. 7, Arist. speaks of πολλοὶ τῶν ἐν τοῖς νόμοις, who dispute the right of enslaving captives made in war. Still less can we, with Suckow (Form. d. plat. Schr. 103 sq.), infer from the plural σοφιστῶν, that Isocrates attributed the Republic and the Laws to different authors; cf. Ueberweg, Plat. Schr. 184 sq. From the statement of Theopompus, quoted p. 38, 94, we cannot gather what Platonic writings he had before him. On the contrary, it appears from Plut. An. Procr. 3, 1; Alex. on Metaph. 1091 a. 27; cf. Arist. De Cœlo, 1, 10, 279 b. 32; and other authorities to be mentioned later on, that Xenocrates noticed the Timæus; according to Suid. Ξενοκρ. he also wrote περὶ τῆς Πλάτωνος πολιτείας; Diog. iv. 82, how-

the succeeding century; and these relate almost entirely to writings which Aristotle, too, distinctly ascribes to Plato. Towards the end of the third century, Aristophanes of Byzantium first arranged a portion of the works in those five Trilogies which we know from Diog. iii. 61 :[14] and fully two centuries later, Thrasylus made a catalogue of them in nine Tetralogies,[15] which catalogue, with a few very unimportant exceptions, contains all the writings transmitted to us as Platonic.[16] Grote[17] thinks we may place entire confidence, not only in the statements of Aristophanes, but even in the catalogue of Thrasylus. It cannot be supposed, he argues, that the school of Athens, which was continued in an

ever, mentions only a treatise π. πολιτείας. Theophrastus refers to the Timæus (Fragm. 28, 34–49 Wimm.,) to the Laws (xi. 915 D). See Fr. 97, 5 (Stobæus, Florilegium 44, 22, end). Eudemus, Eth. Eud. vii. 14, 1247, b. 15, must refer to the Euthydemus (279 D sq., 281 B), inasmuch as what is here quoted as Socratic is to be found there and there only; Eth. Eud. vii. 13, 1246, b. 34, seems to refer to the Protagoras, 352, B, C, and Eth. Eud. iii. 1, 1229, a. 15, to Protag. 360 D; Eth. Eud. vii. 5, 6, 1239, b 13, 1240, b. 17, seems to be connected with the Lysis, 214 C sq., for here the Eudemian text comes nearer the Platonic dialogue than the parallel passage of the Nicomachean Ethics, ix. 10, 1159, b. 7. Aristotle (vide sup. 38, 94) speaks of the Platonic Republic; Dicæarchus of the Phædrus (ap. Diog. iii. 38); Timon of the Timæus (vide p. 20, 38); the first commentary on the latter dialogue was written by Crantor (supra, p. 696 d. 2nd edit.); the Stoic Persæus wrote against Plato's Laws, 260–250 B C. (Diog. vii. 36).

[14] The first included the Republic, Timæus, Critias, the second the Sophist, Politicus, Cratylus, the third the Laws, Minos, Epinomis, the fourth the Theætetus, Euthyphro, Apology; the fifth the Crito, Phædo, the Letters; 'τὰ δ' ἄλλα καθ' ἓν καὶ ἀτάκτως' Suckow, Form. d. plat. Schr. 163, I think wrongly, denies that this division into trilogies really belongs to Aristophanes.

[15] Ap. Diog. iii. 56 sq.

[16] Besides the dialogues mentioned p 46, 5, there are wanting in it only the two small dialogues π. δικαίου and π. ἀρετῆς, the Definitions, and the Letters nos. 14–19, first admitted by Hermann in his edition.

[17] Plato and the other Companions of Socrates, 1, 132 sq.

E 2

unbroken line from its commencement, should not have been completely and accurately informed of all that its founder had written. On the contrary, there can be no doubt that his very handwriting was carefully preserved there; and the members of the Academy were thus in a position to furnish the most trustworthy information to anyone who sought it, concerning the authenticity or the text of a Platonic work. Such an opportunity would surely not have been neglected by Demetrius Phalereus and his successors at the founding of the Alexandrian Library. They would either have procured copies of the original manuscripts of Plato, or have instituted enquiries in Athens as to the authenticity of the works which they received into their collection, causing a catalogue to be made of all the undoubted writings; and since Aristophanes certainly, and Thrasylus probably, followed in their catalogues the Alexandrian tradition, the statements of these writers may be fairly supposed entitled to a high degree of credit. This theory, however, rests wholly upon a series of uncertain presuppositions. It may be that the original manuscripts of Plato, or copies of his works used by himself, were preserved in the Academy, though not a particle of historical evidence on the subject exists; but even supposing such to have been the case, who can guarantee that not only Plato's personal disciples, but their successors, were so convinced of the completeness of their collection, and so jealously watchful over its purity, as to deny admittance to every book not included in it, and represented to them as Platonic? Not to mention that there are many conceivable cases in which the manuscript collection in possession of the school might have to be completed by genuine Platonic works.[18] And granted that the Academy had indeed never admitted any spurious writing into their library, how can we be sure that the Alexandrian librarians were equally scrupulous? They certainly might, on the above presupposition, have informed themselves in Athens as to the works which were there acknowledged to be authentic, but how can we know that they actually did this? There is not the slightest warrant for the assertion; but on the other hand we are told that the high prices paid for writings in Alexandria and Pergamus gave great encouragement to forgery,[19] and that in particular many works were

---

[18] If we suppose that letters of Plato really existed, there is no necessity that copies of them should be found in his literary remains; supposing that the libraries of Speusippus and Xenocrates met with any accident, as might easily have happened during the struggles of the Diadochi for the possession of Athens, or that some of their parts were lost, nothing would have remained but to supply them from without. However, we cannot take into account these possibilities, as has been said it is sufficient that we know nothing as to how Plato's writings were preserved in his school, or what precautions were taken to maintain the collection in its integrity.

[19] Galen in Hippocr. de nat. hom. 1, 42, xv. 105, K. πρὶν γὰρ τοὺς ἐν Ἀλεξανδρείᾳ τε καὶ Περγάμῳ γενέσθαι βασιλεῖς ἐπὶ κτήσει βιβλίων φιλοτιμηθέντας οὐδέπω ψευδῶς ἐπεγέγραπτο σύγγραμμα, λαμβάνειν δ' ἀρξαμένων μισθὸν τῶν κομιζόντων αὐτοῖς σύγγραμμα παλαιοῦ τινος ἀνδρός, οὕτως ἤδη πολλὰ ψευδῶς ἐπιγράφοντες ἐκόμιζον. (Similarly Simpl. in Categ. 2 e. Schol. in Ar. 28, a. infra.) Galen obviously goes too far here in supposing that before the establishment of these two great libraries there had been no forging of books; and still less can we agree with the conclusion of Grote (loc. cit. 155), that as the rivalry of these two libraries first gave occasion for such forgeries, and the library of Pergamus was not founded till 230 B.C., we are not to suppose any forgeries before this time. Of this supposed rivalry Galen says nothing; φιλοτιμεῖσθαι means simply to seek after reputation or glory in anything, to display zeal; Simplicius uses the word σπουδάζειν for it.

falsely attributed to Aristotle, in order that they might be bought by Ptolemy Philadelphus.[20] When we further consider the state of literary criticism in the post Aristotelian period, it seems unreasonable to credit the Alexandrians with having tested the authenticity of works bearing illustrious names, so carefully and accurately as Grote presupposes. The catalogues of Aristophanes and Thrasylus therefore merely prove that the writings they include were held to be Platonic at the time of these grammarians; whether they really were so or not, can only be determined by a particular enquiry into each work, according to the general rules of criticism.

The statements of Aristotle afford a much safer criterion;[21] but even with regard to these, the case is by no means so simple as might be supposed. In the first place, it is sometimes doubtful whether the writing or the passage which refers to a saying of Plato's in truth emanates from Aristotle; and this doubt has already destroyed or weakened the argumentative force of some quotations.[22] But even though the Aristotelian

[20] Cf. Part ii. b. 87, 6, 2nd edit.

[21] A collection of all the references in Aristotle to Plato's writings was attempted by Trendlenburg, Plat de id. et num. doctr. 13 sq.; then in my Platon. Stud. 201 sq Next Suckow (Form. d. plat. Schr 49 sq.), Ueberweg (Unters. plat. Schr. 131 sq.), and Schaarschmidt (Samml. d. plat. Schr. 90 sq.) thoroughly examined these evidences. Still, Bonitz, in his Index Aristotelicus, 598 sq., gives the most exhaustive catalogue of them To this reference is to be made in case of dialogues, the citations from which in what follows are not discussed in detail.

[22] As the citation of the Laws (iv 715, E sq.) at the end of the spurious work π. κόσμου, p. 401; of the Timæus (77 B), π. φυτῶν, 1, 815 a. 21; of the Euthydemus (279 D sq.), in the Eudemian Ethics (vide p. 50, 13). The citation of the Sophist also (254 A) in the xi. Bk. of the Metaphysics c 8, 1064, b. 29, might also be claimed, because not merely is the

authorship of a passage apparently relating to Platonic writings be fully established, the reference is not

second part of this book decidedly spurious, but the genuineness of the first is anything but firmly established (c. 1-8, 1065, a. 26). Still, after repeated examination, I think it is more probably an earlier abstract, perhaps a rough sketch noted down by Aristotle for the purposes of his lectures, rather than a later epitome of Bks. iii. iv. vi. The quotation of the Apology and of the Menexenus, in the 3rd Bk. of the Rhetoric, gives almost more ground for doubt. For though the contents of this book, as a whole, seem sufficiently Aristotelian in character, still the question arises whether, in the form in which we have it, it constituted an original part of Aristotle's Rhetoric, or whether it was not added by a later writer to the first books, perhaps based on notes or a lecture of Aristotle's. In support of the latter supposition, besides other points, might be quoted the fact, that, according to Rhetor. 1, 1, especially p. 1054, b. 16 sq., it seems doubtful whether Aristotle would, on the whole, have treated in his Rhetoric the subjects discussed in the 3rd Bk.; and again, the 3rd Bk. c. 17, returns to the question of the πίστεις, which the first two books had already thoroughly entered into. Especially might we be inclined to suspect a different hand in many of the examples which are accumulated in the 3rd Book and worked out with proportionate detail; and in reference to this, it is worth noticing that quotations, which have already occurred in the first and second books, repeatedly appear in the third book in a more complete form. In i. 9, 1367, b. 8, a saying of the historical Socrates is briefly mentioned (ὥσπερ γὰρ ὁ Σωκρ. ἔλεγεν, οὐ χαλεπὸν Ἀθηναίους ἐν Ἀθηναίοις ἐπαινεῖν;) in Bk. iii. 14, 1415, b. 30, this is more fully quoted from the Menexenus (235 D, 236 A): ὁ γὰρ λέγει Σωκρ. ἐν τῷ ἐπιταφίῳ ἀληθές, ὅτι οὐ χαλεπὸν Ἀθηναίους ἐν Ἀθηναίοις ἐπαινεῖν, ἀλλ' ἐν Λακεδαιμονίοις. Whereas, ii. 23, 1398, a. 15, as an example of a proof, ἐξ ὁρισμοῦ, the following is quoted: οἷον ὅτι τὸ δαιμόνιον οὐδέν ἐστιν ἀλλ' ἢ θεὸς ἢ θεοῦ ἔργον, in iii. 18, 1419, a. 8, we find a quotation of four lines from the Platonic Apology, 27 B–D. The quotation from Theodectes, ii. 23, 1399, b 28, occurs again, III. 15, and is treated of at greater length, from 1416, b. 1-3, we learn the particulars about a passage of the Teucer of Sophocles, which, in 1398, a. 4, was briefly alluded to. Again, it is remarkable that, iii. 14. the Menexenus is denoted by ὁ ἐπιτάφιος (without any specification), while by the like expression, 111, 10, 14, 11, a. 31, the Epitaphios of Lysias is meant. These circumstances certainly give some grounds for doubting whether the fuller quotations of the Apology and Menexenus in the 3rd Bk. of the Rhetoric proceed from Aristotle himself. On the other hand, I cannot agree with Schaarschmidt (Samml. d. plat. Schrf. 383), who remarks, from the passages in Metaph v. 29, 1025, a 6, relative to the Lesser Hippias, that it is

56   *PLATO AND THE OLDER ACADEMY.*

always of a kind that implies an unequivocal recognition of the writings. If not merely the name of the writing is given, but also that of the author; if Aristotle says, 'Plato remarks in the Timæus, Republic,'[23] &c., there can of course be no hesitation as to his meaning. But not unfrequently the writing in which some passage is to be found is named without mention of its author; or conversely, utterances and opinions are ascribed to Plato, and nothing is stated concerning the writings in which they occur; or lastly, reference is made to theories and expressions contained in our Platonic collection, and yet there is no allusion either to Plato as their author, or to a particular writing as their source.[24] It also happens sometimes that a passage from some dialogue is quoted with an express mention of the dialogue, and yet is attributed to Socrates, and not to Plato.[25] In all these cases, the question arises whether or not we can claim Aristotelian evidence for the Platonic origin of the writings concerned; but a portion of them only need occasion us any serious doubt. If Aristotle, in naming a dialogue, remarks, 'Socrates

---

more than improbable that Aristotle himself published the book quoted, especially in the form we have it. Undoubtedly the 6th Bk. of the Metaphysics is proved to be genuine by Aristotle himself (cf. Part ii. b. 58, 2nd edit., and Arist. Gen. et Corr. 11, 10, 336, b. 29, cf. Metaph. v 7)—possibly not as a part of this work, but at any rate as an independent Aristotelian treatise—and there is no reason at all to suppose that we have it merely in the form of a later recasting.

[23] The quotations to which Bonitz in his Index has prefixed *a*.

[24] The three cases denoted by Bonitz b c d.

[25] E g. Gen et Corr. 11, 9, 335, b. 9. οἱ μὲν ἱκανὴν ᾠήθησαν αἰτίαν εἶναι πρὸς τὸ γενέσθαι τὴν τῶν εἰδῶν φύσιν, ὥσπερ ὁ ἐν Φαίδωνι Σωκράτης. Bonitz ranges these cases in the first class, distinguished, however, from those in which Plato is mentioned by the addition of α Σωκρ.

here maintains this or that,' he always means by it that Plato in this dialogue has put the remark into the mouth of Socrates. For not only does he employ the same mode of expression as to writings which he elsewhere most emphatically attributes to Plato,[26] but he never quotes an opinion or a saying of Socrates from any writing that is not in our Platonic collection; though he must certainly have been acquainted with the Socratic dialogues of Xenophon, Æschines, and Antisthenes.[27] Indeed the Socratic utterances are regarded by him as so completely identical with Plato's works, that he even designates the Laws as Socratic,[28] although Socrates never appears in them, and is probably not intended by the Athenian stranger; and he quotes views which were entirely originated by Plato and put in the mouth of his master, simply as the views of Socrates,[29] without any discrimination of the

---

[26] As in the criticism of the Platonic Republic, Polit ii. 1, c 6, 1065, b. 1; Ibid. iv 4, 1291, a. 11 (φησὶ γὰρ ὁ Σωκράτης). viii. 7, 1342, a. 33, b 23, v 12, 1316, a. 1 sqq. (ἐν δὲ τῇ πολιτείᾳ λέγεται μὲν . . . . ὑπὸ τοῦ Σωκράτους, and the like): Gen. et Corr. II, 9, vide previous note. Similarly Polit. II, 4, 1262, b 11, after it has been mentioned that Socrates (i.e the Platonic Socrates in the Republic) wished the State to have the greatest possible unity, come the words, καθάπερ ἐν τοῖς ἐρωτικοῖς ἴσμεν λέγοντα τὸν Ἀριστοφάνην, where Plato's Symposium is meant

[27] Arist. relates in the historic tense (Σωκρ. ᾤετο, ἐζήτει, &c.) many things about Socrates which he may have borrowed from Xenophon or some other source of tradition: but he never quotes in the present tense (Σωκρ. φησὶ, &c) and from a writing mentioned by name, anything Socratic which is not to be found in our Platonic dialogues. In the historic tense there is only one undoubted reference to the Memorabilia of Xenophon, (Mem. i. 2, 54) in Eudemus (Eth. End. vii. 1. 1235, a. 37).

[28] Polit. ii 6, 1265, a. 10 (with reference to the Laws): τὸ μὲν οὖν περιττὸν ἔχουσι πάντες οἱ τοῦ Σωκράτους λόγοι κ τ.λ. In the preceding passage, too, the grammatical subject to 'εἴρηκεν' &c. is Σωκράτης

[29] Cf. Polit. ii. 3, 1261, b. 19,

Platonic from the historic Socrates. If, therefore, a dialogue in our collection is thus treated by Aristotle, we may be certain that he considers it a work of Plato.[30] The same holds good as to dialogues which are cited without the name either of Socrates or Plato.[31] This kind of quotation only presupposes that the writing in question is known to the reader, and will not be mistaken for anything else; we therefore find it employed

21. τοῦτο γὰρ οἴεται ὁ Σωκρ. . . . βούλεται ποιεῖν ὁ Σωκρ. c. 4. 1262, b. 6: δι' ἣν αἰτίαν ὁ Σωκρ. οὕτως οἴεται θεῖν τάττειν, c. 5. 1263, b. 29· αἴτιον δὲ τῷ Σωκράτει τῆς παρακρούσεως χρὴ νομίζειν τῆς ὑπόθεσιν οὐκ οὖσαν ὀρθήν. Polit. viii. 7 1342, b. 23: διὸ καλῶς ἐπιτιμῶσι καὶ τοῦτο Σωκράτει (i.e. the Socr. of the Republic) τῶν περὶ τὴν μουσικήν τινες κ τ.λ.

[30] Ueberweg in contending that the Menexenus in Rhet. iii. 14. 1415, b 30 is not quoted as Platonic, has paid too little attention to the true state of the case. If this citation is really Aristotle's (on this cf. p. 54, 22), we can only conclude that in conformity with his invariable custom he wished here to denote the Menexenus as Platonic, just as much as in the cases of the Republic, the Phædo, and the Symposium quoted at page 57, 26.

[31] As the Timæus, De cœlo iii. 2. 300, b. 17· καθάπερ ἐν τῷ Τιμαίῳ γέγραπται. De Animâ i 3, 406, b. 26. τὸν αὐτὸν δὲ τρόπον (as Democritus) καὶ ὁ Τίμαιος φυσιολογεῖ, and frequently (see Bonitz's Index); the Phædo, Meteorol. ii. 2, 355, b. 32: τὸ δ' ἐν τῷ Φαίδωνι γεγραμμένον . . . ἀδύνατόν ἐστι (I must retract the doubts of my Platon. Stud. 207. as regards the authenticity of this passage); the Phædrus, Rhet iii 7, 1408, b. 20: ὅπερ Γοργίας ἐποίει καὶ τὰ ἐν τῷ Φαίδρῳ; the Meno, Anal. post. 71, a. 29. εἰ δὲ μὴ, τὸ ἐν τῷ Μένωνι ἀπόρημα συμβήσεται. Anal. prior. ii. 21, 67, a. 21: ὁμοίως δὲ καὶ ὁ ἐν τῷ Μένωνι λόγος, ὅτι ἡ μάθησις ἀνάμνησις; the Gorgias, Soph. Elench. 12, 173, a. 7: ὥσπερ καὶ ὁ Καλλικλῆς ἐν τῷ Γοργίᾳ γέγραπται λέγων: the Lesser Hippias, Metaph. v. 29, 1025, a 6· διὸ ὁ ἐν τῷ Ἱππίᾳ λόγος παρακρούεται, &c. Schaarschmidt (Samml d. plat. Schr. 383) says indeed of the latter quotation: 'The writer of the dialogue is here spoken of in a tone of depreciation which we can hardly imagine Aristotle employing with regard to Plato.' However, for the estimation of this assertion it is sufficient to refer to the passages quoted in note 29 from Polit. ii 5; viii. 7. In addition to this Schaarschmidt himself remarks on the same page, 'the condemnatory judgment of Aristotle on the dialogue before us, taken by itself, does not prove that he considered Plato to be the author.' For a further objection to this assertion, vide p. 54, 22.

about other works that are universally famous;[32] but among the philosophic writings which Aristotle mentions in this way, there is none which does not belong to our Platonic collection: the Platonic writings, as before remarked, are the only writings of the Socratic school to which he ever refers. This circumstance makes it extremely probable that Aristotle really intends to ascribe all the writings quoted by him in this form to Plato, otherwise we should certainly have had a right to expect that those which he considered spurious, especially if in their style and treatment they might claim to be Platonic, would not have been introduced without some hint as to the true state of the case. For he could not presuppose this to be necessarily known to his readers.[33]

As to those passages which attribute to Plato or Socrates theories and sayings to be met with in the Platonic writings, but which do not mention the writings, Aristotle himself very often furnishes us with a proof that he is really referring to these by his use of the present tense: 'Plato maintains,' 'Socrates says,' and the like.[34] When he employs this form

[32] E g the Iliad and Odyssee, and many passages of Sophocles and Euripides; cf. Index Aristotelicus under 'Ἰλιάς, 'Οδυσσεία, Σοφοκλῆς, Εὐριπίδης Even the funeral oration of Lysias (§ 60) is quoted Rhet. iii. 10, 1411, a. 31 (on which, however, cf. p 54, 22) merely with the words: οἷον ἐν τῷ ἐπιταφίῳ, and the Μεσσηνιακὸς of Alcidamas, which had been already cited, Rhet i 13, 1373, b. 18, is referred to, II. 23, 1397, a. 11 equally without the author's name.

[33] Schaarschmidt (plat. Schr. 342, 383) is therefore wrong, in my opinion, in denying that the Meno and the Lesser Hippias were attributed to Plato by Aristotle

[34] As Metaph. xii. 6; 1071, b. 32 (Λεύκιππος καὶ Πλάτων) ἀεὶ εἶναί φασι κίνησιν (which acc. to De Cœlo iii. 2, 300, b. 16, comes from the Timæus, 30, A.) Ibid 37, ἀλλὰ μὴν οὐδὲ Πλάτωνί γε οἷόν τε λέγειν ἣν οἴεται ἐνίοτε (Phædr. 245,

of expression, it is a sure indication that he has in his mind those Socratic or Platonic discourses which are laid down in writings;[35] and when we find these very discourses in a work that tradition assures us to be Platonic, it is hardly possible to doubt that this is the work to which the quotation relates. An appeal of this kind to Socratic or Platonic utterances, therefore, if these conditions fully obtain, has no less force than the literal mention of the particular writing, and the express acknowledgment of its Platonic origin. On the other hand, however, we must not conclude that Aristotle, whenever he makes use of the preterite in mentioning a doctrine of Socrates or Plato, refers only indirectly, or not at all,[36] to the writings that contain it. Several cases are here to be distinguished. In the first place, the perfect tense may properly be employed, and is very commonly employed by Aristotle, in quoting the sayings of Plato, or of the Platonic Socrates, from a writing.[37] It is somewhat different with the

C sq. Laws x. 895, E sq) ἀρχὴν εἶναι, τὸ αὐτὸ ἑαυτὸ κινοῦν. ὕστερον γὰρ καὶ ἅμα τῷ οὐρανῷ ἡ ψυχὴ ὥς φησίν (Tim. 34, B sq.). Phys. viii. 1, 251, b 17: Πλάτων δ' αὐτὸν [τὸν χρόνον] γεννᾷ μόνος· ἅμα μὲν γὰρ αὐτὸν τῷ οὐρανῷ γεγονέναι . . φησίν (Tim. 37, D sq). Metaph iii. 5, 1010, b. 12: ὥσπερ καὶ Πλάτων λέγει (Theæt. 171, E 178, C). Top. iv. 2, 122, b. 26: ὡς Πλάτων ὁρίζεται φορὰν τὴν κατὰ τόπον κίνησιν (Theæt 181, C; the same statement occurs also Parm. 138, B sq). Eth. x. 2, 1172, b. 28. τοιούτῳ δὴ λόγῳ καὶ Πλάτων (Phileb. 22, A 60, C sq.) ἀναιρεῖ ὅτι οὐκ ἔστιν ἡδονὴ τἀγαθόν.

[35] As a rule, where the writings are named, the reference is made in the present tense. cf. the quotations in the Index Arist. denoted by a.

[36] As Ueberweg believes, Plat. Schr 140 sq. Cf. on the other side, Bernays apud Schaarschmidt Rhein. Mus. N. F. xviii., 3 sq. Alberti Geist u. Ordn. d. plat. Schr. 54.

[37] E g. Polit. ii. 5, 1264, a 12. οὔτ' εἴρηκεν ὁ Σωκράτης (in the Platonic Republic). Ibid. b. 24: ἡ πολιτεία περὶ ἧς ὁ Σωκρ. εἴρηκεν. c. 6, 1264, b. 28, 36 ἐν τῇ πολιτείᾳ περὶ ὀλίγων πάμπαν διώρικεν ὁ Σωκρ. . . . περὶ τούτων οὐδὲν διώρικεν ὁ Σ.

narrative forms—the imperfect and aorist. These are only used in respect to Socrates when some theory is to be ascribed to the historic Socrates, supposing it to have become known to Aristotle through certain writings.[38] For it might very well be said of the Platonic Socrates that he maintains something (in the present), or that something is in question as said by him (in the perfect), but not that he formerly has said something, because as this ideal person he exists for the reader of the Platonic writings, and for him only, in the present; he has no existence independently of the reader and belonging to the past. If, however, Plato himself is mentioned as having said or thought something, this consideration has no longer any force. His utterances

---

1266, a. 1 : ἐν δὲ τοῖς νόμοις εἴρηται τούτοις c 9. 1271, a. 41 : τῇ ὑποθέσει τοῦ νομοθέτου ἐπιτιμήσειεν ἄν τις, ὅπερ καὶ Πλάτων ἐν τοῖς νόμοις ἐπετετίμηκεν. Top. vi. 3, 140, b 3 : κάθαπερ Πλάτων ὥρισται. Soph. Elench. 12, 173, a. 8 ὁ Καλλικλῆς ἐν τῷ Γοργίᾳ γέγραπται λέγων. Phys. iv. 2, 210, a 1: ὥσπερ ἐν τῷ Τιμαίῳ γέγραφεν. Likewise Gen. et Corr. 1, 8, 325, b. 24: ὥσπερ ἐν τῷ Τιμαίῳ γέγραφε Πλάτων, and frequently.

[38] E g. Eth. N. vii. 3, 1145, b 23 sq.: ὡς ᾤετο Σωκράτης ... Σωκρ. μὲν γὰρ ὅλως ἐμάχετο πρὸς τὸν λόγον κ.τ.λ. Cf. Protag. 352, B sq. Polit. i. 13, 1260, a. 21 : the virtue of the man and of the woman is not the same, κάθαπερ ᾤετο Σωκρ. Cf. Meno 73, A sq So, too, Eth. N. iii 11, 1116, b. 3 the quotation from Socrates, which occurs in Protag. 349 E sq. 360, C sq. is denoted by the past tense ᾠήθη (in the parallel passage in Eth.

Eud. iii 1, 1229, a. 15 by ἔφη), Rhet. iii. 18, 1419, a. 8 sq the conversation between Socrates and Meletus, which Plato narrates Apol 27, B sq, is denoted as historical by the past tenses εἴρηκεν, ἤρετο, ἔφη, &c., and Rhet. ii. 9, 1367, b. 8 the saying that it is easy enough to panegyrize the Athenians in Athens, is attributed to the historical Socrates by the introductory formula ὥσπερ γὰρ ὁ Σωκράτης ἔλεγεν, Rhet. iii. 14, 1415, b. 30, where the same expression is quoted from the Menexenus, the words are quite in conformity with Aristotle's custom : ὁ γὰρ λέγει Σωκρ. ἐν τῷ ἐπιταφίῳ. On the other hand, in Gen et Corr ii. 9, 335, b. 9 (οἱ μὲν ἱκανὴν ᾠήθησαν αἰτίαν εἶναι πρὸς τὸ γενέσθαι τὴν τῶν εἰδῶν φύσιν, ὥσπερ ἐν Φαίδωνι Σωκράτης) we must supply the present οἴεται as the finite verb to ὥσπερ, κ.τ.λ.

are not merely sayings which are present to us in his works, but also acts which he completed in the compilation of those works; in that case, therefore, a historic tense, as well as a present, might be used in quoting them. Though this does not occur very frequently, it is sometimes to be met with,[39] and we have consequently no right to conclude from the use of the preterite in the quotation of a Platonic saying, that it is not derived from any written work.[40]

But there are also many passages in Aristotle where neither Plato nor any one of his dialogues is mentioned, but which have internal evidence to show that Aristotle in writing them had definitely in view particular works of Plato, and which very often allude to these [41] unmistakably, though indirectly. The argu-

[39] Eth. N i 2, 1095, a 32 (εὖ γὰρ καὶ Πλάτων ἠπόρει τοῦτο καὶ ἐζήτει) need not be brought in here, because in this case (besides Republic vi. 511, B) the reference seems rather to oral utterances. But the use of the past tense above remarked occurs decidedly Gen et Corr. ii. 5, 332, a. 29 · ὥσπερ ἐν τῷ Τιμαίῳ Πλάτων ἔγραψεν. Phys. iv. 2, 209, b 15 (Plato, in Timæus 52, A sq.) τὸν τόπον καὶ τὴν χώραν τὸ αὐτὸ ἀπεφήνατο. Polit. ii. 7, 1266, b. 5: Πλάτων δὲ τοὺς νόμους γράφων . . . ᾤετο. Also Gen. et Corr. i. 2, 315, a. 29, the words: Πλάτων μὲν οὖν μόνον περὶ γενέσεως ἐσκέψατο κ.τ λ refer to the Timæus, as we see from what follows (315, b. 30; 316, a. 2 sq.). A similar expression is used De sensu c. 5, 443, b. 30, in referring to a verse from the Phœnissæ of Strattis, ἀληθὲς γὰρ ὅπερ Εὐριπίδην σκώπτων εἶπε Στράττις.

[40] As Ueberweg, Plat. Schr. 153 sq. in remarking on Metaph. vi. 2, 1026, b. 14 and xi. 8, 1064, b. 29 (vide p 399, 2) the past tenses here used, ἔταξεν and εἴρηκε φήσας, (which latter, except as a perfect, cannot be brought under consideration here, in accordance with the above remarks) refer to oral utterances.

[41] The formulæ which Aristotle makes use of here are all pretty much to the same effect, Phys. iv. 7, 214, a. 13: φασί τινες εἶναι τὸ κενὸν τὴν τοῦ σώματος ὕλην (Tim. 52, A sq.), De An. ii. 2, 413, b. 27: τὰ δὲ λοιπὰ μόρια τῆς ψυχῆς . . . οὐκ ἔστι χωριστὰ, καθάπερ τινές φασιν (Tim. 69 c.—though here the reference to a definite passage is questionable); Pol. vii. 7, 1327, b. 38: ὅπερ γὰρ φασί τινες δεῖν ὑπάρ-

mentative value of these passages can only be determined in each case by an appeal to the ordinary rules of criticism. The more perfect is the coincidence

χειν τοῖς φύλαξι κ.τ.λ. (Rep. ii. 375 A sq.); Pol. vii. 10, 1329 b 41: οὔτε κοίνην φαμὲν εἶναι δεῖν τὴν κτῆσιν, ὥσπερ τινὲς εἰρήκασιν (Rep. iii. 416 D); De An. 1, 5, 411, b. 5. λέγουσι δή τινες μεριστὴν αὐτὴν (τὴν ψυχὴν), &c. (Rep. iv. 436 sq.); Part Anim. 11, 6 begin, ἔστι δὲ ὁ μυελὸς ... οὐκ ὥσπερ οἴονταί τινες τῆς γονῆς σπερματικὴ δύναμις (Tim. 86 C?); De Cœlo, iii. 1, 298 b. 33; εἰσὶ δέ τινες, οἳ καὶ πᾶν σῶμα γενητὸν ποιοῦσι, συντιθέντες καὶ διαλύοντες ἐξ ἐπιπέδων καὶ εἰς ἐπίπεδα (Tim. 53 C sq.); De Cœlo, ii 3, 286 b. 27: ἔτι δὲ καὶ οἱ διαιροῦντες εἰς ἐπίπεδα ... μεμαρτυρηκέναι φαίνονται τούτοις &c. (Tim. loc. cit.); De Cœlo, ii. 13, 293 b. 30: ἔνιοι δὲ ... φασὶν αὐτὴν ἵλλεσθαι similarly Ibid 1, 10, 280 a. 28; ... ὥσπερ ἐν τῷ Τιμαίῳ (40 B) γέγραπται; part Anim. iv. 2, 676 b. 22: διόπερ οἱ λέγοντες τὴν φύσιν τῆς χολῆς αἰσθήσεώς τινος εἶναι χάριν, οὐ καλῶς λέγουσιν. φασὶ γὰρ, &c. (Tim. 71 A–D) Pol. vii. 17, 1336 a 34: τὰς δὲ διατάσεις τῶν παίδων καὶ κλαυθμοὺς οὐκ ὀρθῶς ἀπαγορεύουσιν οἱ κωλύοντες ἐν τοῖς νόμοις (Laws, vii. 791 E sq.) By these examples the scruples raised as to Polit. iv. 2, 1289 b. 5, being a reference to Plato (Polit. 303 A), are, so far as concerns the manner of the reference, now settled. Aristotle says there: ἤδη μὲν οὖν τις ἀπεφήνατο καὶ τῶν πρότερον οὕτως, οὐ μὴν εἰς ταὐτὸ βλέψας ἡμῖν. ἐκεῖνος μὲν γὰρ ἔκρινε, πασῶν μὲν [sc. τῶν πολιτειῶν] οὐσῶν

ἐπιεικῶν ... χειρίστην δημοκρατίαν, φαύλων δ' ἀρίστην. Schaarschmidt (Sind. Soph. u. Polit. echt., &c. Rhein. Mus. N. F. xix. p. 2) thinks that he perhaps wishes to give us to understand that he did not know the author of the Politicus, or else that he did not consider it to be Plato's. 'As far as I know, Plato is never cited by him in this way or in any way at all approaching this.' Similarly Ueberweg (Zeitschr. f. Philos. N F. lvii. &c.) says that the Sophist and Politicus are not attested by Aristotle as writings of Plato, but only of τὶς τῶν πρότερον, and Suckow (Form d plat. Schr 87 sq) argues in detail that Aristotle, if he knew and accepted the Politicus as Platonic, could not possibly have failed to mention Plato's name in our passages. Even Stemhart (Ztschr. f. Philos. lviii. 47) finds the anonymous mention of Plato in the Politics so inexplicable that he prefers to attribute the reference in the passage before us to an unknown writer whose views Plato had appropriated. In reality, however, the way in which the passage of the Politicus is here referred to differs from the references to the Republic, Timæus, and Laws before quoted only in this respect, that the author of this dialogue is denoted not by τινὲς or ἔνιοι, but by τὶς in the singular number, that is to say, the definite person, whom Aristotle is thinking about, is more distinctly and clearly referred to than in the other places.

between the passage in Aristotle and the corresponding passage of a Platonic dialogue, and the less reason we have for supposing that the author of the dialogue made use of the Aristotelian writing, the clearer it becomes that the dialogue in question was known to Aristotle, and the greater the probability that this, like other portions of our Platonic collection, similarly quoted and employed, was recognised by him as genuine.

Among the writings that have been transmitted to us as Platonic, those which are most frequently criticised by Aristotle, with continual mention both of the author and the dialogue, are the three great expository works—the Republic, the Timæus, and the Laws. Besides these, the Phædo only is expressly designated by him as a work of Plato.[42] The Phædrus is once named,[43] and its definition of the soul is twice quoted as Platonic.[44] The speech of Aristophanes from the Symposium is treated in a manner that presupposes the authenticity of that dialogue;[45] and the same may be said of the allusions to the Gorgias, Meno, and

---

[42] Metaph. i. 9, 991 b. 3, xiii. 5, 1080, 2 a Gen. et Corr. ii. 9, 335 b. 9 (these three quotations refer to Phædo, 100 B sq.). Further references are given in Index Arist

[43] Rhet. iii. 7 (vide p 58, 31), a passage which gives no occasion for the scruples entertained on p. 55.

[44] Top. vii. 3, 140 h. 3; Metaph. xii. 6, 1071 b. 37. Both places in their statement of this definition coincide more closely with the Phædrus, 245 C, than with the Laws, x. 896 A; that they have borrowed from one and the same writing is shown by the passage in the Metaphysics in its use of the present οἴεται. Cf. p. 59 sq.

[45] Polit. ii. 4, 1262 b. 11: καθάπερ ἐν τοῖς ἐρωτικοῖς λόγοις ἴσμεν λέγοντα τὸν Ἀριστοφάνην. Previously a tenet of the Platonic Republic was mentioned; still it would not follow as a matter of course that the Symposium was also attributed to Plato; it is clear, however, from the remarks on p. 58 sq. that this was the case.

Lesser Hippias.[46] The Theætetus is not actually mentioned, but passages are adduced as from Platonic writings, which are only there to be found.[47] Similarly the Philebus is not named by Aristotle; but in certain passages of his Ethics he evidently has it in mind,[48] and in one of these passages he cites expressly from a Platonic exposition, propositions which the Philebus alone contains.[49] We therefore cannot doubt that he

[46] Cf. p. 58, 30; p. 59, 33; as regards the Meno, also p 61, 38. On the other hand, of all the further parallel passages to the Gorgias quoted in Bonitz, Ind Arist. 598 b. 32 sq, there is not one strong enough to prove its being made use of; Eth. N. vii. 12, 1152 b. 8 refers rather to Speusippus (on whom see 663, 5, 2nd edit.) than to the Gorgias 495 sq, because here it is not asserted that *no* pleasure is a good, but it is merely denied that *every* pleasure is a good.

[47] See p. 59, 34.

[48] Eth. N. vii. 13, p. 1153 a. 13 hardly refers to Phil 53 C, for the remarkable expression αἰσθητὴ γένεσις emphasised there is wanting here. On the other hand, in what precedes, Z. 8 (ἕτερόν τι βέλτιον εἶναι τῆς ἡδονῆς, ὥσπερ τινές φασι, τὸ τέλος τῆς γενέσεως), he refers to Phil. 54 B sq. Possibly the Aristotelian origin of this paragraph is uncertain (cf Part ii. b. 72, 1, 2nd edit.); should it, however, only proceed from Eudemus, its evidence is none the less worthy of consideration. Further cf. my Platon. Stud. 281 sq.

[49] Eth. N. x. 2, 1172 b. 28: τοιούτῳ δὴ λόγῳ καὶ Πλάτων ἀναιρεῖ ὅτι οὐκ ἔστιν ἡδονὴ τἀγαθόν· αἱρετώτερον γὰρ εἶναι τὸν ἡδὺν βίον μετὰ φρονήσεως ἢ χωρίς, εἰ δὲ τὸ μικτὸν κρεῖττον, οὐκ εἶναι τὴν ἡδονὴν τἀγαθόν· οὐδενὸς γὰρ προστεθέντος αὐτὸ τἀγαθὸν αἱρετώτερον γενέσθαι. What is here quoted from Plato, and more particularly, as the present ἀναιρεῖ shows, from a Platonic written treatise, stands line for line, even to the particular expressions, in the Philebus (20 E-22 A, 60 B-61 A). The supposition of Schaarschmidt (Samml. d. plat. Schr 278 sq) is entirely inadmissible (as Georgii Jahrb f. Philol. 1868, vol. 97, 300 sq. clearly shows). He refers the quotation of Aristotle to Protag. 353 C-358 C, instead of the Philebus, and would account for the great conformity of it with the Philebus by supposing the writer of the Philebus to have made use of the passage of Aristotle. Not merely are the expressions different in the Protagoras—there is no mention of φρόνησις, of αἱρετὸν, of the mixed life and of the separation (χωρὶς) of pleasure and knowledge, as in the Philebus,—but there is simply nothing at all that Aristotle quotes from Plato. The Protagoras does not refute the identification of the good with pleasure, by showing that pleasure joined with knowledge is better than pleasure alone; but from the presupposition that the good consists in pleasure (a presupposition, the problematical

was acquainted with this dialogue and recognised its authenticity. There are also in the writings of Aristotle many indications, which sometimes taken independently, sometimes in their coincidence,[50] unmistak-

correctness of which is indeed hinted at, p. 358 B, which, however, Socrates himself makes and never attacks) it is demonstrated that every man does that from which he anticipates for himself most enjoyment and least pain; it is therefore impossible to sin against his better knowledge, through being overcome by pleasure—a tenet which Aristotle loc. cit. does not mention.

[50] Indeed the value of Aristotle's evidence is in a high degree strengthened thereby. In an entire series of passages from different works, widely distant in point of time, Aristotle shows an agreement with two writings in our collection of Plato's works (which, owing to their reciprocal references (Soph. 217 A Polit. ad init.), must stand or fall together), so striking, not only in thought but in expression, that it cannot possibly be attributed merely to accident. He alludes in one (perh. two) of these passages expressly to Plato, in a second (Metaph. xiv. 2; see previous note) clearly enough to a Platonic written treatise, in a third (Polit. iv 2, see p. 62, 41) to a τὶς τῶν πρότερον, in the rest indefinitely to views and assertions, the author of which indeed he does not name, but which he had already before him from various sources. How are these facts to be explained, if Aristotle either did not know the Sophist and Politicus, or did not acknowledge them as Platonic? (two cases, the difference between which Schaarschmidt loc. cit. 98 sq., 237 sq. does not clearly distinguish). The first of these suppositions is disproved by the definite and repeated allusion of Aristotle to his predecessors whose views are here noticed; for it is quite beyond the bounds of probability to suppose either that Aristotle picked up and retailed out of oral tradition or lost writings all that is found in our dialogues, (the mention of which is most simply explained by his having made use of these dialogues,) or that the writer of those dialogues only collected these scattered notices by way of a supplement, either from the same sources as Aristotle, or from his own works. If on the other hand we suppose that the Sophist and Politicus were indeed used by Aristotle, but not acknowledged as Platonic, we shall seek in vain for any explanation of the fact that, Metaph. vi. 2 (xi. 8), he quotes as Platonic a passage which is found in a dialogue recognised by himself to be spurious; or that, Metaph. xiv 2, in his statement of the grounds which gave rise to a far-reaching determination of Platonic doctrines, he follows the thoughts and expressions of a supposititious writing of Plato's in reference to the same subjects; and again that he repeatedly favours a second pseudo-Platonic dialogue with a notice, of which, one would have imagined, he would scarcely have thought such an apocryphal

ably prove that both the Sophist [51] and the Politicus [52]

production worthy, considering that generally (cf. 57) he refers to no Socratic dialogues, except those which are contained in our collection of Plato's works, and consequently, as we must conclude, to such only as he recognised to be Platonic.

[51] The following passages seem to refer to the Sophist: (1) Metaph. vi. 2, 1026, b. 14. διὸ Πλάτων τρόπον τινὰ οὐ κακῶς τὴν σοφιστικὴν περὶ τὸ μὴ ὂν ἔταξεν. If Aristotle here alludes to a Platonic dialogue, this can only be the Sophist, in which 254, A stands the following: the Sophist, ἀποδιδράσκων εἰς τὴν τοῦ μὴ ὄντος σκοτεινότητα, τριβῇ προσαπτόμενος αὐτῆς can with difficulty be caught sight of; and Schaarschmidt is entirely mistaken (Samml. d. plat. Schr. 196) in referring instead of this to the Republic vi. 492 A—494 B, where there is nothing about the relation of Sophistic to the μὴ ὄν. From the same passage comes (2) Metaph. xi. 8, a paragraph which is only another recension of vi. 2, 1064, b. 29: διὸ Πλάτων οὐ κακῶς εἴρηκε φήσας τὸν σοφιστὴν περὶ τὸ μὴ ὂν διατρίβειν. Here the quotation of the Sophist is so perfectly obvious, that even Schaarschmidt allows it (Samml. d. plat. Schr. 101); and even if this part of the Metaphysics does not come from Aristotle (on which vide p. 54, 22), still the passage has its importance as evidence for the reference, which the words in Metaph. vi. 2 had given before. However, there is no need of this evidence; even of itself it is highly improbable that a judgment which occurs in a written treatise handed down as Platonic production worthy, considering and here only, should be quoted by Aristotle as indeed Platonic, but not out of this treatise. (On the past tense ἔταξε cf. p. 62, 39.) Still if this passage stood alone, we might have some doubt. But we find in Aristotle still further express references to the Sophist. (3) In Metaph. xiv. 2, 1088, b. 35, Aristotle remarks, in connection with the question, whether the Ideas and Numbers are composed of certain στοιχεῖα: πολλὰ μὲν οὖν τὰ αἴτια τῆς ἐπὶ ταύτας τὰς οὐσίας ἐκτροπῆς, μάλγιστα δὲ τὸ ἀπορῆσαι ἀρχαικῶς. ἔδοξε γὰρ αὐτοῖς πάντ' ἔσεσθαι ἓν τὰ ὄντα, αὐτὸ τὸ ὄν, εἰ μή τις λύσει καὶ ὁμόσε βαδιεῖται τῷ Παρμενίδου λόγῳ "οὐ γὰρ μήποτε τοῦτο δαῇς εἶναι μὴ ἐόντα," ἀλλ' ἀνάγκη εἶναι τὸ μὴ ὂν δεῖξαι ὅτι ἔστιν. οὕτω γὰρ ἐκ τοῦ ὄντος καὶ ἄλλου τινὸς τὰ ὄντα ἔσεσθαι, εἰ πολλά ἐστιν Cf. 1089, a. 19· ἐκ ποίου οὖν ὄντος καὶ μὴ ὄντος πολλὰ τὰ ὄντα; βούλεται μὲν δὴ τὸ ψεῦδος καὶ ταύτην τὴν φύσιν λέγειν (Alex. λέγει) τὸ οὐκ ὄν. κ τ.λ Now that in this passage Aristotle did not merely (as Schaarschmidt, Rhein. Mus. xviii. 7; Samml. d. Plat. Schr. 105 wishes to make out) intend us to understand Platonic scholars, but, primarily Plato himself, is at once clear from the beginning, in which his object is to display the grounds which gave rise originally to the supposition of elements of the Ideas; for this supposition was undoubtedly first propounded by Plato, and Schaarschmidt loc. cit. is wrong in believing that the reference here cannot be to Plato, inasmuch as the doctrine of Ideas in Aristotle's

F 2

were regarded by him as Platonic; and as the Politicus is plainly referred to in the Laws,[53] it has the further support of all the evidence on the side of the latter.

Metaph. xiii. 4. 1078, b. 12, 1, 6, 987, a. 29, is derived from Socratic and Heraclitean doctrines, whereas the view of the ἔνιοι in our passage [together with another, it runs: πολλὰ μὲν οὖν τὰ αἴτια] is derived from a reference to the Parmenides. There the question is concerned with the Ideas, here with the elements, unity, and the great and small. Further, the reference of the passage before us to Plato follows from the singular βούλεται and (according to Alexander's reading) λέγει; these same expressions, however (cf. p. 59 sq.), show that Arist. is referring to a definite written treatise of Plato's, which can be no other than the Sophist, for in the Sophist only does what we have here occur. Again, though Aristotle, as usual, does not quote word for word, only formulating more precisely what Plato says, in conformity with his supposed meaning (βούλεται), and further on (1089, a 21) adding a reminiscence from lectures or oral disquisitions (See on this point Bonitz ad loc.; Ueberweg, Plat. Schr. 157, f); still the allusion to passages like Soph. 237 A, 241 D, 242 A, 258 D, E, cannot be mistaken (as Pilger, in his Programm ub. d. Athetese des plat Soph. Berl. 1869, p 7, sq, thoroughly proves). (4) It must remain undecided whether Metaph vii 4, 1030, a 25; Rhet. 24, 1402, a 4; Soph. El. 25, 180, a. 32, are to be referred specially to the remarks in the Sophist (258 E, 260 C) about the μὴ ὄν, in De Interpr 11, 21, a. 32 (τὸ δὲ μὴ ὄν, ὅτι δοξαστὸν, οὐκ ἀληθὲς εἰπεῖν ὄν τι), and Soph. El. 5, 167, a. 1 (οἷον εἰ τὸ μὴ ὄν ἐστι δοξαστὸν, ὅτι τὸ μὴ ὂν ἔστιν), it is exceedingly probable, though not strictly proved, that there is an allusion to Soph. 240 D—241, B; for with the point which is expressly emphasised in this passage,—that we cannot use expressions like ψευδῆ δοξάζειν, without asserting ψευδῆ ὡς ἔστιν ἐν δόξαις τε καὶ κατὰ λόγους, and consequently attributing the ὂν to the μὴ ὄν,—parallel passages like Theætet. 189, A. Rep. v., 476, E. 478, B. do not correspond so closely. (5) The reference of Top. vi. 7, 146, a. 22 sq. to Soph. 247 D, is more certain: in the latter passage as an example of a disjunctive definition, which is therefore open to certain objections, is quoted, ὅτι τὸ ὂν τὸ δυνατὸν παθεῖν ἢ ποιῆσαι; in the former also we read: λέγω δὴ τὸ καὶ ὁποιανοῦν κεκτημένον δύναμιν. εἴτ' εἰς τὸ ποιεῖν ἕτερον ὁτιοῦν πεφυκὸς εἴτ' εἰς τὸ παθεῖν. . . . πᾶν τοῦτο ὄντως εἶναι, this is again repeated 248, c. and it is shown that this determination is also applicable to supersensuous existence. It is incredible that so characteristic a definition was propounded earlier by any other philosopher; it seems rather as if it was first put forward by its author in connection with the inquiry introduced in the Sophist, for the purpose of solving the questions there raised, and it is moreover actually brought in as something new and hitherto unknown to the opponents at p. 247 D

It is clear from the Rhetoric that the Apology was acknowledged by Aristotle; but some doubt exists with

[52] The passage of the Politics where Arist. mentions the judgment of one of his predecessors on democracy has been already quoted, p. 62, 41. If we compare with it Polit 303 A: διὸ γέγονε [ἡ τοῦ πλήθους ἀρχὴ] πασῶν μὲν νομίμων τῶν πολιτείων οὐσῶν τούτων χειρίστη, παρανόμων δ'οὐσῶν ξυμπασῶν βελτίστη, the complete harmony in thought; and in words too, as far as can be expected in a quotation from memory; makes it almost unimaginable that Aristotle had any other passage in his mind. Not less decided are the two passages Polit. iii. 15, 16, 1286, a. 7, 1287, a. 33. The first proposes the question: πότερον συμφέρει μᾶλλον ὑπὸ τοῦ ἀρίστου ἀνδρὸς ἄρχεσθαι ἢ ὑπὸ τῶν ἀρίστων νόμων, and remarks δοκοῦσι δὴ τοῖς νομίζουσι συμφέρειν βασιλεύεσθαι τὸ καθόλου μόνον οἱ νόμοι λέγειν, ἀλλ' οὐ πρὸς τὰ προσπίπτοντα ἐπιτάττειν, ὥστ' ἐν ὁτοιῳοῦν τέχνῃ τὸ κατὰ γράμματ' ἄρχειν ἠλίθιον; the second in criticising this view mentions particularly the latter point: τὸ δὲ τῶν τεχνῶν εἶναι δοκεῖ παράδειγμα ψεῦδος, ὅτι τὸ κατὰ γράμματα ἰατρεύεσθαι φαῦλον The assertions here combated are developed at length in the Politicus; p. 294 A. sq., it is shown: τὸ δ'ἄριστον οὐ τοὺς νόμους ἐστὶν ἰσχύειν,[ἀλλ' ἄνδρα τὸν μετὰ φρονήσεως βασιλικόν, and this is supported by the argument that the law lays down the same ordinance for all persons and cases without regard to particular circumstances,—that it is a διὰ παντὸς γιγνομένον ἁπλοῦν, πρὸς τὰ μηδέποτε ἁπλᾶ; and in the further working out of this position occurs (295 B, and previously 293 A) the comparison with the physicians, who do not bind themselves strictly to the rules of their art, when that art itself shows them that under given circumstances a departure therefrom is advisable. We must conclude that this was actually the comparison to which Aristotle loc. cit. alludes, although we do not know that the Politicus was in his possession: for there can be no question as to an accidental coincidence in such a characteristic thought; and it is just as incredible that the author of the Politicus based his own theory, self-consistent as it is, and deduced from Socratico-Platonic pre-suppositions with such consummate accuracy and justness, merely on the passages in Aristotle, and still more incredible that he should have done this without attempting to remove the objections of Aristotle at all. Now Aristotle actually met with the views which he combats: where else can he have found them except in the dialogue before us? For otherwise we must suppose before our Politicus another treatise forming its counterpart, belonging likewise to the Platonic school, and corresponding with it, even in the particulars of the thoughts and the exposition. —Moreover the assertion which Arist. Polit. 1, 1, 1252, a. 7, combats: πολιτικὸν καὶ βασιλικὸν καὶ οἰκονομικὸν καὶ δεσποτικὸν εἶναι τὸν αὐτὸν, is found together with the reason ; ὡς οὐδὲν διαφέρουσαν μεγάλην οἰκίαν ἢ μικρὰν πόλιν, almost word for word in the Politicus 259 B, C; the same asser-

regard to the Menexenus.[54] He nowhere mentions the Parmenides; there is only one minor particular, which may possibly be quoted from it.[55] But if the Philebus really alludes to the Parmenides,[56] the evidence for the one dialogue would indirectly apply to the other. The Protagoras, too, is never specified; but it was apparently known to Aristotle,[57] and used by him as a

ion is repeatedly spoken of by Aristotle, Pol. i. 3, 1253, b. 18, c. 7, beg. vii., 3. 1325, a. 27.— Further parallel passages, the evidence of which is however inferior to those hitherto quoted, are given in the Index Arist.

[53] This follows from a comparison of the Laws, iv. 713 C sq. (on the golden age), with Polit. 271 D sq. Schaarschmidt, however (Samml d. plat. Schr.), thinks the passage of the Laws imitated in the Politicus. In my opinion, the freshness and originality of the exposition in the passage before us is so decided, that the grounds for its spuriousness must be very strong, before we should be justified in looking for the origin of the Politicus in the wider amplifications of the Laws, which even here (713 E) obviously contain an allusion to the Republic (v. 473, c. sq.)

[54] The passages with which we are here concerned were quoted on p. 54, and the grounds on which the citations of the 3rd Bk. of the Rhetoric were called in question were there indicated. Apart from these, however, the use of the Apology is proved by Rhet. 11, 23, although the saying of Socrates, which is quoted 1, 9, with the words Σωκράτης ἔλεγεν may, according to what we have said at p. 60 sq., have come to Aristotle from other quarters, as for instance from the Menexenus. Even if he knew this dialogue, we must still suppose other sources of tradition for Socratic sayings, for he could scarcely have attributed it to the historic Socrates merely on the authority of the Menexenus.

[55] In the passage mentioned p. 59, 34, which certainly may come from the Parmenides as well as from the Theætetus.

[56] I have already supported this in my Platon. Stud. 194, by the argument that the first part of the Parmenides (129 B sq, 130 E sq) is as good as directly cited in the Philebus (14 C, 15 B), and this reason I still think is quite valid. Schaarschmidt (Samml. d. plat. Schr. 277) also agrees with me; he, however, makes use of this supposition in a different direction from that above, and concludes from the spuriousness of the Parmenides, which he believes to be incontestable, that the Philebus likewise cannot be genuine.

[57] The proof is furnished by the passage quoted in Bonitz's Index, Part. Anim. iv. 10, 687, a. 24: people complain ὡς συνέστηκεν οὐ καλῶς ὁ ἄνθρωπος ἀλλὰ χείριστα τῶν ζῴων· ἀνυπόδητόν τε γὰρ αὐτὸν εἶναί φασι καὶ γυμνὸν καὶ οὐκ ἔχοντα ὅπλον πρὸς τὴν ἀλκήν. Cf. Prot.

historical authority.⁵⁸ He seems also to have been acquainted with the Lysis, Charmides, and Laches; though this is not so certain as in the case of the Protagoras.⁵⁹ It is still more doubtful whether or not two passages relate to the Cratylus ⁶⁰ and the Greater Hippias.⁶¹ The Euthydemus is indeed referred to by Eudemus; ⁶² but the fallacies which Aristotle quotes from the sophist of that name ⁶³ are not to be found in the Platonic dialogue; and though certainly on the suppo-

---

21 C (Protagoras's Myth): καὶ ὁρᾷ τὰ μὲν ἄλλα ζῷα ἐμμελῶς πάντων ἔχοντα, τὸν δὲ ἄνθρωπον γυμνόν τε καὶ ἀνυπόδητον καὶ ἄστρωτον καὶ ἄοπλον.

⁵⁸ For instance Prot. 352 B sq. is the source of the account about Socrates Eth. N. vii. 3 ad init., and the notice of Protag. Ethic. N. x. 1, 1164, a. 24 refers to Prot. 328 B sq Also Eth. N. iii. 9, 1115, a. 9 approaches nearer Prot. 358 D than Lach. 198 B.

⁵⁹ Cf. the references in Bonitz's Index Arist. 599 a and the preceding note.

⁶⁰ De An. 1, 2. 405, b. 27 : διὸ καὶ τοῖς ὀνόμασιν ἀκολουθοῦσιν, οἱ μὲν τὸ θερμὸν λέγοντες (sc. τὴν ψυχὴν), ὅτι διὰ τοῦτο καὶ τὸ ζῆν ὠνόμασται, οἱ δὲ τὸ ψυχρὸν διὰ τὴν ἀναπνοὴν καὶ τὴν κατάψυξιν καλεῖσθαι ψυχήν. Crat 399 D: in the name ψυχὴ the consideration seems to have been, ὡς τοῦτο ἄρα, ὅταν παρῇ τῷ σώματι, αἴτιόν ἐστι τοῦ ζῆν αὐτῷ, τὴν τοῦ ἀναπνεῖν δύναμιν παρέχον καὶ ἀναψῦχον.

⁶¹ Hipp. Maj. 298 A, Socrates puts forth the definition tentatively, and immediately shows it to be useless, ὅτι τὸ καλόν ἐστι τὸ δι' ἀκοῆς τε καὶ ὄψεως ἡδύ. The same definition is also mentioned by Aristotle, Top. vi. 7, 146, a. 21 as an example of a faulty disjunctive definition (οἷον τὸ καλὸν τὸ δι' ὄψεως ἢ τὸ δι' ἀκοῆς ἡδύ). He does not, however, say whence he got it, and there is nothing to prevent our supposing that, like the definition quoted in Top v. 5, 135, a. 12, it was originally propounded by some writer of the Sophistic period (some Prodicus or Gorgias), or else by some one unknown to us, and was met with by Aristotle independently of the Hippias, or that it was current in the Academic school (based on Phileb. 51 B sq., or a corresponding oral discussion) and was therefore known to Aristotle just as much as to the author of the Hippias, supposing him to have been other than Plato The statement of it in Aristotle also varies considerably from that in the Hippias, and according to Metaph. v. 29 (vide p. 392, 3) Aristotle seems to have been acquainted with only one Hippias, viz. the Hippias Minor.

⁶² Cf. p. 50, 13.

⁶³ Soph. El. 20, 177, b. 12 sq.; Rhet. 11, 24, 1401, a 26, cf. vol. i. 914, 4, 3rd edit.

sition of its genuineness, we should expect Aristotle to have used it in his examination of fallacies which often brought him in contact with it,[64] this relation of the two expositions is not sufficiently established to serve as proof for the authenticity of the Euthydemus.

If, then, any dialogue in our collection is mentioned by Aristotle as Platonic, or used by him in a manner that presupposes it to be so, this circumstance is greatly in favour of its authenticity. For twenty years before the death of Plato, Aristotle was a member of the Platonic School at Athens; after that event he quitted the city, but returned twelve or thirteen years later for the rest of his life. That during the lifetime of the master any writing should have been falsely regarded as his work, by scholars who were already well instructed on the subject, or had the opportunity at any moment of becoming so, is quite impossible. Even in the generation succeeding his death, while Speusippus and Xenocrates were at the head of the Academy, and Aristotle and other personal disciples of Plato lived in Athens, this could only have occurred under quite peculiar conditions, and to a very limited extent. It is indeed conceivable that some one of the less important dialogues might after the death of Plato have been admitted even by his immediate disciples without previous acquaintance with it, as an earlier work that had escaped their attention, or under certain circumstances as a posthumous bequest. Cases of this kind have occurred in our own times, though we are so much richer than the ancients in resources, and more

[64] Cf. Part I. 910 sq.

practised in literary criticism. It might still more easily happen that an imperfect sketch of Plato's, completed by another after his death—an unfinished writing, worked up by one of his disciples—might be received as wholly genuine, without accurate discrimination of the original from the later ingredients. But it is incredible that such things should frequently have repeated themselves in the first generation after the master's death; or that reputed works of his, which, had they existed, must on account of their importance have been owned during his lifetime by the School, should afterwards have emerged, and have been universally recognised. If the testimony of Aristotle to Platonic writings, so far as it is clear and undoubted, does not absolutely guarantee their authenticity, it is at all events so strong an argument in their favour, that only the weightiest internal evidence should be suffered to countervail it; and if any criticism of the Platonic collection starts from presuppositions requiring the rejection of numerous works recognised by Aristotle, there is enough in this one circumstance to prove these presuppositions incorrect.

But if the evidence of Aristotle has this importance on the side of the writings from which he quotes, can we with certainty conclude that those about which he is silent are spurious? No one would maintain this without some qualification. Aristotle is not passing judgment on Plato's works as a literary historian who is bound to furnish a complete catalogue of them, and to tell all that he knows. Nor does he deal with them as a modern writer of the history of philosophy, whose object it is to combine their whole philosophic content into a representation of the Platonic theory; he only mentions them when occasion offers, in stating his own views, or criticising or opposing those of Plato and Socrates. We must not expect him, therefore, to name everything that is known to him as Platonic, but only such writings as it was necessary or desirable to mention for the purposes of any scientific discussion he might happen to be pursuing. Even this canon, however, must be cautiously applied. Plato's works are for us the sole, or at any rate the principal, source of our knowledge concerning his system: we cannot speak of the Platonic philosophy without continually recurring to them. In the case of Aristotle it was otherwise. He owes his knowledge of the Platonic doctrines in the first place to verbal communication and personal intercourse; in the second place only, to the writings of Plato. They were to him but subsidiary sources; in the exposition of the doctrines, he uses them sometimes for the confirmation of that which he already knows from Plato's oral discourses; but he has no occasion to enter more deeply into their contents except on subjects which were not examined in those discourses. Of such subjects, the most important seem to be the application of philosophical principles to the explanation of nature and to political institutions: hence the numerous quotations from the Republic, the Timæus, and the Laws. The metaphysical bases of the system, on the other hand, are indeed frequently and searchingly criticised by Aristotle, but in by far the greater number of cases on the ground of Plato's discourses: the propædeutic enquiries into the conception of knowledge, true virtue, and the art of governing, love, the right scientific method, and its opposition to the Sophistic teaching, are seldom touched upon. Only one [65] of the many passages from which we derive our knowledge of the theory of ideas is quoted by him; he makes no allusion to what is said on this subject in the Republic, Timæus, Symposium, Phædrus, and Theætetus; nor to the explanations of the Sophist, Parmenides, and Philebus, though there was abundant opportunity for it. Even the well-known discussions of the Republic upon the Good are merely glanced at with an uncertain hint,[66] despite the frequent occasions when they might have been aptly introduced. If we turn to those dialogues the authenticity of which has never been questioned, we find the Protagoras, as before remarked,[67] apparently made use of in some passages, but it is never named, and nothing is quoted from it as Platonic. The Theætetus is twice mentioned, the Gorgias and the Symposium once; and none of these quotations relate to the main content of the dialogues—they are only incidental recollections of certain particulars in them, the notice of which seems entirely fortuitous. All this being considered, we may well hesitate to conclude from Aristotle's silence with regard to any Platonic writing, that he was unacquainted with it;[68] and this so much the more, as we do not even possess the whole of Aristotle's

---

[65] The Phædo 100 B sq., quoted p. 56, 24; p. 64, 42.
[66] Eth. iv. 1, 2, 1095, a. 26 is a reminiscence of Rep. vi. 507 A; vii. 517 C.
[67] p. 70.
[68] As is the case with the Parmenides; Ueberweg. plat. Schr. 176 sq., Schaarschmidt, Samml. d. pl Schr. 164.

works, and some lost writing or fragment might very possibly contain citations from dialogues for which we have now no Aristotelian evidence. It is certainly surprising that Aristotle should assert that Plato never enquired wherein the participation of things in ideas consists;[69] while in the Parmenides (130 E sqq.) the difficulties with which this theory has to contend are clearly pointed out. But it is not more surprising than that he should assail the doctrine of ideas with the question : 'Who formed the things of sense after the pattern of the ideas?'[70]—though it is distinctly stated in the Timæus (28 C sq.) that the Creator of the world did this in looking on the eternal archetypes.[71] Nor, again, that he should maintain, notwithstanding the well-known explanation in the Phædo,[72] often alluded to by himself—notwithstanding the doctrine in the Republic, of the Good being the absolute end of the world—that the final cause is not touched by the ideas.[73] We should have expected that in attacking

---

[69] Metaph. 1, 987, b. 13: τὴν μέντοι γε μέθεξιν ἢ τὴν μίμησιν ἥτις ἂν εἴη τῶν εἰδῶν, ἀφεῖσαν (Plato and the Pythagoreans) ἐν κοινῷ ζητεῖν

[70] Metaph. 1, 9, 991, a. 20: τὸ δὲ λέγειν παραδείγματα αὐτὰ [sc. τὰ εἴδη] εἶναι . . . . κενολογεῖν ἐστι . . . . τί γάρ ἐστι τὸ ἐργαζόμενον πρὸς τὰς ἰδέας ἀποβλέπον; Ibid. 992, a. 24 ; xii. 10, 1075, b. 19. In my Platon. Stud. 215, I have mentioned a similar instance, where Arist. (only incidentally) denies to Plato researches which he had actually made (Gen. et Corr. 1, 2, 315 a., 29 sq.; cf. Tim. 58 D sq , 70 B sq., 73–81).

[71] Or if it should be maintained in the latter case, that the Demiurgus is not a scientific explanation and might therefore have been left out of account by Aristotle, he might just as well waive the difficulties of the Parmenides because no positive determination is there given as to how we are to understand the participation of things in the Ideas.

[72] On which see p. 64, 42.

[73] Metaph. 1, 9, 992, a. 29: οὐδὲ δὴ ὃ περὶ τὰς ἐπιστήμας (so Alex. and Cod. A^b, perhaps, however, ποιήσεις should be read instead of ἐπιστ.) ὁρῶμεν ὂν αἴτιον, διὸ καὶ πᾶς νοῦς καὶ πᾶσα φύσις ποιεῖ, οὐδὲ

Plato about the τρίτος ἄνθρωπος,[74] Aristotle, had he been acquainted with the Parmenides, would have referred to the fact that in that dialogue (132A) the same objection is raised. But might we not also have expected after the further stricture: 'Plato ought then to assume ideas of art productions, mere relations, &c., which he does not,'[75] some such remark as this: 'In his writings he certainly does speak of such ideas?' And in the discussions concerning the Platonic theory of the world-soul,[76] should we not have anticipated some mention of the passage in the Laws about the evil soul,[77] which has given so many handles to criticism? Many other things besides these might reasonably have been looked for on the supposition that the writings of Plato had the same significance, as sources of his doctrines, for Aristotle as for us, and were used by him in a similar manner. But this we have no right to presuppose; and therefore his not alluding to a writing is by no means sufficient to prove that it was unknown to him, or that he did not acknowledge it to be Platonic.

By means of Aristotle's testimony, supplemented sometimes from other quarters,[78] we are thus enabled to ascribe a number of writings to Plato with all the certainty that can be attained in this way.[79] These works acquaint us with the scientific and literary character of their author, and so furnish us with a criterion for the

ταύτης τῆς αἰτίας . . . οὐθὲν ἅπτεται τὰ εἴδη.
[74] Vide on this Part II., b. 220, 1, 2nd edit Platon. Stud. 257.
[75] Cf. Part II b. 217 sq., 2nd edit. and p. 113 sq. of this vol.
[76] De An. 1, 3, 406, b. 25; cf.
p. 635 sq., 2nd edit.
[77] Laws x. 896, 897.
[78] See p 50.
[79] How far this goes was discussed on p. 72 sq.

criticism of other works or portions of works which are either insufficiently supported by external evidence, or in their form or contents are open to suspicion. Great care, however, is necessary in fixing and applying this standard; and in some cases even the most cautious weighing of favourable and adverse considerations cannot insure absolute certainty.[80] In the first place we must decide, on which of the dialogues noticed by Aristotle our Platonic criterion is to be based. If we confine ourselves to those which he expressly attributes to Plato, we shall have only the Republic, the Timæus, the Phædo, and the Laws; and important as these works are, it is questionable whether they represent the scientific and literary individuality of the many-sided Plato exhaustively enough to make everything appear un-Platonic that at all departs from their type. If, on the other hand, we also take into account those writings of which Aristotle makes use without mentioning their author, or from which he quotes something that Plato has said, without naming the dialogue,—we find that the Philebus is as well attested as the Theætetus; the Sophist, Politicus, Meno, and the Lesser Hippias, as the Gorgias and Symposium; and all of them better than the Protagoras, the authenticity of which no one doubts. Our Platonic criterion must, in this case, therefore be considerably wider than that of Ueberweg and Schaarschmidt. Moreover it must not be imagined that each divergence in a dialogue from those works considered normal is necessarily a proof of its spurious-

[80] On what follows cf. the valuable paper of Steinhart, Ztschr. f. Phil. lviii. 55 sq.

ess; these normal works themselves present deviations ne from the other, equal in importance to many that ave formed the basis of adverse judgments. If it be bjected against the Philebus that it wants dramatic veliness, and the flow of conversational development, 1e Protagoras may be charged with meagreness of :ientific content, with the entire failure of the theory f ideas, with the apparent barrenness of result in the 'hole enquiry, and the fatiguing prolixity of the disussion about the verse of Simonides. If the antinomic evelopment of conceptions is peculiar to the Parmenles, and elaborate classifications to the Sophist and 'oliticus,—the Timæus stands alone not only in its heories of the Creator and antemundane matter, the 1athematical construction of the elements, the arith- 1etical division, and distribution of the soul in space, ut in its minute treatment of the whole subject of 'hysics, to which no other dialogue makes an approach. 'he Laws are separated by a far greater interval from he Republic and from the other normal works than rom the Politicus, and in an artistic point of view are pen to much graver criticism than the dialectical dialogues; the later form of the Platonic philosophy, nown to us through Aristotle, has a much more bstruse and formal character than the logical and meaphysical statements of the Laws. We cannot, indeed, ;o quite so far as Grote,[81] who sometimes speaks as if 'lato in none of his works had the least regard to those lready written, and thought nothing of contradicting imself in the most glaring manner, even in one and

[81] Plato, i. 349, 360, 439, 559; ii. 89, 125, iii. 165, 463, 521, 1.

the same dialogue. But we ought not, on the other hand, to forget that so exuberant a spirit as Plato's was not limited for its expression to one particular form; that the purpose of a dialogue might make it necessary to emphasize some points in it, and to pass slightly over others: that the nature of a subject or the readers for whom it was intended might require the style of a work to be more or less ornate, and the treatment to be more or less popular; that much that now seems to us incomprehensible might be explained by special occasions and personal references; that we are not justified in expecting, even from a Plato, nothing but productions of equal finish and importance; that as we might have anticipated, even without the evidence establishing it, during the sixty years of Plato's literary activity both his philosophy and his artistic method underwent a considerable change, and that on this account, if on no other, a standard derived from a portion of his works cannot be applicable to them all without condition or modification. These considerations certainly render a decision concerning the genuineness of Platonic writings, so far as this depends on internal arguments, very difficult and complicated. It is not enough simply to compare one dialogue with others, we must enquire whether Plato, as we know him from his undoubted works, might be supposed to have produced the writing in question at a certain date and under certain circumstances. This of course cannot always be answered with equal assurance, either affirmatively or negatively. It is sometimes hard to distinguish with perfect accuracy the work of a tolerably expert imitator from a less important work of the master; what is un-Platonic from what is unfinished, or the result of Plato's advanced age; and therefore it is almost unavoidable that among the dialogues which can be vouched for as Platonic, or the reverse, others should creep in, with respect to which a certain degree of probability is all we can attain. Those writings, however, on which our knowledge and estimate of the Platonic philosophy chiefly depend, can well maintain their ground in any impartial investigation; while, on the other hand, our general view of Platonism would be very little affected by the genuineness or spuriousness of several of the lesser dialogues.

It is impossible in this place to pursue this subject more particularly, or to discuss the reasons which may be urged for or against the Platonic origin of each work. But it seems necessary to point out those writings on which, as original sources of the Platonic philosophy, our exposition of that philosophy will be founded, if even the critical grounds which determine the position of these writings should not at once be explained, and receive only partial notice hereafter.

Our collection of Platonic works contains, besides those dialogues which even in ancient times were acknowledged to be spurious,[82] thirty-five dialogues, thirteen letters,[83] and a number of definitions, mostly relating to ethics. Among these there are a few—the Protagoras, Phædrus, Symposium, Gorgias, Theætetus, and Republic—the authenticity of which has never been

[82] Cf. p. 49, 10.
[83] On the six others which Hermann has admitted cf. 57, 16.

questioned: the Phædo also has been as little affected by the suspicion of Panætius (if it really existed)[84]—as the Timæus by Schelling's temporary doubt.[85] The genuineness of all these works may be considered as fully established. There are, besides, several other important dialogues—the Philebus, Sophist, Politicus, Parmenides, and Cratylus,—which, in spite of the repeated assaults upon them in modern days,[86] are certainly to be regarded as Platonic—not only on the strength of the Aristotelian testimony which can be cited for

[84] Cf. on this p. 49, 10.

[85] Schelling himself in fact retracted his decision against this dialogue (Philos. u Rel. WW. 1, Abth. vi. 36) subsequently (WW. Abth. vii. 374); previously, however, it had been answered by Bockh (Stud. v. Daub. u Creuzer iii. 28). Its repetition by certain writers, as for instance Weisse (z. Arist. Physik 274, 350, 471, Idee d. Gotth 97) will nowadays lead no one into error. Among the express opponents of this view are Hermann, Plat 699, and Steinhart, vi. 68 sq.

[86] Socher (Pl. Schr. 258-294) was the first to reject as spurious the Sophist, Politicus, and Parmenides, but he met with little support afterwards Suckow (Form d plat. Schr. 1855, p. 78 sq., 86 sq) tried to establish the same charge with regard to the Politicus, as did Ueberweg with regard to the Parmenides (Unters plat. Schr. 1861, p. 176 sq., Jahrb. f. Philol. lxxxv. 1863, p. 97 sq.); Schaarschmidt (Samml. d. plat. Schr. 1866, p. 160 sq., and previously in the Rhein. Mus. f. Philol. vol. xviii. 1; xix. 63 sq.; xx. 321 sq.) extended it from the Parmenides to the Sophist, Politicus, Cratylus, and Philebus, and Ueberweg (Gesch. d. Phil. i. 3, edit. 1867, p 116; Philos. Monatschr. 1869, p. 473 sq.) agreed with him with regard to all these dialogues more or less decidedly; afterwards, however (4th edit. of Gesch. d Phil. p. 124, Zeitschr. f. Philos. lvii. 84), he retracted his opinion so far as to recognise the Cratylus and Philebus, while the Sophist and Politicus he regarded as composed from notes of Plato's oral doctrines. The treatises in which Hayduck, Alberti, Deussen, Peipers, Pilger defend as Platonic the Sophist (Hayduck also the Politicus and Cratylus), Georgii the Philebus, Alberti, Benfey, Lehrs, Suckow, Dreykorn the Cratylus, and Druschke, Neumann, Susemihl, Schramm the Parmenides respectively, are mentioned by Ueberweg, Grundriss, i. 117, 4th edit.: for further details cf. Steinhart, Pl. St. Ztscbr. f. Philos. lviii. 32 sq., 193 sq.; K. Planck on the Parmenides, Jahrb. f. Philol. cv. 433 sq., 529 sq.

most of them,[87] but also on account of conclusive internal evidence.[88] The position of the Laws will be the subject of a future discussion. There is all the less reason to mistrust the Critias,[89] since its contents, so far as they go, are entirely in harmony with the opening of the Timæus. The Meno [90] is protected by a clear reference in the Phædo,[91] as well as by Aristotle's quotations; and though not one of Plato's most perfect dialogues, there is no good reason to suspect its authenticity. The Euthydemus is at any rate made use of by Eudemus,[92] and, though often attacked,[93] may be

[87] See p. 64 sq.

[89] We shall have an opportunity later on, in speaking of the doctrines contained in these works, to examine with more detail one or two of the points which are declared to be not Platonic: to notice all the particular objections of this kind is impossible in the limits of the present treatise I will here merely point out how improbable it is, that works so valuable and written with so much dialectic skill, in spite of all the objections that we can make against them, could ever have been composed by anyone in the Old Academy, which, as we know from Aristotle and other accounts, acquitted itself but poorly in abstruse speculation. The points of view which are to be adopted in the more intimate criticism of the writings have been already discussed, p. 77 sq

[89] As Socher 369 sq.; Suckow 58 sq. against him Susemihl, ahrb. f. Philol. lxxi. 703; Ueberweg, Plat. Schr. 186 sq.

[90] Rejected by Ast, Pl. L. und chr. 394 sq., and Schaarschmidt 42 sq., doubted by Ueberweg in his Grundriss i. 123, 4th edit.

[91] P. 72 E sq Cebes here says that pre-existence and immortality follow also κατ' ἐκεῖνον τὸν λόγον, ... ὃν σὺ (Socr) εἴωθας θαμὰ λέγειν, that μάθησις is nothing but ἀνάμνησις, and he proves this not only in reference to former discourses (ἑνὶ μὲν λόγῳ καλλίστῳ ὅτι, &c.), but by the fact worked out at length in the Meno, viz. that by means of properly arranged questions, we can elicit everything from a man, as is shown, for instance, in the case of geometrical figures. That there is a reference here to an earlier written treatise, which can only be the Meno, will be more obvious from a comparison of this brief allusion to something already known to the reader, with the prolix development of a further reason on p. 73 B sq., which is undoubtedly treated with such detail only because it has not occurred in any dialogue hitherto.

[92] Cf. p. 50, 13. Schaarschmidt, p. 341, has asserted that on the contrary the author of the Euthydemus made use of Aristotle's Sophistical Fallacies. But he has not

easily defended, if we bear in mind the proper design of this dialogue,[94] and sufficiently discriminate between what is seriously intended and what is satirical exaggeration or irony : [95] it would be hard to deny to Plato

proved this, for the coincidence of many of the Sophisms which he quotes is by no means conclusive. It would rather, on this supposition, be very extraordinary that the very fallacy which Aristotle attributes to Euthydemus does not occur in the Platonic Euthydemus (vide p. 71, 63). Should we, however, adopt this supposition, and at the same time assert that the Euthydemus was used in the Politicus (Schaarschmidt, 326), we cannot leave the question undecided as to whether Aristotle had the Politicus, or the author of the Politicus had the Aristotelian treatise, before him. (This, however, Schaarschmidt does, p. 237 f)

[93] Ast, 414, sq. Schaarschmidt, 326 sq.

[94] The object of the Euthydemus (on which Bonitz, Plat. Stud. 11, 28 sq . ought especially to be consulted) is to represent the opposition of Socratic and Sophistic views with regard to their value in the training and education of youth ; and this opposition is brought before us here, not by means of a scientific and detailed statement, but by the actual exposition of the two parties themselves, in the form of a (narrated) drama, or rather of a satyric comedy. In the exposition of this subject Plato had to do, not merely with the views of the elder Sophists and their later developments, but also (as was found probable, Part i. p. 255, 2; 256, 1; cf. 248, 4; 253, 1; 254, 1) with Antisthenes, who seemed to him in true Sophistic fashion to destroy all possibility of cognition, to confuse Socratic with Sophistic views, and thereby spoil them, and with those refiners of language of the stamp of Isocrates (for that he is intended p. 305 B sq. is put beyond doubt after the proofs of Spengel, Abh. d. philos. philol. Kl. of the Acad. of Baireuth, vii. 764 sq), who did not know how to distinguish between Socratic and Sophistic views, and hoped to get rid of the rivalry of the true philosophers if they brought the Sophists into discredit. In conformity with this object, the scientific refutation of the Sophistic views is not touched upon beyond a few allusions, while the Socratic philosophy is expounded only in its simplest practical form—nothing new is propounded nor any speculative views enunciated, which might weaken the impression intended to be conveyed here, and in the eyes of an unphilosophical reader might wear the appearance of Sophistry. If Plato voluntarily exercised this self-restraint at a time when he was already firmly in possession of his doctrine of Ideas (Euthyd. 300 E sq.), he must certainly have had some special inducement ; and the present theory will sufficiently explain the fact.

[95] Supporters as well as opponents of the Euthydemus have not seldom failed to make this distinction. E.g., Schaarschmidt, p. 339, amongst many other censures of the artificiality of this dialogue

on trivial grounds so charming a sketch, abounding in comic power and humour. The Apology, which was known to Aristotle,[96] is as little really doubtful [97] as the Crito: both are perfectly comprehensible if we regard the one as in the main a true statement of facts,[98] and the other as apparently a freer representation of the motives which deterred Socrates from flight. We may consider the Lysis, Charmides, and Laches, with all of which Aristotle seems to have been acquainted, to be youthful productions, written when Plato had not as yet essentially advanced beyond the Socratic standpoint; the Lesser Hippias, which is supported by very

which are not clear to me), takes offence because Ctesippus, 303 A., when the buffoonery of Dionysodorus has reached its height, gives up further opposition, with the words ἀφίσταμαι· ἀμάχω τὼ ἄνδρε, where, however, the irony is palpable. Still more unintelligible, at least in my opinion, is the assertion on p. 334 that the mention of Isocrates as the head of a school (Euthyd. 305 B) is such a flagrant violation of chronology that we cannot attribute it to Plato. If this is an un-Platonic anachronism, what must Schaarschmidt think of the anachronisms in the Symposium, the Gorgias, the Protagoras, and the Laws cf. my treatise on the Anachronisms of the Plat. Dial., Abh. d. Berl. Akad. 1873. Hist.-Phil. Kl. 79 sq.), which, however, he rightly accepts without scruple? But the Euthydemus not only does not mention Isocrates as the head of a school, but does not mention him at all; it simply represents Socrates as drawing a scientific character, in which the reader was to recognise Isocrates. This was just as possible and just as little an anachronism as Schaarschmidt's supposed reference to Antisthenes in the Theætetus. Grote (Plato, vol. i. 559), without doubting the genuineness of the Euthydemus, remarks that Euthydemus is treated as the representative of true philosophy and dialectic, though this is in glaring contradiction with all that precedes. But Plato states nothing of the kind: he merely says certain people regard the Sophists (τοὺς ἀμφὶ Εὐθύδημον) as their rivals, and seek therefore (because they confound the Sophists with the true philosophers) to disparage the philosophers.

[96] Cf. p. 70, 54.
[97] As Ast, 474 sq. 492 sq. decides with his usual confidence · on the other hand Schaarschmidt does not give any decided opinion.
[98] Vide Part i. p. 163, 1, and Ueberweg, Plat. Schr. 237 sq.

decisive Aristotelian evidence, as a first attempt; and the Euthyphro as an occasional writing,[99] of a slight and hasty character. On the other hand, there are so many weighty internal arguments against the Menexenus, that notwithstanding the passages in Aristotle's Rhetoric,[100] it is difficult to believe this work Platonic: if Aristotle really meant to attest it, we might suppose that in this one instance he was deceived by a forgery ventured upon soon after Plato's death.[101] The Ion is probably, and the Greater Hippias and First Alcibiades are still more probably, spurious.[102] The remainder of the dialogues in our collection, the Second Alcibiades, the Theages, the Anterasti, Hippar-

[99] Following the precedent of Hermann, Brandis and Steinhart (differing from my Plat. Stud. 150 in reference to the Hippias Minor), I have endeavoured to prove this in the Ztschr. f. Alterthumsw., 1851, p. 250 sq. The same view is embraced by Susemihl and Munk in the works I have so frequently quoted, also by Stein, Gesch. d. Plat. i. 80 sq., 135 sq., and Ueberweg (Gesch. d. Phil. 4th edit. i. 121 sq.) : on the contrary, Ribbing, Genet. Darst. d. plat Ideenl. ii. 129 sq., 103 sq., decides that the Euthyphro, Laches, Charmides, and Lysis, are genuine, while the Hippias Minor he considers to be spurious. Schaarschmidt (Samml. d. plat. Schr. 382 sq.) rejects the whole five dialogues. The latter is opposed by Bonitz in an exhaustive disquisition Zur. Erkl. plat. Dialoge (Hermes v.), 429 sq., specially with regard to the Laches. On the evidence of Aristotle vide p. 58, 31, 70; on the Euthyphro, Part i. p. 161, 1.
[100] On which cf. 54.
[101] With this judgment as regards the Menexenus, which I have already put forward in my Platonic Stud. 144 sq., following Ast, most of those who have treated the question, besides Grote, have since declared themselves in agreement; the question is discussed with particular thoroughness by Steinhart (Plat. W.W. vi. 372 sq.). I will refrain from entering upon it here, especially as the Menexenus is in no way an independent source for Platonic philosophy; Plato's relation to Rhetoric can in no instance be determined from this dialogue, and, in fact, even if genuine, its scope can only be conceived according to the explanations we give of other dialogues.
[102] Cf. Ztschr. f. Alterthumsw., 1851, p. 256 sq. Nor do I find anything in Munk to contradict this view.

chus, Minos, Clitophon, and Epinomis, have been rightly abandoned almost unanimously by all modern critics with the exception of Grote. It is impossible for a moment to allow any genuineness to the Definitions; and Karsten [103] and Steinhart,[104] following the example of Meiners, Hermann, and others, have conclusively shown that the Letters, as has so often happened, were foisted upon their reputed author at various dates.

It has indeed been questioned whether even the undoubted works of Plato present a true picture of his system. According to some, partly to increase his own importance, partly as a precautionary measure, Plato designedly concealed in his writings the real sense and connection of his doctrines, and only disclosed this in secret to his more confidential pupils.[105] This notion has been, however, since Schleiermacher [106] justly and almost universally abandoned.[107] It can be supported

---

[103] Commentatio. Critica de Platonis quæ feruntur epistolis. Utr. 1864.

[104] Pl. Werke, viii. 279 sq. Pl. L., 9 sq. A review of the earlier literature is given by the first of these passages, and by Karsten in the Introduction.

[105] This is the general opinion of earlier scholars. We may refer once for all to Brucker, 1, 659 sq., who gives a thorough and sensible investigation of the reasons for this concealment and the artifices employed; and Tennemann, System d. Plat. 1, 128 sq. 264, 111, 126, 129. Ast, Plat. Leb. u. Schr. 511, gives further details.

[106] Plato's Werke, 1, 1, 11 sq; cf. Ritter, ii. 178 sq., and Socher, Pl. Schr. 392 sq.

[107] One of its last supporters is Weisse, in the notes to his translation of Aristotle's Physics (pp. 271 sq.; 313, 329 sq.; 403 sqq.; 437 sq.; 445 sq.; 471 sq.), and de Anima, pp. 123-143. Hermann (Ueber Plato's Schrifstell Motive. Ges. Abh. 281 sq.) comes rather close to it when he asserts that we must not look for the nucleus of Plato's doctrine in his writings, and that his literary activity never aimed at establishing and developing an organic system of philosophy. Hermann would hardly say that Plato ignored or gave up

neither on Platonic nor Aristotelian evidence:[108] the assertions of later writers who transferred their concep-

all philosophic scope in his writings. But, according to his view, the writings only contain incidental hints of the real principles of Plato's system, the supra-sensuous doctrine of ideas. The application of the principles to questions and circumstances of the phenomenal world is given in the writings; the enunciation of the principles themselves was reserved for oral discourse. If, however, the inquiries of the Theætetus on the conception of knowledge, the discussions of the Sophist, Parmenides, Philebus, Symposium, Phædo, Republic, and Timæus on the nature of conceptions, the intended exposition in the 'Philosopher,' and, in fact, all the passages from which we are now able to form so complete a representation of the doctrine of Ideas—if these were not meant to expound and establish the principles of the system, it becomes difficult to account for them. They may sometimes exhibit a connection with alien questions; but it would argue little acquaintance with Plato's artistic method to conclude from this that they were introduced only incidentally. And Plato—v. Phædrus, 274 B sqq.—makes no division between the principles and their application. Indeed, it would have been rather preposterous to communicate the application of philosophic principles, by means of his writings, to all the world, even beyond the limits of his school, while he withheld the principles themselves, without which the application could not fail to be misunderstood. Ueberweg (Unters. plat. Schr. 65) brings forward in support of Hermann the fact that the Timæus and other writings give merely brief references to many points of essential importance. But he adds that it is the doctrine of the elements of the ideal world and of the soul that is dismissed with these passing notices, rather than the doctrine of ideas. And how do we know that at the time these treatises were written (there can be no question here, it must be remembered, of the Laws), the former doctrine had received its full development? Hermann eventually finds himself obliged to qualify considerably; and, in fact, his former assertions almost disappear. He allows, p. 298, that the Sophist and Parmenides, for instance, are concerned with philosophic principles; but he would account for this by referring them to an earlier period than the Phædrus. This may be disputed; and, at any rate, is in itself no justification for saying that philosophic principles are only incidentally referred to in Plato's writings. On page 300 he makes a further concession the writings of the Middle Period—the Sophist, &c. — 'are directly motived by scientific instruction, and seek to expound systematically the philosopher's fundamental opinions.' Finally, he contents himself with saying of the later writings, 'We cannot expect to find his highest principles enunciated here in broad unmistakable terms' (no intelligent student would have any such expectations); 'such enunciations were reserved for his oral discourses' (which seems highly im-

tions of the Pythagorean mystical doctrine to Plato,[109] consequently prove nothing. It is besides utterly incredible in itself that a philosopher like Plato should have spent a long life in literary labours, designed not

probable). 'But,' continues Hermann, 'these principles are so stamped upon the dialogues, that none with eyes to see can miss any point of real importance, and the dialogues may be used as trustworthy authorities for his philosophic system.' In these words we have everything we could wish for granted.

[108] The Phædrus, 274 B sqq., cannot be quoted in support. Plato is only showing there that the thing written is of no worth in itself, but only in so far as it helps recollection of the thing spoken. He does not say that the content of what is orally delivered should not be written down, but conversely, that that only should be written which has passed in personal intercourse. The Timæus, 28 C, is not more relevant, for, granted the impossibility of discussing anything except with persons of special knowledge, it does not follow that such discussion may not be in written works. Written works may be designed for specialists, and composed so that only they can understand them. In Ep. Plat. vii. 341 B sq.; 11, 312 D sq., we find for the first time something of the alleged secretiveness, in the assertion that no true philosopher entrusts his real thoughts to writing. But this is only one more proof of the spuriousness of the letters, and there is a great deal required to prove that the seventh letter (with Herm. loc. cit.) is just as authentic as anything that Plato tells us about Socrates. As to Aristotle's frequent quotations from Plato's oral discourses (vide subter, and p. 46, 5), several questions present themselves. First: How far do his accounts vary from the contents of the Platonic writings? Secondly: Are these variations to be ascribed to Plato himself, or to our informant? And, thirdly. May they not be explained by supposing a real change in Plato's way of thought or teaching? We shall discuss these points further on.

[109] E.g., the Platonic letters just quoted, which betray themselves at once by their clumsy exaggerations. The second letter, by the way, says that the Platonic writings were the work of Socrates in his youth. Another instance is Numenius apud Eusebium, Preparatio Evangelica, xiv. 5, 7 (cf. xiii. 5), who says that Plato wrote in a purposely obscure style, as a measure of precaution; Simpl De Anim. 7, loc. cit (of Plato and his pupils); ἐν ἀποῤῥήτοις μόνοις τοῖς ἀξίοις παραδιδόντες τὴν φιλοσοφίαν πρὸς τοὺς ἄλλους διὰ τῶν μαθηματικῶν αὐτὴν ἐπεδείκνυντο ὀνομάτων; cf. Cicero De Universo, 2, who supposes Plato to say (in the Timæus, 28 c), that it is not safe to speak openly of the Deity; and Josephus contra Apionem, 11, 31, cf. Krische Forschungen, 183 sq.

to impart his views, but to hide them; a purpose far more effectually and simply carried out by silence. Further he himself assigns the same content to the written as to the spoken word, when he makes the aim of the one to be the reminding us of the other.[110] And Aristotle could not have been aware of any essential difference between Plato's oral and written teaching, otherwise he would not have based his own exposition and criticism equally on both, without ever drawing attention to the fact that the true sense of the writings could only be determined by the spoken comments of their author. Still less would he have taken the mythical or half mythical portions in a literal manner, only possible to one who had never conceived the idea of a secret doctrine pervading them.[111] Nor can this theory be brought into connection with Plato's habit of indirectly hinting at his opinion and gradually arriving at it, instead of distinctly stating it when formed; with his occasional pursuit, in pure caprice as it might seem, of accidental digressions; with the confessions of ignorance or the doubting questions that, instead of a fixed unequivocal decision, conclude many of the dialogues; or with the method that in particular cases invests philosophic thoughts with the many-coloured veil of the mythus. All this, it is true, is found in Plato; and the reasons for such a method will hereafter disclose themselves. Meanwhile the form of the dialogues will offer no insuperable hindrance to their comprehension by anyone who has penetrated

[110] Phædrus, 276 D; cf. preceding note.

[111] Cf. on this my Plat. Stud. p. 201 sq.

their aim and plan, and learned to consider each in the light of the whole, and as explicable only in its relation to others; nor again is there anything in this form to weaken the belief [112] that in the writings of Plato we have trustworthy records of his philosophy. If, lastly, we find in these writings, side by side with philosophic enquiry, a considerable space allotted to historical description and dramatic imagery, it is yet easy in some cases to separate these elements, in others to recognise the philosophic kernel which they themselves contain.

[11] Cf. also Hegel, Gesch. d. Phil. II. 157 sq. 161 sq.

CHAPTER III.

THE ORDER OF THE PLATONIC WRITINGS.

OUR historical comprehension of the Platonic philosophy would be greatly facilitated did we possess more accurate knowledge of the dates of the several works, and the circumstances which influenced or gave rise to them. We should not only then understand much that now in particular dialogues either escapes our notice or remains a mystery, and be better informed as to their design and treatment, but we should also be in a position to judge with greater certainty of the mutual relations of the several works, and to follow step by step the development of Plato's system, so far as it is reflected in his writings. Unfortunately, however, we have not the means of accomplishing all this. The scanty notices of ancient authors as to the date and purpose of certain works are sometimes so untrustworthy that we cannot at all depend upon them,[1] and

---

[1] This holds good of the assertion (Diog iii. 35, brought in by φασί), that Socrates had heard the Lysis read, and Aristotle (ib. 37, acc. to Phavorinus) had heard the Phædo (presumably at its first publication); of the supposition in Diog. iii. 38 (cf. ibid. 62), Olympiod. v. Plat. 3, that the Phædrus was Plato's first written treatise (Cicero, however, Orat. 13, 42 places it later); of the statement of Athenæus (xi. 505 E), that Gorgias outlived the appearance of the dialogue named after him—of Gellius (N. A. xiv. 3, 3) that Xeno-

sometimes tell us nothing more than we might ourselves have derived from the works.² The information to be obtained from these as to their interconnection, design, and time of composition is necessarily of a very limited character. For as they profess to be records of Socratic dialogues, we find indeed in many of them the date and occasion of the alleged conversation either directly or indirectly given; but as to the time when they themselves were composed they are silent, and we can only in a few cases discover from the setting of a dialogue or from one of those anachronisms which Plato allowed himself with so much poetic license, the earliest date to which it can be assigned, and with some probability that also of its composition.³ It is likewise a consequence of their

phon composed his Cyropædia in opposition to the first two books of the Republic, and of Plutarch (Sol. 32), that Plato's death prevented the completion of the Critias. Cf. Ueberweg, Plat. Schr. 210 sq.

² E.g. Arist. Polit. ii. 6, beginn. and 1265, a. b. remarks that the Laws were composed later than the Republic, and that Plato wished to describe in them a state approaching nearer to actually existing states; but little by little it was brought round again to the ideal state of the Republic.

³ It appears from the beginning of the Theætetus that this dialogue is not earlier than the campaign against Corinth, in which Theætetus took part; but what campaign this was we do not learn (vide p. 18, 31). The Meno (acc. to p. 90, A) and the Symposium (acc. to 193, B) cannot have been composed before B.C. 395 and 385 respectively (for it is very improbable that the passage of the Meno can refer, as Susemihl believes, Jahrb. f. Philol. lxxvii. 854, not to the well-known event mentioned in Xen. Hell. iii. 5, but to some incident which has remained unknown to us; we cannot suppose that this incident, which clearly excited so much attention, could have been twice repeated in the course of a few years; and, moreover, before the successful attack of Agesilaus, Persian politics had no occasion to make such sacrifices in order to gain the goodwill of a Theban partyleader, both dialogues, however, seem to be not far distant from these dates. As to the date of the Menexenus, if it is really Platonic, it must have been written after the Peace of Antalcidas, and cannot by any means be placed before that

dramatic form, that the conversation should often develope itself from apparently accidental circumstances, without any definite theme being proposed; and even where there is such a theme, we still cannot be sure that it is the sole, or even the ultimate, end of the dialogue—the end by which we are to estimate its relations to other works; for the reply to this main question is often interwoven with farther enquiries of such importance and scope that it is impossible to regard them as merely subsidiary to the solution of the more limited problem at first proposed.[4] The final result also seems not unfrequently to be purely negative, consisting in the failure of all attempts to answer some query;[5] and though we cannot with Grote[6] conclude from this that Plato's design never extended beyond the refutation of every dogmatic assertion, and the exposition of that elenchtic method by which

time; the Parmenides, 126, B sq., pre-supposes that Plato's half-brother Pyrilampes, and consequently Plato himself, were no longer very young when this dialogue was written. The Apology, Crito, and Phædo, from what is implied in their contents, cannot come before the death of Socrates, nor the Euthyphro, Theætetus, Meno (according to 94 E), Gorgias (521 C), and Politicus (299 B) before the accusation of Socrates, how much later they are (except in the case of the Meno) cannot be determined by any historical data contained in the dialogues themselves. As regards the Republic, even if there were no other grounds for the supposition, Bk. ix. 577, A sq. makes it to a certain degree probable that this dialogue is earlier than Plato's first Sicilian visit. It no more follows from Bk. i. 336 A that the first book at least was written before the execution of Ismenias, B.C. 382 (Ueberweg, plat. Schr. 221), than that it was written before the death of Perdiccas and Xerxes. Cf. on the foregoing points Ueberweg, loc. cit. 217-265.

[4] E g. (besides the Sophist, Politicus, and Philebus), in the Republic, the working out of which goes far beyond the problem propounded Bk. ii. 367 E

[5] Cf. Prot 361 A; Charm. 175 A sq ; Lach. 199 E; Lys. 223 B; Hipp Min. 376 C ; Meno, 100 B, Theæt. 210 A sqq.; Parm. 166 C.

[6] Plato i 246, 269 sq.; 292, 515, ii. 278, 387 sq. ; 500, 550 sq.

Socrates confounded the fancied knowledge of his interlocutors; and that his criticism and dialectics neither rest on any positive conviction, nor even indirectly lead to any;[7] yet the positive element, that which is wanted to complete the critical discussions, is not always so evident as to be unmistakable. Again, if a dialogue relates to phenomena of the post-Socratic period, and perhaps is partly occasioned by them, Plato can only in the rarest instance[8] allow his Socrates plainly to speak of these phenomena; he is therefore restricted to hints, which were probably sufficiently comprehensible to the majority of his first readers, but may easily be overlooked or misinterpreted by us.[9] The same holds good with regard to the mutual inter-

[7] It is of itself scarcely credible that a philosopher who has created such a perfect system as Plato should have composed a whole series of writings, criticising alien views, without at the same time wishing to do anything towards the establishment of his own; Grote's assertion (i. 269, 292, ii. 563 sq.) that the affirmative and negative currents of his speculation are throughout independent of one another, each of them having its own channel, and that in his positive theories he pays as little regard as Socrates to difficulties and contradictions, which he had developed in the details of polemical discussions, is the natural consequence of his presuppositions, but it is in contradiction to all psychological probability. Consideration shows that many scruples thrown out in one dialogue receive in another the solution which Plato's point of view admits; and if this does not always happen, if many objections which Plato maintains against others might also be maintained against himself, this is simply a phenomenon which occurs in the case of Aristotle and many others as well, because it is generally easier to criticise than to improve—to expose difficulties than to solve them; it does not, however, follow that Plato in his dialectical discussions aimed at no positive result.

[8] Phædr. 278 E, about Isocrates, in the beginning of the Theætetus about Theætetus.

[9] Part i. 214 sq. We found it probable that in the Sophist he referred to the Megarians, Part i. p. 248, 4, 252 sqq.; in the Theætetus, Sophist, Euthydemus to Antisthenes, Part i. 303, 1; in the Philebus to Aristippus, p. 84, 94, in the Euthydemus to Isocrates. Many such allusions may occur in the Platonic writings without being remarked.

dependence of the dialogues. There cannot be a direct allusion in one dialogue to another, unless the same persons appear in both;[10] where this is not the case, the only way in which the later dialogue can point to the earlier is by shortly summing up the results of the former discussions, with the remark that the matter has been already considered.[11] But here again it is easy to make mistakes—to overlook the relation between two dialogues, or to imagine one that does not exist; and even when there is no doubt of such interdependence, the question may still sometimes arise which of the writings is the earlier and which the later. There are thus many difficulties, not only in the way of a decision respecting the motive, aim, and plan of the several dialogues,[12] but even of an enquiry into their order, date, and interdependence. Are they so related to each other as to form one, or perhaps more than one, connected series, or ought we to regard them merely as isolated productions, in which Plato, according as occasion or inclination prompted him, disclosed now one and now another fragment of his system, and brought his theories of life and of the world to bear on various subjects, sometimes even on those which had no direct reference to his philosophy?[13]

[10] E.g. in the Theætetus, Sophist and Politicus, the Republic, Timæus and Critias.

[11] In this way in all probability he refers in the Phædo to the Meno (vide p. 83, 91), in the Philebus to the Parmenides (cf. 70, 56), in the Republic, vi. 505 B, to the Philebus, x. 611 A sq., to the Phædo (vide p. 532, 2nd edit.), vi. 50, 6 C, to the Meno (97 A, D sq.), in the Timæus (51 B sq.), and also in the Symposium (202 A) to the Meno (97 sq) and the Theætetus (200 E sq), in the Laws (v. 739 B sq.; also iv 713 E; cf. Repub. v. 473 C), to the Republic and (iv. 713 C sq.) to the Politicus (vide 70, 53).

[12] A question on which I cannot enter here.

[13] The latter is the view of Socher, p. 43 sq., and, essentially

THE ORDER OF THE PLATONIC WRITINGS. 97

Supposing the former alternative to be the case,—is the connection of the writings the result of calculation and design? Or did it evolve itself naturally in the course of the author's life and mental development? Or were all these causes simultaneously at work, so that the origin and sequence of the Platonic writings should be ascribed partly to the philosopher's mental growth, partly to literary and artistic design, and partly also to accidental occasions? What influence again had each of these moments generally and particularly? And how, lastly, on either of the above presuppositions, are we to decide on the date and succession of the several works? On all these points, as is well known, opinions differ widely. Many of the ancient grammarians and commentators divided the works of Plato into certain groups and classes,[14] according to the affinity of

---

of Ast, p. 38 sqq, not to mention the older scholars, such as Tennemann, Plat. Phil i 137, 264

[14] We get a division according to form in Diog. iii. 49 sq., and Proleg. 17: the divisions are into dramatic, narrative, and mixed dialogues. Diog. himself, loc. cit., approves of a division according to matter; we have one like this given by Albinus, Isagoge in Plat. dial. c. 3, 6 Albinus divides the didactic from the zetetic dialogues (ὑφηγητικοί from ζητητικοί), and subdivides the didactic into theoretic and practical; the zetetic into gymnastic and agonistic. These again have further subdivisions; the theoretic dialogues into physical and logical, the practical dialogues into ethical and political. Under the head of gymnastic dialogues comes the so-called maieutic and peirastic; under that of agonistic the endeictic and anatreptic writings Diogenes makes the same primary division into didactic and zetetic dialogues, but proceeds to a triple subdivision, of the zetetic into physical, ethical (including political), and logical (according to the scheme of διδασκαλία, πρᾶξις, ἀπόδειξις), and of the didactic into gymnastic (peirastic and maientic), elenchtic, and agonistic (anatreptic). Aristophanes too in his determination of the trilogies, into which he divided a part of the Platonic dialogues (vide p. 51, 14), in correspondence with the connection which Plato himself has made between certain of them (Aristophanes' first trilogy is that of the Republic, and this seems to have been the standard which occasioned his whole arrangement).

their form or contents; and by this they apparently meant that they were following, at any rate partially, the order observed by Plato himself.[15] Their assumptions are, however, so arbitrary; Platonic doctrines are grouped from such un-Platonic points of view —the spirit and deeper reference of individual works are so little understood—the spurious is so greatly intermingled with the genuine, that this first attempt to determine the order of the writings was rather deter-

seems to have been directed partly by the relation of the contents of the dialogues, partly by referring to the supposed time of publication. The former, on the other hand, is the only starting point for Thrasyllus' arrangement. This grammarian (particulars about whom are given Part iii. a 542, 3, 2nd edit , and in the authorities quoted there) divides the dialogues (acc. to Diog. iii. 56 sqq., Albin. Isag. 4) in one respect just as Diogenes, into physical, logical, ethical, political, maieutic, peirastic, endeictic, anatreptic. This division, and also the double titles of certain dialogues, taken from their contents (Φαίδων ἢ περὶ ψυχῆς and so forth), he either borrowed from some one else or was the first to introduce; but he further divides the whole of the Platonic writings into the nine following tetralogies:—(1) Euthyphro, Apology, Crito, Phædo; (2) Cratylus, Theætetus, Sophist, Politicus; (3) Parmenides, Philebus, Symposium, Phædrus; (4) the two Alcibiades, Hipparchus, Anterastæ; (5) Theages, Charmides, Laches, Lysis; (6) Euthydemus, Protagoras, Gorgias, Meno; (7) the two Hippiæ, Ion, Menexenus; (8) Clitophon, Republic, Timæus, Critias; (9) Minos, Laws, Epinomis, Letters. The standard in this combination is unmistakably the contents of the writings; only in the first tetralogy the philosophical aims are not so much considered as the reference to the fate of Socrates personally. The existence of a series of different arrangements of the Platonic writings is proved (as Nietzsche remarks, Beitr. z. Quellenkunde d. Diog. Laert., Basel, 1870, 13 sq.) by the fact that Diog. iii. 62 mentions no less than nine dialogues, which were placed by different writers at the beginning of their catalogues, among them the Republic and Euthyphro, with which Aristophanes and Thrasyllus had commenced their lists respectively.

[15] According to Diogenes, Thrasyllus maintained that Plato himself published the dialogues in tetralogies. The much-debated question as to the order in which they should be read is of itself, strictly speaking, a presumption that they were arranged on a definite plan. Cf. Diog. 62, Albin. C 4 sqq.

rent than encouraging;[16] and the same judgment must be passed on those modern attempts which followed in the track of Thrasylus and Albinus.[17] Even Tennemann's enquiries into the chronological order of the Platonic works,[18] useful as they were in their time, are generally superficial in their neglect of any fixed and decisive point of view. The notion of an arrangement based upon the internal connection of the dialogues was first fully and satisfactorily carried out in Schleiermacher's brilliant work. According to this author,[19] Plato, as he certainly considered written instruction inferior to spoken,[20] and yet continued writing to such an extent even in old age, must have manifestly sought to make his writings resemble conversation as much as possible. Now the weak point of written teaching, as he himself intimates, is this: that it must always remain uncertain whether the reader has really apprehended the thought of the writer; and that there is no opportunity for defence against objections, or for the removal of misunderstandings. In order, as far as might be, to remedy these defects, Plato in his writings must have made it a rule so to conduct and plan every enquiry that the reader should be driven either to the origination of the required thought, or to the distinct consciousness of having missed it; and as the plan of

---

[16] Against recent defenders of the Thrasyllic tetralogies, cf. Herm. le Thrasyllo, Ind. lect. Gott. 185⅔. 13 sq.

[17] E.g. Serranus, Petit, Sydenham, Eberhard, and Geddes. With regard to these, it will suffice to refer to Schleiermacher, Pl. W. 1, 1, 24 sq; Ast, 49 sq.; Hermann, 562.

[18] Syst. d plat. Phil. 1, 115 sqq. He and his followers up to Hermann are mentioned by Ueberweg, Unters. d. plat. Schr 7-111.

[19] Loc. cit p 17 sqq.

[20] Phædr. 274 B sqq. Cf Protagoras, 329 A.

each separate dialogue clearly shows this design, there arises a natural sequence and a necessary mutual reference in the dialogues collectively. Plato could make no advance in any dialogue unless he presumed a certain effect to have been produced by its predecessor; consequently that which formed the conclusion of one must be presupposed as the basis and commencement of another. And as he regarded the various philosophical sciences, not as many and separate, but as essentially united and indivisible, there would result from this not many parallel independent orders of Platonic dialogues, but one all-embracing order. In this order, Schleiermacher proceeds to distinguish three divisions: [21] the elementary, the indirectly enquiring, and the expository or constructive dialogues. He does not maintain that the chronological succession of the works must necessarily and minutely correspond with this internal relation, nor that occasionally from some accidental reason that which came earlier in order of thought may not have appeared later in order of time. He claims only that his order should coincide in the main with the chronological order.[22] He allows that secondary works of comparatively less importance are intermingled with the principal dialogues, and he would also make room for those occasional writings which do not lie at all within the sphere of philosophy.[23] These concessions, however, do not affect his general canon.[24]

[21] Loc. cit. p 44 sqq.
[22] Loc. cit. p 27 sq.
[23] 38 sq.
[24] Schleiermacher reckons, in the first class of Plato's writings, the Phædrus, Protagoras, and Parmenides as chief works; the Lysis, Laches, Charmides, and Euthyphro

Ast agrees with Schleiermacher in distinguishing three classes of dialogues;[25] but differs from him considerably in his principle of classification, in his distribution of particular dialogues among the three classes, and in his judgment of their authenticity. Schleiermacher is still more decidedly opposed by Socher[26] and Stallbaum[27] in their attempt at a chronological order,[28] but neither of these writers fully

[25] Socratic, in which the poetic and dramatic element predominates; e.g. the Protagoras, Phædrus, Gorgias, and Phædo; dialectic or Megarian, in which the poetic element is in the background (Theætetus, Sophist, Politicus, Parmenides, Cratylus); purely scientific, or Socratic-Platonic, in which the poetic and dialectic elements interpenetrate reciprocally (Philebus, Symposium, Republic, Timæus, Critias). All the rest he regards as spurious. Cf. the criticisms of Brandis, 1, a. 163.

[26] Loc. cit. p. 41 sqq., &c.

[27] De Platonis vita, ingenio et scriptis (Dialogi selecti, 1827, Tom. i. 2 A; Opera, 1833, Tom. i.) developed, and in some points modified, in the Introductions to single dialogues, and in numerous Dissertations.

[28] Socher assumes four periods in his writings. 1. Up to Socrates' accusation and death: comprising the Theages, Laches, Hippias Minor, 1st Alcibiades, De Virtute, Meno, Cratylus, Euthyphro, Apologia, Crito, Phædo. 2. Up to the establishment of the school in the Academy, comprising the Ion, Euthydemus, Hippias Major, Protagoras, Theætetus, Gorgias, Philebus. 3. From that time to about the 55th or 60th year of Plato's life, to which belong the Phædrus, Menexenus, Symposium, Republic, and Timæus. 4. The period of old age, comprising the Laws. Stallbaum makes three periods: one, up to the time just after Socrates' death, including the Lysis, two Hippiæ, Charmides, Laches, Euthydemus, Cratylus, 1st Alcibiades, Meno, Protagoras, Euthyphro, Ion, Apology, Crito, Gorgias Of these he dates the Charmides about B.C. 405, and the Laches soon after (Plat. Opp. v. i 1834, p. 86, vi. 2, 1836, p. 142); the Euthydemus 403 (loc cit vi. 1, 63, sqq).—Ol. 94, 1; Cratylus. Olympiad 94, 2 (loc.

as secondary works; the Apology and Crito as occasional pieces of essentially historical import, and other minor dialogues as probably spurious In the second class he puts the Gorgias and Theætetus, with the Meno as an appanage, and at a further interval the Euthydemus and Cratylus, then come the Sophist, Politicus, Symposium, Phædo, and Philebus. Some few dialogues are passed over as spurious, or at least doubtful. His third class contains the Republic, Timæus, and Critias; and the Laws, again as an appanage.

established this order, or reduced it to a fixed principle. Hermann was the first to controvert the conclusions of Schleiermacher by a new theory, founded on a definite view of the origin of the Platonic writings;[29] for his predecessor Herbart, while seeking to prove the gradual transformation of the doctrine of ideas by the help of the dialogues,[30] had not applied this point of view to our collection as a whole. Like Schleiermacher, Hermann is convinced that the Platonic writings, collectively, represent a living, organic development; but he seeks the cause of this phenomenon, not in any design or calculation on the part of their author, but in the growth of his mind. They are not, in his opinion, a mere exposition of philosophic development for others, but a direct consequence of Plato's individual development. Plato, he thinks, ripened only

---

cit. v. 2, 26); Alcibiades, at the time when Anytus began his proceedings against Socrates (loc. cit vi. 1, 187); Meno, Olympiad 94, 3 (loc. cit. vi. 2, 20); Protagoras, Olympiad 94, 3 or 4 (Dial. Sel. 11, 2, 16; Opp. vi. 2, 142); Euthyphro, Olympiad 95, 1 = B.C. 399, at the beginning of the prosecution (loc cit); Ion same period (loc. cit iv. 2, 289), and the remaining three, Olympiad 95, 1, soon after Socrates' death (Dial. Sel. 11, 1, 24). His second period ranges between the first and second Sicilian journey, and comprises the Theætetus, Sophist, Politicus, Parmenides, all four written between B.C. 399 and 388, and published immediately afterwards (cf. Rep. pp 28–45; previously, in his treatise De Arg. et Art. Theæt. 12 sqq., and Parm. 290 sq, Stallbaum had dated them two years later); soon after these the Phædrus, followed by the Symposium, a little later than B.C 385 (Dial. Sel. iv. 1, xx. sqq.), then the Phædo, Philebus, and Republic, Olympiads 99–100: (Dial. Sel. iii. 1, lxii. sq.). The third period is between the second Sicilian journey and Plato's death, including the Laws and the Critias, the latter begun before the Laws, but finished after. (Cf. Opp. vii. 377.)

[29] Loc. cit., cf. especially 346 sq., 384 sq., 489 sqq.

[30] In the treatise De Plat. Systematis fundamento, 1808 (Wks xii 61 sqq), but especially in the appendix (ibid. 88 sq · cf. Ueberweg, loc. cit. 38 sq)

gradually, and under the influences of his time; the stadia along his course are marked by the different classes of his writings. The two events of greatest consequence in his mental history are, according to Hermann, the death of Socrates, with its immediate result, Plato's withdrawal to Megara; and his own first journey, which acquainted him with the Pythagorean doctrine.[31] While these indicate the chief periods of his intellectual life and literary activity, they also furnish us with three classes of dialogues—the Socratic or elementary; the dialectic or mediatising; the expository or constructive. The dialogues of the first class, written in part before the death of Socrates, in part immediately after, have a fragmentary, more exclusively elenchtic and protreptic character, confine themselves almost entirely to the Socratic manner, and as yet go no deeper into the fundamental questions of philosophy. The second class is distinguished by greater dryness, less liveliness, less carefulness of form, and by that searching criticism (sometimes approving, sometimes polemical) of the Megaro-Eleatic philosophy, which occupied the time of Plato's sojourn in Megara. In the third period, there is on the one hand, as to style, a return to the freshness and fulness of the first;[32] while on the other, Plato's horizon has

---

[31] Hermann himself says, p. 384, 'the return to his native city and the beginning of his career as teacher in the Academy.' But in what follows he really assigns Plato's acquaintance with Pythagoreanism, acquired on his travels, as the deciding motive in his philosophic development.

[32] Hermann accounts for this, p. 397, as follows: 'It was not till his return to his native city that the reminiscences of his youth could once more rise before his soul.' This would certainly be a remarkable effect of external cir-

been enlarged by the enquiries of the Megarian period, by residence in foreign countries, and especially by the knowledge he there acquired of the Pythagorean philosophy; and from the fusion of all these elements we get the most perfect expositions of his system, in which the Socratic form receives the deepest content, and thus attains its highest ideal.[33] The views of modern writers on this question fluctuate for the most part between Schleiermacher and Hermann. For example, Ritter[34] and Brandis,[35] and more recently Rib-

cumstances on a character like Plato's, but scarcely more remarkable, perhaps, than the influence which Hermann ibid. suspects, of the separation—a separation of a few miles—from the metropolis of Greek classicality, in producing the crudities of the Megarian dialogues.

[33] Hermann gives a full discussion of the Lysis, as the type of the first class, which includes the Lesser Hippias, Ion, 1st Alcibiades, Charmides, Laches, and in completion the Protagoras and Euthydemus. The Apology, Crito, and Gorgias are a transition to the second class, and the Euthyphro, Meno, and Hippias Major come still nearer to it, but its proper representatives are the Theætetus, Sophist, Politicus, and Parmenides. The third class is headed by the Phædrus, as an inaugural lecture at the opening of the Academy. Socher, 307 sq., and Stallbaum, Introd. Phæd. iv. 1, xx sq., had already conceived this to be the position of the Phædrus. The Menexenus is an appendage to this, and the Symposium, Phædo, and Philebus are riper productions of the same period, which is completed by the Republic, Timæus, and Critias The Laws come last, suggested by the experiences of the latter Sicilian journeys.

[34] Ritter, Gesch. d. Phil. ii. 186, attaches only a secondary importance to the enquiry into the order of the Platonic writings, as he impugns the existence of any important difference of doctrine in them, and does not allow a purely Socratic period in Plato's literary activity to the extent to which its recognition is justified. He gives up all certainty of results beforehand, but is inclined to think—agreeing with Schleiermacher's three literary periods—that the Phædrus was written before the Protagoras (an inference from p. 275 sqq., compared with Prot. 329, A, which does not seem decisive to me), and before and after these the Lesser Hippias, Lysis, Laches, Charmides; then the Apology, Crito, Euthyphro; next the Gorgias, Parmenides, Theætetus, Sophist, Politicus, perhaps about the same time the Euthydemus, Meno, and Cratylus, later on, the Phædo, Philebus, and Symposium, and

bing,[36] follow Schleiermacher in the main; Schwegler[37] and Steinhart ally themselves with Hermann;[38]

last the Republic, Timæus (Crit.) and Laws.

[35] Brandis, ii. 152 sqq., defends Schleiermacher's view with much force and acuteness against the attacks of Hermann, without maintaining the former's arrangement in all its details. He would assign the Parmenides to the second literary period, and not place the Meno, Euthydemus, and Cratylus between the Theætetus and Sophist. He sets the Phædrus, however, in the front rank, with Schleiermacher, and next to it the Lysis, Protagoras, Charmides, Laches, Euthyphro; and assents generally to the leading ideas of Schleiermacher's arrangement.

[36] Ribbing, in his 'Genet Darstellung der plat Ideenlehre'(Leipz 1863), the second part of which is devoted to an examination into the genuineness and arrangement of the writings, puts forward the hypothesis that the scientific contents and the scientific form of the Platonic writings must be the standard for their arrangement, and that the order arrived at from this point of view must coincide with their proper chronological order. In accordance with this supposition he marks out, in agreement with Schleiermacher, three classes, among which he divides the particular dialogues in the following way: (1) Socratic Dialogues, i e. such as particularly keep to the Socratic method of philosophizing, and are connected with the Platonic system propædeutically. Phædrus, Protagoras, Charmides (acc. to p. 131 sq. also Lysis), Laches, Euthyphro, Apology, Crito, and as a transition to the second class, Gorgias. (2) Dialectico-theoretic dialogues: Theætetus, Meno, Euthydemus, Cratylus, Sophist, Politicus, Parmenides. (3) Synthetic and progressive dialogues: Symposium, Phædo, Philebus, Republic, with which (p. 117 sq.) the Timæus, together with the Critias and the doubtful Hermocrates, must be connected, though not intimately, on account of their exposition of peculiar views The remaining writings, and amongst these the Laws, Ribbing considers spurious.

[37] Hist. of Phil , 3rd edit. p. 43 sq.

[38] Steinhart arranges the dialogues as follows: 1st, Purely Socratic · Ion, Hippias Major and Minor, 1st Alcibiades (before Alcibiades' second banishment, B C. 406), Lysis, Charmides (at the beginning of the rule of the Thirty, B.C. 404), Laches, Protagoras. Socratic, transitional to the doctrine of Ideas: Euthydemus, B.C. 402 , Meno, 399 ; Euthyphro, Apology, Crito, same year; Gorgias, soon after the beginning of the sojourn at Megara; Cratylus, somewhat later. 2nd, Dialectical : Theætetus, B C. 393, composed perhaps at Cyrene ; Parmenides, probably between the Egyptian and Sicilian journey, Sophist and Politicus, same time or perhaps during the Italian journey. 3rd, Works belonging to Plato's maturity, after his travels in Italy and more exact acquaintance with Pythagorean philosophy the Phædrus, B C. 388; Symposium, 385 ; Phædo, Philebus, Republic, about 367 ; Timæus, Laws In his Life of Plato, however (301, 2, 232 sq), the Meno

Susemihl tries to reconcile both,[39] and similarly Ueberweg,[40] holding that the view of Plato's works, as evincing a gradual development of his philosophy, has no less historical justification than the other view of a methodical design determining the order of the works, demands that the two principles should be to some extent the limit, and to some extent the complement, one of the other. He ultimately inclines very much to the side of Schleiermacher, placing, however, the commencement of Plato's literary career much later than Schleiermacher does, and differing considerably from all his predecessors with regard to the order of the several writings.[41] The theories of Munk and

is placed in the time after Socrates' death: and the Philebus, with Ueberweg in Plato's last period, between the Timæus and the Laws

[39] He agrees with Hermann in saying that at the beginning of his literary career Plato had not his whole system already mapped out. But he does not agree with Hermann's further theory, viz., that Plato was unacquainted with earlier philosophies in Socrates' lifetime, and that therefore the acquaintance shown with Eleatic and Pythagorean doctrines is a decisive criterion of the date of any work. His arrangement, accordingly, is slightly different from his predecessor's, the first series comprises Socratic or propædeutic ethical dialogues,—Hippias Minor, Lysis, Charmides, Laches, Protagoras, Meno (399 B C), Apology, Crito, Gorgias (soon after Socrates' death), Euthyphro (rather later). The 2nd series, dialectic dialogues of indirect teaching: Euthydemus, Cratylus (both perhaps written at Megara), Theætetus (after 394 and the visit to Cyrene), Phædrus (389-8), Sophist, Politicus, Parmenides, Symposium (383-4), Phædo. Third series, constructive dialogues. Philebus, Republic (between 380 and 370), Timæus, Critias, Laws

[40] Enquiry into the Platonic writings, 89-111, 74 sq., 81.

[41] In the above-mentioned work (p. 100 sq 293) with regard to the Protagoras, Lesser Hippias, Lysis, Charmides, and Laches, Ueberweg considers it probable that they were composed in Socrates' lifetime, while the Apology and Crito (p. 246 sq.) were composed immediately after his death. To the same period he thinks the Gorgias must belong (p. 249); the Phædrus on the contrary (252 sq., 101) to the years 377-5 B.C., that the Symposium must have been written 385-4 (219 sq.), not long after the

Weisse stand almost alone. While most commentators since Schleiermacher have based their enquiry into the order of the Platonic books chiefly on the contents, these two writers pay much more attention to the form; Munk taking his criterion of earlier or later authorship from the date to which each dialogue is internally assigned,[42] and Weisse from the distinction of direct and narrated dialogues.[43] A few other authors, who

[42] ...hædrus; the Euthydemus (258, 35), between the Phædrus and the Phædo, the Republic and the Timæus, and still earlier before the Phædo the Meno (281 sq.). The Theætetus Ueberweg (227 sq) places in the year 368, or thereabouts; the Sophist, Politicus, and Philebus (p 204 sq., 275, 171, 290 p.), as also the Laws, in Plato's last years (p. 221, 171) The Parmenides he considers spurious supra 82, 86) These views are modified in the treatise 'Ueber den Gegensatz zwischen Methodikern und Genetikern,' Ztschr f. Philos. . F. cvii 1870, p. 55 sq.: cf. Grundr 1. 121, 4th edit. (besides the statements about the Sophist, Politicus, and Meno, quoted pp 82, 3; 83, 90). Ueberweg now thinks it likely that Plato's writings as a whole belong to the period after the founding of the school in the Academy; and further, as a necessary consequence of this supposition, he deduces the sequence of all the writings without exception from a deliberate and systematic plan; and, finally, in harmony with this, he places the Protagoras and the kindred dialogues between the Symposium and the Republic.
[44] In his treatise: 'The Natural arrangement of the Platonic Writings' (cf. especially p 25 sq.) Munk goes on the supposition that Plato wished to give in the main body of his writings—'in the Socratic cycle —not so much an exposition of his own system, as a complete, detailed, and idealised picture of the life of the true philosopher, Socrates, and as that presupposes a plan in accordance with which he determined the external investiture of the dialogues, so the times of publication show the order in which Plato intended them to be read, and on the whole also that in which they were composed. In particular Munk makes the dialogues of the Socratic cycle follow one another thus, in three divisions: (1) Parmenides,· Protagoras, Charmides, Laches, Gorgias, Ion, Hippias Major, Cratylus, Euthydemus, Symposium ; (2) Phædrus, Philebus, Republic, Timæus, Critias; (3) Meno, Theætetus, Sophist, Politicus, Euthyphro, Apology, Crito, Phædo. Outside the cycle come the dialogues which were composed before Socrates' death, or on special occasions, such as on the one hand Alcibiades I., Lysis, and Hippias II, on the other the Laws and the Menexenus.

[43] Schone (on Plato's Protagoras,

108   *PLATO AND THE OLDER ACADEMY.*

have never sought definitely to establish their theories,[44] can only be shortly mentioned in this place.

1862, p. 8 sq.) wishes to make this distinction the ground of an enquiry into the chronological order of Plato's writings He appeals to the passage in the Republic, iii. 392 C sq, where Plato banishes the drama from his state, and together with lyric poetry allows only narrative poetry, and that too under fixed and limited conditions. With him he combines as standards for judgment, the æsthetic and stylistic points of view, because the style of the particular writings is a more universal and trustworthy criterion of their genuineness and date than their subject matter, and the affinity of style will be very closely connected with the time of production. According to this point of view, as he remarks, the Platonic works will arrange themselves somewhat as follows: (1) Laws, Cratylus, Theætetus, Sophist, Politicus, Philebus, Timæus, Critias, Meno, Phædrus: (2) Menexenus, Apology, Crito, Gorgias, Laches, Charmides, Protagoras, Symposium, Parmenides, Republic, Phædo: the *direct* dialogues are—Gorgias, Cratylus, Critias, Crito, Laches, Meno, Laws, Phædrus, Philebus, Politicus, Sophist, Theætetus, Timæus; the *indirect* are—Charmides, Parmenides, Phædo, Protagoras, Republic, Symposium. The Apology is related to the direct, the Menexenus to the indirect dialogues. The writings not mentioned here Schöne apparently does not allow to be Plato's. He says, however, in his preface that he is indebted to a lecture of Weisse for his fundamental conceptions as to the Platonic question, and also for many details in his treatise.

[44] Suckow, Form d. Plat. Schrift. 508 sq, supposes with Schleiermacher ' an arrangement and sequence of the Platonic dialogues according to deliberate and special aims.' His arrangement, however, widely deviating from Schleiermacher is as follows: (1) Parmenides, Protagoras, Symposium, Phædrus; (2) Republic and Timæus; (3) Philebus, Theætetus, Sophist, Apology, Phædo. (The Politicus and the Laws he considers spurious as regards the remaining dialogues he expresses no opinion.) Stein (Sieb. Bucher z. Gesch. d. Plat. i. 80 sq.) separates the Platonic dialogues into three groups: (1) introductory (Lysis, Phædrus, Symposium); (2) such as work out the system in its particular elements, Ethics (Meno, Protagoras, Charmides, Laches, Euthyphro, Euthydemus), Science (Theætetus), the theory of the Good (Gorgias and Philebus), the theory of Ideas (Parmenides, Sophist, and Politicus), Psychology (Phædo); — (3) the dialogues which construct the State and the system of Nature (Republic, Timæus, Critias, Laws). He regards as supplementary the Apology, Crito, Menexenus, the two Hippiæ, Ion, Alcibiades I., and Cratylus. The relation of this division to the time of the composition of the dialogues he has not yet explained. Rose, De Arist. libr. ord. 25, proposes the following arrangement: Apology, Crito, Alcibiades I., Euthyphro, Laches, Lysis, Charmides, two Hippiæ, Ion, Menexenus, Protagoras, Euthyde-

If we would gain a sure standard for this enquiry, e ostensible date of the dialogues and the historical sition which Socrates occupies in them must not be ken into account; for we have no proof at all that e order which would thus result is the order in iich they were composed, or that Plato ever inaded to portray his master in a continuous, bioaphical manner. Indeed, this assumption is refuted, it only by the indications given in several of the orks as to the time when they were written,[45] but so by the circumstance that the Socrates of Plato scourses of philosophy[46] in exactly the same manner, age and in youth; and during the last years of his fe pursues enquiries which formed the elementary oundwork of dialogues purporting to be earlier.[47] The ct that Plato in the Theætetus explicitly makes loice of the direct dramatic form of conversation to roid the inconveniences of second-hand repetition,[48]

us, Gorgias, Meno, Theætetus, iphist, Cratylus, Parmenides, oliticus, Phædrus, Symposium, iædo, Republic, Timæus, Critias, iilebus, Laws, Epinomis, and as ato's last work a letter composed our 7th and 8th Platonic letters, itten Olymp. 107, 1. Alcibiades . and Theages, if they are inuine, precede the Protagoras.

[45] According to this the Meno, id probably also the Theætetus, ust be earlier than the Symposium id the Timæus vide supra 93, 3; i, 11. According to Munk they are later.

[46] For instance in the Euthydenus, where he is ἤδη πρεσβύτερος 72 B), his philosophic method resembles that in the Protagoras, where he is a young man; and in the Euthyphro, a short time before his death, it resembles that in the Charmides (B.C 432) and the Laches (420 B.C): cf. Grote, I. 191.

[47] Cf. e.g. the relation of the Theætetus to the Parmenides, of the Republic to the Timæus, of the Politicus, Gorgias, Meno, and Euthyphro to the Republic, of the Phædrus to the Symposium Munk perverts these relations in a very unsatisfactory way. Cf. also Susemihl's thorough criticism of Munk's work. Jahrb. fur Philol. lxxvii. 829 sq.

[48] Page 143 B. sq, a passage which can only be explained on

and that he elsewhere more than once connects, either expressly or by an unmistakeable reference, a direct dialogue with an indirect one preceding it,[49] would of itself suffice to rebut the theory of Weisse; for the suppositions that are necessary to countervail this evidence[50] go much farther than is permissible to pure conjecture. Nor have we any right to suppose that Plato gave unconditional preference to the repeated dialogue, except in cases where it was important for the attainment of the required end—to describe with some minuteness the persons, motives, and accompanying circumstances of the conversation;[51] he doubtless, during his whole literary career, employed both forms indifferently, as occasion offered. There are other and more important clues by which we can to some extent determine the chronological order of the writings, and

the supposition that the Theætetus was preceded by other narrated dialogues (as the Lysis, Charmides, and Protagoras)

[49] The Timæus and the Laws to the Republic, the Philebus (supra, 70, 56) to the Parmenides.

[50] That the introduction of the Theætetus is not genuine, that the Republic in an earlier recension had the form of a direct dialogue, that the Laws (in spite of the evidences and proofs mentioned supra, pp. 93, 2; 96, 11) were written before the Republic, but were only acknowledged after Plato's death; Schöne, p. 6 sq

[51] For the passage in the Republic which refers only to dramatic, epic, and lyric poetry, allows no reasoning from analogy as to Plato's procedure in writings which serve quite another aim, the philosophic-didactic. Here the question is not about the imitation of different characters, but about the exposition of philosophic views Should, however, that inference be drawn, we fail to see what advantage the narrated dialogues had in this respect over the direct, inasmuch as the expressions of the Sophists and like persons, at the representation of whom offence might have been taken, in the one just as much as in the other were related in direct speech, consequently διὰ μιμήσεως and not ἁπλῇ διηγήσει (Rep. 392 D). The most unworthy traits which Plato represents, such as the obstinacy and buffoonery of Euthydemus and Dionysodorus, are described by Socrates, just as much as the bluntness of Thrasymachus in Rep. 1. 336 B

also the question whether or not that order arises from conscious design. Such are the references in various dialogues to events in Plato's lifetime: they are, however, but few in number, and point only to the date before, and not after, which a dialogue could not have been written.[52] While, therefore, much valuable information of a particular kind is to be gained from them, they do not nearly suffice for the arrangement of the works as a whole. A further criterion might be found in the development of Plato's literary art. But though first attempts, as a rule, are wont to betray themselves by a certain amount of awkwardness, it does not follow that the artistic excellence of an author's works keeps exact pace with his years. For liveliness of mimetic description and dramatic movement, even delicacy of taste and sensitiveness to form, are with most persons, after a certain age, on the decline; and even before that period, artistic form may be kept in the background by the exigencies of strictly scientific enquiry; the mood of an author, the circumstances in which he writes, the purpose for which particular works were composed, may determine the amount of care bestowed and of finish attained, without affording us a clue as to their relative dates; and again, that which Plato intended for the narrow circle of his personal disciples would probably be less ornate as to style than writings designed to awaken scientific interest in a large and mixed number of readers, and to give them their first introduction to philosophy.[53] On similar grounds,

---

[52] Cf. supra, 93, 3.
[53] The remark in reference to this on p. 80 (as to the genuineness of the writings), finds an analogous

however, the scientific method in each later work is not necessarily more perfect than in the earlier, though, on the whole, the fluctuations may be slighter and the progress more steady and continuous. Although, therefore, in considering the mutual relation of two dialogues, this point of view ought not to be disregarded, in many cases the question cannot be decided by reference to it alone. The philosophic content of the various writings affords a safer test. But here also we must begin by enquiring to what extent and under what conditions the relative dates of the dialogues may be inferred from differences in their contents; and what are the characteristics which show whether an exposition really belongs to an earlier stage of its author's development or was purposely carried less far. Plato's own statements give us no information on this point. In a much criticised passage of the Phædrus (274 C sqq.) he objects to written expositions on the ground that they are not restricted to persons who are capable of understanding them, but come into the hands of every one alike, and are therefore liable to all kinds of

application to the order of composition. Even in the case of poets and artists, the supposition that their more complete works are always their latest would lead to mistakes without end; and though in many of them of course the epochs of their development are shown by marked stylistic peculiarities, still it would be exceedingly difficult for us in most cases to determine these epochs precisely, and to assign to them their proper works, if, as in the case of Plato, we had preserved to us only the works themselves, and not any trustworthy accounts about the time of their origin as well. This difficulty is still greater in dealing with a writer to whom the mere artistic form of his works is not an independent and separate object, but only the means to other aims, which themselves limit the conditions and direction of its application.

misconception and unfounded abuse; he would have them regarded in the light of a mere pastime, useful indeed for reminding those already instructed of what in after years they may have forgotten, but far less valuable than personal influence, by which others are scientifically educated and led to right moral convictions. However important this passage may be in another connection, it affords us no help in determining the order, date, and interdependence of the Platonic writings. We cannot conclude from it, as Schleiermacher does, that Plato in each of the dialogues must have assumed the result of an earlier one—unless it be previously shown that there existed among the dialogues a single inter-connected order; for particular dialogues could serve very well for a reminder of oral discourse, and the thoughts engendered by it, even were there no such connection among them. Nor can we presuppose, with Socher[54] and his followers, that Plato could only have expressed himself in this manner at the time when he had commenced, or was about to commence, his school in the Academy; for, in the first place, there was nothing to hinder his exercising that intellectual influence on others—the planting of words in souls fitted for them—of which he here speaks, even before the establishment of regular teaching in the Academy; and, secondly, it is quite possible that in this passage he is not contrasting his literary activity with that kind of instruction which, as a matter of

---

[54] Plato's Schriften, 307. Likewise Stallbaum, Hermann, Steinhart, Susemihl (Genet. Entwick. i. 286; and further references), Ueberweg (Plat. Schr. 252, 128).

fact, he employed, but with the kind he desired, and, according to the Socratic precedent, kept before him as his ideal.[55] Still less can the quotation from the Phædrus lend support to the theory that the compilation of all the dialogues was bound up with Plato's instructions in the Academy;[56] for, understand it as we will, it only expresses the opinion of the author at that particular time, and we do not know how early it was adopted nor how long retained. That in his more comprehensive works at least, he entered upon subjects which in his oral teaching he either passed over, or dealt with more slightly, is in itself likely, and is confirmed by the citations of Aristotle.[57] If, however, it is impossible, even from this passage, to discover either the principles followed by Plato in the arrangement of his writings, or the time when these were composed, the scientific contents themselves contain evidences by which we can distinguish, with more or less certainty, the earlier from the later works. It cannot, indeed, be expected that Plato should expound his whole system in each individual work: it is, on the contrary, sufficiently clear that he often starts in a preliminary and tentative manner from presuppositions of which he is himself certain. But in all the strictly philosophic writings, the state of his own scientific conviction is sure to be somehow betrayed: he either directly enunciates it, if only by isolated hints, when he is designedly confining an enquiry to a subordinate and

---

[55] In the Protagoras also (347 E, 329 A), which most critics rightly place far earlier (387 B.C.), he contrasts the songs of poets, and books generally, with personal conference. Cf. too the Phædrus.

[56] Ueberweg, Ztschr. f. Philos. lvii. 64.

[57] Cf. page 74.

merely preparatory stage; or he allows it to be indirectly perceived in ordering the whole course of the argument toward a higher aim, and foreshadows in the statement of problems their solution in the spirit of his system. If, therefore, out of a number of works, otherwise related to one another, we find some that are wanting in certain fundamental determinations of Platonism, and do not even indirectly require them; while in others these very determinations unmistakeably appear—we must conclude that at the time when the former were written, these points were not clearly established in Plato's own mind, or at any rate not so clearly as when he wrote the latter. If, again, two writings essentially presuppose the same scientific stand-point, but in one of them it is more definitely stated and more fully evolved; if that which in the one case is only prepared for indirectly, or generally established, in the other is distinctly maintained and carried out into particulars, it is probable that the preparatory and less advanced exposition was purposely meant to precede the more perfect and more systematically developed. The same holds good of Plato's references to the pre-Socratic doctrines. He may indeed have been acquainted with these doctrines to a greater or less extent, without expressly touching on them; but as we find him in the majority of his works either openly concerned with the most important, or at any rate unmistakeably pointing to them, while in others he silently passes them by—it is at least highly probable that the latter, generally speaking, date from a time when he did not bestow much attention on those doctrines, or was much less influenced by them than he afterwards became. Even if we suppose that he purposely abstained from mentioning them, we must still, in the absence of any internal proof to the contrary, consider those writings as the earlier in which such mention does not occur; for in that case the most probable assumption would be that his silence proceeded from a desire to ground his readers thoroughly on a Socratic foundation, before introducing them to the pre-Socratic science.

Lastly, great weight must be allowed to the allusions of one dialogue to another. These allusions indeed, as before remarked,[58] can very seldom take the form of direct citation; yet there are often clear indications that the author intended to bring one of his works into close connection with some other. If in a particular dialogue an enquiry is taken up at a point where in another it is broken off; if thoughts which in the one case are stated problematically or vaguely suggested, in the other are definitely announced and scientifically established; or if, conversely, conceptions and theories are in one place attained only after long search, and are elsewhere treated as acknowledged truths, everything favours the supposition that the one dialogue must be later in date than the other, and intended as the application of its results. The author may either, in the composition of the earlier dialogue, have had the later one in view, or he may himself only have attained to the more advanced stand-point in the interval of time between them. In certain cases it

[58] Pp. 95, 96.

may still be doubtful whether a discussion is related to another as preparatory groundwork or complementary superstructure: in general, however, further enquiry will decide.

If then we attempt to apply these principles to the question before us, we shall find, as might be expected, that none of the theories we have been considering can be rigidly carried out; that the order of the Platonic writings cannot depend wholly either on design and calculation to the exclusion of all the influences arising from external circumstances and Plato's own development; or on the gradual growth of Plato's mind, to the exclusion of any ulterior plan; or, still less, on particular moods, occasions, and impulses. We shall not press the assumptions of Schleiermacher to the extent of supposing that Plato's whole system of philosophy and the writings in which it is contained stood from the first moment of his literary activity complete before his mind, and that during the fifty years or more over which that activity extended he was merely executing the design thus formed in his youth. Even Schleiermacher did not go so far as this; and though he constantly refers the order of the Platonic works too exclusively to conscious design, we shall not very greatly diverge from his real opinion if we suppose that when Plato began to write, he was indeed clear about the fundamental points of his system, and had traced out the general plan by which he meant to unfold it in his writings; that this plan, however, was not at once completed in its details, but that the grand outlines which alone in the commencement floated before him were afterwards gradually filled in—perhaps, also, sometimes in compliance with special circumstances altered and enlarged, according to the growth of his knowledge and the recognition of more definite scientific necessities.[59] On the other hand Hermann's point of view does not involve the conclusion, though he himself seems to arrive at it—that Plato put together his system from outside, mechanically joining piece to piece, and expounding it in writings farther and farther, according as he became acquainted with this or that older school. The same principle of interpretation applies equally on the supposition that he developed the Socratic doctrine from within; and that, instead of his acquaintance with another system of philosophy being the cause of his advance to another stage of his philosophic development, the progress of his own philosophic conviction was in fact the cause of increased attention to his predecessors. Lastly, if, in explaining the origin and sequence of the Platonic writings, we chiefly rely on external circumstances and personal moods,[60] even then we need not, with Grote,[61] pronounce the whole question hopeless, we can still enquire whether the contents of the works do not prove a gradual change in their author's stand-point, or the relation of one dialogue to another. This whole matter, however, is not to be decided on à

---

[59] So Brandis, i. a. 160, defining more precisely Hermann's objections (p. 351) to Schleiermacher's view: 'Plato's creative genius early evolved from the Socratic doctrines the outlines of his future system: clear and precise from the first, their innate strength attained a gradual and regular development.'

[60] Cf. p. 96.

[61] Plato, 1. 186 sq.

priori grounds, but only by careful consideration of the Platonic writings themselves.

Among these writings, then, there are certainly several which not only make passing allusion to phenomena of the time, but are only comprehensible in relation to definite historical events. The chief purpose of the Apology is to give the speech of Socrates in his own defence; that of the Crito, to explain the reasons by which he was deterred from flight out of prison;[62] the Euthyphro seems to have been occasioned by the indictment of Socrates, in conjunction with another concurrent incident;[63] the Euthydemus by the appearance of Antisthenes together with that of Isocrates, and the charges brought by both against Plato.[64] But even in such works as these, which, strictly speaking, are to be considered as occasional, the stand-point of the author is so clearly manifest that we can without difficulty assign them to a particular period of his life. The main purpose, however, of the great majority of the dialogues, be their outer motive what it may, is the representation and establishment of the Platonic philosophy: it is therefore all the more to be expected that we should in some measure be able to trace in them how far Plato at the time of their composition had either himself advanced in the formation of his system, or to what point he then desired to conduct the reader; and on what grounds he assumes that his system might be known to the reader from earlier

---

[62] And at the same time in the defence of his friends against the rumours intimated 44 B.

[63] Part i. 161, 1.

[64] Cf. p. 84, 94.

writings. Now we can discover in one part of these writings, nothing that carries us essentially beyond the Socratic stand-point. In the Lesser Hippias, Lysis, Charmides, Laches, Protagoras, Euthyphro, Apology, Crito, there is as yet not a hint of that doctrine which marks the fundamental distinction between the Platonic and Socratic conceptional Philosophy: the doctrine of the independent existence of ideas, above and beside that of phenomena.[65] Neither do they contain any discussions on Natural Science or Anthropology;[66] the belief in immortality is but doubtfully touched on in the Apology;[67] and the Crito (54 B) only presupposes the popular notions about Hades, without a reference to the more philosophic belief, or to the Pythagorean myths, which later on are hardly ever left unnoticed in passages treating of future retribution. In none of these dialogues does Socrates occupy himself with anything beyond those ethical enquiries, in which, accord-

[65] Socrates' desire in the Euthyphro, 5 D, 6 D, to hear, not merely of some particular ὅσιον, ἀλλ' ἐκεῖνο αὐτὸ τὸ εἶδος, ᾧ πάντα τὰ ὅσιά ἐστι, and his explanation μιᾷ ἰδέᾳ τά τε ἀνόσια ἀνόσια εἶναι καὶ τὰ ὅσια ὅσια (cf. Ritter, ii 208; Steinhart, ii. 195; Susemihl, i. 122), must not be made to prove too much. Socrates had indeed already insisted on the constancy of universal ideas: the separate existence of genera is not, however, hinted at in the Euthyphro. We cannot draw any inferences from the names εἶδος and ἰδέα: whereas in Xenophon universal concepts are called γένη, Plato can express them in the Socratic acceptation by ἰδέα or εἶδος, which after all means merely method or form. Plato in fact is standing on the threshold of the Socratic doctrine of ideas, but has not yet stepped beyond it. Still less can be inferred from the Lysis, 217 C sq.; and even if with Steinhart, i. 232 sq., we discover here the dawn of the doctrine of separate Ideas, we must still allow that the passage, as universally understood, does not pass out of the circle of Socratic tenets.

[66] E.g.: that the Platonic division of the soul is intimated in the Protagoras, 352 B; on which point I cannot agree with Ritter.

[67] Vide Part i. 149.

ing to history, the real Socrates was entirely absorbed; in none does he exhibit more intimate knowledge of the earlier systems,—in none does he cope with other adversaries than those who actually did oppose him, the Sophists. The doctrine of virtue has still the older originally Socratic stamp: the virtue of the wise is alone regarded as virtue, and all particular virtues are reduced to knowledge, without the recognition of an unphilosophical virtue side by side with the philosophical, or the admission of a plurality of virtues, such as we afterwards find.[68] A certain crudity of method is also evident in all these dialogues.[69] The amount of mimetic by-play bears no proportion to the meagreness of the philosophic contents: throughout the dramatic description is lively, while the scientific conversation proceeds laboriously and interruptedly with elementary determinations. Even the Protagoras, with all its artistic excellence, is not free from discussions of fatiguing prolixity, and the explanation of the verse of Simonides (338 E sqq.) especially disturbs the transparency of its plan, and looks very like a piece of youthful ostentation. Finally, if we compare the argument of the Gorgias (495 sqq.) against the identity of the good and pleasure, with that of the Protagoras (351 B sqq.), which leaves this identity still as a hypothesis, it is clear that the latter must be earlier than the former, and consequently than all the dialogues succeeding it.[70] Separately all these indications may

[68] As regards the division between philosophic and ordinary virtue, Meno, 96 D sq.

[69] Only the Apology and the Crito are to be excepted, which are not concerned with philosophical enquiries.

[70] The opposite view is main-

be inconclusive; collectively, they certainly warrant the opinion, that at the time of his composing the above-named works, Plato, as regards the scientific form, was less skilled in the art of developing conceptions; and as regards the contents, was still essentially limited to the scope and results of the Socratic teaching.[71] This

tained by Schöne, Plat. Prot. 88 sq. He wishes to make out that the advance is rather on the side of the Protagoras. He says that whereas the Gorgias identified the ἀγαθόν and the ὠφέλιμον, which is, however, nothing else than the continued εὖ βιῶναι of the Protagoras, it contents itself with a mere apparent difference between ἀγαθόν and ἡδύ; the Protagoras on the other hand abolishes this appearance, and draws out in outspoken eudæmonism the consequence of the Socratic stand-point. However, supposing eudæmonism were really this consequence (we have examined this, Part i. 124 sq.), are we to believe that Plato recognised it as such? According to our subsequent knowledge of his Ethics, certainly not. And is it correct to say that the Gorgias by ὠφέλιμον, which is identified with the good, means merely the same as the εὖ ζῆν of the Protagoras (351 B), viz. ἡδέως βιῶναι continued to the end of life? Surely the discussion with Polus, 474 C sq., refutes this supposition; for although it shows that the right is, indeed, not more agreeable, but more profitable than the wrong, yet it seeks this profit exclusively in the health of the soul (477 A sqq.). Further on, 495 A, the position that ἡδύ and ἀγαθόν are the same, and that all pleasure as such is good, and therefore the very supposition acted upon by Socrates in his whole argument Protag. 351 O, is fundamentally contested. I cannot believe, that after making Socrates refute a principle so decidedly in this passage, in the Republic, in the Philebus, and elsewhere, Plato should, in a later dialogue, make him repeat the same principle without the slightest modification; and the same must, I think, hold good in a still greater degree of the Philebus, which Schöne, following Weisse's theory (supra, p. 107, 43), likewise considers later than the Protagoras

[71] The above holds good also, if we suppose that the object of the Protagoras and the kindred dialogues was not so much the exposition of philosophic theories as the painting of the character of Socrates. For as in this case (leaving out of the question the Apology and the Crito) the question is still not about historical accuracy, but about an ideal picture of Socrates, we must ask why the same man, as regards his philosophical convictions, should be here depicted in so many respects differently from the representations of, e g the Symposium and Phædo; and it would be very difficult to bring forward any sufficient reason for this. if Plato himself as a philosopher took just the same stand-point there as he does here. The truth is, the two sides, the depicting of the

must doubtless have been the case while he remained under the personal influence of Socrates, and we might therefore be inclined to place all these dialogues in the period before or immediately after the death of Socrates.[72] But there are many to which this theory could not be extended without ascribing to the youthful Plato an improbable amount of creative skill in the use of the philosophic dialogue, an artistic form which he had himself introduced; and even if we restrict it to the works already named, it may still be asked [73] whether Plato, while his master was still alive, and everyone might listen to his discourses, would have ascribed to him other discourses of his own invention. This, however, does not make it impossible that Plato may have attempted to compose Socratic dialogues, even in the lifetime of Socrates, and may perhaps have written them down, without allowing them to go beyond the circle of his intimate friends; [74] but it is very unlikely that he should at that time have produced so elaborate a work as the Protagoras, which, by its whole plan and design, was evidently meant for the public. This may more properly perhaps be assigned with the Apology and Crito [75] to the interval between

genuine philosopher and the exposition of a philosophic system, cannot be divided in Plato: he draws Socrates for us in such a way, that he at the same time leaves to him the development which to his mind was the Socratic, that is, the true philosophy.

[72] So Hermann, Steinhart, Susemihl, earlier also Ueberweg, supra, pp. 105, 106.

[73] Cf. Schone, Pl. Protag. 72; Grote, Plato, i. 196 sq (who brings forward my view with less authoritative grounds); with him, Ueberweg agrees in what follows, supra, p 106, 41.

[74] The Hippias may be such an earlier literary experiment: cf. pp. 85, 86.

[75] It is probable that the Apology was published immediately after Socrates' death, perhaps written

the death of Socrates and the commencement of the Egyptian journey;[76] and in conjunction with the

down even before, inasmuch as a faithful report of the speech which Socrates delivered before the tribunal must have been the more easy to Plato, the fresher it was in his remembrance. And indeed it was then that he had the most pressing summons to set right the ideas of his fellow-citizens about his teacher by a narrative of the facts. The latter reason, however, would lead us to place the Crito not much later, the more so because here the interest intimated in the Crito itself is added, namely, to defend the friends of Socrates against the appearance of having done nothing at all to save him. It might certainly appear that Plato could not have spoken of the preparations for Socrates' escape, immediately after his death, without endangering the safety of the parties involved therein. But it is questionable whether, on the whole, the discovery of a plan which remained unaccomplished could have led to prosecutions, and whether the plan was not already known even before the appearance of the Crito; again, we do not know how long Crito out-lived Socrates, and whether Plato does not wish to defend the dead against unfavourable judgments; moreover, if Crito was no longer living, he had greater freedom in referring to him; yet besides Crito, he mentions by name none of the persons implicated (p. 45 B), such as the Theban Simmias and Cebes, who without doubt had already returned home.

[76] A more precise arrangement is impossible from the fact that the particulars of this period of Plato's life are not known. If his stay at Megara could have lasted longer, he might have composed the dialogues in question there. But it has been already remarked, p. 17 sq, that we have no right to make this supposition, and it is a wide departure from authenticated tradition to speak, as Hermann does, of a Megaric period and Megaric dialogues. Ueberweg (Zeitschr. f. Phil. lvii., 1870, p. 76 sq. supra, 106, 41) wishes to put back the Protagoras and the kindred dialogues to 387 B.C., and he believes that for this chronology he finds a strong external support in the fact that Isocrates (Bus. 5), six years after Socrates' death, reproaches the rhetorician Polycrates 'Αλκιβιάδην ἔδωκας αὐτῷ (Socr.) μαθητὴν, ὃν ὑπ' ἐκείνου μὲν οὐδεὶς ᾔσθετο παιδευόμενον, which, after the appearance of the Protagoras, could no longer have been said. But if this assertion is not mere imagination (and certainly in the Busiris, which pays little regard to historical truth, we may very well expect this from Isocrates). it cannot mean to deny the intercourse of Alcibiades with Socrates, but only to deny, what Xenophon also, Mem i. 2. 12 sq. refutes, that his opinions and conduct were motived by the Socratic teaching. That on the other hand he was connected with Socrates for a considerable length of time must also be universally known from Xen. loc. cit. This result, however, is also obtained from the Protagoras: Alcibiades is not here represented as παιδευόμενος ὑπὸ Σωκράτους.

Laches, Charmides, and Lysis, may have been intended as a portrayal of Socrates and his philosophy, which, though full of poetic freedom and invention, was in the main true to nature, and might therefore be used by Aristotle as historical evidence.[77] About the same date, but rather earlier than the Apology, the Euthyphro may have been written with a similar design: unless indeed it belongs to the time of Socrates' trial.[78]

It is otherwise with the Gorgias, Meno, Theætetus, and Euthydemus. These four dialogues, judging from the references in them to contemporary events, must not only be later, and for the most part many years later, than the Protagoras and the death of Socrates;[79] but they also in their scientific content

---

[77] Cf. p 85.

[78] The fact, however, that the view of Plato's literary activity developed above makes him begin, not with epoch-making works, which give a glimpse of all that is to follow, but with essays of smaller scientific pretensions (as Ribbing, Plato's Ideenl. ii. 76 sq. objects), can hardly be construed to his prejudice The same is the case (to say nothing of our great poets) with Kant, Leibnitz, Schelling, and many others. Before Plato had discovered in the theory of Ideas the peculiar principle of his system, which could only have happened after long preparation, he was of necessity limited to the setting forth the Socratic philosophy in detail. That there was need of some practice in the literary form which was first used by him can cause us no surprise: seeing, however, that, so soon after the first experiments, he was able to produce such a work of art as the Protagoras, we have no reason to look in vain for traits of his high genius even in the essays of this period; on the other hand we can hardly imagine how, after the Phædrus, he could have written a Lysis, a Laches, and a Charmides, and also in the Protagoras how he could so entirely have refrained from any reference to the theories which separate his standpoint from the Socratic.

[79] It has been already shown, p. 93, 3; 18, 31; pp 83, 84; that the Meno cannot have been written before 395, nor the Theætetus before 394 B.C., and the Euthydemus gives evidence of the activity of Antisthenes in Athens, and his attacks upon Plato, as well as the attack of Isocrates on the Sophists (cf. on this point also p. 132, 94). Even apart from the obvious allusions, Gorg. 486 A, 508 C sq., 521 B sq., we must

point unmistakeably to a time when Plato had already laid the corner stone of his system in the theory of ideas,[80] when he had appropriated the Pythagorean notions of the transmigration of souls and a retribution after death,[81] and connected them by means of the doctrine of Anamnesis with that theory;[82] with which

suppose the Gorgias to have been written not before Socrates' death: this, however, does not help us much.

[80] In the Euthydemus, 301 A, καλὰ πράγματα are ἕτερα αὐτοῦ γε τοῦ καλοῦ· πάρεστι μέντοι ἑκάστῳ αὐτῶν κάλλος τι. In these words I see not merely, with Steinhart, 'a close approximation to the doctrine of Ideas,' but the actual enunciation of this doctrine The αὐτοκαλὸν, the ideally fair, which, separate from individual things that are fair, gives them their fairness by its present indwelling, is actually the ἰδέα of the καλόν. This enunciation is immediately followed by an objection which Antisthenes appears to have used against the participation of Things in the Ideas: v. Part i. p. 255, 2. The words of the Theætetus, 176 E, are even clearer· παραδειγμάτων ἐν τῷ ὄντι ἑστώτων—cf. 175 C—is a plain assertion of the doctrine, which is expressed in the Parmenides, 132 D, in almost the same words. The 'Here' as the dwelling-place of evil, and the 'There' to which we are told to flee in the Theætetus, 176 A, is another decisive example of Plato's idealism being already formed.

[81] These Pythagorean doctrines are seen clearly, not only in the Meno (v. following note), but in the Gorgias. 508 A of the latter (cf. vol. i. 380, 3) shows its author's acquaintance with Pythagoreism: Gorgias, 393 A, D, Plato employs Philolaus' comparison of the σῶμα to a σῆμα (v. vol i 388, 5), and indicates its source by the words κομψὸς ἀνὴρ ἴσως Σικελός τις ἢ Ἰταλικός. Σικελὸς κομψὸς ἀνὴρ is the beginning of a well-known song of Timocreon's, given in Bergk's Poetæ Lyrici, p. 941 ; and the addition of Ἰταλικὸς points to the Italian philosophers, and in particular to Philolaus of Tarentum. The reference is not quite so clear, 523 A sqq., where the ordinary notions about the judges of the dead, the islands of the Blessed, and Hades, are given. But the belief in immortality appears unequivocally here, as in the Theætetus, 177 A, and in 524 B is connected with the same thoughts as meet us afterwards in the Phædo, 64 C, 80 C. The Gorgias, 525 B sqq., distinguishes between curable and incurable sins, temporal and eternal punishments in the future world; just as later on the Republic, x 615 D sq , does, following Pythagorean doctrines. So we cannot doubt that at the time he wrote the Gorgias, Plato's views of a future state were in the main settled.

[82] Vide the well-known passage in the Meno, which will be noticed further in a subsequent place, 81 A sq. The reference in this to the Pythagorean doctrine of metem-

indeed the whole belief in immortality as he understood it was so bound up that both must have arisen almost simultaneously.[83] Since therefore these dia-

psychosis is perfectly plain, though Plato (with Philolaus, v. Pt. 1. 327, 1) only appeals to Pindar and the Orphic tradition; the proof, as is well known, is in a tenet of the Pythagorean Mathematics—the Pythagorean fundamental theory. And it seems equally clear to me that the doctrine of Reminiscence (ἀνάμνησις) really presupposes that of the Ideas. The objects of reminiscence can only be the universal concepts (ἀληθεία τῶν ὄντων)—the sensuous forms of which meet us in individual things — not individual presentations which we have experienced in our former lives: v. Meno, 86 A, cf. Phædo, 99 E. Plato expresses himself as if the latter were his meaning, but this is merely the same mythical form of exposition which we find elsewhere; he states in the Phædo, 72 E sqq., with unmistakable reference to the Meno, the particular way in which he wishes to be understood. I cannot, any more than Ribbing (Pl. Ideenl. i. 173 sq.) or Steger (Pl Stud. i. 43), agree with Steinhart (loc cit 11, 96; iv. 85, 383, 416) and Susemihl (Genet. Entw. i. 85 sq.) in finding in the Meno an earlier and more immature form of the theory of Reminiscence than in the Phædrus, nor with Schaarschmidt (Samml. d. plat. Schr. 356 sq.), who avails himself of the passage in question as evidence for the spuriousness of the Meno. The Meno says, 81 C, that the soul has learnt everything, inasmuch as it has seen καὶ τὰ ἐνθάδε καὶ τὰ ἐν Ἅδου καὶ πάντα χρήματα Similarly in the Republic and the Timæus in the former (x. 614 E), the souls after their wanderings through the world above and the world beneath are represented as narrating to one another what they have seen in both; in the latter (41 D), each of them before entering into human existence is placed on a planet, in the revolutions of which it contemplates the universe; with the last description, the Phædrus agrees on the whole, although in it the ideas stand for that which the souls see during their journey round the world. The Meno again reckons moral and mathematical truths amongst the things which the soul knows from its pre-existence, 81 C, 82 A sq. Further on (p. 85 E sq.) we are met by the fallacy: If the soul were in possession of knowledge, ὃν ἂν ᾖ χρόνον καὶ ὃν ἂν μὴ ᾖ ἄνθρωπος, it must always be in possession of knowledge. I will not undertake to defend the validity of this conclusion I would rather ask where is the valid conclusion, by which pre-existence is proved, and whether, for example, the method of proof in the Phædo, 70 C sq., has in this respect any advantage over that of the Meno? In point of fact, our 'fallacy' is expressly mentioned in the Phædo, 72 E, as a well-known Socratic evidence for the immortality of the soul.

[83] Plato himself gives his opinions on this connection in

logues occupy themselves quite disproportionately with elementary enquiries into the most universal moral principles, concerning the oneness and teachableness of virtue, the conception of knowledge, and the like; the reason cannot be that Plato had not himself advanced essentially beyond the Socratic stand-point and the earliest beginnings of his own system,—it must lie in methodical calculation. The author here intentionally confines himself to what is elementary, because he wants first to establish this on all sides, to secure the foundation of his building, before raising it higher. His method in the Cratylus, Sophist, Politicus, and Parmenides must be criticised from a similar point of view. These dialogues decidedly presuppose the doctrine of ideas:[84] in the Politicus Plato, besides laying down his theory of government, also gives expression to several important determinations of his natural philosophy,[85] betraying Pythagorean influence

the Phædo, 76 D sq. If there is, he says, a beautiful, a good, &c., and generally if there are ideas, the soul must have already been in existence before birth; if we deny the former position, we cannot grant the latter. He says this in reference to the ἀνάμνησις, which is indeed really a recollection of the ideas. The same, however, holds good of the later proofs for the immortality of the soul's nature (Phædo, 100 B sq.); as throughout he goes upon the relation in which the soul stands to the idea of life; and the conception of the soul in the Phædrus as ἀρχὴ κινήσεως (245 C sq.), all along presupposes the separation of the eternal and essential from the external appearance, which, with Plato, is closely connected with the theory of the absolute reality of the Ideas; the soul in its higher parts lives upon the intuition of the Ideas (247 D, 248 B.)

[84] It will be shown later on how the Sophist and Parmenides establish and carry out this doctrine. For the Cratylus, cf. 439 C sq. (where the expression ὀνειρώττειν can at most only mean that the doctrine is new to the readers, not that it has occurred to Plato only then for the first time), 386 D, 389 B, D, 390 E, 423 E; and the Politicus, 285 E sq., 269 D.

[85] Polit. 269 D sq., we find the opposition of the immutable

THE ORDER OF THE PLATONIC WRITINGS. 129

not only in these, but in other more distinct references to that school of his predecessors.[86] Consequently it cannot be supposed that at the date of these dialogues he had not yet perfected his philosophic principle, nor occupied himself with the Pythagoreans; and though, as to contents and method, he is here most nearly allied with the Eleatic-Megarian philosophy, this merely proves that he desired to lead his readers onward from that starting point, not that he himself had not already passed it.

As little are we compelled, on account of the definite prominence in the Phædrus of the doctrine of ideas, and the changing existences of the soul, to consider that dialogue as later than the Sophist, Statesman, and Parmenides,[87] or even than the Gorgias, Meno, Euthydemus, Cratylus, and Theætetus.[88] It is quite as pos-

divine existence and the mutable corporeal world, and, as a consequence, the assumption of periodical changes in mundane affairs. And in 272 D sq., 271 B sq., we get, in connection with this, the doctrine that each soul in each mundane period has to run through a fixed number of earthly bodies, unless previously transferred to a higher destiny. In 273 B, D, the doctrine of the Timæus on matter is clearly anticipated

[86] In the Cratylus, 400 B sq., we find Philolaus' comparison of σῶμα and σῆμα, which occurred before in the Gorgias. We are farther told that this life is a state of purification. In 405 D, we have the Pythagorean World Harmony; in 403 E, the Platonic doctrine of immortality, which is a reference to Pythagoreism. The Sophist, 252 B, gives us the Pythagorean opposition of the Limited and Unlimited, which meet us again in the Parmenides, 137 D, 143 D sq., 144 E, 158 B sqq., with the addition of a contrast between Odd and Even, One and Many; and, ibid. 143 D sq., the derivation of numbers is a reminiscence of the Pythagoreans. In the Politicus, we have the Pythagorean tenets of the Mean, 284 E sq , and the doctrine of the Unlimited, 273 D.

[87] So Hermann and Steinhart: vide supra, pp. 103, 104,; 105, 38.

[88] As Susemihl vide supra. Deuschle (The Platonic Politicus, p. 4) puts the Phædrus rather earlier, between the Euthydemus and Cratylus.

sible that Plato here mythically foretells convictions which were already in his mind during the writing of those dialogues, but which, for the sake of the systematic evolution of his doctrines, he had for the present set aside: that the Phædrus may thus be the introduction to a longer series of writings, designed from its position to afford the reader a preliminary view of the goal, hereafter to be frequently hidden from his eyes, as he presses towards it by the long and tortuous road of methodical enquiry. This possibility rises into probability if we take into consideration all those traces of youthfulness which others have observed;[89] if we remark that some important points of doctrine are in this work, as in the glow of a first discovery, still wanting in the closer limitation which Plato was afterwards obliged to give them;[90] if we note how, in

[89] In Diog. iii. 38, Olympiodorus 3 (vide p. 92, 1), it is declared to be Plato's first written treatise, by reference to the μειρακιῶδες of its subject—the dithyrambic character of the exposition. Schleiermacher, Pl. W. 1 a 69 sq., gives a more thorough exposition of the youthful character recognisable 'in the whole texture and colour' of the Phædrus. He calls attention to the tendency to writing for display, and the exhibition of the author's own superiority, which is discernible throughout; to the proud lavishness of material seen in the second and third refutation of the dialectic adversary, each of which outdoes its predecessor, only to result in the declaration that his whole literary production, and these speeches with it, are merely play. The Rhetors are discomfited with ostentatious completeness; and at every pause the hyplay breaks out in renewed luxuriance, or an uncalled-for solemnity is imparted to the tone. Such are some of the points noticed by Schleiermacher; and to these we may add that even the famous myth of the Phædrus lacks the intuitive faculty which marks Platonic myths as a rule. The dithyrambic tone of the whole work has none of the repose about it with which, in other dialogues, Plato treats the most exalted themes; it is indeed so signally different from the matured lucidity of the Symposium, that we can scarcely suppose there are only a few years between them.

[90] Courage and Desire, which, according to the Timæus, 42 A, 69 C sq. (cf. Polit. 309 C; Rep. x.

the second part, the elements of the scientific method are as if for the first time laid down, and the name and conception of Dialectic, already familiar to us in the Euthydemus,[91] are introduced as something new;[92] if, in fine, we compare the remarks on rhetoric in the Phædrus with those in the Gorgias:[93] and the judg-

[91] 611 B sqq), compose the mortal soul which only comes into being at the union with the body, are here, 246 A sq , transferred to the pre-existent state, and in 249 D sq we find the Love which is the main theme of the Phædrus conceived only in general terms as the striving after the Ideal, awakened by the action of beauty. Not till we come to the Symposium do we find the addition, that Love is concerned with production in the sphere of beauty

[91] P. 290 C; also Cratylus, 390 C; Soph. 253 D sq.; Polit. 285 D, 287 A.

[92] P 265 C sqq. Dialectic is here described on its formal logical side only, and I cannot agree with Steinhart (Pl. W. iii. 459) in regarding the representation given of it as more mature than that in the Sophist, where, loc. cit., the logical problem of Dialectic is based on the doctrine of the community of concepts. Stallbaum's attempt (De Art. Dial. in Phædro doctr. Lpz. 1853, p. 13) to reconcile the elementary description of Dialectic in the Phædrus with the later enunciation does not satisfy me. He says that the Phædrus only wants to represent Dialectic as the true art of Love. Even if this were so, it would not follow that it should be treated as something new, the very name of which has to be enquired. But there is no justification in the dialogue itself for thus narrowing down the scope of its second part.

[93] The Phædrus, 260 E sqq., shows that Rhetoric is not an art at all, but only a τριβή ἄτεχνος, and we find the same in the Gorgias, 463 A sqq. But the former not only takes no exception to the general description of Rhetoric as having only persuasion for its object (however little this may have been Plato's own view), but makes this description the basis of its argument. The latter contradicts this flatly, 458 E, 504 D sqq., and gives the Rhetor the higher aim of amending and teaching his audience, and because Rhetoric does not satisfy these requirements, it is, in the Theætetus, 201 A, Politicus, 304 C, allowed only a subordinate value, compared with Philosophy, though the Phædrus does not clearly divide the respective methods of the two. In face of these facts (which Ueberweg's remarks, Plat. Schr. 294, fail to display in any other light) I cannot allow much importance either to the criticism of the Phædrus on single Rhetors and their theories (Steinhart, iv. 43), nor to the circumstance which Hermann alone (Plat. 517) regards as decisive, viz. that the Phædrus 270 A passes a judgment on Pericles so much more favourable than the Gorgias 515 C sq. 519 A The former praises him as a

ment on Isocrates with that of the Euthydemus.[94] The opinion therefore seems justifiable that Plato up to the death of Socrates remained generally true to the Socratic manner of philosophy, and therefore in the writings of this period did not essentially advance beyond his teacher; but that in the years immediately

speaker of genius and scientific culture; the latter blames him as a statesman Both this praise and blame are quite compatible (as Krische has already remarked, Plat. Phædr 114 sq.), at any rate just as much as e g. the praise of Homer and other poets, Symp. 209 D, is compatible with expressions such as Gorg. 502 B sq ; Rep ii 377 C sq ; x. 598 D sq ; and even supposing it were otherwise, the question still remains whether the unfavourable judgment is the earlier or the later one: the judgment of the Gorgias is repeated in the Politicus, 303 B sq ; and as Plato always considered democracy to be bad, we cannot see how he ever could have arrived at a different view as regards the statesman who most decidedly had paved the way for it

[94] In the Euthydemus, without mentioning Isocrates, yet with distinct reference to him, his depreciatory judgments as regards the Philosophers (or as he calls them the Eristics, the Sophists) are decidedly rebutted, and the middle position which he himself aimed at between a philosopher and a statesman is shown to be untenable. The Phædrus, on the contrary, 278 E sq., represents Socrates as expressing a hope that Isocrates by virtue of the philosophic tendency of his mind will not merely leave all other orators far behind, but perhaps himself also turn to philosophy. Spengel (Isocrates u. Platon. Abh. d Munchner Akad. philos.-philol. Kl. vii. 1855, p. 729-769 , cf. espec 762 sq.) is certainly right in believing that the Phædrus must have been written before the character of Isocrates had developed in that particular direction which Plato's defence in the Euthydemus challenges—before the hope of still winning him over to the side of philosophy had vanished—and before he had published that series of attacks on the philosophers of his time (including Plato, though neither he nor any other is named) which we have in the speeches against the Sophists, Hel. i-7, Panath. 26-32, π. ἀντιδόσ. 195, 258 sq. Philipp. 12. As Isocrates was born B C. 436, supposing the Phædrus to have been composed 38¼ B.C., he had already, at the time of its composition, attained an age to which this condition clearly no longer applied. The remark of Steinhart, Plat. Leben, 181 sq., intended to meet this conclusion, fails to carry conviction with it, as he finally supports his position with the mere assumption that neither was Plato in the Euthydemus thinking of Isocrates, nor Isocrates of Plato in the speech against the Sophists.

succeeding that event, he discovered in the doctrine of ideas and belief in the soul's immortality the central point of his system, and thenceforward began, according to the announcement in the Phædrus, to develope his convictions in methodical progression. That these convictions became in course of time more clearly defined and more distinctly apprehended—that the horizon of the philosopher gradually enlarged, and his method and form of expression to some extent altered— that his relation to the older schools was not throughout the same—that it was long before his political, and far longer before his cosmical theories were completed as to detail; all this we shall probably find, even if the traces of such a development should be less marked in his writings than it was in fact; but the essential stand-point and general outlines of his doctrine must have been certain to him from the date indicated by the Phædrus, Gorgias, Meno, and Theætetus.

It can hardly be doubted that the Symposium and Phædo are later than the Phædrus, and belong to a time when the philosophy of Plato, and also his artistic power, had reached full maturity;[95] the Philebus, too, can scarcely be assigned to an earlier period. But the difficulty of determining the order of these dialogues with regard to one another, and the exact date of each, is so great that we cannot be surprised if the views of critics differ widely on these questions. Between those dialogues which definitely bring forward

[95] Ast and Socher would place the Phædo immediately after Socrates' death (supra, 101, 25, 28): this supposition, however, has been sufficiently refuted, supra.

the doctrine of ideas and the eternal life of the soul, and those from which it is absent, there must be a considerable interval; and if the former were for the most part not written till after the death of Socrates, we cannot venture to place either of the latter in the period closely succeeding that event.

We may reasonably suppose that the dialogues primarily concerned with the delineation of Socrates and the Socratic philosophy, as Plato then apprehended it, may have been written partly in Megara, partly after his return thence to Athens; that he then went to Egypt and Cyrene; that during this journey or immediately after it he formed the views which led him decidedly beyond the Socratic stand-point,—at any rate then first resolved to proclaim them by his master's mouth; and thus this second epoch of his literary activity might commence about four or five years after Socrates' death. But all this is mere conjecture, and cannot be substantiated.

Among the writings of this time the Phædrus seems to be the earliest.[96] The Gorgias and Meno may have followed; their subject and treatment allying them, more than any dialogues of this class, to the Protagoras.[97] From the well-known anachronism in the Meno,[98] it would appear that this work was published not much later than 495 B.C.[99] The Theætetus is connected with the

[96] My own arguments in favour of this supposition are given p. 130 sq.: cf. 112 sq.
[97] The Euthydemus is omitted, for the reasons given on p. 84.
[98] Cf. p 93, 3.
[99] On the one hand Ismenias is expressly called ὁ νῦν νεωστὶ εἰληφὼς τὰ Πολυκράτους χρήματα, which in this case can only be said from the stand-point of the author, not of Socrates; on the other hand, if the incident was still recent, and Plato's indignation at it still fresh,

THE ORDER OF THE PLATONIC WRITINGS. 135

Meno by its subject-matter; the Meno (89 C sq. 96 D sqq.) reduces the question of the teachableness of virtue to the preliminary question, 'Is virtue knowledge?' but at the same time recognises that virtuous conduct can also spring from right opinion; the Theætetus enquires into the conception of knowledge, and its relation to right opinion. In point of date also, the Theætetus seems to approximate to the Meno. For if it was not written at the time of the Corinthian war, we cannot place it much earlier than 368 B.C.[100] It is, however, very unlikely that Plato should at so late a period have thought so elementary an enquiry to be necessary, for we find him in other dialogues [101] treating the distinction of knowledge and opinion as a thing universally acknowledged, and of which it was sufficient merely to remind his readers. Yet if, on the other hand, we place the Theætetus later than 368 B.C., the greater number of Plato's most comprehensive and important works must be crowded into the two last decades of his life: this is in itself not probable, and it becomes still less so when we remember that in these twenty years occurred the two Sicilian journeys, and the alteration in the Platonic philosophy spoken of by Aristotle; which latter is so entirely untraceable in the writings of Plato that we are forced to assign it to a later date.[102] It is therefore almost certain that the

---

it can easily be imagined how he came to allow this remarkable anachronism.

[100] Cf. p. 18, 31.

[101] Tim. 51 D sq.; Rep. v. 477 A, E; vii. 533 E, Symp. 202 A; also Parmen. 155 D, where, together with ἐπιστήμη, δόξα and αἴσθησις appear, plainly the two concepts, the separation of which from Knowledge is the subject of enquiry in the Theætetus.

[102] The Laws form an exception considering their general attitude

Theætetus must have been written a short time after the Meno; most likely between 392 and 390 B.C.[103] The Sophist is connected with the Theætetus in a manner which seems to show that Plato not only meant in the former to refer his readers expressly to the latter, but also to prepare the way, in the conclusion of the Theætetus, for a further enquiry of a like nature.[104] The Politicus, too, is immediately connected with the Sophist;[105] and there is in both dialogues the announcement of a third discussion on the conception of a philosopher; a promise which Plato, for some reason unknown to us, never fulfilled. If this is not sufficient to prove that all these dialogues were composed in direct sequence, without the interruption of we cannot expect them to touch upon the metaphysics of Plato's later doctrines.

[103] The point which Ueberweg, Plat. Schrift. 227 sqq., lays stress upon in support of his own and Munk's supposition that the Theætetus was written before 368, seems to me much too uncertain to prove anything On the contrary, it harmonizes very well with the common view, that Euclid and Theodorus play a part in the Theætetus; and with them, not long before the time assigned for the composition of the dialogue, Plato had had friendly intercourse. Cf. p. 18, 31.

[104] In the Theætetus, after it has been shown that of the different definitions of Knowledge, ἐπιστήμη, as αἴσθησις, δόξα ἀληθής, δόξα ἀληθὴς μετὰ λόγου, no one is satisfactory (210 A); Socrates says in conclusion that he must now depart to the court; ἕωθεν δὲ, ὦ Θεώδωρε, δεῦρο πάλιν ἀπαντῶμεν. In reference to this, the Sophist opens with the words of Theodorus: κατὰ τὴν χθὲς ὁμολογίαν, ὦ Σώκρατες, ἥκομεν. It is true, the concluding words of the Theætetus would not certainly establish any design of a continuation in further dialogues (Bonitz, Plat. Stud. II., 41 in reference to the end of the Laches and Protagoras); but if Plato has connected them with such a continuation, we may in this case certainly suppose that he refers to them in it; and, again, the beginning of the Sophist would have been unintelligible to his readers if it was separated from the Theætetus by a very great interval and by a series of other dialogues.

[105] Politicus, init.; Sophist, 216 C sq.

other works, it is at any rate clear that Plato when he undertook the Sophist had already planned the Politicus, and he probably allowed himself no great delay in the execution of his design. We cannot be so certain about the Theætetus; but it is unlikely that many years can have intervened between this dialogue and the Sophist; and thus there is some ground for believing that the Sophist and Politicus also were composed before the first Sicilian journey, or about that time.[106]

[106] Ueberweg, Plat. Schrift. 275 sq., following Munk's example, places the Theætetus trilogy far later. His chief evidence lies in the observation that the movement in the Ideas maintained by the Sophist (vide on this point, supra, note 42) must belong to a later form of the doctrine than the view of their absolute immutability which is impugned therein Still, however, the question remains whether the view attacked here is that known to us as Plato's from writings like the Phædo, the Timæus, &c. (cf. p. 215 sq), and whether the view of the Ideas as moving and animated, sinks into the background in the remaining dialogues besides the Sophist (that it is not quite wanting was shown loc. cit.), because he had not yet found it out, or because it lay too far out of the dominant tendency of his thoughts, and the difficulty of bringing it into harmony with other more important designs was too great to allow him to follow it out further; or whether we have in the Sophist really a later form of the doctrine of Ideas, and not rather an attempt (subsequently abandoned) to include motion in the concept of the Ideas. The last supposition, besides the other reasons alleged for the priority of the Sophist to the Parmenides and of the Politicus to the Republic, at once falls to the ground when we consider that in the account of the theory of Ideas known to us from Aristotle the characteristic of motion is wanting throughout, and moreover this deficiency is expressly made an objection to the doctrine (cf Part ii. b. 220, 2nd edit.); so that the Sophist cannot be considered as an exposition of the Ideas in their latest form, but merely as the transition to it. Ueberweg further (p. 290 sq.) thinks that he discerns in the Politicus, as well as in the Phædo, anthropological views which must be later than those of the Timæus. The incorrectness of this remark will be proved later on (in chapter viii.). Finally Schaarschmidt (Samml. d plat. Schrift. 239 sq.) endeavours to point out in the same dialogue a whole series of imitations of the Laws, but I cannot enter upon the theory here in detail; I have, however, not found one out of all the passages which he quotes, which contradicts the supposition that the Politicus

The Parmenides refers to the Sophist,[107] the Philebus to the Parmenides;[108] and both the Philebus and the Politicus[109] are presupposed by the Republic.[110] These dialogues must therefore have succeeded one another in the above order.[111] The precise date of each, and where the Euthydemus and Cratylus came in among them, cannot be ascertained; the Symposium was pro-

is one of Plato's works which preceded the Laws.

[107] I have endeavoured to show the probability of this (in Plat. Stud 186 sq 192 sq.) by a comparison of Parm. 128 E sq with Soph. 253 D, 251 A; Parm. 143 A B, 145 A with Soph. 244 B sq., 254 D sq., Parm. 133 C with Soph. 255 C.

[108] Supra, 70, 56

[109] With regard to the latter I shall content myself with referring to Susemihl, Genet Entw ii. 303 sq and chapter viii of this volume, and with the remark that there seems to me to be no occasion for the conjecture that we have it not in its original shape, but in a second elaboration (Alberti, Jahrb. f Philol Suppl. N F. 1, 166 sq)

[110] When it is said, Rep. vi. 505 B: 'ἀλλὰ μὴν τόδε γε οἶσθα, ὅτι τοῖς μὲν πολλοῖς ἡδονὴ δοκεῖ εἶναι τὸ ἀγαθὸν, τοῖς δὲ κομψοτέροις φρόνησις, when the question which forms the subject of the Philebus is thus discussed here as if it were a well-known one, and the two theories there criticised at length are dismissed with a few remarks, we cannot help seeing here in the Repub. a direct allusion to the Philebus, just as in the above-cited passages of the latter we find an allusion to the Parmenides, in the Phædo, 72 E (supra, p. 83, 91), to the Meno; in the Laws, v. 739 B sq. (cf Plat. Stud. 16 sq.) to the Republic.

[111] Ueberweg, p. 204 sq., observes correctly that in the Sophist, and in a still higher degree in the Philebus (to which the present work refers later on, in chapter vi.), there are many points of agreement with the later form of the doctrine of Ideas as represented by Aristotle. But it does not follow that these dialogues are later than all those in which these points of agreement do not appear in the same way. As soon as the theory of Ideas arrived at a definite completion it must have also comprehended those views with which its later form was connected; but Plato would only have had occasion to bring these views into prominence if the doctrine of Ideas as such had been propounded with the object of a dialectical discussion; while in expositions like the Republic and the Timæus, the chief object of which is the application of the theory of Ideas to the world of morality and the world of nature, they would not be mentioned. Ueberweg, however, himself remarks of the Timæus that the construction of the world-soul goes on the same lines as that in the Sophist and Philebus. Cf. also p. 137, 106.

bably written in 384 B.C.,[112] but this fact gives us little help as to the chronology of the other works, since we cannot with certainty determine the place of the Symposium among the Platonic writings. Possibly Plato may have been prevented by his first Sicilian journey from completing the Trilogy of the Sophist,[113] and after the dialectical labour of the Parmenides he may have set aside his intended enquiry concerning the ideal philosopher, and produced instead in the Symposium and the Phædo those matchless descriptions which show us in the one the wise man enjoying his life, and in the other drawing near to death.[114] The Philebus forms the most direct preparation for the Republic and the Timæus, and therefore we may suppose that in order of time, too, it immediately preceded them. These two dialogues must certainly be assigned to Plato's maturity: [115] the only approximation we can

---

[112] The mention (Symp 193 A) of the Arcadian διοικισμός, which, according to Diodor xv. 12, took place in the autumn of Olymp. 98, 4 (385 B.C), is probably to be explained by supposing Plato to have been induced by the recent impression of that event to commit an anachronism tolerable only in the mouth of Aristophanes, and under the influence of his overflowing humour.

[113] Supra, p. 137.

[114] It will be shown later on (in chap. ix.) that we have no reason for considering, with Ueberweg, that the Phædo was later than the Timæus.

[115] The eeventh Platonic letter (vide p. 17, 30) does actually speak as if Plato had written the Republic before his first Sicilian journey; and in modern times there have been many scholars of note to support the assumption that Aristophanes in the Ecclesiazusæ (Ol. 97, 1, B.C. 391) satirised the Platonic state, getting his materials either from the Republic or from orally delivered doctrines to the same effect. We may name Morgenstern, Spengel, Bergk, Meineke, Tchorzewski, and others; vide the references apud Schnitzer (Aristoph. Werke x. 1264 sq.); Susemihl, loc. cit. ii. 296. But such a doubtful source as the eeventh letter cannot be allowed much weight; and with regard to Aristophanes, I can only agree with Susemihl (to whom I content myself with referring, as he gives the

make to a more precise date is through the fact that the Critias has not only been handed down to us in an unfinished state, but was apparently never anything else than a fragment.[116] This phenomenon argues some external hindrance which prevented the completion of the work, and we are thus led to think of

views of his predecessors in full) that the Platonic Republic is not contemplated in the Ecclesiasuzæ. If the attack was aimed at some definite person, the poet, to make himself intelligible to the mass of his audience, would undoubtedly have marked out this person (in spite of the new laws against ridiculing people on the stage, which still did not restrain others from personalities against Plato, supra, p. 36, 82), as clearly as he had done in a hundred other cases. This is not done; and in verse 578 he says explicitly that 'these projects,' which have been supposed to parody Plato, 'have never yet been set on foot.' Nor do the contents of the play necessitate any reminiscence of Plato ; broadly speaking, it is concerned, as the poet repeats and asserts beyond possibility of mistake, with the same moral and political circumstances as the Knights, Wasps, Lysistrata, and Thesmophoriazusæ, in which there had been no alteration since Thrasybulus was restored. The community of women and goods is brought on the stage as a democratic extreme, not as the mere fancy of an aristocratic doctrinaire. The resemblance to Plato in some particular traits, e.g verse 590 sq., 635 sq., in my opinion (which differs from Susemihl's, ii. 297) is not so special as to preclude the possibility of these traits having arisen quite independently from the supposition of such a community existing on Greek soil. Such particular instances must not be pressed too far, or we shall get at last a connection between Ecclesiasuzæ, 670, ἢν δ' ἀποδύῃ γ' αὐτὸς δώσει, and the corresponding Gospel precept. There is nothing to be said for the supposition (Ueberweg, Plat. Schr. 212 sq.) that Aristophanes had in his eye Plato's oral teaching, for in this case we should all the more expect something to point out that Praxagora was indebted to Plato for her knowledge, or at least (if Aristophanes had suddenly become too cautious to venture what others had ventured and could venture without any danger) to the Philosophers : it is, moreover, very improbable that Plato had at that time so far developed his theory of the State as to require community of wives and the participation of the women in war and government Besides, there is the fact that Ueberweg (loc. cit 128) plainly makes Plato's activity as a teacher begin 3–4 years, at earliest, after the representation of the Ecclesiazusæ. Again, Rep. v. 452 A, 456 C, throughout contains no allusions to any pleasantries which the comedians had already indulged in at the expense of his proposals

[116] Supra, 49, 9.

the two last Sicilian journeys and the troubles they entailed.[117] Even independently of this, we could hardly place the Republic and the Timæus later than the years in which those troubles occurred, or there would not have been time for Plato to write the Laws and to modify his system, as Aristotle tells us he did. Supposing the Republic to have been finished before the second Sicilian journey, therefore in 370-368 B.C., and the Critias to have been interrupted by the third journey in 361-2 B.C.,[118] there would then be an interval sufficient for a comprehensive, thoughtful and artistic work like the former; for studies preparatory to the Timæus, which despite its deficiencies in natural science, and the help derived from Philolaus and other predecessors, must doubtless have occupied a considerable time;[119] and sufficient also to account for the striking difference in tone and style between the two dialogues—a difference not so entirely dependent on the diversity of their contents,[120] as to make a further explanation, from the more advanced age of the author, unwelcome.[121] Plato's experiences in Syra-

[117] Susemihl, Genet. Entw. ii. 503, agrees with this.
[118] On the chronology cf. p. 32 sqq
[119] Before writing the Republic, Plato could not have entered upon these studies, at least if at that time he had not yet conceived the plan of the Timæus: and that this is really so is likely from the fact that the Republic contains no allusion to the persons who appear in the beginning of the Timæus, nor to the dialogue carried on with them.

[120] To which alone Susemihl would here suppose a reference.
[121] The solemn dogmatic tone of the Timæus is partly connected with purposed avoidance of a dialectical treatment, partly with the adoption of the Pythagorean Physics and the writings of Philolaus. Still, however, we cannot maintain that these reasons rendered a lucid exposition throughout impossible; and as, on the other hand, in spite of the difference of subject, similar traits are met with in the Laws, we may con-

cuse may have led him to abandon the further representation of the ideal state, begun in the Critias and designed for Hermocrates; and in its stead, after his own practical failure, to give account to himself and to the world, of the principles which must guide the philosopher in such enterprises; and also to enquire what means under existing circumstances are at his disposal. That this work is later than the Republic and belongs to Plato's old age is beyond question;[122] that he devoted much time to it is also evident, not only because of its compass, which is greater than any other of his works, but from the mass of legislative detail it contains. The Republic too may have occupied him for several years, and it is possible that the different parts may have appeared separately, but this theory has no trustworthy evidence to support it.[123]

jecture that they were in some degree at least owing to Plato's advancing years and increasing inclination to Pythagorean speculations

[122] We shall speak with greater detail on this point later on (in chap. xi). Provisionally may be compared, besides the statements quoted pp. 138, 110, 93, 2, the assertion (in Diog iii. 37, Suid. Φιλόσοφος. Προλεγόμενα τ Πλάτ. Φιλος. c. 24) that Philippus of Opus published the Laws from a rough draft of Plato's.

[123] Its only authority is in the assertion quoted p. 92, 1, in Gellius, that Xenophon composed the Cyropædia in opposition to the Platonic State, lectis ex eo duobus fere libris qui primi in volgus exierant. But this anonymous statement not only lacks authenticity, but carries with it its own refutation. Neither at the end of the second book of the Republic nor in any other passage between the beginning of the first and the end of the third is there a single paragraph which could justify the supposition of a special publication of the part so far finished, and so much at least must have appeared to induce Xenophon to write the Cyropædia; Gellius, however, openly presupposes our division of the books, already familiar to Thrasyllus (Diog. iii. 57) Compare on these questions Susemihl, Genet. Entw. ii. 88 sq., whose judgment is more correct than Ueberweg's, Plat. Schr. 212.

THE ORDER OF THE PLATONIC WRITINGS. 143

Nor is there any proof or likelihood that he recast the dialogue a second time.[124] Modern critics have endeavoured to separate the first and last book from the rest of the work, but neither tradition nor valid internal evidence favours the supposition; while on the other hand the artistic and essential unity which appears throughout is an unanswerable argument to the contrary.[125]

---

[124] According to Diog. iii. 37 Euphorio and Panætius reported: πολλάκις ἐστραμμένην εὑρῆσθαι τὴν ἀρχὴν τῆς πολιτείας. Dionys De Comp. verb. p. 208 f. R; and Quintil. viii. 6, 64, says more precisely: the first four (or according to Dion the first eight) words of the Republic were written in many different arrangements, on a tablet found after Plato's death. But from that we cannot with Dionysius, loc. cit., go so far as to conclude that Plato was engaged in polishing his writings up to the time of his death, we plainly have here to do rather with an experiment before publication to see how the opening words would look in different positions. Still less must we magnify these corrections of style into a separate revision of the whole work.

[125] It was, as is well known, Hermann, Plat. i. 537 sq., who put forward the assertion that the first book was originally a separate and independent work of Plato's first or Socratic period, and was afterwards prepared as an introduction to the Republic, and that the tenth book was only added after a longer period. Also that the 5th, 6th, and 7th books were inserted between the 4th and the 8th book by way of a supplement. However, he has not shown much care in substantiating this sweeping assertion. I will not here enter into particulars, because Hermann's assumption has already been tested, with especial reference to the first book, by Steinhart, Pl W. v. 67 sq., 675 sq, and Susemihl, Genet. Entw. ii 65 sqq. I would only point out that the end (x 608 C sq.) is already prepared for in the introduction (i. 330 D). The discussion on Justice, to which the whole of Ethics and Politics is subordinated, starts from the remark, that only the just man awaits the life in the world to come with tranquillity; and at the end it returns, after settling all the intermediate questions, to the starting point, to find its sublime conclusion in the contemplation of reward in the world to come. This framework at once proves that we have to deal with a single self-consistent work, which with all its freedom in working out the details and additions during the process of elaboration, is still designed in accordance with a definite plan.

CHAPTER IV.

ON THE CHARACTER, METHOD, AND DIVISION OF THE PLATONIC PHILOSOPHY.

THE Platonic philosophy is on the one side the completion of the Socratic; but on the other, an extension and an advance upon it. As Socrates in his philosophic enquiries concerned himself with the moral quite as much as with the intellectual life—as with him right action was inseparably united with right cognition, philosophy with morality and religion, being indeed one and the same thing—so is it in Plato; and as the aim of the one philosopher was to ground intelligence and conduct on conceptual knowledge, so to the other the standard of all action and of all convictions is the contemplation of universal ideas. Plato's views concerning the problem and principle of philosophy thus rest entirely on a Socratic basis. But that which had been with Socrates only a universal axiom became with Plato a system; that which the former had laid down as the principle of knowledge was announced by the latter as the principle of metaphysics. Socrates had sought that conceptual knowledge for which he claimed existence, but he had only reduced to their primary concept particular activities and phenomena in connection with the given case. He had never attempted to gain a whole from scientifically combined concepts, and thus to explain the totality of the Real. He confined himself on principle to ethical enquiries, and even these he pursued, not systematically, but in a merely inductory manner. It was Plato who first expanded the Socratic philosophy into a system, combined its ethics with the earlier natural philosophy, and founded both in dialectics, or the pure science of ideas. But the necessity immediately became apparent of a principle not only to guide thought in the scientific method, but also to interpret material things in their essence and existence. Plato, in transcending the Socratic ethics, transcends also the Socratic acceptation of conceptual knowledge. The cognition of ideas, Socrates had said, is the condition of all true knowledge and right action. Therefore, concludes Plato, logical thought is alone true knowledge. All other ways of knowing—presentation, envisagement—afford no scientific certainty of conviction. But if the knowledge of the idea is alone real knowledge, this can only be, according to Plato, because that alone is a knowledge of the Real; because true Being belongs exclusively to the essence of things presented in the idea, and to all else, in proportion only as it participates in the idea. Thus the idealizing of the concept, which with Socrates had been a logical postulate involving a certain scientific dexterity, dialectical impulse, and dialectical art, was now raised to the objective contemplation of the world, and perfected into a system.

This, however, was impossible without introducing a sharper discrimination between intellectual and moral activity. Their direct and unconditional unity, which Socrates had demanded, can only be maintained so long as no advance is made beyond his general view of the two-sided problems. The moment we proceed to particulars—either, on the one hand, examining the conditions of scientific thought, and directing that thought to subjects of no immediate moral import; or, on the other, fixing the attention more steadily on that which is peculiar to moral activities and their various manifestations—we can no longer conceal from ourselves that there is a difference, as well as a connection, between knowledge and action. It will be shown hereafter that this difference forced itself upon Plato too: herein, however, as in his whole conception of philosophy, he is far less widely separated than Aristotle from his master. He distinguishes more sharply than the one between the moral direction of the will and scientific cognition, but does not therefore, like the other, make philosophy an exclusively theoretical activity. He completes the Socratic ethics not only with dialectical but with physical investigations: the latter, however, never prosper in his hands; and whatever may be the obligations of this branch of enquiry to Plato, it is certain that his genius and zeal for natural science were far inferior to those of Aristotle, and that his achievements in this department bear no comparison with those of his scholar, either in extent of knowledge, acuteness of observation, exactness of interpretation, or fruitfulness of result. He gives to concepts, as separate substances, the reality of Ideas; but in holding Ideas to be the only reality, and material things, as such, to be devoid of essence, and non-existent, he makes impossible to himself the explanation of the phenomenal world. He perfects the conceptual philosophy into a system, but is not impelled, like his successor, to enter deeply into particulars: to him the idea only is the true object of thought; the individual phenomenon possesses no interest. He can indeed make use of it to bring to light the idea in which it participates, but that thorough completeness with which Aristotle works his way through empirical data is not his concern. The study of particulars seems to him scarcely more than an intellectual pastime, and if he has for awhile occupied himself with it, he always returns, as if wearied out, to the contemplation of pure ideas. In this respect, also, he stands midway between Socrates and Aristotle; between the philosopher who first taught the development of the concept from presentation or envisagement, and him who more completely than any other Greek thinker has carried it into all the spheres of actual existence. In the same proportion, however, that Plato advanced beyond Socrates, it was inevitable that he should go back to the pre-Socratic doctrines, and regard as his co-disciples those who were then seeking to apply those theories to the perfecting of the Socratic doctrine. To what an extent he did both is well known. Plato is the first of the Greek philosophers who not merely knew and made use of his predecessors, but consciously completed their principles by means of each other, and bound them all together in one higher principle. What Socrates had taught with regard to the concept of knowledge; Parmenides and Heraclitus, the Megarians and Cynics, on the difference between knowledge and opinion; Heraclitus, Zeno, and the Sophists, on the subjectivity of sense perception—all this he built up into a developed theory of knowledge. The Eleatic principle of Being, and the Heraclitean of Becoming, the doctrine of the unity and that of the multiplicity of things, he has, in his doctrine of Ideas, quite as much blended as opposed; while at the same time he has perfected both by means of the Anaxagorean conception of Spirit, the Megaro-Socratic conception of the Good, and the idealised Pythagorean numbers. These latter, properly understood, appear in the theory of the World-soul, and the Mathematical laws, as the mediating element between the idea and the world of sense. Their one element, the concept of the Unlimited, held absolutely and combined with the Heraclitean view of the sensible world, gives the Platonic definition of Matter. The cosmological part of the Pythagorean system is repeated in Plato's conception of the universe: while in his theory of the elements and of physics proper, Empedocles and Anaxagoras, and more distantly the Atomistic and older Ionic natural philosophies, find their echoes. His psychology is deeply coloured with the teaching of Anaxagoras on the immaterial nature of mind, and with that of Pythagoras on immortality. In his ethics, the Socratic basis can as little be mistaken as, in his politics, his sympathy with the Pythagorean aristocracy. Yet Plato is neither the envious imitator that calumny has called him, nor the irresolute eclectic, who only owed it to favouring circumstances that what was scattered about in earlier systems united in him to form a harmonious whole. We may say more truly that this blending of the rays of hitherto isolated genius into one focus is the work of his originality and the fruit of his philosophic principle. The Socratic conceptual philosophy is from the outset directed to the contemplation of things in all their aspects, the dialectic combination of those various definitions of which now one, and now another, is mistaken by a one-sided apprehension for the whole—to the reduction of the multiplicity of experience to its permanent base.[1] Plato applies this method universally, seeking not merely the essential nature of moral activities, but the essential nature of the Real. He is thus inevitably directed towards the assumptions of his predecessors, which had all started from some true perception; but while these assumptions had related entirely and exclusively to one another, Plato's scientific principles required that he should fuse them all into a higher and more comprehensive theory of the world. As therefore Plato's knowledge of the earlier doctrines gave him the most decided impulse in the development of the Socratic teaching, it was conversely that development which alone enabled him to use the combined achievements of the other philosophers for his own system. The Socratic conceptual philosophy was transplanted by him into the fruitful and well-tilled soil of the previous natural

[1] Cf. Part i. page 93, 95 sqq.

philosophy, thence to appropriate to itself all kindred matter; and in thus permeating the older speculation with the spirit of Socrates, purifying and reforming it by dialectic, which was itself extended to metaphysical speculation,—in thus perfecting ethics by natural philosophy, and natural philosophy by ethics—Plato has accomplished one of the greatest intellectual creations ever known. Philosophy could not indeed permanently remain in the form then given to it. Aristotle soon made very essential alterations in the theories of his master; the older Academy itself could not maintain them in their purity, and the later systems that thought to reproduce the system of Plato were self-deceived. But this is precisely Plato's greatness,—that he was able to give the progress of Philosophy an impulse so powerful, so far transcending the limits of his own system, and to proclaim the deepest principle of all right speculation—the Idealism of thought—with such energy, such freshness of youthful enthusiasm, that to him, despite all his scientific deficiencies, belongs the honour of for ever-conferring philosophic consecration on those in whom that principle lives.

In Plato's scientific method, also, we recognise the deepening, the purification and the progress of the Socratic philosophy. From the principle of conceptual knowledge arises, as its immediate consequence, that dialectic of which Socrates must be considered the author.[2] But while Socrates contented himself with developing

---

[2] The dialectic of Zeno and the Sophists differs in being concerned with refutation only: Socrates uses dialectic as a real agent in defining the concept.

the concept out of mere envisagement, Plato further demanded that conceptual science should be drawn out by methodical classification into a system; while Socrates, in forming concepts, starts from the contingencies of the given case, and never goes beyond the particular, Plato requires that thought shall rise, by continued analysis, from conditioned to unconditioned, from the phenomenon to the idea, from particular ideas to the highest and most universal. The Socratic dialectic only set itself to gain the art of right thinking for the immediate use of individuals, to purify their crude presentations into concepts: the practice of dialectic was therefore at the same time education; intellectual and moral activity coincided, as much for the work of the philosopher in itself as for its effect on others. The Platonic dialectic, on the other hand, was subservient to the formation of a system : it has, therefore, as compared with the Socratic, larger outlines and a more fixed form. What in the one was a matter of personal discipline, in the other becomes conscious method reduced to general rules; whereas the former aimed at educating individuals by true concepts, the latter seeks out the nature and connection of concepts in themselves: it enquires not merely into moral problems and activities, but into the essential nature of the Real, proposing as its end a scientific representation of the universe. But Plato does not go so far in this direction as Aristotle; the technicalities of logic were not formed by him, as by his pupil, into an exact, minutely particularising theory; neither for the derivation nor for the systematic application of concepts does he summon to his aid such a mass of experimental material. He cares far less for that equal spread of scientific knowledge into all departments which Aristotle desired, than for the contemplation of the idea as such. He regards the Empirical partly as a mere help to the attainment of the Idea—a ladder to be left behind if we would gain the heights of thought; partly as a type of the nature and inherent force of the ideas—a world of shadows, to which the Philosopher only temporarily descends, forthwith to return into the region of light and of pure being.[3] Whereas, therefore, Socrates in the main confines himself to a search for concepts, the cognition of which is for him moral education; whereas Aristotle extends induction and demonstration, purely in the interests of science, over all the Actual,—the special peculiarity of Plato is that moral education, intellectual teaching, and, in science itself, the formation of concepts and their development, in spite of partial separation, are yet, with him, internally held together and united by their common aim, both leading to that contemplation of the idea, which is at the same time life in the idea.[4] This position is not indeed invariable. We see, in the dialogues, Socratic induction at first decidedly predominating over the constructive element, then both intermingling, and, lastly, inductive preparation receding before systematic deduction; corresponding to which there is also a gradual change from the form of conversation to that of continued exposition. But the fundamental character of the method is never

[3] Vide especially Rep. vi. 511 A sq.; vii. 514 A sqq.
[4] Cf. my Plat. Stnd. p. 23 sq.

effaced; and however deeply Plato may sometimes go into particulars, his ultimate design is only to exhibit with all possible clearness and directness the Idea shining through the phenomenon; to point out its reflection in the finite; to fill with its light not only the intellect, but the whole man.

This speciality in the philosophy of Plato explains the form which he selected for its communication. An artistic nature was indispensable for the production of such a philosophy; conversely, this philosophy would infallibly demand to be informed artistically. The phenomenon, placed in such direct relation to the idea, becomes a beautiful phenomenon; the perception of the idea in the phenomenon an æsthetic perception.[5] Where science and life so completely interpenetrate one another, as with Plato, science can only impart itself in lively description; and as the communicating medium is ideal, this description will necessarily be poetical. At the same time, however, the exposition must be dialectical, if it is to correspond with the subject matter of conceptual philosophy. Plato satisfies both these requirements in the philosophic dialogue, by means of which he occupies a middle position between the personal converse of Socrates and the purely scientific continuous exposition of Aristotle.[6] The Socratic conversation is here idealised, the contingency of its motives

---

[5] It is thus (says Plato himself in the Phædrus, 250 B, D; Symp. 206 D), that the philosophic idea first dawns upon the consciousness.

[6] Aristotle chose the dialogue form only for popular writings, and apparently only in his Platonic period.

and conduct is corrected by a stricter method—the defects of personalities are covered by artistic treatment. Yet the speciality of verbal intercourse, the reciprocal kindling of thought, is still retained. Philosophy is set forth, not merely as a doctrine, but as a living power, in the person of the true philosopher, and a moral and artistic effect is thus produced, of a kind that would have been impossible to bare scientific enquiry. Unbroken discourse is doubtless better suited to the latter ; and Plato himself shows this, for in proportion as his scientific discussions gain in depth and scope, they lose in freedom of conversational movement. In the earlier works, this freedom not unfrequently disturbs the clearness of the logic, while in the dialectical dialogues of the middle order it is more and more subordinated to the logical development of thought. In the later writings, dialogue is indeed employed with the accustomed skill for introductory discussions or personal delineations;[7] but so far as the exposition of the system is concerned it sinks into a mere form, and in the Timæus is discarded at the very commencement.[8] We need not, with Hermann,[9] conclude from this that the form of dialogue had for Plato a merely external value; that, in fact, it was like some favourite and traditional fashion of dress

[7] E.g. in the Symposium, Phædo, and first two books of the Republic.

[8] Cf., on Plato's oral instruction, pp. 25-2, and Hermann, Plat. 352. Steinhart (Plat. W. vi. 44) explains the withdrawal of the dialogue form in the Timæus and Critias by saying that their subject was not adapted for dialogic exposition. This does not really contradict what has been observed above. Even where dialogue is employed throughout, there are many parts open to the same objection.

[9] Loc cit. 352, 354 sq. Ges. Abhdl. 285 sqq.

inherited from his predecessors, adopted in his first attempts as a Socratic pupil, and then adhered to out of piety and loyal attachment, in opposition to general usage. He certainly had an external motive for the choice of this form in the conversations of his master, and a pattern for its artistic treatment in dramatic poetry, especially such as dealt with reflections, morals, and manners, like that of Epicharmus,[10] Sophron,[11] and Euripides; but it cannot be proved [12] that before his time dialogue was already much in vogue for philosophic exposition; and even if it could, we might still be sure that Plato, independent and creative as he was, and endowed with rare artistic feeling, would

[10] Vide vol. i. page 362 sqq.
[11] Cf. page 8, note 11.
[12] Zeno, Sophron, and Alexamenus of Teos are named as predecessors of Plato. It is hardly probable, however, that Zeno used the dialogue form (vide vol. i. page 494); the Prolegomena, c. 5, end, name Parmenides with him: an addition no doubt due to the Platonic Parmenides. Of Sophron, whom Diogenes (iii. 18) says he copied, Aristotle remarks (Poetics, c. 1, 1447, b 9). οὐδὲν γὰρ ἂν ἔχοιμεν ὀνομάσαι κοινὸν τοὺς Σώφρονος καὶ Ξενάρχου μίμους καὶ τοὺς Σωκρατικοὺς λόγους. These mimes may indeed have been written in prose (Arist. ap. Athen. xi. 505 C), but are no proof of the existence of philosophic dialogues. Finally, Alexamenus may have written 'Socratic conversations,' but they must have been very unlike the Platonic dialogues, as Aristotle (ap. Athen. loc. cit.) classes them with Sophron's mimes as prose tales, λόγοι καὶ μιμήσεις (cf. on the passage Suckow's Form. d. Plat. Schr p 50 sq). And this solitary instance of dialogue being used before Plato by a writer so little known and so unimportant cannot go far to prove that the dialogic treatment of philosophic material was 'established and popular.' Indeed, it only became so through the Socratic school, in which the dialogue form was common enough. Vide Part i. pp. 198, 1; 204, 3; 205, 8, 206, 1; 207, 2; 242, 7; not to speak of the Memorabilia (with regard to the Diatribes of Aristippus, we do not know whether they were composed in dialogue form, and we are equally ignorant whether his twenty-five dialogues were genuine. v. p. 298). It is plain that the prevalence of dialogue in the Socratic school was due to its master. Perhaps, however, when Plato wrote his first pieces, there were not, as yet, many Socratic dialogues extant. Xen. Mem. iv. 3, 2, cannot be alleged to prove the opposite.

never on such purely external grounds have held to a form all his life long, even when it was most irksome to him; that mere antiquity would not have determined him in its choice, nor custom in its persistent employment, unless there had been the closest internal connection between that form and his whole conception of philosophy. What this connection was Plato himself points out,[13] when in the Phædrus (275 D) he censures writing, as compared with speech, with its inability to defend itself, and its openness to all attacks and misconceptions; for if this censure holds good of written exposition in general, Plato must have been conscious that even his dialogues could not entirely escape it. Yet, on the other hand, his conviction of the advantages of speech presupposes the design of appropriating as far as possible those advantages to his writing, that 'image of the living and animated word;'[14] and if those advantages, in Plato's opinion, depend upon the art of scientific dialogue,[15] we may

[13] Cf. Schleiermacher, Plat W. i. a. 17 sqq.; Brandis, Gr.-rom. Phil. vi. a. 154, 158 sqq.

[14] Phædrus, 276 A

[15] Phædrus, 276 E: πολὺ δ' οἶμαι, καλλίων σπουδὴ περὶ αὐτὰ γίγνεται, ὅταν τις τῇ διαλεκτικῇ τέχνῃ χρώμενος λαβὼν ψυχὴν προσήκουσαν φυτεύῃ τε καὶ σπείρῃ μετ' ἐπιστήμης λόγους, &c. Dialectic is first defined by Plato (Phædr. 266 B) only as the art of forming logical concepts and of making divisions. Its most suitable form was dialogue, as we may see from the explanation of διαλεκτικὴ as the art of scientific question and answer (Rep vii. 531 E, 534 B, D; Cratylus, 390 C), from the etymology given in Philebus, 57 E; Rep. vii. 532 A; vi. 511 B (against which the derivation ap. Xen. Mem. iv. 5, 12, proves nothing), and from the opposition between dialectic and rhetoric, in the Phædrus, loc. cit. And this is expressly affirmed in the Protagoras, p. 328 E sqq., where people are censured for purely continuous discourse, because, like books, they cannot either answer or ask questions, and are therefore deficient in those advantages which the Phædrus ascribes to oral instruction (Hermann's infelicitous conjecture, οὐχ ὥσπερ βιβλία, com-

reasonably derive from this his own application of that art. But the dialogues themselves manifest beyond possibility of mistake the design of compelling the reader, by their peculiar form, to the independent origination of thoughts. 'Why should there so often be found in them, after the destruction of imaginary knowledge by the essentially Socratic method of proving ignorance, only isolated and apparently unconnected lines of enquiry? why should some of these be hidden by others? why should the argument at last resolve itself in apparent contradictions? unless Plato presupposes his reader to be capable of completing by his own active participation what is wanting in any given enquiry, of discovering the central point in that enquiry, and of subordinating all the rest to that one point—presupposes also that only such a reader will attain any conviction of having understood at all.'[16] The above-named peculiarities are unfavourable to the systematic objective development of science. Since, therefore, Plato has employed them with the most consummate art and the most deliberate intention, he must have had a special reason for it, and this can only be that he considered objective exposition as generally insufficient, and sought instead for some other manner which should stimulate the reader to possess knowledge as a self-generated thing, in which objective instruction should be conditioned by previous

pletely misses the sense of the passage). The dialogue is accordingly recommended (348 C) as the best medium of instruction, and the retention of the dialogue form repeatedly insisted on, as opposed to the Sophistic declamations: cf. 334 C sqq.

[16] A quotation from Brandis, loc. cit. 159 sqq, with which I fully agree.

subjective culture. If this were the design of Plato, and he were at the same time convinced that the form of dialogue suited it better than continuous discourse, it naturally follows that he would select that form for his writings. Thought is to him a conversation of the soul with itself;[17] philosophic communication, an engendering of truth in another; the logical element is therefore essentially dialogical. His writings, too, were probably in the first instance designed, not for the general public,[18] but for his friends, to whom he himself would have imparted them: they were intended to remind those friends of the substance of the scientific conversations he was accustomed to carry on with them, or perhaps as a substitute for these.[19] What therefore could be more natural than that he should adopt the form of their usual intercourse—that of the Socratic dialogue?[20] Stricter science, in the sequel, wisely abandoned this form; but for Plato it was according to nature, and he stands alone and unapproached among all writers of philosophic dialogues,

[17] Sophist, 263 E: διάνοια μὲν καὶ λόγος ταὐτόν· πλὴν ὁ μὲν ἐντὸς τῆς ψυχῆς πρὸς αὐτὴν διάλογος ἄνευ φωνῆς γενόμενος τοῦτ' αὐτὸ ἡμῖν ἐπωνομάσθη διάνοια . . τὸ δέ γ' ἀπ' ἐκείνης ῥεῦμα διὰ τοῦ στόματος ἰὸν μετὰ φθόγγου κέκληται λόγος. Cf. Theæt. 189 E.

[18] There was as yet no bookselling in our sense of the term, although the first beginnings of it seem to come in that period. The usual method of making a work known was by means of recitation, which method Plato would have employed (vide p. 27, 56). The question arises whether Plato's writings had attained a circulation extending beyond his own school before his death. After that event, Hermodorus is taxed with having made a trade of selling Plato's writings; cf. the passages quoted in chapter xiv.

[19] Vide p. 112.

[20] From their original determination in this form we can partly explain the freedom with which Plato in his dialogues makes use of and characterises living personages of his acquaintance, e g. his brothers in the Republic and in the introduction to the Parmenides.

before and after him, because in the case of no other writer did the conditions under which his dialogues were produced exist in similar measure—in his person that rare combination of intellectual and artistic gifts, in his philosophy that equal perfection and inner fusion of the theoretical and practical, of the philosophic Eros, and of dialectic.

The central point of the dialogues is Socrates. Not only does he appear in most of them as the leader in conversation, in the rest as an acute and important listener and occasional speaker, but his personality is pre-eminently the bond which artistically unites the several pieces; and some of the most powerful and most delightful of the dialogues are devoted quite as much to the painting of this personality as to the philosophic development of doctrine.[21] This trait is primarily a tribute of gratitude and veneration offered by the disciple to his master. Plato is conscious that he owes to Socrates what is best in his spiritual life, and under this conviction, gives back to him in his writings the noblest fruits of the borrowed seed as his own. That Socrates should be brought forward was necessary, too, on artistic grounds; for the unity of the Platonic doctrine, and the intimate connection of all the writings devoted to it, could in no way be more artistically represented than by their association with one and the same personality; and that the personality of Socrates was far more suitable than any other; that a nobler, pleasanter picture—a picture more capable of idealisa-

---

[21] Socrates is only omitted in the Laws, the last of Plato's works; and the omission is but one of its peculiarities.

tion—resulted from Plato's placing his opinions in the mouth of Socrates, instead of enunciating them himself, needs no proof.

His procedure has doubtless another and a deeper reason, rooted in the foundations of his manner of thought. Philosophy, according to his acceptation, being not merely a set of doctrines but the perfecting of the whole spiritual life; and science, not a finished, communicable system, apart from the person that knows, but personal activity and mental development,—true philosophy could only be represented in the perfect philosopher, in the personality, words, and demeanour of Socrates.[22] This view of philosophy is closely connected with another trait, by which Plato's literary individuality is marked with special clearness. This is his employment of myths, which he loves to combine with philosophic enquiry, and especially to bring forward for the opening or conclusion of a discussion.[23]

[22] Cf the striking observations of Baur, in his 'Socrates and Christ,' Tubingen Journal, 1837, 3, 97-121

[23] I subjoin for convenience sake a list of all that properly belongs to this class · Protagoras, 320 C sqq., on Prometheus and Epimetheus and the origin of political virtue, perhaps from some writing of Protagoras, v. vol. i. page 575 sq.;—Politicus, 269 C sqq, the changing world-periods : cf. the Laws, iv. 713, 13 sq., for a short mythic picture of the Golden Age; —Timæus, 21 A sq., and Critias, the cosmic revolutions, the Atlantides, and Athenians ;—Symposium, 189 D sq.. Aristophanes' tale of how the difference in sex arose :—Ibid. 203 A sq., the begetting of Eros. Republic, iii. 414 D sqq., triple classification of men;—Phædrus, 246 A sqq.; Meno, 81 A sqq ; Gorgias, 523 A sqq.; Phædo, 110 B sqq ; Republic, x. 614 B sq., Timæus, 41 A sqq., the Soul, its pre-existence, wanderings, its condition hereafter, its recollection of previous perceptions. The whole investiture of the Timæus is also mythic—the Demiurgus, together with the subordinate gods, and all the history of the creation of the world; so is the Name-giver of the Cratylus. I shall go more at length into the import of these myths in their proper places. The short narratives of the Cicadas and of Theuth have no esoteric

Here, however, another motive comes into play. On the one side, the mythus is the expression of the religious and poetical character of the Platonic philosophy.[24] Plato makes use of the traditions of the popular faith and of the mysteries (in which beneath the veil of fable he divines a deeper meaning) for the artistic representation of his ideas; he also extends and multiplies them by original inventions, which rise from the transparent personification of philosophic conceptions, into lively epic description fully and exuberantly drawn out. But, on the other side, the mythus is not a mere garment, thrown over a thought that had previously existed in a purely scientific shape; in many cases it is for Plato a positive necessity, and his masterly use of it is a consequence of the fact, that he does not turn back upon the path of reflection to seek a picture for his thought, but that from the very outset, like a creative artist, he thinks in pictures: that the mythus does not reiterate that which the author has elsewhere dialectically expressed, but seizes by anticipation, as with a presentiment, that for which logical expression is still wanting. The Platonic myths, in short, almost always point to a gap in scientific knowledge: they are introduced where something has to be set forth, which the philosopher indeed acknowledges as true, but which he has no means of

reference to philosophic doctrines. Phædr. 259 A sq. 274 C sq The legend of Gyges, Rep. xi. 359 D sq., is used by Plato for the elucidation of a position, but is not introduced in his own name. Rep. vii. 514 sqq., is an allegory, out of which a myth could be constructed, but the narrative form is wanting.

[24] On the religious signification of the Platonic myths, cf. Baur, loc. cit. 91 sqq.; Theol. Stud. u. Krit. 1837, 3, 552 sqq.

establishing scientifically.[25] This takes place chiefly in two cases: (1) when it is required to explain the origin of material things, the methodical derivation of which is impossible, according to the presuppositions of Plato's system;[26] and (2) when circumstances are to be described which have no analogy with our present experience, and which cannot be more exactly delineated. The first is found in the mythological cosmogony of the Timæus;[27] the second in the narrations concerning the future life and the primeval history of man; for the essential purport of these latter is also the determination of the state in which human society would find itself under altered, ideal conditions. When Plato in these cases adopts the mythical representation, he indirectly confesses that his ordinary style would be impossible to him. His myths are consequently not only a proof of his artistic ability, and an effect of the intimate relation still subsisting between his philosophy and his poetry, but they also betray the boundaries of his methodical thought. However admirable in themselves, therefore, they are, in a scientific point of view, rather a sign of

---

[25] Plato himself shows this in his eschatologic myths: Phædo, 114 D; Gorg. 523 A, 527 A; and Timæus, 29 D, 59 C, he speaks of the εἰκὼs μῦθοs. Stumpf (Verh. d. Plat. Gott. z. idee d. Gut. 37) confounds the myth with allegory in asserting (though he retracts the assertion virtually, p. 100), that 'the myth excludes probability, because, if taken literally, it could only be false, while it could only be true if understood in its general sense.' This cannot be got out of Plato's words, and is in itself mistaken. The signification of a myth is simply whatever the author wishes to express by it: but must this be invariably true?

[26] As will be shown in its proper place.

[27] The Name-giver of the Cratylus and the φυτουργὸs τῆs κλίνηs of Republic, x. 597 B sqq., belong to this class.

MYTHS.

weakness than of strength: they indicate the point at which it becomes evident that as yet he cannot be wholly a philosopher, because he is still too much of a poet.[28]

[28] Cf. Hegel's remarks, History of Philosophy, ii 163 sqq. A. Jahn (Dissertatio Platonica, Bern, 1839, p. 20 sqq) has rather strengthened than refuted Hegel's position, though his perverse philosophic assumptions have done much to obscure the simple understanding of the case; e.g. the arbitrary and unsatisfactory division of the myths (ibid 31 sq) into theological, psychological, cosmogonical, and physical—a division that reminds us of Sallust's de Mundo, c. 4. Deuschle (Plat Sprachphil. 38 sqq, Ueber plat. Mythen, 3 sqq.) is much more satisfactory on the nature and import of Plato's myths, and Susemihl (Genet. Entw. i. 228, 283 sq) and Steinhart (Pl W. vi. 73) in the main agree with him He shows that the Platonic envisagement of the world, and the method of its development, was essentially ontological, not genetic; and that, therefore, Platonic philosophy was not concerned, even if it had been able, to explain the genesis of the Existent. The Become, however, forced itself into consideration; and some form had to be found at once capable of a speculative content, and demonstrating by its unphilosophic stamp the nothingness of the experiential substratum. This form was the mythus, 'the value and charm of which' (as Steinhart says, loc cit.) 'lie in that mysterious union of Being and Becoming, which, unattainable by cognition, may only be grasped by imagination and feeling,' the essential import of which is 'to give a pictorial envisagement, where pure thought can no longer help us, of the transition of the Idea into phenomena.' We may, therefore, expect a mythical representation 'wherever' (Deuschle, Plat. M. 10) 'Plato's doctrine involves a difficulty between true Being and a process of Becoming: the former belongs to intellectual investigation; the latter has to be brought before us by an envisagement which fills up its outlines.' While acknowledging the ingenuity of these deductions, I am prevented by the following reasons from giving full adhesion to the theory First, I cannot concede that Plato uses mythic representation *only* when he has to explain a process of Becoming. For (even to pass over Phædr 259 A sq, 274 C sq., and 247 C, 250 B, Rep. x. 597 B, where the Ideas themselves are thus treated) the myths in the Symposium and Politicus (as will be shown further on) are not concerned with the explanation of anything Become; in the former the object is to give a description of Eros—a definition through concepts—which might just as well have been given in purely dialectic form. But artistic considerations decided Plato to clothe his thought in the light and transparent envelopment of the mythus. In the Politicus, he merely follows out the position that the reduction of statecraft to the pastoral art is at most applicable only to the golden

164   PLATO AND THE OLDER ACADEMY.

Plato's more comprehensive and methodical development of philosophy necessitates also a clearer distinction of its several branches with him than with earlier philosophers. Yet the dividing lines are not so sharply drawn in his writings as in those of Aristotle; nor is the precise determination of each branch quite certain.[29] Modern writers have not unfrequently ascribed to Plato classifications which are manifestly alien to him;[30] and the same is true of the previously

---

age, and that, applied to our own times, it is wrong and overlooks the real distinction between the two. All the philosophic opinions contained in the myth of the Statesman might have been dispensed with as far as its immediate object is concerned. Again, the myth of Rep. iii. does not stand in the place of an explanation. On this account, then, I cannot concede to Deuschle (Plat. M. 12) that a myth like that of the Symposium is necessary on philosophic grounds, though I entirely acknowledge its artistic propriety Generally speaking, we shall find it best not to press the philosophical construction too much, not to confine too strictly poetical invention. As regards the scientific worth of the Platonic myths, I do not think my judgment on them overthrown by the remark (Plat. Sprach. phil. 38) that this exposition was necessary to Plato from his point of view. This I have endeavoured to prove myself: and the assertion that the deficiencies of Plato's scientific procedure come into prominence in this very need of a mythical exposition is no contradiction. Deuschle, plat. M. 4, virtually admits this. Fuller enquiries into the Platonic myths are given in Alb. Fischer De Mythis Plat. (Königsb. 1865), 27 sq.; Ueberweg, Grundr. i. 129. To these must now be added Volquardsen on the Platonic myths, Schlesw. 1871. Fischer's classification of the myths into poetical and philosophical (loc. cit.) is inexact, because, if we understand by the first the purely poetical (for they are all poetical on the whole, else they would not be myths), this class must be limited to the Phædr. 259 (of the Cicadas); Phædr. 274 C eq (about Theuth) is a didactic narrative, though without any philosophic content. Of the other instances placed by Fischer in this class, Rep. ii. 359 D eq is no myth at all, while Prot. 230 C sqq, and Symp. 189 D sqq., express definite philosophic suppositions. The further division of the philosophic myths into ontological, methodic, cosmological, psychological, and political, is at once useless and inaccurate, inasmuch as not unfrequently several of these elements are treated in the same myth.

[29] Cf. on what follows Ritter, ii. 244 sqq.

[30] E.g. the division into a general

mentioned attempts [31] of the old grammarians to arrange his works according to their contents. Though the external evidence in its favour is insufficient,[32] there is far more to be said for the theory that he divided the whole subject matter of philosophy into three parts: Dialectics (or Logic), Physics, and Ethics.[33] For not only is this distribution presupposed by Aristotle [34] and employed by Xenocrates,[35] but the most important of the dialogues, in regard to their main subject, fall into three corresponding groups; though scarcely one dialogue is wholly contained in either.

and an applied part: (Marbach, Gesch. d. Phil. i. 215, who further subdivides the latter into Physics and Ethics; similarly Schleiermacher, Gesch. d Phil. 98, speaks of a 'twofold direction of cognition to unity and totality, and in the latter to Physics and Ethics,' to Plato himself is attributed merely the threefold division into Dialectics, Physics, and Ethics); a distinction which nowhere occurs. Nor again do we find a distinction between theoretical and practical philosophy: (Krug, Gesch. d. alt Phil. 209; Buhle, Gesch. d. Phil. ii. 70 sq.; and Tenneman, Plat. Phil. i. 240 sqq., add as a third division Logic or Dialectics, by which, however, they only understand the theory of cognition). Van Heusde's distinction of a *philosophia pulcri, veri et justi*, is entirely modern and unplatonic.

[31] P 97, 14

[32] See preceding note. The eclectic Antiochus is not an original source in questions of the Platonic philosophy; and this is true without exception of the writers of the second and third century of the Christian era

[33] Cic. Acad i 5, 19, who, acc. to c. 4, 14 (cf Fin v 3, 8, 4, 9), follows Antiochus in this instance. Diog. iii 56: to Physics Socrates added Ethics, and Plato Dialectics (more correctly Apul. Dogm. Plat. 3. he had Ethics and Dialectics from Socrates). Atticus ap. Euseb. pr Ev. xi 2, 2 sqq., Apul loc. cit., both of whom, however, show their untrustworthiness, in ranging Theology and the doctrine of Ideas under Physics; so also Aristocl apud Euseb. loc. cit 3 6, and Alcinous Isag. c. 7, who mentions the three divisions of dialectical, theoretical, and practical philosophy. Sextus Math vii. 16, after detailing the three parts of philosophy, says far more circumspectly: ὧν δυνάμει μὲν Πλάτων ἐστὶν ἀρχηγὸς .... ῥητότατα δὲ οἱ περὶ τὸν Ξενοκράτη καὶ οἱ ἀπὸ τοῦ περιπάτου ἔτι δὲ οἱ ἀπὸ τῆς στοᾶς ἔχονται τῆσδε τῆς διαιρέσεως.

[34] Top. i. 14, 105 b. 19; cf. Anal. Post. i. 33, end.

[35] See note 33.

The Timæus, and, so far as Anthropology may be classed under Physics, the Phædo also, is physical as to contents; the Republic, Politicus, Philebus, Gorgias, ethical; the Theætetus, Sophist and Parmenides, dialectical. We may therefore venture to derive this division from Plato, though it is never brought forward in his writings,[36] and at any rate cannot be proved in the case of his oral discourses. But, however applicable it may be, it does not exhaust the philosophic content of the dialogues. It has already been pointed out that in these the Socratic induction,—discussion for scientific preparation and moral education,—is combined with systematic development of doctrine, and at first even asserts itself to a far greater extent. What place, then, is to be assigned to such arguments? Where are we to arrange all those refutations of popular opinion and of customary virtue, of the Sophists and their Eudæmonistic theories—all those passages which treat of the conception and the method of knowledge, the oneness of virtue, and the relation of knowledge to moral action, of philosophic love and the stages of its development? It is usual to place one part of them under Dialectic, another under Ethics. But by this procedure, either the coherent exposition of these

[36] By Dialectic Plato understands Philosophy generally, as will be shown more thoroughly later on. He acknowledges a strictly scientific procedure only where pure concepts are dealt with; and, therefore, the limitation of Dialectic to the doctrine of true existences is not opposed to his views He does not know the names Physics and Ethics. Instead of the latter he would rather say Politics· cf Polit. 303 E, 305 E, 259 B; and Euthydem. 291 C sqq.; Gorg. 464 B.

DIVISION OF PLATO'S SYSTEM. 167

sciences is interrupted by elementary discussions which Plato, even where he introduces them, has left far behind—or the enquiries concerning true knowledge and right action, always in him so closely intermingled, are forced widely apart. To renounce an articulate division of the exposition based on the contents, and to adhere only to the conjectural arrangement of the dialogues,[37] seems unadvisable; for if we thus gain a true representation of the order in which Plato propounded his thoughts, we get none of their internal connection; and it is evident from the frequent discussion in widely distant dialogues of one and the same thought, that the two orders do not necessarily coincide. Unless we would follow Plato even in his repetitions—in the want of perfect systematic clearness inseparable from his manner of explanation—we must, in considering dialogues which are the stronghold of any particular doctrine, adduce all parallel instances from among the other dialogues. But if in this manner the order of the writings be once abandoned, we have no longer any reason for adhering to it at all; the problem will rather be to place ourselves at the inner source and centre of the Platonic system, and to rally round this nucleus the elements of that system, according to their internal relation in the mind of their author.[38] On this subject Plato himself (Rep. vi. 511 B)

[37] A commencement may be found in Brandis, cf. loc. cit. p. 182, 192: afterwards, however, he returns to an arrangement according to matter, which in the main agrees with the ordinary one.

[38] I need not protest that in these remarks I do not disparage the worth of investigations into the sequence and respective relations of the Platonic dialogues, or accede to the sweeping sentence of Hegel against such inquiries (Gesch. d. Phil. xi. 156),

gives us a pregnant hint. The highest division of the thinkable, he says, and the proper object of philosophy is this: 'What the reason as such attains by means of the dialectic faculty, using the hypotheses not as first principles, but merely as hypotheses, like steps and points of departure,[39] in order to reach out from them to the unconditioned, the first principle of all things; and laying hold of this, and then of that which follows from it, it again descends to the last step; so that it nowhere makes use of any sensible object, but proceeds wholly from ideas, through ideas, to ideas.' In this passage, and also in a noteworthy passage of Aristotle,[40] a double way is clearly traced out for thought: the way from beneath, upward; and that from above, downward: the inductive ascent to the idea, effected by the cancelling of final hypotheses, and the systematic descent from the idea to the particular. Now we already know that these two ways correspond with the two elements united in the doctrine of Plato, and also distinguishable from each other in his literary exposition. We therefore pursue this indication, con-

superficially reiterated by Marbach (Gesch. d. Phil. 1. 198). These investigations are in their proper place of the highest value, but, in an exposition of the Platonic system, merely literary points must be subordinated to questions of the philosophic connexion.

[39] Properly, 'onsets,' ὁρμαί: but here the word seems to signify not so much the actual onset, as the starting-point. Similarly Symp. 211 C: ὥσπερ ἐπαναβαθμοῖς χρώμενον [τοῖς πολλοῖς καλοῖς].

[40] Eth. N. i. 2, 1095 a. 32: εὖ γὰρ καὶ Πλάτων ἠπόρει τοῦτο καὶ ἐζήτει, πότερον ἀπὸ τῶν ἀρχῶν, ἢ ἐπὶ τὰς ἀρχὰς ἐστὶν ἡ ὁδός, ὥσπερ ἐν τῷ σταδίῳ ἀπὸ τῶν ἀθλοθετῶν ἐπὶ τὸ πέρας ἢ ἀνάπαλιν. This expression seems to refer to Plato's procedure in oral instruction. The words ἠπόρει καὶ ἐζήτει are suitable neither to the passage in the Republic nor to the analogous (though not coincident) passage in the Phædo, 101 D. Cf. the reference later on from Phædr. 265 D sqq.

sidering in the following pages, first the propædeutic groundwork, and then the systematic construction of the Platonic theory. This latter, again, may be divided into Dialectics, Physics, and Ethics.[41]

[41] It needs no proof to show that these three divisions could only have been arranged in the order given above, and the reverse order adopted by Freis, Gesch. d. Phil. i. § 58 sqq., requires as little refutation as his assertion (loc. cit. p. 288), that Plato, as a true Socratic, was occupied entirely with practical philosophy, and in his method did not go beyond the epagogic process.

CHAPTER V.

THE PROPÆDEUTIC GROUNDWORK OF THE PLATONIC DOCTRINE.

SPEAKING generally. Plato's Propædeutic consists in applying destructive criticism to the unphilosophical point of view, and demonstrating the necessity of true philosophy. In particular, three stages may be distinguished in this process. Ordinary consciousness forms the point of departure. By the dialectical analysis of the presuppositions, which were regarded by ordinary consciousness as primary and certain truths, we next arrive at the negative result of the Sophists.[1] When this has been surmounted, and not till then, the philosophic point of view can be positively evolved.

Plato has refuted the position of ordinary consciousness both on its theoretical and on its practical side. In theory, ordinary consciousness may be generally defined as the Envisaging Consciousness (Vorstellendes Bewusstsein); or, more exactly to discriminate its elements, it apprehends truth partly as Sensuous Perception, and partly as Envisagement (Vorstellen) in the

[1] Grote's objections (Plato, i. 259 sq) have been answered, Part i. p. 157.

narrower sense—Opinion, or what a man conceives (δόξα).[2]

In opposition to this, Plato shows in the Theætetus that Knowledge (ἐπιστήμη) is something different from Perception (sensation, αἴσθησις) and Right Opinion. Perception is not Knowledge, for (Theæt. 151 E) Perception is only the manner in which things appear to us (φαντασία): if, therefore, Knowledge consisted in Perception, it would follow that for each man that must be true which appears to him true—the principle of the Sophists, the refutation of which we shall presently consider. Perception shows us the self-same object in the most contradictory manner: at one time great, at another small; now hard, now soft; now straight, now crooked: how then can it be regarded as equally true with thought, which abolishes these contradictions?[3] But even Right Opinion is not Knowledge; inasmuch as Knowledge is to be sought in the activity of the soul as such, and not in yielding ourselves to external impressions[4]—Opinion is inadequate to the problem of Knowledge. If Right Opinion (this by way of indirect proof) were indeed Knowledge, the possibility of False Opinion would be inexplicable. For in the first place, False Opinion could relate neither to what is known nor to what is unknown: of the former we have Right Opinion, of the latter (if Knowledge and Opinion be really

---

[2] Cf. Rep. v. 475 E sqq., and passages to be presently cited.
[3] Rep. iii. 523 E sq.; x. 602 C sq.
[4] Theæt. 187 A: ὅμως δὲ τοσοῦτόν γε προβεβήκαμεν, ὥστε μὴ ζητεῖν αὐτὴν (τὴν ἐπιστήμην) ἐν αἰσθήσει τὸ παράπαν, ἀλλ' ἐν ἐκείνῳ τῷ ὀνόματι, ὅτι ποτ' ἔχει ἡ ψυχὴ ὅταν αὐτὴ καθ' αὑτὴν πραγματεύηται περὶ τὰ ὄντα.

identical) none at all.[5] Further, if we suppose False Opinion to be an opinion corresponding to no object, this would presuppose that the non-existent might be conceived; but that is impossible, since every notion is a notion of something that exists. If it be made to consist in the mistaking of one notion for another (ἀλλοδοξία), it is equally inconceivable that a man should mistake one thing that he knows, by virtue of his very knowledge, for some other thing that he knows, or even for something he does not know.[6] That is to say, Knowledge and Right Opinion cannot be the same, for Right Opinion does not exclude the possibility of False, and Knowledge does exclude it;[7] Opinion can be

---

[5] Vide 187 C sq.

[6] Vide 189 B–200 D; and specially the end of this section. Briefly, the drift of the whole—in particular of the elaborate comparisons of the soul to a wax-tablet and to a dove-cot—is to show that in supposing the identity of Knowledge and Right Opinion there is an incorrect combination of an opinion with a perception, not a confusion of the concepts themselves, and that, therefore, such a supposition is incorrect. In refuting what is false, Plato generally gives hints of the truth; and we find a series of acute and striking remarks in the course of his demonstration, specially in the distinction (afterwards so productive in Aristotle's hands) between actual and potential knowledge, and in the dictum that error is based, not in our particular opinions about or envisagements of things, but in an incorrect combination of these; in the case of sensible things, an incorrect combination of the pictures our memory makes with our perceptions: 190 B sq. Steinhart (Pl. W. iii. 44, 93 sq.) lays such stress on this positive side of the dialogue as to assert that 'the genetic development of the process of thought' is to be recognised in it, as well as the refutation of error as to the nature of Knowledge. I cannot agree with him here: there is no investigation into the genesis of Knowledge; and even its nature is only indirectly hinted at in separating it from Perception and Opinion.

[7] On the other hand, Bonitz (Plat. Stud. i. 69 sq) thinks that the question at 187 B, 200 C, is not as to the possibility of error, but the explanation of what goes on in the soul when error arises. To me the point seems to lie in the demonstration that if δόξα ἀληθής coincided with ἐπιστήμη, δόξα ψευδής would be inexplicable; so Theætetus' definition of ἐπιστήμη as δόξα ἀληθής is refuted apago-

true or false—Knowledge only true: we cannot know falsely, but only know or not know.[8] This diversity may also be proved by experience, for Knowledge is only produced by instruction; Right Opinion, on the contrary, not unfrequently, as by rhetoricians, through mere persuasion. Knowledge, therefore, cannot lie in the sphere of Opinion, but must belong to some specifically different activity.[9] For the same reason, it cannot be defined [10] as Right Opinion along with an explanation (λόγος); for whatever may be comprehended in the explanation, if this itself does not start from a cognition, but only from a right envisagement, its addition can never transmute Opinion into Knowledge.[11] The

gically. This view, in my opinion, is favoured by the fact that it, and it alone, can bring the section we are discussing into harmony with the theme of the whole dialogue. Regarded in any other light, this section becomes an unmotived episode of disproportionate length, interrupting the enquiry into the concept of ἐπιστήμη. And the subsequent progress of the dialogue confirms my explanation. The difficulties with which the explanation of False Opinion has to contend come back finally to the contradiction: 'what I know I must at the same time not know, or must confound with something else;' cf. p 199 C sq.; 196 C et alibi. But the contradiction disappears as soon as the supposition of 187 C (that the opposite of δόξα ψευδής, δόξα ἀληθής coincides with ἐπιστήμη) is given up. Right Opinion (δόξα ἀληθής) may (as Plato says in the Meno, 97 E; Tim. 51 E) pass into error; Knowledge (ἐπιστήμη) cannot.

[8] This is directly enunciated by the Gorgias, 454 D: ἆρ' ἔστι τις— πίστις ψευδὴς καὶ ἀληθής; φαίης ἂν, ὡς ἐγὼ οἶμαι. Ναί· τί δέ; ἐπιστήμη ἐστὶ ψευδὴς καὶ ἀληθής; Οὐδαμῶς. Δῆλον γὰρ αὖ ὅτι οὐ ταὐτόν ἐστιν Πίστις is here equivalent to the δόξα of other passages, cf. Rep. iii 534 A sq. (infra, note 14), where that part of δόξα which relates to Reality as distinguished from mere pictures of things is called πίστις, and ibid. v. 477 E: ὁμολόγεις μὴ τὸ αὐτὸ εἶναι ἐπιστήμην τε καὶ δόξαν. Πῶς γὰρ ἂν ἔφη, τό γε ἀναμάρτητον τῷ μὴ ἀναμαρτήτῳ ταὐτὸν ποτέ τις νοῦν ἔχων τιθείη;

[9] Cf. Schleiermacher, Platon's Werke. ii. 1, 176.

[10] With Antisthenes, v Part i. p. 252 sq.

[11] V 201 C–210. I cannot here go into the details of the argument; v. Susemihl, i. 199 sq.; Steinhart, ii. 81 sq. Hermann's opinion (Plat. 498, 659, repeated by Alberti, z. Dialektik d. Pl., Jahn's Jahrb. Suppl., New Series,

174   *PLATO AND THE OLDER ACADEMY.*

Meno tells [12] us wherein they differ: Opinion lacks intelligent insight into the necessity of the thing: it is consequently, even if true, an uncertain and variable possession. Knowledge alone, by supplying this want, guarantees abiding cognition of truth. And summing up all previous discussions, the Timæus (51 E) declares that Knowledge is implanted in us by instruction, Right Opinion by persuasion; [13] the one is always accompanied by true reason, the other is without reason; the one is not to be moved by persuasion, the other may be moved; and lastly, every man may be said to participate in Right Opinion, but in Reason only the gods, and very few men. The Republic,[14] in a more objective manner, proves the inferior worth of Opinion, in that Knowledge has pure Being for its subject-matter, Opinion only something intermediate between Being and Non-Being: consequently Opinion must itself be intermediate between Knowledge and Ignorance. This ex-

---

i. 123, and favoured by Susemihl, p. 207 and Steinhart, p. 85) that the position apparently disputed really contains Plato's own view, contradicts the obvious sense of the passage. Right Opinion, according to Plato, becomes Knowledge, not through any explanation in Antisthenes' sense, but through cognition of causes (αἰτίας λογισμῷ, Meno, 98 A).

[12] 97 sq; cf. Symp. 202 A; Rep. vi. 506 C The same characteristic distinguishes τέχνη from ἐμπειρία in the Gorgias, 465 A.

[13] Gorgias, 454 E.

[14] V 476 D-478 D. Cf. Symp. 202 A, Phileb. 59 A sq. Similarly in Rep. vi. 509 D sq; vii. 533 E sq., the domain of the Visible and of Becoming is assigned to Opinion, that of the Intellectual and of Being to Knowledge. The further subdivision of δόξα into opinion about (or envisagement of) real things on the one hand (πίστις) and their mere pictures on the other (εἰκασία) is made to parallel the subdivision of Knowledge into symbolic and pure Knowledge: v. p 510 D. In other places Plato puts αἴσθησις side by side with δόξα, e g. in the Parmenides, 155 D; Timæus, 28 B; 37 B; besides the Theætetus. Cf. also the passage (to be noticed presently) in Aristotle, De Anima, i. 2, 404 b. 21.

position to some extent presupposes the distinction between Knowledge and Opinion, and in some degree depends on limitations which belong to the further development of the system.

That which in the sphere of theory is the antithesis of Opinion and Knowledge, becomes in practice the antithesis of common and philosophic Virtue.[15] Ordinary virtue is even formally insufficient: it is a mere matter of custom, without clear understanding; allowing itself to be guided by Opinion instead of Knowledge. It thus becomes a plurality of individual activities, which are bound together by no internal unity; nay, which even partially contradict one another. It is also deficient in content, partly in making evil as well as good its aim; partly in desiring the good, not for its own sake but on extraneous grounds. In all these relations Plato finds a higher conception of morality to be necessary.

Customary virtue arises from habit; it is action without intelligent insight into the causes of that action;[16] it depends on Right Opinion, not on Knowledge:[17] whence it evidently follows that the possession of such virtue is not combined with the capacity for imparting it to others; and that according to the usual view, or at any rate the usual practice, there are no teachers of

---

[15] Cf. following note.

[16] Meno, 99 A sq. et al.; Phædo, 82 A: οἱ τὴν δημοτικὴν τε καὶ πολιτικὴν ἀρετὴν ἐπιτετηδευκότες, ἣν δὴ καλοῦσι σωφροσύνην τε καὶ δικαιοσύνην ἐξ ἔθους τε καὶ μελέτης γεγονυῖαν ἄνευ φιλοσοφίας τε καὶ νοῦ. Rep. x. 619 C (of one who has brought unhappiness on himself by an unwise choice in his second life): εἶναι δὲ αὐτὸν τῶν ἐκ τοῦ οὐρανοῦ ἡκόντων, ἐν τεταγμένῃ πολιτείᾳ ἐν τῷ προτέρῳ βίῳ βεβιωκότα, ἔθει ἄνευ φιλοσοφίας ἀρετῆς μετειληφότα. Cf. Rep. iii. 402 A; vii. 522 A.

[17] Meno, 97 sq.; especially 99 A-C; Rep. vii. 534 C.

virtue [18]—for those who profess to be teachers (the Sophists) are, as we shall presently see, recognised as such neither by Plato, nor by the popular verdict.[19] For the same reason this virtue has in itself no warranty of its own continuance; its origin and subsistence are dependent on chance and circumstances. All who are content with it, the famous statesmen of ancient Athens not excepted, are virtuous only by the Divine appointment; that is to say, they owe their virtue to accident;[20] they stand on no essentially higher ground

---

[18] Protagoras, 319 B sq.; Meno, 87 B sq.; 93 sqq.

[19] Meno, 91 B sq., where Anytus represents the men of δημοτικὴ ἀρετή.

[20] This view of the θεία μοῖρα was enunciated by Ritter, ii 472, and opposed by Hermann (Jahn's Archiv 1840, p. 56 sq.; cf. Plat. 484), Susemihl (Genet. Ent. i. 71), Fenerlein (Sittenl. d. Alterth. 82), Schaarschmidt (Samml. d. Plat. Sch. 350), and Stallbaum (Vind. loci leg. Plat. 22 sq.). It may be easily explained and supported. The expression denotes any divine dispensation, either in the disposition of outward circumstances, or in the natural endowments and inward motives of individuals. We see the former exemplified in Socrates' words (Phædo, 58 E): μηδ᾽ εἰς Ἅιδου ἰόντα ἄνευ θείας μοίρας ἰέναι, ἀλλὰ κἀκεῖσε ἀφικόμενον εὖ πράξειν· the latter in Rep. vi. 492 E, where it is said that with ordinary human endowments no one can be saved for philosophy in the present corruption of States; but ὅ τι περ ἂν σωθῇ τε καὶ γένηται οἷον δεῖ ἐν τοιαύτῃ καταστάσει πολιτείων, θεοῦ μοῖραν αὐτὸ σῶσαι λέγων οὐ κακῶς ἐρεῖς (Schaarschmidt gives an inexact account of this in making Plato say that if a moral character does appear in the world, it is only through divine aid; the question is not of the world in general, but of the existing κατάστασις τῶν πολιτειῶν.) Here the divine dispensation includes both ways of help: the extraordinary endowment of the individual, and the favourable disposition of outward circumstances, which unite to preserve him from the bad influence of a corrupt state; cf. ibid. 496 B sq. Similarly, in Plato's Apology, 33 C (vide Part i. 49, 5), the dreams and oracles urging Socrates to occupy himself with philosophy are attributed to θεία μοῖρα. In other passages the expression is applied to natural disposition, natural excellence of any sort, θεία μοῖρα properly denoting the divine in man, the divine inheritance which is his, because of his kinship to the gods (e.g in Prot. 322 A; Phædrus, 230 A). In this sense the true ruler who has been brought to right practical knowledge

than soothsayers and poets, and all those who produce what is true and beautiful from mere inspiration (μανία,

(ἐπιστήμη) by an unusually happy natural disposition, and has learnt to act correspondingly, is said (Laws, ix. 875 C) to be θείᾳ μοίρᾳ γεννηθείς. The same or a similar designation for the natural disposition of men is found in Xen. Mem ii. 3, 18; Arist Eth. Ni x. 10, 1179 b. 21, as pointed out by Hermann, loc. cit. p. 56; cf. also Epinomis, 985 A. In all these instances, θεία μοῖρα is simply used of the derivation of some fact from divine causation, without excluding conscious human activity; thus knowledge itself may be ultimately referred to divine dispensation, as in Rep. vi 492 E; Laws, ix. 875 C. In other places, θεία μοῖρα is opposed to ἐπιστήμη, when a thing is spoken of as due, not to conscious human activity motived by knowledge, but to mere natural disposition, to circumstances, or to some inspiration of which no clear account can be given. Thus in Rep. ii. 366 C, θείᾳ φύσει (essentially equivalent to θείᾳ μοίρᾳ) and ἐπιστήμη are opposed in the words ('all love injustice') πλὴν εἴ τις θείᾳ φύσει δυσχεραίνων τὸ ἀδικεῖν ἢ ἐπιστήμην λαβὼν ἀπέχεται αὐτοῦ. Similarly, in the Laws, i. 642 C, θείᾳ μοίρᾳ is made parallel to αὐτοφυῶς, as opposed to ἀνάγκη the man who is righteous at Athens, we are there told, must be really and unmistakably righteous, for there is no compulsion in the laws or institutions to keep him so, and he must be simply following the dictates of his own nature. Here, as in Rep. vi. 492 E (v. supra), the θείᾳ μοίρᾳ must denote the virtue of an individual in an evilly constituted state, as an exception only ascribable to a special dispensation of providence. Analogous to this is the opposition we find in the Phædrus, 244 C sq., between prophetic inspiration, which is spoken of in terms of praise as resulting θείᾳ μοίρᾳ, and the ζήτησις τῶν ἐμφρόνων: the same opposition is used in the Ion, 534 B, with reference to poetic inspiration: poets are said to utter themselves οὐ τέχνῃ ἀλλὰ θείᾳ μοίρᾳ: and we may compare the similar expressions of the Apology, 22 C, ὅτι οὐ σοφίᾳ ποιοῖεν ἃ ποιοῖεν, ἀλλὰ φύσει τινὶ καὶ ἐνθουσιάζοντες κ.τ.λ., and Laws, iii. 682 A. In the Meno, the contrast to knowledge and to virtue dependent on knowledge denoted by θείᾳ μοίρᾳ is clear. the great statesmen of old, we read in 99 B sq., achieved their business by pure εὐδοξίᾳ, οὐ σοφίᾳ τινὶ σόφοι ὄντες: as far as their wisdom went, they were on a level with soothsayers, &c (οὐδὲν διαφερόντος ἔχοντες πρὸς τὸ φρονεῖν ἢ οἱ χρησμῳδοὶ κ.τ.λ.), who often hit the truth unconsciously (νοῦν μὴ ἔχοντες—μηδὲν εἰδότες ὧν λέγουσιν). Virtue comes to those who cannot impart it to others by teaching, θείᾳ μοίρᾳ ἄνευ νοῦ: he who can so impart it may be compared to Tiresias: οἷος πέπνυται, αἱ δὲ σκιαὶ ἀίσσουσιν. A virtue to which such expressions are applicable is so far below philosophic morality, that if Plato in the Meno derived the latter from θεία μοῖρα, he 'could not' (v. Feuerlein, loc. cit.) 'have been clear in his own

ἐνθουσιασμός).[21] On this account Plato (Rep. x. 619 D) makes the majority of those, who through unphilosophic virtue have gained the heavenly blessedness, fail on their re-entrance into this world; and in the Phædo (82 A) he says, satirically, that they have the cheerful prospect of being placed in the course of their transmigrations among bees, wasps, ants, or some other well-

mind as to the derivation of virtue ;' and Hermann's assertion (loc cit. p. 61 sq.) that in the persons of whom Plato is here speaking, the imperfections of customary virtue are supposed to be complemented by divine aid, *ita ut, si quis divinitus regatur, eum non minus firmiter incedere significet, quam qui rationem ducem habeat*, is altogether untenable. The passage in the Politicue, which he quotes to support his view (309 C), is not to the point: it deals not with the virtue discussed in the Meno, but with philosophic virtue, if right opinion (ἀληθὴς δόξα), as to Right and Wrong, duly substantiated (μετὰ βεβαιώσεως), has been appropriated by the soul, then (according to the Politicus) the moral faculties of the soul are bound together by a divine bond. It is precisely in virtue of this confirmation (δεσμὸς) that, according to the Meno, 97 E sq., right opinion becomes knowledge. Finally, I cannot admit that Steinhart has given an adequate account of Plato's view, Pl. W. II. 118 According to him, in practical life, even where cognition fails, or is incomplete, Plato would say that the element of divinity in man, combined with the correct practical judgment that experience gives, is able to produce a solidity and certainty of moral action, commendable in its sphere, having its source, equally with the higher virtue, in the divine life. It is precisely this certainty of moral action that Plato, loc. cit., denies to any virtue not based on knowledge ; yet there is no contradiction in his deriving customary virtue from a divine dispensation, and we need see no irony in the expression (as Morgenstern, Stallbaum, and others do; cf. Hermann, loc. cit. p. 52 A, 4); he recognises the disposition of God in the fact that virtue has not yet died out of the world, careless as men are of its preservation by means of thorough teaching—just as in Rep. VI. 492 E, he ascribes the appearance now and then in corrupt states of a genuine philosopher to the mercy of heaven. Customary virtue, then, though not absolutely a thing of chance, is such to those who possess it, because they have not the means of producing it by scientific method in others, or of keeping it safe (Meno, 97 E sq.; 100 A); and it is only in this sense that I have here, and in my Platonic Studies, p. 109, spoken of θεία μοῖρα as at all approximating to chance.

[21] Meno, 96 D to end; cf. Apology, 21 B sq.

regulated race—perhaps even once again in the ranks of peaceful citizens. The only means of delivering virtue from this sphere of contingency is to ground it upon knowledge. The theoretic apprehension of morality alone contains the cause of moral practice: All desire the good; even when they desire evil, they do this only because they mistake evil for good. Consequently where there is true knowledge of that which is good and useful, there of necessity must be also moral will; for it is altogether inconceivable that anyone should knowingly and designedly strive after that which is hurtful to him. All sins arise from ignorance, all right action from cognition of the right;[22] no one is voluntarily bad.[23] While, therefore, want of knowledge is usually made an excuse for crimes, Plato is so little of that opinion, that he rather maintains with Socrates, that it is better to err designedly than undesignedly:[24] that, for example, the involuntary lie or self-deception is much worse than conscious deception of others, and that every organ for the attainment of truth is wanting[25] to the

[22] Prot. 352–357, 358 C; Gorg. 466 D; 468 E; Meno, 77 B sq.; Theæt. 176 C sq.; Euthyd. 279 D sq., where εὐτυχία is reduced to wisdom. The eudæmonistic premises that may seem to underlie any of these passages must be taken as κατ' ἄνθρωπον; where Plato gives us unconditional enunciation of his own views, the eudæmonistic basis of morals is most decidedly rejected.

[23] Tim. 86 D; vide beginning of next chapter.

[24] We get this fully enunciated only in the Hippias Minor, of which this assertion forms the theme; but it is clearly to be seen in other places, v. previous and two following notes, and Part i p 123, 1.

[25] Rep. vii. 535 D: οὐκοῦν καὶ πρὸς ἀλήθειαν ταὐτὸν τοῦτο ἀνάπηρον ψυχὴν θήσομεν, ἣ ἂν τὸ μὲν ἑκούσιον ψεῦδος μισῇ καὶ χαλεπῶς φέρῃ αὐτή τε καὶ ἑτέρων ψευδομένων ὑπεραγανακτῇ, τὸ δ' ἀκούσιον εὐκόλως προσδέχηται καὶ ἁμαθαίνουσά που ἁλισκομένη μὴ ἀγανακτῇ, ἀλλ' εὐχερῶς ὥσπερ θηρίον ὕειον ἐν ἀμαθίᾳ μολύνηται. Cf. ibid. ii. 382.

180 *PLATO AND THE OLDER ACADEMY.*

man who only avoids the one, and not in a far greater degree the other. Hence, however, the farther consequence simultaneously follows—that the faults of the wise are not real faults, but only infringements of the ordinary code of morals, justifiable from a higher standpoint.[26]

With this want of self-consciousness on the part of conventional virtue is closely connected its view of morality as a plurality of particular activities, not as one and self-identical in all its various expressions. As against this, Plato, like Socrates, maintains (what naturally results from the reduction of virtue to knowledge) the unity of all virtue; and he establishes this position by the argument that virtues can be contradistinguished neither by means of the persons who possess them, nor yet by their own content: not by the former, for that which makes virtue to be virtue must be the same in all;[27] and equally not by the latter, for the content of virtue consists only in knowledge of the good in science or intelligence.[28] It will

[26] Vide Part i. p. 123; and Hippias Minor, 376 B. ὁ ἄρα ἑκὼν ἁμαρτάνων εἴπερ τίς ἐστιν οὗτος οὐκ ἂν ἄλλος εἴη ἢ ὁ ἀγαθός.

[27] Meno, 71 D sq.

[28] Plato repeats this Socratic dictum in his earlier dialogues, specially in the Protagoras. The assertion that δικαιοσύνη, σωφροσύνη, ὁσιότης, σοφία, and ἀνδρεία are so many parts of virtue is met (329 C–333 B) by several objections, more subtle than convincing, but seriously meant by Plato: then in 349 B the question is taken up afresh; and, as Protagoras concedes that the first four of the virtues mentioned resemble each other, but maintains that Courage is altogether diverse from each of them, he is shown (358 C sq.): (1) that no one chooses what he deems an evil rather than good; (2) that fear is the expectation of evil; (3) that, therefore, no one chooses what he deems fearful; (4) that the distinction between the courageous and the timid comes to the one knowing, and the other not knowing, what is fearful and what not; and that, therefore, Courage is σοφία τῶν δεινῶν καὶ μὴ δεινῶν. A definition identical with this (noticed

hereafter be shown that Plato, notwithstanding, again assumes certain distinctions of virtues, without prejudice, however, to their essential unity; but he probably arrived at that determination (which is to be found in the Republic alone [29]) only in the later development of

Part i. p. 120, 3) is combated by Socrates in the Laches, 198 A sq. But the objection brought against it there is, that courage, so defined, cannot be a part of virtue along with other parts, because we cannot know what is to be feared and what not, without knowing generally what is good and what evil; and such knowledge embraces all virtues. This plainly does not amount to a rejection of the definition as useless: the point enunciated is, that the different virtues are not a series of independent qualities, but merely different forms of virtue as a whole, and the essence of virtue, according to the well-known Socratic doctrine, resides in cognition of the good In the Charmides, again, 173 A sq., where a doubt is raised as to the usefulness of σωφροσύνη, regarded as self-knowledge, and therefore knowledge of our knowledge, there is not really any objection raised to the reduction of σωφροσύνη to knowledge; we are only shown that the relation of knowledge to happiness requires a more exact determination than that hitherto given.

[29] Bonitz (Hermes, v. 444 sq.) thinks that the definition of courage in the Laches virtually coincides with the later definition of the Republic. Taking the definition of 192 D (φρόνιμος καρτερία) in connection with 194 E and 199 B sq. (where virtue is said to consist in knowing what is good and what bad), we get the concept of courage, he thinks, as equivalent to constancy dependent on moral insight. This connection seems to me, however, to be reading more into the dialogue than is there properly. In 192 D sq. Socrates does not merely combat the notion that an unintelligent hardihood deserves the name of courage, but shows further that even to define the latter as φρόνιμος καρτερία is incorrect. The arguments he uses to prove this may perhaps be, even from the Socratic-Platonic point of view, not irrefutable, but there is nothing to show that they are not seriously meant. Courage is proved to be neither a καρτερία φρόνιμος nor an ἄφρων καρτέρησις: we can but conclude that its essence is not καρτερία at all On the other hand, the really Socratic definition proposed by Nicias, as has been remarked, is not unconditionally disputed; it is shown to be irreconcilable with the supposition that courage is merely a part of virtue, but we are not told whether the fault lies in that supposition or in Nicias' definition. The former, in my opinion, is Plato's meaning, judging from the point of view he adopts in the Protagoras; so that the positive side of the question (hinted at by the apparently resultless discussion of the Laches) is given by the Socratic principle, that courage, like all virtue, is reducible to knowledge—the knowledge of the good.

his system. But if traditional virtue is imperfect because wanting in discernment of its true essential nature and the internal coherence of its parts, it is so no less with regard to its contents and motives. For the generally received principle of doing good to friends and evil to enemies, makes not only the doing of good but of evil to be virtuous;[30] and the incentives to virtue are usually derived, not from itself, but from external ends of advantage or pleasure.[31] True virtue, however, allows neither the one nor the other. He who is really virtuous will do evil to no one, for the good can only *do* good;[32] and as little will such a man do good for the attainment by his virtue of ulterior advantages present or future. For to be valiant through fear, and temperate through intemperance, is to love virtue for the sake of vice. This is only a mimicry of true virtue, a slavish virtue in which there is nothing genuine or sound—a justice which has self-interest for its heart's core, and is chiefly prevented by weakness from breaking out into open wrong.[33] True

---

[30] Meno, 71 E; Crito, 49 B sq.; Rep i. 334 B. Cf Part 1. p. 142 sq

[31] Phædo, 68 D sq ; 82 C; Rep. ii. 362 E sq. Justice is recommended only because of the reward it wins from men and gods, in this world and the next, not for its own sake; indeed, the happiness of the unjust is the subject of praise and envy, and even the gods are believed to be not inexorable to their sacrifices.

[32] Rep. i. 334 B sq.; Crito loc. cit. It is only from the point of view of universal consciousness that Plato (Phil. 49 D) regards joy at an enemy's misfortune as allowable; cf. Susemihl, ii. 38: here he is repeating a Socratic definition, v. Part i. p. 142, 3.

[33] Plato shows (Rep. ii. 365 A. sq) that the most reckless self-seeking is a strict consequence from the motives generally adduced for justice; and in Rep. vi. 492 A sq , he points out that the masses which in political assemblies rule states and statesmen are the only real perverters of youth,—the great Sophists,—whom the so-called Sophists merely follow, in

virtue, on the contrary, consists in a man's freeing himself from all these motives, and regarding knowledge as the coin for which all else must be exchanged.[34]

What Plato, therefore, blames in the ordinary point of view is its general want of consciousness regarding its own action, and the contradiction in which it is consequently involved; it is satisfied with a truth containing error, and a virtue containing vice. This very contradiction the Sophists had pointed out, and employed for the bewildering of the popular conscience; but instead of proceeding to a more thorough establishment of knowledge and morality, they stopped short at this negative result, and only positivized the unconditional validity of subjective opinion and will. We have shown in the foregoing pages that Plato builds on quite another foundation, and pursues quite another end. We shall now turn to consider his procedure in the scientific refutation of the Sophists. We may again distinguish a theoretic and a practical side. The theoretic principle of the Sophists may be generally expressed in the proposition, 'Man is the measure of all things.' Theoretically regarded, the import of this proposition is: 'that is true for every man which appears to him true;' practically, 'that is right for every

---

studying and pandering to their inclinations. Sophistic ethics, in his opinion, are the simple consequence of the ethics of custom.

[34] Phædo, 68 B sq., 82 C; 83 E; Rep. x. 612 A. The first, specially, of these passages is one of the purest and most beautiful that Plato ever wrote. One is tempted to quote many kindred passages, perhaps I may be allowed to refer to the noble places in Spinoza, Eth. pr. 41; Ep. 34, p. 503.

man which seems to him right.' Both principles were thoroughly refuted by Plato.

As against the theoretic principle, he adduces [35] first the experimental fact that judgments about the future at any rate have often no truth even for the person that judges; but in his opinion the decisive proof is that such a principle would destroy all possibility of knowledge. If all is truth that appears true to the individual, there can be no truth at all; for of every proposition, and of this among the rest, the contrary would be equally true: there can consequently be no distinction of knowledge and ignorance, wisdom and folly, virtue and vice; all must be in accordance with the doctrine of Heraclitus, in constant flux, so that all attributes, and equally their opposites,[36] may be predicated of each particular. Above all, upon this hypothesis, that must remain unknown which forms the sole true subject-matter of knowledge—the essence of things (the οὐσία)—for this is unattainable by the sensuous perception to which Protagoras restricts us; there could be nothing absolutely self-evident and fixed—nothing in itself beautiful, true, and good; therefore, also, no knowledge of truth. Truth and science can only be spoken of when they are sought, not in sensuous experience, but in the soul's pure energizing in the sphere of true Being. Plato has expressed himself more fully with regard to the ethical code of the Sophists, for the combating of which the Cyrenaic doctrine of pleasure

[35] Theæt. 170 A; 172 B; 177 C–137 A; Cratyl 386 A sq.; 439 C sq.

[36] Similarly Aristotle (Metaph. iv. 4, 5) refutes the doctrine of Heraclitus and Protagoras as denying the principle of contradiction.

SOPHISTIC ETHICS. 185

(coupled by him with the foregoing) gave an opening. It is first criticised in the Gorgias [37] in its association with the Rhetoric of the Sophists. On their side it is here maintained that the greatest happiness consists in the power of doing what one likes, and that this happiness is also the natural object of our actions; for natural right is only the right of the stronger. The Platonic Socrates shows, on the contrary, that to do what one likes (ἃ δοκεῖ τινι) is in itself no happiness, but only to do what one wills (ἃ βούλεται): this alone will really benefit the doer, for all will the good. But the good is not pleasure, as common opinion admits, when it discriminates between the beautiful and the pleasant, the shameful and the unpleasant. This is required by the nature of the case; for good and evil exclude one another—pleasure and pain mutually presuppose each other; pleasure and pain belong equally to the good and to the bad man—goodness and badness do not. So far, therefore, from pleasure being the highest good, and the striving after pleasure the universal right, it is, conversely, better to suffer wrong than to do it—to be cured of evil by punishment than to remain unpunished; for that only can be good which is just.[38]

The argument[39] in the Philebus establishes the same conclusion more fully, but on that very account

[37] Cf. specially 466 C–479 E; 488 B–508 C. The conversation with the politician Callicles belongs to the refutation of the Sophistic principle, as I have shown in vol. i. p. 922, 6. According to Plato, Sophistic ethics are only the enunciation in general principles of what the world is accustomed to do without talking about it: v. supra, p. 182, 33. Cf. Part i. p. 23.

[38] Cf. Theæt. 176 D sq. As to the apparently different exposition of the Protagoras, v. p. 188, 46.

[39] Specially 23 B–55 C.

belongs rather to the objective part of the system. The question here discussed is, Whether pleasure or knowledge be the highest good? the former the principle of the Sophists; the latter that of Socrates, and more definitely of the Megarians and Cynics. The answer imports that to perfect happiness both are requisite, but that knowledge is incomparably the higher and the more nearly related to the absolute good. The main line in the proof of this proposition is marked by the observation that pleasure belongs to the sphere of Becoming;[40] the good, on the contrary, must be an absolute and essential existence: that all Becoming has Being for its end, but the good is itself the highest end; that pleasure is most nearly akin to the Unlimited (Material); knowledge to the Divine Reason as the ordering and forming cause. Plato further draws attention to the fact that pleasure and pain are not seldom based upon a mere optical delusion; that pleasure in most cases only occurs in conjunction with its contrary, pain:[41] that the intensest sensations of pleasure arise from a state of bodily or mental disease. Discarding such, there remains as unmixed pleasure only the theoretic enjoyment of sensuous beauty, of

---

[40] Cf Rep. ix. 583 E: τὸ ἡδὺ ἐν ψυχῇ γιγνόμενον καὶ τὸ λυπηρὸν κίνησίς τις ἀμφοτέρω ἐστιν. Tim. 64.

[41] Wehrmann (Plat. de summ. bon. doctr. p. 49 sq.) thinks that Plato cannot be here speaking of the feeling of pleasure as such, and would, therefore, understand, by ἡδονὴ, Desire. There is no hint of this in Plato's words; indeed, in the Philebus, 27 E, 41 D, ἡδονὴ is shown to be the feeling of pleasure unmistakably by its opposition to λύπη. It is without limit (or indefinite), because always combined with its opposite (v. supra, and Phædo, p. 60 B; Phædrus, 258 E), and hence containing the possibility of continual increase, in proportion as it frees itself from that opposite.

which, however, Plato elsewhere declares (Tim. 47 A sqq.) that its true worth lies only in forming the indispensable groundwork of thought, and which, even in the Philebus, he decidedly places after knowledge. Lastly, in the Republic, we find an agreement with these discussions, and an evident reference to them in the remarks as to the doctrine of pleasure (vi. 505 C). Even the adherents of that doctrine must admit that there are bad pleasures, while at the same time they hold pleasure to be the good: this is nothing less than to declare good and evil to be the same thing. Similarly, in another passage [42]—' The philosopher only has true happiness, for his pleasure alone consists in being filled with something real; that is the sole pleasure which is unalloyed, and bound to no conditioning pain. The question whether justice is more profitable than injustice, is as absurd as would be the enquiry—is it better to be sick or well?' [43]

The refutation (in the Republic [44]) of the Sophistic assertion that justice is merely the interest of the ruler, by the exclusion of paid service from the art of government, is only a special application of the distinction between relative and absolute good; for this is manifestly grounded on the universal presupposition that the end of moral activity must be in, and not outside, itself. And when, finally, the superiority of justice to injustice is proved [45] from the argument that the just

[42] Ix. 583 B; 587 A, and the previous quotations from 376 E, onwards.
[43] Rep. iv. 445 A sq.
[44] Rep. i 339-347.
[45] 348 B sq., where, however, the clearness of the thought (correct in itself) is marred by the equivocal use of the word πλεονεκτεῖν, the propriety of which I cannot recognise with Susemihl, ii. 101.

only tries to get the better of the unjust, but the latter is at strife both with the just and unjust; and, therefore, that without justice no social polity and no common action would be possible—for not even a band of robbers could entirely do without this virtue—the practical principle of the Sophist is refuted in the same manner as the theoretical has already been refuted. As no knowledge is possible if instead of the concept of the thing, the opinion of each individual holds good, so no reasonable and teleological action is possible if the individual will and advantage become law, instead of being subordinated to a law of universal validity.[46]

[46] The exposition given above seems to be contradicted by the treatment of the ethical question in the Protagoras. To support his definition of courage as σοφία τῶν δεινῶν καὶ μὴ δεινῶν (360 D), Socrates asserts (350 B) that ἡδέως ζῆν is coincident with εὖ ζῆν, or the ἀγαθὸν—ἀηδῶς ζῆν with the κακόν. Protagoras objects that not every ἡδὺ is an ἀγαθὸν, nor every ἀνιαρὸν a κακόν. To this the answer is, 353 C sqq., that the Pleasant is called evil only when productive of greater unpleasantness, the Unpleasant is called good only when productive of greater pleasantness; and that the art of living consists in rightly estimating the proportions of Pleasure and Pain resultant—not merely with reference to the present but the future—from our actions. If, with Grote (Plato, ii. 78 sq.; 120, 559; i. 540), we here recognise the positive expression of Plato's own conviction, we are obliged to concede the existence of an irreconcilable contradiction between the Protagoras and the other Dialogues, specially the Gorgias. We might, however, well hesitate to ascribe such inconsistency to Plato, even if we held with Grote that the sensualist theory of the Protagoras were correct in itself. The Crito and the Apology, which can scarcely be younger, at all events not much younger, works than the Protagoras, enunciate views which are incompatible with Grote's interpretation of that dialogue (cf. p. 128). Plato shows that the theories put in Socrates' mouth in the Protagoras are not his ultimatum, by the repeated reference to the πολλοὶ (351 C, 353 E), who are mainly concerned—showing them that they have no right to assume the possibility of doing evil knowingly, because evil, in the end, is always harmful to man. But why this is so, is not said: it remains undecided whether the Pleasure, which is to form the standard of the good, is sensuous pleasure (to which the concept of ἡδονὴ in the Philebus is limited), or that higher contentment which arises from the healthi-

SOPHISTIC ETHICS.

The fundamental defect, then, in the Sophistic Ethics appears to be this: that by its doctrine of pleasure it sets the transitory in place of the permanent, appearance in place of essence, ends which are relative, and therefore always changing into their opposites, in place of the one absolute, self-consistent end. The polemic against their theoretic principle had established exactly the same point. Their doctrine in general is therefore apprehended by Plato as the consummated perversion of the right view of the world, the systematic supplanting of Essence by show or appearance; of true knowledge by appearance-knowledge; of moral action by a debased utilitarianism, in bondage to finite ends; it is (according to the definition at the conclusion of the Sophist) the art of giving, by means of quibbling criticism, an appearance of knowledge, where none is possessed, and when there is full consciousness of the deficiency: and so Rhetoric, the general application of Sophistic doctrine, is the art of producing glamour in whole masses of people, with the same show that Sophistic uses to glamour individuals.[47] Or if we take both together, the art of the Sophists consists in the study and dexterous management of that Great Beast, the people,[48] in all its moods and tempers.

ness of the soul. This question is not discussed till we get to the Gorgias and the later Dialogues, nor is the Good expressly distinguished from the Pleasant (v. supr. p. 121, 70). We thus see an advance in the development of Plato's Ethics, not so much in contrast as in scientific elaboration. Eudæmonism such as Grote attributes to Plato, is alien even to the Protagoras.

[47] V. Soph. 268 B; Phædrus, 261 A sq.; Gorg. 455 A; 462 B-466 A. The Euthydemus is a satire on the Eristic of the Sophists. Cf. vol. i 885, 910 sq.

[48] Rep. vi. 493.

The Sophist neither understands nor professes virtue:[49] he is nothing better than a huckster and craftsman, who praises his wares indiscriminately, no matter how they may be made;[50] and the Rhetorician, instead of being a leader of the people, degrades himself into their slave.[51] In place of instructing the ignorant (which he, as possessing knowledge, ought to do), and improving the morally lost and neglected, he, being ignorant, uses ignorance to induce persuasion, and basely flatters folly and greed.[52] Sophistry and Rhetoric therefore, far from being true arts, are rather to be described as mere knacks (ἐμπειρίαι), or, still more accurately, as parts of the art of flattery,—as spurious arts, which are just as truly caricatures of law-giving and the administration of justice as the arts of dress and cookery are caricatures of gymnastic and medicine.[53] There is only a passing exception to this judgment when Plato in the Sophist (231 B sqq.) glances at the sifting and purgative efficacy of Sophistic, but he immediately retracts the observation, as doing it too much honour.

If such be a true account of what usually passes for Philosophy, and if the position of unphilosophic consciousness be equally inadequate, where, in contra-

[49] Meno, 96 A sq.; with which cf. all the dialogues contrasting the Sophistic and Socratic theories of virtue: e.g. Hippias Minor, Protagoras, Gorgias, the first book of the Republic, and ibid. vi. 495 C sqq.
[50] Prot. 313 C sqq.; Soph. 223 B-226 A; Rep. vi. 495 C sq.
[51] Gorg. 517 B sq. This judgment applied equally to the most famous Athenian statesmen, we are told, ibid. 515 C sqq.
[52] Gorg. 458 E sq.; 463 A sq.; 504 D sq. Cf. Theæt. 201 A sq.; Polit. 304 C.
[53] Gorg. 462 B sq. Demagogy is compared to Cookery by Aristophanes, Equites, 215 sq.

distinction to both, shall we seek for true Philosophy?

It has already been shown that Plato gives to the idea of Philosophy a far larger signification than that to which we are now accustomed: while we understand by it only a definite manner of thought, it is to him quite as essentially a concern of life; nay, this practical element is the first, the universal groundwork, without which he cannot conceive the theoretic element at all. Herein he closely resembles Socrates, whose philosophy entirely coincided with his personal character; and though Plato transcended this narrowness of the Socratic view in order to develope the idea into a system, he himself never apprehended Philosophy in so exclusively a theoretic light as Aristotle.[54] If therefore we would understand his determinations of the essence and problem of Philosophy, we must begin with its derivation from practical necessity, with the description of the philosophic impulse. The theoretic form of Philosophy, the philosophic method, will occupy only the second place; thirdly, and arising from both, we get Plato's collective view of Philosophy, and the philosophic education of men.

The general groundwork of Philosophy is the philosophic impulse. But as with Socrates this never took the purely theoretic form of an intellectual impulse, but simultaneously with the personal acquisition of knowledge aimed directly at the engendering of knowledge and virtue in others; so with Plato it is essentially related to the practical realisation of truth, and

[54] Cf. pp. 144, 146.

is therefore more exactly defined as generative impulse or Eros. Philosophy, according to him, springs, like all higher life, from inspiration or enthusiasm (μανία).[55] When the remembrance of the archetypes which the soul beheld in its heavenly existence awakens in it at sight of the earthly copies, it is possessed with a wondering delight, is beside itself and falls into an ecstasy;[56] and herein,—in the overpowering contrast of the Idea with the Phenomenon,—lies the ultimate ground of that wonder which Plato calls the beginning of Philosophy:[57] of that bewilderment, that burning pain which consumes every noble spirit when first the presentiment of a higher than itself arises in it,[58]—of that singularity and maladroitness in worldly matters, which to the superficial gaze is the most striking trait in the philosopher.[59] The reason that this ideal enthusiasm assumes the form of love is said in the Phædrus (250 B, D) to be the special brightness

[55] Religious or artistic inspiration generally is called frenzy in Greek. Cf. quotations in vol. i. 651, 1; 759, 3; and Heraclitus on p. Plat. Pyth. orac. c. 6, p. 397.

[56] Phædr. 244 A sq.; 249 D; Ion, 251 B. The unconditioned praise given in the former of these passages to divine inspiration is in keeping with the dithyrambic tone of the speech: it is, however, considerably modified by other places, like Apology, 22 C, Meno, 99 B sq; Timæus, 71 E sq. (cf. Ion, 534 B); and the Phædrus itself, 248 D.

[57] Theæt. 155 D; cf. Arist. Metaph. 1. 2; 982 b. 12. This wonder is, loc. cit., derived from the intuition of the various contradictions encompassing ordinary notions or envisagements. It is precisely these in which the Idea announces itself indirectly.

[58] Phædr. 251 A sq.; Symp. 215 D sq. (v. Part i. p. 153); 218 A sq.; Theæt. 149 A, 151 A; Rep. vii. 515 E; Meno, 80 A.

[59] Theæt. 173 C sqq.; 175 B, E; Rep. vii. 516 E–517 D. We get the type of this philosophic ἀτοπία in Socrates. in it he is the complete philosophic ἐρωτικὸς, ἔρως personified, indeed; v. Symp. 215 A sq., 221 D sq., and my translation, Part i. p. 86. Cf. Schwegler, on the Composition of Plato's Symposium, p 9 sqq.; Steinhart, Pl. W. iv. 258, &c.

which distinguishes the visible copies of the beautiful above those of all other ideas: therefore it is that they make the strongest impression on the mind. In the Symposium, this phenomenon is more precisely accounted for by the striving after immortality of mortal nature: having none of the divine unchangeableness, it feels the necessity of sustaining itself by continual self-propagation. This propagative impulse is love.[60] Love therefore on the one side springs from the higher, divinely related nature of man,[61]—it is the yearning to become like the immortal. But on the other, it is no more than a yearning, not yet possession; thus far it presupposes a want, and belongs only to the finite, not to the perfect divine Essence.[62] Love is consequently a middle term between having and not having,— the transition from the one to the other; Eros is the son of Penia and Poros.[63] The object of this yearning endeavour is, in general, the Good; or more exactly, the possession of the Good,—of happiness; for happiness is what all men desire. And therefore it aims at immortality, because with the desire for happiness is directly given the wish that the possession of the Good may be eternal.[64] So Love is, generally speaking, the endeavour of the finite to expand itself to infinity, to fill itself with what is eternal and imperishable, to generate something enduring. The external condition of Love's existence is the presence

---

[60] Symp. 206 B sq.; cf. Laws, vi. 773 E, iv. 721 B sq.

[61] Poros, the father of Eros, is called the son of Metis; v. note 66.

[62] Loc. cit. 202 B sq.; 203 E sq.

[63] Loc. cit. 199 C-204 B.

[64] Loc. cit. 204 E-200 A.

of Beauty,[65] for this alone by its harmonious form, corresponding to the desire in ourselves, awakes desire for the infinite.[66] But Love is as various as Beauty, in kind and degree: he does not reveal himself from the beginning fully and perfectly; rising step by step from incompleteness to completeness, he is realised in a graduated series of different forms. The first is the love of beautiful shapes,—of one, and then of all: a higher step is the love of beautiful souls, which ope-

[65] Loc. cit 206 C sq.-209 B; cf. Phædr. 250 B. D.

[66] The above may serve to explain the Myth in Symp. 203. Eros is a δαίμων, one of the beings midway between mortals and immortals, mediating between them. Accordingly, he is at once poor and rich, ugly and full of love for the beautiful, knowing nothing and ever striving after knowledge; uniting the most contradictory qualities, because in Love the finite and the infinite sides of our nature meet and find their unity. He is the son of Penia and Poros, because Love springs partly from man's need, partly from that higher faculty, which makes him able to get the thing needed; (πόρος is not Wealth, but Getting, Industry). His father is called a son of Metis, because all gain or getting is the fruit of wit or cunning, and this particular gain, the gain of higher good, springs from the reasonable spiritual nature of man. And Eros is born on Aphrodite's birthday, because it is the revelation of the Beautiful that first awakens Love, soliciting the higher in human nature to fructify the lower, finite, needing element, and unite with it in the struggle towards the Good (cf. 203 C with 206 C sq.). These are the main features of the doctrine, laid down clearly enough in the myth, and hitherto pretty generally agreed on (v. Susemihl, i. 393 sq., with his quotations; and Deuschle, Plat Myth. p. 13), with only unimportant differences of interpretation in details. Anything beyond this I class as poetic ornament, and I cannot, therefore, agree with the meaning seen by Susemihl, loc. cit., in the garden of Zeus and the drunkenness of Poros Still less can I accept the interpretation given by Jahn (with the partial approval of Brandis, ii. a. 422 sq.) in his Dissertationes Platonicæ, 64 sq; 249 sq., which is really a return to the Neo-Platonic expositions collected with learned industry by him on p. 136 sq. (cf. Steinhart, Plat. W. iv. 388 sq.) According to Jahn, Metis means the divine reason, Poros and Aphrodite the Ideae of the Good and the Beautiful, Penia Matter, and Eros the human soul. This interpretation is as clearly excluded as the right one is unmistakably enunciated by what in the dialogue precedes and follows about Eros without metaphor.

rates in moral words and efforts, in works of education, art, and legislation : a third is the love of beautiful sciences—the seeking out of beauty wherever it may be found; the highest of all is the love which rises up to the pure, shapeless, eternal and unchangeable beauty, unmixed with aught finite or material,—to the Idea, which brings forth true knowledge and true virtue, and which alone attains the goal of Eros—immortality.[67] If this be the first adequate realisation of that for which Eros strives, then plainly he has been aiming at nothing else from the very beginning; all subordinate stages of his satisfaction were but imperfect and uncertain attempts to seize on the Idea in its copies.[68] Eros therefore, in his true nature, is the philosophic impulse, the striving for the representation of absolute beauty,—the struggle to inform the Finite with the Idea by means of speculative knowledge and a

[67] Symp. 208 E-212 A. In the less fully developed exposition of the Phædrus, 249 D sq., this distinction is barely hinted at, and the philosophic ἔρως is still in immediate connection with παιδεραστία in the good sense.

[68] This circumstance is overlooked by Deuschle, Plat. Myth. 30, where he objects, as against the comparison of ἔρως with the philosophic impulse, that the former only coincides with the latter in its highest completion. The proper object of Love, according to Plato, is primarily the Beautiful as such, the Eternal, the Idea; this can at first be only apprehended in its sensuous and finite copies, and the lover gets only by degrees any insight into the aim and scope of what he does. But this does not alter the case; the lower forms of love are only first steps to (Symp 211 B sq.), or, if continued in, misunderstandings of, the true philosophic Eros. Properly, it is always the Good and the enduring possession of the Good that all eravo (Symp. 205 D sq.; Phædr 249 D sq). Immortality itself (the business, according to Plato, of all, even sensuous love) is only to be won through a philosophic life (Phædr. 248 E; 256 A sq.; Symp. 212 A, &c). Plato does not merely understand by philosophy scientific investigation, but, so far as it bears relation to Truth and Reality, every branch of human activity.

o 2

philosophic life; and all delight in any particular beauty is to be considered as a moment only, in the development of this impulse.[69]

The philosophic impulse is then, in the first place, a striving for the possession of truth: but if we further enquire as to the means of attaining this possession, Plato answers (somewhat unexpectedly for his ordinary enthusiastic admirers)—The dialectic method.[70] All other moral and spiritual training—that whole course of preparation, which the Symposium has described to us, and the Republic will more exactly describe—leads but to the threshold of philosophy: through her proper domain, Dialectic alone can guide us. That this must

[69] Besides the Phædrus and the Symposium, the Lysis deserves mention here; cf. chap. ii. 99. The result of the enquiry into the concept of φίλος, p. 219 A, is τὸ οὔτε κακὸν οὔτε ἀγαθὸν ἄρα διὰ τὸ κακὸν καὶ τὸ ἐχθρὸν τοῦ ἀγαθοῦ φίλον ἐστὶν ἕνεκα τοῦ ἀγαθοῦ καὶ φίλου. And this formula suits the doctrine of the Symposium on Eros completely. Love, according to the Symposium, springs from a defect and a need (διὰ τὸ κακὸν, therefore, or as we have it more precisely in the Lysis, 218 C, διὰ κακοῦ παρουσίαν), directs itself, for the sake of the absolute Good and Godlike (ἕνεκα τοῦ ἀγαθοῦ), towards Beauty in eternal Existence (τοῦ ἀγαθοῦ φίλον), and belongs only to a being standing midway between Finite and Infinite (the οὔτε κακὸν οὔτε ἀγαθόν). And in p. 218 A we find the dictum of Symposium 203, E sq.—that the Gods, or the wise in general, do not philosophize, nor do the utterly ignorant, but only those who are midway between both—given in almost the same words If we are not to suppose that, at the time of writing the Lysis, Plato had found the leading thoughts of his later system, there remains the hypothesis, that the psychological analysis which is the basis of his later exposition had even then led him up to the point attainable from Socratic principles, but the further metaphysical elucidation of these psychological phenomena did not come till afterwards. This view might gain some confirmation from the fact that the Symposium 199 C sq. makes Socrates say only what we get in the Lysis, whereas all advance on that is put in the mouth of Diotima This circumstance, however, cannot be pressed far.

[70] Steger, Die Platonische Dialektik (Plat. Stud. i. Instr. 1869, p. 33 sq.), where passages in point are fully given.

be superadded to the philosophic impulse is first announced in the Phædrus, the representation of Eros in the earlier part of that dialogue being followed by an enquiry into the art of discourse further on.[71] And though at first the necessity of the latter method is established (261 C) on the wholly external ground that without it the end of eloquence, namely the guidance of souls, cannot be attained—yet in the course of the argument this external view is again discarded (266 B, 270 D). The Sophist, going more deeply into the matter (251 A, 253 E), shows that as some concepts allow, and others resist, mutual combination, there must necessarily be a science of Combination of Concepts,—that is, Dialectic. The Philebus declares this science (16 B sqq.) to be the highest gift of the gods and the true fire of Prometheus, without which no workmanlike treatment of any subject is possible. Concerning the essential nature of Dialectic, we must premise that its object is exclusively the Idea: it is the instrument by means of which the pure Idea is freed from all sensuous form and presupposition, and developed.[72] It is therefore peculiar to the

[71] V. Schleiermacher, Introd. to the Phædrus, esp. p. 65 sq.

[72] Rep. vi. 511 B (v. supra, 167): τὸ τοίνυν ἕτερον μάνθανε τμῆμα τοῦ νοητοῦ λέγοντά με τοῦτο, οὗ αὐτὸς ὁ λόγος ἅπτεται τῇ τοῦ διαλέγεσθαι δυνάμει, τὰς ὑποθέσεις ποιούμενος οὐκ ἀρχὰς, ἀλλὰ τῷ ὄντι ὑποθέσεις, οἷον ἐπιβάσεις τε καὶ ὁρμὰς, ἵνα μέχρι τοῦ ἀνυποθέτου ἐπὶ τὴν τοῦ παντὸς ἀρχὴν ἰὼν, ἁψάμενος αὐτῆς, πάλιν αὖ ἐχόμενος τῶν ἐκείνης ἐχομένων, οὕτως ἐπὶ τελευτὴν καταβαίνῃ αἰσθητῷ παντάπασιν οὐδενὶ προσχρώμενος, ἀλλ' εἴδεσιν αὐτοῖς δι' αὐτῶν εἰς αὐτὰ καὶ τελευτᾷ εἰς εἴδη. Rep. vii. 532 A: ὅταν τις τῷ διαλέγεσθαι ἐπιχειρῇ ἄνευ πασῶν τῶν αἰσθήσεων διὰ τοῦ λόγου ἐπ' αὐτὸ ὃ ἔστιν ἕκαστον ὁρμᾷ, κἂν μὴ ἀποστῇ πρὶν ἂν αὐτὸ ὃ ἔστιν ἀγαθὸν αὐτῇ νοήσει λάβῃ, ἐπ' αὐτῷ γίγνεται τῷ τοῦ νοητοῦ τέλει. . . . Τί οὖν; οὐ διαλεκτικὴν ταύτην τὴν πορείαν καλεῖς; Ibid. 533 C: ἡ διαλεκτικὴ μέθοδος

philosopher;[73] for he alone can recognise Being in itself—the essence and concept of things,[74] and by this knowledge can regulate all other arts and sciences.[75] Dialectic has a double task—συναγωγή and διαίρεσις —the Formation of concepts and their Classification.[76] The first reduces the Many of experience to one Genus, the second divides this Genus organically into its Species, without breaking any of its natural articulations, or overlooking one division that really exists. He who is skilled to recognise the One concept pervading the Many and Divided—and, conversely, to carry out the one concept methodically through the whole graduated scale of its sub-kinds

μόνη ταύτῃ πορεύεται, τὰς ὑποθέσεις ἀναιροῦσα ἐπ' αὐτὴν τὴν ἀρχὴν κ.τ.λ. Phileb 58 A. Dialectic is ἡ περὶ τὸ ὂν καὶ τὸ ὄντως καὶ τὸ κατὰ ταὐτὸν ἀεὶ πεφυκὸς ἐπιστήμη. Cf. following notes.

[73] Soph. 253 E: ἀλλὰ μὴν τό γε διαλεκτικὸν οὐκ ἄλλῳ δώσεις, ὡς ἐγᾦμαι, πλὴν τῷ καθαρῶς τε καὶ δικαίως φιλοσοφοῦντι. Cf. Phædr. 278 D.

[74] Rep v. end; vi. 484 B.

[75] Phileb. 58 A. Dialectic is the science ἡ πᾶσαν τὴν γε νῦν λεγομένην (Arithmetic, Geometry, &c.) γνοίη. Euthyd. 290 B sq.: οἱ δ' αὖ γεωμέτραι καὶ ἀστρονόμοι καὶ οἱ λογιστικοί—παραδιδόασι δήπου τοῖς διαλεκτικοῖς καταχρῆσθαι αὐτῶν τοῖς εὑρήμασιν, ὅσοι γε αὐτῶν μὴ παντάπασιν ἀνόητοί εἰσιν. Cratyl. 390 C: the Dialectician has to overlook the activity of the νομοθέτης (here = ὀνοματοθέτης). The Politicus, 305 B sq , gives the Statesman's art the same relation to all practical arts; but as the Republic (v. 473 C and passim) identifies the true ruler with the true philosopher, we may transfer the assertion to philosophy.

[76] Heyder (Comparison of the Aristotelian and Hegelian Dialectic, i. 49 sq.) is wrong in adding to these, as a third element, the Combination of Concepts. The passages to be presently quoted from the Phædrus, Philebus, and Sophist plainly show that Plato regards the business of Dialectic as finished in the determination and division of concepts. The Sophist specially shows that the knowledge of the universality of concepts is given in division; and it would be contradictory to Plato's view to say that division limits off concepts from all others, while combination of concepts gives them their due relations to others. The Sophist tells us that this relation is given by showing how far the concepts are identical or different, i.e. by their spheres being limited off from each other.

down to particulars, and, as a consequence of this procedure, to establish the mutual relations of concepts, and the possibility or impossibility of their combination—he is the true workman in Dialectic.[77]

Of these two elements of Dialectic, one, the Formation of concepts, had already been apprehended by Socrates, whose philosophic merit is essentially based on this fact. Plato throughout presupposes this Socratic induction, and his own method with regard to it is generally distinguished from that of his master only by its more technical and conscious use. In the Concept, the *What* of things is to be determined; not this or that quality only in them must be given, but

[77] Phædr. 265 D sq. (cf. 261 E, and specially 273 D, 277 B), the art of speech has two essential elements. εἰς μίαν τε ἰδέαν συνορῶντα ἄγειν τὰ πολλαχῇ διεσπαρμένα, ἵν' ἕκαστον ὁριζόμενος δῆλον ποίῃ περὶ οὗ ἂν ἀεὶ διδάσκειν ἐθέλῃ —and πάλιν κατ' εἴδη δύνασθαι τέμνειν, κατ' ἄρθρα ᾗ πέφυκε, καὶ μὴ ἐπιχειρεῖν καταγνῶναι κακοῦ μαγείρου τρόπῳ χρώμενον . . . καὶ τοὺς δυναμένους αὐτὸ δρᾶν εἰ μὲν ὀρθῶς ἢ μὴ προσαγορεύω, θεὸς οἶδε, καλῶ δὲ οὖν μέχρι τοῦδε διαλεκτικούς. Soph. 253 B sq.: ἆρ' οὐ μετ' ἐπιστήμης τινὸς ἀναγκαῖον διὰ τῶν λόγων πορεύεσθαι τὸν ὀρθῶς μέλλοντα δείξειν ποῖα ποίοις συμφωνεῖ τῶν γενῶν καὶ ποῖα ἄλληλα οὐ δέχεται, καὶ δὴ καὶ διὰ πάντων εἰ συνέχοντα ἅττ' ἐστίν, ὥστε συμμίγνυσθαι δυνατὰ εἶναι, καὶ πάλιν ἐν ταῖς διαιρέσεσιν εἰ δι' ὅλων ἕτερα τῆς διαιρέσεως αἴτια;—τὸ κατὰ γένη διαιρεῖσθαι καὶ μήτε ταὐτὸν εἶδος ἕτερον ἡγήσασθαι μήθ' ἕτερον ὂν ταὐτὸν, μῶν οὐ τῆς διαλεκτικῆς φήσομεν ἐπιστήμης εἶναι;—οὐκοῦν ὅγε τοῦτο δυνατὸς δρᾶν μίαν ἰδέαν διὰ πολλῶν, ἑνὸς ἑκάστου κειμένου χωρὶς, πάντῃ διατεταμένην ἱκανῶς διαισθάνεται, καὶ πολλὰς ἑτέρας ὑπὸ μιᾶς ἔξωθεν περιεχομένας, καὶ μίαν αὖ δι' ὅλων πολλῶν ἐν ἑνὶ ξυνημμένην, καὶ πολλὰς χωρὶς πάντῃ διωρισμένας· τοῦτο δ' ἔστιν, ᾗ τε κοινωνεῖν ἕκαστα δύναται, καὶ ὅπῃ μὴ, διακρίνειν κατὰ γένος ἐπίστασθαι. Polit. 285 A; Phileb. 16 C sq.; vide subter, note 92. Only one of the elements here united in the concept of Dialectic is brought into prominence by Republic vii. 537 C. The disposition towards Dialectic, we are there told, consists in the ability to bring particulars under a concept—ὁ συνοπτικὸς διαλεκτικός, ὁ δὲ μὴ, οὔ—and in x. 596 A, the peculiarity of dialectic process is described as the seeking one general concept under which to bring the Many. Cf. Rep. vii. 531 E-534 B, D; Cratyl. 390 C. The dialectician is the man who

the marks that distinguish them from all others;[78] not the contingent in them, but the essential;[79] for with that only is Science concerned.[80] But the essence of things consists solely in that wherein all belonging to the same class agree, in the common attribute. The determination of the concept is therefore something quite other than the enumeration of the multiplicity comprehended within that concept: it has to do with that which is equally present in all particulars and individuals; with the Universal, without which no particular can be understood, because it is contained in each particular and is presupposed by it.[81] Briefly, then, the concept must determine the Essence of

can give account of his convictions in question and answer, and this ability comes from λόγον ἑκάστων λαμβάνειν τῆς οὐσίας.

[78] Theæt 208 D; Polit. 285 A.

[79] V. e.g. Meno, 71 B: ὃ δὲ μὴ οἶδα τί ἐστι, πῶς ἂν ὁποῖόν γέ τι εἰδείην; Euthyph. 11 A: κινδυνεύεις, ὦ Εὐθύφρον, ἐρωτώμενος τὸ ὅσιον ὅτι ποτ' ἔστι, τὴν μὲν οὐσίαν μοι αὐτοῦ οὐ βούλεσθαι δηλῶσαι, πάθος δέ τι περὶ αὐτοῦ λέγειν. Gorg. 448 B sqq., where Polus is asked what Gorgias is, and on answering that his art is the sovereign art, is informed that the question is not ποία τις εἴη ἡ Γοργίου τέχνη, ἀλλὰ τίς.

[80] V. supr. p. 175 sq. On this point, and the nature of real Being, fuller details in the exposition of the theory of Ideas.

[81] Meno, 71 D sq. Socrates asks what Virtue is. Meno replies that the virtue of man is so and so, the virtue of woman so and so, &c, and is brought up by Socrates saying that he does not want a σμῆνος ἀρετῶν, but the μία ἀρετή, not a Virtue, but Virtue (73 E); or, in other words (72 E), he wants that in which the virtue of man, woman, &c. is not separate, but one and the same. So Theæt. 146 C sqq., where to Socrates' question, what Knowledge is, Theætetus at first answers with an enumeration of the various sorts of knowledge, and is then told that he was not asked τίνων ἡ ἐπιστήμη, οὐδ' ὁπόσαι τινές· οὐ γὰρ ἀριθμῆσαι αὐτὰς βουλόμενοι ἠρόμεθα, ἀλλὰ γνῶναι ἐπιστήμην αὐτὸ ὅ τί ποτ' ἐστίν: the thought of any special form of knowledge always presupposes the general concept of knowledge—σκυτικὴ is ἐπιστήμη ὑποδημάτων; with no concept of ἐπιστήμη in general, there can be no concept of σκυτικὴ ἐπιστήμη in particular. Cf. Euthyph. 5 D, 6 D (the enquiry is into the αὐτὸ αὐτῷ ὅμοιον καὶ ἔχον μίαν τινὰ ἰδέαν—the εἶδος αὐτὸ ᾧ πάντα τὰ ὅσια ὅσιά ἐστιν), Lach. 191 D sq., and supr. p. 198.

DIALECTIC, FORMATION OF CONCEPTS. 201

things, by establishing the distinguishing characteristics of Classes. For this purpose Plato, following his master, starts as much as possible from the known and universally acknowledged. He will not only express the truth, but will do so in such a manner that others may be convinced by it:[82] and he therefore requires that the progress of knowledge be brought about through examples, so that we may understand the unknown from the known, and learn to recognise in the unknown, characteristics elsewhere familiar to us.[83] This procedure is very usual with Plato.[84] It brings with it a danger already perceived by Socrates. When we start from individual observations and examples, and above all from individual experiences, we must take care lest our concepts represent only particular sides of the objects in question, and not the whole of their essence. Socrates tried to escape this danger by means of that dialectical comparison of the different cases, in which we have learned to recognise one of the most important peculiarities of his method. The skill of Plato in this dialectic is also well known, and even

---

[82] Meno, 75 D: δεῖ δὴ πραότερόν πως καὶ διαλεκτικώτερον ἀποκρίνεσθαι. ἔστι δὲ ἴσως τὸ διαλεκτικώτερον, μὴ μόνον τἀληθῆ ἀποκρίνεσθαι, ἀλλὰ καὶ δι' ἐκείνων ὧν ἂν προσομολογῇ εἰδέναι ὁ ἐρωτώμενος. Cf. the quotations as to Socrates, Part i. pp. 102, 1; 109.

[83] Polit. 277 E sqq.; as children in learning to read go wrong over the same letters, in complicated words, as they read easily in simple ones, so with us in regard to the στοιχεῖα τῶν πάντων: and we must do as is done in teaching—ἀνάγειν πρῶτον ἐπ' ἐκεῖνα ἐν οἷς ταὐτὰ ταῦτα ὀρθῶς ἐδόξαζον, ἀνάγοντας δὲ τιθέναι παρὰ τὰ μήπω γιγνωσκόμενα καὶ παραβάλλοντας ἐνδεικνύναι τὴν αὐτὴν ὁμοιότητα καὶ φύσιν ἐν ἀμφοτέραις οὖσαν ταῖς συμπλοκαῖς κ.τ.λ, and the use of examples is that, by putting together related cases, we get to recognise an unknown as identical with a known.

[84] So Gorg. 448 B sq, 449 D; Meno 73 E sqq.; Theæt 146 D sqq; Polit. 279 A sqq.

his earliest works show him to have been in this respect the apt disciple of Socrates. But as he has given to the Socratic philosophy in general a more scientific form, so in this particular he requires a stricter procedure. The truth of the conceptual determination is not merely to be tested by individual instances which are always selected with a certain arbitrariness, but each assumption is to be developed in all its positive and negative consequences to prove its admissibility and necessity: all the results that may arise, on the one hand from itself, and on the other from the opposite hypothesis, are to be drawn out, and in this way we are to ascertain whether it is compatible with, and therefore required by, that which is elsewhere acknowledged as truth. This is that hypothetic discussion of the concept which Plato so emphatically recommends as dialectic training, on the ground that thus alone can the correctness of presuppositions be perfectly tested.[85]

[85] The principal passage to refer to is the Parmenides, 135 C sqq Socrates has been brought into perplexity by the objections to the theory of Ideas, and Parmenides says to him: πρῴ γὰρ, πρὶν γυμνασθῆναι, ὦ Σώκρατες, ὁρίζεσθαι ἐπιχειρεῖς καλόν τέ τι καὶ δίκαιον καὶ ἀγαθὸν καὶ ἓν ἕκαστον τῶν εἰδῶν·
... καλὴ μὲν οὖν καὶ θεία, εὖ ἴσθι, ἡ ὁρμὴ ἣν ὁρμᾷς ἐπὶ τοὺς λόγους ἕλκυσον δὲ σαυτὸν καὶ γύμνασαι μᾶλλον διὰ τῆς δοκούσης ἀχρήστου εἶναι καὶ καλουμένης ὑπὸ τῶν πολλῶν ἀδολεσχίας, ἕως ἔτι νέος εἶ· εἰ δὲ μή, σὲ διαφεύξεται ἡ ἀλήθεια. Τίς οὖν ὁ τρόπος, φάναι, ὦ Παρμενίδη, τῆς γυμνασίας; Οὗτος, εἰπεῖν, ὅνπερ ἤκουσας Ζήνωνος (the indirect proof of an assumption by development of its consequences), χρὴ δὲ καὶ τόδε ἔτι πρὸς τούτῳ ποιεῖν, μὴ μόνον εἰ ἔστιν ἕκαστον ὑποθέμενον σκοπεῖν τὰ συμβαίνοντα ἐκ τῆς ὑποθέσεως, ἀλλὰ καὶ εἰ μή ἐστι τὸ αὐτὸ τοῦτο ὑποτίθεσθαι εἰ βούλει μᾶλλον γυμνασθῆναι. And of this the whole of the second part of the Parmenides gives a detailed illustration. Cf. Phædo, 101 D: εἰ δέ τις αὐτῆς τῆς ὑποθέσεως ἔχοιτο, χαίρειν ἐῴης ἂν καὶ οὐκ ἀποκρίναιο, ἕως ἂν τὰ ἀπ' ἐκείνης ὁρμηθέντα σκέψαιο, εἴ σοι ἀλλήλοις ξυμφωνεῖ ἢ διαφωνεῖ, ἐπειδὴ δὲ ἐκείνης αὐτῆς δέοι σε διδόναι λόγον, ὡσαύτως ἂν διδοίης, ἄλλην αὖ ὑπόθεσιν ὑποθέμενος, ἥτις τῶν ἄνωθεν βελτίστη φαίνοιτο, ἕως ἐπί τι ἱκανὸν ἔλθοις, ἅμα δὲ οὐκ ἂν φύροιο, ὥσπερ οἱ ἀντιλογικοὶ περί τε τῆς ἀρχῆς διαλεγόμενος καὶ τῶν ἐξ ἐκεί-

The method seems to have been motived not only by the Socratic teaching, but also by the Eleatic dialectic as worked out by Zeno;[86] Zeno, however, only aims at refuting the ordinary notions by inference; Plato, as a true Socratic, has for his ultimate end a positive result, an exhaustive definition of the concept. And as he insists that with each assumption its opposite also shall be thoroughly sifted, in the manner described—his method where fully carried out, as in the Parmenides, takes the form of an antinomic exposition, the ultimate aim of which is, by refuting one-sided presuppositions, to establish those that are true. But however great may be the value set by Plato upon this hypothetic development of the concept, it is still, as he himself says, only a preparation, or, more exactly, a moment in the dialectic method—a part of that which Aristotle

νης ὡρμημένων, εἴπερ βούλοιώ τι τῶν ὄντων εὑρεῖν. (P. 100 A treats, not of the proof of the principles, but their application to particulars.) Meno, 86 E. συγχώρησον ἐξ ὑποθέσεως αὐτὸ σκοπεῖσθαι... λέγω δὲ τὸ ἐξ ὑποθέσεως ὧδε, ὥσπερ οἱ γεωμέτραι πολλάκις σκοποῦνται .. εἰ μέν ἐστι τοῦτο τὸ χωρίον τοιοῦτον οἷον παρὰ τὴν δοθεῖσαν αὐτὸν γραμμὴν παρατείναντα ἐλλείπειν τοιούτῳ χωρίῳ, οἷον ἂν αὐτὸ τὸ παρατεταμένον ᾖ ἄλλο τι συμβαίνειν μοι δοκεῖ, καὶ ἄλλο αὖ, εἰ ἀδύνατόν ἐστι ταῦτα παθεῖν. Cf Rep. vii. 534 B sq. There is only an apparent contradiction in the Cratylus, 436 C sq., where the remark μέγιστον δέ σοι ἔστω τεκμήριον ὅτι οὐκ ἔσφαλται τῆς ἀληθείας ὁ τιθέμενος· οὐ γὰρ ἄν ποτε οὕτω ξύμφωνα ἦν αὐτῷ ἅπαντα is met by the answer: ἀλλὰ τοῦτο μὲν, ὦ 'γαθὲ Κρατύλε, οὐδέν ἐστιν ἀπολόγημα· εἰ γὰρ τὸ πρῶτον σφαλεὶς ὁ τιθέμενος τἆλλα ἤδη πρὸς τοῦτ' ἐβιάζετο καὶ αὐτῷ ξυμφωνεῖν ἠνάγκαζεν, οὐδὲν ἄτοπον... τὰ λοιπὰ πάμπολλα ἤδη ὄντα ἑπόμενα ὁμολογεῖν ἀλλήλοις· δεῖ δὴ περὶ τῆς ἀρχῆς παντὸς πράγματος παντὶ ἀνδρὶ τὸν πολὺν λόγον εἶναι καὶ τὴν πολλὴν σκέψιν, εἴτε ὀρθῶς εἴτε μὴ ὑπόκειται· ἐκείνης δὲ ἐξετασθείσης ἱκανῶς, τὰ λοιπὰ ἐκείνῃ φαίνεσθαι ἑπόμενα· for it is afterwards shown that Cratylus' onesided supposition becomes involved in contradictions in its consequence—because the ἀρχὴ has no real proof.

[86] This he shows by the introduction and investiture of the Parmenides: the whole procedure of the dialogue reminds one forcibly of Zeno's method. Cf vol. i. 494, 496 sqq.

calls induction: for its aim is to enquire into the truth of concepts, and to make possible their right definition. If the presuppositions of unphilosophic consciousness are subjected to this treatment, they are refuted and annulled in the Idea; if it is applied to philosophic propositions, as in the Parmenides, these receive their dialectical establishment and more exact determination: but if by this process we have arrived at the Idea as the Unconditioned—the indirect development of thought must give place to the direct, the analytic to the synthetic.[87]

We have remarked before that the speciality of the Synthetic method lies, according to Plato, in Classification or Division. As the Concept expresses the common attribute wherein a number of things agree, Division expresses the differences by which a class is

---

[87] Brandis (Gr.-röm. Phil. ii. a. 264) calls this ἐξ ὑποθέσεως σκοπεῖν a higher process of dialectic completing Division. He has generally brought out this side of Plato's dialectic acutely and correctly; but I cannot agree with him here. The object is not to find a corrective for Division, but to determine the truth of the ὑποθέσεις, i e. the right mental grasp of the Concepts on which an enquiry proceeds: and this is exemplified in the Meno, the Parmenides, and the Protagoras before them, 329 C sqq. And again, this ἐξ ὑποθέσεως σκοπεῖν seems to me not to be essentially separate from the elements of Dialectic above mentioned (formation of Concepts, and Division), but to belong to the former of them, as the critico-dialectical test of rightly applied Induction. I cannot either agree with Heyder (Comparison of Aristotelian and Hegelian Dialectic, i. 99 sqq.–113 sqq.) in thinking that the hypothetic-dialectic process aims not so much at the introduction and verification of means whereby Concepts in themselves are explained or limited, as at the introduction and verification of certain Combinations of Concepts. Apart from what I have observed (note 76), this view will not agree with Plato's own explanations, that throughout, the object of this process is only to test the ὑποθέσεις, the correctness of the leading Concepts. Heyder cannot quote Arist. Metaph. xiii. 4, 1078 b. 25 on his side, and with as little reason can he appeal to the procedure of Plato's Parmenides, which is expressly concerned with investigating the Concepts of Unity and Being.

separated into its kinds.[88] He, therefore, who would make a right division must not introduce arbitrary distinctions into things, but seek out those already existing in them—the natural articulations of the conceptual group.[89] For this purpose two things are to be observed: that the division is to be according to real differences of Kind, not merely Quantitative disparity; and that the intermediate links by which the lower kinds are connected with the higher are not to be passed over.[90] The former is necessary in order to obtain a logical, and not a merely external division;[91] the latter, that we may judge rightly the relation of concepts, and learn to combine the unity of the class with the multi-

---

[88] Phædr. 265 E (v. p. 199?); Polit. 285 A. διὰ δὲ τὸ μὴ κατ' εἴδη συνειθίσθαι σκοπεῖν διαιρουμένους ταυτά τε τοσοῦτον διαφέροντα ξυμβάλλουσιν εὐθὺς εἰς ταὐτὸν ὅμοια νομίσαντες, καὶ τοὐναντίον αὖ τούτου δρῶσιν ἕτερα οὐ κατὰ μέρη διαιροῦντες, δέον, ὅταν μὲν τὴν τῶν πολλῶν τις πρότερον αἴσθηται κοινωνίαν, μὴ προαφίστασθαι πρὶν ἂν ἐν αὐτῇ τὰς διαφορὰς ἴδῃ πάσας, ὁπόσαι περ ἐν εἴδεσι κεῖνται, τὰς δὲ αὖ παντοδαπὰς ἀνομοιότητας, ὅταν ἐν πλήθεσιν ὀφθῶσι, μὴ δυνατὸν εἶναι δυσωπούμενον παύεσθαι, πρὶν ἂν ξύμπαντα τὰ οἰκεῖα ἐντὸς μιᾶς ὁμοιότητος ἔρξας γένους τινὸς οὐσίᾳ περιβάληται.

[89] This is the τέμνειν κατ' ἄρθρα so often insisted on by Plato: Phædr. loc. cit. Ibid. 272 D: κατ' εἴδη τε διαιρεῖσθαι τὰ ὄντα καὶ μιᾷ ἰδέᾳ καθ' ἓν ἕκαστον περιλαμβάνειν. 277 B: καθ' αὑτό τε πᾶν ὁρίζεσθαι... ὁρισάμενός τε πάλιν κατ' εἴδη μέχρι τοῦ ἀτμήτου τέμνειν. Polit. 287 C: κατὰ μέλη τοίνυν αὐτὰς οἷον ἱερεῖον διαιρώμεθα. Rep. v. 454 A: the main reason of Eristic error is τὸ μὴ δύνασθαι κατ' εἴδη διαιρούμενοι τὸ λεγόμενον ἐπισκοπεῖν, ἀλλὰ κατ' αὐτὸ τὸ ὄνομα διώκειν τοῦ λεχθέντος τὴν ἐναντίωσιν, Cf. note 92.

[90] Polit. 262 A: μὴ σμικρὸν μόριον ἓν πρὸς μεγάλα καὶ πολλὰ ἀφαιρῶμεν, μηδὲ εἴδους χωρίς· ἀλλὰ τὸ μέρος ἅμα εἶδος ἐχέτω.

[91] Cf. foregoing note and Polit. 263 A sqq: γένος καὶ μέρος ὡς οὐ ταὐτόν ἐστον, ἀλλ' ἕτερον ἀλλήλοιν ...εἶδός τε καὶ μέρος ἕτερον ἀλλήλων εἶναι...ὡς εἶδος μὲν ὅταν ᾖ του, καὶ μέρος αὐτὸ ἀναγκαῖον εἶναι τοῦ πράγματος, ὅτουπερ ἂν εἶδος λέγηται· μέρος δὲ εἶδος οὐδεμία ἀνάγκη. We get a hint of this distinction in the Protagoras, 329 D, in the question (anticipating Aristotle's distinction of ὁμοιομερὲς and ἀνομοιομερὲς) whether the alleged parts of virtue are as distinct as the parts of the face (nose and mouth, for instance), or only ὥσπερ τὰ τοῦ χρυσοῦ μόρια οὐδὲν διαφέρει τὰ ἕτερα τῶν ἑτέρων ἀλλήλων καὶ τοῦ ὅλου, ἀλλ' ἢ μεγέθει καὶ σμικρότητι.

plicity of that which is comprehended under it.[92] The first is conditioned by the second; for only by a regular progression from universal to particular can we be sure that the kinds are rightly determined, and that merely collective concepts are not confounded with concepts of kind.[93] The problem is to survey logically, by means of a complete and methodical

---

[92] Phileb. 16 C: it is one of the most important discoveries, a true fire of Prometheus for science, ὡς ἐξ ἑνὸς μὲν καὶ ἐκ πολλῶν ὄντων τῶν ἀεὶ λεγομένων εἶναι, πέρας δὲ καὶ ἀπειρίαν ἐν αὑτοῖς ξύμφυτον ἐχόντων. δεῖν οὖν ἡμᾶς τούτων οὕτω διακεκοσμημένων ἀεὶ μίαν ἰδέαν περὶ παντὸς ἑκάστοτε θεμένους ζητεῖν· εὑρήσειν γὰρ ἐνοῦσαν· ἐὰν οὖν μεταλάβωμεν, μετὰ μίαν δύο εἴ πως εἰσί, σκοπεῖν, εἰ δὲ μή, τρεῖς ἤ τινα ἄλλον ἀριθμὸν καὶ τῶν ἐν ἐκείνων ἕκαστον (we should either read κ. τῶν ἐν ἐκείνῳ ἕκ. with Stallbaum, ad loc., or καὶ ἓν ἐκείνων ἕκαστον) πάλιν ὡσαύτως, μέχρι περ ἂν τὸ κατ' ἀρχὰς ἓν μὴ ὅτι ἓν καὶ πολλὰ καὶ ἄπειρά ἐστι μόνον ἴδῃ τις, ἀλλὰ καὶ ὅποσα· τὴν δὲ τοῦ ἀπείρου ἰδέαν πρὸς τὸ πλῆθος μὴ προσφέρειν, πρὶν ἄν τις τὸν ἀριθμὸν αὐτοῦ πάντα κατίδῃ τὸν μεταξὺ τοῦ ἀπείρου τε καὶ τοῦ ἑνός· τότε δ' ἤδη τὸ ἓν ἕκαστον τῶν πάντων εἰς τὸ ἄπειρον μεθέντα χαίρειν ἐᾶν. This is revealed of the gods: οἱ δὲ νῦν τῶν ἀνθρώπων σοφοὶ ἓν μέν, ὅπως ἂν τύχωσι τί πολλὰ θᾶττον καὶ βραδύτερον ποιοῦσι τοῦ δέοντος, μετὰ δὲ τὸ ἓν ἄπειρα εὐθύς· τὰ δὲ μέσα αὐτοὺς ἐκφεύγει, οἷς διακεχώρισται τό τε διαλεκτικῶς πάλιν καὶ τὸ ἐριστικῶς ἡμᾶς ποιεῖσθαι πρὸς ἀλλήλους τοὺς λόγους (with the latter cf. ibid. 15 D; Phædr. 261 D; Rep. vii. 539 B). Schaarschmidt, Samml. d. plat. Schr. 298 sq. tries to show in this place a misunderstanding of Aristotle's statements as to the elements of the Ideas, and a consequent proof of the spuriousness of the Philebus. It has been, however, already pointed out (p. 398 sq.) that Aristotle used the Philebus as a work of Plato's; and Schaarschmidt's objection really rests on an incorrect interpretation of the passage before us. We have not to do here with the question as to the final metaphysical elements of things (still less, as Schaarschmidt says, with those of material things as such), but simply with the logical perception that in all Being there is unity and multiplicity, so far as on one side every class of existent may be reduced to one generic concept, and on the other every generic concept is brought before us in a multiplicity of individuals. This multiplicity is not merely an unlimited multiplicity (ἄπειρος), but also a limited, in so far as the generic concept resolves itself, not directly into an indeterminate number of individuals, but into a determinate number of species and subordinate species in succession: the indeterminate manifold of individuals, susceptible of no further articulation, only begins with the lowest limit of this conceptual division. I fail to see anything un-Platonic in this.

enumeration of its divisions and subdivisions, the whole area included under a class; to follow all the ramifications of the concepts to the point where their regular co-articulated series ends and the indefinite multiplicity of the phenomenon begins. By this method it is shown whether concepts are identical or diverse, in what respect they fall or do not fall under the same higher idea; how far they are consequently allied or opposed, capable of combination or the reverse,—in a word, their reciprocal relation is established, and we are enabled by this knowledge to make a methodical descent from the highest universal to the particular, to the very confines of the ideal world.[94] But while insisting on the continuity of the progression and the completeness of all intermediate links, Plato as constantly urges that we should start from the simplest divisions. What he prefers, therefore, is bisection, which becomes quadrisection, when two grounds of division cross:[95] but where such a classification is impracticable, some other must be chosen which approaches dichotomy as nearly as the given case will allow.[96]

---

[93] Polit. 262 B (cf. 264 A)· a more hasty procedure has something wrong about it; ἀλλὰ γὰρ, ὦ φίλε, λεπτουργεῖν (to go immediately into details) οὐκ ἀσφαλές, διὰ μέσων δὲ ἀσφαλέστερον ἰέναι τέμνοντας, καὶ μᾶλλον ἰδέαις ἄν τις προστυγχάνοι. τοῦτο δὲ διαφέρει τὸ πᾶν πρὸς τὰς ζητήσεις. An example of this faulty procedure is then given in the division of mankind into Hellenes and Barbarians, in which one step is taken from the most universal to the most particular, and the mistake is made of treating the infinitely various races of non-Greeks as one race.

[94] V. supr. notes 92 and 72. Plato has no fixed phrase for the division of Genus and Species expressed in this and the related passages: γένος (which is not frequent) and εἶδος are equivalents with him (e.g. Soph. 253 D; Polit. 262 D sq.; 263 A; vid. supr. note 91), and in Tim. 57 C sq. he absolutely uses the former = species, the latter = genus: τὰν τοῖς εἴδεσι γένη.

[95] κατὰ πλάτος and κατὰ μῆκος τέμνειν. Soph. 266 A.

A completed logical system is not to be found in Plato; and neither by inferences from his own method, nor by combination of single incidental expressions, are we justified in supplying this want. The whole gist of the question is, How far did he enunciate the laws of thought (which, in common with every reasoning man, he must certainly have followed)—in the shape of logical rules, and systematise those individual observations concerning the forms and conditions of our thought which occasionally obtruded themselves upon him—into a distinct theory? This he has only done in the two points that have just been considered. For the rest, his writings do indeed contain hints and germs of the later logic, but no comprehensive combination and development of these. Thus he sometimes says that all our convictions must agree;[96] that contradictory determinations cannot at the same time belong to one and the same thing:[98] that it is a proof of error, if concerning the same thing the opposite in the same reference is affirmed.[99] He also declares that knowledge

---

[96] Phileb. loc. cit.; Polit. 287 C· κατὰ μέλη τοίνυν αὐτὰς ... διαιρώμεθα, ἐπειδὴ δίχα ἀδυνατοῦμεν· δεῖ γὰρ εἰς τὸν ἐγγύτατα ὅτι μάλιστα τέμνειν ἀριθμὸν ἀεί. The Sophist (218 D-231 E-235 B sq.; 264 C sqq.) gives elaborate instances of dichotomy carried out in detail: cf. Polit. 258 B-267 C; 279 C sqq.

[97] E g. Phædo, 100 A; Laws, v. 746 C.

[98] Rep. iv. 436 B: δῆλον ὅτι ταὐτὸν τἀναντία ποιεῖν ἢ πάσχειν κατὰ ταὐτόν γε καὶ πρὸς ταὐτὸν οὐκ ἐθελήσει ἅμα, ὥστε ἐάν που εὑρίσκωμεν ἐν αὐτοῖς ταῦτα γιγνόμενα, εἰσόμεθα ὅτι οὐ ταὐτὸν ἦν ἀλλὰ πλείω. Phædo,

162 D; 103 C, Theæt. 190 B. In the world of phenomena, opposite properties are seen combined in one subject: but. according to Plato, as will be shown presently, these properties do not belong to the things simultaneously: they are detached in the flux of Becoming and the subjects themselves are not simple but composite substances: so the properties are not, strictly speaking, found together in One and the Same. Cf. Rep. loc. cit.; Phædo, 102 D sqq.; Parm. 128 E sqq.; Soph. 258 E sqq.

[99] Soph. 230 B, Rep. x. 602 E.

can only exist when we are conscious of the reasons for our assumptions.[100] But though we may here recognise the two laws of modern logic—the Law of Contradictories and that of the Sufficient Reason,[101] Plato nowhere says that all rules of thought may be reduced to these two propositions. He has indeed enunciated them, but he has not yet placed them as the most universal principles at the apex of the science of thought. Further, when he investigates the nature of concepts, the combination in them of the One and the Many, the possibility of their being connected, their mutual compatibility and incompatibility, the relations of Genus and Species,—in all this he considers concepts, not as the product of our thought, but as something actually and absolutely existing independently of it: Logic is still veiled in Metaphysics. These enquiries, and others connected with them, into the conditions of truth and error, we must for that reason relegate to another place. In the remark that all discourse consists in the union of the concept of a predicate with that of a subject;[102] and that thought, as discourse without sound, is nothing else than affirming or denying,[103] we can trace

---

[100] Cf. p. 174 and Tim. 28 A.

[101] Tennemann, Syst. d. plat. Phil. ii. 217 sqq.; Brandis, ii. a. 266 sq.

[102] Soph. 259 E: if the combination of concepts is denied (as by Antisthenes), the possibility of discourse is taken away· διὰ γὰρ τὴν ἀλλήλων τῶν εἰδῶν συμπλοκὴν ὁ λόγος γέγονεν ἡμῖν. Ibid. 26 B. mere ὀνόματα, like Lion, Goat, Horse, and mere verbs like βαδίζει, τρέχει, καθεύδει, give no continued meaning: this is only given by the combination of the ὄνομα denoting an οὐσία with the ῥῆμα expressing a doing or not doing.

[104] Theæt. 189 E: τὸ δὲ διανοεῖσθαι ἆρ' ὅπερ ἐγὼ καλεῖς... λόγον ὃν αὐτὴ πρὸς αὑτὴν ἡ ψυχὴ διεξέρχεται... αὐτὴ ἑαυτὴν ἐρωτῶσα καὶ ἀποκρινομένη καὶ φάσκουσα καὶ οὐ φάσκουσα. So Soph. 263 E (v. supr. p. 158, 17), and immediately, καὶ μὴν ἐν λόγοις αὐτοὶ ἴσμεν ὄν... φάσιν τε καὶ ἀπόφασιν—opinion (δόξα) is therefore an affirmation or denial without discourse.

only the first, though very important, beginnings of the theory of judgments. Still less can a doctrine of syllogisms be derived from Platonic intimations;[104] and though, in the method of divisions, there is foreshadowed the demonstrative process by which Aristotle descends from the universal to the particular, we must remember that it is precisely the syllogistic medium of this progression that is here wanting.[105] On the whole, therefore, though we cannot but recognise in Plato essential elements of the Aristotelian logic, it would be a mistake to force these out of their original connection in order to construct from them a Platonic logic on a later model.[106]

In relation to his scientific method, Plato also discusses the question of the significance of language for Philosophy. An opening for such a discussion was given him on several sides.[107] Among the older philosophers, Heraclitus especially had laid stress on lin-

[104] E.g. the passages quoted p. 174, 12; cf. Polit. 280 A; Crat. 412 A; Phileb. 11 B.

[105] Aristotle speaks clearly as to the difference of the two methods, Anal. Prior. i. 31; Anal. Post. ii. 5. He calls Division οἷον ἀσθενὴς συλλογισμὸς, and points out that its defect lies in the minor being assumed without demonstration (e.g. ἄνθρωπος ζῷον, ἄνθρωπος πεζόν). He is therefore enabled to say (Soph Elench. 34, 183 b 34), without disparagement of Plato's Division, that the subjects treated of in the Topics (among which the Conclusion stands in the first series —here the Conclusion of Probability—) have never before received any scientific discussion.

[106] Tennemann makes this mistake, loc. cit. pp. 214–259 though he observes correctly enough that we must not (as Engel does in his Enquiry into a method of developing the Logic of Plato's Dialogues) lay down, in an exposition of his logic, all the rules actually followed by Plato. Prantl's procedure (Gesch. d. Log. i. 59 sqq.) is much more accurate

[107] Cf. on what follows Classen, De Gramm. Gr. Primordiis (Bonn, 1829), p. 15 sqq.; Lersch, Sprachphilos. der Alten, i. 10 sqq.; ii. 4 sqq.; Steinhart, Pl. WW. ii. 535 sq.; Steinthal, Gesch. d. Sprachwissensch. bei Gr. u. Röm. 72 sqq.

guistic expression;[108] and indeed the Greeks in general, with their quick wit and ready tongues, were fond of deriving and playing upon the words they used.[109] Various sophists had afterwards occupied themselves with philosophical questions,[110] while at the same time the Sophistic art of disputation necessitated a closer study of forms of speech, and the relation of expression to thought.[111] Of the same date are also extant enquiries of Democritus concerning Speech;[112] and it is clear from the Platonic Cratylus that in the school of Heraclitus the principle that everything has its natural name, and from names the nature of things is infallibly to be known[113]—had led to endless and most arbitrary play upon etymologies. This seems to have been likewise the case in the School of Anaxagoras.[114] Among the Socra-

---

[108] We cannot, however, point out any really scientific enunciation of his on speech (cf. vol. 1. 588, 2), and even Schuster (Heracl. 318 sq.) does not appear to have made much of this point Even if Heraclitus did say that speech was given to men by the gods, or remarked incidentally that the very name shows the Being of the thing (both of which are possible), this would not warrant our ascribing to him a definite theory of speech. Still less can any such thing be sought for in Pythagoras or his school: cf loc. cit. 410, 1.

[109] Cf the instances quoted by Lersch, iii 3 sqq. from poets.

[110] Cf. vol. 1. 932 sq.

[111] V. loc. cit. 913 sq : cf. p 903.

[112] Cf. vol. i. 745, 1: and Diog. ix. 48, who names some of Democritus' writings on verbal expression.

[113] Crat 383 A; 428 E sqq.; 435 D; 438 C; 439 A, 440 C; Lersch, i. 30; and Lassalle, Heracl. ii. 394. compare Hippocr. De Arte, ii. b. i. 7 K: τὰ μὲν γὰρ ὀνόματα φύσιος νομοθετήματα ἐστι. But we cannot draw any inferences from this as to Heraclitus' doctrines · as Steinthal, loc cit. 90, remarks, Hippocrates continues, τὰ δὲ εἴδεα οὐ νομοθετήματα ἀλλὰ βλαστήματα; he knows the doctrine of Ideas, and, with Plato (v. subt. p. 213), attaches greater importance to the knowledge of concepts than the knowledge of names. We have no right to derive what he says on the latter from Heraclitus, especially with the Cratylus as a much more obvious source for him to draw on.

[114] Crat 412 C sqq. Plato here says that the name of the δίκαιον is thus explained by the supporters of an universal flux in things

tics, Antisthenes had written on names and languages as connected with his dialectical theories.[115] And to say nothing of these predecessors, it was necessary for a philosopher like Plato,[116] who distinctly acknowledged the close affinity between speech and thought, to make up his mind as to the significance of language for knowledge. It was of the greatest consequence to the Ideal philosophy to ascertain what worth attached to words, and how far a true imitation of things might be recognised in them. His ultimate conclusion, however, is only this: that Philosophy must go her own way independently of Philology. In the Cratylus[117] he shows that language is by no means to be regarded as the product of an arbitrary enactment, of which each man may dispose as he likes: for if there be any truth, and if everything has its determinate essence, those names alone can be true which, corresponding to the nature of things, instruct us with regard to their essence;[118] which, in other words, rightly imitate things. This is the problem of speech: to provide us with a picture, not of the external phenomenon, but of the

there is a something which pervades the flux, and ἐπιτροπεύει τὰ ἄλλα πάντα διαιιόν; and the name Δία is connected with this If we inquire what this is, one answer will be, the Sun; another Fire, a third, not Fire itself, but τὸ θερμὸν τὸ ἐν τῷ πυρὶ ἐνόν: while a fourth, ridiculing them all, will make the δίκαιον equivalent to Anaxagoras' νοῦς. Cf. Pt. i. 804, 1. Plato seems to have some definite treatise in view which brought all these etymologies together; for Hermogenes says, 413 D, φαίνει μοι, ὦ Σώκρατες, ταῦτα μὲν ἀκηκοέναι τοῦ καὶ οὐκ αὐτοσχεδιάζειν.

[115] Cf. part i. p. 250, 7.

[116] V. supr. p. 158, 17, and note 103 of this chapter.

[117] Cf. on the interpretation of this dialogue Schleiermacher, Pl. W. ii. 2, 1 sqq, Brandis, ii. A 284 sqq.; Steinhart, Pl. W. ii. 543 sqq., and specially Deuschle, Die Plat. Sprachphil. (Marb. 1852), who is followed almost throughout by Susemihl, Genet. Entw. 144 sqq.

[118] V 385 E-390 A.

essence of things;[119] and this it accomplishes by expressing the properties of things in sounds, which require corresponding conditions and movements on the part of the organ of speech.[120] On the other hand, however, as Plato remarks, we must not forget that a picture never completely reproduces its subject; and that as in painting, that other art of imitation, there are better and worse artists, so also the makers of words may have committed mistakes which perhaps may run through a whole language.[121] This may explain why particular words are not always logically formed,[122] and why, as a whole, they do not represent one and the same view of the world. There are many etymologies, for instance, on which the Heraclitean doctrine of the flux of all things is based;[123] but against all of them others might be advanced with equal conclusiveness to support the opposite view.[124] Accordingly we must allow that caprice, custom, and common consent have each had a share in language,[125] and we must consequently give up seeking in words a knowledge of things.[126] As the first naming presupposes a knowledge of the things named,[127] we must, like the first word-makers, turn our attention, not to names, but rather to the things themselves,[128] and acknowledge the dialectian to be the superior critic, who has to overlook the work of the language-maker,

---

[119] 422 C–424 A; 430 A, E.
[120] Motion, e.g. by R, smoothness by L; size by A, &c. pp 424 A–427 D.
[121] 428 D–433 B; 436 B–D.
[122] 434 C sq.
[123] We get a parody of the Heraclitic style in the purposely exaggerated and extravagant etymologies which are accumulated and pushed to the absurdest lengths in 391 D–421 E, and 426 C.
[124] 436 E–437 D.
[125] 434 E–435 C
[126] 435 D–436 B; 438 C sq.
[127] 437 E sqq.
[128] 439 A sq; 440 C sq.

and decide on the correctness or incorrectness of the names bestowed.[129] Dialectic alone is that which governs and perfects all other arts: and philological enquiries only afford another confirmation of this truth.[130]

We have now considered separately the two conditions of philosophic activity,—philosophic impulse and philosophic method. It remains to show how, in the union of these, Philosophy as a whole developes itself in man. Plato, after some imperfect and partial hints in the Symposium,[131] gives a full representation of this process in the Republic. The groundwork of all culture and education is here said to be Music (in the larger sense given to the word by the Greeks) and Gymnastic: a harmonious blending of the two will temper the soul aright, and free it alike from effeminacy and rudeness.[132] The chief thing, however, and the only direct preparation for Philosophy is Music. The ultimate aim of all musical education is that children growing up in a healthy moral atmosphere should get a taste for all that is good and noble, and accustom

---

[129] 389 A–390 E.

[130] Deuschle, loc cit. pp. 8–20, points out all that is strictly grammatical in Plato, besides these philological discussions: some points are borrowed from his predecessors, others are Plato's own. Among them are the distinction of ὄνομα and ῥῆμα (Soph. 259 E; 261 E sqq.: v. supr. note 102; Theæt. 206 D; Crat. 399 B; 425 A; 431 B, and passim: cf. Eudemus ap. Simpl. Phys. 21 b. Deuschle points out that the ῥῆμα is not merely the verb in the sense of Time, but every denotation of the predicate, loc. cit. p. 8 sq.: so Claassen, loc cit. p. 45 sq.): the concept of ἐπωνυμία (Parm. 131 A; Phædo, 103 B, et sæpius); the division of the letters into Vowels, Semivowels, and Mutes (Phileb. 18 B sq; Crat 424 C; cf. Theæt. 203 B); Number (Soph. 237 E), Tenses of the Verb (Parm. 151 E–155 D; 141 D, alibi); Active and Passive (Soph. 219 B; Phil. 26 E).

[131] V. supra, 193 sq.

[132] Rep. ii. 376 E sqq., and especially iii 410 B sqq.; cf. Tim. 87 C sqq.

themselves to practise it.[133] Musical education must result in love of beauty, which is in its nature pure and undisturbed by sensuous admixture.[134] (Here, also, Eros is the beginning of philosophy.) This education, however, is as yet without intelligence (λόγος), a thing of mere habit;[135] its fruit is at first ordinary virtue, guided by Right Opinion; not philosophic virtue, ruled by scientific Knowledge.[136] To attain this, scientific education must be added to musical. But the highest object of science is the Idea of the Good; and the inclination of the spirit to this Idea is its highest problem. The turning towards true existence is in the beginning as painful to the spiritual eye as the vision of full sunlight to one who has lived all his life in a dark cavern. On the other hand, he who is accustomed to the contemplation of Being will at first only grope about uncertainly in the twilight of the world of phenomena, and so for a while appear to those who inhabit it as an ignorant and incapable person. The inference is, not that this turning to perfect truth should be unattempted, but only that it should be accomplished by natural gradations.[137] These stages or steps are formed by all the sciences, which, pointing out the inherence of

[133] ἵν' ὥσπερ ἐν ὑγιεινῷ τόπῳ οἰκοῦντες οἱ νέοι ἀπὸ παντὸς ὠφελῶνται, ὁπόθεν ἂν αὐτοῖς ἀπὸ τῶν καλῶν ἔργων ἢ πρὸς ὄψιν ἢ πρὸς ἀκοήν τι προσβάλῃ, ὥσπερ αὔρα φέρουσα ἀπὸ χρηστῶν τόπων ὑγίειαν. καὶ εὐθὺς ἐκ παιδίων λανθάνῃ εἰς ὁμοιότητά τε καὶ φιλίαν καὶ ξυμφωνίαν τῷ καλῷ λόγῳ ἄγουσα Rep. iii. 401 C.

[134] Rep 402 D sqq.; 403 C: δεῖ δέ που τελευτᾶν τὰ μουσικὰ εἰς τὰ τοῦ καλοῦ ἐρωτικά.

[135] Cf. note 133; Rep. iii. 402 A; vii. 522 A (musical education is ἔθεσι παιδεύουσα .. οὐκ ἐπιστήμην παραδιδοῦσα .. μάθημα οὐδὲν ἦν ἐν αὐτῇ).

[136] Cf Symp 202 A, and supra, p. 175 sq.

[137] Rep. vi. 504 E sqq.; vii. 514 A–519 B; cf. Theæt. 173 C sq; 175 B sq.

thought even in the sensuous form, at the same time induce consciousness of the inadequacy and contradictoriness of the sensuous Perception. The mathematical sciences, e.g. (including Mechanics, Astronomy, and Acoustics), are a middle term between the ordinary Perception or Opinion attaching to Sense, and pure sciences, just as their object, according to Plato, stands midway between the Idea and the Phenomenon. They are distinguished from Opinion, as being occupied with the Essence of things, with the common and invariable basis which underlies the plurality of different and contradictory perceptions. And they are distinguished from science in the narrower acceptation, as making known the Idea, not purely in itself, but in the objects of Sense; they are therefore still fettered to certain dogmatic premises, instead of dialectically accounting for these, and thus cancelling them in the first principle of all, itself without presupposition.[138] If, however, the mathematical sciences are to be of any real use, they must be treated in some other than the usual manner. Instead of being pursued only for practical ends, and in their application to the corporeal, the transition from Sense to Thought must be upheld as their proper aim; the pure contemplation of number, magnitude, and the like, must be made their main object; in a word, they must be used philosophically and not empirically.[139] In that case they

---

[138] Rep. vi. 510 B sq; vii. 523 A-533 E; and Symp. 210 C sq; 211 C.

[139] Rep. vii. 525 B sqq.; 527 A; 529, 531 B; Phileb. 56 D sq. (v. subt. note 158), 62 A; cf Tim. 91 D; Phædo, 100 B sqq. On Plato as a mathematician, v. my Pl. St. 357.

necessarily lead to Dialectic, which, as the highest and best of sciences, forms the coping stone of all the rest; which alone comprehends all other sciences, and teaches their right application.[140]

In the whole of this exposition, the unity and internal relation of the theoretical and practical, the two constituent parts which together form the essence of Philosophy, are set forth with more than usual decision. Elsewhere Philosophy is viewed, now as Eros, now as Dialectic: here it is most positively affirmed, that while mere love of beauty is inadequate without scientific culture, scientific culture is impossible without love of beauty: they are mutually related as different stages of one process. Philosophic love consummates itself in scientific contemplation.[141] Science, on the other hand, is not a mere concern of the intellect, but is also practical in its nature, occupied not with the external accumulation of knowledge, but with the turning of the spiritual eye, and the whole man, to the Ideal.[142] As they are one in principle,[143] they ulti-

---

[140] V. notes 72 and 159.

[141] V. supra, p. 69 sq. and Symp. 209 E sq., where the contemplation of the pure Idea is discussed as the completion of the Art of Love.

[142] Rep. vii 518 B: (δεῖ δὴ ἡμᾶς νομίσαι) τὴν παιδείαν οὐχ οἴαν τινες ἐπαγγελλόμενοί φασιν εἶναι τοιαύτην καὶ εἶναι φασὶ δέ που οὐκ ἐνούσης ἐν τῇ ψυχῇ ἐπιστήμης σφεῖς ἐντιθέναι, οἷον τυφλοῖς ὀφθαλμοῖς ὄψιν ἐντιθέντες... ὁ δέ γε νῦν λόγος .. σημαίνει, ταύτην τὴν ἐνοῦσαν ἑκάστου δύναμιν ἐν τῇ ψυχῇ καὶ τὸ ὄργανον, ᾧ καταμανθάνει ἕκαστος, οἷον εἰ ὄμμα μὴ δυνατὸν ἦν ἄλλως ἢ ξὺν ὅλῳ τῷ σώματι στρέφειν πρὸς τὸ φανὸν ἐκ τοῦ σκοτώδους, οὕτω ξὺν ὅλῃ τῇ ψυχῇ ἐκ τοῦ γιγνομένου περιστρεπτέον εἶναι, ἕως ἂν εἰς τὸ ὂν καὶ τοῦ ὄντος τὸ φανότατον δυνατὴ γένηται ἀνασχέσθαι θεωμένη· τοῦτο δ' εἶναί φαμεν τἀγαθόν. The problem is not ἐμποιῆσαι αὐτῷ τὸ ὁρᾶν, ἀλλ' ὡς ἔχοντι μὲν αὐτό, οὐκ ὀρθῶς δὲ τετραμμένῳ οὐδὲ βλέποντι οἷ ἔδει, τοῦτο διαμηχανήσασθαι. 533 C· ἡ διαλεκτικὴ μέθοδος μόνη ταύτῃ πορεύεται τὰς ὑποθέσεις ἀναιροῦσα ἐπ' αὐτὴν τὴν ἀρχὴν ἵνα βεβαιώσηται, καὶ τῷ ὄντι ἐν βορβόρῳ βαρβαρικῷ τινι τὸ τῆς ψυχῆς ὄμμα κατορωρυγ-

mately coincide in their working and manifestation. In the Symposium,[144] the pain of the philosophic new birth is represented as an effect of philosophic love; here it appears as a consequence of the dialectical ascent to the Idea. In the Phædrus, philosophic love is described as a μανία; in this place the same is virtually said of close attention to Dialectic; Dialectic at first causes unfitness for the affairs of practical life: and it is the very essence of μανία, that to the eye dazzled with the vision of the Ideal finite associations and relations should disappear.[145] Practice and theory are thus absolutely conjoined. He alone [146] is capable of philosophic cognition who has early learned the renunciation of things sensuous; conversely in the Republic (x. 611 D), Philosophy appears as the raising of the whole man out of the ocean of sense, as the scraping off of the shells and weeds that have overgrown the soul; and in the Phædo (64 sq.), as the complete liberation from the dominion of the body—the death of the inner man : thought being set forth as the means of this liberation, since by it we rise above sensible impressions. In Philosophy, then, there is no longer any opposition of theory and practice, and the different kinds of theoretic activity unite into a whole. All the various forms of knowledge —Perception, Opinion, intelligent Reflection—are but

μένον ἠρέμα ἕλκει καὶ ἀνάγει ἄνω, συνερίθοις καὶ συμπεριαγωγοῖς χρωμένη αἷς διήλθομεν τέχναις Cf. ibid. 514 A sq ; 517 B; Theæt. 175 B sq.; Soph 254 A.

[143] Science, according to Plato (as will be shown later on in the anthropology) is essentially nothing but reminiscence of the Idea ; and Eros (cf. supra) is the same.

[144] 215 E sqq ; v Part i. 153.
[145] Cf. supra, p. 191.
[146] Cf. Rep. vii. 519 A sq.

stages of philosophic or reasoned Knowledge.[147] They stand to this last, therefore, in a double relation. On the one hand, they must be transcended if true Knowledge is to be attained. He who would behold the absolutely real must free himself from the body; he must renounce the senses, which draw us away from

[147] Aristotle, De An. i. 2, 404 b. 22, thus gives Plato's enumeration of the stages of theoretic consciousness: (Πλάτων) νοῦν μὲν τὸ ἕν, ἐπιστήμην δὲ τὰ δύο· μοναχῶς γὰρ ἐφ' ἕν· τὸν δὲ τοῦ ἐπιπέδου ἀριθμὸν (triad) δόξαν, αἴσθησιν δὲ τὸν τοῦ στερεοῦ (four). For further details on the passage, v. chap. 7, note 103, and my Plat. St. 227 sq. So in the dialogues, Perception and Opinion, or Envisagement, are assigned to the unscientific consciousness, directed towards the phenomenal world (v. supra, p 70 sq); and the ἐπιστήμαι are noticed (Symp. 210 C, Phil. 66 B; cf. Rep. ix. 585 C) as the next preliminary stage of pure thought, or Dialectic· the highest stage is called νοῦς (Tim. 51 D), and νοῦς καὶ φρόνησις (Phil. loc cit.). In Symp. 210 C, 211 C, it appears as ἐπιστήμη or μάθημα; but Plato draws a clear distinction between the one ἐπιστήμη, directed towards the pure Idea, and the other ἐπιστῆμαι, which are merely preparatory to it. The most exact correspondence with Aristotle's exposition is found in the Timæus, 37 B: δόξαι and πίστεις are there assigned to the Sensuous and Mutable (πίστις is used alone, 29 C), while νοῦς and ἐπιστήμη (ἀλήθεια, 29 C) belong to the Intelligible and Immutable. Rep. vi. 509 D sq.; vii. 533 E eq. is only a partial deviation from this: ἐπιστήμη there stands first (νοῦς or νόησις are equivalents), διάνοια second, πίστις third, εἰκασία fourth. The first two, dealing with the Invisible, are combined under the name of νόησις: the two others, dealing with the Visible, under the name of δόξα. Plato himself tells us that ἐπιστήμη here is the same as νοῦς elsewhere (as in Symp loc. cit. and Phædo, 247 C). Διάνοια corresponds to the Aristotelian ἐπιστήμη, as is clearly shown by Rep 533 D; 510 B sqq; 511 D sq There is a confusion here between the division elsewhere given of Knowledge based on Opinion and another division, not so important from Plato's point of view—vide note 14 By διάνοια or ἐπιστήμη Plato means (as Brandis observes) exclusively mathematical science. This is expressly stated, Rep. vi. 510 B sq.; 511 C sq, and is a natural consequence of his doctrines: mathematical laws are to him (vide subter) the sole mediating elements between Idea and Phenomenon; and therefore only a knowledge of these laws can mediate between Opinion or Envisagement and the science of the Idea. In enumerations like the above Plato allows himself considerable laxity, as may be seen from the Philebus, 66 B, besides the places already quoted. The terminology is a matter of indifference. Rep. vii. 533 D.

pure contemplation, and intervene darkling between the spirit and truth;[148] he must turn his eyes away from shadows and direct them to true Being,[149] must rise from the irrational Envisagement to Reason:[150] he must remember that eyes and ears were given us, not that we might revel in sensuous sights and sounds, but to lead us, through the perception of the heavenly motions and of audible harmony, to order and harmony in the soul's movements.[151] We must not stop short at conditioned, mathematical thought, which makes use of certain presuppositions, but does not analyse them.[152] But, on the other hand, the sensuous Phenomenon is at any rate a copy of the Idea, and thus serves to awaken in us the recollection of the Idea:[153] Right Opinion is only distinguished from Knowledge by the want of dialectic establishment.[154] The mathematical sciences, too, are, in Plato's view, the most direct and indispensable preliminaries of Dialectic; for they represent in sensible form the concepts which the philosopher contemplated in their purity.[155] It is therefore one and the same matter with which the different intellectual activities have to do, only that this matter is not apprehended by all as equally perfect and unalloyed. That which is true in the sensuous Perception, in Opinion and in reflective Thought, is included in

[148] Phædo, 65 A-67 B; 67 D; Rep. vii. 532 A
[149] Rep. vii. 514 sq.
[150] Tim. 28 A; 51 D sq.; cf. supra, 174.
[151] Tim. 47 A sq
[152] Rep. vi. 510 B sq.; vii. 533 C; cf. note 72, p. 215 sq.
[153] Phædr. 250 D sq.; Symp. 210 A, Phædo, 75 A sq.
[154] V supra, 174. On account of this connection, Right Opinion is actually set by the side of Knowledge and commended: e.g. Theæt. 202 D; Phileb. 66 B; Rep. ix. 585 C, Laws, x. 896
[155] Cf. p. 215 sq.

Philosophy as pure thought: the Idea is there grasped whole and entire, its confused and partial appropriation having already given to the lower forms of knowledge an import, and a relative share in truth.[156] Philosophy is consequently not one science among others, but Science absolutely, the only adequate manner of knowing; and all the particular sciences [157] must fall under this, so soon as they are rightly treated. They thus belong to the propædeutic of Philosophy,[158] and find in Dialectic their end; and they are worthless in proportion and as long as they are withheld from the use of the dialectician.[159] Nay, even the handicraft arts—con-

---

[156] As will be proved in the following sections.

[157] Confined, however, in Plato, as we have seen, to the mathematical branches.

[158] Rep. vii. 525 B: the guardians are to be admonished, ἐπὶ λογιστικὴν ἰέναι καὶ ἀνθάπτεσθαι αὐτῆς μὴ ἰδιωτικῶς, ἀλλ' ἕως ἂν ἐπὶ θέαν τῆς τῶν ἀριθμῶν φύσεως ἀφίκωνται τῇ νοήσει αὐτῇ· they are (525 D) no longer ὁρατὰ ἢ ἁπτὰ σώματα ἔχοντας ἀριθμοὺς προτείνεσθαι, but τὸ ἓν ἴσον τε ἕκαστον πᾶν παντὶ καὶ οὐδὲ σμικρὸν διαφέρον, μόριόν τε ἔχον ἐν ἑαυτῷ οὐδέν. Astronomy rightly studied is to use the course of the stars (529 C sq) only as an example τῶν ἀληθινῶν, ἃς τὸ ὂν τάχος καὶ ἡ οὖσα βραδυτὴς ἐν τῷ ἀληθινῷ καὶ πᾶσι τοῖς ἀληθέσι σχήμασι φοράς τε πρὸς ἄλληλα φέρεται καὶ τὰ ἐνόντα φέρει. Phileb. 56 D. οἱ μὲν γάρ που μονάδας ἀνίσους καταριθμοῦνται τῶν περὶ ἀριθμόν, οἷον στρατόπεδα δύο καὶ βοῦς δύο καὶ δύο τὰ σμικρότατα ἢ καὶ τὰ πάντων μέγιστα· οἱ δ' οὐκ ἄν ποτε αὐτοῖς συνακολουθήσειαν, εἰ μὴ μονάδα μονάδος ἑκάστης τῶν μυρίων μηδεμίαν ἄλλην ἄλλης διαφέρουσάν τις θήσει—and the mathematical sciences thus treated are αἱ περὶ τὴν τῶν ὄντως φιλοσοφούντων ὁρμήν. Ibid. 57 C. For further details, v. supra.

[159] Rep vii. 534 E: ἆρ' οὖν δοκεῖ σοι ὥσπερ θριγκὸς (coping stone) τοῖς μαθήμασιν ἡ διαλεκτικὴ ἡμῖν ἐπάνω κεῖσθαι, κ.τ.λ Ibid. 531 C: οἶμαι δέ γ' ἦν δ' ἐγώ, καὶ ἡ τούτων πάντων ὧν διεληλύθαμεν μέθοδος ἐὰν μὲν ἐπὶ τὴν ἀλλήλων κοινωνίαν ἀφίκηται καὶ ξυγγένειαν, καὶ ξυλλογισθῇ ταῦτα, ᾗ ἐστιν ἀλλήλοις οἰκεῖα, φέρειν τι αὐτῶν εἰς ἃ βουλόμεθα τὴν πραγματείαν καὶ οὐκ ἀνόνητα πονεῖσθαι, εἰ δὲ μὴ ἀνόνητα Cf. note 75. Ribbing's idea that Plato here 'identifies' mathematics with Dialectic, is, I think, sufficiently disproved by foregoing remarks Mathematics with him are only a preliminary to Dialectic, not Dialectic itself: they have to do with similar subjects—number, magnitude, motion, &c.—but are differentiated by the method of procedure.

temptuously as the Republic repudiates them,[160] and however little worth Plato in reality allowed to them—even they, by virtue of their relative share in truth elsewhere conceded, belong likewise to the first stages of Philosophy.[161]

Philosophy is therefore, in a word, the focus which unites all the scattered rays of truth in human opinion and action;[162] it is the absolute consummation of the spiritual life generally, the royal art sought in the Euthydemus[163] by Socrates, in which making or producing, and knowledge of the use of that which is made, coincide.

Plato is, however, quite aware that Philosophy is never fully and perfectly represented in actuality. As early as the Phædrus we find him desiring that no man shall be called wise, but only at most a lover of wisdom, for God alone is wise.[164] So in the Parmenides (134 C) he declares that God alone has perfect knowledge: and on that ground he claims for men, in a celebrated passage of the Theætetus (176 B), not divinity, but only the greatest possible likeness to God. Still less does it appear to him conceivable that the soul in this earthly life, among the incessantly disturbing influences of the body, should attain the pure intuition of truth:[165] even the endeavour for wisdom or the philosophic impulse, he derives not merely from the inclina-

[160] Vii. 522 B; vi. 495 D.
[161] Symp 209 A; Phileb. 55 C sqq.: cf. Ritter, Gesch. d. Phil ii. 237.
[162] Cf. Rep. v. 473 B: τὸν φιλόσοφον σοφίας φήσομεν ἐπιθυμητὴν εἶναι οὐ τῆς μὲν τῆς δ' οὔ, ἀλλὰ πάσης.
[163] 289 B; 291 B.
[164] 278 D· cf. Symp 203 E: θεῶν οὐδεὶς φιλοσοφεῖ οὐδ' ἐπιθυμεῖ σοφὸς γενέσθαι· ἔστι γάρ.
[165] Phædo, 66 B sqq.

tion of man towards wisdom, but also from the feeling of ignorance : [166] and he confesses that the highest object of knowledge, the Good or God, is only to be arrived at with difficulty, and only to be beheld at specially favourable moments.[167] Yet it by no means follows from this that what he himself calls Philosophy is to him but an impracticable ideal—that he gives to the Divine science alone that high significance and unbounded range, and regards human science, on the contrary, as a manner of mental life, side by side with other activities equally good and useful. It is assuredly human science developing itself, by a long series of means, out of the philosophic impulse, to which in the Symposium and Republic he assigns so lofty a place; for the engendering of which he gives detailed directions; on which he grounds the whole organism of his state; without which, as a ruling power, he sees no period to human misery. The philosophic sobriety and moderation of our own times, thankful for any crumbs that may be left for thought—was unknown to Plato. To him Philosophy is the totality of all mental activities in their completed development, the only adequate realization of reasonable human nature, the queen whom all other realms must serve, and of whom alone they hold in fief their allotted share of truth. Whether or not this view is well founded, whether Plato conceives the idea of Philosophy with sufficient clearness, whether he does not over-estimate the compass of human intellectual powers, or rightly determines the

[166] V. supra, pp. 192, 193.
[167] Rep. vi. 506 E, vii. 517 B; Tim. 28 C; Phædr. 248 A.

relation of spiritual activities and the limits of the different spheres of life—this is not the place to enquire.

For the further development of the Platonic system, we distinguish, in accordance with the foregoing observations—*Dialectic*, or the doctrine of the Idea—*Physics*, or the doctrine of the Phenomenon of the Idea in nature—*Ethics*, or the doctrine of its representation in human action. The question as to the relation of the Platonic Philosophy to Religion and Art will afterwards be supplementarily considered.

CHAPTER VI.

DIALECTIC, OR THE DOCTRINE OF IDEAS.

According to Plato, the specific and primary subject-matter of Philosophy consists, as already shown, in Ideas; for they alone contain true Being, the Essence of things. The enquiry into Ideas, which is Dialectic in the narrower sense, must therefore come first in the construction of his system: on that foundation only can a philosophic view of nature and of human life be built up. This enquiry is threefold: (1) Concerning the derivation of Ideas; (2) their Universal Concept; and (3) their expansion into an organised Plurality, a World of Ideas.

I. *The Establishment of the Doctrine of Ideas.*—The theory of Ideas is primarily connected with the Socratic-Platonic theory of the nature of Knowledge. Concepts alone guarantee true Knowledge. But in the same proportion that truth belongs to our opinions (for Plato, like other philosophers, starts with this assumption [1]), reality must belong to their object, and

[1] Parmenides had already said that Non-being cannot be thought or expressed, that only Being could be thought (see vol. i. 470, 1). This tenet was frequently taken advantage of by the Sophists, in order to prove that false opinion is impossible (ib. 905, 3, 4). Similarly the so-called Hippocr. De Arte, c. ii b. i. 7 Kuhn. τὰ μὲν ἐόντα ἀεὶ ὁρᾶταί τε καὶ γινώσκεται, τὰ δὲ μὴ ἐόντα οὔτε ὁρᾶται οὔτε γινώσκεται.

vice versâ. That which may be known is, that which cannot be known is not. In the same measure that a thing exists, it is also knowable. Absolute Being is therefore absolutely knowable; absolute Non-being, absolutely unknowable;[2] that which, uniting in itself Being and Non-being, lies in the midst between the absolutely real and the absolutely unreal,—must have a kind of knowledge corresponding to it, intermediate between Knowledge and Ignorance; it is not the province of Knowledge but of Opinion.[3] As certainly, therefore, as Knowledge is something other than Opinion,[4] so must also the object of Knowledge be other than that of Opinion: the former is an unconditioned reality; the latter a something to which Being and Non-being equally belong. If Opinion refers to the Material, our concepts can only refer to that which is Immaterial; and to this alone can a full and true existence be attributed.[5] Plato thus expressly de-

---

[2] We shall find this later on in the case of matter.

[3] Rep. v. 476 E sq.; vi. 511 E. Cf. supra, p. 175 sq. Plato clearly expresses his agreement with the fundamental position that it is impossible to conceive Non-being (loc. cit. 478 B: ἆρ' οὖν τὸ μὴ ὂν δοξάζει; ἢ ἀδύνατον καὶ δοξάσαι τὸ μὴ ὄν; ἐννόει δέ· οὐχ ὁ δοξάζων ἐπί τι φέρει τὴν δόξαν; ἢ οἷόν τε αὖ δοξάζειν μέν, δοξάζειν δὲ μηδέν, &c. Similarly Theæt. 188 D sqq. (cf. Parm. 132 B, 142 A, 164 A), and his attack on the sophistical conclusion just mentioned is not directed against the major proposition: he allows that there can be no notion of Non-being, but denies that error is the notion of Non-being as such. He refers error to the notion of relative Non-being or Other-being—to the confusion and incorrect association of notions. Theæt. 189 B sq , Soph. 261 A sq · further details subter

[4] Cf. note 147, and p 170 sqq.

[5] Rep. v. 477 B: ἆρ' οὖν λέγομέν τι δόξαν εἶναι, Πῶς γὰρ οὔ, πότερον ἄλλην δύναμιν ἐπιστήμης ἢ τὴν αὐτήν; Ἄλλην. Ἐπ' ἄλλῳ ἄρα τέτακται δόξα καὶ ἐπ' ἄλλῳ ἐπιστήμη, κατὰ τὴν ἄλλην δύναμιν ἑκατέρα τὴν αὑτῆς. Οὕτω. οὐκοῦν ἐπιστήμη μὲν ἐπὶ τῷ ὄντι πέφυκε γνῶναι ὡς ἔστι τὸ ὄν; opinion, on the other hand (478 D), belongs to something which being at the same time existent and non-existent, is between

signates the distinction between Knowledge and Right Opinion, as the point on which our decision concerning the reality of Ideas depends. If they are identical, we can only assume the existence of the Corporeal; but if they are different, we must ascribe to Ideas, which are underived, unchangeable and imperishable,—apprehended not by the senses but by reason alone,—an absolute and independent existence.[6] The reality of Ideas seems to him the direct and inevitable consequence of the Socratic philosophy of Concepts. Knowledge can only be employed on true existence, on the colourless, shapeless, immaterial Essence which the spirit alone beholds.[7] If there is any Knowledge at all, there must also be a fixed and invariable object of Knowledge,—an object that exists not only for us and by reason of us, but in and for itself. Only the Invariable can be known. We can attribute no quality to that which is conceived as constantly changing.[8]

the εἰλικρινῶς ὄν and the πάντως μὴ ὄν.

[6] Tim 51 B: the question is: ἆρ' ἔστι τι πῦρ αὐτὸ ἐφ' ἑαυτοῦ καὶ πάντα περὶ ὧν λέγομεν οὕτως αὐτὰ καθ' αὑτὰ ὄντα ἕκαστα, ἢ ταῦτα ἅπερ βλέπομεν, &c. μόνα ἐστὶ τοιαύτην ἔχοντα ἀλήθειαν, ἄλλα δὲ οὐκ ἔστι παρὰ ταῦτα οὐδαμῇ οὐδαμῶς, ἀλλὰ μάτην ἑκάστοτε εἶναί τί φαμεν εἶδος ἑκάστου νοητόν, τὸ δὲ οὐδὲν ἄρ' ἦν πλὴν λόγος: this question is not to be discussed more fully in this place; εἰ δέ τις ὅρος ὁρισθεὶς μέγας διὰ βραχέων φανείη, τοῦτο μάλιστ' ἐγκαιριώτατον γένοιτ' ἄν. ὧδε οὖν τήν γ' ἐμὴν αὐτὸς τίθεμαι ψῆφον· εἰ μὲν νοῦς καὶ δόξα ἀληθής ἐστον δύο γένη, παντάπασιν εἶναι καθ' αὑτὰ ταῦτα, ἀναίσθητα ὑφ' ἡμῶν εἴδη, νοούμενα μόνον· εἰ δ', ὥς τισι φαίνεται, δόξα ἀληθὴς νοῦ διαφέρει τὸ μηδέν, πάνθ' ὁπόσ' αὖ διὰ τοῦ σώματος αἰσθανόμεθα, θετέον βεβαιότατα. δύο δὲ λεκτέον ἐκείνω (here follows what was quoted, p. 495). τούτων δὲ οὕτως ἐχόντων ὁμολογητέον ἓν μὲν εἶναι τὸ κατὰ ταὐτὰ εἶδος ἔχον, ἀγέννητον καὶ ἀνώλεθρον, οὔτε εἰς ἑαυτό· εἰσδεχόμενον ἄλλο ἄλλοθεν οὔτε αὐτὸ εἰς ἄλλο ποι ἰόν, ἀόρατον δὲ καὶ ἄλλων ἀναίσθητον, τοῦτο ὃ δὴ νόησις εἴληχεν ἐπισκοπεῖν τὸ δ' ὁμώνυμον ὅμοιόν τε ἐκείνῳ δεύτερον, αἰσθητόν, γεννητόν, πεφορημένον ἀεί γιγνόμενόν τε ἔν τινι τόπῳ καὶ πάλιν ἐκεῖθεν ἀπολλύμενον, δόξῃ μετ' αἰσθήσεως περιληπτόν.

[7] Phædr. 247 C.

[8] Crat. 386 D; 439 C sq.; Soph.

Therefore to deny the reality of Ideas is altogether to annihilate the possibility of scientific enquiry.[9] What is here derived from the idea of Knowledge, Plato also deduces from the contemplation of Being; and, as the doctrine of Ideas is, on the one side, a result of the Socratic philosophy, on the other, it follows from the teaching of Heraclitus and the Eleatics. As Ideas are to Opinion in the region of Knowledge, so is true Existence to Phenomena,—the Immaterial to the Material—in the region of Being. The Sensible, then, is a something Becoming, but the end of Becoming is Being.[10] The Sensible is many and divided; but these many things become what they are, only by reason of that which is common to them all; and this common element must be distinct from the particulars, nor can any notion of it be abstracted from individuals, for these never show us that common quality itself, but only an imperfect copy.[11] No individual presents its essence purely, but each possesses its own qualities in combination with their opposites. The manifold just is also unjust,—the manifold beautiful, ugly; and so on. This totality is therefore to be regarded as a middle-term between Being and Non-being: pure and full reality

---

249 B sq.; Phileb 58 A. Cf. also the remarks, p 174, on the mutability of Right Opinion and the immutability of Knowledge, and vol. i. 602, on the consequences of the doctrine of the flux of all things which are drawn out in the Cratylus.

[9] Parmen. 135 B sq.

[10] Phil 54 B: φημὶ δὴ γενέσεως μὲν ἕνεκα φάρμακά τε καὶ πάντα ὄργανα καὶ πᾶσαν ὕλην παρατίθεσθαι πᾶσιν, ἑκάστην δὲ γένεσιν ἄλλην ἄλλης οὐσίας τινὸς ἑκάστης ἕνεκα γίγνεσθαι, ξύμπασαν δὲ γένεσιν οὐσίας ἕνεκα· γίγνεσθαι ξυμπάσης. The doctrine of Flux and the partial non-existence of the sensible will be discussed at greater length in the beginning of the next chapter.

[11] Parm. 132 A; Phædo, 74 A sqq.

DOCTRINE OF IDEAS. ITS ESTABLISHMENT.

can only be conceded to the one absolute self-identical beauty or justice, exalted above all opposition and restriction.[12] We must distinguish between that which ever is and never becomes (Tim. 27 D) and that which is ever in process of Becoming and never arrives at Being. The one, remaining always self-identical, can be apprehended by rational Thought;—the other, arising and passing away, without ever really being, can only be the subject of Opinion and Perception without Reason: the former is the prototype, the latter the copy. The contemplation of Nature leads us to these prototypes; for the world is perfect and beautiful, simply because it is fashioned after an eternal and unchangeable pattern.[13] Things can only be understood by us in relation to their ultimate aim; their true causes are those by means of which they become good and fair; and this they are, because they participate in beauty and goodness itself, in absolute Existence.[14] Our moral life, too, presupposes moral prototypes, the perception of which must guide us, so that our actions may tend towards right ends.[15] There is, in short, nothing in the

---

[12] Rep. v. 479 A sq., vii. 524 C; Phædo, loc cit. 78 D sq., 103 B.

[13] Tim 28 A–29 A; 30 C.

[14] Cf. the passages of the Phædo and Timæus (viz. 46 C sq.; 68 E and 100 B–E respectively) to be noticed later on.

[15] Phædo, 247 D; 250 B sq, in his sketch of the world of Ideas, Plato expressly particularises the αὐτὴ δικαιοσύνη, σωφροσύνη, ἐπιστήμη, together with the Idea of beauty; Theæt. 176 E, he speaks of the παραδείγματα ἐν τῷ ὄντι ἑστῶτα, τοῦ μὲν θείου εὐδαιμονεστάτου, τοῦ δὲ ἀθέου ἀθλιωτάτου Parm. 130 B; Phædo, 65 D, Rep v. 476 A, of the Idea of the δίκαιον, καλὸν, ἀγαθόν, &c.; and the highest ot all Ideas to Plato is, as we shall find, that of the Good. Still (as Ribbing remarks, Pl. Ideenl. 1 316 sq) we cannot conclude that the practical Ideas alone or at any rate in preference to the others, formed the starting point of the doctrine of Ideas. In the Parmenides (loc. cit.) and Phædo (78 D; 101 A sqq.), together with or even before the Idea of justice, those of simi-

world which does not point us to the Idea; nothing which has not in the Idea the cause of its existence, and of such perfection as belongs to it. The dialectical exposition of this necessity of the theory of Ideas is attempted in the Sophist, and more fully in the Parmenides. The first proves, as against the doctrine of an original plurality of Being, from the concept of Being itself, that the All, in so far as Being belongs to it, is also One;[16] as against Materialism, from the facts

larity, equality, unity, plurality, duality, greatness, &c., are mentioned, and from the passages quoted in the preceding note we see how great was the influence of Plato's teleology on the formation of the theory of Ideas It was not merely on the basis of a definite kind of hypostasized concepts that this doctrine arose, but from the universal conviction that in all existence and becoming the thought given by its concept was the only true reality.

[16] 243 D, Plato asks those who suppose two original existences (the warm and the cold and the like). τί ποτε ἄρα τοῦτ' ἐπ' ἀμφοῖν φθέγγεσθε, λέγοντες ἄμφω καὶ ἑκάτερον εἶναι; τί τὸ εἶναι τοῦτο ὑπολάβωμεν ὑμῶν; πότερον τρίτον παρὰ τὰ δύο ἐκεῖνα, καὶ τρία τὸ πᾶν, ἀλλὰ μὴ δύο ἔτι καθ' ὑμᾶς τιθῶμεν; (That this is not so is not expressly proved, nor had Plato any need of proof, because the triplicity of existence directly contradicts its supposed duality, and the existent as such is only one, although it is a third together with the two elements.) οὐ γάρ που τοῖν γε δυοῖν καλοῦντες θάτερον ὂν (calling only the one of them an existing thing, as Parmenides and the Atomists; cf. Pt. i. 479 sq.; 687 sqq) ἀμφότερα ὁμοίως εἶναι λέγετε· σχεδὸν μὲν γὰρ ἀμφοτέρως (i.e. whether we call only the one or only the other an existing thing) ἕν, ἀλλ' οὐ δύο εἴτην. Ἀληθῆ λέγεις. Ἀλλ' ἄρα τὰ ἄμφω βούλεσθε καλεῖν ὄν; Ἴσως. Ἀλλ', ὦ φίλοι, φήσομεν, κἂν οὕτω τὰ δύο λέγοιτ' ἂν σαφέστατα ἕν. Ὀρθότατα εἴρηκας. By this explanation the above view seems to me to be perfectly justified. It might indeed be objected (Bonitz, Plat. Stud. ii. 51) that the possibility mentioned by Plato in the above passage—that existence itself is separate from the two elements—is overlooked. This supposition, it is true, is not expressly contradicted by Plato, apparently from the reasons indicated above; but his design in mentioning it can only be to show the untenability of the assertion of an original duality of existence in any sense that could possibly be assigned to it In the case before us, this is done by showing the contradiction such an assumption involves (viz. the necessity of three existents instead of the presupposed two) The same argument would apply with equal force

of moral and mental conditions, that there must be some other Being than that of Sense.[17] The Parmenides takes up the question more generally and from a logical point of view (Parm. 137), developing both hypotheses,—'the One is' and 'the One is not'—in their consequences. From the Being of the One, contradictions arise conditionally; from the Non-being of the One, absolutely. It is thus proved that without the One Being, neither the thought of the One, nor the Being of the Many, would be possible: however inadequate may be the Eleatic view of the One Being, and however necessary it may be to rise from this abstract Unity excluding Plurality, to the comprehensive Unity of the Idea.[18] The proper connection of the Platonic doctrine, however, is more clearly marked in other expositions.

The theory of Ideas, then, is grounded on these two main points of view, that, to its author, neither true Knowledge nor true Being seems possible without the Reality of Ideas. These points of view overlap, and are mingled in Plato's expositions; for the reason why Knowledge is impossible without Ideas is this: that

against the assumption of three, four, or any additional quantity whatsoever, of original elements: and we have really an indirect assertion here of what has been directly stated in the two other cases, that the originally existent, *qua* existent, can only be one.

[17] 246 E sq.; cf. Theæt. 155 E, where those who would allow nothing to be real, ἢ οὗ ἂν δύνωνται ἀπρὶξ τοῖν χεροῖν λαβέσθαι, πράξεις δὲ καὶ γενέσεις καὶ πᾶν τὸ ἀόρατον οὐκ ἀποδεχόμενοι ὡς ἐν οὐσίας μέρει, are treated with unqualified contempt.

[18] This view of the Parmenides, which I first propounded in my Plat Stud 159 sqq and defended in the first edition of the present work, part 1. p. 346 sqq, I cannot substantiate with greater detail in this place; besides the dissertations mentioned above, cf. Suscmihl Genet. Entw. 1. 341 sqq.; Ribbing, loc cit. 221 sqq.

sensible existence wants permanence and self-consistency, without which Knowledge is unthinkable. And that the material phenomenon has no true Being is proved by the impossibility of knowing it ideally. The same conclusion is reached by the Platonic proofs of the theory as represented by Aristotle in his work on Ideas,[19] so far as we are acquainted with that work.[20] The first of these, the λόγοι ἐκ τῶν ἐπιστημῶν, coincides with the proof above developed—that all Knowledge refers to the permanent, self-identical Ideas. The second, τὸ ἓν ἐπὶ πολλῶν, is based on the proposition that the Universal which is in all particulars of the same Genus, must itself be distinct from these. The third (τὸ νοεῖν τι φθαρέντων), which is closely connected with the second, proves the independent existence of Ideas, by the argument that the universal concept remains in the soul even if the phenomenon be destroyed. Two other proofs, adduced by Alexander,—that things to which the same predicates belong, must be copied from the same archetype, and that things which are like one another can only be so by reason of participation in one Universal,—concur with those already quoted from Parm. 132 and Phædo 74. The doctrine of Ideas therefore is ultimately based upon the conviction that Reality belongs not to the Phenomenon with its self-contradictory divisions and variability, but to the Essence of things in its unity and identity; not to the sensibly perceived but to the logically thought.

[19] Cf. my Plat. Stud. p. 232 sq., and Schwegler and Bonitz ad loc. Arist.

[20] From Arist. Mstaph. i. 9, 990 b. 8 sqq. 22, and Alex. ad locum.

The theory being thus derived, we can also see how the hypothesis of Ideas connects itself with Plato's historical position. Besides his relation to Socrates, Aristotle refers us to the influence of the Heraclitean philosophy, and also to that of the Pythagoreans and Eleatics. 'These systems,' he says,[21] 'were followed by the enquiries of Plato, which indeed on most points were allied with the Pythagoreans, but in some particulars diverged from the Italian philosophy. From his youth he agreed with Cratylus and the Heracliteans, that all things sensible are in continual flux, and that no knowledge of them is possible; and he remained true to that doctrine. At the same time, however, he embraced the Socratic philosophy, which occupied itself with Ethical investigations to the exclusion of natural science, yet in these sought out the universal and applied itself primarily to determination of concepts; and so Plato came to the conclusion that this procedure must refer to something different from Sense, for sensible things cannot be universally defined, being always liable to change. These classes of existence, then, he called Ideas; concerning sensible things, he maintained that they subsist side by side with Ideas, and are named after them, for the Manifold which bears like name with the Ideas is such by virtue of participation in the Ideas. This last definition is only a different expression of the Pythagorean tenet, that things are the copies of numbers.' 'Moreover,' continues Aristotle at the conclusion of the chapter, 'he assigns respectively to his two elements,—to the One and to

---

[21] Metaph. i. 6, beginn. Cf. xiii. 9; 1086 a. 35 sqq.

Matter,—the causes of good and evil: in which he was anticipated by some of the earlier philosophers, as Empedocles and Anaxagoras.' This passage sums up nearly all the elements from which the Platonic theory of Ideas was historically developed; the Eleatics and Megarians might, however, have been more expressly mentioned. The Socratic demand for conceptual knowledge unmistakably forms the starting point of the theory; but Plato, by the utilization of all that the earlier philosophy offered, and in the direction which it traced out for him, enlarged this ground; his greatness, indeed, consists in his having been able to draw forth the result of the whole previous development, and shape from the given elements an entirely new creation. Socrates had declared that all true knowledge must rest upon right concepts: he had recognised in this conceptual knowledge the rule of all action; he had shown that Nature herself could only be explained by the concept of an End. Plato follows him in these convictions, and combines with them what earlier philosophers—Parmenides and Heraclitus, Empedocles and Democritus—had taught on the uncertainty of the senses, and on the difference of rational Cognition from Opinion [22]—together with Anaxagoras' doctrines of the world-forming mind, and the intelligent disposition of all things.[23] With those older philo-

---

[22] See above, p. 170 sqq., with which compare vol. i p. 476 sq; 583 sq.; 651; 741 sq.

[23] Plato himself, Phædo, 97 B sq. (vide vol. 1. 811); Phileb. 28 C, sqq, tells us what importance he attached to this doctrine, and what conclusions he drew from it, and at the same time how he regretted the absence of its further development in Anaxagoras.

sophers, their view of knowledge was only a consequence of their metaphysics; Plato, on the contrary, reduces Socrates' principles on scientific method to the metaphysical ideas they presuppose. He asks, How is the Real to be conceived by us, if only reasoning thought assures a true cognition of the Real? To this question Parmenides had already replied; The one eternal invariable Essence can alone be regarded as the Real. And a similar answer was given by Plato's fellow-disciple Euclides, who may possibly have anticipated Plato in the formation of his system.[24] Plato was drawn to such a view by several influences. In the first place, it seemed to him a direct result of the Socratic theory of conceptual knowledge that something real should correspond to our concepts, and that this should excel all else in reality as far as science excels all other ways of knowing in truth.[25] Similarly it became clear that the object of our thought must not be sought in the phenomenon.[26] This, however, ensued still more definitely from the Heraclitean doctrines of the flux of all things; for the permanent element, to which our ideas relate, could not lie in the sphere of unconditional change.[27] The Eleatic arguments against Plurality and Mutation were at any rate so far acknowledged by Plato that he excluded from true Being that unregulated movement and unlimited Multiplicity—not comprehended in the unity of the Idea, not co-articulated according to fixed differences of kind—which the world of Sense appeared

[24] Vide Part i. p. 218 sq.
[25] Vide supra, p. 225 sq.
[26] Ibid p. 226.
[27] Ibid. p. 228.

to him to offer.[28] And Parmenides, having already, on these grounds, denied to Being all sensible properties, and the Pythagoreans having, in their numbers, declared that which is not palpable to the senses to be the Essence of things [29]—Plato may have been all the more inclined to maintain the same of the Immaterial which forms the subject-matter of our concepts. Nor, lastly, must we estimate too lightly the influence of that æsthetic view of the world which was always uppermost in Plato's artistic spirit. As the Greek everywhere loves clear limitation, firmly outlined forms, definiteness, visibility, as in his mythology he places before us the whole contents of moral and natural life embodied in plastic shapes,—so does Plato feel the necessity of translating the matter of his thought out of the abstract form of the concept into the concrete form of an ideal vision. It does not satisfy him that our reason should distinguish the qualifying realities embodied in things,—that *we* should separate them from the connection in which we perceive them; they must also exist in themselves apart from this inter-connection; they must condense into independent essences, concepts must become Ideas. The doctrine of Ideas thus appears as a truly Greek creation,

---

[28] Vide loc. cit. and note 92. Further details will be given in the paragraph on Matter.

[29] We shall find an opportunity later on to return to the importance attached by Plato to the Pythagorean doctrines of numbers. Aristotle's statement, Metaph. 1. 6 beginn. that Plato had in most points adhered to the Pythagoreans, goes too far. Asclepius (ad loc. Metaph.) corrects Aristotle, but is also mistaken in his assertion that 'he ought to have said in all points, for Plato was a thorough Pythagorean.' The same statement was frequently made in the Neo-Pythagorean and Neo-Platonic schools.

and, more particularly, as a fruit of that union between the Socratic and pre-Socratic philosophy, which was accomplished in Plato's comprehensive mind. The Ideas are the Socratic concepts, elevated from rules of knowledge into metaphysical principles, and applied to the speculations of natural philosophy concerning the essence and grounds of Existence.[30]

II. *The Concept of Ideas.*—If, then, we would be clear as to the general concept and nature of Ideas, it primarily follows from the preceding discussion that they are that which, as unconditioned Reality, is unaffected by the change and partial non-being of the phenomenon, and, as uniform and self-identical, is untouched by the multiplicity and contradictions of concrete existence.[31] Plato takes for this permanent and

---

[30] Further particulars on the relation of the doctrine of Ideas to earlier philosophic theories will be given presently. Schleiermacher, Gesch. d. Phil. 104, combats the above-mentioned Aristotelian explanation, and wishes to refer the Ideas to a combination between Heraclitus and Anaxagoras—to a remodelling of the doctrine of homœomeries. This theory is entirely without historical justification Herbert, more correctly (in his treatise, which will still repay perusal, De Plat. systematis fundamento, Werke, xii. 63 sq), sees in the doctrine of Ideas a combination of Eleatic and Heraclitean elements, but leaves entirely out of account the main point, viz. the Socratic conceptual philosophy. The formula in which he sums up the gist of his view: *Divide Heracliti* γένεσιν οὐσίᾳ *Parmenidis: habebis ideas Platonis* (for which—in spite of Ueberweg, Unters. plat. Schr. 40—we could just as well say conversely *divide* οὐσίαν *Parmenidis,* &c.), is better adapted to the Atomistic doctrine than to that of Ideas : vide vol. i. 687 sqq.

[31] In the first reference Plato calls the Ideas οὐσία (Phædr. 247 C; Crat. 386 D, Phædo, 78 D ; Parm 135 A); ἀΐδιος οὐσία (Tim. 37 E); ἀεὶ ὄν (ibid. 27 D); ὄντως ὄν, ὄντως ὄντα (Phædr 247 C, E ; Rep. x. 597 D). παντελῶς ὄν (Soph 248 E; Rep. v. 477 A); κατὰ ταὐτὰ ὄν, ὡσαύτως ὄν, ἀεὶ κατὰ ταὐτὰ ἔχον ἀκινήτως (Tim. 35 A , 38 A; Phædo, 78 D, cf. Soph 248 B); the adjective αὐτὸς or αὐτὸ ὅ ἐστι (Phædr. 247 D; Theæt. 175 C; Crat. 389 D; Soph. 225 C; Parm. 130 B, 133 D: 134 D; Phædo, 65 D sq.; 78 D; 100 C; Phileb. 62 A; Rep. vi.

self-identical element (as the name of Ideas shows [32]) the Universal or Genus — that which is conceived by us in general concepts. This alone it is which as early as the Theætetus appears as the Essence of things and the sole object of science; [33] with the

507 B; 493 E; Tim. 51 B; is an equivalent term; cf. Arist. Metaph. iii 2; 997 b. 8; vii. 16, 1040 b. 32; Eth. Nich. i. 4; 1096 b. 34. Other passages may be found Ind. Aristot. 124 b. 52 sqq. Parm. 132 C the Ideas are designated as ἕν, in Phileb. 15 A sq. as ἑνάδες or μονάδες.

[32] εἶδος and ἰδέα (for which μορφή is used Phædo, 103 E; 104 D; Phileb. 12 C) signify in Plato generally any form or shape, especially, however, species or genus (for as yet these were not distinguished, vide note 94), and from a subjective point of view the Idea or general concept; e.g. Euthyphro, 6 D; Gorg. 454 E; Theæt. 148 D; Meno, 72 C; Phædr 249 B; 265 D; Soph. 253 D; Parm. 129 C; 132 A–D; Symp. 205 B; 210 B; Rep. v. 454 A; vi 507 B; viii. 544 D; Phileb 15 D; 23 D; 32 C; cf. Ast, Lex. Plat.; Brandis, gr. röm. Phil. ii. 221 sqq. According to Aristotle, Metaph 1. 6 (supra, p. 233), Plato seems to have established this usage. Both ancients and moderns have in vain tried to discover any distinction in the signification of the two expressions. Seneca. e.g has the assertion, of course not original, that ἰδέα is the *exemplar*, εἶδος the *forma ab exemplari sumta* —the archetype and the copy respectively. Further development of this is found in the Neo-Platonist Johannes Diaconus, Alleg. in Hes.

Theog. 452 Ox., who was indebted to Proclus for his knowledge. He says that ἰδέα with a simple ι signifies the purely simple, the αὐτοέν, the αὐτοδυάς, &c., εἶδος with a diphthong τὰ σύνδετα ἐκ ψυχῆς τε καὶ σώματος ἢ μορφῆς (add καὶ ὕλης). These are, of course, mere fictions. I cannot agree with Richter (De Id. Plat 28 sq) and Schleiermacher (Gesch. d. Phil. 104), who would make εἶδος signify the concept of a species, ἰδέα the archetype; nor with the view of Deuschle (Plat Sprachphil. 73), and Susemihl (Genet. Entw 122), that in εἶδος we are to understand the subjective concept, in ἰδέα the objective fundamental form (Steinhart inverts this order, but acknowledges both the expressions to be essentially the same). A comparison of the above and other passages proves that Plato makes no distinction at all between the two, as regards their scientific meaning; cf. e g Parm 132 A sq.; 135 B.

[33] Theæt. 185 B, after several concepts have been mentioned: ταῦτα δὴ πάντα διὰ τίνος περὶ αὐτοῖν διανοεῖ; οὔτε γὰρ δι' ἀκοῆς οὔτε δι' ὄψεως οἷόν τε τὸ κοινὸν λαμβάνειν περὶ αὐτῶν. Ibid C: ἡ δὲ διὰ τίνος δύναμις τό τ' ἐπὶ πᾶσι κοινὸν καὶ τὸ ἐπὶ τούτοις δηλοῖ σοι; 186 D (with reference to this passage): ἐν μὲν ἄρα τοῖς παθήμασιν (sensible impressions) οὐκ ἔνι ἐπιστήμη, ἐν δὲ τῷ περὶ ἐκείνων συλλογισμῷ· οὐσίας

search for which, according to the Phædrus, all Knowledge begins;[34] which the Parmenides describes as alone true Being;[35] to say nothing of the above-quoted distinct and reiterated declarations. Plato,[36] therefore, expressly defines the Idea as that which is common to the Many of like name; Aristotle similarly defines it [37] as the ἓν ἐπὶ πολλῶν, and on this founds his objection that it is a contradiction to assume the Universal as Substance and, in so far, as a particular.[38] The view of modern criticism [39] that Ideas

γὰρ καὶ ἀληθείας ἐνταῦθα μέν, ὡς ἔοικε, δυνατὸν ἅψασθαι, ἐκεῖ δὲ ἀδύνατον.

[34] Phædr. 265 D (vide p. 199, where further proofs are adduced); ibid. 249 B

[35] E.g. 132 C. where the εἶδος is designated as the ἓν ὃ ἐπὶ πᾶσι τὸ νόημα ἐπὸν νοεῖ, μίαν τινὰ οὖσαν ἰδέαν, the ἓν ἀεὶ ὂν τὸ αὐτὸ ἐπὶ πᾶσιν. 135 A : ὡς ἔστι γένος τι ἑκάστου καὶ οὐσία αὐτὴ καθ' αὑτήν. Cf Rep. vi. 507 B . πολλὰ καλά ... καὶ πολλὰ ἀγαθὰ καὶ ἕκαστα οὕτως εἶναί φαμέν τε καὶ διορίζομεν τῷ λόγῳ ... καὶ αὐτὸ δὴ καλὸν καὶ αὐτὸ ἀγαθὸν καὶ οὕτω περὶ πάντων, ἃ τότε ὡς πολλὰ ἐτίθεμεν, πάλιν αὖ κατ' ἰδέαν μίαν ἑκάστου ὡς μιᾶς οὔσης τιθέντες ὃ ἔστιν ἕκαστον προσαγορεύομεν .. καὶ τὰ μὲν δὴ ὁρᾶσθαί φαμεν, νοεῖσθαι δ' οὔ, τὰς δ' αὖ ἰδέας νοεῖσθαι μὲν ὁρᾶσθαι δ' οὔ. Tim. 31 A starts on the same supposition that for every plurality an Idea must be assumed as unity.

[36] Rep. x. 596 A · εἶδος γάρ πού τι ἓν ἕκαστον εἰώθαμεν τίθεσθαι περὶ ἕκαστα τὰ πολλὰ οἷς ταὐτὸν ὄνομα ἐπιφέρομεν. Ritter (ii. 306 ; cf. 303 A 3) translates this passage: 'An Idea is assigned to each thing which we designate as a number of things by the same name,' and he infers that, inasmuch as not merely every individual but also every attribute, every condition, and every relation, and even the variable, can be set forth in names, and every name signifies an Idea, therefore the Idea cannot merely express general concepts. Here however the main point is neglected ; viz. that what the Idea corresponds to is the ὄνομα common to many things.

[37] Metaph. i. 9, 990 b. 6 (xiii. 4, 1079 a. 2): καθ' ἕκαστον γὰρ ὁμωνυμόν τί ἐστι (ἐν τοῖς εἴδεσι) καὶ παρὰ τὰς οὐσίας (i.e. οὐσίαι in the Aristotelian sense, substances) τῶν τε (? cf. Bonitz ad loc.) ἄλλων ὧν ἐστιν ἓν ἐπὶ πολλῶν. Hence in what follows the ἓν ἐπὶ πολλῶν is mentioned under the Platonic evidences for the doctrine of Ideas, vide p. 232. Cf. Metaph xiii. 4, 1078 b 30 ἀλλ' ὁ μὲν Σωκράτης τὰ καθόλου οὐ χωριστὰ ἐποίει οὐδὲ τοὺς ὁρισμούς· οἱ δ' ἐχώρισαν καὶ τὰ τοιαῦτα τῶν ὄντων ἰδέας προσηγόρευσαν. Ib. 1079 a. 9, 32 ; Anal. post. i. 11 beginn.

[38] Metaph. vii 16, 1040 b. 26 sqq.; xiii. 9, 1086 a. 31 sqq.

[39] Ritter, loc cit., with whom Volquardsen agrees, Plat. Idee. d.

240   PLATO AND THE OLDER ACADEMY.

contain not only the Universal in the sense we associate with the word, but also the individual, besides being incapable of proof, is thus evidently opposed to Plato's clear definitions. This Universal, which is the idea, he conceives as separate from the world of Phenomena, as absolutely existing Substance.[40] It is the heavenly sphere, in which alone lies the field of truth, in which the gods and pure souls behold colourless, shapeless, incorporeal Existence;[41] the justice, tem-

---

pers. Geist. 17 sq., without, however, adducing anything new. Ritter brings the following points in support of his view: (1) what has already been refuted, note 36. (2) The fact that in Crat. 386 D and elsewhere a permanent existence is attributed not merely to things, but also to the actions or activities of things. From this, however, it does not follow that these activities individually—as distinct from their general concepts—go to form the content of the respective Ideas. (3) That according to Plato the soul is non-sensible and imperishable. But this is far from proving that it is an Idea. (4) That according to Theæt. 184 D, the individual soul is considered as an Idea, and (Phædo, 102 B) what Simmias is and what Socrates is, is distinguished from what is both of them. The latter passage, however, rather goes against Ritter, for what Simmias is and what Socrates is,—i.e. their individual existence,—is here separated from the Idea or common element in which both partake. In the first passage (Theæt. 184 D), certainly the argument is that the single experiences of sense coincide εἰς μίαν τινὰ ἰδέαν, εἴτε ψυχὴν εἴτε ὅ τι δεῖ καλεῖν. but the latter qualification only proves that in the present case we have not to deal with the stricter philosophic usage of ἰδέα or εἶδος. The word stands in an indefinite sense, just as in Tim. 28 A, 49 A, 52 A (where matter is called an εἶδος); 59 C, 69 C, 70 C, 71 A; Rep vi. 507 E, &c., and also in the passage Theæt. 157 C, wrongly cited by Ritter on his side. It is distinctly stated (Phædo, 103 E, 104 C, 105 C sq.) that the soul is not an Idea in the proper sense of the term. Vide infra

[40] This word, taken in the original Aristotelian sense, signifies generally anything subsisting for itself, forming no inherent part or attribute of anything else, and having no need of any substratum separate from itself. Of course if we understand by substance, as Herbart does (loc. cit. Werke, xii 76), that which contains several mutable properties, itself remaining constant in the permutations of these properties, we have every reason for combating as he does the assertion that the Ideas are substances.

[41] Phædr. 247 C sq.

perance, and science that are exalted above all Becoming, and exist not in another, but in their own pure Essence. The true Beauty is in no living creature in earth or heaven or anywhere else, but remains in its purity everlastingly for itself and by itself, in one form (αὐτὸ καθ' αὑτὸ μεθ' αὑτοῦ μονοειδὲς ἀεὶ ὄν), unmoved by the changes of that which participates in it.[42] The Essence of things exists absolutely for itself, one in kind, and subject to no vicissitude.[43] The Ideas stand as the eternal prototypes of Being—all other things are copied from them.[44] Purely for themselves (αὐτὰ καθ' αὑτὰ), and divided from that which has part in them (χωρὶς), they are in the intelligible sphere (τόπος νοητὸς) to be beheld not with eyes, but by thought alone;[45] visible things are but their adumbrations:[46] phenomena, we might say, are relative; the Ideas alone

[42] Symp. 211 A. Steinhart (Pl. Wk. iii. 424, 441; iv. 254, 641), following the Neo-Platonists (cf. vol. iii. b. 695; 723, 3, 2nd ed.), says: 'The Ideas must not be confounded with the general concepts of the understanding'—'in the Symposium (loc. cit.) they are most decidedly distinguished from generic concepts:'—'the concept of Species becomes an Idea only so far as it participates in the Ideal concept of Genus.' I agree with Bonitz (Plat. Stud. ii 75 sq.) and others in opposing these views. The content of the Ideas is given by general concepts,—hypostatised by Plato—without any difference being made between Ideal and other concepts; nor are Species excluded from the sphere of Ideas every Species, except the *infima species*, may be regarded as a Genus. Cf further, Rep. vi. 511 C (v sup. p. 168); Parmen. 130 C sq.; Phileb. 16 C (v. sup. 206, 92); and subsequent remarks on the extent of the World of Ideas.

[43] Phædo, 78 D: ἀεὶ αὐτῶν ἕκαστον ὃ ἔστι, μονοειδὲς ὃν αὐτὸ καθ' αὑτό, ὡσαύτως κατὰ ταὐτὰ ἔχει καὶ οὐδέποτε οὐδαμῇ οὐδαμῶς ἀλλοίωσιν οὐδεμίαν ἐνδέχεται. Phileb. 15 B; Tim 51 B; vide note 6.

[44] Tim 28 A; Parm. 132 D; Theæt. 176 E.

[45] P. 556, Pt. i.; Parmen. 128 E; 130 B sq.; 135 A; Phædo, 100 B, Rep. vi. 507 B (vide note 35).

[46] They are represented as such in the famous allegory of the Cave-dwellers, Rep. vii.. 514 B sq., 516 E; 517 D.

are absolute.[47] In a word, the Ideas are, to use an illustration of Aristotle's, χωρισταί:[48] — i.e. there belongs to them a Being entirely independent of, and different from, the Being of things: they are self-subsistent entities.[49] Consequently, those theories which have confused the Platonic Ideas with sensible substances, hypostasized images of the fancy (ideals), or with subjective conceptions, are neither of them correct. The first[50] is now pretty generally abandoned, and has been already refuted by the preceding quotations from the Phædrus, Symposium, and Republic: we might also refer to the assertion of the Timæus (52 B), that only the copy of the Idea—in general, the Becoming, not the truly Existing—is in space; together with the corroborative testimony of Aristotle.[51] It may be said

[47] Plato draws a distinction in a general logical sense between the καθ' αὑτὸ and the πρός τι cf. Soph. 255 C (ἀλλ' οἶμαί σε συγχωρεῖν τῶν ὄντων τὰ μὲν αὐτὰ καθ' αὑτά, τὰ δὲ πρὸς ἄλληλα ἀεὶ λέγεσθαι), also Parm. 133 C, Rep. iv. 438 A Hermodorus, ap. Simpl. Phys. 54 b. says: τῶν ὄντων τὰ μὲν καθ' αὑτὰ εἶναι λέγει [Πλάτων], ὡς ἄνθρωπον καὶ ἵππον, τὰ δὲ πρὸς ἕτερα, καὶ τούτων τὰ μὲν ὡς πρὸς ἐναντία, ὡς ἀγαθὸν κακῷ, τὰ δὲ ὡς πρός τι. But although this logical distinction extends as such through both worlds —the world of sense and the world of Ideas (cf. on the Idea of the Relative, subter, note 126) — in a metaphysical sense the Idea alone is an absolute. It is, as we have just been told, αὐτὸ καθ' αὑτό; while of the phænomenon of sense it is said ἑτέρου τινὸς ἀεὶ φέρεται φάντασμα, διὰ ταῦτα ἐν ἑτέρῳ προσήκει τινὶ γίγνεσθαι (Tim. 52 C). The latter is a relative, only a copy of the Idea—has its existence only in and through this relation.

[48] Metaph. i. 9, 991 b. 2; xiii. 9, 1086 a. 31 sq., xiii. 4, vide p. 554, 1; Phys. ii. 2, 193, b. 35; cf. Anal. Post. i. 77 a. 5; Metaph. i. 6, 987 b. 8, 29; and my Plat. Stud. 230.

[49] οὐσίαι as Aristotle calls them: cf. Metaph. i.9, 990 b. 30, 991 b. 1; iii. 6, 1002 b. 29; vii. 16, 1040 b. 26. How this determination harmonises with the other, that things exist only in and through the Ideas, will be discussed later on.

[50] Tiedemann, Geist d. spek. Phil. ii. 91 sq., where by 'substances' are understood sensible substances; cf. Van Heusde, Init. Phil. Plat. ii. 3, 30, 40.

[51] Phys. iv. 1, 209 b. 33: Πλάτωνι μέντοι λεκτέον ... διὰ τί οὐκ ἐν τόπῳ τὰ εἴδη. iii 4, 203 a. 8:

that Plato speaks of the super-mundane sphere, and that his disciple describes Ideas as αἰσθητὰ ἀΐδια.[52] But the figurative character of the former representation is too apparent to allow of its serving as proof; and Aristotle's remark is clearly not intended to convey Plato's own view, but to disprove it by its consequence.[53] The other supposition, that the Platonic Ideas are subjective thoughts, is more prevalent. Hardly anyone would now regard them as mere conceptions of *human* reason;[54] but it has been maintained, even recently, that they have no absolute existence, but are only the thoughts of God.[55] This theory is as untrue as the

Πλάτων δὲ ἔξω [τοῦ οὐρανοῦ] μὲν οὐδὲν εἶναι σῶμα, οὐδὲ τὰς ἰδέας, διὰ τὸ μηδέπου εἶναι αὐτάς

[52] Arist. Metaph. iii, 2, 997 b. 5 sq.; cf vii. 16, 1040 b. 30.

[53] Cf Plat. Stud. p. 231.

[54] Melanchthon, Opp. ed. Bretsch. xiii. 520; Buble, Gesch. d. Phil. ii. 96 sq.; Tennemann, Syst. d. Plat. Phil. ii. 118 sq. (cf. Gesch. d. Phil. ii. 296 sqq.), who makes the Ideas (viewed as archetypes of things), notions or envisagements; viewed as in the spirit of man, works of the Deity. Plat ii. 125, iii. 11 sq., 155 sq; Gesch. d. Phil. ii. 369 sqq.

[55] This theory is met with in antiquity among the later Platonists, and is general in Neo-Platonism (cf. vol. iii. a. 726; b. 105; 411 sq.; 469; 571,5; 694; 723, 3, 2nd edit.). There, however, it was connected with the belief in the substantiality of the Ideas, and it was not observed that the two theories are contradictory. The same view of the doctrine of Ideas is common among the Platonizing realists of the middle ages Among the moderns, cf. Meiners, Gesch. d. Wissensch. ii. 803; Stallbaum, Plat. Tim. 40, Parm. 269 sqq.; Richter, De Id. Plat. 21 sq., 36 sq.; Trendelenburg, De Philebi Cons. 17 sq. The latter says that the Ideas are *formæ a mente artifice susceptæ*, creations of the divine reason, *quæ cogitando ita ideas gignat, ut sint, quia cogitentur*, and when they are described as absolute and as χωρισταί, the meaning merely is that they continue in the thoughts of the Divinity independent of the vicissitudes of phænomenal appearance Cf, to the same effect, Rettig, Αἰτία in the Philebus, &c. (Bern, 1866), 24 sq ; Volquardsen, loc. cit. p. 16 sq., who, to support his view, quotes certain dicta from Rep. iv. 435, not to be found there at all. Kuhn, De Dialecticâ Plat. p. 9, 47 sq, approximates to this view in supposing that the Ideas (as was held by the Neo-Platonists) subsist in

other and is altogether wanting in proof. Plato's having been led to the doctrine of Ideas by his enquiry into the nature of knowledge proves nothing; indeed, it is more in agreement with the objective derivation of Ideas.[56] The description of the Ideas as archetypes, according to which Divine Reason fashioned the world,[57] or again, as the objects which human Reason contemplates,[58] does not make them mere products of divine or human Reason. The Ideas are here presupposed by the activity of Reason, just as external things are presupposed by the activity of the sense which perceives them. Nor can this theory be deduced from the passage in the Philebus (28 D, 30 C), where the royal mind of Zeus is said to be the power which orders and governs all. Zeus here stands for the soul of the universe; that which he governs is the world,[59] and reason, as is remarked, belongs to him from the cause above him—the Idea,[60] which is accordingly treated not as the creation, but as the condition of the reason that thinks it. The proposition in the Parmenides (134 C) that God has knowledge in itself is not more conclusive; for this having is expressly described as participation, and the gods, not God, are spoken of[61] as the possessors of that

God as the most perfectly real existence, and at the same time are comprehended by his thoughts. Similarly Ebben, Plat. id. doctr. 78 sqq.
[56] Supra, p. 228 sq.
[57] Tim. 28 A; Rep. x. 596 A sq; Phædr 247 A.
[58] Tim. 52 A, and frequently.
[59] Τόδε τὸ καλούμενον ὅλον, the κόσμος καὶ ἥλιος καὶ σελήνη καὶ ἀστέρες καὶ πᾶσα ἡ περιφορά, the ἐνιαυτοί τε καὶ ὧραι καὶ μῆνες.
[60] I shall return to this later on.
[61] οὐκιῦν εἴπερ τι ἄλλο αὐτῆς ἐπιστήμης μετέχει, οὐκ ἄν τινα μᾶλλον ἢ θεὸν φαίης ἔχειν τὴν ἀκριβεστάτην ἐπιστήμην, . . . οὐκοῦν εἰ παρὰ τῷ θεῷ αὕτη ἐστίν . . . ἡ ἀκριβεστάτη ἐπιστήμη . . . ἐκεῖνοι . . .

CONCEPT OF IDEAS. 245

knowledge. It is impossible to deduce from the passage that the Idea of knowledge as such exists only in the divine thought. And though, lastly, in the Republic (x. 597 B) God is called the Artist (ποιητὴς), or Creator (φυτουργὸς), who has created the 'Bed-in-itself,' the Idea of the bed; it by no means follows from this that that Idea is only a thought of God, and has no existence except in the divine thought.[62] We must remember that this is not intended for a strictly philosophic explanation of the origin of Ideas;[63] and, that the Deity with Plato (as we shall presently find) is convertible with the highest Idea. Derived Ideas may very fairly be called his creations without involving the existence of the Idea only in the thought, and by the thought of a personality distinct from itself.[64]

The substantiality of Ideas is certified not only by the testimony of Aristotle, but also by the above-cited

οὔτε γιγνώσκουσι τὰ ἀνθρώπεια πράγματα θεοὶ ὄντες.

[62] When we say, God made the world, we do not assert that the world is merely a thought of God.

[63] With the Greeks, as everywhere else, whatever is not made by man (and consequently all the works of Nature) is referred to the Divinity. So here, the κλίνη ἐν τῇ φύσει οὖσα is as such made by God. But this is merely the explanation of popular religion, a figure of speech used just as easily by those who expressly deny the attribute of ποιεῖν to the Divinity, as Aristotle does (cf De Cœlo, 1. 4, 271 a. 33, Eth. N. x. 9, 1179 a. 24; i. 10, 1099 b. 11; and on the other hand the passages quoted vol. ii b. 276 sq 2nd edit); so that we cannot make it any real criterion of scientific views. This is particularly true of the case before us; for the sake of symmetry, three different κλινοποιοί must exist, to correspond to the three different sorts of κλίναι.

[64] Hermann has therefore no reason for discovering in this passage an entirely new development of the doctrine of Ideas, and an evidence for the later composition of the tenth book of the Republic (Plat. 540, 695); cf. Susemihl, Genet. Entw. ii. 262 sq, Steinhart, iv. 258.

Platonic passages. Ideas which exist absolutely, in no other, but purely for themselves, which remain for ever the Archetypes of things, uncreated and imperishable, according to which even the divine intelligence moves itself, cannot at the same time be creatures of that intelligence subsisting only in it,[65] owing their existence to it alone. The eternity of Ideas is proclaimed by Plato most emphatically, and regarded as the most essential of the characteristics by which they are to be discriminated from the phenomenon.[66] How then can they be likewise thoughts which first sprang from the thinking soul? This difficulty is not obviated by saying[67] that the origin of Ideas from the Divine Mind is not to be thought of as an origin in time: for not only an origin in time, but all and every origin is denied to them by Plato.[68] Again, Plato

---

[65] Cf. e.g. the passage of the Symposium, 211 A. Could Plato have thus maintained that the Idea of the Beautiful existed absolutely in none other, if his own opinion had been that it did exist only in some other, viz. the divine, understanding?

[66] E.g. Tim 27 D ἔστιν οὖν δὴ κατ᾽ ἐμὴν δόξαν πρῶτον διαιρετέον τόδε· τί τὸ ὂν ἀεὶ γένεσιν δὲ οὐκ ἔχον, καὶ τί τὸ γιγνόμενον μὲν ἀεὶ ὂν δὲ οὐδέποτε, &c. Ibid 28 C, Symp. 210 E. Aristotle frequently designates the Ideas as eternal; e.g. Metaph. i. 9, 990 b. 33, 991 a. 26; iii. 2, 997 b. 5 sqq.

[67] Trendelenburg. loc cit. 20; Stumpf. Verh. d. plat. Gott. zur Idee d. Guten, 78 sq.

[68] E.g. Tim 28 C τόδε δὲ οὖν πάλιν ἐπισκεπτέον περὶ αὐτοῦ (sc. τοῦ κόσμου), πρὸς πότερον τῶν παραδειγμάτων ὁ τεκταινόμενος αὐτὸν ἀπειργάζετο, πότερον πρὸς τὸ κατὰ ταὐτὰ καὶ ὡσαύτως ἔχον ἢ πρὸς τὸ γεγονός. So in what follows: the creator of the world looked only πρὸς τὸ ἀίδιον not πρὸς τὸ γεγονός. We see plainly that Eternity and immutability of existence on the one hand, and Becoming on the other, are to Plato opposite and contradictory antitheses; the thought that anything could spring into being and yet be eternal and unchangeable, which is Trendelenburg's view of the Ideas, is quite beyond Plato's intellectual horizon. Cf. Phileb. 15 B μίαν ἑκάστην (each Idea), οὖσαν ἀεὶ τὴν αὐτὴν καὶ μήτε γένεσιν μήτε ὄλεθρον προσδεχομένην. Further details, supra, note 6, p. 228 sq.

himself mentions the supposition that Ideas may be merely thoughts, having no other existence than in the soul ; and sets it aside with the observation, that if it were so, everything that participates in them must be a thinking subject ;[69] it is self-evident, he says, that absolute entities as such cannot exist in us.[70] And in another place,[71] he expressly guards himself against the notion that the Idea of beauty is a 'speech or a knowledge.' Nor can Aristotle have been aware that the Platonic Ideas were the thoughts of the Essence of things, and not this Essence itself. Not only does he never imply that they have their abode merely in human or Divine thought,[72] but he describes them with all possible distinctness as self-subsistent substances ;[73] and on this presupposition, subjects them to a criticism which would be utterly groundless, and

[69] Parm. 132 B ; cf. Tim. 51 C. It has been already remarked, Pt. i. p. 254, 1, end, that Plato here has in his mind the nominalism of Antisthenes.

[70] Parm 133 C: οἶμαι ἂν καὶ σὲ καὶ ἄλλον, ὅστις αὐτήν τινα καθ' αὑτὴν ἑκάστου οὐσίαν τίθεται εἶναι, ὁμολογῆσαι ἂν πρῶτον μὲν μηδεμίαν αὐτῶν εἶναι ἐν ἡμῖν. πῶς γὰρ ἂν αὐτὴ καθ' αὑτὴν ἔτι εἴη;

[71] Symp. 211 A.

[72] Aristotle nowhere describes the Ideas either as thoughts simply, or as thoughts of the Divinity; but, as we have already seen, he expressly calls them eternal substances. Can we, however, imagine that if he had known anything of the theory discussed above, he would have neglected to object to the doctrine of Ideas the contradiction between this determination and the other?

[73] This is clear from the passages cited supra, notes 48 and 48, and indeed from the single expression χωριστός, to explain which as Trendelenburg does (vide note 55) is made absolutely impossible by Aristotelian usage and by the connection in which it is used of the Platonic Ideas. Cf e.g. (not to cite the whole of the passages adduced, Ind. Arist. 860 a. 35 sq.) Metaph. vii. 16, 1040 b. 26 sq., xiii. 9. 1086 a 31 sqq., where he charges the doctrine of Ideas with a contradiction, in that the Ideas as concepts must be general and as χωρισταί individual. With Trendelenburg's interpretation of χωριστὸς this criticism is objectless : the archetypes in the thoughts of God anterior to individual Being can only be general concepts.

must throughout have taken quite another turn, if he had understood by Ideas either concepts abstracted by us from things, or such prototypes as preceded things only in the creative mind of God.[74] It is equally evident that he was unacquainted with any theory of the Ideas being the creations of the Deity.[75] We are, therefore, fully justified in asserting that Plato held the Ideas neither as the thoughts of man nor of God.[76]

But if the Real, which is the object of thought, must be a substantial entity, it cannot on that very account be conceived in the manner of the Eleatics, as Unity without Multiplicity, Permanence without Motion. If

[74] As regards the first of the above supposed cases (viz that the Ideas are the concepts of human intelligence), this will be at once conceded. And as to the second not the slightest doubt can remain. Of all the objections of Aristotle against the doctrine of Ideas (a review of them is given, Pt. 1. b. 216 sq. 2nd edit.), there is not a single one which does not lose its force as soon as we understand by the Platonic Ideas, not substantial and self-subsisting concepts, but the thoughts of the Divinity expressing the essence of certain things

[75] This definition is never mentioned either in his account of the doctrine of Ideas, or in his criticism of it, though the question was obvious (had he been aware of it)—How does the creation of the Ideas agree with their eternity? (an eternity so strongly emphasized by Aristotle) Plato, in the disquisitions which Aristotle had heard, seems never to have referred to the Deity (vide p. 76, 70) as the agent through whom the Ideas are copied in things; still less would he have done so in order to explain the origin of the Ideas themselves, which were at once eternal and without origin.

[76] If we say with Stallbaum (Parm. 269, cf. 272; Tim. 41)· *ideas esse sempiternas numinis divini cogitationes, in quibus inest ipsa rerum essentia ita quidem, ut quales res cogitantur, tales etiam sint et vi sua consistant . . . in ideis veram οὐσίαν contineri,* the question at once arises: Have the Ideas the essence of things merely as content and object, so that they themselves are distinct therefrom as subjective and objective, or are they actually the substance of things? And how can they be so if they are the thoughts of the divinity? Must not we admit in full the inference by means of which Plato (Parm. loc. cit) refutes the supposition that the Ideas are mere thoughts· ἢ ἐκ νοημάτων ἕκαστον εἶναι καὶ πάντα νοεῖν, ἢ νοήματα ὄντα ἀνόητα εἶναι?

the All is established as One, nothing (as shown in the Sophist [77]) can be predicated of it; for as soon as we combine a predicate with a subject, a name with a thing, we at once introduce a plurality. If we say the One is, we speak of the One and of Being as of two things; if we name the One or Being, we distinguish this naming from the thing named. Neither can Being be a whole,[78] for the conception of a whole involves that of parts; the whole is not pure Unity, but a Plurality, the parts of which stand in relation to Unity. If Unity be predicated of Being, and Being thus becomes a Whole, Unity is therein discriminated from Being; we have then consequently instead of One Being, two—the One and Being. If Unity does not belong to Being, and Being is therefore not a Whole, then, supposing the conception of Whole to have a real import (the Whole as such exists), Being lacks the existence that belongs to the Whole, and is so far Non-existent. If it be maintained that there is no Whole, then Being would be deprived of magnitude, nor could it, generally speaking, be or become anything.[79] But still less can the All be assumed as merely Multiplicity.[80] The right course must be to admit both Unity and Multiplicity. How are they to be reconciled? Only, as before shown, by the theory of the communion of concepts. If no combination of concepts were

---

[77] 244 B–245 E.
[78] Which must be the case according to Parmenides. Vide Pt. i. 471, 1; 473.
[79] Cf. as to the train of thought of the above passages Ribbing, Plat. Ideenl. i. 196 sq.; Petersen, De Soph. Plat. ord. (Kiel 1871), p. 9 sq., 38 sq.; and the authorities there quoted. It is impossible for me to substantiate my view in detail here.
[80] Vide p. 228 sq.

possible, no attribute could be predicated of anything different from the thing itself:[81] we could, therefore, only say of Being that it exists; in no relation, that it does not exist: whence, as a farther consequence, the Unity of all Being inevitably follows. This presupposition is, however, untrue, as indeed it must be, if speech and knowledge in general are to be possible.[82] Closer investigation convinces us that certain concepts exclude, while others are compatible with, and even presuppose, each other. With the concept of Being, for example, all those concepts are compatible which express any determination of Being, even when these are mutually exclusive, as Rest and Motion. So far, then, as concepts may be combined, the being denoted by one of them belongs to the other. So far as they are different, or mutually exclusive, the Being denoted by one does not belong to the other; consequently the Being of the one is the Non-being of the other.[83] And as each concept may be combined with many others, but, as a concept, is at the same time different from all others, so to each in many relations there belongs Existence, but in an infinite number, Non-existence.[84] The Non-existent, therefore

---

[81] The assertion of Antisthenes; vide Part I. p. 252.

[82] 259 D sq.; 251 B sq.

[83] Motion e.g can be united with Being, because it *is*; it is, however, at the same time ἕτερον τοῦ ὄντος, for its concept is different from that of Being: οὐκοῦν δὴ σαφῶς ἡ κίνησις ὄντως οὐκ ὄν ἐστι καὶ ὄν, ἐπείπερ τοῦ ὄντος μετέχει. 256 D; 254 D.

[84] 256 D · ἔστιν ἄρα ἐξ ἀνάγκης τὸ μὴ ὂν ἐπί τε κινήσεως εἶναι καὶ κατὰ πάντα τὰ γένη. κατὰ πάντα γὰρ ἡ θατέρου φύσις ἕτερον ἀπεργαζομένη τοῦ ὄντος ἕκαστον οὐκ ὂν ποιεῖ, καὶ ξύμπαντα δὴ κατὰ ταῦτα οὕτως οὐκ ὄντα ὀρθῶς ἐροῦμεν, καὶ πάλιν, ὅτι μετέχει τοῦ ὄντος, εἶναί τε καὶ ὄντα ... περὶ ἕκαστον ἄρα τῶν εἰδῶν πολὺ μέν ἐστι τὸ ὄν, ἄπειρον δὲ πλήθει τὸ μὴ ὄν.

CONCEPT OF IDEAS.

is as well as the Existent; for Non-being is itself a Being, namely the Being of the Other (and therefore not absolute, but relative Non-being, the negation of a determinate Being) and thus in every Being there is also a Non-being,—the Difference.[85]

That is to say: the veritably Existent is not pure but determinate Being: there is not merely One Existent but many; and these many stand reciprocally in the most various relations of identity and difference, exclusion and communion.[86]

The Parmenides attains the same result, by a more abstract and thoroughgoing dialectic discussion.[87] The two propositions from which the second part of this dialogue starts, 'The One is' and 'The One is not,' affirm the same as the two assumptions refuted in the Sophist—'The All is One,' and 'The All is Many.' Both these propositions are reduced *ad absurdum* by the derivation of contradictory conse-

---

[85] Cf on this particularly 256 E–259 B; 260 C

[86] It is contrary to Plato's clear and definite opinion to reduce the doctrine of the κοινωνία τῶν γενῶν to 'the possibility of some things connecting themselves with others in the being of the individual,' as Stumpf does (Verh. d plat Gott z. Idee d. Gut 48 sq) The question put was (p. 251 D), not whether a thing can partake in several Ideas at the same time, but whether οὐσία, κίνησις, στάσις can enter into communion with one another. We are then shown that if it is absolutely denied that κίνησις and στάσις partake in οὐσία, the consequence is that they *are* not; if it is absolutely affirmed, then (not, as we should have expected, that anything in motion may at the same time be at rest, but) κίνησίς τε αὐτὴ παντάπασιν ἵσταιτ' ἂν, καὶ στάσις πάλιν αὐτὴ κινοῖτο, and so throughout, e.g. 254 B sq., 254 D · κίνησις and στάσις are ἀμίκτω πρὸς ἀλλήλω, Being on the contrary μικτὸν ἀμφοῖν· ἔστον γὰρ ἄμφω που, 255 A sq.: neither κίνησις nor στάσις is ταὐτὸν or θάτερον. 255 sq.: κίνησις is ἕτερον στάσεως· it participates in Being, in ταὐτὸν and θάτερον, without being identical with them · it *is*, and it is α ταὐτὸν or ἕτερον, &c.

[87] With respect to which cf. supra, note 187.

quences; and the inference is that true Being must be defined as a Unity including in itself Multiplicity. But at the same time, from the manner in which the concept of Being is regarded in this apagogic proof, and from the contradictions which arise from that view, it is intimated that this true Being is essentially different from empirical Being, which, bounded by time and space, has no real Unity. With this exposition is closely allied that of the Philebus [88] (14 C, 17 A), which unmistakably refers to it. The result of the earlier enquiries is here briefly summed up in the assertion that the One is Many, and the Many, One; and this holds good, not only of that which arises and passes away (τὸ γιγνόμενον καὶ ἀπολλύμενον), but also of pure concepts;—they also are compounded of One and Many, and have in themselves limit, and unlimitedness. Hence one and the same thing appears to thought, now as One, now as Many.[89] Plato therefore declares true Existence to be only the Eternal, Self-identical, Indivisible, Uncontained by space; but on the other hand, he does not conceive it, with the Eleatics, as one Universal Substance, but as a multiplicity of substances, of which each without detriment to its Unity combines in itself a Plurality

---

[88] Vide p. 70, 56.

[89] 15 B· the question is not whether a subject can unite in itself many attributes or a whole many parts—on this people are now agreed—but about simple or unit-concepts, πρῶτον μὲν εἴ τινας δεῖ τοιαύτας εἶναι μονάδας ὑπολαμβάνειν ἀληθῶς οὔσας· εἶτα πῶς αὖ ταύτας, μίαν ἑκάστην οὖσαν ἀεὶ τὴν αὐτὴν καὶ μήτε γένεσιν μήτε ὄλεθρον προσδεχομένην, ὅμως εἶναι βεβαιότατα μίαν ταύτην· μετὰ δὲ τοῦτ' ἐν τοῖς γιγνομένοις αὖ καὶ ἀπείροις εἴτε διεσπασμένην καὶ πολλὰ γεγονυῖαν θετέον, εἴθ' ὅλην αὐτὴν αὑτῆς χωρίς, ὃ δὴ πάντων ἀδυνατώτατον φαίνοιτ' ἂν, ταὐτὸν καὶ ἓν ἅμα ἐν ἑνί τε καὶ πολλοῖς γίγνεσθαι. Cf. quotation on p. 206, 92

CONCEPT OF IDEAS. 253

of relations and determinations.[90] This was required by the origin of the theory of Ideas; the Socratic concepts, which form the logical germ of Ideas, arose from the dialectical combination of the different sides and qualities of things into one. And such a definition was indispensable to Plato; there would be an end of any participation of things in Ideas, as well as of any combination of concepts, if these were to be regarded as Unity without Difference.[91] This, then,

[90] There is no objection to Ribbing's view (Plat. Ideenl. 1. 336), that every Idea is 'also a concrete existence,' allowing that 'concrete' here has its true meaning, not of sensible being or individual existence, but simply (as in Hegel, when he speaks of the concrete concept) of the universally Determined. On the other hand, I cannot see what Ribbing has to object from a historical point of view against my assertion that the Platonic Ideas are the universal, nor do I find any explanation in the detailed discussion of the matter, loc. cit. p 325 sq, 355 sq. By saying that the Ideas are the universal, we mean that every Idea contains that which occurs equally in several individual things; these individual things may be more or fewer, and the scope of the Ideas may be accordingly greater or less. It has already (p. 237 sq.) been incontrovertibly proved from Plato himself that this is the Platonic doctrine, nor indeed does Ribbing combat it, loc. cit. 374. It is, therefore, inconsistent of him to say (ibid.): 'Plato no more intended to define the universal by the Ideas than to define the individual as the really existing, he wished simply to show the necessity of a constant Being as separate from Becoming.' That the latter was his intention is beyond all doubt, but (as undeniably shown by his most definite explanations) he knew that this constant Being was only to be found in the universal existence of genera. He hypostasizes this universal; he attributes to it, as we shall find, even intelligence and life, and, generally, determinations which we are accustomed to attribute to individuals only. But we cannot say that he was still undecided as to its universality or not; we can only say that to him these determinations did not seem incompatible with the nature of that which is thought of in general concepts.

[91] Plato himself emphasizes this point of view. In the above-quoted passages of the Sophist he proves that the combination of concepts and the recognition of a Manifold in them are mutual conditions, and in the Philebus, loc. cit., he finds the key to the problem of the simple or unit-concept compre-

is the point at which the metaphysical doctrine of Plato most definitely diverges from that of the Eleatics, and shows that its concern is not the denial but the explanation of Actual existence (des Gegebenen).

The union in Ideas of the One and the Many was also expressed by describing the Ideas as numbers.[92] This view must have belonged to Plato's later development: it has no place in his writings. We can distinguish between his scientific and empirical treatment of numbers as well as of Mathematics in general;[93] but his pure Mathematics is primarily a preparatory stage of Dialectic, the numbers with which it has to do are not Ideal, but mathematical numbers; not identical with Ideas, but intermediate between them and the things of sense.[94] Side by side with numbers, the Ideas of numbers are also spoken of,[95] but only in the same sense that Ideas generally are opposed

hending the Many of the phenomenon, in the position that the actual includes unity and plurality, finiteness and infinity. In the Parmenides, too, after the speculations about the participation of things in the Ideas (130 E sq.), we find that dialectical discussion of which the last result is (vide p. 251) a progress from the pure Being of the Eleatics to the expanded and manifold Idea. More details on this point will be given later on.

[92] Cf. my Plat. Stud. p. 239 sq., 236 nt.; Trendelenburg, Plat de Id. et Numeris doctrina ex Arist. illustr. p. 71 sq., Comm. in Arist. de An. p. 232; Brandis, in Rhein. Mus. ii. (1828) 562 sq.: Gr. - Röm. Phil. ii. a. 315 sq.; Ravaisson, Essai sur la Métaphysique d'Aristote, i. 176 sq.; Schwegler and Bonitz, ad loc., Metaph. (xiii. 6 sq ; Susemihl, Genet. Entw. ii. 525 sq).

[93] See p. 216

[94] The so-called numbers in which (Phileb. 56 D), unlike units, as e.g. two armies or two oxen are numbered together, the $\dot{\alpha}\rho\iota\theta\mu o\grave{\iota}$ $\dot{o}\rho\alpha\tau\grave{\alpha}\ \mathring{\eta}\ \dot{\alpha}\pi\tau\grave{\alpha}\ \sigma\acute{\omega}\mu\alpha\tau\alpha\ \check{\epsilon}\chi o\nu\tau\epsilon s$ (Rep vii 525 D); the $\dot{\alpha}\rho\iota\theta\mu o\grave{\iota}\ \alpha\grave{\iota}\sigma\theta\eta\tau o\grave{\iota}$, as Arist. calls them, Metaph. i. 8, end ; xiv. 3, 1090 b. 36; cf. c. 5. 1092 b. 22 ($\dot{\alpha}\rho\ \sigma\omega\mu\alpha\tau\iota\kappa o\grave{\iota}$).

[95] Rep. v. 479 B, Phædo, 101 C.

to things: so that under the totality of Ideas, Ideas of numbers also appear,—not that Ideas in general are represented as numbers, or that all Ideas, as such, are at the same time denoted as being numbers. Aristotle likewise points out that the doctrine of Ideas was in its origin independent of the doctrine of numbers.[96] The germs only of Plato's later view may be perceived in some passages of the dialogues. The Philebus declares the Pythagorean doctrine of the universal Combination of the One and the Many, of the Limit and Unlimitedness, to be the keystone of Dialectic;[97] this dialogue, therefore, applies to concepts those laws which the Pythagoreans had demonstrated in numbers. Plato further[98] recognises in numbers and mathematical relations the connecting link between the Idea and the Phenomenon. Numbers represent the Ideas to us as the measure of the Corporeal and of that which is contained in Space: and if a symbolical expression had to be employed instead of a purely logical one, it was most obvious to express the Idea and its determinations in arithmetical formulæ. The actual blending of the two was first asserted by Aristotle. According to his representation, the Platonic Ideas are nothing but numbers,[99] and when Plato

[96] Metaph. xiii. 4, 1078 b. 9 : περὶ δὲ τῶν ἰδεῶν πρῶτον αὐτὴν τὴν κατὰ τὴν ἰδέαν δόξαν ἐπισκεπτέον, μηθὲν συνάπτοντας πρὸς τὴν τῶν ἀριθμῶν φύσιν, ἀλλ' ὡς ὑπέλαβον ἐξ ἀρχῆς οἱ πρῶτοι τὰς ἰδέας φήσαντες εἶναι.

[97] Vide p. 206, 92.

[98] As will be shown later on, in chap. vii.

[99] E.g. Metaph. i. 6, 987 b. 20 sq.; c 8, end; c. 9, 991 b. 9 sqq.; xiii. 6 sq Further details in the following note, and Plat. Stud 239. Theophrastus, Metaph. 313 Br. (Fragm. 12, 13, Wimm.), refers to the same form of the doctrine Πλάτων .. εἰς τὰς ἰδέας ἀνάπτων, ταύτας δ' εἰς τοὺς ἀριθμοὺς, ἐκ δὲ τούτων εἰς τὰς ἀρχάς.

said that things are what they are by reason of participation in Ideas, he only departed from the Pythagorean doctrine in distinguishing between mathematical and Ideal numbers,[100] and separating the latter, as to their existence, from things perceptible to sense.[101] The more exact distinction between the two kinds of numbers is this: that the mathematical consist of homogeneous unities, which can therefore be reckoned together, each with each, whereas with the Ideal numbers this is not the case:[102] consequently the former express merely quantitative, the latter, logical determinations. In the one, each number is like each in kind, and only different in quantity; whereas in the other, each is discriminated from each qualitatively. But a definite succession is also involved in the logical distinction of numbers. As the lower concepts are conditioned by the higher, the numbers corresponding to them must also be conditioned; those which express the most universal and fundamental Ideas must precede all others. The Ideal numbers have therefore, as distinguished from the mathematical, this specific characteristic,—that in them there is a Before and After;[103] that is, a fixed succession. Though this

---

[100] ἀριθμοὶ εἰδητικοί (Metaph. xiii. 9, 1086 a. 5, xiv. 2, 1088 b 34 c 3, 1090 b 35), ἀρ τῶν εἰδῶν (ibid. xiii. 7, 1081 a. 21, c. 8, 1083 b. 3; xiv. 3, 1090 b. 33), ἀρ. νοητοί (ibid. 1. 8, end), πρῶτοι ἀρ. (ibid. xiii. 6, 1080 b. 22. c. 7, 1081 a. 21 sqq.; xiv. 4, beginn.). The expression, i. 6, 987 b. 34, is questionable.

[101] Metaph. i 6; especially p. 987 a. 29 b. 22 sq.

[102] Aristotle expressly treats of this distinction, Metaph. xiii. 6-8; namely, c. 6, beginn. c. 8, 1083 a. 31 Cf. Plat. Stud. 240 sq

[103] In my Platonic studies, 243 sqq., I referred this expression with Trendelenburg to the mathematical numbers, and consequently agreed with his conjecture, that in Metaph. xiii. 6, 1080 b. 11 (οἱ μὲν ἀμφοτέρους φασὶν εἶναι τοὺς ἀριθμούς, τὸν μὲν ἔχοντα τὸ πρότερον

THE IDEAS AS NUMBERS. 257

form of doctrine was in great favour with the older Academy, and though much quibbling and scholastic

καὶ ὕστερον τὰς ἰδέας, τὸν δὲ μαθηματικὸν παρὰ τὰς ἰδέας) a μή has fallen out before ἔχοντα I must now, however, concede to Brandis, as Trendelenburg does, that this supposition is inadmissible, not merely because the manuscripts and commentators know nothing of it, but also because Priority and Posteriority are attributed to Ideal and not to mathematical number. In Metaph. xiii. 6, 1080 a. 16, from the premiss· τὸ μὲν πρῶτόν τι αὐτοῦ [τοῦ ἀριθμοῦ] τὸ δ' ἐχόμενον, ἕτερον ὂν τῷ εἴδει ἕκαστον, we get the conclusion. καὶ τοῦτο ἢ ἐπὶ τῶν μονάδων εὐθὺς ὑπάρχει καὶ ἔστιν ἀσύμβλητος ὁποιαοῦν μονὰς ὁποιαοῦν μόναδι; so that those numbers are heterogeneous (ἀσύμβλητοι), of which, on account of their diversity in concept, the one is earlier, the other later. So we find in c. 7, 1081 a. 17· if all units were heterogeneous, there could be not only no mathematical, but no Ideal number οὐ γὰρ ἔσται ἡ δυὰς πρώτη ... ἔπειτα οἱ ἑξῆς ἀριθμοί. Hence a Before and After is supposed in the Ideal numbers. This is still plainer in what follows, and Z. 35 sqq., where both times the μονάδες πρότεραι καὶ ὕστεραι are substituted for the μονάδες ἀσύμβλητοι (cf. also c. 8, 1083 a. 33) So too 1081 b. 28, where, in reference to the πρώτη δυὰς, &c., it is asked: τίνα τρόπον ἐκ προτέρων μονάδων καὶ ὑστέρων συγκεῖνται; further, p. 1082, a. 26 sq., is very clear, Aristotle objects, as against the Platonic theory of Ideal numbers, that not merely all whole numbers, but the parts of them as well, must

stand in the relation of Priority and Posteriority; that they must, therefore, be Ideas, and that an Idea must consequently be composed of several Ideas (e g. the Ideal Eight of two Ideal Fours). Further on, 1082 b. 19 sq., we read: if there is an ἀριθμὸς πρῶτος καὶ δεύτερος, then the units in the Three-by-itself cannot be homogeneous with those in the Two-by-itself (ἀδιάφοροι = σύμβλητοι), and c 8, 1083 a. 6, the supposition that the units of the Ideal numbers are heterogeneous (διάφοροι = ἀσύμβλητοι) is met by the question Whether they differ quantitatively or qualitatively, and whether, supposing the former to be the case, αἱ πρῶται μείζους ἢ ἐλάττους καὶ αἱ ὕστερον ἐπιδιδόασιν ἢ τοὐναντίον; Finally, p. 1083 b 32, it is inferred that, as unity is prior to duality, unity must (according to Platonic doctrine) be the Idea of duality. Here, then, the Ideas stand in the relation of Priority and Posteriority. From these passages it is clear that with Aristotle the πρότερον καὶ ὕστερον marks the peculiarity of the Ideal numbers, and at the same time some light is thrown on the meaning of that expression. That number is prior out of which another proceeds, the number two e.g is prior to the number four, four is prior to eight; for the Four proceeds from the Ideal Two and the δυὰς ἀόριστος, and from these the Eight proceeds (Metaph. xiii. 7, 1081 b 21, 1082; a. 33), only not (cf. Arist ibid.) κατὰ πρόσθεσιν, as if the Two were contained in the Four, but by γέννησις (what-

S

pedantry have been expended upon the relation of numbers to Ideas,[104] it can only have had a secondary impor-

ever may be the exact meaning of that mysterious phrase), so that one number has the other as its product. The Before and After, therefore, signifies the relation of the factor to the product, of the conditioning to the conditioned. In support of this interpretation Trendelenburg (Plat. de id. doct. p. 81) rightly refers to Metaph v. 11, 1019 a : τὰ μὲν δὴ οὕτω λέγεται πρότερα καὶ ὕστερα· τὰ δὲ κατὰ φύσιν καὶ οὐσίαν, ὅσα ἐνδέχεται εἶναι ἄνευ ἄλλων, ἐκεῖνα δὲ ἄνευ ἐκείνων, μή (cf. Phys. viii. 7, 260 b. 17; Eth. Eudem. ι. 8; Theophr. Metaph. ii. p. 308, 12 Br., where the ἀρχαί correspond to the πρότερα and τὰ ὑπὸ τὰς ἀρχὰς to the ὕστερα) ᾗ διαιρέσει ἐχρήσατο Πλάτων. Cf also Categ. c. 12: πρότερον ἑτέρου ἕτερον λέγεται τετραχῶς, πρῶτον μὲν καὶ κυριώτατα κατὰ χρόνον.. δεύτερον δὲ τὸ μὴ ἀντιστρέφον κατὰ τὴν τοῦ εἶναι ἀκολούθησιν, οἷον τὸ ἓν τῶν δύο πρότερον· δυοῖν μὲν γὰρ ὄντων ἀκολουθεῖ εὐθὺς τὸ ἓν εἶναι, ἑνὸς δὲ ὄντος οὐκ ἀναγκαῖον δύο εἶναι, &c. Plato, Parm 153 B· πάντων ἄρα τὸ ἓν πρῶτον γέγονε τῶν ἀριθμὸν ἐχόντων... πρῶτον δέ γε, οἶμαι, γεγονὸς πρότερον γέγονε, τὰ δὲ ἄλλα ὕστερον. The consideration which formerly made me doubtful of this, viz. that, according to Metaph. iii. 3, 999 a. 12, there is no Before or After in individuals (ἄτομα), I no longer consider of any importance. Though these are conditioned by some other individual thing, still in individual existences (into which the lowest concepts of species finally resolve themselves—and it is these alone which Aristotle is considering, cf. p. 998 b 14 sqq.) we find, not the relation of Conditioning to Conditioned, of, higher to lower concept, but a logical co-ordination. But how can this view of the Before and After be reconciled with the statement (Metaph. iii. 3, 999 a. 6, Eth. iv. 1, 4, 1096 a. 17; Eth. Eud. i 8, 1218 a.; cf. my Plat Stud. p 243 sq) that Plato and his school supposed no Ideas of things in which there is a Before and After? Against Brandis' expedient, of taking the πρότερον καὶ ὕστερον in these passages in a different sense to that of those previously quoted, viz. here, as signifying numerical, in Metaph. xiii. as signifying conceptual sequence, I must repeat my former objection (which Susemihl, loc. cit. ii 527, has not succeeded in refuting) that a technical expression like πρότερον καὶ ὕστερον used by the same writer in the same way and in analogous connection, cannot possibly have opposite meanings. Hitherto everything proves satisfactorily that the expression, 'Things in which there is a Before and an After,' was the standing denotation in the Platonic school for the peculiarity of certain numbers. How could this expression be used to signify the exactly opposite peculiarity of another class? The difficulty comes before us in another way. If we ask why no Ideas were presupposed of things in which there is a Before and an After, Aristotle answers: Because things which are separated in species,

tancein its bearing on Plato's original system,—otherwise more decided traces of it must have been somewhere

but at the same time stand in a definite relation of sequence, so that one of them is always first, another second, &c. cannot be reduced to any common concept. This reason is stated, Polit iii. 1, 1275 a 34 sqq. Δεῖ δὲ μὴ λανθάνειν, ὅτι τῶν πραγμάτων ἐν οἷς τὰ ὑποκείμενα διαφέρει τῷ εἴδει, καὶ τὸ μὲν αὐτῶν ἐστι πρῶτον τὸ δὲ δεύτερον τὸ δ' ἐχόμενον, ἢ τοπαράπαν οὐδέν ἐστιν, ᾗ τοιαῦτα, τὸ κοινόν, ἢ γλίσχρως. This is just the case in the constitutions of states: they are εἴδει διαφέρουσαι ἀλλήλων, at the same time, however, αἱ μὲν ὕστεραι αἱ δὲ πρότεραι; for the perverted are necessarily later than the good states, from the deterioration of which they take their rise. The question, therefore, cannot be answered according to the concept of the πολίτης by any adequate definition—no characteristic mark can be given which is applicable to all. On the same ground, Aristotle, Eth N. loc. cit., supports an objection against an Idea of the Good. The originators of the theory of Ideas, he says, οὐκ ἐποίουν ἰδέας ἐν οἷς τὸ πρότερον καὶ τὸ ὕστερον ἔλεγον, διόπερ οὐδὲ τῶν ἀριθμῶν ἰδέαν κατεσκεύαζον. Accordingly, they ought to suppose no Idea of the Good; for the Good occurs in all the categories; there is a Substantial Good (Divinity and Nous), a Qualitative, a Quantitative, a Relative Good, &c., the Substantial, however, precedes the Qualitative, &c.; the Good, therefore, falls under the determination of the Before and the After,

ὥστ' οὐκ ἂν εἴη κοινή τις ἐπὶ τούτων ἰδέα (or as it is put subsequently: δῆλον ὡς οὐκ ἂν εἴη κοινόν τι καθόλου καὶ ἕν). For the same reasons, numbers, if they stand as conceptually separate in the relation of the Before and the After, can be reduced to no common concept, and therefore to no Idea. But it is in this relation that the Ideal numbers stand, and the Ideal numbers only. There is consequently no Idea which includes them all in itself. Each is an Idea by itself (cf Metaph. vii. 11, 1036 b. 15, where the following statement is put in the mouth of the advocates of the doctrine of Ideas: ἔνια μὲν γὰρ εἶναι ταὐτὰ τὸ εἶδος καὶ οὗ τὸ εἶδος, οἷον δυάδα—the αὐτοδυὰς—καὶ τὸ εἶδος δυάδος), which includes in itself a plurality of homogeneous things (e g the Ideal duality, the αὐτοδυὰς, includes all mathematical dualities), but all of them together have no Idea above themselves, as they cannot be brought under a common concept. The Ideal two, three, four, &c, are specifically distinct; they are not coordinated as species in juxta-position, but are to be subordinated as prior and posterior, conditioning and conditioned, they therefore cannot be looked upon merely as separate expressions of one Idea, the Idea of number. Eth. Eud. i. 8, also contains a reference to the doctrine of Ideal numbers ἔτι ἐν ὅσοις ὑπάρχει τὸ πρότερον καὶ ὕστερον, οὐκ ἔστι κοινόν τι παρὰ ταῦτα καὶ τοῦτο χωριστόν· εἴη γὰρ ἄν τι τοῦ πρώτου πρότερον· πρότερον γὰρ τὸ

found in his works. The main point, to him, is the thought which underlies the doctrine of numbers—that,

κοινὸν καὶ χωριστὸν διὰ τὸ ἀναιρουμένου τοῦ κοινοῦ ἀναιρεῖσθαι τὸ πρῶτον. οἷον εἰ τὸ διπλάσιον πρῶτον τῶν πολλαπλασίων, οὐκ ἐνδέχεται τὸ πολλαπλάσιον τὸ κοινῇ κατηγορούμενον εἶναι χωριστόν. ἔσται γὰρ πον διπλασίου πρότερον, εἰ συμβαίνει τὸ κοινὸν εἶναι τὴν ἰδέαν. In the words, τὸ διπλάσιον, &c., Eudemus undoubtedly had in view the Platonic theory of the indefinite duad from which, through its connection with the unit, the πρώτη δυὰς must proceed as the first actual number (Metaph xiii. 7, 1081 a 14, 21, 1081 b. 1 sqq.). The only peculiarity is that in order to prove the impossibility of an Idea of that in which there is a Before and an After, he lays stress on the supposed separate existence of the Ideas. In Metaph iii. 3, this reference to the Platonic Ideal numbers appears to me to hold good; although Bonitz (Arist. Metaph. ii. 153 sq. 251), while agreeing generally with the above explanation, here and v. 11 (ibid.) denies it, with the concurrence of Bonghi (Metafisica d'Arist. 115 sq., 253 sq.) and Susemihl. Aristotle raises the question, whether the γένη or the ἐνυπάρχοντα (the material elements of things) are to be considered as ἀρχαί, and remarks among other objections to the first of these suppositions. ἔτι ἐν οἷς τὸ πρότερον καὶ ὕστερόν ἐστι, οὐχ οἷόν τε τὸ ἐπὶ τούτων εἶναί τι παρὰ ταῦτα. οἷον εἰ πρώτη τῶν ἀριθμῶν ἡ δυὰς, οὐκ ἔσται τις ἀριθμὸς παρὰ τὰ εἴδη τῶν ἀριθμῶν· ὁμοίως δὲ οὐδὲ σχῆμα παρὰ τὰ εἴδη τῶν σχημάτων. Still less, in any other cases, will the γένη be παρὰ τὰ εἴδη. τούτων γὰρ δοκεῖ μάλιστα εἶναι γένη. Moreover, of those cases ἔπον τὸ μὲν βέλτιον τὸ δὲ χεῖρον, there can be no γένος, for the better is always prior. Aristotle is speaking quite generally, but in the example that he quotes: οἷον εἰ πρώτη τῶν ἀριθμῶν ἡ δυὰς, he seems to have the πρῶτος δυὰς in his mind (Metaph. xiii. 7, 1081 a. 23 b. 4), which alone is qualified to be an example of that in which the Before and After is, this being supposed to exist only in the Ideal numbers However, the interpretation of these words is of no importance to the present question. I cannot agree with Susemihl, loc. cit., that 'neither Eudemus nor Aristotle would have expressly proved the impossibility of Ideas of the Ideal numhers, because the impossibility is self-evident.' It is not proved, either in Eth. Eud. i. 8. or Metaph iii. 3, that there are no Ideas of the Ideal numbers. In the former passage it is shown that there are no Ideas of the things in which the Before and After is, and the numbers are merely taken as an example, but not the only possible example. In the latter there is no proving at all; it is laid down as something acknowledged, and again illustrated by the numbers, only by way of example And it is far from being self-evident that there can be no . Ideas of Ideas; indeed, Aristotle Metaph i 9, 991 a 29 sq., xiii. 5, 1079 b 3, remarks that Ideas of Ideas are a necessary consequence of the doctrine of Ideas. Still less can I concede to Susemihl that my view

in Reality, Unity and Multiplicity must be organically combined.

Plato is opposed to the distinctionless Unity of the Eleatic Substance. He declares himself equally against its motionless Invariability: and here he is in collision with his friend Euclides, who at that time appears to have admitted the Plurality of Being, while he denied to it all motion and activity.[105] This view, says Plato, would make Being incognizable for us, and in itself lifeless and irrational. If we are to participate in Being, we must act upon it, or be acted upon by it: if we are to know Being, a capacity on its side of suffering ($\pi\acute{a}\sigma\chi\varepsilon\iota\nu$, the power of becoming known) must correspond to our faculty of knowledge. And suffering without motion is impossible.[106] If true

is inadmissible in the passage of Eth. iv. 1, 4. Susemihl thinks that, as the Good, an Idea of which the Idea of the Good is, is not itself this Idea, the numbers of which Plato supposes no Idea, cannot themselves be the Ideal numbers. But because the separate kinds of the Good, which Plato reduces to one Idea, are not themselves Ideas, we can by no means infer that the numbers which he does not reduce to one Idea, are likewise not Ideas. However, in the comparison of the several kinds of Good with the several numbers, the point is not whether one or the other are Ideas or not, but only that in both the Before and the After is found. Aristotle says that whatever stands in the relation of the Before and the After, has, according to Plato, no Idea. But not merely do the numbers (as Plato supposes) stand in this relation, but also the several kinds of the Good. Therefore, there can no more be any Idea of these than, according to Plato, there can be of the numbers. This conclusion remains equally valid, whether Plato says of the Ideal or the mathematical numbers, that they stand in the relation of the Before and the After, and therefore can be reduced to no Idea.

[104] Particulars on this point below.

[105] Cf. Part i. p. 218 sq.

[106] Soph 248 A sqq.; Grote (Plato, ii 439 sqq.) has mistaken Plato's meaning in trying to prove that Plato here represents the Ideas as something relative—existing merely in relation to the knowing subject—and that he thereby returns to the theory of Protagoras, refuted in the Theætetus Plato does not say that the existence of the Ideas is conditioned by our knowledge of them;

Existence is not to be without mind and reason, it must also have life, soul, and motion.[107] We cannot deny to it all permanence of Being, if knowledge is to be possible; yet we must not conceive it as absolutely unmoved,[108] but as possessing reason, life, and energy. The concept of Being must be reduced to that of Power.[109] Ideas are described as something 'energetic.'

what he asserts is merely that the Ideas, among other attributes, have the attribute of being known by us. If we follow Grote we must suppose that in speaking of a knowledge of the Absolute or of the deity, we are at the same time making them into relatives of some sort.

[107] Loc. cit. 248 E sq.: Τί δὲ πρὸς Διός; ὡς ἀληθῶς κίνησιν καὶ ζωὴν καὶ ψυχὴν καὶ φρόνησιν ἢ ῥᾳδίως πεισθησόμεθα τῷ παντελῶς ὄντι μὴ παρεῖναι, μηδὲ ζῆν αὐτὸ μηδὲ φρονεῖν, ἀλλὰ σεμνὸν καὶ ἅγιον, νοῦν οὐκ ἔχον, ἀκίνητον ἑστὸς εἶναι;—Δεινὸν μέντ' ἂν, ὦ ξένε, λόγον συγχωροῖμεν.—'Αλλὰ νοῦν μὲν ἔχειν, ζωὴν δὲ μὴ φῶμεν;—Καὶ πῶς;—'Αλλὰ ταῦτα μὲν ἀμφότερα ἔνοντ' αὐτῷ λέγομεν, οὐ μὴν ἐν ψυχῇ γε φήσομεν αὐτὸ ἔχειν αὐτά; καὶ τίν' ἂν ἕτερον ἔχοι τρόπον;—'Αλλὰ δῆτα νοῦν μὲν καὶ ζωὴν καὶ ψυχὴν ἀκίνητον μέντοι τὸ παράπαν ἔμψυχον ὂν ἑστάναι;—Πάντα ἔμοιγε ἄλογα ταῦτ' εἶναι φαίνεται. It is impossible to understand this passage as Hermann does, viz. that intellect and motion are declared to be *a* true Being, but are not attributed to *all* true Being.

[108] Loc. cit. 249 B sq.: ξυμβαίνει δ' οὖν, ὦ Θεαίτητε, ἀκινήτων τε ὄντων νοῦν μηδενὶ περὶ μηδενὸς εἶναι μηδαμοῦ . . τῷ δὴ φιλοσόφῳ . πᾶσα, ὡς ἔοικεν, ἀνάγκη διὰ ταῦτα, μήτε τῶν ἓν ἢ καὶ τὰ πολλὰ εἴδη λεγόντων τὸ πᾶν ἑστηκὸς ἀποδέχεσθαι, κ.τ.λ.

[109] Loc. cit. 247 D Plato meets the Materialists with the fundamental position: λέγω δὴ τὸ καὶ ὁποιανοῦν κεκτημένον δύναμιν εἴτ' εἰς τὸ ποιεῖν ἕτερον ὁτιοῦν πεφυκὸς εἴτ' εἰς τὸ παθεῖν καὶ σμικρότατον ὑπὸ τοῦ φαυλοτάτου, κἂν εἰ μόνον εἰσάπαξ, πᾶν τοῦτο ὄντως εἶναι · τίθεμαι γὰρ ὅρον ὁρίζειν τὰ ὄντα, ὡς ἔστιν οὐκ ἄλλο τι πλὴν δύναμις. Even this position, we are told, 248 C. is not conceded by the Megarians, because doing and suffering belong merely to Becoming, and as the above instances will hold good on the other side, the determination that the existent is nothing else than δύναμις, is proved quite generally of all that is real and actual. I cannot agree with Deuschle (Plat. Sprach. phil. 35) that we are to understand by δύναμις not power, but possibility of entering into relation with anything else. In the first place we can scarcely believe that Plato defined the ὄντως ὂν by the concept of possibility, the very concept to which Aristotle reduces the Platonic μὴ ὄν, Matter. Again, no single passage is to be found in Plato where δύναμις signifies mere possibility; it invariably means power or ability wherever it stands in a connec-

THE IDEAS AS POWERS. 263

in the Phædo, where they are made the proper and only efficient causes of things;[110] and still more definitely

tion analogous to that under discussion. Finally, Plato himself explains unmistakably what meaning he attached to the expression, in Rep. v. 477 C: φήσομεν δυνάμεις γένος τι τῶν ὄντων, αἷς δὴ καὶ ἡμεῖς δυνάμεθα ἃ δυνάμεθα καὶ ἄλλο τῶν ὅ τι περ ἂν δύνηται, οἷον λέγω ὄψιν καὶ ἀκοήν, etc. Each of these δυνάμεις is something colourless and shapeless, generally speaking something not an object of sense, only known in its operations, i.e. in a word, *power*. Stumpf, again (Verh. d. plat. Got. z. Idee d. Guten. 19, 30) asserts that Plato nowhere calls the Ideas efficient and operative causes; that Soph. 248, D sq. he attributes to them merely the passive motion of becoming known, not the faculty of putting something else in motion. This latter passage is quite irrelevant: for though Plato proves that the Ideas, in so far as they are known, suffer or are passive and therefore also moved, they are not excluded from the possibility of having active as well as passive faculties. Stumpf, in order to support his view (to say nothing of the passages which I quote from the Republic and the Philebus), is obliged to pervert the perfectly clear enunciation of the Phædo (quoted in the following note) and the definite statement of Aristotle: while with regard to the Sophist he has to maintain that soul is attributed to the Ideas only 'in a broad sense,'—as having self-movement, but not the faculty of operating on anything else. But even this self-movement is an activity, and presupposes an active power.

[110] 95 E, Socrates passes on to speak of the doctrine of Ideas with the remark: we have now περὶ γενέσεως καὶ φθορᾶς τὴν αἰτίαν διαπραγματεύσασθαι. In his youth he had been addicted to natural philosophy, to searching out the causes of things, διὰ τί γίγνεται ἕκαστον καὶ διὰ τί ἀπόλλυται καὶ διὰ τί ἔστι; he gave it up, however, without having attained any satisfaction. Hence he was all the more sanguine about the Nous of Anaxagoras. As a cosmoplastic Mind must adjust everything for the best, he had hoped to hear from Anaxagoras the final cause of all things. In this hope, however, he was miserably deceived; instead of intellectual causes Anaxagoras had only mentioned material causes. But in reality these are merely the indispensable means (ἐκεῖνο ἄνευ οὗ τὸ αἴτιον οὐκ ἄν ποτ' εἴη αἴτιον): the actual and only operative causes are the final causes (τὴν δὲ τοῦ ὡς οἷόν τε βέλτιστα [-ον] αὐτὰ [he is speaking of the heavenly bodies] τεθῆναι δύναμιν οὕτω νῦν κεῖσθαι, ταύτην οὔτε ζητοῦσιν οὔτε τινα οἴονται δαιμονίαν ἰσχὺν ἔχειν . . . καὶ ὡς ἀληθῶς τἀγαθὸν καὶ δέον ξυνδεῖν καὶ ξυνέχειν οὐδὲν οἴονται, 99 B). As then no one has proved these causes to be in things, he has himself looked for them in the Ideas, and so supposes that it is the presence of the Idea (the καλὸν αὐτό, etc.) of anything which makes a thing what it is. In the whole of this explanation not merely is there no distinction drawn between the

in the Philebus, where Plato ascribes to the highest cause (by which we can only understand Ideas),[111]

conceptual, the efficient, and the final cause, but all three are clearly enunciated as one and the same. The Ideas, or, in Aristotelian terminology, the conceptual or formal causes, are to do just what Plato sought for in vain in Anaxagoras, viz to bring out the ἄριστον and βέλτιστον; they coincide with the final causes. Plato declares his unwillingness to have anything to do with any other causes besides these (100, D: τὰ μὴν ἄλλα χαίρειν ἐῶ, ταράττομαι γὰρ ἐν τοῖς ἄλλοις πᾶσι, τοῦτο δὲ ἁπλῶς καὶ ἀτέχνως καὶ ἴσως εὐήθως ἔχω παρ' ἐμαυτῷ ὅτι οὐκ ἄλλο τι ποιεῖ [that which is beautiful] καλὸν ἢ ἡ ἐκείνου τοῦ καλοῦ εἴτε παρουσία εἴτε κοινωνία εἴτε ὅπῃ δὴ καὶ ὅπως προσγενομένη· οὐ γὰρ ἔτι τοῦτο διϊσχυρίζομαι, ἀλλ' ὅτι τῷ καλῷ πάντα τὰ καλὰ γίγνεται καλά). They are sufficient for him, nor does he find any further principle necessary; they are, as Aristotle says, in the passages quoted, p. 398, 1, on the occasion of the passage before us, καὶ τοῦ εἶναι καὶ τοῦ γίγνεσθαι αἴτια, αἴτια καὶ γενέσεως καὶ φθορᾶς.

[111] Plato (Philebus, 23 C sqq.; cf 16 C) makes a fourfold division: the Finite, the Infinite, the Compound of the two, and the Cause of the Compound. He goes on to describe the Infinite in such a way that we can only understand by it the so-called Platonic Matter. By the Compound of the two he means the world of sense, in so far as it is ordered by definite proportions, the γένεσις εἰς οὐσίαν ἐκ τῶν μετὰ τοῦ πέρατος ἀπειργασμένων μέτρων. Brandis (gr.-rom. Phil. ii. a. 332), Steinhart (Pl. W. iv. 641), Susemihl (Genet Entw. ii. 13), and Rettig (Αἰτία in the Philebus, &c. Bern. 1866, p. 18 sq) refer the Finite to the Idea, the fourth principle, the Cause, must, they think, signify the Divinity—either as identical with the Idea of the Good, or (as Rettig would have it) the creator of this and all other Ideas But with regard to the first of these suppositions: Would Plato, who otherwise always opposes the Ideal world, as a whole, to the phenomenal world, have made in this one case such a total distinction between the highest Idea and the derivative Ideas, as to place them in two quite separate classes, and to parallel the distinction between them by that between Idea and phenomenon? If, on the other hand, we understand by αἰτία the Divinity as the creator of Ideas distinct and separate from the Idea of the Good, this view is not only opposed by all the reasons (to be discussed later on) which favour the actual equalisation of the Good and the Divinity, but also obliges us to refer the Good to the sphere of the πέρας, whereas, acc. to Rep. vi. 508 E sqq, it is elevated above all being and knowledge as the αἰτία ἐπιστήμης καὶ ἀληθείας. In the Philebus (64 C sqq.) it is clearly described as the Cause of the Compound; even a product of the good, νοῦς and ἐπιστήμη, (28 C sqq.; 31 A) is classed with the αἰτία And Plato's de-

reason and wisdom ; and thence deduces the adaptation of means to ends in the economy of the universe.[112]

scription of the πέρας is not at all suitable to the Ideas. To the finite (p. 25 A, D) must belong everything which does not admit (δέχεσθαι) of more or less, but only of the opposite determinations, πρῶτον μὲν τὸ ἴσον καὶ ἰσότητα, μετὰ δὲ τὸ ἴσον τὸ διπλάσιον καὶ πᾶν ὅτι περ ἂν πρὸς ἀριθμὸν ἀριθμὸς ἢ μέτρον ἢ πρὸς μέτρον, that is to say, everything which is capable of exact numerical and metrical determination The sphere of mathematical relations is thus clearly denoted by what would be a very imperfect description of the Ideal world. The field of the Ideas is in no way limited to numerical and metrical determinations. And it is improbable that this point of view is emphasised 'merely in opposition to the ἄπειρον without excluding the other determinations of the Ideas' (Brandis, loc. cit.), because Plato clearly intends to give an accurate and universally valid enunciation of what we are to think of under the different principles. Further, as νοῦς and ἐπιστήμη are reckoned not under the πέρας, but under the fourth principle, the αἰτία (v. sup.) and as according to a well-known fundamental principle of Plato's (supra, p. 225 sq) the value and truth of knowledge depend on the nature of its object, the Ideas, (which are the highest object of contemplation for νοῦς, and through the possession of which knowledge as such originates), cannot be placed a degree lower, in the sphere of the πέρας. Finally, 27 D sqq., the preference is given to the composite life of pleasure and knowledge, because it belongs to the τρίτον γένος, ξυμπάντων τῶν ἀπείρων ὑπὸ τοῦ πέρατος δεδεμένων This preference of the compound to the πέρας will not harmonise with the supposition, that we are to think of the Ideas under the latter principle The fact that Plato elsewhere (Phædo, 74 A sqq., 78 D, 100 D sq.; Rep. v. 479 A sqq) makes use of the Equal, the Double, &c , as examples to elucidate the distinction between the Idea and the things in which the Idea occurs (Rettig, p. 15), is irrelevant; in similar passages he makes use of other Ideas (the Just, the Beautiful, the Great, the Small, &c), in a similar way; this has nothing to do with the present question. Rettig is also wrong in saying (p. 19) that 'the πέρας cannot signify the mathematical πέρας, for the πέρας, according to 23 E, has different kinds, whereas quantity alone cannot establish differences of kind.' The latter statement is signally mistaken: the πέρας in numbers is different from that in figures, and that in tones or movements is different again. Plato says, 23 E, 26 C, sq., not that the Infinite and the Finite, but that the Infinite and the Mixed, are split up and divided in many ways, whereas τό γε πέρας οὔτε πολλὰ εἶχεν, οὔτ' ἐδυσκολαίνομεν ὡς οὐκ ἦν ἓν φύσει. Rettig (p 16),—to quote one only of the many passages which he brings against me,—represents the well-known place in Aristox. Harm. El. 11, 30 Meib. (subter, note 166)

We shall also find that the Idea of the Good is at the same time the highest efficient cause, the infinite Reason; and Aristotle, as we see from his writings,

as being on his side, because the πέρας here is put in the same position as, according to Plato's expositions elsewhere, is held by Dialectic or the doctrine of Ideas I cannot, however, see how he understands the words: καὶ τὸ πέρας ὅτι ἀγαθόν ἐστιν ἕν τὸ πέρας is evidently adverbial, and means 'finally;' but Rettig seems to have considered it to be the subject of a sentence which in this connection would go thoroughly against the sense I cannot give up the view which I endeavoured to establish in my Plat. Stud. 248 sqq., and with which in the meanwhile others have agreed (e g. Siebeck Unters. z. Phil. d. Gr. 89 sqq ; Schneider, d mat. Princ. d. plat. Phil. 14), viz that it is not the πέρας but the αἴτιον, which in the passage before us fills the place otherwise occupied by the Ideas. If this is described as the world-creating intellect, it merely shows that to Plato νοῦς and the Idea coincide in the latter reference; and the two positions, —'everything is the work of intellect (νοῦς),' and 'everything is what it is through the Idea,' mean the same This is seen unmistakably in the enunciations of the Phædo, noticed above. My view at once clears up Schaarschmidt's objection against the Philebus (Samml. d plat. Schr. 294 sqq.) that there is no reference in it to the Ideas. He objects further that a mixture of the Finite and the Infinite is impossible, because the πέρας would be destroyed by the entrance of the ἄπειρον. This objection arises from a misunderstanding the Philebus says (loc. cit.) that the ἄπειρον admits of the More and Less, &c., the πέρας, on the contrary, only admits of the opposite (cf ou this meaning of δέχεσθαι Tim. 52 A). As to the assertion that the Finite and the Infinite cannot exist together in things, Plato states the exact contrary (supra, p. 206, 92) Finally, Schaarschmidt (ibid. 295) would find in the expression γένος used for the ἄπειρον, &c , not merely a departure from Platonic usage, but a proof that 'these are, to the author of the dialogue, not world-forming Powers but only subjective pictures of Thought.' He is satisfactorily answered by Schneider (loc. cit p. 4), who refers to Tim. 48 E sq ; 50 C , 52 A.

[112] The αἰτία, which, p. 26 E sqq., is also called the ποιοῦν or δημιουργοῦν, is described p. 30 A sqq, as κοσμοῦσα τε καὶ συντάττουσα ἐνιαυτούς τε καὶ ὥρας καὶ μῆνας, σοφία καὶ νοῦς λεγομένη δικαιότατ' ἄν. (It has been already shown, 28 C sqq ; cf. 22 C, that νοῦς adjusted the world and still regulates it) It is in all things, it invests us with the soul, which (as Socrates said, Xen. Mem. i. 4, 8) must have its origin from the soul of the universe, just as our body from the body of the universe, and from it springs all knowledge; through it the universe itself is endowed with its soul and intellect, 30 D . οὐκοῦν

knew of no efficient cause as held by his master above and beside Ideas.[113] We cannot doubt that Plato meant to set forth in Ideas not merely the archetypes and essence of all true Existence, but energetic powers; that he regarded them as living and active, intelligent and reasonable. Nor is this view prejudiced by his distinguishing, in mythical or popular language, the efficient cause from Ideas.[114] This is a necessary

ἐν μὲν τῇ τοῦ Διὸς ἐρεῖς φύσει βασιλικὴν μὲν ψυχὴν βασιλικὸν δὲ νοῦν ἐγγίγνεσθαι διὰ τὴν τῆς αἰτίας δύναμιν, ἐν δὲ ἄλλοις ἄλλα καλά. Cf. subter, note 172

[113] Aristotle frequently objects to the doctrine of Ideas, that it wants an efficient principle. E.g. Gen. et Corr. ii. 9, 335 b 7 sqq · generation and decay presuppose matter and form, δεῖ δὲ προσεῖναι καὶ τὴν τρίτην, ἣν ἅπαντες μὲν ὀνειρώττυυσι, λέγει δ' οὐδείς, ἀλλ' οἱ μὲν ἱκανὴν ᾠήθησαν αἰτίαν εἶναι πρὸς τὸ γίνεσθαι τὴν τῶν εἰδῶν φύσιν, ὥσπερ ὁ ἐν Φαίδωνι Σωκράτης, &c. Metaph. i 9, 991 a 19 sq. (xiii. 5, 1079 b. 23): the Ideas cannot be the causes of things: τὸ δὲ λέγειν παραδείγματα αὐτὰ εἶναι καὶ μετέχειν αὐτῶν τἆλλα κενολογεῖν ἐστι καὶ μεταφορὰς λέγειν ποιητικάς. τί γάρ ἐστι τὸ ἐργαζόμενον πρὸς τὰς ἰδέας ἀποβλέπον; Ibid 992 a. 24 sqq.; viii. 6, 1045 b. 7; xii. 6, 1071 b 14. It is remarkable that Aristotle here takes no notice of the explanation of the Timæus —probably because he attached no scientific value to it, owing to its mystical character And his expressions make it highly probable that Plato in his oral discourses never mentioned special efficient causes in conjunction with the Ideas. Cf. p. 76 on this point.

[114] Plato, as is well known, often speaks of the Divinity and its activity in the world, he calls God the author of all good and of good only (Rep. ii. 379 A sqq.); he says that all things, lifeless and living, must have been produced by God, and not by a blind and unconscious power of nature (Soph. 265 C; cf. Phileb. 28 C sqq); he extols the care of the Divinity or of the gods for mankind, the righteousness of the divine government of the world (Phædo, 62 B, D, Rep. x. 612 E sq.; Laws, x. 899 D sqq , iv. 715 E. &c.); he says that to imitate God is the highest object for mankind (Theæt. 176 B and further below). Such popular expressions, however, cannot prove much; his scientific conception of the Divinity is the really important thing Is the Divinity actually a second cause together with the Idea, or merely another expression for the causality of the Idea? The fact of God being called the author of the Ideas is of little weight, as has been shown p. 245. The explanation of the Timæus, which makes

result of the system: if Ideas are the only true and primary Reality, an equally primary efficient cause beside and together with themselves is impossible. They are the efficient principle that imparts Being to things, and as this Being is of a kind that can only be explained by Reason working to an end, Reason must be conceded to them. This position was certainly open to criticism. It was a difficult problem to conceive classes as self-existent substances; but it was far more difficult to endow these unchangeable entities with motion, life, and thought; to suppose them as moved, and yet as invariable and not subject to Becoming;[115] as powers, in spite of their absoluteness, operating in things. The soul which Plato in the Sophist attributes to pure Being, he afterwards places midway between the world of Sense and the world of

the world-creator build up the universe on the pattern of the Ideas, is, as we shall find later on, so mystical in all its parts that no dogmatic conclusions can be drawn from it. Phædr. 247 D, where θεὸς is merely *a* god, proves nothing, and Parm. 134 C sqq. not much more

[115] Deuschle has very rightly (Jahn's Jahrbb. B. lxxi. p. 176 sq.) called attention to a difficulty involved in the question how the ideas can partake in Motion without partaking in Becoming, and how the soul can be that which is absolutely moved and at the same time have an eternal nature. This question, as Deuschle rightly recognises, is to be answered by the fact that with Plato the Idea of motion is superior to that of Becoming, and that therefore all Becoming is to be considered as a motion, but not every motion as a Becoming. If Plato in isolated passages (Theæt. 181 C sq.; Parm. 138 B, where ἀλλοίωσις and φορὰ are separated as two distinct kinds of motion) assumes a concept of motion which is not applicable to the Ideas at all, and only improperly to the soul, we must be content to make allowance for a mere inaccuracy which might easily have been corrected by a more exact determination. The actual difficulty, however, of imagining motion without change, is not removed.

THE IDEAS AS POWERS.

Ideas. So far, however, as the two points of view came into collision, the dynamical aspect must necessarily, with Plato, have been overpowered by the ontological. His whole philosophy is from the outset directed far less to the explanation of Becoming, than to the consideration of Being; the concepts hypostasized in the Ideas represent to us primarily that which is permanent in the vicissitude of phenomena, not the causes of that vicissitude. If Plato conceives them as living powers, this is only a concession forced from him by the facts of natural and spiritual life. But it is antagonistic to the main current of his system, and cannot be harmonized with his other theories respecting Ideas. We can easily understand how in his attempt at a comprehensive establishment of his doctrine of Ideas, this thought was not excluded. Such a determination naturally resulted from the universal presuppositions of that doctrine; and we therefore find traces of it, as has been shown, in other dialogues besides the Sophist.[116] But the difficulties

[116] Schaarschmidt, loc cit. 204 sq., sees in the above-mentioned discussion a distinct proof for the spuriousness of the Sophist. But this is only taking one side of the case into consideration. It is of course a contradiction to attribute motion, life, &c. to the Ideas, and at the same time (as in the passage mentioned, p. 241 sq) to assert that they are capable of no change whatever But it is a contradiction, in which Plato must have become involved as soon as ever he tried to reconcile the two fundamental determinations of his doctrine of Ideas,—viz. that the Ideas on the one hand do not come into contact with the mutability, partiality. and incompleteness of sensible Being, while on the other hand they are the only original reality and the only source of all reality for derivative Being. It is just the same as with the theological problem, which has so often involved the greatest thinkers in flagrant contradictions, — the problem how to imagine the Divinity as at once a creative in-

270 PLATO AND THE OLDER ACADEMY.

which it involved were too great to allow of much progress in this direction.[117] Although, therefore, the necessity of regarding Ideas not only as archetypes, but as efficient causes, was constantly obtruding itself

telligence and an absolute existence elevated above all incompleteness and mutability. The contradiction in the Platonic expressions is not to be denied, but we cannot say how Plato should have undertaken to escape from the contradiction on his own presuppositions Its occurrence, however, does not justify the denial of a Platonic origin to a dialogue which shows such obvious traces of Plato's genius, and which has such distinct Aristotelian and even (indirectly) Platonic evidence in its favour. In Rep. vii. 529 D, Plato speaks of the φοραὶ ἃs τὸ ὂν τάχος καὶ ἡ οὖσα βραδυτὴs φέρεται. It would not follow that all other Ideas are moved even if the ὂν τάχος were the Idea of swiftness; but it does follow that Plato did not think motion incompatible with the immutability of the ὄν. He has, moreover (as Peipers, Philol xxix 4, 711 sq., rightly observes), attributed motion to νοῦs (Tim. 47 B; 89 A; 34 A; 77 B; Symp. x 897 C, 898 A), though he could not have meant either of the motions described in the preceding note, or have considered νοῦs to be moved in the sense in which things of sense are, in opposition to the Ideas. What we are really to understand by this motion of νοῦs he does not tell us. We must, after all, credit Plato with the remarkable and unde- niably false argument 248 C, sq. (if οὐσία is known, it πάσχει, for if knowing is a ποιεῖν, becoming known is a πάσχειν), just as much as with many other difficulties in his writings; e.g. the dictum that we cannot imagine a μὴ ὂν (Theæt. 189 A; Rep. i. 478 B; Soph. 240 D sq.), or the argument Rep. i. 349 B sqq, which turns on the ambiguous meaning of πλέον ἔχειν, the derivation of the elements Tim. 31 B sq, and the like.

[117] In this point seems to lie the explanation of the fact that the predicates, which Plato lays claim to for them, are not attributed to the Ideas with such definiteness in any other dialogue. This exposition does not show us the latest form of the Platonic doctrine of ideas, as Ueberweg thinks (Unters. plat. Schr. 275 sq.; vide p. 106, 41), but is one from which Plato so far subsequently departed as not to pursue the road here indicated any further without entirely giving up the movement and life (the efficient δύναμις) of the Ideas. In the latest form of the doctrine of Ideas known to us from the accounts of Aristotle this point of view recedes altogether. It has been already proved, p. 136 sq, that all evidence from other sources forbids our reckoning the Sophist amongst Plato's last works.

upon him, he could never really carry out this thought; he preferred to explain the phenomenal world by those mythical representations which poorly compensate for the gaps in the scientific development. So much the more productive, however, for Plato's system is the other determination, that Unity and Multiplicity are combined in the Ideas. This alone enabled him to set in the place of the abstract Eleatic One, the concrete unity of the Socratic concept; to join concepts dialectically, and to place them in a positive relation to phenomena, where only a negative relation had existed. The Plurality of the phenomenon is sustained and comprehended by the Unity of the Concept. Only because he acknowledges Plurality in the Unity of the Concept has he the right to maintain not only One Idea, but a multiplicity of logically co-articulated Ideas—a World of Ideas.

III. *The World of Ideas.*—Plato hardly ever speaks of the Idea, but always of Ideas in the plural.[118] However little he himself would have allowed us to say so,[119] the Ideas, arising out of the Socratic concepts, are, like them, abstracted from experience. They represent primarily a particular; and thought can only ascend step by step from this particular to the uni-

[118] As Ritter rightly remarks (Gott. Anz. 1840, 20, St. S. 188); only it does not follow from this that in explaining the Platonic doctrine we are not to speak of the Idea to express generally the concept connected with the word εἶδος or ἰδέα, as Aristotle does, e.g. Metaph xii. 4, 1079 b. 9. Plato himself speaks of τὸ εἶδος not only where (e g. Parm. 131 A; Phædo, 103 E) he is treating of a definite Idea, but also where he is treating of the concept of the εἶδος generally: Polit 263 B· cf.Symp. 210 B, Phædr 249 B

[119] Cf. on this point, p. 228.

versal, from the lower concepts to the higher. But the concepts being hypostasized, the particular in them cannot be so cancelled in the universal that collective concepts shall at last be reduced to one Highest principle, or several such, and, according to their whole contents, be derived from these principles, as moments of their logical development. Each concept is something absolutely self-subsistent; and, the reciprocal interdependence of concepts (like the interconnection of concepts with phenomena, to be considered presently) has only the form of participation and communion.[120] Plato's design does not extend to a purely *à priori* construction; it only embraces a complete logical arrangement of the Ideas which he himself has found by means of induction, or, if we prefer the expression, by means of Recollection, developing itself in the region of Sense.[121]

Of these Ideas there is an indefinite number.[122] Since every generic and specific concept is, according to Plato, something substantial,—an Idea,—there must be as many Ideas as there are Genera and Species.[123] And since Ideas alone are the Real by virtue of which all things are what they are, there can be nothing, and there can be imagined nothing, of which there is no Idea. Such a thing would be altogether non-existent, and that which is absolutely non-existent cannot be conceived.[124] It seems therefore to Plato a culpable

---

[120] Supra, p. 249 sq.
[121] Cf. p. 204 sqq.
[122] Arist Metaph. i. 9, init : οἱ δὲ τὰς ἰδέας αἰτίας τιθέμενοι πρῶτον μὲν ζητοῦντες τωνδὶ τῶν ὄντων λάβειν τὰς αἰτίας ἕτερα τούτοις ἴσα τὸν ἀριθμὸν ἐκόμισαν, &c.
[123] Supra, p. 237, sq.
[124] Supra, p. 225, sq.

want of philosophic maturity, that there should be any hesitation in assigning Ideas even to the very meanest things.[125] He himself reduces to their Ideas not only those things which are great and perfect, but also the smallest and most worthless: not only natural objects but artistic productions; not only substances, but mere conceptions of quality and relation; activities and ways of life, mathematical figures and grammatical forms. He recognises Ideas of hair and of dirt, of the table and of the bed, of Greatness and of Smallness, of Likeness and Unlikeness, of the Double, &c.; an Idea of the noun, even Ideas of Non-Being and of that which is in its nature the direct contradictory of the Idea, Evil and Vice.[126] In a word, there is absolutely nothing which

---

[125] In the well-known passage Parm. 130 B sqq. After Socrates has spoken of the Ideas of Similarity, the One, the Many, Righteousness, Beauty, the Good, Parmenides asks him whether he supposes a self-subsisting Idea of man, or of fire or water, and then whether he supposes an idea of hairs, dirt, &c Socrates, already embarrassed by the first of these questions, thinks that he must answer the second in the negative. Parmenides, however, tells him by way of advice: νέος γὰρ εἶ ἔτι, ὦ Σώκρατες, καὶ οὔ πώ σου ἀντείληπται ἡ φιλοσοφία ὡς ἔτι ἀντιλήψεται κατ' ἐμὴν δόξαν, ὅτε οὐδὲν αὐτῶν ἀτιμάσεις· νῦν δὲ ἔτι πρὸς ἀνθρώπων ἀποβλέπεις δόξας διὰ τὴν ἡλικίαν

[126] The proofs, for the most part mentioned by Ritter, ii 302 sqq, are to be found in the following passages besides those just quoted: Tim. 51 B (the fire καθ' αὑτὸ, which is distinct from visible fires, the same holds good of the remaining elements); Rep. x. 596 A, 597 C sq. (the Idea of a bed, the κλίνη ὄντως οὖσα, ἐκείνη ὃ ἔστι κλίνη, the Idea of a table); Crat. 389 B (the Idea of a shuttle, αὐτὸ ὃ ἔστι κερκίς); Parm 133 C, D (the αὐτὸς δεσπότης, ὃ ἔστι δεσπότης and the αὐτὸς δοῦλος ὃ ἔστι δοῦλος), Phædo, 65 D (the δίκαιον, καλὸν, ἀγαθὸν αὐτὸ, the οὐσία of Health, Greatness, and Strength); ibid. 100 D sqq (the Beautiful καθ' αὑτὸ, Greatness, Smallness, Plurality, Unity, Duality, καθ' αὑτό); Rep. v. 479 A sq. (the Beautiful, the Just, the Double, the Great, the Small, the Heavy, the Light, καθ' αὑτὸ. In vii. 529 D, by the motions of actual swiftness and slowness in the actual numbers and the actual figures are meant, as the context shows, not the Ideas, but the intuitions of pure mathematics, which, however,

has not its Idea. Wherever a uniform Character of several phenomena can be proved to exist, the sphere

in this place are not distinguished clearly enough from the corresponding Ideas). Phileb. 62 A (αὐτῆς δικαιοσύνης ὅ τι ἔστι ... κύκλου καὶ σφαίρας αὐτῆς τῆς θείας); Phædr. 247 D (the αὐτὴ δικαιοσύνη, σωφροσύνη, ἐπιστήμη, the ἐν τῷ ὅ ἐστιν ὂν ὄντως ἐπιστήμη οὖσα); Crat. 389 D; 390 F (αὐτὸ ἐκεῖνο, ὃ ἔστιν ὄνομα . . τὸ τῇ φύσει ὂν ὄνομα); ibid. 423 E (the οὐσία of colour and sound); ibid. 386 D (all things, and consequently all activities, have an οὐσία βέβαιος); Theæt. 176 E (παραδειγμάτων ἐν τῷ ὄντι ἑστώτων, τοῦ μὲν θείου εὐδαιμονεστάτου, τοῦ δὲ ἀθέου ἀθλιωτάτου, cf. the παραδείγματα βίων, Rep. x. 617 D, 618 A, which of course taken by themselves would prove nothing on account of the mythical character of this exposition); Soph. 254 C sqq. (the most general εἶδη, the ὄν, στάσις, κίνησις, ταὐτὸν and θάτερον); ibid. 258 C (δεῖ θαρρύντα ἤδη λέγειν ὅτι τὸ μὴ ὂν βεβαίως ἔστι τὴν αὐτοῦ φύσιν ἔχον . . . ἐνάριθμον τῶν πολλῶν ὄντων εἶδος ἕν; cf. 254 D· τὸ μὴ ὂν . . . ὡς ἔστιν ὄντως μὴ ὄν); Rep v 476 A · καὶ περὶ δικαίου καὶ ἀδίκου καὶ ἀγαθοῦ καὶ κακοῦ καὶ πάντων τῶν εἰδῶν περὶ ὁ αὐτὸς λόγος, αὐτὸ μὲν ἓν ἕκαστον εἶναι, &c., cf. ibid. iii. 402 C: πρὶν ἂν τὰ τῆς σωφροσύνης εἴδη καὶ ἀνδρείας, &c , καὶ τὰ τούτων αὖ ἐναντία πανταχοῦ περιφερόμενα γνωρίζομεν, and Theæt. 186 A: to those things which the soul contemplates without the aid of sense, belong the ὅμοιον and the ἀνόμοιον, the ταὐτὸν and ἕτερον, the καλὸν καὶ αἰσχρὸν, the ἀγαθὸν καὶ κακόν. Susemihl (Genet. Entw.

ii. 197) would make out that not merely the Ideas of the bad, but also the Ideas of special virtues are simply a provisional supposition, because the latter only belong to appearance, and because the Ideas of the bad would be in direct contradiction to the doctrine that God is only the cause of the good. But Plato, as we see, supposed Ideas of many things which belong only to appearance ; and if the Ideas of the bad or of Non-being entangle us in contradiction, such a contradiction does not, any more than the other instances objected by Aristotle, justify us in departing from Plato's definite statements where the statements are supported by the consequences of Plato's doctrine. If there is an Idea corresponding to every concept, this must unavoidably hold good of the concepts of badness, Non-being, &c. The Idea of Being ought not to give us greater offence than any other. As Bonitz (plat. Stud. ii. 82) rightly remarks, reality as such (Being itself) does not belong to the essence of things represented in the Ideas, though Plato scarcely makes this distinction. According to his original supposition, there is an Idea corresponding to every general concept without exception. This Idea is the content of the concept, and one of the most general concepts is that of Being. Again Plato speaks of the μονάς (Phædo, 101 C), in which everything must participate in order to be one, although unity is given with the concept of the thing just as directly as Being. Bonitz

of Ideas extends. Only where that uniform character ceases, and the unity and permanence of the Concept fall asunder in the conceptless plurality and absolute unrest of Becoming,—the Ideal World finds its limit.[127] Plato seems subsequently to have become somewhat confused, as well he might, as to these deductions from his theory. According to Aristotle, he assumed no Ideas of things artificially made, nor of negation and relation;[128] but the original point of view was in

finds the Idea of Being explicable enough, but he does not think it was required by the consequences of the doctrine of Ideas Schaarschmidt (Samml. d. plat. Schr. 202) sees in it something which cannot be attributed to Plato, but which might just as well be maintained of the Ideas of the table, bed, βίος ἄθεος, unity, &c., and would actually be maintained, even if they occurred in the Sophist or Parmenides instead of the Republic, Phædo, and Theætetus

[127] That Plato did suppose such a limit, is clear from Phileb. 16 C sq, not to mention other passages, vide p. 206, 92. To this point Ritter. loc. cit, rightly refers Tim. 66 D: περὶ δὲ δὴ τὴν τῶν μυκτήρων δύναμιν εἴδη μὲν οὐκ ἔνι· τὸ γὰρ τῶν ὀσμῶν πᾶν ἡμιγενές, εἴδει δὲ οὐδενὶ ξυμβέβηκε ξυμμετρία πρὸς τό τινα σχεῖν ὀσμήν. Distinctions of kinds of smell are here denied, because smell always has to do with an incomplete and undetermined Becoming,—because it belongs, as is said in what follows, only to a transient moment.

[128] Metaph. xii. 3, 1070 a. 13 sqq.; in many things, as e.g. in artistic products, the form cannot exist except in conjunction with the matter; if this is at all possible, it is only met with in natural products: διὸ δὴ οὐ κακῶς ὁ Πλάτων ἔφη, ὅτι εἴδη ἐστὶν ὁπόσα φύσει (that there are just as many Ideas as there are kinds of natural products. The fact would remain the same even if Plato's name did not originally stand in the text, but was first introduced from Alexander, as Rose (Arist. libr. ord. 151) conjectures with great probability, for in any case Plato is meant). Ibid. 1, 9, 991 b 6 πολλὰ γίγνεται ἕτερα, οἷον οἰκία καὶ δακτύλιος, ὧν οὔ φαμεν εἴδη εἶναι. Ibid. 990 b 8 sqq., the evidences for the doctrine of Ideas are (1) not valid, (2) would lead to Ideas of things of which we (i.e. the Platonic schools—Aristotle in his criticism of the doctrines of Ideas is unintentionally communicative) presuppose no Ideas; κατά τε γὰρ τοὺς λόγους τοὺς ἐκ τῶν ἐπιστημῶν εἴδη ἔσται πάντων ὅσων ἐπιστῆμαί εἰσι (which was actually Plato's original intention, according to the above account), καὶ κατὰ τὸ ἓν ἐπὶ πολλῶν καὶ τῶν ἀποφάσεων ... ἔτι δὲ οἱ ἀκριβέστεροι τῶν λόγων οἱ μὲν τῶν πρός τι ποιοῦσιν

these cases abandoned. In this way many difficulties were evaded, but others arose in their place which were not less dangerous to his system.

Ideas, as we already know, are related to one another, not merely as a multiplicity, but more precisely, as parts of a whole. What holds good of concepts, must also hold good of the entities that are thought in concepts. They form a graduated series, descending in ordered coarticulation, and a sequence of natural subdivisions, from the highest Genera to the lowest Species, from the most universal to the most particular.[129] In all conceivable ways they cross, combine, exclude, or participate in, each other.[130] It is the task of science fully to represent this system, to rise from the particular to the most universal principles, to descend again from these to the particular, to define all middle terms that intervene, to ascertain all relations of concepts.[131] Plato did not aim at a purely dia-

ἰδέας, ὧν οὔ φαμεν εἶναι καθ' αὐτὸ γένος, &c (which, in spite of Ebben's objection, Plat. id. doct. p. 96 sq., can only mean . 'of which there can be no self-subsisting forms,' i.e. no Ideas). Ibid. Z. 27 (xiii. 4, 1079 a. 24) Xenocrates according to Proclus in Perm. 136, Cons. defined the Ideas as αἰτία παραδειγματικὴ τῶν κατὰ φύσιν ἀεὶ συνεστώτων. From this, as Proclus remarks, it would follow that there are no Ideas of the products of art or of things contrary to nature. A similar definition is attributed to Plato in the exposition of Platonic doctrine, ap. Diog. iii. 77, which is possibly throughout inauthentic. This view is common among the later Platonists and was then, naturally enough, attributed to Plato, cf. the scholia on the passage of the Metaph. and vol iii. (2nd edit.), z. 726 b. 470; 695; 723, 3, the references to Alcinous, Plotinus, Syrian, Proclus. Still, even Aristotle mentions (in speaking of Health in itself) the Idea of a mere concept of an attribute, Metaph. iii. 2, 997 b. 8: αὐτὸ γὰρ ἄνθρωπόν φασιν εἶναι καὶ ἵππον καὶ ὑγίειαν (they speak of an αὐτοάνθρωπος, &c.).

[129] Cf p. 204 sqq , and the quotations from Rep. vi. on pp. 168, 196.

[130] Vide p. 248 sq.

[131] Phileb. 16 C sqq.; Rep vi. 511 B; Soph. 253 B sqq.; vide pp. 196, 205.

THE WORLD OF IDEAS. 277

dectical construction; he argues rather from several given concepts;[132] yet he demands that by an exhaustive enumeration and comparison of the sum total of collective concepts, a science comprehending the whole world of Ideas shall be attained.

He himself, however, made but a small beginning in this direction.[133] He names as examples of universal concepts, Being and Non-being, Likeness and Unlikeness, Sameness and Difference, Unity and Number, Straightness and Crookedness.[134] He uses the categories of Quality,[135] of Quantity,[136] of Relation;[137] and according to Hermodorus,[138] distinguishes among the last

---

[132] So in the expositions which follow the idea of an immanent dialectic, Soph. 244 B sqq., Parm. 142 B sqq.; in both the separation of the One and the Existent is supposed, and further inferences are drawn from this supposition.

[133] Cf. on what follows, Trendelenburg, Hist. Beiträge zur Phil. 1 205 sqq.; Prantl, Gesch. der Logik, i. 73 sq.

[134] Theæt. 184 C. The discussions of the Parmenides, 137 sqq., are occupied with similar concepts, and a further series such as the concept of the Whole and the Parts, Motion and Rest, Finite and Infinite. Cf. my Plat. Stud. 169.

[135] Theæt. 182 A, where the expression ποιότης is brought in with an apology as something new, Rep iv 38 A sqq. (vide note 6), where a distinction is drawn between the ποιόν τι and the αὐτὸ ἕκαστον; Crat. 432 A sq, between qualitative and quantitative determinations (of number). Phileb. 37 C; Soph. 262 E.

[136] Soph. 245 D: every ὅλον is a ποσόν Phil 24 C sq. the More and Less, the σφόδρα and ἠρέμα, make the ποσόν (determined magnitude) impossible.

[137] Soph. 255 C τῶν ὄντων τὰ μὲν αὐτὰ καθ' αὑτά, τὰ δὲ πρὸς ἄλληλα ἀεὶ λέγεσθαι . . . τὸ δ' ἕτερον ἀεὶ πρὸς ἕτερον, &c. Rep. iv. 438 A: ὅσα γ' ἐστὶ τοιαῦτα οἷα εἶναί του, τὰ μὲν ποιὰ ἄττα ποιοῦ τινός ἐστιν, τὰ δ' αὐτὰ ἕκαστα αὐτοῦ ἑκάστου μόνον, Science e.g. proceeds on knowledge simply, definite science (ποιά τις ἐπιστήμη) on definite knowledge. Parm. 133 C, and the quotation from Hermodorus, p. 241, 47.

[138] In the passage apud Simpl. Phys 54 b just mentioned, after the words quoted pp. 214, 47, Hermodorus goes on to say . of that which is πρὸς ἕτερα, the one is ὡς πρὸς ἐναντία, the other ὡς πρός τι, καὶ τούτων τὰ μὲν ὡς ὡρισμένα, τὰ δὲ ὡς ἀόριστα. This latter distinction he explains in the words (which I quote at length, because I shall have to return to them later on). καὶ τὸ μὲν ὡς μέγα

several kinds. The distinction of the Absolute and Relative forms the logical groundwork of his whole system; for the Idea exists in and for itself; the Phenomenon, and to the fullest extent, Matter, only in relation to something else.[139] He further affirms that in all Reality, Unity and Multiplicity, Limit and Unlimitedness, Identity and Difference, Being and Non-being are combined.[140] He determines the concept of Being by the two characteristics of doing and suffering.[141] He instances in the Sophist,[142] Being, Rest, and Motion (to which Sameness and Difference are afterwards added), as the most important generic concepts; and, at the same time, determines which of these are compatible with, and which exclude, each other. He

πρὸς μικρὸν λεγόμενα πάντα ἔχειν (sc. λέγει Πλάτων) τὸ μᾶλλον καὶ τὸ ἧττον. ἔστι γὰρ μᾶλλον εἶναι μεῖζον καὶ ἔλαττον εἰς ἄπειρον φερόμενα. ὡσαύτως δὲ καὶ πλατύτερον καὶ στενότερον [στενώτ.], καὶ βαθύτερον [βαρυτ] καὶ κουφότερον, καὶ πάντα τὰ οὕτω λεγόμενα εἰς ἄπειρον. τὰ δὲ ὡς τὸ ἴσον καὶ τὸ μέσον καὶ ἡρμοσμένον λεγόμενα οὐκ ἔχειν τὸ μᾶλλον καὶ τὸ ἧττυν, τὰ δὲ ἐναντία τούτων ἔχειν. ἔστι γὰρ μᾶλλον ἄνισον ἀνίσου καὶ κινούμενον κινουμένου καὶ ἀνάρμοστον ἀναρμόστου. ὥστε ἀμφοτέρων αὐτῶν [αὐτῶν should either be excised or altered into τούτων] τῶν συζυγιῶν πάντα [perhaps κατὰ πάντα], πλὴν τοῦ ἑνὸς στοιχείου τὸ μᾶλλον καὶ ἧττον δεδεγμένον [-ων], ἄστακτον [ἄστατον] καὶ ἄπειρον καὶ ἄμορφον καὶ οὐκ ὂν τὸ τοιοῦτον λέγεσθαι κατὰ ἀπόφασιν τοῦ ὄντος. τῷ τοιούτῳ δὲ οὐ προσήκειν οὔτε ἀρχῆς οὔτε οὐσίας, ἀλλ' ἐν ἀκρισίᾳ τινὶ φέρεσθαι The last position (as that just quoted,

from Dercyllides) is again given with unimportant variations, p. 56. b : ὥστε ἄστατον καὶ ἄμυρφον καὶ ἄπειρον καὶ οὐκ ὂν τὸ τοιοῦτο λέγεσθαι κατὰ ἀπόφασιν τοῦ ὄντος τῷ τοιούτῳ δὲ οὐ προσήκει οὔτε ἀρχῆς οὔτε οὐσίας, ἀλλ' ἐν ἀκρασίᾳ (for which ἀκρισίᾳ is the better reading) τινὶ φέρεσθαι. Of the distinctions here made, that of the πρὸς ἕτερα into the πρὸς ἐναντία and the πρός τι, is not found in the Platonic writings, though this need not be any reason for mistrusting the statement of Hermodorus ; on the other hand, the opposition of ὡρισμένα and ἀόριστα together with a more detailed description of the latter is met with again lower down.

[139] Cf. p. 241, 47, and the quotations to be made later on as to the phænomenal world and matter.

[140] Vide p. 204 sq.; 249 sq.

[141] Vide p. 262, 109.

[142] 254 C sqq.: cf. supra. 249, sq.

THE WORLD OF IDEAS. 279

discriminates in the Republic [143] between the knowing subject and the thing known, Knowledge and Reality, Science and Being. But though in these and similar definitions [144] the germs of the Aristotelian theory of Categories are clearly discernible, yet in none of the specified places does Plato attempt a complete catalogue of the highest concepts or an arrangement of them according to their internal relation. This want would have been ill supplied by the numerical system, which, when the fusion of Ideas with the Pythagorean numbers had begun, he subsequently attempted by deriving numbers from Unity and indefinite Duality,[145] —even had this derivation been more fully accomplished than was actually the case.[146]

In designating the point in which the graduated series of Being terminates, Plato is more explicit. The highest of all Ideas is the Idea of the Good. As in the visible world, the sun brings forth simultaneously knowledge and life,—as he enlightens the eye

[143] Vi. 508 E sqq; vide p. 269, 116.

[144] E.g. Tim. 37 A, where Plut. (Procr. an. 23, 3, p 1023), sees the first sketch of the ten categories.

[145] Arist. Metaph. xiii. 7, 1081 a 14, 21 b. 17 sqq.; 31, 1082 a. 13 b 30, xiv. 3, 1091 a. 4, 1, 9, 990 b. 19: cf. my Plat. Stud. 220, sqq. 242. We shall have to speak of the ἀόριστος δυάς in treating of the doctrine of matter.

[146] According to Arist. ibid. xii. 8, 1073 a. 18; xiii. 8, 1084 a 12 Phys. iii 6, 206 b 32, it is in any case limited to the first ten numbers, and perhaps did not go so far, for Aristotle does not express himself quite clearly. Aristotle's objection (Metaph. xiv. 4, beginn.) against the supporters of the Ideal numbers, viz. that they do not derive the first odd number, seems to refer, as Bonitz ad loc. supposes, simply to the fact that they did not account for the origin of the first odd number, the unit, whereas (acc. to the passage before us and xiii. 7, 1081 a. 21) they did try to derive the first duality. And as the unit is the root of all odd numbers, what holds good of it holds good indirectly of the odd generally. According to Metaph. xiii. 7, the Platonic school regarded other odd numbers, for instance, three, as derived.

280   *PLATO AND THE OLDER ACADEMY.*

and reveals things seen, while everywhere causing growth and increase; so in the super-sensuous world, the Good is the source of Being and of Science, of Truth and of Knowledge: and as the sun is higher than light and the eye, so is the Good higher than Being and Science.[147] But this definition has its difficulties. In the whole treatment of the question in the Philebus, we can only understand by the Good the goal of human activity,—that which is the highest Good for men.[148] As there is an express reference to this dialogue in the passage above quoted from the Republic,[149] it might seem as if here, too, the Idea of

---

[147] Rep. vi. 508 E, after the digression about the sun: τοῦτο τοίνυν τὸ τὴν ἀλήθειαν (real existence, actuality) παρέχον τοῖς γιγνωσκομένοις, καὶ τῷ γιγνώσκοντι τὴν δύναμιν ἀποδιδὸν τὴν τοῦ ἀγαθοῦ ἰδέαν φάθι εἶναι αἰτίαν δ' ἐπιστήμης οὖσαν καὶ ἀληθείας, ὡς γιγνωσκομένης μὲν διανοοῦ, οὕτω δὲ καλῶν ἀμφοτέρων ὄντων, γνώσεώς τε καὶ ἀληθείας, ἄλλο καὶ κάλλιον ἔτι τούτων ἡγούμενος αὐτὸ ὀρθῶς ἡγήσει· ἐπιστήμην δὲ καὶ ἀλήθειαν, ὥσπερ ἐκεῖ φῶς τε καὶ ὄψιν ἡλιοειδῆ μὲν νομίζειν ὀρθόν, ἥλιον δὲ ἡγεῖσθαι οὐκ ὀρθῶς ἔχει, οὕτω καὶ ἐνταῦθα ἀγαθοειδῆ μὲν νομίζειν ταῦτ' ἀμφότερα ὀρθόν, ἀγαθὸν δὲ ἡγεῖσθαι ὁπότερον αὐτῶν οὐκ ὀρθόν, ἀλλ' ἔτι μειζόνως τιμητέον τὴν τοῦ ἀγαθοῦ ἕξιν . . .   καὶ τοῖς γιγνωσκομένοις τοίνυν μὴ μόνον τὸ γιγνώσκεσθαι φάναι ὑπὸ τοῦ ἀγαθοῦ παρεῖναι, ἀλλὰ καὶ τὸ εἶναί τε καὶ τὴν οὐσίαν ὑπ' ἐκείνου αὐτοῖς προσεῖναι, οὐκ οὐσίας ὄντος τοῦ ἀγαθοῦ, ἀλλ' ἔτι ἐπέκεινα τῆς οὐσίας πρεσβείᾳ καὶ δυνάμει ὑπερέχοντος.

[148] At the very beginning the question is so put that the one side asserts: ἀγαθὸν εἶναι τὸ χαίρειν πᾶσι ζῴοις καὶ τὴν ἡδονὴν &c., the other τὸ φρονεῖν καὶ τὸ νοεῖν καὶ τὸ μεμνῆσθαι &c τῆς γε ἡδονῆς ἀμείνω καὶ λῴω γίγνεσθαι ξύμπασιν . . . ὠφελιμώτατον ἁπάντων εἶναι πᾶσι. So the object is (p. 11 D) ἕξιν ψυχῆς ἀποφαίνειν τινὰ τὴν δυναμένην ἀνθρώποις πᾶσι τὸν βίον εὐδαίμονα παρέχειν the one considers ἡδονὴ as this ἕξις, the other, φρόνησις. So again 14 B, 19 C (τί τῶν ἀνθρωπίνων κτημάτων ἄριστον); 20 B sqq.; cf. 27 D, where a life combining wisdom and pleasure is pronounced to be the Good, 66 A sqq., where the elements of the perfect life (the κτῆμα πρῶτον, δεύτερον &c) are enumerated. Subsequently the original question is enlarged into (64 A) the general one: τί ποτε ἔν τε ἀνθρώπῳ καὶ τῷ παντὶ πέφυκεν ἀγαθόν;

[149] After Socrates has observed that the Idea of the Good is the highest object of knowledge, he continues with unmistakable re-

the Good were set forth only as the goal of an activity (which in this case could not be merely human activity)—as the ultimate end of the world, or typical concept to which the divine intelligence looked, and by which it was guided in the framing of the world.[150] According to this view, the Idea of the Good might still be held as something real and substantial,[151] but it could not be an efficient cause; and it must be distinguished in such a manner from the Deity that either the Idea must be related to the Deity or the Deity to the Idea, as the conditioning to the conditioned. The former, supposing the Idea of the Good to be the genus under which the Deity is contained;[152] the latter if it expressed a work or a thought of God,[153] or even an inherent determination of His essence.[154] But Plato's

ference to the Philebus, 505 B ἀλλὰ μὴν καὶ τόδε γε οἶσθα, ὅτι τοῖς μὲν πολλοῖς ἡδονὴ δοκεῖ εἶναι τὸ ἀγαθόν, τοῖς δὲ κομψοτέροις φρόνησις; and then, after a short refutation of both views, 506 B, the question with which the above-mentioned exposition was introduced, is wound up thus: ἀλλὰ σὺ δή, ὦ Σώκρατες, πότερον ἐπιστήμην τὸ ἀγαθὸν φῇς εἶναι, ἢ ἡδονήν, ἢ ἄλλο τι παρὰ ταῦτα; in the middle of this statement the remark again occurs, 509 A · Socrates does not consider pleasure to be the Good.

[150] Van Heusde, Init. Phil. Plat. ii. 3, 88 sqq.; Hermann, Ind lect. Marb. 182⅔ (printed in Jahn's and Seebode's Archiv, i. 622 sq.); Vindiciæ Disput. de Idea boni, Marb. 1839 (A. u. d. T, Vindiciæ Platonicæ, Marb. 1840); Stallbaum in Phileb. Prolegg. (1820), xxxiv, lxxxix; Plat. Tim. 46 sqq.; Plat. Parm 272, Trendelenburg, De Philebi Consilio (1837), 17 sq.; Wehrmann, Plato de s. bono doctr. 70 sq Martin, Etudes sur le Timée, i. 9 sqq speaks less definitely for the separation of the Divinity from the Idea of the Good; he supposes that Plato sometimes identified the two, as, for instance, in the Republic.

[151] As Hermann and Trendelenburg.

[152] So Trendelenburg, loc. cit. with reference to Timæus, 30 A

[153] Orges, Comparat. Plat. et Arist libr. de rep. (Berl. 1843), 23 sqq.: the Idea of the Good is the power and completeness of God displaying itself in things; Ebben, Plat ideær. doctr. (Bonn, 1849), p. 65, says it is an attribute of God—viz. that which displays itself in the limitation of the unlimited.

[154] This supposition is fre

own declarations forbid the assumption. If it is the Idea of the Good which imparts to things their Being, to intelligence its capacity for knowledge, if it is called the cause of all truth and beauty, the parent of light, the source of reality and reason,[155] it is not merely the end but the ground of all Being, efficient force, cause absolute.[156] Plato cannot have contemplated another and a separate efficient cause; or in this place, where he is specifying the ultimate ground of all things, and the supreme object of knowledge,[157] it must necessarily have been mentioned.[158] He says clearly in the Philebus that the Divine Reason is none other than the Good;[159] and in the Timæus, he so speaks

quently found with regard to the Ideas generally: vide p. 266 sq.

[155] Rep. loc. cit. and vii. 517 B· "ἃ δ' οὖν ἐμοὶ φαινόμενα οὕτω φαίνεται, ἐν τῷ γνωστῷ τελευταία ἡ τοῦ ἀγαθοῦ ἰδέα καὶ μόγις ὁρᾶσθαι, ὀφθεῖσα δὲ συλλογιστέα εἶναι ὡς ἄρα πᾶσι πάντων αὕτη ὀρθῶν τε καὶ καλῶν αἰτία, ἔν τε ὁρατῷ φῶς καὶ τὸν τούτου κύριον τεκοῦσα, ἔν τε νοητῷ αὐτὴ κυρία ἀλήθειαν καὶ νοῦν παρασχομένη, καὶ ὅτι δεῖ ταύτην ἰδεῖν τὸν μέλλοντα ἐμφρόνως πράξειν ἢ ἰδίᾳ ἢ δημοσίᾳ.

[156] As the Ideas are generally, vide p. 263 sqq.

[157] The μέγιστον μάθημα as it is called, vi. 505 A.

[158] It has been already remarked, p. 255 sq., that he has mentioned no such causes in any scientific connection with the Ideas.

[159] 22 C. Socrates has proved that pleasure could not be the good; but again knowledge without pleasure is not sufficient; and then he goes on ὡς μὲν τοίνυν τὴν γε Φιλήβου θεὸν οὐ δεῖ δια-νοεῖσθαι ταὐτὸν καὶ τἀγαθὸν, ἱκανῶς εἰρῆσθαί μοι δοκεῖ.—οὐδὲ γὰρ, Philebus replies, ὁ σὸς νοῦς, ὦ Σώκρατες, ἔστι τἀγαθὸν, ἀλλ' ἕξει ταὐτὰ ἐγκλήματα —τάχ' ἂν, is the answer, ὦ Φίληβε, ὅ γε ἐμός· οὐ μέντοι τόν γε ἀληθινὸν ἅμα καὶ θεῖον οἶμαι νοῦν ἀλλ' ἄλλως πως ἔχειν. Hermann, Vindic. 18, mistakes the meaning of this passage in saying that the answer applies only to the last words of Philebus, the comparison of intellect with pleasure. Neither of them is itself the Good, and only in this sense could Socrates admit the assertion of Philebus of the human intellect. Its further extension he could not allow because (as he has hinted 11 D, and followed out in detail, 28 A sqq.) in men the intellect is more nearly related to the Good than pleasure, consequently what he denies of the divine intellect is that it is separate from the Good. Nor again can we say with Wehrmann (p 80) that God is here described

of the Creator, that in order to get a consistent meaning we must abandon the notion of His being separate from the Ideas, from which He is said to have copied the universe.[160] This hypothesis seems indeed to be required by the whole inter-connection of the Platonic doctrine. For in whatever way we may conceive the relation of God to a world of Ideas distinct from Himself, we are everywhere met by insuperable obstacles. Are we to suppose the Ideas to be thoughts or creations of God? or are they to be immanent determinations of His Essence? The one theory would imperil their eternity and self-dependence; the other, their absolute existence;[161] and both would make the Idea of the Good, which, according to Plato, is the Highest of the Thinkable, something derived. Not this

as the Good or the principle of all Good, but that the Good is not described as divinity or intellect, the Good is only one side of the divine being If this were so, the Good could not, at the same time, be a self-subsisting Idea, as it must be according to the Republic: Plato, however, not merely says that the divine intellect is the Good, but that it is ταὐτὸν καὶ τἀγαθόν.

[160] E.g. Rep. vii. (vide note 155), the Idea of the Good is described as the summit of the supra-sensuous world and the cause of all things, which is only perceived with difficulty. So Tim. 28 C, the Divinity as the αἴτιον is thus spoken of: τὸν μὲν οὖν ποιητὴν καὶ πατέρα τοῦδε τοῦ παντὸς εὑρεῖν τε ἔργον καὶ εὑρόντα εἰς πάντας ἀδύνατον λέγειν, and Tim. 37 A it is called τῶν νοητῶν ἀεί τε ὄντων ἄριστον (the words are to be thus connected, vide Stallbaum), and there is just as little mention of the Divinity there as there is of the Good here Further, whereas according to Tim. 28 A, C the Creator of the world looks to the archetype in order to make the world like it, he himself appears as this archetype 29 F, 92 B (where the world is called εἰκὼν τοῦ νοητοῦ [sc. θεοῦ] θεὸς αἰσθητός). The same statements are made with regard both to the Divinity and the Idea, and both change places. When finally, 37 C, the world is called τῶν ἀϊδίων θεῶν ἄγαλμα by the eternal gods as distinguished from the gods that become, we can only understand the Ideas; and then the ἀεὶ ὢν θεὸς (Tim. 34 A) becomes identical with the highest Idea.

[161] Cf. p. 240 sq on this point.

Idea, but the Deity to whom it belonged or by whom it was engendered, would be the First and Highest. But neither a thought nor an attribute, nor a creature of God, could be called by Plato an Idea; since no thought is possible except through an intuition of the Idea; no creation except by the imitation of the Idea; no quality or attribute except through participation in the Idea.[162] Are we then on the contrary to suppose God to be a product of Ideas? an individual that participates in the Idea of the Good? In that case He would not be the Absolute Eternal God, but only one of the 'created gods.' He would stand to Ideas in the same relation that the spirits of the stars and the souls of men stand to them. Or, lastly, are we to assume [163] that He exists side by side with the Ideas as a special, independent principle? that He neither brought them forth, nor was brought forth by them, and that His activity essentially consists in working out the combination of Ideas with Phenomena,—in forming the world according to Ideas? In favour of this view it may be urged, not only that Plato so expresses himself in the Timæus, but that there are important reasons for such a theory in his system. Though he himself would not have admitted it, his Ideas are undeniably wanting in the moving principle that impels them to the Phenomenon.[164] This want appears to be supplied by the concept of Deity; indeed in the Timæus the World-framer is only required, because there would otherwise be no efficient cause. So far, we might hope by this

[162] Cf. p. 242 sqq.
[163] With Hermann.
[164] Cf. p. 268 sq. Further details below.

view to avoid essential difficulties. But we shall only have prepared for ourselves others near at hand. Could Plato really have placed his highest principles so dualistically in juxtaposition, without attempting to combine them? If Ideas alone are true Reality, can another essence side by side with them, distinct from them, and equally original, find a place? Must it not rather hold good of the Deity (as of all things except the Idea) that He is what He is, only through participation in the Idea? which is in no way compatible with the concept of God. All things considered, we may say that the Unity of the Platonic system can only be established on the supposition that Plato in his own belief never really separated the efficient from the logical cause, the Deity from the highest Idea, that of the Good. But it has been already shown [165] that he identifies them, that he attributes efficient power and designing reason, sometimes to Ideas in general, sometimes to the highest Idea in particular. This is confirmed by the statement that in the oral discourses of his later life the supreme Unity is designated as the Good; [166]

---

[165] See p. 281 sq , 263 sq.

[166] Aristox. Harm Elem 11, beginn. p. 30, Meib.: καθάπερ Ἀριστοτέλης ἀεὶ διηγεῖτο, τοὺς πλείστους τῶν ἀκουσάντων παρὰ Πλάτωνος τὴν περὶ τἀγαθοῦ ἀκρόασιν παθεῖν· προσιέναι μὲν γὰρ ἕκαστον ὑπολαμβάνοντα λήψεσθαί τι τῶν νομιζομένων ἀνθρωπίνων ἀγαθῶν· ὅτε δὲ φανείησαν οἱ λόγοι περὶ μαθημάτων καὶ ἀριθμῶν καὶ γεωμετρίας καὶ ἀστρολογίας, καὶ τὸ πέρας, ὅτι ἀγαθόν ἐστι ἓν, παντελῶς, οἶμαι, παράδοξόν τι ἐφαίνετο αὐτοῖς. Arist. Metaph. xiv. 4, 1091 b. 13: τῶν δὲ τὰς ἀκινήτους οὐσίας εἶναι λεγόντων οἱ μέν φασιν αὐτὸ τὸ ἓν τὸ ἀγαθὸν αὐτὸ εἶναι, which the Pseudo-Alexander ad loc. refers to Plato. Ibid. i. 6, end. Plato considered the one as the basis of Good, matter as the basis of evil; with which we may connect the words of c. 4, p. 985 a. 9: τὸ τῶν ἀγαθῶν ἁπάντων αἴτιον αὐτὸ τἀγαθόν ἐστι. Theophrastus also

for this supreme Unity must have been identical with God. It is mentioned, too, as a departure of Speusippus from the doctrine of his Master, that he distinguished the Divine Reason from the One and the Good.[167] The same view is presupposed by Aristotle when he says that Plato recognised only two kinds of causes, the formal or conceptual, and the material cause:[168] and on this he grounds his complaint that Plato omits to state who forms things according to Ideas.[169] To us it may certainly sound incomprehensible that a theological concept like the concept of the Good, should not merely be generally hypostasized, but positively declared to be the highest active energy and reason. We are accustomed to conceive of Reason only in the form of personality, which it would seem impossible to attribute to an idea. But it may be questioned whether all this appeared so inconceivable to Plato, as it appears to us, with our altered modes of thought. The mind that could allow relative determinations, the Same, the Great, the Small, &c., to precede as ideal entities the things in which we perceive them, could also make an aim into a self-

---

recognises the identity of the Good and the Divinity in Plato, in saying of him apud Simpl. Phys. 6 b. m (Fragm. 48 Wunm): δύο τὰς ἀρχὰς βούλεται ποιεῖν, τὸ μὲν ὑποκείμενον ὡς ὕλην, ὁ προσαγορεύει πανδεχὲς, τὸ δ' ὡς αἴτιον καὶ κινοῦν, ὃ περιάπτει τῇ τοῦ θεοῦ καὶ τῇ τἀγαθοῦ δυνάμει.

[167] Stobæus. Ekl. i. 58: Σπεύσιππος [θεὸν ἀπεφήνατο] τὸν νοῦν, οὔτε τῷ ἑνὶ οὔτε τῷ ἀγαθῷ τὸν αὐτὸν, ἰδιοφυῆ δέ. In the words οὔτε, &c Krische, Forsch. i. 256, rightly points out that Speusippus must have opposed himself to modes of thought which he had found previously in Plato, and which put νοῦς on a level with the One and the Good.

[168] Metaph i. 6, 988 a. 8· φανερὸν δ' ἐκ τῶν εἰρημένων ὅτι δυοῖν αἰτίαιν μόνον κέχρηται, τῇ τε τοῦ τί ἐστι καὶ τῇ κατὰ τὴν ὕλην. Theophr. preceding note.

[169] Vide p. 76, 70, sq

THE GOOD.

subsistent Reality, and the absolute aim and end, or the Good, into absolute Cause and absolute Being.[170] That step once taken, it is not surprising that the Good, like all the other Ideas in their own spheres, should have been invested with further qualities such as Power, Activity and Reason, without which it could not be that infinite essential nature at all. But what relation it then bears to personality, is a question which Plato probably never definitely proposed to himself. The ancients were generally wanting in the distinct concept of personality, and Reason was not seldom apprehended as universal world-intellect, hovering uncertainly between personal existence and impersonal.[171] Plato says indeed that Reason can be imparted to no essence without a soul, and he accordingly makes reason inherent even in the Cosmos by means of the soul.[172] But in the first place, we cannot con-

[170] That this must lead to many disadvantages is shown in the case before us. We have thus to explain, e g the mixture above remarked (p 280 sq.), of the highest Good with the metaphysical concept of the absolute. The concept of the Good is abstracted from human life, it signifies that which is advantageous to mankind (as it did to Socrates). Plato then generalises it into the concept of the absolute, but its original meaning is continually playing into it: hence the confusion; neither the ethical nor the metaphysical concept of the Good is attained in its simplicity. Further difficulties arise (cf. Brandis, 11. a. 327 sq.) when we ask how the Idea of the Good is the cause of all other Ideas of the sensible world? The answer, however, can only be the same which we have had to the more general question as to the causality of the Ideas: viz that here we have an instance of the inadequacy of the system, which Plato himself indirectly acknowledged by the silence in which he passes by the critical points.

[171] Vide the remarks in vol. 1. p. 808, and subsequent observations on Aristotle's concept of God

[172] Tim. 30 B· λογισάμενος οὖν εὕρισκεν [ὁ θεὸς] ἐκ τῶν κατὰ φύσιν ὁρατῶν οὐδὲν ἀνόητον τοῦ νοῦν ἔχοντος ὅλον ὅλου κάλλιον ἔσεσθαί ποτε ἔργον, νοῦν δ' αὖ χωρὶς ψυχῆς ἀδύνατον παραγενέσθαι τῳ· διὰ δὴ τὸν λογισμὸν τόνδε νοῦν μὲν ἐν ψυχῇ ψυχὴν δὲ ἐν σώματι ξυνιστὰς τὸ πᾶν

clude from this that the Divine Reason in itself exists as a soul; for however inseparably they may be bound together, the World-soul is always a principle distinct from and subordinate to Reason, which only combines with it, because in no other way could Reason impart itself to the world; [173] and in the next place, a personality in the specific sense can scarcely be ascribed to the World-soul. Still less can we derive such a principle from the logical application of the Platonic hypotheses about God. If an original existence belong alone to the Universal, God, as the most original, must also be the most universal; [174] if separate individuals

ξυνετεκταίνετο. In the light of this passage we must explain Phileb. 30 C: σοφία μὴν καὶ νοῦς ἄνευ ψυχῆς οὐκ ἄν ποτε γενοίσθην Οὐ γὰρ οὖν. Οὐκοῦν ἐν μὲν τῇ τοῦ Διὸς, &c. Vide p. 266, 112. The question here is not as to intellect in its supramundane existence, but intellect in so far as it is immanent in the universe (or as it is mythically expressed, in the nature of Zeus); the supramundane intellect is, however, separated from that which dwells in the world, when it is said that Zeus possesses a kingly soul and a kingly understanding διὰ τὴν τῆς αἰτίας δύναμιν. Deity, in the absolute sense, cannot have its reason imparted to it by some extraneous cause. The same holds good of Tim. 37 C; reason and knowledge are only in the soul, and 46 D: τῶν γὰρ ὄντων ᾧ νοῦν μόνῳ κτᾶσθαι προσήκει, λεκτέον ψυχήν. Here also the question asked is not whether νοῦς as such can be imagined without soul, but whether it can be immanent in anything other than the soul, and the only thing denied is that reason can belong to the corporeal.

[173] Tim. 35 A sqq. Plato certainly explains himself otherwise, Soph. 248 E sq. (vide p. 262, 107); this expression, however, is not to be identified with the confused theories of the Timæus, it is merely an inaccuracy which was subsequently corrected by Plato himself.

[174] Stumpf, Verh. d plat. Gott. z. idee d. Gut. 94, raises the objection that, as the Ideas are hypostasised and therefore separate from things and from one another, the Idea of the Good must be the most individual, and the Platonic God must be absolutely transcendent and individual. But substantiality and individuality are not identical to Plato, though they are to Aristotle. It is Aristotle's well-grounded and repeated objection against the theory of Ideas that the Ideas ought to be the universal to the individuals,— the genera, whereas they cannot

are what they are only by participation in a higher, that essence which has no higher above it cannot be a separate individual : if the soul is contra-distinguished from the Idea by its relation to the material world (by the share which the Unlimited has in it), a soul cannot be attributed to the Idea as such, nor consequently to God, who is identical with the highest Idea. Plato has nowhere expressly drawn out these consequences, but, on the other hand, he has done nothing to guard against them. He often speaks of God as a person; and we have no right to see in this only a conscious adaptation of his language to the popular religious notions. Such a mode of representation was, as before remarked, indispensable to him (on account of the immobility of Ideas) in order to explain phenomena; and all that he says concerning the perfection of God, divine Providence, and the care of the Gods for men,[175] gives the impression, not that he is deliberately translating philosophic ideas into a language grown strange to him, but rather that he himself shares the religious belief, and holds it in the main to be well founded. Yet he never tries to reconcile these religious notions more definitely with his scientific conceptions, or to demonstrate their mutual compatibility. We can therefore only conclude that he was unconscious of the problem.[176] In his scientific enquiry into the highest

---

be so as χωρισταί. It has already been shown, p. 237 sq., that the Platonic Ideas are the hypostasised concepts of genus But the highest Idea as such must be necessarily the highest genus, and consequently the most universal.

[175] Vide p. 267, 114.

[176] This Rihbing, Plat. Ideenl. i. 370 sqq., candidly admits, though he will not allow that the Ideas are the universal, and that therefore

causes he confined himself to the Ideas, and when, as in the Timæus, he found it necessary to introduce the Deity side by side with them, he does so without proof or accurate definition, but merely as a presupposition of faith.[177] For his personal needs,[178] and for practical application, he held to the belief in Gods, purifying it indeed in the spirit of his philosophy,[179] but not investigating very narrowly its relation to the doctrine of Ideas; contenting himself with the thought that both asserted the same truth; that the Ideas were truly divine, and that the highest Idea coincided with the highest Deity.[180] The difficulties besetting the com-

the predication of personality would contradict their concept. Whether this supposition is 'honourable to the philosopher' (as Stumpf, loc. cit., maintains against me) or not, is not the question which the historical enquirer has to put; we have simply to discover what can be proved, or at least made probable. It is certainly not improbable that even Plato was unconscious of a problem which remained a secret to all antiquity up to the time of Plotinus, and that he overlooked the difficulty in which the theory of Ideas involved him just as much as many others which lay nearer to hand.

[177] Tim. 28 A sqq. it is proved that the world must have a cause, for, as being corporeal, it came into existence, τῷ δ' αὖ γενομένῳ φαμὲν ὑπ' αἰτίου τινὸς ἀνάγκην εἶναι γενέσθαι. It is not, however, shown further that this αἴτιον is reducible to a ποιητής, πατήρ, δημιουργός; we have here dogmatic beliefs and scientific ideas set simply down side by side.

[178] This is unmistakably the real point, and so far I agree with Deuschle's remark (Plato, Mythen, 16 sq.) that to Plato's mind the personal God had a meaning beyond a mere mythical personification. This, however, holds good, not only of a God, but also of the gods

[179] On this point more exact details will be given later on

[180] But does not this make Plato a pantheist? Even if this were so, it would be no great misfortune, and still less a valid objection against the result of an historical enquiry. This, however, is not the question here, and the title which Rettig has given to his treatise, 'Αἰτία in the Philebus the personal Divinity of Plato or Plato no pantheist,' implies a very vague conception of pantheism. If Plato had repudiated the personality of the divinity, he would still not be a pantheist. In his latest principles he has neither removed the dualism of the Idea

parison of things so essentially different seem to have been overlooked by Plato, as by many another philosopher before and since his time.[181]

In thus determining the highest Being as the Good, and as Reason assigning an end, Plato apprehends it as the creative principle, revealing itself in the Phenomenon: because God is good, He formed the world.[182]

and so-called Matter, nor the separation of the Ideas from things and of the Ideas from one another. But the statement against which Rettig takes the field does not assert that Plato repudiated the personality of the divinity, but merely that he did not enquire into the question of personality.

[181] The view above developed, that the Idea of the Good is identical with the divinity, is found with different modifications of detail, which affect the question of the personality of the Platonic God (not to mention the Neo-Platonists), in Herbart, Einleit. in d. phil. WW. i. 248, Plat. Syst. fund. ibid. xii. 78; Schleiermacher. Pl. WW. ii. C 134; Ritter, Gesch. d. Phil. ii. 311 sq.; Preller, Hist. phil. gr.-röm. 2 A p. 249; Bonitz, Disputatt. Plat. 5 sqq.; Brandis, ii. a. 322 sqq.; Schwegler, Gesch. d. Phil. 3 A 56; Strumpell, Gesch d. theor Phil d Gr. 131; Ueberweg, Rhein Mus. ix. 69 sqq.; Susemihl, Genet. Entw. i. 360, ii. 22, 196, 202; Steinhart, Pl. WW. iv. 644 sq., 659, v 214 sq., 258, 689 sq., vi. 86, Stumpf, loc. cit.; Ribbing, Plat Ideenl. i. 370 sqq. (Other authorities apud Stallbaum, Plat. Tim. 47.) I cannot, however, for the reasons above stated, agree with Steinhart (iv. 645), in referring Phileb. 30 A, C to the divinity in an absolute sense. In Phædr 246 C, which he also quotes, Plato is not expressing his own views on the divinity, but simply the ordinary opinion, which he declares to be mistaken. It appears to me a very improbable conjecture of Steinhart's (vi. 87 sq.,) that Plato distinguished between a principle of rest or permanency and an efficient principle of motion, an objective and subjective, an Ideal and a real side in the divine Being—the former the Idea of the Good, the latter, Spirit. Both forms of statement are found in Plato, but he does not in any way indicate that different sides of the divine principle are thereby intended All the objections of Rettig, Volquardsen, &c. to my view, so far as they seemed to me to be of any importance, will be found to have been noticed either with or without express reference.

[182] Tim. 29 D. λέγωμεν δὴ δι' ἥν τινα αἰτίαν γένεσιν καὶ τὸ πᾶν τόδε ὁ ξυνιστὰς ξυνέστησεν, ἀγαθὸς ἦν ἀγαθῷ δὲ οὐδεὶς περὶ οὐδενὸς οὐδέποτε ἐγγίγνεται φθόνος (the very same important position which Plato brings as an objection, Phædr. 247 A, to the θεῖον φθονερὸν of the popular creed).

The doctrine of Ideas is in this way connected with the study of the Cosmos,—Dialectics with Physics.

τούτου δ' ἐκτὸς ὢν πάντα ὅτι μάλιστα γενέσθαι ἐβουλήθη παραλήσια ἑαυτῷ ... βουληθεὶς γὰρ ὁ θεὸς ἀγαθὰ μὲν πάντα, φλαῦρον δὲ μηδὲν εἶναι κατὰ δύναμιν, οὕτω δὴ πᾶν ὅσον ἦν ὁρατὸν παραλαβὼν οὐχ ἡσυχίαν ἄγον, ἀλλὰ κινούμενον πλημμελῶς καὶ ἀτάκτως, εἰς τάξιν αὐτὸ ἤγαγεν ἐκ τῆς ἀταξίας, ἡγησάμενος ἐκεῖνο τούτου πάντως ἄμεινον.

CHAPTER VII.

PHYSICS.

THE GENERAL CAUSES OF THE WORLD OF PHENOMENA.

UNDER the name of Physics we include all discussions relating to the sphere of natural existence; on the general causes of the world of Phenomena, as contradistinguished from the world of Ideas; on the Cosmos and its parts; and on Man. The first of these enquiries has three divisions: (1) the universal groundwork of the Sensuous as such, namely Matter; (2) the relation of the Sensuous to the Idea; (3) that which mediatises between the world of Ideas and that of Sense— the World-soul.

1. *Matter.* To understand Plato's doctrine of Matter, we must look back to his doctrine of Ideas. Plato considers Ideas as the only true existence: he regards the sensible Phenomenon as a middle-term between Being and Non-Being; that to which only a transition from Being to Non-Being, and from Non-Being to Being, only a Becoming, and never a Being, can belong. In the Phenomenon the Idea is never purely presented to us, but always intermingled with its opposite, confusedly, broken up in a Plurality

of individuals, hidden beneath the material veil.[1] The Phenomenon is not an absolute self-dependent existence, but all its Being is Being for another, by means of another, in relation to another, for the sake of another.[2] The objects of Sense are therefore, in a word, only a shadow and mimicry of true Existence. That which in the latter is One, in the former is Many and Divided; what there exists purely for and by itself is here in, and by reason of, another; what is there Being, is here Becoming. But how is this metamorphosis of the Idea in the Phenomenon brought about? The cause of it cannot lie in the Ideas themselves; these, even if they enter into a community of existence, still remain individually distinct, without interminglement, each in its own specific essence: an Idea cannot coalesce with its opposite or pass over into it.[3] Therefore, if one Idea

[1] Vide supra and Rep. vii. 524 C, vi. 493 E, 476 A, 477 A: Symp. 211 E, 207 D; Polit. 269 D.

[2] Symp. 211 A, where archetypal Beauty in opposition to phænomenal beauty (τὰ πολλὰ καλὰ) is described as οὐ τῇ μὲν καλόν, τῇ δ' αἰσχρόν, οὐδὲ τοτὲ μὲν, τοτὲ δ' οὒ, οὐδὲ πρὸς μὲν τὸ καλὸν πρὸς δὲ τὸ αἰσχρὸν οὐδ' ἔνθα μὲν καλόν, ἔνθα δ' αἰσχρόν, ὥς τισὶ μὲν ὂν καλόν, τισὶ δὲ αἰσχρόν. Phileb. 54 C, vide chap. ii. n. 10. Tim. 52 C: εἰκόνι μὲν (sensible appearance), ἐπείπερ οὐδ' αὐτὸ τοῦτο ἐφ' ᾧ γέγονεν (the Actual, for the exposition of which it serves) ἑαυτῆς ἐστιν, ἑτέρου δέ τινος ἀεὶ φέρεται φάντασμα, διὰ ταῦτα ἐν ἑτέρῳ προσήκει τινὶ γίγνεσθαι, οὐσίας ἁμωσγέπως ἀντεχομένην, ἢ μηδὲν τὸ παράπαν αὐτὴν εἶναι. Cf. Rep v. 476 A; Phædo, 102 B sq.; also Crat. 386 D; Theæt. 160 B, in which latter passage, however, Plato is not speaking in his own name

[3] Phædo, 102 D sqq.. ἐμοὶ γὰρ φαίνεται οὐ μόνον αὐτὸ τὸ μέγεθος οὐδέποτ' ἐθέλειν ἅμα μέγα καὶ σμικρὸν εἶναι, &c, ὡς δ' αὔτως καὶ τὸ σμικρὸν τὸ ἐν ἡμῖν οὐκ ἐθέλει ποτὲ μέγα γίγνεσθαι οὐδὲ ἄλλο οὐδὲν τῶν ἐναντίων, &c. To this it is objected that Socrates himself had just said that opposites come from opposites, to which it is replied: τότε μὲν γὰρ ἐλέγετο ἐκ τοῦ ἐναντίου πράγματος τὸ ἐναντίον πρᾶγμα γίγνεσθαι, νῦν δὲ ὅτι αὐτὸ τὸ ἐναντίον ἑαυτῷ ἐναντίον οὐκ ἄν ποτε γένοιτο, &c. Cf. Soph. 252 D, 255 A.

goes through many other Ideas, and includes them in itself,[4] each must still maintain its unchanged identity,[5] after its own fashion. One concept allows itself to combine with another, only so far as it is identical with that other.[6] Sensible objects on the other hand, in contradistinction from Ideas, are capable of assuming not only similar, but also opposite conditions; and this is so essential in them, that Plato plainly says there is not one of them which is not at the same time its own opposite, the existence of which is not simultaneously its non-existence.[7] This imperfection of the Phenomenon cannot spring from the Idea: it rather proves that necessity as well as Reason is the cause of the world, and that this irrational cause cannot entirely be overcome by Reason.[8] Consequently to explain Sense as such, a special principle must be assumed, and this principle must be the direct contrary of the Idea, for it is precisely the contradiction between the Phenomenon and the Idea which has to be derived from it. It must contain the cause of the Non-being, the divisibility, the mutability of the Phenomenon, and only this; for whatever is real, one, and permanent, origi-

[4] Soph. 253 D, vide chap. v. note 78.
[5] Phileb. 15 B (vide note 88) Cf. pp 228, 240. It will be shown presently that Repub. v. 476 A does not contradict this view.
[6] Soph. 255 E sqq., vide p 249.
[7] Rep. v. 479 A (vide p. 224); Phædo, 102.
[8] Tim. 48 A : μεμιγμένη γὰρ οὖν ἡ τοῦδε τοῦ κόσμου γένεσις ἐξ ἀνάγκης τε καὶ νοῦ συστάσεως ἐγεν-νήθη · νοῦ δὲ ἀνάγκης ἄρχοντος τῷ πείθειν αὐτὴν τῶν γιγνομένων τὰ πλεῖστα ἐπὶ τὸ βέλτιστον ἄγειν, ταύτῃ κατὰ ταῦτά τε δι' ἀνάγκης ἡττωμένης ὑπὸ πειθοῦς ἔμφρονος οὕτω κατ' ἀρχὰς ξυνίστατο τόδε τὸ πᾶν. εἴ τις οὖν ᾗ γέγονε κατὰ ταῦτα ὄντως ἐρεῖ, μικτέον καὶ τὸ τῆς πλανωμένης εἶδος αἰτίας, ᾗ φέρειν πέφυκεν Cf. Tim. 56 C, 68 E; Theæt. 176 A.

nates exclusively with the Idea. Therefore if the Idea be the purely Existent, this principle will be the purely Non-existent; if the one be uniform and invariable Essence, the other must be absolute division and absolute change. This principle is what is usually, though not in Platonic phraseology,[9] termed by us Platonic Matter.

[9] The word ὕλη in Plato bears the same signification as in ordinary speech. it means a 'wood,' 'timber,' and sometimes generally 'material.' The later philosophic application of the word to signify the abstract concept of material substratum is expressed by Plato, so far as he has that concept at all, in other ways. This holds good of Tim. 69 A, where, after a discussion on the two kinds of causes to be mentioned later on, we read· ὅτ' οὖν δὴ τὰ νῦν οἶον τέκτοσιν ἡμῖν ὕλη παράκειται τὰ τῶν αἰτίων γένη διυλασμένα (or -λισμένα): 'since we have the different kinds of causes set out before us, as carpenters have their timber,' and Phileb. 54 B (supra, chap. vi. n 10). The context gives no occasion for understanding ὕλη, with Susemihl, Genet. Entw. ii. 43, and Wohlstein, Mat. w. Weltseele (Marb 1863), p. 7, as 'matter in general,' and not rather (on the analogy of φάρμακα and ὄργανα) in the sense of raw material. The so-called Timæus of Locri uses ὕλη (93 A sqq, 97 F), where Plato (Timæus, 48 E sqq.) has ὑποδοχὴ γενέσεως, φύσις τὰ πάντα σώματα δεχομένη, δεξαμένη, ἐκμαγεῖον, ἐκεῖνο ἐν ᾧ γίγνεται, χώρα, τόπος, &c. Ὕλη, as a technical philosophic term, is first met with in Aristotle, and is frequently used in his exposition of the Platonic doctrine. It does not, however, follow that he had heard the word from Plato's own lips in the oral discourses; for, as is well known, Aristotle does not hesitate to enunciate the views of earlier thinkers in his own terminology. In Phys. iv 2, 209 b ii. 210 a. 1, he says: Plato in the Timæus (where, however, this denotation never occurs) calls ὕλη the μεθεκτικὸν, in the ἄγραφα δόγματα It is the Great and Small If we consider how foreign the word is to the Timæns, how closely its usage in Aristotle is connected with the peculiar leading ideas of his system, and how little it is suitable to Plato, who did not, like his scholars, seek for the basis of the corporeal in a positive substratum; and if again we observe that, for the reasons given above, it could not have occurred in the ἄγραφα δόγματα, and that Theophrastus (in the passage quoted chap. vi. note 165) does not appear to know the term as Platonic, it will seem far from probable that Plato introduced it into philosophic language Although therefore I shall make use of Aristotle's term for the sake of brevity, I do not wish it to be considered as Platonic. Σῶμα may be more correctly regarded as an ordinary Platonic

MATTER. 297

A description of it is given in the Philebus and Timæus.[10] The Philebus (24 E) designates the universal substratum of the sensible Phenomenon as the Unlimited, and ascribes to it 'all that is capable of more and less, of stronger and weaker, and of excess;' that is to say, the Unlimited is that within which no fixed and exact determination is possible, the element of conceptless existence, of change, which never arrives at Being and permanence.[11] The Timæus (48 E) enters

denotation of the corporeal, in its general character and as distinguished from the spiritual. It occurs in this sense, Soph. 246 A–248 A; Polit. 269 D, 273 B (where Schaarschmidt, Samml. d. plat. Schr. 210, thinks he finds an evidence of spuriousness in this 'un-Platonic' signification of the word), and also Phileb. 29 C. cf. 64 B, and particularly (together with the equivalent σωματοειδές, in Tim. 28 B) 31 B, 34 B, 35 A, 36 D, 50 B. The concept of σῶμα, however, does not coincide with that of matter: the σῶμα is visible and palpable, and this presupposes that it consists of the elements (Tim. 28 B, 31 B sqq); the so-called matter, on the contrary, is anterior to the elementary bodies, yet it has none of their determinations in itself, and is therefore not perceptible to the senses The πανδεχὲς becomes the σῶμα because it admits the form of the four elements.

[10] In the passage quoted p. 263, 110.

[11] Cf. Tim. 27 D, where it is said of the sensible as a whole, that it is γιγνόμενον μὲν ἀεὶ ὂν δὲ οὐδέποτε . . . δόξῃ μετ' αἰσθήσεως ἀλόγου δοξαστὸν, γιγνόμενον καὶ ἀπολλύμενον, ὄντως δὲ οὐδέποτε ὄν. Wohlstein, loc. cit. 3 sq. 8 sq., would understand by the γιγνόμενον ἀεὶ in this passage not the world but matter, and would refer the γεννητὸν παράδειγμα mentioned in what follows (28 B, 29 A) to matter also. Against the first of these suppositions there is the circumstance that the γιγνόμενον ἀεὶ is not merely perceptible and presentable but also subject to becoming and perishing. Matter, according to Plato (cf. note 14), is neither. A complete and accurate consideration of the passage will show both suppositions to be equally untenable. With respect to the γιγνόμενον ἀεὶ it is remarked that it must have an author. The question follows, What archetype the author used in its creation? That which is fashioned after an archetype is itself neither the archetype nor the material in which it is fashioned. Nor can the material be identified with the archetype which it is to represent, as Wohlstein maintains By the γεννητὸν παράδειγμα is not meant anything which actually preceded the creation of the world; it is merely something laid down hypothetically. Instead of saying, 'the creator fashioned the world on an

more into detail. Plato here distinguishes first the archetypical, self-identical Essence—Ideas. Secondly, comes that which is imitated from them, the sensible Phenomenon. In the third place we have that which is at once the groundwork and the receptacle of all Becoming, the common element which underlies all corporeal elements and all determinate matter. In the ceaseless flux of all these forms in the circle of Becoming this common element runs through them as their permanent substratum: it is the something in which they become, and to which they return. It is never represented in them purely, but only under a particular form;[12] it is the impressible mass (ἐκμαγεῖον) out of which they were all formed, but which, for that very reason, must itself be without specific quality or definite form. That such an element must be presupposed, Plato proves from the continual flux of things sensible, the constant passing of the elements one into another. This he says would be impossible if the determinate kinds of matter in themselves were something real, a Something, and not merely modifications of one common and therefore necessarily indeterminate third Something.[13] That Something he more precisely describes as an invisible and shapeless nature, capable of

eternal archetype,' Plato says 'he fashioned it not according to the Becoming, but according to the Eternal.'

[12] 49 D sq.: we must not call any definite material (as fire, water, &c.) a τόδε or τοῦτο, but only a τοιοῦτον, because they are always passing into one another: φεύγει γὰρ οὐχ ὑπόμενον τὴν τοῦ τόδε καὶ τοῦτο καὶ τὴν τῷδε καὶ πᾶσαν ὅση μόνιμα ὡς ὄντα αὐτὰ ἐνδείκνυται φάσις. . . . ἐν ᾧ δὲ ἐγγιγνόμενα ἀεὶ ἕκαστον αὐτῶν φαντάζεται καὶ πάλιν ἐκεῖθεν ἀπόλλυται, μόνον ἐκεῖνο αὖ προσαγορεύειν τῷ τε τοῦτο καὶ τῷ τόδε προσχρωμένους. ὀνόματα, κ.τ.λ.

[13] 49 B sqq. We have already met with something similar in Diogenes of Apollonia, vol. i. p. 219.

taking any shape;[14] as Space, which, itself eternal and imperishable, provides a home for all Becoming; as the Other, in which all Becoming must be, in order to exist at all; while true Existence, as in itself sole, cannot enter a sphere so entirely different from itself.[15] The statements of Plato's disciples are all to this effect. According to Aristotle, Plato in his discourses reduced Matter to the Unlimited, or, as he usually says, to the

[14] 50 A sqq; e.g. as gold continually transformed into all possible figures would still be called gold, so with the nature (φύσις) which admits all bodies in itself. ταὐτὸν αὐτὴν ἀεὶ προσρητέον· ἐκ γὰρ τῆς ἑαυτῆς τὸ παράπα· οὐκ ἐξίσταται δυνάμεως. δέχεταί τε γὰρ ἀεὶ τὰ πάντα, καὶ μορφὴν οὐδεμίαν ποτὲ οὐδενὶ τῶν εἰσιόντων ὁμοίαν εἴληφεν οὐδαμῇ οὐδαμῶς· ἐκμαγεῖον γὰρ φύσει παντὶ κεῖται, κινούμενόν τε καὶ διασχηματιζόμενον ὑπὸ τῶν εἰσιόντων, φαίνεται δὲ δι' ἐκεῖνα ἄλλοτε ἀλλοῖον. τὰ δὲ εἰσιόντα καὶ ἐξιόντα τῶν ὄντων ἀεὶ μιμήματα (that which enters into that nature is in each case the copy of the Ideas), τυπωθέντα ἀπ' αὐτῶν τρόπον τινὰ δύσφραστον καὶ θαυμαστόν. . . . That in which an impression is to be taken must in itself be ἄμορφον ἐκείνων ἁπασῶν τῶν ἰδέων, ὅσας μέλλοι δέχεσθαί ποθεν. If it already had any of these forms, it would give back the impression badly Just as we make the oil, out of which ointments are to be prepared, scentless, and the wax formless which we intend to mould, ταὐτὸν οὖν καὶ τῷ τὰ τῶν πάντων ἀεί τε ὄντων κατὰ πᾶν ἑαυτοῦ (in each of its parts) πολλάκις ἀφομοιώματα καλῶς μέλλοντι δέχεσθαι πάντων ἐκτὸς αὐτῷ προσήκει πεφυκέναι τῶν εἰδῶν. διὸ δὴ τὴν τοῦ γεγονότος ὁρατοῦ καὶ πάντως αἰσθητοῦ μητέρα καὶ ὑποδοχὴν μήτε γῆν μήτε ἀέρα μήτε πῦρ μήτε ὕδωρ λέγωμεν, μήτε ὅσα ἐκ τούτων μήτε ἐξ ὧν ταῦτα γέγονεν ἀλλ' ἀνόρατον εἶδός τι καὶ ἄμορφον, πανδεχές, μεταλαμβάνον δὲ ἀπορώτατά πῃ τοῦ νοητοῦ καὶ δυσαλωτότατον αὐτὸ λέγοντες οὐ ψευσόμεθα. The correct view is simply that: πῦρ μὲν ἑκάστοτε αὐτοῦ τὸ πεπυρωμένον μέρος φαίνεσθαι, τὸ δὲ ὑγρανθὲν ὕδωρ, κ τ λ.

[15] 52 A sq.: ὁμολογητέον, ἓν μὲν εἶναι τὸ κατὰ ταὐτὰ εἶδος ἔχον, ἀγέννητον καὶ ἀνώλεθρον, &c. . . . τὸ δὲ ὁμώνυμον ὅμοιόν τε ἐκείνῳ (sensible Being) δεύτερον . . . τρίτον δὲ αὖ γένος ὂν τὸ τῆς χώρας ἀεί, φθορὰν οὐ προσδεχόμενον, ἕδραν δὲ παρέχον ὅσα ἔχει γένεσιν πᾶσιν, αὐτὸ δὲ μετ' ἀναισθησίας ἁπτὸν λογισμῷ τινι νόθῳ, μόγις πιστόν, πρὸς ὃ δὴ καὶ ὀνειροπολοῦμεν βλέποντες, καί φαμεν ἀναγκαῖον εἶναί που τὸ ὂν ἅπαν ἔν τινι τόπῳ καὶ κατέχον χώραν τινά, τὸ δὲ μήτε ἐν γῇ μήτε που κατ' οὐρανὸν οὐδὲν εἶναι . . . τἀληθὲς, ὡς εἰκόνι μὲν, κ.τ.λ. (vide note 2) . . . οὗτος μὲν οὖν δὴ παρὰ τῆς ἐμῆς ψήφου λογισθεὶς ἐν κεφαλαίῳ δεδόσθω λόγος, ὄν τε καὶ χώραν καὶ γένεσιν εἶναι τρία τριχῇ καὶ πρὶν οὐρανὸν γενέσθαι.

300   *PLATO AND THE OLDER ACADEMY.*

Great and Small, in order thus to express that its specific essence consists, not in fixed, self-identical, Ideally defined properties, but only in extensive or intensive quantity; that it is capable of enlargement and diminution, of increase and decrease to an indefinite extent.[16] Hermodorus says he described it as all that stands in the relation of Great and Small, that has in itself an endless gradation of more and less, that falls under the category of the inconstant, the infinite, the formless, the Non-existent, and as such can neither be called a principle nor a Being.[17] What then are we to gather from these statements was Plato's real opinion? It was once generally supposed that Plato taught the existence of an eternal corporeal Matter, or, at any rate, of a corporeal Matter that preceded the creation of the world. Aristotle first gave occasion to this view,[18] though he does not share it; among later writers it is almost universal, and in modern times it has found many noteworthy supporters,[19] though not a few [20] opponents.[21] Much may be urged in its favour.

[16] Phys. iii. 4, 203 a. 15 c. 6, 306 b. 27; iv. 2, 209 b. 33, 1, 9, 192 a. 11; Metaph. i. 6, 987 b. 20 sqq. 1, 7, 988 a. 25; iii. 3, 998 b 10. This statement is more fully discussed in my Plat. Stud. p. 217 sqq., and later on in this chapter.

[17] In the statement of Dercylides as to Hermodorus (borrowed from Simplicius), vide p. 277, 137, which is quoted in detail in my Diatribe de Hermodoro, p. 20 sqq., and again by Susemihl, Genet. Entw. ii. 522 sqq. The quotation from Eudemus, vol. i. 302–3, 3rd edit., agrees with this.

[18] Vide p. 283, 160.

[19] Bonitz, Disput. Platonicæ, 65 sq.; Brandis, Gr.-röm. Phil ii. a. 295 sqq ; Stallbaum, Plat. Tim. p. 43, 205 sqq.; Reinhold, Gesch. d. Phil. i. 125; Hegel, Gesch. der Phil. ii. 231 sq.; Strumpell, Gesch. d theor. Phil. d. Gr. 144 sqq ; Ueberweg ub. d. pl. Welts., Rhein -Mus. ix. 57 sqq.; Volquardsen Idee. d. pers. Geist. 70 sq.; Schneider, D. Mat. Princ. d. plat. Metaph. (Gera, 1872) 11 sq , Wohlstein, Mat. u. Welts. 11 sq , &c.

[20] Böckh, in Daub and Creuzer's Studien, iii. 26 sqq., Ritter,

The groundwork of sensuous existence is undoubtedly described in the Timæus as a material substratum;— it is that in which all particular forms of matter arise, and into which they resolve themselves;[22] it is compared with the unhewn mass out of which the artist fashions his figures; it is set forth as the τοῦτο and τόδε, which, never departing from its own nature, assumes sometimes the form of fire, sometimes that of water, &c.: lastly, mention is made of something visible, which, before the beginning of the world, had, in the restlessness of lawless motion, the forms and qualities of all elements confusedly and uncertainly in itself.[23] But this last enunciation contradicts others too palpably to be maintained. Plato repeatedly de-

---

Gesch. der Phil. ii. 345, sq.; Preller, Hist phil. Gr.-röm. 257; Schleiermacher, Gesch. der Phil. p. 105; Steinhart, Plat. W. vi. 115 sqq.; Susemihl, Genet. Entw. ii. 405 sqq.; Ribbing, Plat. Ideenl. i. 333 sq.; Siebeck, Unters. z. Phil. d. Gr. 103 sqq Cf. my Plat. Stnd. 212, 225.

[21] Marbach, Gesch. der Phil. i. p. 113 sq , and Sigwart, Gesch. der Phil. i. 117 sqq., express themselves vaguely. Ast (über die Materie in Tim. Abhandl. der Munchener Akad. i. 45-54) does not clearly state his own views as to Plato's meaning

[22] Vide supra. 298. The statement Tim. 51 A, that the ὑποδοχὴ τοῦ γεγονότος is neither one of the four elements, μήτε ὅσα ἐκ τούτων μήτε ἐξ ὧν ταῦτα γέγονεν, is merely intended to exclude the notion of any definite matter: the individual sensible things are what come into being from the elements. By 'that out of which these become' we are not merely to understand the triangles (vide chap. viii.) of which Plato composes the elements. The expression seems designedly general, to suit any other supposition which represents the elements as derived, e.g. the theories of the Atomists and of Anaxagoras. There is no real question as to what the elements are composed of. The object is rather to guard against any confusion of the primal substratum with the components of the elements (determined in form or quality), whatever they may be.

[23] Tim. 30 A, vide p. 291, 181; 52 D sqq. 69 B; cf. Polit 269 D, 273 B: τούτων δὲ αὐτῷ [τῷ κόσμῳ] τὸ σωματοειδὲς τῆς συγκράσεως αἴτιον, τὸ τῆς πάλαι ποτὲ φύσεως σύντροφον, ὅτι πολλῆς ἦν μετέχον ἀταξίας πρὶν εἰς τὸν νῦν κόσμον ἀφικέσθαι.

clares that the common substratum of all elementary forms must be entirely formless. Here beginnings of configuration are attributed to it. Elsewhere he holds that all the visible was originally created.[24] According to this passage, a visible something existed before the creation of the world.[25] He makes all motion in the corporeal to come from the soul. Here inanimate matter is said to be continually moved. These contradictions are not to be evaded by the distinction of a double matter;[26] (a primitive matter which, as wholly shapeless, is likewise invisible and uncorporeal,—and a

---

[24] Tim. 28 B

[25] The expedient, which Stallbaum (Plat. Tim. 205 sqq) and apparently also Volquardsen (loc. cit 70 sq.) adopt in the supposition that God first made matter and then fashioned the world out of it, is thoroughly inadmissible Had this been Plato's meaning he must somewhere or other have declared it; but there is not a single passage in which a creation of matter is taught or hinted at (on Tim. 52 D, cf. note 27), nor does Aristotle know anything about it; the Timæus rather distinguishes the foundation of the corporeal from all Becoming: the archetype is one, the copy is two, γένεσιν ἔχον καὶ ὁρατὸν, the ὑποδοχὴ γενέσεως, three (48 E); ἅπαν ὅσονπερ ἔχῃ γένεσιν (49 E, vide note 12) is a mere τοιοῦτον, not a τόδε; the ἕδραν παρέχον ὅσα ἔχει γένεσιν πᾶσιν is separated from the αἰσθητὸν and γεννητὸν (52 A, vide note 15). One is fashioned by God: of the other it is said that he has received it to form it into the world (30 A: πᾶν ὅσον ἦν ὁρατὸν παραλαβών 68 E. ταῦτα δὴ πάντα τότε ταύτῃ πεφυκότα ἐξ ἀνάγκης ὁ .. δημιουργὸς ... παρελάμβανεν, ἡνίκα τὸν αὐτάρκη τε καὶ τὸν τελεώτατον θεὸν ἐγέννα). Expressions like this cannot mean that God created it for this end and then formed it: and Plato could not possibly have assumed this. Supposing that there were in the world no element in its essence and origin independent of the divine causality, the limitation of that causality by necessity, and the opposition of νοῦς and ἀνάγκη, so expressly emphasised by Plato, would have no foundation, for (Politicus, 273 B) only good is communicated to the world by its author, everything incomplete and bad can only originate from its corporeal nature. Were this likewise the work of the Divinity, there could be, on Plato's theory, no such thing as evil in the world.

[26] Ueberweg, Rhein. Mus. ix. 62. Siebeck loc. cit. is opposed to him.

secondary matter, which even before the creation of the world was to a certain extent formed). Not only does Plato give no hint of such a distinction,[27] but he expressly excludes it, by attributing to the same substratum—which at first, before the Deity has begun to set it in order, is described as entirely without properties—an unregulated motion, and those beginnings of elementary forms, which it is difficult to conceive as originating prior to the framing of the Cosmos.[28] This point must therefore belong to the mythical expressions in which the Timæus abounds.[29] It is the ancient notion of Chaos which Plato temporarily appropriates,

---

[27] Tim. 52 D (supra, note 15 end) might perhaps suggest itself; where by γένεσις, as distinguished from χώρα, the so-called secondary matter might be understood. But the comparison of p. 50 C (γένη τριττά, τὸ μὲν γιγνόμενον, τὸ δ' ἐν ᾧ γίγνεται, τὸ δ' ὅθεν ἀφομοιούμενον φύεται τὸ γιγνόμενον) and 52 A (supra, note 15 beginning) proves that the γένεσις applies to that which is fashioned on the model of the ideas—the word of sense. This would of course not be anterior to the world; Plato does not say that the γιγνόμενον was before the world, but simply that the ὄν, the χώρα, and the γένεσις are distinct (τρία τριχῇ), and were always so, i.e. they are distinct in concept.

[28] Tim. 48 E, Plato says: besides the previous two classes (εἴδη), the παράδειγμα and the μίμημα παραδείγματος, there is a third, the ὑποδοχὴ or τιθήνη γενέσεως. After having shown that all determinate matter, in its continual interchange and transition, presupposes such an unchangeable substratum, he repeats, 50 C (vide previous note), his enumeration and explains that none of the forms and attributes which it is to appropriate can belong to that substratum; then, 52 A (vide note 15), he again recurs to the same classification, which, 52 D (ibid. end), is repeated a third time, and immediately adds the words: τὴν δὲ δὴ γενέσεως τιθήνην ὑγραινομένην, καὶ πυρουμένην, &c. παντοδαπὴν μὲν ἰδεῖν φαίνεσθαι, διὰ δὲ τὸ μηθ' ὁμοίων δυνάμεων μήτε ἰσορρόπων ἐμπίπλασθαι κατ' οὐδὲν αὐτῆς ἰσορροπεῖν, &c. Here it is obvious that the τιθήνη is the substratum previously described as entirely formless, which however cannot possibly be liquid, fiery, &c., before it has taken the forms of the elementary bodies.

[29] So, according to Bockh, loc. cit., with all that goes beyond the theory of matter in this dialogue.

replacing it by something else when he has to explain himself more definitely. The rest has more weight, but is still not decisive; even if that which underlies all determinate matter, as substratum and as cause of its apparent constitution, be, according to our view, Matter alone, it may still be asked whether that view is shared by Plato. He constantly declares, and the Timæus reiterates the declaration (27 D), that only to the Idea does true existence belong; but how can he maintain this if Matter be set beside the Idea, as a second substance, equally eternal, and according to its essential nature equally permanent and self-identical, in all the vicissitude of its forms? So far, however, from doing so, Plato designates matter with sufficient clearness as the Non-existent. According to the Timæus, it is neither to be apprehended by Thought, like the Idea; nor by Perception, like the sensible Phenomenon.[30] Since, then, true Being, according to Plato, is absolutely knowable, while that which is intermediate between Being and Non-being is the object of perception, and Non-being is wholly unknowable,[31]—it follows that Matter can only belong to Non-being. And the same inference is deducible from the definition of sense as a middle term between Being and Non-being.[32] If all the Being of Sense arises from participation in Ideas,[33] that can only be Non-being whereby Sense and Ideas are contradistinguished from each other. Plato, however, has expressed himself still

[30] 52 A sq.; vide note 15.
[31] Vide p. 266, 225
[32] Rep. v. 477 A, 479 B sq, x. 597 A.
[33] Rep. v. 479, vi. 509 B, vii. 517 C sq.; Phædo, 74 A sq.; 76 D, 100 D; Symp. 211 B; Parm. 129 A, 130 B

more clearly: 'That in which all things appear, grow up and decay, is Space.'[34] It is, therefore, that Third Element which, side by side with Ideas and the Phenomenal world, is required as the universal groundwork of the latter.[35] It is conceived, not as a mass filling space, but as Space itself—the Empty, which receives into itself the forms of the corporeal. Hence the Timæus never speaks of this groundwork of the sensibly-perceptible as that *out of* which, but always as that *in* which, things have become.[36] Aristotle, too, agrees with this; his testimony is all the more weighty, as his inclination to fit in the views of others under

---

[34] Cf with Tim. 49 E: (ἐν ᾧ δὲ ἐγγιγνόμενα ἀεὶ ἕκαστα αὐτῶν φαντάζεται καὶ πάλιν ἐκεῖθεν ἀπόλλυται) ibid. 52 A: (τὸ αἰσθητὸν) γιγνόμενόν τε ἔν τινι τόπῳ καὶ πάλιν ἐκεῖθεν ἀπολλύμενον.

[35] Loc. cit.: τρίτον δὲ αὖ γένος ὂν τὸ τῆς χώρας ἀεὶ φθορὰν οὐ προσδεχόμενον, ἕδραν δὲ παρέχον ὅσα ἔχει γένεσιν πᾶσιν, κ.τ.λ.; vide note 15. Tim. 53 D: οὗτος μὲν οὖν δὴ παρὰ τῆς ἐμῆς ψήφου λογισθεὶς ἐν κεφαλαίῳ δεδόσθω λόγος, ὅν τε καὶ χώραν καὶ γένεσιν εἶναι, &c. It is unimportant whether we translate χώρα here by 'space,' or with Schneider (d. mat. Princ. d. plat. Metaph. 12) by 'place,' for place just as well as space can be imagined empty or full. The only point here is whether it is a full or an empty space, which, according to Plato, forms the original substratum of the corporeal world. But as Plato expressly marks the χώρα as the sphere of all Becoming, we need not give it the more limited signification of Place (i e. determined space), rather than the general one of Space. Plato himself, according to Aristotle, did not distinguish between χώρα and τόπος: v. subter, note 39.

[36] He says, 50 A, 53 A, of the elements, that things are fashioned ἐξ αὐτῶν, for they have determined forms, they are bodies (which is not the case with the δεξαμένη; cf. note 9, end), and therefore constituent parts of things. With respect to that which precedes the elements as their general substratum, it is merely said, 49 E, 50 C–E, 52 A–B, that it is that ἐν ᾧ γίγνεται, the ἐκδεχόμενον πάντα γένη ἐν αὐτῷ &c. Such an expression, repeated six times, cannot be unintentional, but can only be explained on the view enunciated above. What, again, is the meaning of the statement, 50 A (supra, note 14), in a comparison, that as the figures which we make ἐκ χρυσοῦ are all gold, so it is with the φύσις τὰ πάντα σώματα δεχομένη, it is to be considered in all of them as one and the same? In both cases the substratum remains

categories of his system would have disposed him rather to ascribe to his master the notion of Matter as a positive principle side by side with the Idea, in opposition to Plato's real meaning, than to deny, without historical reason, that Plato held such an opinion. Aristotle, however, assures us that Plato made the Unlimited (ἄπειρον) a principle, not in the sense in which 'unlimited' might be the predicate of another substratum, but so that the Unlimited should itself be subject.[37] He distinguishes his own view of Matter from the Platonic view, by the definition that while Plato regards Matter as wholly and absolutely Non-being, he himself regards it as only relatively so: (κατὰ συμβεβηκός). To Plato negation (στέρησις) is the essence of Matter; to Aristotle it is only a quality of Matter.[38] As to the oral discourses, Aristotle makes it appear that in these, far more than in the Timæus, Plato avoided the appearance of presupposing a positive Matter; since he merely designates the Great-and-Small as that which receives Ideas into itself.[39] But

the same, in spite of the multiplicity and change of its forms; but it does not follow that this substratum is in one case that *out* of which, and in the other that *in* which, the things become

[37] Phys. iii. 4, 203 a 3 · πάντες (τὸ ἄπειρον) ὡς ἀρχήν τινα τιθέασι τῶν ὄντων, οἱ μὲν, ὥσπερ οἱ Πυθαγόρειοι καὶ Πλάτων, καθ' αὑτό, οὐχ ὡς συμβεβηκός τινι ἑτέρῳ, ἀλλ' οὐσίαν αὐτὸ ὂν τὸ ἄπειρον.

[38] Phys. i. 9; vide my Plat. Stud. p 223 sqq. Ebben's objections to my elucidation of this passage (De Plat. id. doctr. 41 sqq.) scarcely need detailed examination.

[39] Phys. iv. 2, 209 b. ii. 33: Πλάτων τὴν ὕλην καὶ τὴν χώραν ταὐτό φησίν εἶναι ἐν τῷ Τιμαίῳ · τὸ γὰρ μεταληπτικὸν καὶ τὴν χώραν ἓν καὶ ταὐτόν. ἄλλον δὲ τρόπον ἐκεῖ τε λέγων τὸ μεταληπτικὸν καὶ ἐν τοῖς λεγομένοις ἀγράφοις δόγμασιν (on which cf. chap. ii note 7) ὅμως τὸν τόπον καὶ τὴν χώραν τὸ αὐτὸ ἀπεφήνατο . . Πλάτωνι μέντοι λεκτέον . . . διὰ τί οὐκ ἐν τόπῳ τὰ εἴδη καὶ οἱ ἀριθμοί, εἴπερ τὸ μεθεκτικὸν ὁ τόπος, εἴτε τοῦ μεγάλου καὶ τοῦ μικροῦ ὄντος τοῦ μεθεκτικοῦ εἴτε τῆς ὕλης, ὥσπερ ἐν τῷ Τιμαίῳ

the most striking proof of the correctness of this view is given by Plato himself in his mathematical construction of the Elements.[40] A philosopher who should conceive of a mass filling space, assuming different forms, and thus changing into the several elements, could only seek for the ultimate constituents of these elements in the smallest bodies. Plato, however, supposes the Elements to be composed of planes, and, in their passage into each other, to resolve themselves into planes. Thus he makes bodies to originate not from atoms primarily, but from figures, by means of the mathematical limitation of empty space.[41]

γέγραφεν. Plato in the Timæus does not use the expression ὕλη (vide note 9), but he describes the basis of the sensible in such a way that Aristotle ascribes that denotation to him. As he expressly makes an exception in the case of the ἄγραφα δόγματα, there can have been no description in them similar to that of the Timæus; Metaph. ι. 7, 988 a. 25, the Great-and-Small are expressly denoted as a ὕλη ἀσώματος, and Phys iv. 7, 214 a. 13, Aristotle says: διὸ φασί τινες εἶναι τὸ κενὸν τὴν τοῦ σώματος ὕλην, οἷπερ καὶ τὸν τόπον, which certainly refers to the Platonic school, and probably to Plato himself. Plato had actually described the χώρα as the τόπος of all perceptible existences (in the passage Tim. 52 A sq, quoted in note 15 and note 34).

[40] This point, which is decisive for the present question, and too little considered by the supporters of a corporeal primary matter in Plato (as Susemihl, loc. cit. 409, remarks) will be discussed in greater detail below.

[41] Teichmuller's objections (Stud. z. Gesch. d. Begr. 328 sq.) to the above view seem to me to prove little : 'Matter, according to Plato, is the basis of motion and change; but this does not apply to space.' But the basis of motion with Plato is the soul; matter so called is only basis of Becoming, of the shifting change between opposed conditions. Why should not this basis, on Plato's theory, reside in the fact that, that which, according to its conceptual essence is something ordered and regulated, becomes, when it admits the form of space, something unlimited and therefore un-ordered? 'It could not be said of space' (vide note 15) 'that we perceive matter as in a dream when we say that everything must be in a determined place.' But Plato does not say that 'we perceive matter as in a dream'; he says that the χώρα is that in reference to which we imagine (ὀνειροπολοῦμεν) that everything must be in a place somewhere, whereas this is not true of the actually existing.

For these reasons we cannot admit that Plato held a corporeal primary Matter. But it does not follow that Ritter [42] is right in assuming him to have regarded the sensuous notion as something merely subjective. According to Ritter, all Ideas (with the exception of the highest) possess only a limited existence. This involves the hypothesis of a limited knowledge which does not adequately distinguish the pure essence of

The expression ὀνειρώττειν does not imply that χώρα cannot be perceived in the waking state, but that we imagine what holds good only of sensible being, to hold good of all being generally. Teichmuller's final objection is that Plato's description elsewhere of matter does not apply to space. This in a certain sense is correct; the delineation of the antemundane chaotic matter (mentioned supra) cannot be transferred unchanged to the concept given in the passage before us. But Teichmuller, like all who deny to Plato the notion of such matter, is forced to reckon this delineation amongst the mythical elements of the exposition. On the other hand, as regards Plato's manner of envisagement, I cannot see the impossibility of saying that space becomes watery or fiery (τὴν δὲ δὴ γενέσεως τιθήνην ὑγραινομένην καὶ πυρουμένην, 52 D). In the formation of the elements, the πανδεχὲς becomes water, fire, &c. simply through a determined fashioning in space. This paragraph, however, by which every theory of Platonic matter has to establish its correctness, Teichmuller passes by unnoticed. He believes (p. 332 sq.) that Plato determines matter, just as Aristotle did afterwards, to be Potentiality (δύναμις). The only proof which he quotes to support his view, Tim. 50 B, does not prove it in the least. It is there said of the φύσις τὰ πάντα σώματα δεχομένη (vide note 14). ταὐτὸν αὐτὴν ἀεὶ προσρητέον· ἐκ γὰρ τῆς ἑαυτῆς τὸ παράπαν οὐκ ἐξίσταται δυνάμεως. A determined δύναμις (here identical with φύσις), i.e. a determined property, is certainly thus attributed to it; and according to what follows this consists in its being the πανδεχές. But we cannot conclude that in its essence it is nothing else than δύναμις; whether δύναμις is understood as the potentiality to become everything, or the power to produce everything. In Teichmuller's further remarks, there is nothing to prove that, 'according to Plato, the essence of matter is the potentiality of the Idea, or mere possibility, and nothing more.'

[42] Gesch. d. Phil. ii 363–378; vide especially p. 369, 374 sqq. Similarly Fries Gesch. der Phil. i. 295, 306, 336, 351, and Maguire, An Essay on the Platonic Idea (Lond. 1866), 102 sq, who, however, has strangely misunderstood the words (Tim. 52 B) τὸ δὲ μήτ' ἐν γῇ, κ.τ.λ.

things, and only apprehends Ideas partially. Hence the notion of an existence in which the Ideas are intermingled, and their absolute Being becomes a merely relative Being. Intelligent natures, however, strive for perfect knowledge; and thus the notion of Becoming appears to arise. The sensuous notion, therefore, results from the imperfection of Ideas in their separation from one another; the world of Sense exists only in relation to the sentient subject. So the Platonic theory of Matter would be in effect identical with that of Leibnitz,—sensible existence would be only the product of confused notion or opinion. Of this line of thought (as Ritter himself admits [43]) there are, in the Platonic writings, only 'very obscure indications,' and even these, on closer consideration, disappear. Plato certainly says that there is a κοινωνία of Ideas; and that in the sensuous notion and sensuous existence Ideas intermingle with each other.[44] But he nowhere makes the communion of concepts, as such, contain the ground of this intermingling. Even in the Republic (v. 476 A)[45] it is only asserted that, beside the combination of concepts with the corporeal and Becoming, their combination among themselves might make it appear as if the concept, which is essentially One, were a Plurality. But

[43] Loc. cit. p. 370.
[44] E.g. Rep. vii. 524 C: μέγα μὴν καὶ ὄψις καὶ σμικρὸν ἑώρα, φαμέν, ἀλλ' οὐ κεχωρισμένον, ἀλλὰ συγκεχυμένον τι. Cf. Rep v. 479 A; vide pp 228, 295.
[45] Πάντων τῶν εἰδῶν περὶ ὃ αὐτὸς λόγος, αὐτὸ μὲν ἓν ἕκαστον εἶναι, τῇ δὲ τῶν πράξεων καὶ σωμάτων καὶ ἀλλήλων κοινωνίᾳ πανταχοῦ φανταζόμενα πολλὰ φαίνεσθαι ἕκαστον, i.e. one and the same concept appears in different places; the concept of unity, for instance, not merely in the separate individuals of most widely different kinds, but in all the concepts which participate in it; hence the appearance of unity as such being manifold.

as this only happens in the case of persons unacquainted with the dialectical discrimination of Ideas,[46] it must result from the incapacity of the individual to distinguish the copy from the prototype, the thing participating from that in which it participates.[47] Nothing is said as to the origin of that distinction. If we bring other passages to our aid, we shall find that Plato, so far from deriving material existence merely from the sensuous notion, rather derives the sensuous notion from the nature of the corporeal. According to the Phædo, it is the union of soul with body which hinders us from a pure cognition:[48] at our entrance into this life, by means of that union, we have sipped the draught of Lethe and forgotten the Ideas.[49] At the beginning of its earthly existence, the soul loses reason in the ebb and flow of sensation; not until this has abated, does it once more partake of reason:[50] and then, only by disengaging itself inwardly from the body.[51] The soul cannot hope for the full possession of reason till it is wholly freed from this lower life and exists in itself alone.[52] The tone and connection of these enunciations being almost wholly didactic, we ought not to

[46] Soph. 253 D; Phileb. 15 D.
[47] Rep. v. 476 C ὁ οὖν καλὰ μὲν πράγματα νομίζων, αὐτὸ δὲ κάλλος μήτε νομίζων, μήτε, ἄν τις ἡγῆται ἐπὶ τὴν γνῶσιν αὐτοῦ, δυνάμενος ἕπεσθαι, ὄναρ ἢ ὕπαρ δοκεῖ σοι ζῆν; σκόπει δέ· τὸ ὀνειρώττειν ἆρα οὐ τόδε ἐστὶν, ἐάν τε ἐν ὕπνῳ τις, ἐάν τε ἐγρηγορὼς τὸ ὅμοιόν τῳ μὴ ὅμοιον ἀλλ' αὐτὸ ἡγῆται εἶναι ᾧ ἔοικεν; ⟨.. τί δὲ, ὁ τἀναντία τούτων ἡγούμενός τέ τι αὐτὸ καλὸν καὶ δυνάμενος καθορᾶν καὶ αὐτὸ καὶ τὰ ἐκείνου μετέχοντα, καὶ οὔτε τὰ μετέχοντα αὐτὸ οὔτε αὐτὸ τὰ μετέχοντα ἡγούμενος, ὕπαρ ἢ ὄναρ αὖ καὶ οὗτος δοκεῖ σοι ζῆν,

[48] Phædo, 66 B sqq. Cf. ibid. 65 A; Rep x. 611 B.
[49] Phædo, 76 D; Rep x. 621 A.
[50] Tim. 44 A· καὶ διὰ δὴ πάντα ταῦτα τὰ παθήματα (the previously described αἰσθήσεις) νῦν κατ' ἀρχάς τε ἄνους ψυχὴ γίγνεται τὸ πρῶτον, ὅταν εἰς σῶμα ἐνδεθῇ θνητόν, &c
[51] Phædo, 64 A, 65 E, 67 A; Tim. 42 B sq
[52] Phædo, 66 E, 67 B.

consider them mythical and exaggerated unless they are contradicted by definite counter-explanations. But this is not the case. Plato's having recognised in the sensuous perception a means for attaining the knowledge of truth, proves nothing.[53] The sensuous perception is such a means only so far as the sensuous element in it is abstracted, and a return made to the Idea that is revealed in it. On Ritter's theory Plato must have derived the sensuous notion from the communion of Ideas with each other, and from the manner in which this communion is presented by particular Ideas or souls,[54]—the sensible phenomenon being afterwards derived solely from the perception of sense. So far from this, Plato takes the opposite course, and explains the intermingling of Ideas from the nature of the sensuous notion, and the nature of the sensuous notion from that of sensuous existence. Such is the only explanation given in the Philebus and Timæus : and Aristotle knows of no other.[55] Indeed, as Brandis well remarks,[56] the subjective idealism which Ritter ascribes to Plato is altogether foreign to antiquity, and must necessarily be so from its whole point of view; it presupposes a consciousness of the importance of subjectivity, too one-sided and powerful for any but modern times.

If, then, the Universal, the basis of sensible existence, is neither a material substratum, nor a mere phantasy of the subjective notion, what is it ? Plato, in the passages

[53] Ritter, p. 350.
[54] Ritter's theory of souls being Ideas, and its incorrectness, I have already adverted to (preceding chapter). His view of matter, however, can be adopted, with slight modifications, apart from that theory, and no further stress need be laid here upon the point.
[55] See my Plat. Stud. p. 216 sqq.
[56] Gr.-rom. Phil. ii. a. 297.

quoted above, tells us himself, and Aristotle agrees with him. The groundwork of all material existence is the Unlimited—i.e. Unlimitedness, the Great-and-Small—conceived not as predicate, but as subject; not, however, to be described as corporeal substance; the Non-existent, i.e. Non-being;[57] that is to say, empty Space, as the condition of separation and division. In the place of an eternal Matter we must therefore suppose the mere form of Materiality, the form of Existence in Space and of Motion; and when the Timæus speaks of a Matter restlessly moved, before the creation of the world, this only expresses the thought that separation and Becoming are the essential forms of all sensible existence. These forms Plato would have us regard as something objective, present in the sensible Phenomenon itself, not merely in our notion. On the other hand, Matter can have no reality or substantiality of its own, for all reality is in Ideas. It remains, therefore, to explain Matter as the negation of the reality supposed in Ideas; as the Non-being of the Idea, into which the latter cannot enter without dissolving its Unity in Multiplicity, its Permanence in the flux of Becoming, its definiteness in the unlimited possibility of augmentation and diminution, its self-identity in an internal contradiction, its absolute Being in a combination of Being and Non-being. This concept is certainly hard to realise. Putting aside the question whether a Space without a substratum in Space—a Non-being, which exists apart from the notion

[57] For the μὴ ὂν cannot here be the predicate of a subject separate from it.

of it—is thinkable; reserving to another place the enquiry about the participation of this Non-being in Ideas, and passing by all the objections which might be raised from without, against this portion of the Platonic doctrine,—there are still two considerations which from its own point of view cannot be overlooked. One is the relation of Matter to our knowledge; the other its relation to things. That which absolutely is not, Plato maintains[58] cannot be conceived; consequently, if Matter is absolute Non-existence, the notion of it must also be impossible. It cannot be the object of perception (as he says himself[59]), for perception shows us only determinate forms of Matter, not the pure formless ground of all the material, only a τοιοῦτον, not the τόδε. But still less can it be the object of thought, for thought has to do only with the truly existent, not with the Non-existent. And it is impossible to see how we arrive at the notion of this substratum, if it is neither in a condition to be perceived nor thought. It is only a veiled expression of this perplexity when Plato says that it is apprehended by a kind of spurious reason; [60] and when he adds that it is very hard to comprehend, the embarrassment is

---

[58] Vide p. 226.

[59] Tim. 51 A, 52 B (vide notes 14 and 15), where it is called ἀνόρατον, μετ' ἀναισθησίας ἁπτὸν, 49 D sq (supra, note 12).

[60] 52 B· μετ' ἀναισθησίας ἁπτὸν λογισμῷ τινι νόθῳ. In what this 'spurious thinking' consists Plato himself can hardly explain. he makes use of this strange expression from inability to bring the notion of Matter under any of his categories. Tim. Socr. 94 B, understands him to mean a knowledge by analogy (λογισμῷ νόθῳ, τῷ μήπω κατ' ἐνθυωρίαν νοῆσθαι, ἀλλὰ κατ' ἀναλογίαν); and so Alex. Aphrod. Qu. nat. i. 1, p. 14; Simpl. Phys. 49 b u. Plotin. ii. 4, 10, p. 164 (i. 118 Kirchh.), interprets the expression as abstract thought, the ἀοριστία resulting from the removal of all sensible attributes.

openly confessed.[61] The fact is that, when we abstract all the particular qualities of that which is sensibly perceived, and seek for its common property, we find that it is only something thought, a universal concept; which, according to Plato's presuppositions, is precisely what it cannot be. The same result follows if we keep in view the import of Matter for the Being of things. Inasmuch as Matter is absolutely non-existent, and the sensible phenomenon is a middle term between Being and Non-being, an inferior proportion of reality must belong to Matter as compared with the sensible Phenomenon: to the one, a half-reality; to the other, none at all. But Matter is also to be the permanent principle,—that which, in the vicissitude of sensuous properties, maintains itself as something essential and self-identical.[62] It is the Objective, to which the images of Ideas reflecting themselves in the Phenomenon must cleave, in order to take hold, and become participant in Being.[63] It is that irrational remainder which is always left when we abstract from things that which in them is the copy of the Idea. However little reality may be conceded to it, it has the power of receiving the Idea, at least for its manifestation in the flux of Becoming and the externality of existence in Space,[64] and also of occasioning the vicissitude of birth and decay.[65] These characteristics certainly

---

[61] Loc. cit.: [τὸ τῆς χώρας] μόγις πιστόν, κ.τ.λ. (vide note 15), 49 A: νῦν δὲ ὁ λόγος ἔοικεν εἰσαναγκάζειν χαλεπὸν καὶ ἀμυδρὸν εἶδος ἐπιχειρεῖν λόγοις ἐμφανίσαι

[62] The τόδε and τοῦτο, which are equivalent; vide notes 12 and 14.

[63] 52 C; vide notes 2 and 3.

[64] Cf. subsequent remarks in this chapter and in chap. x. on the relation of reason to natural necessity, on the origin of the latter and on evil.

[65] Cf. the quotations from Eu-

carry us far beyond the concept of mere Space, and give to Matter, instead of Non-being, a Being which, in its very permanence, has a certain similarity to that of the Idea. That which Plato adduces [66] as the special characteristic of true Being,—the power to do and to suffer,—is also attributed to Matter, when it is described as a cause restraining the operations of reason.[67] And this may help to explain those expressions in the Timæus, which represent the groundwork of sense not as mere capability of extension, but as a mass contained in Space. But we must abide by the results we have just obtained. Plato's real view, according to his plain statement, tends to deny all Being to Matter, to abolish the notion of extended substance in the concept of mere extension. This was necessitated by the first general principles of his system. Whatever contradicts this view (so far as Plato seriously means it) we must regard as an involuntary concession to facts, which refused to give way to his theory.[68]

II. *The Relation of Sensible Objects to the Idea.*—The above conception of Platonic Matter explains, on one side at least, Plato's theory as to the relation of material things to the Idea. It is usually believed that, to Plato, the world of sense and that of Ideas stood over against each other, as two separate spheres,

demus and Hermodorus, note 17, and p 277, 137.

[66] Vide p. 262, 108.

[67] τὸ τῆς πλανωμένης αἰτίας εἶδος, Tim. 48 A.

[68] I cannot, however, appeal to the passage (Soph 242 D) quoted by Teichmuller (Stud. z. Gesch. d. Begr. 137) as evidence against the dualistic character of the Platonic system. In that passage the question is not as to dualism in general, but as to the assumption of two or three material principles, and especially as to the half-mythical cosmogonies of Pherecydes and (apparently) of Parmenides in the second part of his poem.

316   PLATO AND THE OLDER ACADEMY.

two substantially different classes of existence. The objections of Aristotle to the theory of Ideas [69] are chiefly grounded on this hypothesis, to which Plato has undoubtedly given occasion by what he says of the existence of Ideas for themselves and as archetypes. We must nevertheless question its correctness. Plato himself asks [70] how it is possible that Ideas can be in the Becoming, and in the unlimited Many, without losing their Unity and Invariability? And he shows with what difficulties this enquiry is beset. Whether it be assumed that the whole Idea is in each of the many participating in it, or that in each there is only a part of the Idea, in either case the Idea would be divided.[71] Again, if the doctrine of Ideas be founded on the necessity of assuming a common concept for all Multiplicity, a common concept must be likewise assumed for and above the Idea and its synonymous phenomena:—and so on *ad infinitum*.[72] This difficulty presents itself again on the supposition that the communion of things with Ideas consists in the imitation of the one from the other.[73] Lastly, if it be maintained that the Ideas are that which they are, for themselves absolutely,—it would seem that they could never have reference to us or become known by us, but only refer to themselves.[74] These ob-

[69] Cf. Pt. ii. b. 216 sqq., 2nd edit.
[70] Phileb. 15 B; vide p. 252, 89.
[71] Phileb. loc. cit. Parm. 130 E–131 E.
[72] Parm. 131 E sq. The same objection, often made by Aristotle, is usually expressed by saying that the doctrine of Ideas necessitates the supposition of a τρίτος ἄνθρωπος. Vide infra.
[73] Parm. 132 D sqq. Cf. Alexander's quotation from Eudemus (Schol. in Arist. 566 a. 11. b. 15).
[74] Parm. 133 B sqq.

jections to the doctrine of Ideas would not have been suggested by Plato, had he not been convinced that his theory was unaffected by them. How then from his own point of view could he seek their solution? The answer lies in his view of the nature of material things. As he ascribed to the Material no specific reality, distinct from that of the Ideas, but places all reality, simply and solely, in the Idea, and regards Non-being as the special property of the world of sense, all difficulties in this form vanish. He does not require any Third between the Idea and the Phenomenon, for they are not two separate substances, standing side by side with one another; the Idea alone is the Substantial. He need not fear that the Idea should be divided, because of the participation of the Many in it, for this plurality is nothing truly real. Nor need he consider how the Idea, as existing for itself, can at the same time stand in relation to the Phenomenon; for as the Phenomenon, so far as it exists, is immanent in the Idea,—as its allotted share of Being is only the Being of the Idea in it,—so the Being of Ideas, and their reference to one another, is in itself their reference to the Phenomenon; and the Being of the Phenomenon is its reference to the Ideas.[75] While, therefore, in places where he has no occasion to develope more precisely his view of the nature of material things, Plato may adhere to the ordinary notion, and represent the Ideas as archetypes, over against which the copies stand, with a reality of their own, like a second world side by side with ours—in

[75] Cf. Plat. Stud. p. 181.

318 PLATO AND THE OLDER ACADEMY.

reality, he is still only expressing the qualitative distinction between real and merely phenomenal existence. He is only giving the metaphysical difference between the world of Ideas and the world of sense; not an actual partition of the two, in which each attains its specific reality, and the sum total of Being is divided between them. It is one and the same Being which is contemplated whole and pure in the Idea—imperfect and turbid in the sensible Phenomenon. The unity of the Idea appears [76] in objects of sense as Multiplicity; the Phenomenon is (Rep. vii. 514) only the adumbration of the Idea,[77] only the multiform diffusion of its rays in that which, by itself, is the dark and empty space of the Unlimited. But whether this opinion is intrinsically tenable, and whether the above-mentioned difficulties as to the theory of Ideas do not, after all, reappear in an altered form, is another question which will come before us further on.[78]

---

[76] Rep. v. 476 A; Phil. 15 B. See note 47.

[77] Cf. the well-known allegory of the prisoners in the cave, Rep. vii. 514 sqq., according to which the objects of sensible perception stand to true existences in the relation of the shadows to the bodies, when we take any object of sensible perception for something real, we are simply taking the shadows for the things themselves.

[78] The view developed above is essentially accepted by Susemihl, Genet. Entw. i. 352, Deuschle, Plat. Sprachphil. 27 sq.; Ribbing, Plat. Ideenl. i. 252, 262, 333, 360 sq.; and is combated by Stumpf, Verh. d. plat. Gott. z. Idee d. Guten, 23 sqq., and others. It is well known that Plato ascribes a being (and that too of a particular kind) not merely to Ideas but to souls and sensible things. We have seen (note 15) that, together with the Ideas and the corporeal world, he mentions space as a third class of Being: and he considers the Becoming and change of sensible things an objective incident. Aristotle, therefore, with whom the reality of the latter was an article of faith, in representing the εἴδη as χωριστά, as a second world besides the sensible world, had sufficient justification in the Platonic doctrine. The Ideas may be independent of and uninfluenced by the phenomenon, and there may be something in the phenomenon which

All that we have said, however, concerns only one side of the relation of the Phenomenon to the Idea: the negative aspect, in which the self-subsistence of sensible things is cancelled, and the Phenomenon is reduced to the Idea, as its substance. The other side is far more difficult. If the world of sense, as such, have so little reality; if, apart from its participation in the Idea, it be even regarded as non-existent, how is this Non-existence generally thinkable beside the absolute Being of the Idea, and how can it be explained from the point of view of the Ideas? To this question the Platonic system as such contains no answer. The separates it from the Idea. But, as was shown above, it does not follow that the phenomenon has equally an existence in and for itself; that its being does not rise into that of the Ideas; that consequently it exists without the Ideas, just as the Ideas exist without it. I do not assert that the Platonic view on the relation of things to the Ideas is exhausted by the explanation of the immanence of the one in the other. I merely say that this expresses one side of the doctrine; the other side, the distinction of things from the Ideas, the separateness of sensible being, which makes the Ideas something beyond the world of sense, εἴδη χωριστά, can not only not be explained by that determination, but cannot even be brought into harmony with it. An objector therefore must not be contented with showing that the latter determinations are to be found in Plato (which I do not deny), but must prove that the others are not to be found and are not needed by the universal presuppositions of his system. To prove this is impossible so long as the passages above quoted are allowed to stand, and so long as the oft-repeated explanation (that only the Ideas have real Being, and are the object of knowledge, and that all the attributes of things, in short all the reality that they have, is imparted to them by the Ideas) holds good. If it seems impossible to attribute such a contradiction to Plato, we may ask how Plato could have proceeded in order to escape it on the suppositions of his system; and why this contradiction is less possible than the others which Aristotle has so forcibly pointed out. And we may notice that even Spinoza, whose conclusions otherwise are educed with the utmost rigour, continually involves himself in analogous contradictions, explaining the plurality of things and finitude generally as something which vanishes under reflective contemplation (*sub æternitatis specie*), and yet as an objective reality, not merely a *datum* in our envisagement.

assumption, side by side with the Ideas, of a second real principle which should contain the ground of finite existence, Plato has made impossible, by maintaining that reality belongs alone to the Idea. Neither can he derive the finite from the Ideas themselves—for what should determine the Idea to assume the form of Non-being instead of its perfect Being, and to break up the unity of its essence into partition in space? He allows, indeed, that in each individual concept, as such, there is an infinity of Non-being; but this is quite other than the Non-being of material existence. The Non-being in the Ideas is only the distinction of Ideas from one another,—the Non-being of sensible objects, on the contrary, is the distinction of the Phenomenon from the Idea. The former completes itself by means of the reciprocal relation of the Ideas, so that the Ideal world, taken as a whole, includes in itself all reality, and has abolished all Non-being. The latter is the essential and constant boundary of the finite, by reason of which each Idea appears (not only in relation to other Ideas, but in itself) as a multiplicity, consequently in part non-existent, inseparably combined with the contrary of itself. Again, therefore, it is impossible to point out in Plato any actual derivation of the phenomenon from the Ideas. We can but enquire whether he ever sought to establish such an interconnection, and if so, how he attempted it.

We get our first hint on this subject from the fact that the Idea of the Good is placed at the apex of the system,—or that God, as the Timæus expresses it,[79]

[79] 29 D sq ; vide p. 291, note 181.

formed the world because He was good. This thought, fully developed, would lead to such a concept of God as would make it essential in Him to manifest Himself in the Finite. Plato, however, for reasons deducible from the foregoing pages, could not thus develope it. The only conclusion he draws is that God brought into order the lawlessly moved mass of visible things, in which Matter, or the Finite, is already generally presupposed. To explain this latter, the Timæus can only appeal to necessity.[80] Of the Divine causality, on the contrary, it is assumed, that it could bring forth nothing but perfection.[81] Similarly the Theætetus (176 A) declares: Evil can never cease, for there must always be something opposite to good; and as this can have no place with the gods, it necessarily hovers about in mortal nature and in our world. And the Politicus (269 C) speaks to the same effect, of the alternation of cycles, following of necessity from the corporeal nature of the universe. All this, however, does not bring the question a single step nearer its answer, for this necessity is only another expression for the nature of the Finite,—which is here presupposed and not derived. In vain do we seek among the writings of Plato, for any express mention of such a derivation. We are therefore forced to construct one

[80] 46 D, 56 C, 68 D sq, and especially 47 F sq.
[81] At least in 41 C. The fundamental position propounded, 30 A, in another connection (θέμις οὔτ'ἦν οὔτ' ἔστι τῷ ἀρίστῳ δρᾶν ἄλλο πλὴν τὸ κάλλιστον), is applied to mean that God Himself can produce no mortal creation, and the whole distinction, to be mentioned later on, between that which νοῦς and that which ἀνάγκη has done in the world, points that way. Cf. Polit. 209 E sq. It will be shown below that no evil comes from God (chap. xii.).

from the whole tenor of his system. How Ritter has attempted to do this we have already seen, but were unable to agree with him. Aristotle seems to point out another way. According to him,[82] the Great-and-Small (or the Unlimited) is not merely the Matter of sensible objects but also of the Ideas: from its union with the One arise Ideas or intelligible numbers.[83] If we adhere to this view, Materiality, in which the specific property of the sensible phenomenon consists, would be accounted for, by means of the participation

[82] Metaph. i. 6, 987 b. 18 sqq. (where in the sentence so often quoted, ἐξ ἐκείνων, &c., the words τὰ εἴδη are to be struck out). 988 a. 8 sqq., xi. 2, 1060 b. 6, xiv. 1, 1087 b. 12; Phys. iii. 4, 203 a. 3-16, iv. 2, 209 b. 33 According to Simpl. Phys. 32 b. m. 104, b m. cf. 117 a. m. (Schol. in Ar. 334 b. 25, 362 a. 7, 368 a. 30), other Platonists, e.g Speusippus, Xenocrates, Heraclides, Hestiæus, gave a similar account, following the Platonic discourses on the Good. On the Great-and-Small of the early part of this chapter, and on the whole doctrine, cf my Plat. Stud. 216 sqq., 252 sqq., 291 sqq; Brandis, ii. a. 307 sqq.

[83] V. p. 253 sqq. The indefinite duad together with the unit is mentioned instead of the Great-and-Small as the material element (Alex. ad Metaph. i. 6, 987 b. 33; i. 9, 990 b. 17. Idem apud Simpl. Phys. 32 b. m., 104 b.; Porphyr. and Simpl. ibid.). Plato himself, however, seems to have used this exposition only with reference to numbers: the indefinite or the Great-and-Small of number is the even, the duad, which is called the δυὰς ἀόριστος, is distinction from the number two. (Cf. Arist Metaph. xiii. 7, 1081 a. 13 sqq., b 17 sqq. 31, 1082 a 13, b 30 c. q 1085 b. 7, xiv 3, 1091 a. 4, 1, 9, 990 b. 19; Alex. ad Metaph. i. 6; Schol. 551 b. 19; Ps. Alex. ad Metaph. 1085 b. 4, and my Plat. Stud 220 sqq., with the results of which Brandis (ii. a. 310) and Schwegler (Ariet Metaph. iii. 64) agree). On the other hand we see from Theophrastus, Metaph. (Frag. xii Wimm.) 12, 33, that the indefinite duad was made use of in the Platonic schools, like the ἄπειρον of the Pythagoreans, as the basis of everything finite and sensible. Instead of the term Great-and-Small, we find the Many and Few, the More and Less, Plurality, the Unlike, the Other, used to represent the material element (Arist. Metaph. xiv. 1, 1087 b. 4 sqq.). Each of these is added as Platonic to the disputed determinations of the Platonists, cf. on Unity and Plurality, Phileb. 16 c.; on the Like and Unlike, Tim. 27 D sq., Phil. 25 A, Parm 161 c. sq.; on the Unit and the θάτερον, Parmenides, Tim. 35 A, Soph. 254 E sqq.; on the More and Less, the Many and Few, Phileb. 24 E.

of the world of sense in the Ideas, and the difficulty of explaining the origin of material existence from Ideas would be removed.[84] But it is removed only to return in greater force. It is certainly more comprehensible that things should have in them Ideas in conjunction with the material element, but it is all the less easy to see how there can belong to Ideas, which are to consist of the same elements as material things, an existence essentially different from sensible existence. It is in effect to cut away the ground from under the whole Ideal theory, and at the same time to leave the world of sense, as distinguished from that of the Ideas, unexplained and unexplainable. And the same may be urged against the attempt [85] to explain the difference of the sensible, and the super-sensible world, by making Ideas originate from the immediate activity of the One, and sensible things out of the common material primary cause by means of the activity of Ideas.[86] If it is the same One, and the same Unlimited which in a first combination produces Ideas, and in a second, brought about by Ideas, produces sensible things, it is impossible to see where the extension and variability come from, which belong to sensible things,

[84] Stallbaum (Proll. in Tim 44; Parm. 136 sqq.) thinks that Platonic matter can be explained as simply equivalent to the eternal or infinite, which is also the matter of the Ideas

[85] Brandis, Gr.-rom. Phil. ii. b. 622; cf i. a 307 sq.

[86] Arist. Metaph. i. 6, 988 a. 10 (following the quotation, chap. ii. 167): τὰ γὰρ εἴδη τοῦ τί ἐστιν αἰτία τοῖς ἄλλοις τοῖς δ' εἴδεσι τὸ ἕν. καὶ (sc. φανερὸν) τίς; ἡ ὕλη ἡ ὑποκειμένη, καθ' ἧς τὰ εἴδη μὲν ἐπὶ τῶν αἰσθητῶν τὸ δὲ ἓν ἐν τοῖς εἴδεσι λέγεται (of which in that place the Ideas, here the One is predicted, so far as they contribute properties, definiteness of form), ὅτι αὕτη δυάς ἐστι, τὸ μέγα καὶ τὸ μικρόν.

but not to Ideas. The essential difference of Idea and phenomenon is still unaccounted for. There would be only one way out of the difficulty: to assume with Weisse [87] that the same elements constitute Ideal and finite Being, but in diverse relation; that in Ideas, the One rules and encompasses Matter, in the world of sense, it is overcome and embraced by Matter. But how is this perversion of the original relation of the two principles brought about? We can only retreat upon an inexplicable deterioration of a part of the Ideas.[88] But neither the Platonic nor the Aristotelian writings give the least hint of such a deterioration. The only passage which might be adduced in support of it, the Platonic doctrine of the sinking down of the soul into corporeality, has not this universal cosmical import, and presupposes the existence of a material world. If this way, however, be closed, it is no longer possible to ascribe to Plato the doctrine that the same Matter which is the groundwork of sensible existence, is also in the Ideas. Together with Matter, he must have transferred to the Ideal world Becoming, extension, and all that the Philebus predicates of the Unlimited, and the Timæus of the Universally-recipient. But in so doing he would have abandoned all ground for the assumption of Ideas, and for the distinction of sensible objects from the Idea. He would have flatly contra-

[87] De Plat. et Arist. in constit. summ. philos. princ. differentia (Lpz. 1828), 21 sqq. and in many passages of his notes on Aristotle's Physics and De Animâ; cf. my Plat. Stud. p. 293.

[88] Stallbaum's remark loc. cit. that the sensible is simply the copy, the Ideas the archetype, explains nothing; the question is, how the incompleteness of the copy can be reconciled with the equality of the elements in the Ideas and the sensible thing.

dicted the proposition, quoted by Aristotle,[89] that the Ideas are not in space. The groundwork of things sensible, which Plato describes in the Timæus, was necessary, because without it the specific difference between the world of Ideas and that of sense could not be explained. It was to provide a home for the Becoming and corporeal,—the visible and the sensible;[90] to be the place for the copies of the Idea, which, as copies merely, must exist in another;[91] it is the ground of change and of extension, the cause of the resistance experienced by the Idea in natural necessity.[92] How then can it be at the same time the element which forms the Ideas and Ideal numbers by receiving Unity into itself? Would not the Ideas directly become something extended? Would not that be true of them which Plato expressly denies[93]—that they are in another—namely in space? From these considerations it seems safer to charge Aristotle with a misunderstanding of the Platonic doctrine into which he might easily fall, rather than Plato with a contradiction that utterly destroys the coherence of his system. That Plato spoke of the Unlimited, or the Great-and-Small, in reference to Ideas, we may well believe. He actually does so in his writings. In the

---

[89] V. p. 242, 50.
[90] 49 A, 50 B, 51 A, 52 A.
[91] 52 B; vide notes 15 and 2
[92] Tim 47 E sqq. Details on this point later on.
[93] Vide supra, p. 240 eqq., but particularly the passage just quoted Tim 52 B; it is true only of the copy of Real Existence, that everything must be somewhere, for only this is in something else; τῷ δὲ ὄντως ὄντι βοηθὸς ὁ δι' ἀκριβείας ἀληθὴς λόγος, ὡς ἕως ἄν τι τὸ μὲν ἄλλο ᾖ, τὸ δὲ ἄλλο, οὐδέτερον ἐν οὐδετέρῳ ποτὲ γεγενημένον ἓν ἅμα ταὐτὸν καὶ δύο γενήσεσθον. Plato could not have expressed more definitely the independence of matter and the Idea.

Philebus (16 C) after he has said, at first quite universally, and expressly including pure Ideas (15 A), that all things have in them by nature limits and unlimitedness, he subsequently, referring to this, divides existence into Limited and Unlimited, and then describes the unlimited (24 A *sqq.*) in a manner that could not apply to the Idea, but only to the Unlimited in the material sense. Similarly in the Sophist (256 E) he remarks, in regard to the infinity of negative elements and class-qualities, that there is in every Idea plurality of Being and infinity of Non-being. There is no doubt a confusion here in Plato's language; and so far as this always presupposes confusion of thought, we must admit that he has not distinguished with sufficient clearness the elements of Plurality and Difference in the Ideas, from the cause out of which arise the divisibility and mutability of phenomena. But that he, therefore, transferred the Unlimited, in the same sense in which it is the specific property of sensible existence, to Ideas also, or that he actually called it the Matter of Ideas, we are not justified in asserting. Aristotle, however, makes no such allusion to a difference between the Matter of Ideas and that of sensible things, as modern critics have professed to find in him,[94] and the theory is positively excluded by his

---

[94] Ueberweg, Rhein. Mus. ix. 64 sqq who cannot convince himself that Plato identified the Indefinite in the Ideas with the material of sensible things, and also refuses to recognise it in the accounts given by Aristotle. These accounts, he says, designate the One and the Great-and-Small as the elements of all things; but this does not prevent the homonymous elements being considered as specifically distinct, at the same time as their generic similarity is recognised. In the Ideas, the first element is the One in the highest sense, the Idea of the good or the Divinity. The second is the θάτερον

whole exposition.[95] We can, therefore, only suppose that, on this particular question, he somewhat misap-

or the separation of the Ideas from one another. In mathematics, the former is the number one, the latter is arithmetically the indefinite duad, geometrically space, in corporeal substances, the former is the ἔνυλον εἶδος (determined qualities), the latter matter. The same view is supported by Stumpf loc. cit 77 sq.

[95] Aristotle often mentions the ἄπειρον or the μέγα καὶ μικρὸν as the ὕλη of the ideas; but he nowhere gives us to understand that this is an ἄπειρον of a different sort or the same ἄπειρον in a different way to that of sensible things. One and the same ἄπειρον is in both. Cf. Phys. iii. 4, 203 a. 9: τὸ μέντοι ἄπειρον καὶ ἐν τοῖς αἰσθητοῖς καὶ ἐν ἐκείναις [ταῖς ἰδέαις] εἶναι. i. 6, 987 b. 18: Plato considered the στοιχεῖα of the Ideas as the στοιχεῖα of all things: ὡς μὲν οὖν ὕλην τὸ μέγα καὶ τὸ μικρὸν εἶναι ἀρχὰς, ὡς δ' οὐσίαν τὸ ἕν. Ibid. 988 a. 11, vide note 86. Metaph xi. 2, 1060 b. 6 · τοῖς ... ἐκ τοῦ ἑνὸς καὶ τῆς ὕλης τὸν ἀριθμὸν (viz. the Ideal number or the Idea) γεννῶσι πρῶτον. xiv. 1, 1087 b. 12. the Platonists do not correctly define the ἀρχαὶ or στοιχεῖα οἱ μὲν τὸ μέγα καὶ τὸ μικρὸν λέγοντες μετὰ τοῦ ἑνὸς τρία ταῦτα στοιχεῖα τῶν ἀριθμῶν, τὰ μὲν δύο ὕλην τὸ δ' ἓν τὴν μορφήν. Stumpf loc. cit. remarks on this that, according to Aristotle, the ἕν the immediate cause only for the Ideas, and 'the same explanation holds good of the μέγα καὶ μικρόν.' I cannot understand how the Great-and-Small can possibly be called 'the immediate cause for the Ideas only;'

there is nothing in the things of sense that can supply its place as the Idea in them supplies the place of the One. Nor can I agree with Stumpf's conclusion. It is much more probable that Aristotle, had he meant that the ἄπειρον stands in different relation to sensible things from that in which it stands to the Ideas, would have said so, just as he does say in reference to the One. But in Metaph. 1. 6, 988, a. 11. (vide note 1), he says of one and the same ὕλη, the Great-and-Small—that in the Ideas, the One in things, the Idea, is assigned as the determination of form; and though in Phys. i. 4, 6, 203, a. 15, 206, b. 27 he ascribes two ἄπειρα to Plato, in so far as Plato breaks up the ἄπειρον into the Great-and-Small, there is not a word of different sorts of Great-and-Small in his accounts of Plato's doctrine as to the matter of Bodies. He says that in the Platonic school (and perhaps even with Plato himself) the Long and Short, the Broad and Narrow, the Deep and Shallow, were placed under the derivation of lengths, surfaces, and bodies respectively, instead of the Generic Concept comprehending them, viz the Great-and-Small (Metaph i. 9, 992 a. 10; xiii. 9, 1085 a 9). But he nowhere states that for the derivation of physical bodies the Great-and-Small was replaced by any other concept (such as that of the Full and Void). On the contrary, he meets Plato with the question, How can the Ideas be out of space, when the Great and Small, or Matter, is the μεθεκτικὸν = space?

prehended Plato. If such a view seem to impugn too disrespectfully the historical credibility of the Stagirite,[96] we must remember that the vagueness of Platonic doctrine would be very likely to cause a misapprehension of its real meaning in the mind of one who everywhere sought for fixed and accurately defined concepts. The physical part of the system which obliged Plato to determine the concept of Matter more accurately, and to distinguish the corporeally Unlimited from the element of plurality in the Ideas,—was, if we may judge from his quotations, chiefly known to Aristotle from the Timæus; and similar and even more striking misconstructions of Platonic expressions can be traced to him, with regard to many writings that still exist.[97] He points out himself that Plato described the Great-

(Phys. iv. 2, 209 b. 33.) In Metaph. i. 9, 992, b. 7 he draws the inference that if the ὑπεροχή and ἔλλειψις (equivalent to the Great-and-Small) are causes of motion, the Ideas also must be moved. Metaph. xiv. 3, 1090 b. 32 (where cf. Bonitz on the text), in opposition to Plato, he asks, whence the mathematical numbers are derived If from the Great-and-Small, they will be identical with the Ideal numbers. Phys. iii. 6 end. he concludes that if the ἄπειρον is the comprehensive principle in sensible things, καὶ ἐν τοῖς νοητοῖς τὸ μέγα καὶ τὸ μικρὸν ἔδει περιέχειν τὰ νοητά. These objections and inferences would be impossible if Aristotle had not supposed that the Great-and-Small, which is intended to be an element of the Ideas, was identical with the cause of extent and motion in bodies, or if he had known anything of its distinction from the Great-and-Small in mathematical numbers 'Aristotle could not possibly,' says Stumpf, 'have charged Plato with such a contradiction, as that the matter of the Ideas was identical with that of sensible things, while the Ideas themselves were not in space; still less would he have left this contradiction unnoticed in his criticism of the doctrine of Ideas.' But a mere glance shows that he has done both; he has charged Plato with the contradiction in question, and has made use of it in criticising the Ideas

[96] Brandis loc. cit. p. 322; Stallbaum in Jahn and Seebode's Jahrb. 1842, xxxv 1, 63.

[97] Cf my Plat. Stud. p. 200-16, an enquiry too little considered by the uncompromising partisans of Aristotelian accounts of Plato's philosophy.

and-Small, as the element of Ideas, differently from the Matter of the Timæus.[98] Even the defenders of Aristotle are forced to admit that he mistook the import of Plato's doctrine on several essential points.[99] It is true that Plato's disciples themselves acknow-

---

[98] Phys. iv. 2; vide notes 39 and 9. I no longer appeal to Metaph. i. 6, 987 b. 33, as the words there, ἔξω τῶν πρώτων, are too vague in their meaning, and Bonitz ad loc. has proved that my former reference of them to the Ideal numbers is unlikely. Probably these words, for which no suitable sense can be found, are an interpolation.

[99] Weisse ad Arist. Phys p. 448: 'It is remarkable that none of his followers, not even Aristotle, understood the meaning of this theory [of the derivation of Ideas], and its full signification.' Ibid. p. 472 sqq. the identification of the Great-and-Small with space (consequently with the ὕλη of the Timæus) is mentioned among Aristotle's misunderstandings. Stallbaum (Jahn's Jahrb. 1842, xxxv. 1, 65 sq.) admits that 'Aristotle may have mistaken the true sense of the Platonic doctrines,' that not unfrequently 'he attributes to them a meaning which is in direct contradiction to Plato's,' and particularly that the 'objective being' of the Ideas is falsely 'converted into the ὕλη and to some extent into a material substance,' though at the same time it must be conceded 'that Aristotle has not foisted anything foreign on Plato, but has actually transmitted to us accounts, by means of which it becomes possible to comprehend and partly fill up Plato's scientific foundation of the doctrine of Ideas.' But is not this 'attributing a meaning quite contradictory to Plato's true meaning,' foisting something foreign on Plato? Stallbaum (p 64) consoles himself with the fact that Plato applied the expression 'the one and the infinite' to the Ideas as well as to sensible things. But 'his meaning was indisputably not that the content or the matter is the same in all and everything.' In the Ideas 'the infinite is the being of the Ideas in their indeterminate state, which is without any determined predicate and therefore cannot be thought of or known by itself particularly;'—'but with sensible things the case is quite different;'—'for in them the infinite is the unregulated and indeterminate principle of the sensible matter.' This whole defence amounts, as we see, to the fact that Aristotle made use of Platonic expressions, but probably attributed to them a sense completely contradictory to their real meaning. The philological correctness of the word is maintained, where the real point is its true meaning in the exposition of philosophical opinions. Brandis does not go quite so far; he concedes, that though Aristotle cannot misunderstand any of Plato's fundamental doctrine, 'he has failed to notice in his criticism the principles and aim of the theories, and has regarded their mythical dress or complement not as such, but as integral parts of doctrine.' This grants nearly all that we require.

ledged the doctrines attributed to him by Aristotle,[100] but it is equally true that in so doing they departed from true Platonism, and, especially, almost forgot the theory of Ideas, confounding it with the Pythagorean doctrine of Numbers.[101] It is far more unlikely that Plato should himself have applied his theory in a way that was virtually its destruction, than that his disciples, Aristotle among the rest, should, in the same manner, and for the same reasons, have departed from its original meaning. These reasons lay, on the one side, in the obscurity and discontinuity of the Platonic doctrine; and, on the other, in the dogmatic apprehension by his followers of indefinite and often merely figurative expressions. With this not only Speusippus and Xenocrates, but Aristotle himself, judging from his procedure in other cases, may be charged. It is quite possible that Plato in his later years may have recognised more clearly than at first the gap left by his system between the Ideas and Actuality; and he may have attempted to fill it up more definitely. He may, therefore, have pointed out that even in Ideas there is an infinite plurality, and designated this plurality by the name of the Unlimited or the Great-and-Small. He may have observed that as sensible things are ordered according to numerical proportions, so Ideas in a certain sense might be called Numbers. He may, further, have derived particular numbers from

---

[100] Brandis, i. a 322
[101] The evidence for this is given below; as a preliminary I may merely refer to Metaph. i. 9, 992 a. 3: γέγονε τὰ μαθήματα τοῖς νῦν ἡ φιλοσοφία, φασκόντων τῶν ἄλλων χάριν αὐτὰ δεῖν πραγματεύεσθαι, and the expressions of Metaph. xiii. 9, 1086 a. 2, xiv. 2, 1088 b. 34.

NO DERIVATION OF THE SENSIBLE. 331

Unity and Plurality, the universal elements of Ideas,[102] and he may have reduced certain concepts to numbers.[103]

[102] Vide p. 279, 145, 146; and note 83 of the present chapter.

[103] Arist De An. i. 2, 404 b. 18: in accordance with the principle that like is known through like, we conclude that the soul must be composed out of the elements of all things, inasmuch as it could not otherwise know everything. This was the doctrine of Empedocles; and of Plato in the Timæus: Ὁμοίως δὲ καὶ ἐν τοῖς περὶ φιλοσοφίας λεγομένοις διωρίσθη, αὐτὸ μὲν τὸ ζῷον ἐξ αὐτῆς τῆς τοῦ ἑνὸς ἰδέας καὶ τοῦ πρώτου μήκους καὶ πλάτους καὶ βάθους, τὰ δὲ ἄλλα ὁμοιοτρόπως. ἔτι δὲ καὶ ἄλλως, νοῦν μὲν τὸ ἕν, ἐπιστήμην δὲ τὰ δύο. μοναχῶς γὰρ ἐφ᾽ ἕν· τὸν δὲ τοῦ ἐπιπέδου ἀριθμὸν δόξαν, αἴσθησιν δὲ τὸν τοῦ στερεοῦ· οἱ μὲν γὰρ ἀριθμοὶ τὰ εἴδη αὐτὰ καὶ αἱ ἀρχαὶ ἐλέγοντο, εἰσὶ δ᾽ ἐκ τῶν στοιχείων. κρίνεται δὲ τὰ πράγματα τὰ μὲν νῷ, τὰ δ᾽ ἐπιστήμῃ, τὰ δὲ δόξῃ τὰ δ᾽ αἰσθήσει· εἴδη δ᾽ οἱ ἀριθμοὶ οὗτοι τῶν πραγμάτων. Metaph. xiii. 8, 1084 a. 12: ἀλλὰ μὴν εἰ μέχρι τῆς δεκάδος ὁ ἀριθμός, ὥσπερ τινές φασι, πρῶτον μὲν ταχὺ ἐπιλείψει τὰ εἴδη· οἷον εἰ ἔστιν ἡ τριὰς αὐτοάνθρωπος, τίς ἔσται ἀριθμὸς αὐτόιππος. Still, it does not follow that Plato himself or one of his scholars referred the Idea of man to the number three; this is simply an example chosen by Aristotle, to show the absurdity of the Platonic identification of Ideas and numbers. Nor must we conclude too much from the passage of the De Anima. As has been already shown, vol. i. 349, from this and other passages, Plato derived the line from the number two, superficies from three, and body from four. He compares reason with unity, knowledge with duality, &c., and he therefore calls the former the unit and the latter the number two, &c., following out this Pythagorean symbolism, whilst to each act of cognition he assigns a higher number, further removed from unity, belonging to sensible and corporeal things, in proportion as the act of cognition is further removed from the single intuition of the Idea and turns to the manifold and corporeal (cf. p. 219, 147). Finally he asserts that the Idea of living Being (on which cf. Tim. 30, c. 39, E 28 c.) is composed of the Idea of the unit and the Ideas of the corporeal, and the rest of living beings (ζῷα is to be supplied with ἄλλα), each in its kind, are composed out of corresponding elements. By the ἄλλα ζῷα we may either understand actual living beings, or more probably (according to Tim. 30, c. 39), the Ideas of separate living beings comprehended under the Idea of the αὐτοζῷον. So much may be concluded from the statement of Aristotle. Everything besides is his own addition. We cannot therefore assert that Plato himself compared reason with unity, reflection with duality, &c., because he believed the soul capable of knowing everything, only if it had in itself in the numbers the elements of all things. Aristotle is the first who propounded that theory and combined it with the further determination that the numbers are the principles of things. We must not attribute to the statements about the αὐτο-

He may, lastly, have ceased to insist upon the difference between the world of sense and that of Ideas, side by side with the analogy between them. All this would be quite possible without belying his main philosophic position, and Aristotle may so far have transmitted to us his propositions on these subjects with literal correctness. But it is incredible that Plato should have intended in these propositions to annul the distinction between the Unlimited in space, and that plurality which is also in the Ideas. If his disciple so understood them, he must be charged, not indeed with false witness as to his master's words, but with a view of them that is too external, too dogmatic, too little observant of the spirit and interconnection of the Platonic philosophy.[104]

We must then abandon the hope of finding in Plato

ζῷον the object for which Aristotle used it. These seem rather to have sprung from the consideration, that just as living beings are composed of soul and body, there must also be in the Idea a something corresponding to the soul, and a something corresponding to the body. But as Aristotle usually looks for the most remote traces of every doctrine in his predecessors, he recognises the doctrine of the soul including all principles in itself (as necessary to its universal power of cognition), wherever it is composed of the most general elements of things. (The explanations of Simplicius, De An. 7 loc. cit., and Philoponus, De An. C 2, m. sqq., of the passage περὶ ψυχῆς is not from the Aristotelian treatise π. φιλοσοφίας, as Simpl. himself gives us to understand; still, both consider this treatise to be the same as that on the Good.)—I cannot here enter further into the treatise on the Soul, nor the explanations, somewhat different from my own, to be found in Trendelenburg (Plat. de id. et num. doctr. 85 sqq.; in Arist. de an 220-234); Brandis (perd. Arist. libr. 48-61; Rhein. Mus. ii. 1828, 568 sqq.); Bonitz (Disputatt. Plat. 79 sqq.); Stallbaum (Plat. Parm. 280 sq.); Susemihl (Genet. Darst. ii. 543 sq.). Cf. my Plat. Stud. 227 sq., 271 sqq. on the subject; it is unnecessary here to discuss some variations in the present exposition from my earlier views.

[104] Amongst others who express themselves to this effect are Bonitz Arist. Metaph. ii. 94; Susemihl, Genet. Entw. 541 sqq., 550 sqq.; Ribbing, Plat. Ideenl. i. 396.

a derivation of the Sensible from the Idea; and this is to acknowledge that his system is involved in a contradiction, inextricable from its own point of view; a contradiction already latent in the concept of Ideas, but which only at this stage becomes fully apparent. The Idea, according to Plato, is to contain all reality, yet at the same time there must belong to the phenomenon not merely the existence accorded to it by reason of the Idea, but, together with this, a kind of existence that cannot be derived from the Idea. The Idea is to be therefore on the one hand the sole reality, and substance of the phemonenon; on the other, it is to exist for itself, it is not to enter into the plurality and vicissitude of sensible objects, and not to require the latter for its realization. But if the phenomenon is not a moment of the Idea itself, if a Being belongs to it which is not by reason of the Idea, then the Idea has not all Being in itself; and though that which distinguishes the phenomenon from it may be defined as Non-being, it is not in truth absolute Unreality, otherwise it could not have the power of circumscribing the Being of the Idea in the phenomenon, and of separating it in Divisibility and Becoming. Neither is the phenomenon in that ease absolutely immanent in the Idea, for that which makes it a phenomenon cannot be derived from the Idea. Plato, in his original design, unmistakeably intended to represent the Idea as the sole Reality, and all other Being as a Being contained in the Idea. He was unable, however, to carry out this design: in attempting to do so, he comes to the conclusion that the Idea has in the phenomenon a limit, a something impenetrable, external to itself. The cause of this lies in the abstract view of the Idea as an absolutely existent, self-completed substance, which does not require the phenomenon for its realization. In excluding the phenomenon from itself, the Idea as such receives limits from the phenomenon; the Idea remains on one side, the phenomenon on the other, and the presupposed immanence of both is transformed into their dualism and the transcendency of the Idea. Here there is certainly a contradiction: the fault, however, does not lie in our representation, but in the subject of it. It was inevitable that so defective a beginning should be refuted by its result; and in acknowledging this contradiction, we state only the objective matter of fact and the internal historical connection; for it was this very contradiction by which Aristotle took hold of the Platonic principle and developed it into a new form of thought.[105]

[105] The case, of course, is altered, if Teichmüller (Stud. z. Gesch. d. Begr. 280 sqq.) is right in seeing in the above statement 'the most striking indirect proof of the incorrectness of a view which leads to such inextricable contradictions.' He would escape this contradiction by representing Plato as a pure Pantheist. To use Teichmüller's own rather infelicitous phraseology, Plato must be understood 'in an Athanasian, not an Arian, sense' I e. the Intelligible forms only the immanent soul of the Becoming, the world is the continuous birth of the Deity (who is at once its father and son), and so the transcendence of the Ideas as opposed to the phenomenon is entirely abolished (p. 154–166 sq). Plato's system is 'a Pantheistic Hylozoism and Monism.' (p. 254). We may certainly call for proof of such assertions, in the face, not only of all previous expositions of Platonic philosophy, but of Plato's own enunciations in a contrary direction. But Teichmüller scarcely seeks to give us one We can see plainly from our investigations, as far as they have hitherto gone, that there is an element in Plato's system, which, taken separately, might lead to Teichmüller's position; but we also see that it is counterbalanced by another, which prevents it from becoming dominant. If we keep exclusively to the position that things are what they are

NO DERIVATION OF THE SENSIBLE. 335

As with the origin of the world of Sense, so with regard to its subsistence. Plato is as little able to explain satisfactorily the co-existence of the Idea and the phenomenon, as the derivation of the one from the other. It is perfectly comprehensible from his point of view that the Idea should have room beside the phenomenon, for no specific reality is to belong to the latter, by which the reality of the Idea could be circumscribed. But it is, on that very account, all the less easy to understand how the phenomenon finds room beside the Idea—how an existence can be ascribed to it, if all reality lies in the Idea. Plato here summons to his aid the theory of participation: things are all that they are only by participating in the Idea.[106] But as Aristotle complains,[107] he has scarcely

only through the presence of the Ideas, Teichmuller's conclusions are unavoidable. If we consider that Plato's doctrine of Ideas arose out of the sharp distinction between the Constant and the Changing, the immutable Existence and the mutable contradictory phenomenon, and that it never enabled him to explain the latter from the former, we are forced to allow a residuum of Reality in things not derivable from the Idea; and the world of sense appears as a second world, with a Reality of its own, as opposed to the world of Concepts, which latter, according to the original view of the doctrine of Ideas, is yet the sole Reality. The Ideas have passed from being the immanent Existence in things into something transcendental. It is the part of historical investigation to grapple with such a contradiction, but not to remove it by ignoring one-half of the Platonic doctrine. The relation to the world assigned by Teichmüller (p. 245 sqq) to the Platonic Deity is rather attributed by Plato to the World-soul The World-soul is inserted between the Ideas and the phenomenal-world, because such a relation was unsuitable to the former.

[106] Parm. 129 A, 130 E; Phædo, 100 C sqq.; Symp. 211 B; Rep. v. 476 A; Euthyd. 301 A &c. This relation is expressed by μεταλαμβάνειν, μετέχειν, μέθεξις, παρουσία, κοινωνία.

[107] Metaph. 1. 6, 987 b, 9: according to Plato the things of sense are named after the Ideas (i.e. they receive their attributes from them): κατὰ μέθεξιν γὰρ εἶναι τὰ πολλὰ τῶν συνωνύμων τοῖς εἴδεσιν (the many which are synonymous with the Ideas exist only through participation in the Ideas; cf. Plat. Stud. 234; Schwegler and Bonitz ad

made an attempt to determine that concept accurately; and in all that he says on the subject, this perplexity is clearly to be noted. He refers indeed to some of the difficulties involved in the notion of participation, while pointing out the way to solve them;[108] but the main question—how the one essence can combine with that which is absolutely divided, the permanent with that which is restlessly changing, the uncontained in space with the contained, the wholly real with the non-existent, to form the unity of the phenomenon, and how they are mutually related in this combination—is left unanswered. It is only evident that even in his most mature period, however settled might be his conviction as to the participation of things in Ideas, he could find no adequate formula for it.[109] Nor is it any real explanation, to represent the Ideas as the patterns which are imitated in phenomena.[110] The objection,[111] that the likeness of the copy to the archetype would only be possible by their

loc.). τὴν δὲ μέθεξιν τοὔνομα μόνον μετέβαλεν· οἱ μὲν γὰρ Πυθαγόρειοι μιμήσει τὰ ὄντα φασὶν εἶναι τῶν ἀριθμῶν, Πλάτων δὲ μεθέξει, τοὔνομα μεταβαλών. τὴν μέντοι γε μέθεξιν ἢ τὴν μίμησιν, ἥτις ἂν εἴη τῶν εἰδῶν, ἀφεῖσαν ἐν κοινῷ ζητεῖν. Ibid. c. 9, 991 a. 20 (vide p. 266, 112).

[108] Vide supra, p. 316 sq.

[109] Cf. Phædo, 100 D (see preceding chapter, note 109). Tim. 50 C (vide p. 299, 14): the forms which enter into matter bear the impress of the Ideas τρόπον τινὰ δύσφραστον καὶ θαυμαστόν. Ibid. 51 A: the basis of all determined bodies is an εἶδος ἄμορφον, πανδεχές, μεταλαμβάνον δὲ ἀπορώτατά πῃ τοῦ νοητοῦ—the latter words do not state that matter in and by itself is a νοητὸν in a certain sense, but they are to be interpreted in the light of 50 C.

[110] Theæt. 176; Crat. 389 A sq.; Parm. 132 C sqq.; Phædr. 250 A; Rep. vi 500 E; ix. 592 B, Tim. 28 A sqq., 30 C sqq., 48 E. The attributes of things are the copy of the Ideas, and so far, Plato says, (Tim. 50 C, 51 B), the corporeal admits in itself the μιμήματα of the Ideas; and, as the things themselves thereby become like the Ideas, they can be directly called imitations of them (μιμήματα), as Tim. 49 A; cf. 30 C.

[111] Parm. loc. cit.

NO DERIVATION OF THE SENSIBLE.

common participation in an Idea separate from them both, is easily removed;[112] but the question of Aristotle[113] as to the efficient Cause which imitates things from Ideas is much more serious. Here Plato, as far as his philosophic concepts are concerned, leaves us entirely at fault; in place of scientific explanation, we have the popular notion of the Framer of the world, who fashions Matter like a human artist, only with the wondrous might of a God. According to Plato, the Ideas are indeed the archetypes of material things, but they are at the same time their essence and their reality. Things are only copied from Ideas in so far as they participate in them. Consequently, if their participation in Ideas remains unexplained, this want cannot be supplied by what is said of their being imitated from the Idea. So far then as the things of sense are the manifestation and copy of the Idea, they must be determined by the Idea; so far as they have in Matter a specific principle in themselves, they are at the same time determined by Necessity; for though the world is the work of Reason,[114] it cannot be denied that in its origin there was, side by side with Reason, another blindly acting cause; and even the Creator could not make his work absolutely perfect, but only as good as was permitted by the nature of the Finite.[115]

---

[112] Vide supra, p 317 sq.
[113] Vide p. 266, 112.
[114] Cf., besides the following note, Soph. 235 C sq., Phileb. 28 C sqq.; Laws, x. 897 B sqq, and supra, preceding chapter, notes 111, 158, 171.
[115] Tim 48 A (vide supra, note 6). 46 C. ταῦτ' οὖν πάντα ἔστι τῶν ξυναιτίων, οἷς θεὸς ὑπηρετοῦσι χρῆται τὴν τοῦ ἀρίστου κατὰ τὸ δυνατὸν (this has occurred p 30 A) ἰδέαν ἀποτελῶν. 46 E: λεκτέα μὲν ἀμφότερα τὰ τῶν αἰτιῶν γένη, χωρὶς δὲ ὅσαι μετὰ νοῦ καλῶν καὶ ἀγαθῶν δημιουργοὶ καὶ ὅσαι μονωθεῖσαι φρονήσεως τὸ τυχὸν ἄτακτον ἑκάστοτε ἐξεργάζονται. 56 C, &c.; vide fol-

Reason has no higher law in its working than the Idea of the Good, that highest Idea from which all others arise, and by which they are ruled: material things, as the work of Reason, must be explained from the Idea of the Good, that is, teleologically. That in them which resists this explanation, is to be regarded as the product of mechanical causes — the work of natural necessity. These two kinds of causes are in no way to be compared: the specific and essential grounds of material things are final causes; the physical grounds

lowing note. Cf. further the quotations in the last chapter, and Polit 273 C (τὸ τῆς παλαιᾶς ἀναρμοστίας πάθος, which by its growth in the world left to itself, introduces a continual decrease of the good, and an increase of the bad, and would bring the world to dissolution if it were not for the interference of the divinity in the ἄπειρος τόπος τῆς ἀνομοιότητος) It will be shown later on how this gives rise to a bad World-soul in the Laws. Still, Plutarch's opinion (Procreat. Anim in Tim C 5 sqq.), which is followed by Stallbaum, Plat. Polit. 100; Martin, Etudes i 355, 369, and Ueberweg, Rhein. Mus. ix 76, 79, viz. that Plato in the earlier writings derived the bad and evil from this and not from matter, is not correct, even if, with Stallbaum the one World-soul, *quem rerum divinarum invasit incuria*, is put in the place of the bad World-soul. The Politicus, 269 D sq., derives the confused condition of the world from the nature of the corporeal; and again, 273 B, we find τούτων δὲ (the declension from completeness in the world) αὐτῷ τὸ σωματοειδὲς τῆς συγκράσεως αἴτιον, τὸ τῆς πάλαι ποτὲ φύσεως ξύντροφον,

ὅτι πολλῆς ἦν μετέχον ἀταξίας πρὶν εἰς τὸν νῦν κόσμον ἀφικέσθαι. The Timæus makes no mention of a bad World-soul, but (46 E) we find express mention of the corporeal (47 E), matter and material causes are spoken of as τὰ δι' ἀνάγκης γιγνόμενα, τὸ τῆς πλανωμένης εἶδος αἰτίας, 52 D sq , to matter are ascribed heterogeneous powers and an unregulated motion, before the formation of the world; whereas from the soul are derived only order and proportion. The visible, to which the soul (acc to 37 A) does not belong, is represented as ordered by God, the soul as the cause of regulated movement is formed not from an older unregulated soul, but from the Ideal and corporeal substance Phædr. 245 D sq.: the world directing soul, not the unregulated, is unbecome. It is therefore no misunderstanding of Plato's doctrine when Arist. Phys. 1 9, 192 a. 15, speaks of its κακοποιὸν with reference to the Platonic matter, and Eudemus (acc. to Plat. loc. cit. 7, 3) accuses Plato of calling the same principle at one time μήτηρ καὶ τιθήνη, and at another representing it as αἰτία καὶ ἀρχὴ κακῶν. Cf. Steinhart, vi. 95.

PARTICIPATION IN THE IDEAS. 339

are to be considered as merely concurrent causes, or, more precisely, means to Reason that is working to an end.[116] But still they are not so powerless as to be altogether obedient instruments of Reason. We have already seen that Matter in spite of its Non-being, hinders and disfigures the Idea in the phenomenon; here, Plato speaks of a resistance of Necessity to Reason —a resistance which yields only partially to the per-

---

[116] Phædo, 96 A sqq. (cf. p. 10, 18), Socrates blames the Physicists, particularly Anaxagoras, because they wish to explain all things merely out of air, æther, wind, water, and the like, instead of demonstrating their proper reason teleologically; for if Mind (νοῦς) is the creator of the world, it must have arranged everything in the best possible way: ἐκ δὴ τοῦ λόγου τούτου οὐδὲν ἄλλο σκοπεῖν προσήκειν ἀνθρώπῳ ... ἀλλ᾽ ἢ τὸ ἄριστον καὶ τὸ βέλτιστον Having learnt Anaxagoras' doctrine of νοῦς, he hoped that with regard to the formation of the earth, for instance, and all other points, he would ἐπεκδιηγήσεσθαι τὴν αἰτίαν καὶ τὴν ἀνάγκην, λέγοντα τὸ ἄμεινον καὶ ὅτι αὐτὴν ἄμεινον ἦν τοιαύτην εἶναι .. καὶ εἴ μοι ταῦτα ἀποφαίνοιτο παρεσκευάσμην ὡς οὐκέτι ποθεσόμενος αἰτίας ἄλλο εἶδος, &c. In this expectation, however, he was entirely deceived; Anaxagoras, like all the rest, spoke merely of physical, not final, causes. This procedure, however, is no better than if one were to say, 'Socrates acts in all things reasonably,' and then mentioned his sinews and bones as the reason of his acts. ἀλλ᾽ αἴτια μὲν τὰ τοιαῦτα καλεῖν λίαν ἄτοπον· εἰ δέ τις λέγοι ὅτι ἄνευ τοῦ τοιαῦτα ἔχειν .. οὐκ ἂν οἷός τ᾽ ἦν ποιεῖν τὰ δόξαντά μοι, ἀληθῆ ἂν λέγοι· ὡς μέντοι διὰ ταῦτα ποιῶ ἃ ποιῶ καὶ ταῦτα νῷ πράττω, ἀλλ᾽ οὐ τῇ τοῦ βελτίστου αἱρέσει, πολλὴ ἂν καὶ μακρὰ ῥᾳθυμία εἴη τοῦ λόγου. τὸ γὰρ μὴ διελέσθαι οἷόν τ᾽ εἶναι ὅτι ἄλλο μέν τί ἐστι τὸ αἴτιον τῷ ὄντι, ἄλλο δ᾽ ἐκεῖνο ἄνευ οὗ τὸ αἴτιον οὐκ ἄν ποτ᾽ εἴη αἴτιον, &c. (cf. p. 262, 109) Tim. 46 C (vide preceding note). 46 D τὸν δὲ νοῦ καὶ ἐπιστήμης ἐραστὴν ἀνάγκη τὰς τῆς ἔμφρονος φύσεως αἰτίας πρώτας μεταδιώκειν, ὅσαι δὲ ὑπ᾽ ἄλλων μὲν κινουμένων ἕτερα δὲ ἐξ ἀνάγκης κινούντων γίγνονται, δευτέρας, &c. (preceding note). 48 A (vide p 227, 8), 68 E (at the end of the review of the physical distinctions and causes of things). ταῦτα δὴ πάντα τότε ταύτῃ πεφυκότα ἐξ ἀνάγκης ὁ τοῦ καλλίστου τε καὶ ἀρίστου δημιουργὸς ἐν τοῖς γιγνομένοις παρελάμβανεν ... χρώμενος μὲν ταῖς περὶ ταῦτα αἰτίαις ὑπηρετούσαις, τὸ δὲ εὖ τεκταινόμενος ἐν πᾶσι τοῖς γιγνομένοις αὐτός· διὸ δὴ χρὴ δύ᾽ αἰτίας εἴδη διορίζεσθαι, τὸ μὲν ἀναγκαῖον, τὸ δὲ θεῖον, καὶ τὸ μὲν θεῖον ἐν ἅπασι ζητεῖν κτήσεως ἕνεκα εὐδαίμονος βίου, καθ᾽ ὅσον ἡμῶν ἡ φύσις ἐνδέχεται, τὸ δὲ ἀναγκαῖον ἐκείνων χάριν, λογιζόμενον, ὡς ἄνευ τούτων οὐ δυνατὰ αὐτὰ ἐκεῖνα, ἐφ᾽ οἷς σπουδάζομεν, μόνα κατανοεῖν οὐδ᾽ αὖ λαβεῖν οὐδ᾽ ἄλλως πως μετασχεῖν.

suasion of Reason, and so prevented the Creator from producing a thoroughly perfect work.[117] In the same way, as we shall presently find,[118] it is the body which hinders man from pure knowledge, which calls forth in him evil desires, and moral disorder of every kind. Aristotle, indeed, plainly says that Plato held Matter as the cause of evil.[119] To comprehend both causes in one—to recognise in natural Necessity the proper work of Reason, and the positive medium (not merely the limitation and negative condition) of its working—is impossible to him, in this dualism.[120] But his teleology preserves in the main the external character of the Socratic view of Nature, though the end of Nature is no longer exclusively the welfare of men, but the Good, Beauty, Proportion, and Order.[121] The natural world and the forces of Nature are thus related to

[117] Tim 48 A (supra, p. 227, 8) Ibid. 56 C (on the formation of the elements). καὶ δὴ καὶ τὸ τῶν ἀναλογιῶν .. τὸν θεὸν, ὅπη περ ἡ τῆς ἀνάγκης ἑκοῦσα πεισθεῖσά τε φύσις ὑπεῖκε, ταύτῃ πάντῃ δι' ἀκριβείας ἀποτελεσθεισῶν ὑπ' αὐτοῦ ξυνηρμόσθαι ταῦτα ἀνὰ λόγον. Cf. Theophr. Metaph 33 (vol. i. 314, 3)

[118] Pp 227, 241 sq.

[119] Metaph. i. 6, end, it is said of Plato, ἔτι δὲ τὴν τοῦ εὖ καὶ τοκακῶς αἰτίαν τοῖς στοιχείοις (the unit and matter) ἀπέδωκεν ἑκατέροις ἑκατέραν, and Phys. i. 9, 192 a. 14 Aristotle, as already remarked, speaks in Plato's sense of the κακοποιὸν of matter.

[120] Cf., also, Rep. ii. 379 C. οὐδ' ἄρα, ἦν δ' ἐγὼ, ὁ θεὸς, ἐπειδὴ ἀγαθὸς, πάντων ἂν εἴη αἴτιος, ὡς οἱ πολλοὶ λέγουσιν, ἀλλ' ὀλίγων μὲν τοῖς ἀνθρώποις αἴτιος, πολλῶν δὲ ἀναίτιος· πολλῷ γὰρ ἐλάττω τἀγαθὰ τῶν κακῶν ἡμῖν · καὶ τῶν μὲν ἀγαθῶν οὐδένα ἄλλον αἰτιατέον τῶν δὲ κακῶν ἄλλ' ἄττα δεῖ ζητεῖν τὰ αἴτια (by which primarily, though not exclusively, the human will is to be understood). Polit. 273 D σμικρὰ μὲν τἀγαθὰ, πολλὴν δὲ τὴν τῶν ἐναντίων κρᾶσιν ἐπεγκεραννύμενος (ὁ κόσμος). Theæt. 176 A (infra, chap. x. note 6)

[121] Cf. Phileb. 28 C sq., 30 A sqq., 64 C sqq.; Phædo, loc. cit., Tim 29 E sq. In other passages the reference to the interests of mankind comes forward more strongly; particularly in the last part of the Timæus, the contents of which naturally lead us to expect this.

consequences external to themselves:[122] hence there was a special necessity that Plato should here use not only personification, but mythical language, with regard to efficient causes. Aristotle was the first to conceive the notion of inner activity working to an end; and even he leaves much to be desired in his scientific view of this activity, and still more in its application.

Although, however, Plato did not succeed in overcoming the dualism of the idea and the phenomenon, he yet attempts, while presupposing this dualism, to point out the middle terms by means of which the Idea and the phenomenon are combined. And this he perceives in mathematical proportions, or the World-soul.

III. *The World-soul.*[123] As God desired that the world should be framed in the best possible manner, says the Timæus,[124] He considered that nothing unintelligent, taken as a whole, could ever be better than the intelligent; and that intelligence ($νοῦς$) could not exist in anything which was devoid of soul. For this reason He put the intelligence of the world into a soul,

---

[122] Cf. on this the quotations in note 116, particularly Phædo, 98 B sqq.

[123] Böckh, On the formation of the World-soul in the Timæus; Daub and Creuzer's Studien, iii. 34 sqq. (now Kl. Schr.iii. 109 sqq.); Enquiry into Plato's Cosmic System (1852), p 18 sq.; Brandis, De perd. Arist. libr. 64, Rhein. Mus. ii. 1828, p. 579; Gr -rom. Phil. ii. a. 361 sqq ; Stallbaum, Schola crit. et hist. sup. loco Tim. 1837; Plat. Tim. p. 134 sqq.; Ritter ii. 365 sq 396, Trendl. Plat. de id. et num. doctr. 52, 95 , Bonitz, Disputatt Plat. 47 sqq.; Martin Études, i. 346 sqq., Ueberweg, Ueber die plat. Weltseele, Rhein. Mus. f. Phil. ix. 37 sqq., Steinhart, Pl. WW. vi. 94–104, Susemihl, Genet. Entw. ii. 352 sq.; Philologus,ii. Supplementbl. (1863), p 219 sqq.; Wohlstein, Mat und Weltseele, Marb. 1863; Wohlrab, Quid Pl. de An. mundi elementis docuerit, Dresd. 1872.

[124] 30 B; cf. supra, p. 228, 171.

and the soul in the world as into a body. He prepared the soul as follows. Before He had formed the corporeal elements, He compounded out of the indivisible and self-identical substance and also out of the divisible and corporeal, a third nature intermediate between them. Having mingled in this substance the Same and the Other, he divided the whole according to the cardinal numbers of the harmonic and astronomical systems,[125]

[125] 35 A: τῆς ἀμερίστου καὶ ἀεὶ κατὰ ταὐτὰ ἐχούσης οὐσίας καὶ τῆς αὖ περὶ τὰ σώματα γιγνομένης μεριστῆς τρίτον ἐξ ἀμφοῖν ἐν μέσῳ ξυνεκεράσατο οὐσίας εἶδος τῆς τε ταὐτοῦ φύσεως αὖ [πέρι] καὶ τῆς θατέρου, καὶ κατὰ ταῦτα ξυνέστησεν ἐν μέσῳ τοῦ τε ἀμεροῦς αὐτῶν καὶ τοῦ κατὰ τὰ σώματα μεριστοῦ. καὶ τρία λαβὼν αὐτὰ ὄντα συνεκεράσατο εἰς μίαν πάντα ἰδέαν, τὴν θατέρου φύσιν δύσμικτον οὖσαν εἰς ταὐτὸν ξυναρμόττων βίᾳ· μιγνὺς δὲ μετὰ τῆς οὐσίας καὶ ἐκ τριῶν ποιησάμενος ἕν, πάλιν ὅλον τοῦτο μοίρας ὅσας προσῆκε διένειμεν, ἑκάστην δὲ ἔκ τε ταὐτοῦ καὶ θατέρου καὶ τῆς οὐσίας μεμιγμένην, &c. In the interpretation suggested in the text, I have gone on the lately universal supposition that the unmeaning πέρι, here enclosed in brackets, is to be struck out. On the other hand, I believe that we must retain the αὖ before it, which Stallbaum ad loc. changes into ὄν, and Bonitz, Hermann (in his edition), and Susemihl agree in wishing to remove, not merely because this is the easiest explanation of the insertion of πέρι (from the preceding αὖ περί), but because the separation of the ταὐτὸν and θάτερον from the ἀμέριστον and the μεριστὸν, thus expressed is really Platonic. Although the ταὐτὸν is connected with the Divided, and the θάτερον with the Undivided, they in no way coincide; both pairs of concepts have a separate import, and in their combination give two classifications which cross each other. The ταὐτὸν and θάτερον both occur in the Indivisible and the Divisible, in the Idea and the Corporeal, and are found in intellectual as well as sensible knowledge (Tim. 37 A sq.; Soph. 255 C sqq., vide pp. 250, 278). The soul is indebted to the ἀμέριστον for its power of knowing the Ideal, to the μεριστὸν for its power of knowing the sensible, to the ταὐτὸν for its ability to conceive (in sensible and Ideal alike) the relation of identity, to the θάτερον for its ability (equally in both) to conceive the relation of difference (see on this point Tim. loc. cit. together with the elucidation of the passage later on in this chapter. Sensible perception is here represented as proceeding from the κύκλος θατέρου, thought from the κύκλος ταὐτοῦ; but this does not prove that the θάτερον is identical with the αἰσθητὸν, and the ταὐτὸν with the νοητόν; the circle of the ταὐτὸν is, according to p. 36 C, that in which the fixed stars move, the circle of the θάτερον, with its seven-

and formed from the entire compound, by a longitudinal bisection, the circle of the heaven of fixed stars, and that of the planets.[126]

In this representation the mythical and imaginative element is at once apparent. The division and spreading out of the World-soul in space, prior to the formation of the corporeal; its origin from a chemical admixture, the entirely material treatment even of the Immaterial, can never have been seriously intended by Plato; otherwise he would deserve all the censure,

---

fold divisions, that in which the planets move. Each of these circles, however, according to 35 B, cf. note 137, is composed in all its parts out of the ταὐτὸν, the θάτερον, and οὐσία). In order to express this different import of the two pairs, Plato keeps them apart in his exposition. Ueberweg correctly points out, p. 41 sq., that the substance of the World-soul is formed by a kind of chemical mixture out of the ἀμέριστον and the μεριστόν; both are completely blended and no longer appear in it separately. The ταὐτὸν and θάτερον do appear separately, both according to the passage before us, and 37 A. Only these two are mentioned as parts of the World-soul, together with οὐσία, the Indivisible and the Divisible are merely elements of οὐσία. (Cf. Martin, i. 358 sqq; Steinhart, vi 243, on the other hand, Susemihl, Wohlrab, and others consider with Bockh that the ταὐτὸν and θάτερον are identical in signification with the μεριστὸν and ἀμέριστον.) The genitives τῆς ἀμερίστου—μεριστῆς appear to me to depend on the following ἐν μέσῳ; the genitive τῆς τε ταὐτοῦ φυσ., &c. on ἐξ: so that the sense is: Between the divisible and indivisible substance he mixed a third, composed out of the two, and further also (αὖ) composed out of the nature of the ταὐτὸν and θάτερον, and formed it so as to stand midway between the indivisible part of them, and the part which can be divided in bodies. Instead of τοῦ τε ἀμεροῦς αὐτῶν Steinhart loc cit. would read, with Proclus in Tim 187 E, τοῦ τε ἀμεροῦς αὐτοῦ; but in the present passage Plato had no occasion to speak of the Indivisible καθ' αὐτό. Wohlrab, p. 10, on the other hand, would refer the αὐτοῦ to the τρίτον οὐσίας εἶδος; but it is hard to see how this could be placed between the ἀμερὲς and the μεριστὸν in it, consequently between its own elements. Susemihl's conjecture (Philol. Anzeiger, v. 672), that αὐτῶν is to be changed into αὐτὸ, is more likely. I cannot here enter more fully into the various interpretations of the present passage, given most fully by Susemihl in the Philologus, and by Wohlrab

[126] Further details on this point, p. 212.

which Aristotle,[127] strangely mistaking the mythical form, casts upon this portion of the Timæus. With regard to his real scientific views, it is first of all undisputed (and the Timæus places it beyond a doubt) that he held the cosmos to be a living creature, and attributed to it not only a soul, but the most perfect and most intelligent soul. This conviction partly resulted from the universal consideration of the relations between the soul and the body—partly from the particular contemplation of nature and the human mind. If God created a world, He must have made it as perfect as possible, and this perfection must belong to the Universe which contains in itself all essential natures, in greater measure than to any of its parts.[128] But the intelligent is always more perfect than the unintelligent, and intelligence cannot dwell in any being, except by means of a soul. If, therefore, the world is the most perfect of all created beings, it must, as possessing the most perfect intelligence, possess also the most perfect soul [129] All that is moved by another must be preceded by a Self-moved; this alone is the beginning of motion. But all the corporeal is moved by another, the soul on the contrary is nothing else than the self-moving motion.[130] The soul is consequently prior to the body; and that which belongs to the soul is prior to the corporeal. Reason and art are older than that which is generally called nature; and this name itself is in truth far more applicable to the soul than to the body. The same must also

---

[127] De An. i, 2, 406 b. 25 sqq.
[128] Tim. 30 A, C sq., 37 A, 92 end.
[129] Vide p. 238, 171.
[130] ἡ δυναμένη αὐτὴ αὑτὴν κινεῖν κίνησις. Laws, 896 A.

hold good with regard to the Cosmos. In this also, the soul must be the first and governing principle; the body the secondary and subservient.[131] Or if we consider more particularly the constitution of the universe, there is shown in its whole economy, such a comprehensive adaptation of means to ends, and, especially in the motion of the stars, such an admirable regularity, that it is impossible to doubt the Reason and wisdom that rule in it. But where, except in the soul of the world, can this Reason have its dwelling? [132] The same universal mind or reason proclaims itself, lastly, in our own spirit: for just as there is nothing in our body which is not derived from the body of the world, so says Plato (with Socrates),[133] there could be in us no soul, if there were none in the universe. And as the corporeal elements in the universe are incomparably more glorious, mighty, and perfect than in our body, so must the soul of the world proportionately transcend our soul in perfection.[134] In a word, therefore, the World-soul is necessary, because only through it can Reason impart itself to the corporeal; it is the indispensable intermediate principle between the Idea and

[131] Laws, x. 891 E–896 E. The leading idea of this proof has, however, been already expressed in the Phædrus, 245 C · μόνον δὴ τὸ αὐτὸ κινοῦν (the soul), ἅτε οὐκ ἀπολεῖπον ἑαυτὸ, οὔ ποτε λήγει κινούμενον, ἀλλὰ καὶ τοῖς ἄλλοις ὅσα κινεῖται τοῦτο πηγὴ καὶ ἀρχὴ κινήσεως. Cf. Crat. 400 A; Tim. 34 B · God did not form the soul after the body, οὐ γὰρ ἂν ἄρχεσθαι πρεσβύτερον ὑπὸ νεωτέρου ξυνέρξας εἴασεν . . . ὁ δὲ καὶ γενέσει καὶ ἀρετῇ προτέραν καὶ πρεσβυτέραν ψυχὴν σώματος ὡς δεσπότιν καὶ ἄρξουσαν ἀρξομένου ξυνεστήσατο.

[132] Phileb. 30 A sqq. (p. 264, 111) So, 28 D sq., the stars and their motions were appealed to, to prove that not chance, but reason and intellect govern the world. Cf. Tim. 47 A sqq.; Soph. 265 C sq.; Laws, x. 897 B sqq.

[133] Vide part i p. 147, 1.

[134] Phileb. 29 A sqq., and supra, loc. cit.

the phenomenon. As such, it is, on the one side, the cause of all regulated motion, and of all the configuration thence proceeding; on the other it is the source of all spiritual life and especially of all knowledge, for knowledge, according to Plato, is that which distinguishes man from the beasts.[135] These are the points of view from which he starts in his description of the World-soul. It is compounded of the indivisible and of the divisible essence; that is to say, it combines the sole Idea with the sensible phenomenon, by uniting in itself the specific qualities of both.[136] It is incorporeal, like the Idea; but is at the same time, related to the corporeal; it stands over against the unlimited Multiplicity of phenomena as its ideal Unity: against its lawless vicissitude as the permanent element which introduces into it fixed proportion and law. But it is

---

[135] Cf. Phædr. 249 B.

[136] Tim. 35 A, Plato says distinctly that the οὐσία ἀμέριστος denotes the Ideal, the οὐσία μεριστή the Corporeal; while he repeatedly calls the latter περὶ τὰ σώματα μεριστή, and describes the former just as he previously, 27 D, described the Ideas (there: ἀεὶ κατὰ ταὐτὰ ἐχούσης οὐσίας; here. ἀεὶ κατὰ ταὐτὰ ὄν). It does not follow that the Ideas as such, and sensible things as such, are in the World-soul; Plato simply says that the substance of the World-soul is a mixture of the sensible and the Ideal substance. The substance of the sensible and the Ideal is something different from the individual Ideas, and the individual sensible things (cf Ueberweg, p. 54 sq.); it signifies (as Simpl. De An. 6 b. o. rightly remarks) merely the νοητὸς and αἰσθητὸς ὅρος, the γενικὰ στοιχεῖα τοῦ ὄντος, the element of the Ideal and the Sensible, the universal essence of it. After the deduction of figurative expressions (as Simpl. loc. cit. 72 b. o. virtually acknowledges), the general result is that the soul stands midway between Sensible and Ideal, and partakes in both. Plato speaks of a participation of the soul in the Idea. In the Phædo, 105 B sqq, et sæpius, Martin, i. 355 sqq. explains the μεριστὸν as the un-ordered soul; the ἀμέριστον as the νοῦς which emanates from God. The former supposition has been already refuted, note 115; the idea of an emanation is quite un-Platonic.

not, like the Idea, altogether outside this multiplicity; being involved, as the Soul of the body, in space, and as the primary cause of motion, in vicissitude. The union of the Same and the Other with this substance of Soul has reference to the combination of uniformity and change in the motion of the heavenly bodies;[137] of comparison and difference in knowledge.[138] In the revolution of the heaven of fixed stars, and in the rational cognition, the element of the Same predominates; in the movement of the planets and in the sensuous notion that of the other. We must not, however, restrict any of these phenomena to either of these two elements, nor must we in this half allegorical delineation seek a complete and developed system, or be too anxious and precise about its connection with other theoretic determinations.[139] The division of the

---

[137] 36 C, the motion of the heaven of the fixed stars is assigned (ἐπεφήμισεν) to the ταὐτὸν, that of the planets to the θάτερον. Plato, however, cannot mean that in the former there is no mutability, and in the latter no fixedness. Without mutability no motion at all, without fixedness no regulated motion is imaginable; but (Soph. 255 B), both these qualities are attributed to motion, and the Politicus, 269 D indicates the element of mutability in the motion of the universe; while (Tim. 35 B), in the division of the World-soul it is expressly remarked that each of its parts is composed out of οὐσία, ταὐτὸν, and θάτερον; and (37 A sq.), the knowledge both of Identity and Difference is ascribed to the circle of the ταὐτὸν and that of the θάτερον alike. The meaning is that in the sphere of the fixed stars the ταὐτὸν, in that of the planets the θάτερον, is predominant, as Plut. 24, 6 says.

[138] 37 A sqq.

[139] Ancient and modern commentators have combined the ταὐτὸν and θάτερον of the Timæus in different ways with the other wellknown principles of the Platonic system. Modern interpreters usually presuppose the identity of the ταὐτὸν with the ἀμέριστον, and of the θάτερον with the μεριστόν. Ritter, especially (ii. 366, 396), understands the Ideal by the ταὐτὸν, and the Material by the θάτερον, so too, Stallbaum (Plat. Tim. 136 sq)—who compares the former with the Finite, the latter with the Infinite—and most of the commentators. Tennemann (Plat. Phil. iii. 66) understands Unity and Plurality or Mutability; Böckh

soul as to its whole substance, according to the relations of the harmonic and astronomical systems,[140] implies

(loc. cit. 34 sqq.; cf. Cosmic system of Pl. p 19), Unity and the indefinite duad, which is more Platonic, instead of the duad; Trendelenburg (Plat. de id et num. doctr. 95), Ueberweg (54 sq), and apparently Brandis (Gr.-röm. Phil. ii. a. 366), would say the Infinite or the Great and Small I cannot agree unconditionally with the latter explanations of the μεριστὸν and the ἀμέριστον. The mixture of these two elementary principles must clearly represent the soul as something midway between the Ideas and sensible things. But this is not favoured either by the theory that it is composed out of Unity and Duality, or the theory that it is composed out of the Unit and the Infinite. Unity and Duality are merely the elements of number (according to the later form of the doctrine, of ideal, as well as mathematical number), the Unit and the Infinite, conversely, must exist in everything, Sensible and Ideal alike. Ueberweg's expedient, of supposing a threefold Unit, and a threefold Infinite (of which only the second the mathematical unit and the mathematical or, more accurately, the spatial infinite are to be taken as elements of the world-soul), has been already refuted, p. 327 sq. My own view is that the ἀμέριστον denotes the Ideal, the μεριστὸν the Corporeal. To say that these two are in all things (as Plut. c. 3, 3; and Martin, i. 379, object) is only correct if we include the soul, by means of which the Sensible participates in the Idea, in our reckoning. It has been already proved, p. 343, that the ταὐτὸν and θάτερον do not coincide with the ἀμέριστον and the μεριστὸν. And the Greek interpreters as a rule (Procl. Tim. 187 C, says not all), distinguish the two, e.g. Xenocrates and Crantor ap Plut. c. 1-3; Proclus 181 C sqq., 187 A sqq.; Simpl. de an. 6 b. u.; Philop. De an. C 2, D 7; Tim. Locr. 95 E (the details of these explanations are to be found in the passages themselves and in Martin, i. 371 sqq.: Steinhart vi. 243). Plutarch too, c. 25, 3, agrees in distinguishing them; by the μεριστὸν, however, he understands (c. 6)—as does Martin, i. 355 sq., not matter, but the ordered soul, which even before the formation of the world, moved the Material, and became the World-soul through its association with Reason (the ἀμέριστον: cf. note 115). Timæus of Locri (96 A) makes two motive powers out of the ταὐτὸν and θάτερον by an arbitrary limitation of their meaning. The suppositions of Brandis in the two older treatises, that the Great-and-Small is meant by the μεριστὸν and ἀμέριστον, or the ταὐτὸν and θάτερον, and the kindred theory of Stallbaum, sup loco Tim. p. 6 sqq., who would understand the indefinite duad or (sic) 'the Ideal and the corporeally Infinite,' have been refuted by Bonitz, p. 53, those of Herbart (Emil. in die Phil. W. i. 251), and Bonitz (p. 68 sqq. and cf. Martin, i. 358 sqq), viz. that the soul is composed out of the Ideas of Identity, Difference, and Being, by Ueberweg, pp. 46-54. Even Plutarch, c. 23, shows that the soul is not an Idea.

[140] Tim. 35 B-36 B; Bœckh loc.

that the soul comprehends all proportion and measure primarily in itself: it is wholly number and harmony,

cit pp 43–81 (cf metr. Pind. 203 sqq), following Crantor, Eudoxus and Plutarch, gives an exhaustive elucidation of this passage, and a catalogue of the ancient interpreters as far as they are known to us All the moderns follow his example, e g. Stallbaum ad loc.; Brandis, i. 457 sqq.; ii a 363 sq.; Martin, i. 383 sqq.; ii. 35 sq.; Müller, in his review, p 263 sqq.; Steinhart, vi. 99 sqq; Susemihl, Genet. Entw. ii. 357 sqq., and others, though not all with equal understanding. Briefly, Plato represents the collective World-soul as divided into seven parts, which stand to one another as 1, 2, 3, 4, 9, 8, 27, that is to say the two and three follow unity, and then the squares and cubes of two and three. Both these series of numbers, that progressing in the proportion of 1 : 2, and that in the proportion of 1 · 3 (the διπλάσια and τριπλάσια διαστήματα), are then further completed in such a way that between each two terms of the system two means are inserted, an arithmetical and a harmonic; i.e. one which is greater by the same number as that by which it is less than the larger term; and one such that its difference from the smaller divided by the smaller equals its difference from the larger divided by the larger (cf vol i. 348, 3) If this requirement is satisfied, and the smallest number put as unity, which will allow the expression of the rest of the series in whole numbers, we get the following scheme. (The second number of each series gives the harmonic, the third the arithmetical mean.) (A) For the διπλάσια διαστήματα:

Proportion of—
1 : 2) 384 512 576 768
2 : 4) 768 1024 1152 1536
4 . 8) 1536 2048 2304 3072;
(B) for the τριπλάσια διαστήματα:
Proportion of—
1 : 3) 384 576 768 1152
3 : 9) 1152 1728 2304 3456
9 : 27) 3456 5184 6912 10368.
According to this scheme, in the series of the διπλάσια διαστήματα, the first of the four numbers of each series stands to the second (e g 384 · 512), and the third to the fourth (576 · 768) as 3 : 4; the second to the third (512 : 576) as 8 : 9. In the series of the τριπλάσια διαστήματα, the first stands to the second (384 : 576), and the third to the fourth (768 1152) as 2 3; the second to the third (576 : 768) as 3 : 4. Hence (Tim. 36 A sq) arise the proportions 2 : 3, 3 : 4, 8 9 The first two of these fill up the τριπλάσια. the second and third the διπλάσια διαστήματα. If we try to reduce the proportion 3 · 4 to the proportion 8 · 9, which serves to complete it, we find our progress arrested; but if we advance from the number 384 in the proportion of 8 . 9, we get the numbers $432 = \frac{9}{8} \times 384$, and $486 = \frac{9}{8} \times 432$; for the remainder, instead of the proportion 8 : 9, we get only 486 : 512 = 243 256 The same holds good of the resolution of the proportion 2 3 through the proportion 8 . 9, 2 : 3 is greater than 3 · 4 by the interval 8 · 9. All the proportions depending on the fundamental proportion 2 : 3 and 3 : 4 can be resolved into the two proportions 8 . 9 and 243 : 256. If this process be applied to the

and from it spring all numerical definition and all harmony in the world: for with Plato, as with the

whole of the numbers in the above scheme, we get the following results:—

384	} 8 : 9	2048	} 256 : 273⅔
432		2187	
486	} 8 : 9	2304	} 243 : 256
512	} 243 : 256	2592	} 8 : 9
576	} 8 : 9	2916	} 8 : 9
648	} 8 : 9	3072	} 243 : 256
729	} 8 : 9	3456	} 8 : 9
768	} 243 : 256	3888	} 8 : 9
864	} 8 : 9	4374	} 8 : 9
972	} 8 : 9	4608	} 243 : 256
1024	} 243 : 256	5184	} 8 : 9
1152	} 8 : 9	5832	} 8 : 9
1296	} 8 : 9	6561	} 8 : 9
1458	} 8 : 9	6912	} 243 : 256
1536	} 243 : 256	7776	} 8 : 9
1728	} 8 : 9	8748	} 8 : 9
1944	} 8 : 9	9216	} 243 : 256
2048	} 243 : 256	10368	} 8 : 9

In this series, derived from the first three numbers, Plato recognises the fundamental determinations of the astronomical and harmonic system. In the former, according to his of course entirely arbitrary supposition (Tim. 36 D; cf. 38 D; Rep. x. 617 A sq.), the distances of the planets depend upon the numbers two and three, and their powers; the sun, Venus, Mercury, Mars, Jupiter, Saturn are respectively 2, 3, 4, 8, 9, 27 times as far from the earth as the moon. So in the harmonic system. The eight tones of the octachord stand according to a diatonic classification, the strings going from lowest to highest, and consequently the tones are numbered from the high to the low (which is not always the case, e.g. Arist. Metaph. v. ii. 1018, b. 28, x 7, 1057, a. 22, the procedure is from the ὑπάτη through the μέση to the νήτη) in the following proportion —

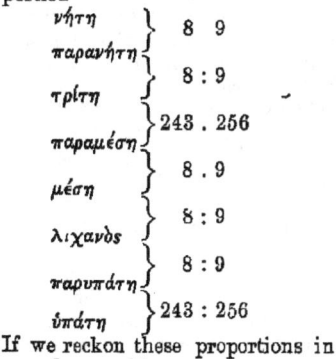

νήτη	} 8 : 9
παρανήτη	} 8 : 9
τρίτη	} 243 : 256
παραμέση	} 8 : 9
μέση	} 8 : 9
λιχανός	} 8 : 9
παρυπάτη	} 243 : 256
ὑπάτη	

If we reckon these proportions in accordance with a single measure for all eight tones, and make the higher tone the lesser (as is usual with the ancients, because the height of the tone, as is well known, stands in inverse proportion to the length of the sounding-string with equal thickness and tension, or because, as Bockh supposes, loc. cit. 49, the higher tone requires just as many vibrations in a lesser time. I cannot, however, find this in the passages quoted by Bockh, and in any case the first method of measurement seems to me to be the original), we obtain the following formula: if the tone of the νήτη be set down as = 384, then the παρανήτη = 432, the τρίτη = 486, the

Pythagoreans, musical harmony and the system of the heavenly bodies are the principal revelations of the invisible numbers and their accord.[141] In this respect,

παραμέση = 512, the μέση = 576, the λιχανὸς = 648, the παρυπάτη = 729, the ὑπάτη = 768 (Other numbers would result, if we put down the larger number for the higher tone and the smaller for the deeper, as we should do in determining the proportion of the tone according to the number of its vibrations Then if the ὑπάτη were put down at 486, we should have for the παρυπάτη 512; for the λιχανὸς 576; for the μέση 648, for the παραμέση 729; for the τρίτη 768; for the παρανήτη 864; for the νήτη 972. But clearly this is not Plato's way of reckoning, and Martin, i. 395 is mistaken in believing that Plato intended to assign the larger numbers particularly to the higher tones, because, acc. to Tim. 67 B; 80 A sq., with Aristotle and others he considers them to be quicker than the lower tones. As Martin himself remarks, even those old musicians who knew that the higher tones consist of more parts than the lower or produce more vibrations in the air, do not invariably do this, because they calculate the proportion of the tone according to the length of the strings Others, of course, e.g. Arist ap. Plut. Mus. 23, 5; Arist. Problem xvii. 23, Plut an. procr. 18, 4 sq, 19, 1, assign the larger number to the higher tone. Further details on this point are to be found in Martin, loc. cit.) The fundamental proportions of the above scale, as the Pythagoreans had already taught (see vol. i. 305 –i. 345 sq.), are the octave (διὰ πασῶν), or the proportion 1 : 2 (λόγος διπλάσιος), the fifth (διὰ πέντε), in Philolaus (δι' ὀξειῶν), or 2 : 3 (ἡμιόλιον), the fourth (διὰ τεσσάρων, in Philol. συλλαβή), or 3 : 4 (ἐπίτριτον), the tone, or 8 : 9, and the lesser semi-tone, or 243 : 256 (this lesser half of a tone is called in Philolaus δίεσις, later λεῖμμα, the greater = 256 : 273¾ is called ἀποτομή). From the νήτη to the παραμέση, and from the μέση to the ὑπάτη is a fourth, from the νήτη to the μέση, and from the παραμέση to the ὑπάτη is a fifth, the distance of the particular strings amounts partly to a tone, partly to a λεῖμμα. It is obvious that these are the same proportions which form the basis of the series of numbers. All the derivative tones (e g. the διὰ πασῶν καὶ διὰ πέντε = 1 : 3, and the δὶς διὰ πασῶν = 1 : 4) can easily be shown in it (cf Plat. an. procr. 14, 2), and it contains in itself a system of four octaves, a fifth and a tone, the sequence of the tones likewise comes quite right, if with Böckh and the pseudo-Timæus (who can only on this supposition give the sum of the numbers in question as 114,695) we interpolate the number 6144 between the numbers 5832 and 6561. This number is distant a λεῖμμα from 5832, and an ἀποτομή from 6561. Then there remains only the unimportant anomaly that two tones (2048 · 2304 and 6144 6912) are resolved into a semi-tone, and that in the fourth octave (3072 : 6144) the fifth preceding the fourth.

[141] Cf. Rep. vii. 527 D sq.; 529 C sqq; 530 D; Tim. 47 A sqq.; and vol. i. 374.

therefore, the World-soul has the same import and comprehension as that which Plato, in the Philebus, calls the Limit, and Aristotle represents him as calling the Mathematical principle. For of the Limit it is said [142] that the whole sphere of number and measure belongs to it; and Aristotle assigns to the Mathematical principle the same place that is occupied in the Timæus by the World-soul: it stands midway between material objects and the Ideas.[143] It is quite in harmony with this, that Plato should make the Mathematical sciences, and these alone, form the transition from the sensible perception to the contemplation of the Idea;[144] for in conformity with his principles, this pre-supposes that as these sciences themselves lie in the midst between the sensible notion and pure thought,[145] so must their object lie between the phenomenon and the Idea. The two concepts, however, are certainly distinct in their points of departure and in their apprehension. The notion of the World-soul, starting from the contemplation of Life and motion, represents primarily the efficient powers in the universe, conceived in the manner of the human soul: the Mathematical principle represents the formal determination of things, accord-

[142] 25 A; vide p. 264.

[143] Metaph. i. 6, 987 a. 14· ἔτι δὲ παρὰ τὰ αἰσθητὰ καὶ τὰ εἴδη τὰ μαθηματικὰ τῶν πραγμάτων εἶναί φησι μεταξὺ, διαφέροντα τῶν μὲν αἰσθητῶν τῷ ἀΐδια καὶ ἀκίνητα εἶναι, τῶν δ' εἰδῶν τῷ τὰ μὲν πόλλ' ἄττα ὅμοια εἶναι τὸ δὲ εἶδος αὐτὸ ἓν ἕκαστον μόνον. (Similarly in the shorter allusions 1, 9, 991 a. 4, vii.; 2, 1028 b. 18, xi; 1, 1059 b. 6.) The expression ἀκίνητα is, however, inaccurate; in Plato neither the World-soul nor, acc. to Rep. vii. 529 C sq. (supra, p 221, 158), the mathematical principle is absolutely unmoved, they are only free from Becoming and the changeability of Becoming.

[144] Vide p. 215.

[145] Cf. p. 225.

ing to number and measure.[146] But as in the Platonic Ideas, the highest efficient and the highest formal causes coincide, and are divided only temporarily and in inexact description, so it is here. The World-soul comprehends in itself all mathematical proportions in unity; and occupies the position, which according to the Philebus and to Aristotle, is exclusively filled by the Mathematical principle. Though we should not be justified in assuming that Plato has expressly identified them, and must indeed acknowledge that the problem of finding a middle term between Idea and phenomenon is apprehended in the two doctrines from different sides (this middle term being regarded in the concept of the soul from the point of view of living force, as cause of motion and of opinion, while in the concept of the mathematical principle it appears as a specific form of Being); yet both have ultimately the same signification, and take the same place in the Platonic system.[147] They show us the Idea in reference to the world of sense; and the world of sense embraced

[146] On this depends Plutarch's objection, De an. procr. 23, 1, to the theory that the soul is either a number or a space· μήτε τοῖς πέρασι μήτε τοῖς ἀριθμοῖς μεθὲν ἴχνος ἐνυπάρχειν ἐκείνης τῆς δυνάμεως, ᾗ τὸ αἰσθητὸν ἡ ψυχὴ πέφυκε κρίνειν· neither thought nor conception nor sensation can be derived from units, lines, or superficies, v. note 154.

[147] So Siebeck, Unters. z. Phil. d. Gr. 101 sq. The fact that in the Phileb. 30 A, C, the World-soul is especially mentioned together with the πέρας (by which I understand the mathematical standard of determination), goes neither against my explanation of the πέρας, nor against the correctness of the connection given above. I do not, of course, suppose that Plato expressly identified the mathematical principle and the World-soul, so I am not concerned with Rettig's citation (p. 20, Αἰτία in the Philebus) of this passage as against the assumption 'that πέρας means the World-soul.'

by firmly limited relations. In mathematical forms, the unity of the Idea does indeed separate into plurality; but these forms are not subject to the vicissitude of sensible things.[148] The Soul enters into the corporeal and its motion, but the soul itself is not corporeal.[149] While all that is corporeal is moved by another, the soul is the self-moved, and moves everything else,[150] and though distinct from the Idea, the soul is of all things most closely related to it.[151] Strictly speaking, we should go a step further, and declare both the World-soul and mathematical forms to be the Idea itself, as the formal determination and motive principle of the material world. For as Matter as such is the Non-existent, the Real in the soul can only be the Idea. But the same reasons which obliged Plato to separate the Idea from the phenomenon, necessitated also the distinction of the soul from the Idea: the soul is derived, the Idea original; the soul is generated, the Idea eternal; the Soul is a particular, the Idea a universal;[152] the Idea is absolute reality, the soul only participates in reality.[153] As the Ideas are placed side by side with one another, although, properly speaking, the lower must be contained in the higher, and all in the highest; as the world of sense is set beside the Ideas, although, in so far as it possesses reality, it is immanent in them, so the Soul appears as a Third between

---

[148] V. note 143.
[149] Soph. 246 E sqq.; Phædo, 79 A sq.; Tim. 36 E et alibi.
[150] V. supra, p. 345.
[151] Phædo, 79 A sq. D (where the subject of discussion is the human soul), but acc. to Tim. 41 D, this must hold good even more of the World-soul. Rep x. 611 E.
[152] So, too, mathematical things in relation to the Idea; vide passages quoted, note 143, from Aristotle.
[153] See p. 346 sq., p. 239, 39.

the Idea and the phenomenon, instead of merely representing that side of the Idea, which is turned to the phenomenon; and we find that the mathematical forms still retain a place beside the soul, while at the same time mathematical proportions are within it.[154]

[154] The old Platonists reckoned the soul for the most part among mathematical things, only they were not agreed as to whether its nature was arithmetical or geometrical, a number or a magnitude. The former was the view of Xenocrates, who, as we shall see later on, defined it as a self-moving number. So (acc to Proclus in Tim. 187 B) did Aristander, Numenius, and many others; and to this view belongs the statement (Diog iii. 67) that Plato attributed to the soul an ἀρχὴ ἀριθμητική, to the body an ἀρχὴ γεωμετρική, which, however, hardly agrees with what immediately follows, where the soul is defined as ἰδέα τοῦ πάντη διαστατοῦ πνεύματος. The other view belongs not only to Severus, as mentioned by Proclus loc. cit, but to Speusippus and Posidonius. The former of these imagined its Being as in space (ἐν ἰδέᾳ τοῦ πάντη διαστατοῦ, Stob. Ekl. 1. 862); the latter defined it more precisely as ἰδέα τοῦ πάντη διαστατοῦ καθ' ἀριθμὸν συνεστῶσα ἁρμονίαν περιέχοντα (Plut. an. procr 22, 1, who, however, wrongly understands the ἰδέα τ. π. διαστ. as an Idea, whereas it must rather mean a formation of that which is in space fashioned according to harmonic numbers). In the first view, the elements of the soul, the ἀμέριστον and μεριστὸν, would be referred to the Unit and the indefinite duad; in the second, to the Point and the intermediate Space (Procl. loc. cit., whose statement with regard to Xenocrates will receive further confirmation) Posidonius, however, refers them to the νοητὸν and spatial magnitude (τὴν τῶν περάτων οὐσίαν περὶ τὰ σώματα, the limitation of bodies in space). Aristotle, De An. 1, 3, 407, a. 2, objects to Plato that in the Timæus he makes the soul a magnitude. Ueberweg, loc cit 56, 74 sq. holds the same view. The soul according to Ueberweg is a mathematical magnitude, and in space; of its elements, the ταὐτὸν signifies number, the θάτερον space, which admits of all figures; and this space is the principle of motion in secondary matter, and, as such, the irrational soul (v. note 115) The quarrel of Xenocrates and Speusippus seems to show that Plato had not expressed himself definitely in favour of one view or the other. Aristotle had to form his doctrine as to the soul from the Timæus alone, for his quotation De An. 1, 2 (supra, p. 256, 103), from the Discourses on Philosophy is irrelevant to the present question. The probable conclusion to be drawn from the Timæus is that the soul, in spite of its incorporeality and invisibility, is envisaged as being diffused through the body of the World-whole. Such envisagements of the relation of soul to body, especially in an animated treatment of the subject,

The activity of the Soul is partly motion, partly intelligence.[155] It is the first principle of all motion, for it alone is the Self-moving, and in moving itself it also moves the body.[156] The Phædrus says that the soul has the care of the inanimate, traverses the world and is its ruler.[157] The more fanciful imagery of the

are scarcely to be avoided, but I cannot believe Plato to have represented it as a magnitude in space, in the direct manner Ueberweg supposes. All the expressions which can be quoted in favour of his view are veiled in a mythical and symbolical twilight which forbids our conceiving them as dogmatic. No one takes the division of the world-soul into eight circles, and all the connected details, as a literal expression of Plato's belief; nor can the general supposition (only used in that allegorical exposition), that the soul is extended in space and divisible in space, be strictly pressed. Otherwise we should be obliged to consider the soul, not merely as something extended, but as something corporeal; anything filling space and yet not material can be no more split up and bent into circles than it can be mixed in a caldron (Tim. 41 D). From the exposition of the Timæus we can really infer nothing, simply because we should infer too much. In itself, however, it is incredible that Plato, who considers the fact of filling space to be the distinguishing sign of Body, should have expressly attributed the same quality to the incorporeal, standing in as close connection with the Idea as the soul He might rather have called the soul a number; but as this determination is unanimously quoted as peculiar to Xenocrates, we cannot, of course, ascribe it to Plato. The most probable view is that Plato did not expressly declare himself on this point, and left the relation of the soul to the mathematical principle generally in that indeterminate state which our text presupposes.

[155] Cf Arist De An. i 2.
[156] Vide note 131. Phædr. 245 D sq. κινήσεως μὲν ἀρχὴ τὸ αὐτὸ αὐτὸ κινοῦν . ψυχῆς οὐσίαν τε καὶ λόγον τοῦτον αὐτόν τις λέγων οὐκ αἰσχυνεῖται . . . μὴ ἄλλο τι εἶναι τὸ αὐτὸ ἑαυτὸ κινοῦν ἢ ψυχήν.
[157] 246 B: πᾶσα ἡ ψυχὴ παντὸς ἐπιμελεῖται τοῦ ἀψύχου, πάντα δὲ οὐρανὸν περιπολεῖ, ἄλλοτ' ἐν ἄλλοις εἴδεσι γιγνομένη. τελέα μὲν οὖν οὖσα καὶ ἐπτερωμένη μετεωροπορεῖ τε καὶ πάντα τὸν κόσμον διοικεῖ. ἡ δὲ πτερορρυήσασα φέρεται, &c. A question may possibly arise, whether we are to understand the πᾶσα ψυχὴ as the whole collective soul,— i.e. the soul of the All, or (with Susemihl, ii 399, and others) each individual soul. In favour of the first view we have besides the πᾶσα ἡ ψυχὴ (for which also πᾶσα ψυχὴ occurs) the words παντὸς ἐπιμελεῖται τοῦ ἀψύχου . . . . πάντα τὸν κόσμον διοικεῖ, for each individual soul supposes only its body, and all individual souls collectively suppose only their collective body; whereas the soul of the universe, and it only, cares for everything

Timæus is to the same effect. The entire World-soul, we are told, was divided lengthwise into two parts; and these two halves were bent into an outer and an inner circle, of which the outer is named the circle of the Same; the inner, that of the Other. These circles, laid obliquely within each other, are the scaffolding of the World system: the circle of the Same is the sphere of fixed stars; the circle of the Other forms by further division the seven spheres of the planets. In the circular revolution of these spheres the soul, turning in itself, moves; it is interfused everywhere from the centre of the universe to the circumference, and envelopes it externally; and as all the corporeal is built into these spheres, the soul effects also the motion of the corporeal.[158] As Plato's real opinion, however, we can only maintain this much, that the soul—diffused throughout the universe and by virtue of its nature, ceaselessly self-moving, according to fixed laws—causes the division as well as the motion of matter in the heavenly spheres: and that its harmony and life are revealed in the order and courses of the stars. The Timæus also connects the intelligence of the World-soul with its motion and harmonious distribution. By reason of its composition (37, A ff), and because it is divided and bound together in itself according to harmonical proportion—because it at last returns into itself by its circular motion,—it tells itself

inanimate, including inorganic nature. Here, however, though less clearly than in the Timæus, the soul of the All is thought of as including and embracing the collectivity of the individual souls in itself.

[158] 34 B, 36 B–E. The astronomical part of this exposition will be discussed later on.

throughout its whole essence of all that it touches in its course, whether Divisible or Indivisible: in what respect it is the same, and in what diverse, whether and how it is related to Being or Becoming. But this speech, spreading itself soundlessly in the sphere of the Self-moved, generates knowledge. If the faculty of perception is touched by it and the announcement comes to the soul from the circle of the Other,[159] then true notions and opinions arise;[160] if it is signified to thought, from the circle of the Same, rational cognition and intelligent knowledge are the result. Here again the literal and figurative are freely intermingled, and Plato himself might, perhaps, scarcely be able to define with accuracy where his representation ceases to be dogmatic and begins to be mythical. He is doubtless in earnest [161] when he ascribes to the world a soul, and to this soul the most perfect intelligence that can belong to aught created; and though the more precise concept of personality hardly applies to this soul,[162] yet in all that he says on the subject, he abun-

[159] In 37 B, αἰσθητικόν, the reading of one of Bekker's MSS., is to be adopted instead of αἰσθητόν (as is shown by the opposition of λογιστικόν), and it is to this that the αὐτοῦ τὴν ψυχήν of our text refers. The αἰσθητικόν must signify, not the faculty of perception, but the subject capable of perception, which, however, can, at the same time, be one admitting of thought, a λογιστικόν. It is, however, more convenient to read αὐτόν [sc. τὸν λόγον]; then the αἰσθητικόν may be the faculty of perception, and the whole passage receives a more natural colouring. In the above, therefore, I follow this conjecture. The expressions περὶ τὸ αἰσθητὸν γίγνεσθαι, περὶ τὸ λογιστικὸν εἶναι are generally referred to the objects of the λόγος (cf. Stallbaum in loc.), but this tends to embarrassment with the λογιστικόν, which ought to be νοητόν to meet this view.

[160] On these stages of cognition cf. p 279 sq.

[161] V. pp. 325 sqq ; 288, 172; 266, 112.

[162] What can we understand by a personality which comprises

dantly shows that he himself conceives it as analogous to the human soul. The question which to us would immediately occur, how far the World-soul possesses self-consciousness and will, he has scarcely even raised.[163] It sounds to us strange that the intellectual activity of this soul should coincide with the revolution in space of the heavens; that reason and science should be assigned to the sphere of fixed stars, and opinion to that of the planets. Even Plato probably did not intend this exposition to be taken literally;[164] yet he has certainly brought knowledge and the movement of the soul into a connection which must have made any accurate definition almost as difficult to him as to ourselves. He regards knowledge as a motion returning into itself, and ascribes to the World-soul a knowledge of all that is in itself and in the world, just because there belongs to it this perfect motion in and around itself. Other philosophers had similarly combined knowledge and motion,[165] and Plato elsewhere compares them in a way that shows us that he conceived them to be governed by analogous laws.[166] The same holds good

numberless other existences, and those too possessed of life and soul? How could the soul be a World-soul, unless it were in relation with all parts of the world, just as the human soul is with the parts of the body?

[163] Cf. p. 266.

[164] If we take the passage just quoted from Tim. 37 B as it stands, the result would be that Right Opinion is brought about by the motion of the planetary circle, Thought and Knowledge by that of the fixed stars. No clear idea, however, can be got out of this, whether we understand Thought and Opinion to be the Thought and Opinion of the human soul, or of the World-soul. We can hardly suppose that Plato would have attributed to the World-soul, besides Thought, mere Opinion, even though it were Right Opinion.

[165] E.g. Anaxagoras and Diogenes, vide vol. i. 804 sq., 220; cf. Arist. De An 1. 2, 405 a. 13, 21.

[166] In Tim. 34 B is mentioned the circular motion τῶν ἑπτὰ [κινήσεων] τὴν περὶ νοῦν καὶ φρόνησιν μάλιστα

of the mathematical partition of the Soul. As Plato expressed the differences of knowledge by means of numbers,[167] he might also place knowledge generally, in combination with number. The infinite Many, as Philolaus had already taught,[168] becomes cognisable by being reduced through number and measure to definite proportions. Plato derives the knowledge of the World-soul from its harmonious distribution of parts, as well as from its composition and motion,[169] and this is in the main his real opinion. The Soul could not know material things did it not bear within itself, in harmonic proportions, the principle of all determination and order. As its motion is regulated by number, so is its knowledge; and as in the one case it effects the transition of the Idea to the phenomenon and brings the unlimited plurality of material things into subjection to the Idea,—so in the other it combines Unity and Multiplicity, the cognition of Reason and the perception of Sense.

οὖσαν, similarly 39 C, 40 A. Laws. x. 898 A: εἶναί τε αὐτὴν τῇ τοῦ νοῦ περιόδῳ πάντως ὡς δυνατὸν οἰκειοτάτην τε καὶ ὁμοίαν .... κατὰ ταὐτὰ δήπου καὶ ὡσαύτως καὶ ἐν τῷ αὐτῷ καὶ περὶ τὰ αὐτὰ καὶ πρὸς τὰ αὐτὰ καὶ ἕνα λόγον καὶ τάξιν μίαν ἄμφω κινεῖσθαι; and Tim. 77 B, 89 A, 90 C sq., cf. 43 D, 44 D, 47 D, thought is described simply as a motion, and more particularly a circular motion (περιφορὰ) of the soul

[167] Vide p. 219, 147, and p. 256, 103.

[168] Vide vol. i. 294, 1.

[169] Tim. 37 A: ἅτε .... ἀνὰ λόγον μερισθεῖσα καὶ ξυνδεθεῖσα.

CHAPTER VIII.

THE WORLD-SYSTEM AND ITS PARTS.

THE foregoing pages contain the leading thoughts of the Platonic view of Nature. The World is the phenomenon of the Idea in Space and in Time,—the sensible and variable copy of the Eternal: it is the common product of the Divine Reason and of Natural Necessity, of the Idea and of Matter. That which mediatises between them, the proximate cause of all order, motion, life, and knowledge, is the Soul.

The Timæus shows how, from these causes, the origin and economy of the universe are to be explained; and to do so, it enters deeply into the particulars of phenomena. It may well be conceived, however, from the character of Plato's genius, that these enquiries into natural science would be little to his taste: accordingly we find, not merely that the Timæus alone of his writings discusses this subject, but that it does not seem to have been pursued even in his oral discourses.

Aristotle, at any rate, appeals for this portion of his theory solely to the Timæus. But Plato himself declares that he esteems such discussions as inferior in value to more general philosophic enquiry. Our words, he says, are constituted like the objects they describe. Only the doctrine of invariable Being can lay claim to perfect certainty and exactitude; where the mere phenomenon of true Reality is in question, we must be content with probability instead of strict truth.[1] These things are therefore rather a matter of intellectual pastime than of serious philosophic investigation.[2] Perhaps he is not quite in earnest,[3] but from these remarks we may infer that Plato was to some extent aware of his weakness in natural science, and at the same time believed that from the nature of the subject, greater certainty in such enquiries was hardly to be attained. On his philosophy, indeed, the bearing of his own enquiries in this direction is unimportant:

---

[1] Tim. 29 B sq.; cf. 44 C, 56 C, 57 D, 67 D, 68 D, 90 E Even in the important questions about matter and the unity of the world Plato uses this caution. Tim. 48 D (on the text cf. Böckh, Kl. Schr. iii. 239), he says that about the Sensible as the εἰκών of true Being, only εἰκότες λόγοι are possible, i e. such as are like the truth, but not the truth itself, just as an εἰκών is that which is like a thing, but is not the thing itself. That which is merely like the truth—merely probable—includes not only scientific suppositions, but also (as Susemihl Genet., Entw. ii. 321 points out) mythical expositions. Plato himself clearly gives us to understand this in the passages already quoted, p. 485, 1; he says, however, in the Phædo, 114 D, at the end of his eschatological myth: it would in truth be foolish ταῦτα διισχυρίσασθαι οὕτως ἔχειν ... ὅτι

μέντοι ἢ ταῦτ' ἐστὶν ἢ τοιαῦτ' ἄττα ... τοῦτο καὶ πρέπειν μοι δοκεῖ, κ.τ λ. This myth, then, cannot indeed lay claim to complete truth, but to a certain probability, and the same result is derived from Gorg. 527 A. Cf. 523 A.

[2] Tim. 59 C: τἆλλα δὲ τῶν τοιούτων οὐδὲν ποικίλον ἔτι διαλογίσασθαι, τὴν τῶν εἰκότων μύθων μεταδιώκοντα ἰδέαν, ἣν ὅταν τις ἀναπαύσεως ἕνεκα, τοὺς περὶ τῶν ὄντων ἀεὶ καταθέμενος λόγους, τοὺς γενέσεως περὶ διαθεώμενος εἰκότας ἀμεταμέλητον ἡδονὴν κτᾶται, μέτριον ἂν ἐν τῷ βίῳ παιδιὰν καὶ φρόνιμον ποιοῖτο.

[3] παιδία, at least in the passage just quoted, recalls the corresponding and clearly exaggerated expression of Phædr. 265 C, 276 D, and the whole depreciatory treatment of physical science is in harmony with the solemn tone of the Timæus

they contain Ideas and observations, which are sometimes ingenious and sometimes puerile, interesting no doubt for the history of natural science, but for that of philosophy in great measure valueless, because of their slight connection with Plato's philosophic principles. Much appears to be borrowed from others, especially from Philolaus, and probably Democritus. Three main points have, however, a more universal importance : these are, the Origin of the World, the derivation of the Elements, and the concept of the World-System.

I. *The Origin of the World.*—This is described in the Timæus as a mechanical construction. The universal Architect resolves to make the totality of the visible as perfect as possible, by forming a created nature after the eternal archetype of the living essential nature. For this purpose, He first mingles the World-soul, and divides it in its circles. Then He binds the chaotic, fluent matter into the primary forms of the four elements. From these He prepares the system of the universe—building matter into the scaffolding of the World-soul. In its various parts He places the stars, to be the dividers of Time. Lastly, that nothing might be wanting to the perfection of the world, He forms living beings.[4]

Now the mythical character of this description generally cannot be doubted, but it is not easy to determine how far the mythus extends. We have already in reference to this subject spoken of the Creator, of the Soul, and of Matter : we are now more immediately concerned with the question whether, and to what

[4] See x. 27 E–57 D.

extent, Plato seriously maintains the beginning of the world in time, and its gradual formation.[5] On the one hand, not only does this seem to be required by the whole tone of the Timæus, but it appears to result still more definitely from the explanation (28 B), that the world as corporeal, must have become; for all sensible and corporeal things are subject to Becoming. On the other hand, however, this assumption involves us in a series of glaring contradictions. For if all that is corporeal must have become, or been created, this must

[5] The views of the first Platonic scholars were divided on this point —Aristotle (De cœlo, i. 10, 280 a. 28; iv. 2, 300 b. 16; Phys. viii. 1, 251 b. 17, Metaph. xii. 3, 1071 b. 31, 37, De An. i. 3, 406 b. 25 sqq.) in his criticism of the Platonic cosmogony takes the Timæus literally throughout and considers the temporal origin of the world, the World-soul, and time, to be Plato's real meaning. Still even he says (Gen. et corr. ii. 1, 329 a, 13) that Plato did not clearly explain whether matter can exist otherwise than in the form of the four elements; and that if this question be answered in the negative, the beginning of the world must also be denied. Another view (acc. to Arist. De cœlo, i. 10, 279 b 32) was, that Plato represented the formation of the world as a temporal act merely for the sake of clearness. We learn from Simpl. ad loc. Schol. in Arist. 488 b. 15 (whose statement is repeated by others, 489 a. 6, 9); Pseudo-Alex. ad Metaph. 1091 a. 27; Plut. procr. an. 3, 1, that Xenocrates availed himself of this expedient; and was followed by Crantor and Eudorus (Plut. loc. cit. and c. 4, 1), Taurus ap. Philop. De ætern. mundi, vi. 21, and most of the Platonists who inclined to Pythagorean views—the Neo-Platonists without exception. On the other hand, Theophrastus (Fragm. 28 sq; Wimm ap. Philop. loc. cit. vi. 8, 31, 27) rejects this supposition— though not so decidedly as Aristotle—and with him Alexander ap. Philop. vi. 27, and apparently the whole Peripatetic school agree. Among the Platonists, Plutarch, loc cit. and Atticus (on whom see vol. iii. a. 722, 2nd edit) endeavour to prove that the theory of the world being without a beginning is foreign to Plato. Among the moderns Böckh (On the World-soul, p. 23 sq) has repeated the view of Xenocrates; and is followed by Brandis (ii. a. 356 sq., 365), Steinhart (Plat. WW. vi. 68 sqq., 94 sq.), Susemihl (Genet. Entw. ii 326 sqq.), and others, together with my Plat. St. 208 sqq. and the 1st ed. of the present work. Martin, Etudes i 355, 370 sq., 377; ii. 179 sqq.; Ueberweg. Rhein. Mus. ix. 76, 79; Plat Schr. 287 sq.; Stumpf, Verh. d. plat. Gott. z. Idee d. Gut. 36 sqq declare in favour of Plutarch's view.

also hold good of Matter; yet Matter is supposed to precede the creation of the world, and (30 A) is represented in this its ante-mundane condition as something already visible. But if we are to include the notion of an eternal matter in the mythical portion of the dialogue, where is our warranty that the creation of the world is not part of the same, and that the proper meaning of the latter theory may not be the metaphysical dependence of the finite on the Eternal? The dogmatic form in which it is proved argues little; for the point is primarily to show, not a chronological beginning, but an Author of the world.[6] And we constantly find Plato adopting this dogmatic tone [7]

[6] Cf. Tim. 28 B· σκεπτέον δ' οὖν περὶ αὐτοῦ πρῶτον ... πότερον ἦν ἀεί, γενέσεως ἀρχὴν ἔχων οὐδεμίαν, ἢ γέγονεν, ἀπ' ἀρχῆς τινος ἀρξάμενος. γέγονεν ... τῷ δ' αὖ γενομένῳ φαμὲν ὑπ' αἰτίου τινὸς ἀνάγκην εἶναι γενέσθαι

[7] E.g. Polit. 269 C. Here the necessity of a periodical alternation between the self-motion of the world and its motion by divine agency (the starting-point of the well-known cosmological myth) is insisted on as dogmatically and with the same apparent earnestness as the necessity of a beginning of the world in the Timæus. 'The corporeal cannot possibly be always the same The world has a body It must consequently change, and this change consists in its revolution. But it is impossible that it should continually revolve of itself. The ἡγούμενον τῶν κινουμένων πάντων alone has this power And its nature does not allow (οὐ θέμις) that it should be moved first in one direction and then in another by this ἡγούμενον. The world, therefore, can neither always move itself nor always be moved by the divinity. Nor can two gods move it in opposite ways. The only conclusion remaining is that at one time it is moved by God, and at another being left alone, it moves in an opposite direction of itself.' This is just as didactic as the passage of the Timæus, and can be made to give just as valid and formal conclusions as Stumpf has derived from the latter passage (loc. cit. 38 f.). But can we conclude from it that Plato really considered the world as alternately moved by the divinity, and again (in an opposite direction, and with a complete change of relations) by its ἔμφυτος ἐπιθυμία, while he lays down in question and answer that with the changed direction of the world's revolution the life of the things in it must also suffer a change?

in places where it is impossible he can be stating his real and literal meaning. We cannot, it is true, rely much on inferences from the Platonic writings, never perhaps drawn by Plato himself;[8] but the case is different with the assertion in Timæus (37 D, 38 C), that Time first began with the world. This assertion

---

Again, if there is any one point in the Platonic system established by the most distinct explanations on the part of its author, it is the doctrine that the Ideas are uncreated. Yet, as we have seen supra, p. 226, 3, Plato speaks of God as the creator of the Ideas; and in his lectures explained his views as to their origin in such a way that Aristotle (as in the question of the formation of the world) regards a γένεσις τῶν ἀριθμῶν not as merely τοῦ θεωρῆσαι ἕνεκεν. (Metaph xiv 4 beginn.) That the ἀριθμοί here are to be understood as the Ideal numbers, and that the passage refers not to the Platonists only, but to Plato himself, is shown from Alex. and Metaph. i. 6, 987, b. 33; Schol. 551 a. 38 sqq., besides all our other authorities for this doctrine of Plato's. The literal interpreters of the cosmogony in the Timæus might appeal confidently to Plato's own explanation if the words (Tim. 26 D) τὸ μὴ πλασθέντα μῦθον ἀλλ' ἀληθινὸν λόγον εἶναι πάμμεγά που. were applied to it. Stumpf, indeed, loc. cit., thinks that he can support his theory by these words. But, as a glance will show, they refer, not to the picture of the formation of the world, but to Critias' narrative of the struggle between the Athenians and the Atlantids This is a πλασθεὶς μῦθος if ever there was one, and yet Plato expressly says it is not. The discrepancies before mentioned (p. 301 sq.), in his expressions as to Matter, and in the discussion of the Protagoras, quoted p. 188, 46, might also be adduced to show how little the apparently didactic tone of a passage justifies us in considering everything in it to be Plato's scientific conviction, and how many reasons there are, in a question like the present, for thinking twice before we commit ourselves to an assertion (Ueberweg, plat. Schr. 287 sq.), more suited to a theological apologist than a historical enquirer. If Plato (Tim. 28 B) declared himself for a created world, believing all the while that it was eternal (which, however, the passage itself does not suppose unconditionally), 'then,' says Ueberweg, 'we can only characterise his position by terms which we are heartily ashamed of applying to him He must either have been a hypocrite or a fool.' Which of the two was he when he wrote the above quoted passage of the Politicus, or when he ventured to declare the fable of the people of Atlantis to be true history?

[8] That e.g. the world, if God (Tim 29 E) created it out of goodness, must be just as eternal as the goodness of God.

is perfectly logical if a beginning of the world be assumed, for that which alone previously existed,—the world of Ideas, is not in Time,—and empty Time is nothing. But it is all the more difficult to see how notwithstanding this, Plato can always speak of that which was before the formation of the world,[9] while he nevertheless acknowledges (37 E sqq.) that this Before and After are only possible in Time.[10] The unoriginated pre-existence of the soul which Plato taught,[11] excludes a beginning of the world; for the Soul is itself a part of the world, and cannot be conceived without the body which it forms and animates. These contradictions may not suffice to prove that Plato deliberately made use of the theory of a historical creation as being in itself untrue, retaining as his own belief that the world had no beginning; but they at least show that the theory was not brought forward by him didactically, as part of his doctrine; that it was regarded as one of the presentations he occasionally employed without feeling moved to investigate or to pronounce upon them definitely.

This view is countenanced not only by the fact that many disciples of Plato have explained the origin of the world in Time as merely figurative investiture;[12] but also by the whole composition of the Timæus. For

[9] Tim 30 A, 34 B, C, 52 D, 53 B.
[10] Phædr. 245 D sqq., Meno, 86 A; Phædo, 106 D; Rep. x. 611; A, &c., cf Laws, vi. 781 E, where the supposition that mankind is without beginning or end is viewed as at least possible and even probable.
[11] The theory that it is not the World-soul sketched in the Timæus, but the unregulated soul of the Laws that is without beginning, has been refuted, p. 338, 115. The Phædrus expressly designates the soul, which it has proved to be without beginning, as the mover of heaven.
[12] See note 5.

the formation of the universe, instead of following the chronological sequence of its parts, as would be the case in a historical narration, is represented altogether according to ideal moments. Plato speaks first very fully of the works of Reason in the world, then (47 E sqq.) of the works of Necessity; and lastly, of the world itself (69 sqq.), as the common product of both these causes. In the first of these divisions, we are told of the composition of the corporeal elements, before that of the World-soul which preceded this process; and we find that the same object, because it may be regarded from two different points of view, is doubly represented—like the above-mentioned origin of the elements. Thus by its very form, this representation shows that it was designed to set forth not so much the historical order of events in the creation—as the universal causes and constituents of the World as it now exists. The mythical element, therefore, becomes strongest at those points where something historically new is introduced (30 B, 35 B, 36 B, 37 B, 41 A, &c.).[13]

II. *The formation of the Elements.*—The establishment of a well-ordered universe required that all bodies should be reducible to the four elements.[14] But here the two ways of regarding the elements—the teleological and the physical—directly

---

[13] The fact of Aristotle's taking Plato's exposition literally is no proof Similar misconceptions of the mythical form are common in him; see my Plat. Stud. p. 207. The doubts there expressed against the meteorology I now retract.

[14] Plato was the first to use the name στοιχεῖον, according to Eudemus (ap. Simpl. Phys. 2 a, u.; Schol. in Arist. 322 a, 8), and Phavorinus, ap. Diog. iii. 24. He gave the same name to his most general causes, the unit and the Great-and-Small (Arist. Metaph. xiv. 1, 1087 b. 13).

encounter one another. From the teleological point of view the Timæus (31 B sqq.) says: The world being corporeal, must of necessity be also visible and tangible: it could not be visible without fire, nor tangible without earth, which is the ground of all that is solid. Midway between these, however, there must be a third element which combines them; and as the fairest combination is Proportion, this Third must stand in proportion to both. If planes only were concerned, one mean would be sufficient, but as bodies are in question, two are necessary.[15] We thus obtain

[15] After Plato loc. cit. has shown that the body of the world must consist of fire and earth, he continues: Two always require a third as their δεσμὸς ἐν μέσῳ ἀμφοῖν ξυναγωγός; the most beautiful δεσμὸς is the proportion (ἀναλογία) found where, out of three ἀριθμοί, ὄγκοι, or δυνάμεις (here, as in Theæt. 147 D sqq, not 'powers,' but 'roots'), the second stands to the third as the first to the second, and to the first as the third to the second. Εἰ μὲν οὖν ἐπίπεδον μὲν, βάθος δὲ μηδὲν ἔχον ἔδει γίγνεσθαι τὸ τοῦ παντὸς σῶμα, μία μεσότης ἂν ἐξήρκει τά τε μεθ' ἑαυτῆς ξυνδεῖν καὶ ἑαυτήν· νῦν δὲ .... στερεοειδῆ γὰρ αὐτὸν προσῆκεν εἶναι, τὰ δὲ στερεὰ μία μὲν οὐδέποτε, δύο δὲ ἀεὶ μεσότητες ξυναρμόττουσιν, and therefore God has put water and air between fire and earth, and assigned to them the relations stated above. This passage gives rise to considerable difficulties, even apart from the erroneous artificiality of the whole deduction. It is true (as Bockh shows, De Plat. corp. mund. fabrica, reprinted with valuable additions in his Klein. Schr. iii. 229-265) that, under certain determinations which we must suppose Plato assumed, between any two ἐπίπεδα there is one mean proportional, and between any two solids two proportionals, whether the expressions ἐπίπεδον and στερεὸν be understood in a geometrical or in an arithmetical sense In the former case it is clear that not only between any two squares but also between any two plane rectilineal figures similar to one another there is one mean proportional, between any two cubes and any two parallelopipeds similar to one another there are two mean proportionals. In the latter, not only between any two square numbers, but also between any two plane numbers (i.e. numbers with two factors) there is one rational proportional, and not only between any two cubic numbers but also between any two solid numbers generally (i e. formed out of three factors) there are two rational proportionals, provided that the factors of the one number stand to one another in the same relation as those of the second

four elements, which among them form one proportion; so that fire is related to air, as air to water; and air to water, as water to earth.

number. (E.g. between the square numbers $2 \times 2 = 4$ and $3 \times 3 = 9$ there is the proportional number $2 \times 3 = 6 : 4 : 6 = 6 : 9$; between the plane non-square numbers $2 \times 3 = 6$ and $4 \times 6 = 24$ the proportional number 2×6 or 3×4, because $6 : 12 = 12 : 24$. Between the cubic numbers $2 \times 2 \times 2 = 8$ and $3 \times 3 \times 3 = 27$ occur the two numbers $2 \times 2 \times 3 = 12$ and $2 \times 3 \times 3 = 18$, because $8 : 12 = 12 : 18 = 18 : 27$; between the non-cubic solid numbers $4 \times 6 \times 8 = 192$ and $6 \times 9 \times 12 = 648$ occur the two numbers $4 \times 6 \times 12$ or $4 \times 9 \times 8$ or $6 \times 6 \times 8 = 288$ and $4 \times 9 \times 12$ or $6 \times 9 \times 8$ or $6 \times 6 \times 12 = 432$, because $192 : 288 = 288 : 432 = 432 : 648$; the same holds good in the analogous cases in planes and solids) But Plato asserts, not merely that there is one mean proportional between any two planes and two between any two solids. but that the latter are by no means bound by one $\mu\epsilon\sigma\acute{o}\tau\eta s$. Such a generality, however, is not correct; as between two similar planes or plane numbers under certain circumstances there occur two further mean proportionals besides the one mean (e.g. between $2^2 = 4$ and $16^2 = 256$ there come, not only $2 \times 16 = 32$, but also $4^2 = 16$ and $8^2 = 64$, because both $4 : 32 = 32 : 256$ and $4 : 16 = 16 : 64 = 64 : 256$), so between two similar solids and two analogously formed solid numbers, together with the two proportionals which always lie between them, there occurs one besides in certain cases. If two solid numbers are at the same time analogously formed plane numbers, there result between them, not only two mean proportionals, but one besides (e.g. between $2^3 = 8$ and $8^3 = 512$ there are the two proportionals 32 and 128, and also the one mean 64, because $8 = 1 \times 8$ and $512 = 8 \times 64$; between these comes 8×8, or what is the same thing 1×64); and if the roots of two cubic numbers have a mean proportional which can be expressed in whole numbers, the cube of the latter is the mean proportional between the former. (This is the case, e.g between $4^3 = 64$ and $9^3 = 729$; their mean proportionals are not only $4 \times 4 \times 9 = 144$ and $4 \times 9 \times 9 = 324$, but also 6^3, for as $4 : 6 = 6 : 9$, $4^3 : 6^3 = 6^3 : 9^3$, i e $64 : 216 = 216 : 729$ So again, between $5^3 = 125$ and $20^3 = 8000$ there are the two proportionals 500 and 2000, and also the one proportional 1000, for as $5 : 10 = 10 : 20$, $5^3 : 10^3 = 10^3 : 20^3$, i e $125 : 1000 = 1000 : 8000$.) We cannot suppose that this was unknown to Plato How then are we to explain his assertion that the $\sigma\tau\epsilon\rho\epsilon\grave{a}$ never have a $\mu\epsilon\sigma\acute{o}\tau\eta s$ between them? The simplest explanation would be to translate his words: 'Solids are never connected by *one* $\mu\epsilon\sigma\acute{o}\tau\eta s$, but always by two at least.' And this explanation might indeed be defended by examples, e.g. Arist. Metaph ix 5, 1048 a. 8, c. 8, 1050 b. 33, xii 3, 1070 a. 18, and others. It is, however, almost too simple; as Plato loc. cit. wishes to prove that two intermediate terms must be inserted between fire and earth, his object is to show, not merely that at

THE ELEMENTS.

This, though Plato may have seriously intended it, is in reality but a flight of fancy.[16] The four ele-

least two terms, but that neither more nor less than two terms occur between two solids; and as the two proportionals between certain ἐπίπεδα belong to a different series from that to which the one occurring in all of them belongs, and the one proportional between certain στερεά belongs to a different series from that to which the two proportionals occurring in all belong, we should still have that which Plato denies within each of those proportionals Ancient and modern interpreters therefore seek variously to limit Plato's statement to such στερεά as have actually only two proportionals between them. (See the Review in Martin, Etudes, i. 337 sqq.) Nicomachus, for example (Arithm. ii. 24, p. 69), understands by them, not merely cubic numbers generally, but still more definitely κύβοι συνεχεῖς (1^3, 2^3, 3^3, &c.), and by the plane numbers he understands τετράγωνα συνεχῆ. Of such numbers of course the position holds good without exception: between 2^2 and 3^2, 3^2 and 4^2, &c. there is only one rational mean proportional, between 2^3 and 3^3, 3^3 and 4^3, &c there are only two. But if Plato meant only these special cases, he would not have expressed himself so generally, and he must have given some reasons why fire and earth were to be exclusively regarded in the light of this analogy Martin, who exhaustively refutes the elucidations of Stallbaum and Cousin (Muller, Pl WW. vi. 259 sqq. can hardly be brought under consideration), wishes to make out that by ἐπίπεδα are meant only the numbers which have two factors, and by the στερεά only the numbers which have three prime numbers as factors; Kónitzer (Ueb. d. Elementarkörper nach Pl. Tim. 1846, p 13 sqq.) would limit them still closer to the squares and cubes of prime numbers. With this elucidation Susemihl, Genet. Entw. ii. 347 sq. agrees, and Bockh (d. Kosm Syst. Pl. 17) allowed himself to be won over to it. In the end, however, he returned to his original view (Kl. Schr. iii. 253 sqq), seeing no justification for the limitation of Plato's statement to the plane and solid numbers derived from prime numbers, and the further limitation to square and cubic numbers He appeals to the fact that in the cases where there are two proportionals besides the one mean between two planes or plane numbers, and one proportional besides the two means between solids or solid numbers, these latter do not proceed from the geometrical or arithmetical construction, and that two plane numbers can only have two rational proportionals between them, if they are at the same time similar solid bodies, and two solid numbers can only have one rational proportional, if they are at the same time similar plane numbers. This solution seems to me to be the best. If there are two proportionals between ἐπίπεδα and one between στερεά, this is merely accidental, and it does not follow that the one are ἐπίπεδα, the other στερεά, and Plato accordingly thinks that this case may be left out in his construction of the elements.

[16] Hegel, Gesch. d. Phil. ii. 221

ments are only in appearance derived and placed in a certain order, by means of an external reference of aim, and a false arithmetical analogy. This order proceeds from the rarer and lighter to the denser and heavier; and the idea of a geometrical proportion could not properly be applied to it.[17] Still more remarkable is the physical derivation of the elements.[18] Plato here repeats Philolaus'[19] theory, that the fundamental form of fire is the Tetrahedron; of air, the Octahedron; of water, the Icosahedron; and of earth, the Cube:[20] the fifth regular figure, the Dodecahedron, he does not connect with an element.[21] By compounding these

sqq., is unnecessarily surprised at this, and misinterprets it.

[17] Ancient and modern commentators fall into contradictions as soon as they try to prove the existence and extent of a proportion between the four elements of the same kind as that between the terms of a quadruple arithmetical proportion.

[18] Tim 53 C sqq.; cf. Martin, ii. 234 sqq.

[19] See vol. i. 350 sqq.

[20] Plato, 55 D sqq., enumerates the considerations which led him to adopt this classification; viz. mobility, magnitude, weight, greater or less capability of penetrating other bodies.

[21] He merely says, 55 C· ἔτι δὲ οὔσης ξυστάσεως μιᾶς πέμπτης ἐπὶ τὸ πᾶν ὁ θεὸς αὐτῇ κατεχρήσατο ἐκεῖνο διαζωγραφῶν. What is the meaning of διαζωγραφεῖν, and what part is played by the dodecahedron? Susemihl, ii. 413, explains: 'He painted the universe with figures;' and refers this painting to the adornment of the heavens with stars (Tim. 40 A; Rep. vii. 529 C), to which the dodecahedron might be applied, as coming nearest to the sphere. The stars (Rep. vii. 529 D sqq.) are not perfect spheres, but (on the analogy of the δωδεκάσκυτοι σφαῖραι, to which the earth is compared, Phædo, 100 B) approach, like the universe, the form of the dodecahedron It seems more natural to refer the διαζωγραφεῖν (which is not necessarily colour-painting) to the plan or design of the world which preceded its formation The world and the stars too are spherical in form, and while the earth (Tim. 33 B, 40 A) is a perfect sphere, the dodecahedron is of all regular solids that which nearest approaches to the sphere, that on which a sphere can be most easily described, and that therefore which could be most readily laid down as the plan of the world. The dodecahedron of the present passage used to be taken as the plan of the æther; Philolaus seems to have been of this opinion (cf. vol. i. 350 sq.);

THE ELEMENTS. 373

bodies themselves, not out of corporeal atoms, but out of planes of a certain kind,[22]—by again resolving

and with him the Platonic Epinomis, 981 C, and Xenocrates, who, ap. Simpl. Phys. 205 b Schol in Arist. 427 a. 15, attributes this view to Plato. Although the later interpreters follow him in this view (see Martin, iii. 140 sq), we cannot agree with him as to the form of the doctrine contained in the Platonic writings In the Phædo, 109 B sq , 111 A sq. (cf. Crat 109 B), Plato understands by æther, in accordance with ordinary usage, the purer air lying next to our atmosphere, and still more definitely he says, Tim. 58 D: ἀέρος τὸ ἐναγέστατον ἐπίκλην αἰθὴρ καλούμενος. The æther is not a fifth element with him. He could not admit the dodecahedron (as Martin proves, ii. 245 sqq) in its construction of the elements, because it is bounded, not by triangles, but equilateral pentagons, which again are composed neither (as Stallbaum thinks, ad loc.) of equilateral nor of rectangular triangles of one of the two Platonic elementary forms. The conclusion is, that the theory which constructs the elementary bodies out of triangles, and explains the transition of one element into another by the separation and different combination of its elementary triangles, belongs originally to Plato and not to Philolaus, who classes the dodecahedron as an elementary form with the four other bodies. The form which this theory takes in Plato must be foreign to Philolaus, because Plato's reduction of matter to pure space is unknown to him. Plato himself clearly gives us to understand that this discovery is his own, when he introduces the enquiry about the material primal cause and the formation of the four elements, Tim. 48 B, with the remark: νῦν γὰρ οὐδείς πω γένεσιν αὐτῶν μεμήνυκεν, ἀλλ' ὡς εἰδόσι, πῦρ ὅ τί ποτέ ἐστι καὶ ἕκαστον αὐτῶν, λέγομεν ἀρχὰς αὐτὰ τιθέμενοι, στοιχεῖα τοῦ παντός.

[22] All superficies, he says, 53 C sqq., consist of triangles, and all triangles arise out of two different right-angled triangles, the isosceles and the scalene; of the scalene, however, the best and consequently the most congenial for the formation of the elements is that of which the lesser cathetus is half as large as the hypothenuse. Out of six such triangles arises an equilateral triangle, and out of four isosceles triangles arises a square. Out of the square is formed the cube, out of equilateral triangles the three remaining bodies. (Therefore, 54 B sq. : τρίγωνα ἐξ ὧν τὰ

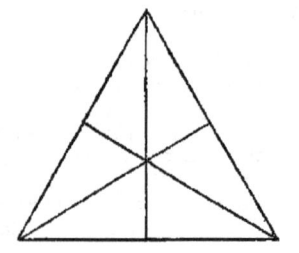

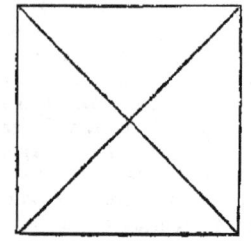

them ultimately into triangles, in the transition of the elements [23] one into another,—he clearly shows that the ground which underlies them is not a Matter that fills space, but space itself. From this ground these determinate bodies are to be formed in such a manner that certain parts of space are mathematically limited, and comprehended in definite figures.[24] Not

σώματα μεμηχάνηται .... ἐκ τοῦ ἰσοσκελοῦς τριγώνου ξυναρμοσθέν) The fact that he here attributes to the square four and not two, to the equilateral triangle six and not two elementary triangles, is accounted for by his wish to resolve them into their smallest parts (cf. Tim. 48 B). For this purpose he divided the equilateral triangle by the perpendicular, and the square by the diagonal (cf. Martin, ii. 239: according to Plutarch the Pythagoreans emphasised the threefold bisection of the equilateral triangle by its perpendicular as an important quality of it; see vol. i. 337, 2). From the combination of the elements which he assumes Plato infers that only a part of them change into one another; v. next note

[23] 54 C: not all the elements pass into one another, but only the three higher: ἐκ γὰρ ἑνὸς ἅπαντα πεφυκότα λυθέντων τε τῶν μειζόνων πολλὰ σμικρὰ ἐκ τῶν αὐτῶν ξυστήσεται, δεχόμενα τὰ προσήκοντα ἑαυτοῖς σχήματα, καὶ σμικρὰ ὅταν αὖ πολλὰ κατὰ τὰ τρίγωνα διασπαρῇ, γενόμενος εἷς ἀριθμὸς ἑνὸς ὄγκου μέγα ἀποτελέσειεν ἂν ἄλλο εἶδος ἕν. From this point of view the subject is further treated, 56 D sqq. If one element is split up by another of smaller parts, or a smaller mass of the latter crushed by a larger mass of the former, or if again the elementary bodies of the smaller are united by the pressure of the larger, then out of one part of water arise two parts of air and one part of fire, out of one part of air two parts of fire, and *vice versâ*; the transition of one element into another is brought about by the elementary triangles out of which it is composed being loosened from one another, and by a new combination being formed of the elementary bodies in a different numerical proportion The whole conception is put in a clear light by Plato's words, 81 B sq, on the nourishment, growth, old age, and death of the living being.

[24] If Plato presupposed for his construction of the elements a Material in the ordinary sense, he must either have viewed it as a qualitatively equable and quantitatively undistinguished mass, out of which the elements arose, because certain parts of this mass transiently take the form of the elementary bodies—cube, tetrahedron, &c. (in which case there would be not the slightest reason why every element could not come out of every other); or he must have supposed that at the formation of the elements the mass was made in the form of corporeal elements for all time. But then

indivisible bodies, but indivisible surfaces, are supposed as the primary constituents of the corporeal.[25] These produce the smallest bodies by combining with certain figures. Bodies are therefore not only limited by planes, but also compounded out of them;[26] a Matter which assumes corporeal figures is not recognised.

From the difference of their figures quantitative distinctions also arise in these elemental bodies. Of those which consist of triangles of the same kind, each is greater or less, according to the number of such triangles which it contains.[27] Similar differences are found within particular elements. The triangles

any transition of one element into another would be impossible, and what according to Plato is true only of the earth, but according to Empedocles of the elements, and to Democritus of the atoms—viz. that they may intermingle with, but cannot change into, one another—must hold good of all of them. In neither case could he speak of the resolution of the elements into triangles, and their formation out of triangles, in the way we have seen.

[25] Martin, in his otherwise excellent exposition, ii. 241 sq., is not quite right in saying (with Simpl. De Cœlo, Schol in Ar. 510 a. 37; Philop gen et corr. 47 a. o): *Si chacune des figures planes qu'il décrit est supposée avoir quelque épaisseur . . . . . . comme des feuilles minces d'un métal quelconque, taillées suivant les figures qu'il décrit, et si l'on suppose ces feuilles réunies de manière à présenter l'apparence extérieure des quatre corps solides dont il parle, mais à laisser l'intérieur complètement vide, toutes les transformations indiquées s'expliquent parfaitement. . . . . , . . . Nous considérons donc les triangles et les carrés de Platon comme des feuilles minces de matière corporelle.* Plato does not, as Martin believes, inaccurately call plane bodies planes; he is thinking of actual planes, which, however, he treats as plane bodies. This is easily explained, if mathematical abstractions are once taken as something real—more real than matter.

[26] So too Aristotle, who here understands the Platonic doctrines quite correctly: De Cœlo, iii. 1, 298 b. 33. Ibid. c. 7, 8; 305 a. 35, 306 a. sqq., gen. et corr. i. 2, 315 b. 30 sqq. ii. 1, 329 a. 21 sq; cf Alex Aphr. Quæst nat. ii 13, against the variant opinion of many Platonists

[27] 54 C, 56 A, D. How the earth stands to the three other elements as regards the magnitude of its smallest bodily parts is not here stated: but as it is the heaviest element, it must have the largest parts. Cf. 60 E.

of each sort (and consequently also the elemental bodies consisting of an equal number of such triangles) differ in magnitude,[28] and thus from the beginning there is a diversity in kinds of matter, which, coupled with the mixture of these kinds in unequal proportions, perfectly explains the infinite multiplicity of things.

The elemental composition of bodies regulates their distribution in space. Each element has its natural place in the universe, to which it tends, and in which, in regard to its preponderating mass, it has its dwelling.[29] Lightness and heaviness are therefore relative terms, the signification of which changes according to position: on earth, the earthly element appears the heavier; in the fiery sphere, fire.[30] There can never be

---

[28] 57 C sq.; this can be reconciled with the previous quotation, by supposing (with Martin, ii. 254) that the largest part of fire is never so large as the smallest part of air, &c.

[29] 52 D sqq., 57 B sqq. Plato here derives the separation of matter in space from the original motion of matter; the result is that the lighter rises and the heavier sinks, just as in the winnowing of corn. But immediately after, he explains, 57 E sq., the motion itself as purely physical, springing out of the dissimilarity of the elements. It is, however, difficult to conceive how elementary distinctions and properties could have come into matter before God divided the latter into elementary forms, from which alone the distinctions can proceed. We may, therefore, class this point amongst the mythical parts of the Timæus; cf. p. 391 sq., 364 sq.

[30] From 56 B we might infer that Plato identified heaviness and lightness with greatness and smallness. Fire, he says, is the lightest of the three superior elements, because it consists of the smallest number of equal-sized parts, and similarly the two others in proportion. Hence the further notion, that just as smallness is merely a smaller amount of greatness, so lightness is only a smaller amount of heaviness. Everything tends to the mean, that which has large parts tends to it more powerfully than that which has smaller parts. So the latter is moved upward not of its own nature, but by the pressure of heavy bodies. (So Democritus; v. vol. i. 701, 713.) Plato himself, however, expressly rejects the supposition, 62 C sqq., that

THE ELEMENTS. 377

a complete separation of material substances. The external orbit of the universe, being circular and continuous, presses together the bodies contained in it,[31] and will not allow of any empty space between them.[32] Consequently the smaller bodies are crowded into the interstices of the greater, and there results a continual mixture of the different kinds of matter.[33] The perpetual motion and decomposition of the elements is a consequence of this admixture. As long as an elemental body is among its kindred, it remains unchanged; for among bodies which are similar and uniform none can change, or be changed by, another. If, on the contrary, smaller proportions of one element are

everything moves downward by nature, and upward only as a consequence of some compulsion In the universe, there is no up and down, only an inner and an outer; nor does he imagine any general striving towards the mean,—certainly not a universal attraction of all matter. He simply says that every element has its natural place, out of which it can be removed only by force, to this force it offers greater opposition the greater its mass. The natural place of all bodies is the κάτω. Towards this they strive; and the heaviness of a body consists merely in its striving to unite itself with what is congenial (or to prevent its separation from it). Ritter, ii. 400, wrongly infers from Tim 61 C, that the elements have sensation together with this striving; the words αἴσθησιν ὑπάρχειν δεῖ signify (as Stallbaum rightly explains) that they must be an object of sensation.

[31] Cf. vol. i. 374, 2, 637 (Empsd. v. 133).

[32] 58 A sqq., 60 C. Empedocles and Anaxagoras, following the Eleatics (see vol. i. 472, 2; 516; 620, 2; 803, 1), had denied Void. Hence a double difficulty to Plato First, his four elementary bodies never fill up any space so completely that no intermediate space is left (Arist. de Cœlo, iii. 8, beginn.), to say nothing of the fact that no sphere can be entirely filled out by rectilineal figures. And the resolution of an elementary body into its component triangles must produce a void each time, as there was nothing between them (Martin, ii. 255 sq.). Plato must either have disregarded these difficulties (which, in the case of the first, would have been strange for a mathematician to do), or else he does not mean to deny void absolutely, but merely to assert that no space remains void which can at all be taken possession of by a body.

[33] 58 A sq.

contained in greater proportions of another, in consequence of the universal pressure they are crushed or cut up;[34] and their constituent parts must either pass over into the form of the stronger element, or make their escape to their kindred element in their natural place. Thus there is a perpetual ebb and flow of the elements: the diversity of Matter is the cause of its constant motion.[35] The sum of the four elements constitutes the universe. (Tim. 32 C sqq.)

[34] Further details on this resolution of the elements, 60 E sqq.

[35] 56 C-58, C (with 57 E: κίνησιν εἰς ἀνωμαλότητα ἀεὶ τιθῶμεν, cf. the quotation Pt. i. 302-3). This doctrine of the elements is followed by a discussion of separate phenomena, remarkable for its acuteness, though naturally insufficient for the demands of modern knowledge. He treats next, 58 C sqq, of the different kinds of fire, air, and particularly water, under which he includes liquid (ὕδωρ ὑγρόν), but also what is fusible (ὕδ. χυτόν), the metals, and then ice, hail, snow, hoar frost, the juice of plants (particularly wine), oil, honey, ὀπὸς (not opium, as Martin thinks, ii. 262, but the acids obtained from plants to curdle milk, so called in Homer). Further, 60 B sqq. he treats of the various kinds of earth, stone, bricks, natron, lava, glass, wax. &c.; 61 D sqq., of warmth, and cold, hardness and softness, heaviness and lightness; 64 A sq. of the conditions under which any thing becomes the object of sensations of pleasure or pain; 65 B sqq. of the qualities of things perceptible by taste; 66 D sqq. on smells, which all arise either in the transition of air into water, or of water into air; in the former case they are called ὀμίχλη, in the latter καπνός: 67 A sqq. cf. 80 A sq. treats of tones; 67 C-69 A (cf. Meno, 76 C sq), of colours. To explain these phenomena Plato starts from his pre-suppositions as to the fundamental parts of the elements. He seeks to show who the separate bodies, according to the composition of their smallest parts and the extent of the intermediate space, at one time admit air and fire to pass through, but are burst by water, at another time forbid the entrance of water and admit fire. Hence he concludes that the two former are destructible by water, and the latter by fire. He explains the hardening of molten metals, the freezing of water, the condensation of earth into stone, and the like, by supposing that the parts of fire and water contained in them, passing out and seeking their natural place, press the surrounding air against the materials in question, and so condense them. Similarly (79 E-80 C; cf. Martin, ii. 342 sqq), he tries to explain the downward motion of lightning, the apparently attractive power of

THE ELEMENTS. 379

III. *The World-System.*—The further description of the universe contains much that is of a specific character, distinguishing it from the theories of Anaxagoras and Democritus, as also from the system of Philolaus; though in its whole spirit it greatly resembles the latter. The shape of the universe is that of a globe.[36] Within this globe three divisions are to be distinguished, answering to the three Pythagorean regions of the world, though they are not actually identified with them by Plato. The earth is placed as a round ball in the centre,[37] at the axis of the universe. Then follow the sun, the moon, and the five other planets, in circles described around the earth, and arranged according to the intervals of the harmonic system. The heaven of fixed stars, one undivided

---

amber and the magnet, and other phenomena. He observes that every sensation depends upon a motion of the object which occasions it, this motion is transmitted through the intervening space to the senses, and further to the soul, &c. I cannot here enter further into this portion of the dialogue; much useful matter is given by Martin, ii. 254–294; Steinhart, vi. 251 sq.; Susemihl, ii. 425 sq, 432 sqq.

[36] This is so according to the Tim. 33 B sqq because the sphere is the most perfect figure, and because the universe needs no limbs.

[37] 40 B (with which cf. Bockh, Cosm˙ Syst Plat. p. 59 sqq, Klein. Schr. iii. 294 sqq): cf. 62 E, Phædo, 108 E. The statement of Theophrastus apud Plut. quæst. Plat. viii. 1, p. 1006; Numa, c. ii. —viz. that Plato in his later years regretted having made the earth the middle point of the universe in the Timæus, because this belonged to a better, i.e. the central fire—is with good reason suspected by Martin, ii. 91, and Bockh, Cosm. Syst. 144 sqq., because (1) it rests merely on a report which might easily have been transferred to Plato by Academics of Pythagorean tendencies (Arist. De Cœlo, ii. 13–293 a. 27); because (2) even the latest works of Plato display no trace of any such opinion, and (3) the Epinomis, which was composed by the editor of the laws—one of Plato's most strictly astronomical pupils, and designed for the astronomical completion of this latter dialogue—is acquainted only with the geocentric system of the Timæus: see 986 A sqq., 990 A sq.

sphere, forms the outermost circle.[38] The earth is immovable.[39] The heaven of fixed stars turns in one day

[38] 36 B sqq., 40 A sq. (On the distance of the planets, cf. p. 350.) Besides the above conceptions, Gruppe, Kosm. Syst. d. Gr. 125, would attribute to Plato the doctrines of the epicycle, and the eccentric; cf. against him Bockh, Kosm. Syst. 126 sq. A different system from that of the Timæus (viz. the Philolaic system) has been suspected in the Phædrus, 246 E sqq.; I think, however, that Susemihl, Genet. Entw. i. 234 sq. is right in limiting the influence of Philolaus to a few traits. I cannot agree with Martin (ii. 138 sq., 114), and Stallbaum (in mythum Plat. de div. amoris ortu, cf. Susemihl in Jahn's Jahrb. lxxv, 589 sq.), in trying to make out the twelve gods of the Phædrus by adding the three regions of water, air, and æther to the earth, and the eight circles of the stars. Plato would not have called these elements gods, and the description of moving does not suit them. The twelve gods of the popular religion are meant, and astronomical determinations are transferred to them. Consequently we can draw no conclusion from the passage. Further details apud Susemihl.

[39] Bockh has shown that this is Plato's real meaning, De Plat. Syst. Cœl. glob. p. vi. sqq. (1810), and subsequently in his treatise on the Cosmic system of Plato, pp. 14, 75, and Kl. Schr. loc. cit. (in opposition to Gruppe, die Kosm. Syst. d. Gr. 1851, p. 1 sqq. and Grote, Plato's doctrine of the rotation of the earth, 1860, cf. Plato, iii. 257; Martin, vi. 86 sqq., and Susemihl in Jahn's Jahrb. lxxv, 598 sq. against a follower of Gruppe). This becomes in the highest degree probable from the circumstance that Plato, Tim. 39 B, derives day and night from the motion of the heaven of the fixed stars, and, 38 C sqq., 39 B; Rep. x. 616 C sqq., throughout he reckons the sun among the planets; by the former the daily, and by the latter the yearly motion of the earth is kept up. It might be said that we could account for the motion of the constellations by supposing that, together with the daily revolution of the firmament and the individual motions of the planets, there is also a revolution of the earth, either from east to west, or west to east, but far less rapid than that of the heaven of the fixed stars. But Plato has nowhere suggested this idea, nor made the least effort to explain the phenomena on such a supposition. There was nothing to induce him to make such an artificial and far-fetched hypothesis. The Timæus, 34 A sq., 36 B sqq. 38 E sq, 40 A, always speaks of two motions only of the whole heaven and the planets, and the Phædo, 109 A, undoubtedly treats the earth as at rest. Bockh, Kosm. Syst. 63 sqq., proves that Tim 40 B does not contradict this view: εἰλλομένην there means not 'revolving' but 'formed into a ball.' In the Laws, vii. 822, we have the same statement as Tim. 39 A. Aristotle certainly says De Cœlo, ii. 13, 293, b. 30: ἔνιοι δὲ καὶ κειμένην ἐπὶ τοῦ κέντρου φασὶν αὐτὴν (the earth) ἴλλεσθαι καὶ κινεῖσθαι περὶ τὸν διὰ παντὸς τεταμένον πόλον, ὥσπερ

around the axis of the universe, in the direction of the equator, from east to west; and the circles comprehended in it are likewise carried round with the same motion. They themselves, however, move in various periods of revolution (increasing according to their distance) around the earth, in the plane of the Ecliptic, from west to east. Their courses are therefore, properly speaking, not circles, but spirals; and as those which have the shortest periods move the quickest in a direction opposed to the motion of the whole, it appears as if they remained the furthest behind this motion. The swiftest look like the slowest: those

ἐν τῷ Τιμαίῳ γέγραπται, and κινεῖσθαι (as Prantl shows in his edition, p 311) cannot be removed from the text (with two MSS. and Bekker), because it recurs c. 14 begin. unanimously attested. There are many things against Böckh's view (loc cit 76 sqq.) that the mention of the Timæus (ὥσπερ . . . . γεγρ.) refers only to the Ἴλλεσθαι (or εἰλεῖσθαι), and not to the additional κινεῖσθαι, and that Aristotle here meant to attribute the assertion that the earth moves round the axis of the universe not to Plato himself, but to others unknown to us It only does not follow from this that Plato supposed a revolution of the earth round an axis, whether daily or in a longer space of time. I cannot approve of the conjecture (Prantl, loc cit., Susemihl. Genet Entw. ii 380 sq) that Plato ascribed to the earth at least a vibrating motion towards the axis of the universe, and that this is what the κινεῖσθαι of Aristotle refers to. Aristotle, as is clearly shown by c. 14, 296 a. 34 sq , 7, means a motion from west to east corresponding to the individual movement of the planets; the Timæus, on the contrary, says nothing about a motion of the earth. Since, then, this word cannot be removed from the passage of Aristotle, we can only acknowledge that in this case Aristotle misunderstood the words of the Timæus, perhaps led to do so by some Platonists who took the passage in that way. This was quite possible from the words, and Plato is even thus credited with far less extravagance than we find in the Meteorology, ii. 2, 355 b 32 sqq. The passage of the Timæus, ap. Cic. Acad ii. 39, 123 (perhaps from Heraclides; see Part 1. p. 687, 4, 2nd edit) refers to a daily revolution of the earth round its axis Cf Teichmuller, Stud. z. Gesch. d. Begriffe, 238 sqq., whose explanation agrees in its results with the above, which was written before the appearance of his work.

which overtake the others in the direction of west to east, appear in the contrary direction, to be overtaken by them.[40]

These motions of the heavenly bodies give rise to Time, which is nothing else than the duration of their periods.[41] A complete cosmical period, or perfect year, has elapsed, when all the planetary circles at the end of their revolution have arrived at the same point of the heaven of fixed stars, from which they set out.[42] The duration of this cosmical year Plato fixes, not according to astronomical calculation, but by arbitrary conjecture, at ten thousand years:[43] and he seems to

---

[40] Tim. 36 B sqq, 39 B sqq.: cf. Rep x 617 A sq ; Laws, vii. 822 A sq.; also Epinom. 986 E sq., and Böckh, Kosm. Syst. 16–59, Martin. ii. 42 sq., 80 sq As regards the time of the planets' revolution, Plato supposes it the same for the sun, Venus, and Mercury (this is the order in which he puts them, reckoning outwards) The motion of the heaven of the fixed stars is denoted as ἐπὶ δεξιά, Tim. 36 C, of the planets as ἐπ' ἀριστερά, plainly in order that the more complete motion may be ascribed to the more complete objects. In this Plato must have by an artifice contented himself with the ordinary usage which makes the east the right and the west the left side of the world The motion from east to west is therefore towards the left, and *vice versâ*. V. Böckh, p. 28 sqq. Laws, vi 760 D; on another occasion, Epin. 987 B, in an astronomical reference, the east is treated as the right side.

[41] Tim. 37 D–38 C, 39 B sqq

Hence the tenet here that time was created with the world (see p. 669). Ibid on the distinction between endless time and eternity. Maguire's (Pl. Id. 103, see chap. vii. 42) assertion, that Plato considered time as something merely subjective is entirely without foundation.

[42] 39 D

[43] This duration of the year of the world (pre-supposed Rep. vii. 546 B, as will be shown later on) is expressed more definitely in the statement (Phædr. 248 C, E, 249 B, Rep. x. 615 A C, 621 D), that the souls which have not fallen remain free from the body throughout one revolution of the universe, while the others enter into human life ten times, and after each period of life among men have to complete a period of 1000 years (strictly speaking, the period would be 11,000 years, but the inaccuracy must be attributed to the myth). Hence the curious assertion, Tim. 23 D sq , that the oldest historical recollection does not

connect with it, periodical changes in the condition of the world.[44] The particular heavenly bodies are so inserted in their orbits that they never change their place in them: the forward motion around the universal centre is not to be ascribed to these bodies as such, but to their circles.[45] Plato, however, gives to each of them a movement around its own axis,[46] but this assumption

reach beyond 9000 years. Other calculations of the great years are not to be taken as Platonic (cf. Martin, ii 80). Plato is so evidently giving a round number with his usual mixture of dogmatism and symbolism, that to connect his great year, as Steinhart does, vi. 102, with observations on the advance of the equinoxes, is beside the question. Cf. Susemihl, Phil. xv 423 sq., Gen. Ent. ii 360, 379

[44] Polit 269 C sqq., where of course (cf. Tim. 36 E, and elsewhere) Plato is not in earnest in supposing that God from time to time withdraws from the government of the world · Tim. 22 B sqq., 23 D; Laws, iii. 677 A sqq.

[45] This is clear from Tim. 36 B sqq., 38 C, 40 A sq. But it is not quite clear how we are to conceive this circle itself. The description mentioned p 358, depicts the circles of the planets as small bands bent into a circle, and the circle of the fixed stars as a band of the same kind, only much broader; doubtless Plato imagined the latter (as it appears to the eye) as a sphere, and the circles of the planets only as linear or like a band.

[46] Tim. 40 A: κινήσεις δὲ δύο προσῆψεν ἑκάστῳ, τὴν μὲν ἐν τῷ αὐτῷ κατὰ ταὐτὰ περὶ τῶν αὐτῶν ἀεὶ τὰ αὐτὰ ἑαυτῷ διανοουμένῳ, τὴν δὲ εἰς τὸ πρόσθεν ὑπὸ τῆς ταὐτοῦ καὶ ὁμοίου περιφορᾶς κρατουμένῳ. Plato says this of the fixed stars; whether he intended that it should hold good of the planets is questionable. In favour of this view we might allege that the motion which Plato considers to be peculiar to reason (cf p. 358 sq) must also belong to the planets: for they are rational beings or visible gods And acc. to p. 40 B (where I cannot agree with Susemihl's explanation, Philol xv. 426) they are fashioned according to the fixed stars (κατ' ἐκεῖνα γέγονεν). These reasons, however, are not decisive The planets may be fashioned according to the fixed stars without at the same time resembling them in all points; and Plato himself, loc cit., distinctly indicates their difference, in that the one κατὰ ταὐτὰ ἐν ταὐτῷ στρεφόμενα ἀεὶ μένει, while the others are τρεπόμενα καὶ πλάνην ἴσχοντα, which rather means that the latter are without motion ἐν ταὐτῷ. In the case of the fixed stars reason is connected with their reflex motion, but even the earth, 40 C, is designated as a divinity, although it has not that motion (as Susemihl rightly remarks, loc. cit.); and this also holds good of the central fire of the Pythagoreans and the 'Εστία of the Phædrus (247 A). As only two and not

is manifestly the result, not of astronomical observation, but of speculative theory.[47] The stars must revolve around themselves, because this is the motion of reason,[48] and they must partake in reason. Far from seeing, like Anaxagoras and Democritus, only dead masses in the heavenly bodies, Plato regards them as living beings, whose souls must be higher and diviner than human souls, in proportion as their bodies are brighter and fairer than ours.[49] In this he is evidently influenced by the even and regular motion, in which the stars as nearly as possible follow pure mathematical laws.[50] If the soul is, generally, the moving principle, the most perfect soul must be where there is the

three motions are mentioned in the case of the planets (38 C sqq.), I think (with Steinhart, vi. 109; Susemihl, loc. cit. and Genet. Entw. ii 385) that Plato more probably attributed to the planets the motion on their own axes which Martin, Etudes, ii. 83, and Bockh, Kosm. Syst. 59, with Proclus, ascribe to them. The planets do not, like the fixed stars, belong to the κύκλος ταὐτοῦ, but to the κύκλος θατέρου (see p. 358).

[47] There is no phenomenon which they serve to explain, nor any law known to Plato from which they could be derived; and the coruscation of the fixed stars, which Susemihl mentions loc cit. could at the most have been considered merely as a confirmation but not as the proper ground of the theory.

[48] See p. 359 sq. and note 2, the words περὶ τ. αὐτ. ... διανοουμένῳ.

[49] Tim. 38 E, 39 E sqq.: there are four kinds of vital existences; the first is the heavenly, belonging to the gods. The Demiurgus formed this for the most part out of fire, so that it might be as beautiful and bright to look upon as possible, and gave it the round form of the universe, and the motions discussed above: ἐξ ἧς δὴ τῆς αἰτίας γέγονεν ὅσ' ἀπλανῆ τῶν ἄστρων ζῷα θεῖα ὄντα καὶ ἀίδια καὶ κατὰ ταὐτὰ ἐν ταὐτῷ στρεφόμενα ἀεὶ μένει· τὰ δὲ τρεπόμενα ... κατ' ἐκεῖνα γέγονεν. Cf. Laws, x. 886 D, 898 D sqq., xii. 966 D sqq.; Crat. 397 C.

[50] As Plato says, Rep. vii. 530 A, even the stars cannot correspond to mathematical rules quite perfectly, and without any deviation, because after all they are visible, and have a body. He thus seems to have noticed that the phenomena do not altogether agree with his astronomical system; but instead of giving an astronomical solution of the difficulty (which was indeed impossible to him), he cuts the knot by a mere theory.

most perfect motion; and if the motive power in the Soul is accompanied by the faculty of knowledge, the highest knowledge must belong to that soul which by a perfectly regular motion of body evinces the highest reason.[51] If the Cosmos, absolutely uniform and harmonious, circling about itself, possesses the most divine and most reasonable soul, those parts of the Cosmos which most nearly approximate to it in form and motion will most largely participate in this privilege. The stars are therefore the noblest and most intelligent of all created natures; they are the created gods,[52] as the universe is the one created God. Man may learn how to regulate the lawless movements of his soul by their unchanging courses:[53] he himself is not to be compared with them in worth and perfection. So strongly was the Greek deification of nature at work, even in the philosopher who did more than anyone else to turn away the thought of his nation from the many-coloured multiplicity of the phenomenon to a colourless conceptual world beyond. As to the personality of these gods, and whether thought combined with self-consciousness belongs to them, in the same way as to man, Plato seems never to have enquired.[54]

[51] Cf. p. 344 sq. Hence in Laws, x. 898, D sqq. (on the basis of the pyschology developed loc. cit.), it is shown that the stars are gods. (There is nothing in the passage about the animation of the years, months, and seasons, such as Teichmuller, Stud. z. Gesch. d. Begr. 362, finds in 899 B, and by which he would make out that the animation of the stars is not to be taken literally; the passage simply says that souls—those of the stars—are πάντων τούτων αἴτιαι.)

[52] θεοὶ ὁρατοὶ καὶ γεννητοί, Tim. 40 D, cf 41 A sqq, and supra, note 49.

[53] Tim. 47 B sq.

[54] Teichmuller (Stud. z Gesch. d. Begr. 185 sq.; cf. 353 sqq.) says that Plato's created (gewordene) gods are merely metaphorical: meaning that the Ideas of the gods, just as the Ideas of mortal beings,

386   *PLATO AND THE OLDER ACADEMY.*

The Timæus[55] sums up the result of its whole cosmogony in the concept of the world as the perfect ζῶον. Made like the Idea of the Living One (the αὐ-

are contained in the Idea of the animal. He can of course appeal to the difficulty which results as soon as ever we endeavour to determine precisely the conception of the spiritual individuality of the stars, as well as to the obviously mythical elements which run through the narrative of their creation (39 E sq., 42 A sq.). But similar difficulties arise in very many doctrinal determinations without giving us any right to reject them as un-Platonic; as e g. in the doctrine of the World-soul, and of the three parts of the human soul, &c. If the narrative of the origin of the stars bears the same mythical character as the whole cosmogony of the Timæus, it does not follow that Plato is not in earnest in what he says about its intelligence and divinity, not only here but also in the Laws. He speaks of the formation of the world in an equally mythical way, but he does not therefore doubt that the world is the most perfect revelation of the Idea,—the *become* God. He tells us myth after myth about the origin and destiny of the human soul; but who can dispute that the soul is to him the divine in man, the seat of the intellect? Plato distinctly gives us to understand that the case is essentially different with the divinity of the stars, and with the divinity of the purely mythical gods Chromos, Rhea, &c. In the well-known passage of Tim 40 E sq., he refuses with withering irony to express his views about these, as he has just done in the case of the former; and Teichmul-ler himself has correctly enunciated the reasons which, according to the above, induced Plato, as they did Aristotle and other philosophers afterwards, to suppose that the stars are animated by an intellect far higher than that of men. Where the tenets, which a philosopher expresses with all definiteness, so clearly proceed from pre-suppositions acknowledged by him, we cannot doubt that they correspond to his actual opinions. Plato certainly does not in the least endeavour to form for us a more precise conception of the animation of the stars. He does not tell us whether he attributes to them a self-consciousness, sensibility, or will, whether, in short, he imagines their life to be personal or not. But has he made any such scientific statement with reference to the World-soul or the Divinity? Has he accurately analysed human self-consciousness? Whenever the doctrines of an ancient philosopher give us occasion to ask questions, to which we find no answers in that philosopher's works, our first enquiry should always be whether he ever proposed these questions to himself; and in the present case we are not justified in assuming this.

[55] 30 C sqq., 36 E, 37 C, 39 E, 34 A sq , 68 E, 92 end. Cf. beginning of the Critias. This exposition might, to a great extent, have been borrowed from Philolaus, if we could depend upon the genuineness of the fragments in Stob. Ecl. i. 420, the beginning of which has many points of similarity with Tim. 32 C sqq., 37 A,

το ζῷον), so far as the created can be like the Eternal, comprehending in its body the totality of the corporeal, participating, by means of its soul, in individual and endless life and in divine reason, never growing old nor passing away,[56] the Cosmos is the best of things created, the perfect copy of the everlasting and invisible God: itself a blessed God, sole in its kind, sufficing to itself and in need of no other. In this description we cannot fail to recognise the characteristic of the ancient view of the world. Even Plato is far too deeply penetrated with the glory of Nature to despise her as the Non-Divine, or to rank her as the unspiritual, below human self-consciousness. As the heavenly bodies are visible gods, so the universe is to him the One visible God which comprehends in itself all other created gods, and by reason of the perfection and intelligence of its nature occupies the place of Zeus.[57] According to Plato it is above all things necessary to this perfection of the Cosmos, that as the Idea of the Living includes in itself all living beings, so the world, as its copy, should also include them.[58] They fall, however, under two classes: the mortal and the immortal. Of the latter we have already spoken and shall have again to speak. The former, on account of the peculiar connexion in which the Platonic theory places all other living creatures with man, will lead us at once to Anthropology.

[38] C. Cf., however, vol. i 317, 4; 359, 1.

[56] In itself the world, and also the created gods, are not necessarily indissoluble, since everything which has come into being can pass away. But only their creator could destroy them; and this he would not wish to do by reason of his goodness. Tim. 32 C, 38 B, 41 A Cf. p. 400 sq.

[57] See p. 112, 171, and 266.

[58] Tim. 39 E, 41 B, 69 C, 92 end.

CHAPTER IX.

MAN.

PLATO has discussed the nature of the soul and of man both mythically and scientifically. In more or less mythical language, he speaks of the origin and pre-existence of souls, of their condition after death, and of Recollection (ἀνάμνησις). His enquiries into the divisions of the soul, and the interdependence of spiritual and corporeal life, are conducted in a more exclusively scientific manner. Our attention must first be directed to the mythical and half-mythical representations; for even the more strictly scientific utterances often receive their fullest elucidation from these. But we must previously glance at the general concept of the Soul, as determined by Plato.

We are told in the Timæus (41 sqq.) that when the Creator had formed the Universe as a whole and the godlike natures in it (the stars), He commanded the created gods to produce mortal beings. They therefore fashioned the human body and the mortal part of the soul. He Himself prepared its immortal part in the same cup in which He had before fashioned the World-soul. The materials and the mixture were the same, only in less purity. This means, if we abstract the form of the representation, that the essence of the human soul, conceived apart from its union with the body, is the same as that of the World-soul, except for the difference of the derived from the original, the part from the whole.[1] If then the World-soul is, with regard to Being in general, the mediatising principle between the Idea and the Phenomenon, the first form of existence of the Idea in multiplicity, this must also hold good of the human soul. Though not itself the Idea,[2] it is so closely combined with the Idea that it cannot be conceived without it. Reason cannot impart itself to any nature except through the instrumentality of the soul;[3] conversely, it is so entirely essential in the soul to participate in the Idea of life, that death can never enter it.[4] Hence the soul is expressly defined as the self-moved.[5] But this it can only be so far as its essence is specifically different from that of the body, and akin to that of the Idea; for life and motion originally belong to the Idea, and all life, even of derived existence, comes from it.[6] The Idea, in contradistinction to the plurality of Sensible things, is absolutely uniform and self-identical, and, in contradistinction to their transitoriness, is absolutely eternal. The soul, in its true nature, is without end or begin-

---

[1] Phileb. 30 A: τὸ παρ' ἡμῖν σῶμα ἆρ' οὐ ψυχὴν φήσομεν ἔχειν; Δῆλον ὅτι φήσομεν. Πόθεν, ὦ φίλε Πρώταρχε, λαβὸν, εἴπερ μὴ τό γε τοῦ παντὸς σῶμα ἔμψυχον ὂν ἐτύγχανε, ταὐτά γε ἔχον τούτῳ καὶ ἔτι πάντῃ καλλίονα. (Cf. supra, p. 266, 112). The human soul as well as the world-soul is said to have the two circles of the ταὐτὸν and θάτερον in itself, and is divided according to the harmonic system (Tim 43 C sq., 42 C), which is to be understood in the sense explained previously (p. 346, sqq., 358 sq.).

[2] See p. 239, 39.

[3] See p. 172, 287.

[4] Phædo, 105 C, 106 D; cf. 102 D sqq.

[5] See p. 345.

[6] See p. 261, sqq.

ning, free from all multiplicity, inequality, and compositeness.[7] More precise explanations than these, in regard to the universal concept of the soul, we vainly seek in Plato.

This high position, however, only belongs to the soul, as contemplated in its pure essential nature without reference to the disturbing influence of the body. The soul's present condition is so little adapted to that essential nature, that Plato can only account for it by a departure of the souls from their original state; and he finds no consolation for its imperfection, except in a prospective return to that state.

The Creator of the world (so the Timæus continues, 41 D sqq.) formed in the beginning as many souls as there were stars,[8] and placed each soul in a star,[9]

---

[7] Rep. x. 611 B sq.; Phædo, 78 B sqq., the results of which investigation are (x. 80 B) comprehended in the words: τῷ μὲν θείῳ καὶ ἀθανάτῳ καὶ νοητῷ καὶ μονοειδεῖ καὶ ἀδιαλύτῳ καὶ ἀεὶ ὡσαύτως καὶ κατὰ ταὐτὰ ἔχοντι αὑτῷ ὁμοιότατον εἶναι ψυχήν. Cf. Laws, 899 D: ὅτι μὲν ἡγεῖ θεοὺς συγγένειά τις ἴσως τε θεία πρὸς τὸ ξύμφυτον ἄγει

[8] Susemihl, Genet. Entw. ii. 396, understands by this that the creator of the world divided the whole collective soul-substance into as many parts as there are fixed stars, appointed one of these parts to each of the latter, and caused the individual souls, in their transplantation to the earth and the planets, to proceed from these parts. As far as Plato's scientific views are concerned, the meaning of such an entirely mythical point would be indifferent. As the question, however, has actually been raised, I cannot concur with the view just quoted. The creator forms ψυχὰς ἰσαρίθμους τοῖς ἄστροις, displays the universe to them, and proclaims the law of their future existence. In my opinion, none but the individual souls can be meant. The number need cause no difficulty; that of the souls is meant to be limited (see below), that of the stars, on the other hand, is always considered incalculable. The fact that, according to this view, 'every (fixed) star would have only one reasonable inhabitant,' is of no importance whatever. The question here is not about the inhabitants of the fixed stars; the souls are merely divided amongst the stars for a time, in order that they may contemplate the world from them (as in Phædr. 246 E sqq., only in a different way).

[9] In this case, however, we can

ordaining that they should thence contemplate the universe, and afterwards be implanted in bodies. At first, all were to come into the world alike, as men. Whoever should overcome the senses in this bodily existence should again return to a blessed existence in his star. Whoever did not accomplish this, should assume at the second birth the form of a woman; but, in case of continued wickedness, he should sink down among beasts,[10] and not be released from this wandering until, by conquest over his lower nature, his soul had regained its original perfection. In accordance with this decree, the souls were distributed, some on the earth, some on the planets,[11] and the created gods fashioned for them bodies, and the mortal parts of the soul.

This exposition differs from the much earlier one of the Phædrus (246 sqq.) as follows. The entrance of souls into bodies, which the Timæus primarily derives from a universal cosmic law, is in the Phædrus ultimately reduced to a decline of the souls from their destiny. Hence the mortal part, which the Timæus only allows to approach the immortal soul when it

only think of the fixed stars, because this transposition of each soul to its definite star is clearly distinguished from its subsequent transplantation to the planets. 41 E, 42 D (overlooked by Martin, ii. 151).

[10] There is a further development of this point, Tim. 90 E sqq.

[11] This point, standing quite separately in Plato (and thoroughly misunderstood by Martin, loc. cit.), cannot be taken otherwise than as asserting that the planets have inhabitants just as the earth has; for the expression 42 D prevents our supposing that the human souls come to the planets first and then to the earth. Anaxagoras, and Philolaus before Plato, had supposed the moon to be inhabited (see vol. i. 820, 366); Plato seems to follow them. To understand Rep. ix. 592 B as referring to inhabitants of another world is very hazardous.

enters the body, is, with regard to both its components, Courage and Desire,[12] already attributed to the soul in the pre-existent state: there would otherwise be nothing to mislead souls to their fall.[13] In other respects, the fundamental ideas of both dialogues are the same. If a soul, overcoming Desire, follows the choir of the gods

[12] The whole description proves that these two qualities are to be understood by the two horses of the soul, Phædr. 246 A; cf also 247 E, 253 D sqq., 255 E sq. All that is brought against this view from the Timæus (Hermann, De part. an. immort. sec. Plat. Gött. 1850–1, p. 10, following Hermias in Phædr. p. 126) would prove nothing at all, even supposing that it was not a mythical exposition. Why might not Plato have altered his views? To explain the horses of the soul as equivalent to the elements of the soul mentioned in the Timæus, as Hermann does, after Hermias, is more than improbable. These parts of the soul will be discussed later on.

[13] I cannot concur with Susemihl's supposition (Genet. Entw. i 232, ii. 398; Philol. xv. 417 sqq.) that Plato imagines the souls to be clothed with a sidereal body previous to the earthly life. In the Timæus 41 C. sq., 42 E, only the souls, and these only in their immortal part, are fashioned by the Demiurgus; these souls are transported into the fixed stars, and only afterwards do they obtain a body,—not perhaps earthly, but simply a body—and with this the sensible powers of the soul (42 A · ὅποτε δὴ σώμασιν ἐμφυτευθεῖεν ἐξ ἀνάγκης ... πρῶτον μὲν αἴσθησιν ἀναγκαῖον εἴη μίαν πᾶσιν ἐκ βιαίων παθημάτων ξύμφυτον γίγνεσθαι, &c.) begin. Of a superterrestrial body Plato not only says nothing (as he must necessarily have done if he supposed it to exist), but positively excludes the notion by the whole character of his exposition This body must have been created by the inferior gods, and their activity only commences with the creation of the earthly body; αἴσθησις too would have been inseparable from it, and αἴσθησις only originates with the earthly body. Nor is there anything in the Phædrus, 245 C sqq., about a sidereal body: it is the souls themselves which throng and push and lose their plumage, &c. We might of course say that incorporeal souls could not live in the stars, but just as little could they wander about the heavens and raise their heads into the sphere above the heavens, according to the fable of the Phædrus. We cannot expect that such mythical traits should be thoroughly consistent with one another and in harmony with the serious determinations of the Platonic doctrine We are not justified in attributing determinate theories to Plato simply because they are required in a purely mythical exposition.

up to the super-celestial place to behold pure entities, it remains for a period of 10,000 years,—one revolution of the universe,—free from the body: but those souls which neglect to do this, and forget their highest nature, sink down to the earth. At their first birth, all, as stated in the Phædrus, are implanted in human, and male, bodies; only their lots vary according to their merit. After death, all are judged, and placed for a thousand years, some as a punishment under the earth, some as a reward in heaven. This period having elapsed, they have again to choose,—the evil as well as the good,—a new kind of life; and in this choice, human souls pass into beasts, or from beasts back into human bodies. Those alone who thrice in succession have spent their lives in the pursuit of wisdom, are allowed to return, after the three thousand years, to the super-celestial abode. The latter part of this representation is confirmed by the Republic.[14] The souls after death are there said to come into a place where they are judged: the just are led away thence to the right, into heaven; the unjust to the left, beneath the earth. Both, as a tenfold reward of their deeds, have to accomplish a journey of a thousand years, which for the one is full of sorrow, for the other of blessed visions.[15] At the end of his thousand years, each soul has again to select an earthly lot, either human or animal, and only the very greatest sinners are cast for

[14] x. 613 E sqq. In vi. 498 D a future return to life was already supposed.

[15] In 615 C the question is brought forward, which afterwards caused so much trouble to Christian dogmatism, viz the fate of children who die young. Plato refuses to enter into it

ever into Tartarus.[16] The Politicus [17] also recognises a periodical entrance of souls into bodies.

The Gorgias (523 sqq.) gives a detailed account of the future judgment, again with the qualification that incorrigible sinners are to be everlastingly punished: and the Phædo (109 sqq.), with much cosmological imagery, describes the state after death in the same way. Here four lots are distinguished (113 D sqq.): that of ordinary goodness, of incurable wickedness, of curable wickedness, and of extraordinary holiness. People of the first class find themselves in a condition which, though happy, is still subject to purification; those of the second are eternally punished; those of the third temporarily.[18] Those who are remarkable for goodness attain to perfect bliss, the highest grade of which—entire freedom from the body—is the portion of the true philosopher alone.[19] This passage is to be taken in connection with the former one, Phædo (80 sqq.), which makes the return of the greater number of souls into corporeal life (as men or animals) a necessary consequence of their attachment to the things of sense. But the Gorgias not only represents much more strongly than the Phædo the distinction of

[16] The peculiar touch here added—that at such persons the abyss of the world beneath roared—is a remodelling of a Pythagorean notion; cf. vol. i. 389, 3.

[17] 272 E; cf. 271 B sq., the development of details is here of course different, but the general doctrine the same as elsewhere.

[18] Brandis, Gr.-röm. Phil. ii. a. 448, is mistaken in trying to find here (114 A) a belief in the efficacy of intercession for the departed. The idea is rather that the offender is punished until he has expiated his offence, and propitiated the injured person; there is nothing about intercession.

[19] A similar division of a fourfold state of recompense is referred to in the passage from the Laws, x. 904 B sqq. quoted p. 409.

ordinary from philosophical virtue, and its importance in determining future conditions, but contains a somewhat different eschatology. According to the other descriptions, the departed spirits appear immediately after death before the bar of judgment, and only resume a body at the end of a thousand years. Here, the souls that hanker after sensible things are said to hover as shadows around the graves, until their desire draws them again into new bodies.[20]

Plato employs the same method in the doctrine of Recollection, to explain the phenomena of the present life. The possibility of learning, he says,[21] would be incomprehensible, the sophistic objection that one cannot learn that which is known, nor seek that which is unknown,[22] would be unanswerable, if the unknown were not in some other relation to the known; something namely that man has once known and then again forgotten. Experience shows this to be actually the case. How could mathematical and other truths be extracted merely by questions from a person to whom they had hitherto been entirely strange, if they were not previously latent in him? How could sensible things remind us of universal concepts if the latter were not known to us independently of the former? They cannot be abstracted from the things themselves, for no particular represents its essence exactly and completely. But if these concepts and cognitions are given us

[20] 108 A does not really balance this variation, in spite of the reference to the former passage.
[21] Phædr. 249 B sq.; Meno, 80 D sqq ; Phædo, 72 E sqq.: cf. Tim. 41 E.
[22] See vol. i. 912; Prantl, Gesch. d. Log. i. 23.

before any presentation has been appropriated, we cannot have acquired them in this life, but must have brought them with us from a previous life.[23] The facts of learning, and of conceptual knowledge are only to be explained by the pre-existence of the soul. This doctrine alone makes Thought, distinguishing characteristic of human nature,[24] comprehensible to us.

That the above descriptions as they stand were regarded by Plato not as dogmatic teaching but as myths, it scarcely required his express assertions[25] to prove: this is unmistakably shown by the contradictions not only between one dialogue and another, but often in the very same; the careless prodigality with which historical and physical wonders are heaped together; the occasional intermingling of irony;[26] and the precise detailing of particularities that are beyond all human ken. But he no less clearly asserts that these myths were viewed by him not as mere myths, but also as hints of the truth, worth serious consideration;[27]

---

[23] The expression which Aristotle, De an. iii. 4, 429 a. 27, quotes, though without Plato's name, and which Philop. De an. ii. 5 a., though only conjecturally, refers to Plato, seems to imply this original possession of the Ideas. εὖ δὴ οἱ λέγοντες τὴν ψυχὴν εἶναι τόπον εἰδῶν. Perhaps, however, he has in mind the more general view, on which cf. p. 287, 172.

[24] Phædr. loc. cit.; only a human soul can come into a human body, because it alone has heard truth: δεῖ γὰρ ἄνθρωπον ξυνιέναι κατ' εἶδος λεγόμενον ἐκ πολλῶν ἰὸν αἰσθήσεων εἰς ἓν λογισμῷ ξυναιρούμενον· τοῦτο δέ ἐστιν ἀνάμνησις ἐκείνων, ἅ ποτ' εἶδεν ἡμῶν ἡ ψυχή, &c.

[25] Phædo, 114 D; Rep. x. 621 B; Meno, 86 B.

[26] Cf. Phædo, 82 A; Tim. 91 D; Rep. x. 620.

[27] Georg. 523 A; Phædo, loc. cit.: τὸ μὲν οὖν ταῦτα διισχυρίσασθαι οὕτως ἔχειν, ὡς ἐγὼ διελήλυθα, οὐ πρέπει νοῦν ἔχοντι ἀνδρί. ὅτι μέντοι ἢ ταῦτ' ἐστὶν ἢ τοιαῦτ' ἄττα περὶ τὰς ψυχὰς ἡμῶν καὶ τὰς οἰκήσεις, ἐπεί περ ἀθάνατόν γε ἡ ψυχὴ φαίνεται οὖσα, ταῦτα καὶ πρέπειν μοι δοκεῖ καὶ ἄξιον κινδυνεῦσαι οἰομένῳ οὕτως ἔχειν.

and he therefore combines with them moral exhortations which he never would have grounded on uncertain fables.[28] It is difficult, however, to make out precisely where that which is intended to be dogmatic ends, and that which is mythical begins. Plato himself was manifestly in uncertainty, and for that very reason betakes himself to the myth. The doctrine of immortality is the point, the strictly dogmatic signification of which can least be doubted. Not only in the Phædo, but in the Phædrus and Republic, too, it is the subject of a complete philosophic demonstration. But this demonstration is directly founded on the concept of the soul, as determined by the whole inter-connection of the Platonic system. The soul in its Idea is that to the essence of which life belongs: at no moment, therefore, can it be conceived as not living. This ontological proof of immortality sums up all the separate proofs in the Phædo,[29] and is brought forward in

[28] Phædo, loc. cit.; Georg. 526 D, 527 B sq.; Rep. x. 618 B sq., 621 B.

[29] The details in the Phædo about immortality appear to form a series of distinct evidences and considerations. If, however, we look into them more closely, we see that they all depend on one thought. The consciousness of the Ideal Being of the human soul (which is above growth and decay) is here exhibited in its advance to an ever clearer scientific certainty, in its establishment with each new step on deeper and firmer convictions. In the end we get (64 A–69 E) as a general pre-supposition of philosophic endeavour—a postulate of the philosophic consciousness—that all philosophising is a loosing of the soul from the body, a kind of death; and consequently that the soul arrives at its determination, the cognition of truth, only after the separation from the body, i.e. only after death. (Whether this exposition be called a proof or not is, I think, of no importance, the Platonic Socrates, 63 B E, makes use of it as a justification of his belief in a happy life after death.) Plato himself, however, 69 E sq., suggests that this kind of foundation is not sufficient; hence in a second part (70 C–84 B) he produces some other proofs.

the Phædrus, where it is shown that as the soul is ever in motion and is the first beginning of all motion, it must be indestructible as well as underived.[30] The proof which Plato considers complete and incontestable. This proof is brought in by refuting the notion that the soul is merely the harmony of its body (90 C-95 A). After (95 A-102 A) showing that the starting-point lies in the doctrine of Ideas (upon which all the previous discussions ultimately hinge), Plato develops the final argument as above (102 A-107 B): 'A concept can never pass into its opposite, nor can a thing which has a definite concept belonging to its being admit the entrance of its opposite. But life belongs to the being of the soul, consequently it cannot admit the opposite of this, viz. death. Therefore it is immortal and imperishable.' I cannot here enter into details as to the different views which have been entertained on the composition of the Phædo, and its arguments for the immortality of the soul. Cf., however, Schleiermacher, Plat. WW. ii. 3, 13 sq.; Baur, Sokrates und Christus (Tub. Ztschr. 1837, 3), 114 sq; Steinhart, Pl. WW. iv. 114 sq. (who, however, concedes too much to Hermann's mistaken assertion that the proofs of the Phædo exhibit the development of Plato's convictions on this subject, Herm. Plat. 528 sq —See, on the other side, Rettig. ub Pl. Phædo, Bern, 1845, p. 27 sqq.); Bonitz, z. Erkl. platon. Dialogu, Hermes, v. 413 sqq Further details apud Ueberweg, Gesch. d. Phil. i. 135 sq

from the nature of the soul itself, to demonstrate that which he expounded merely as an immediate pre-supposition of philosophic life and endeavour. These proofs are all distinguished from the decisive and incontestable proof of the last part, by the fact that they do not proceed from the concept of the soul as such, but from individual analogies and facts, by which immortality may be inferred with a high degree of probability, but not with the unquestionable certainty which Plato attributes to his chief argument. It is proved first of all (70 C-72 D) that as everything originates from its opposite, the living must originate from the dead, as the dead from the living; the dead must therefore exist. It is then shown (72 E-77 A) that the generation of new notions, and the formation of general concepts, are to be understood merely as Reminiscence, and are to be explained from a previous possession of those notions, and an existence prior to the present. And (according to the doctrine of the origination of the living from the dead) this prior existence must find its correspondence in an existence after death. Finally (78 B-81 A), from a comparison of the soul with the body, the result is obtained that the soul belongs to the class of simple and unchangeable things: and these are not liable to dissolution. Still even these proofs are found to be insufficient (85 D, 88 B sq). A third division, distinct from the previous sections, introduces us to

[30] 245 C . ψυχὴ πᾶσα ἀθάνατος. τὸ γὰρ ἀεικίνητον ἀθάνατον, &c.

same argument is used in the Republic,[31] where it is said that the destruction of a thing is caused by its own inherent evil. But the evil of the soul, that is moral evil, does not weaken its faculty of life. If the soul could be destroyed at all, vice, says Plato, would have destroyed it; as this is not the case, we see that an absolutely indestructible life is inherent in it. In a word, the nature of the soul guarantees that it cannot cease to live: it is the immediate cause of all life and motion; and though both may be borrowed by the soul from a higher, namely the Idea, yet it is[32] only by means of the soul that the Idea can impart itself to the Corporeal.[33] Therefore, in proportion as it is

The soul is ἀρχὴ κινήσεως· ἀρχὴ δὲ ἀγένητον. ἐξ ἀρχῆς γὰρ ἀνάγκη πᾶν τὸ γιγνόμενον γίγνεσθαι, αὐτὴν δὲ μηδ' ἐξ ἑνός· εἰ γὰρ ἔκ του ἀρχὴ γίγνοιτο, οὐκ ἂν ἐξ ἀρχῆς γίγνοιτο. ἐπειδὴ δὲ ἀγένητόν ἐστι, καὶ ἀδιάφθορον αὐτὸ ἀνάγκη εἶναι (cf. supra p. 344) . . . . ἀθανάτου δὲ πεφασμένον τοῦ ὑφ' ἑαυτοῦ κινουμένου, ψυχῆς οὐσίαν τε καὶ λόγον τοῦτον αὐτόν τις λέγων οὐκ αἰσχυνεῖται. πᾶν γὰρ σῶμα ᾧ μὲν ἔξωθεν τὸ κινεῖσθαι, ἄψυχον, ᾧ δὲ ἔνδοθεν αὐτῷ ἐξ αὐτοῦ, ἔμψυχον, ὡς ταύτης οὔσης φύσεως ψυχῆς· εἰ δ' ἔστι τοῦτο οὕτως ἔχον, μὴ ἄλλο τι εἶναι τὸ αὐτὸ ἑαυτὸ κινοῦν ἢ ψυχήν, ἐξ ἀνάγκης ἀγένητόν τε καὶ ἀθάνατον ψυχὴ ἂν εἴη.

[31] x 608 D sqq. Cf Phædo, 92 E sq., and Steinhart, v. 262 sq.

[32] See p. 288, 172

[33] The Phædrus designates the soul itself as the ἀρχὴ κινήσεως, without saying that it is indebted only to participation in the Idea of life and the Ideal Cause for its motive power (Phædo, 105 C; Phileb. 30 B sq.; see p 266, 112), and that it therefore belongs to the conditioned and derivative, or, as the Timæus puts it, that it was produced by God together with the rest of the world. This is of no importance to the present question, but still there is a difference: the exposition of the Phædrus is less precise and developed than that of the later dialogues. I cannot agree with Ueberweg (Unters plat. Schr. 282 sqq.) that the Timæus differs from the Phædo in its view of the Being of the soul. Tim. 41 A, the creator of the world says to the created gods τὸ μὲν οὖν δὴ δεθὲν πᾶν λυτόν, τό γε μὴν καλῶς ἁρμοσθὲν καὶ ἔχον εὖ λύειν ἐθέλειν κακοῦ· δι' ἃ καὶ ἐπείπερ γεγένησθε, ἀθάνατοι μὲν οὐκ ἐστὲ οὐδ' ἄλυτοι τὸ πάμπαν, οὔτι μὲν δὴ λυθήσεσθέ γε οὐδὲ τεύξεσθε θανάτου μοίρας, τῆς ἐμῆς βουλήσεως μείζονος ἔτι θεσμοῦ καὶ κυριωτέρου λαχόντες ἐκείνων, οἷς ὅτ' ἐγίγνεσθε ξυνεδεῖσθε.

necessary that the Idea in the universe should be manifested in the phenomenon, the soul, as the medium of

Hence Ueberweg concludes that as the soul according to the Timæus has also an origin and a composition, the principle τὸ δεθὲν πᾶν λυτὸν must hold good of it. The soul cannot, therefore, be immortal by nature, but only by the will of God. A comparison of this exposition with that of the Phædrus and the Phædo shows, says Ueberweg, that the Timæus stands between these two and forms the transition from the one to the other. The Phædrus presupposes the perishableness of everything conditioned, and therefore explains the soul as something unconditioned, an ἀρχή, in order to vindicate its immortality. The Phædo, on the other hand, considers the soul to be conditioned by the Idea of life, and accordingly gives up the perishableness of everything conditioned; it allows that such a thing may be imperishable, provided it stand in an essential relation to the Idea of life. The Timæus agrees with the Phædrus as to the perishableness of everything conditioned, and with the Phædo in saying that the soul is a conditioned thing. Hence it denies any natural immortality to the soul; and for this reason it may be considered earlier than the Phædo. But in making this combination Ueberweg ought to have paid some attention to the Republic, which he has left quite out of consideration. The Republic, which is prior to the Timæus, distinctly refers to the discussions of the Phædo, 69 C–72 B. and 78 B – 81 A (cf. especially Rep. 611 A with Phædo, 72 A sq., 611 B with Phædo, 78 B sq.), the substance of which is referred to here so briefly only because it was detailed elsewhere. And in the words: ὅτι μὲν τοίνυν ἀθάνατον ἡ ψυχὴ καὶ ὁ ἄρτι λόγος καὶ οἱ ἄλλοι ἀναγκάσειαν ἄν, we are clearly referred to further proofs known to the reader, which can only be those of the Phædo. In the argument above mentioned, 608 D sqq , it is evidently assumed that the soul is imperishable by nature, this being the only reason why its οἰκεία πονηρία is incapable of killing it. Again, it is incorrect to say that the principle τὸ δεθὲν πᾶν λυτὸν is given up in the Phædo. It is stated just as definitely there as in the Timæus (Ph. 78 B : τῷ μὲν ξυντιθέντι τε καὶ ξυνθέτῳ ὄντι φύσει προσήκει τοῦτο πάσχειν, διαιρεθῆναι ταύτῃ ᾗπερ ξυννετέθη· εἰ δέ τι τυγχάνει ὂν ἀξύνθετον, τούτῳ μόνῳ προσήκει μὴ πάσχειν ταῦτα εἴπερ τῳ ἄλλῳ), and is repeated. Republic, 611 B. The Republic and Timæus, as well as the Phædo, add that the soul is not a σύνθετον, but a simple Being, and they prove its immortality immediately from this simplicity. The Phædo (80 B· ψυχῇ δὲ αὖ τὸ παράπαν ἀδιαλύτῳ εἶναι ἢ ἐγγύς τι τούτου) does not omit to intimate that the indissolubility of the soul is not so unconditioned and original as that of the Idea. Is this really different in the Timæus? Θυμὸς and ἐπιθυμία are first (42 A, 69 C) associated with the soul on its entry into the body, but they do not belong to its original Being, which outlasts death. If we want to know this Being we must, as Republic 611 B sq. expressly remarks, leave them out of the question. By its transient connection with

PRE-EXISTENCE AND IMMORTALITY. 401

this manifestation, is also necessary; and as it is impossible that the universe and its motion can ever

them it does not become anything composite. This would only be the case according to Phædrus, 246 A sq. Ueberweg believes that the Phædrus agrees with the Timæus as to the perishableness of everything conditioned. But the Timæus does not speak of the conditioned any more than the Phædo or Republic it speaks of the composite. Is the soul to be considered as composite, and therefore dissoluble, in the Timæus, because, according to a mythical exposition, it is formed out of its elements? (see p. 342 sq.) We might say in favour of this view that the principle πᾶν δεθὲν λυτὸν is adduced not merely, 41 A, with reference to the composition of the stars out of the corporeal elements (40 A; cf. 42 E sq.), but also presupposed, 43 D. One of the soul's circles is there said to be utterly confined by the throng of sensible perceptions at the entry of the soul into the body. This is the circle of identity (Thought), the ταὐτὸν. The other circle (Opinion) is so confused, ὥστε τὰς τοῦ διπλασίου καὶ τριπλασίου τρεῖς ἑκατέρας ἀποστάσεις καὶ τὰς τῶν ἡμιολίων καὶ ἐπιτρίτων καὶ ἐπογδόων μεσότητας καὶ ξυνδέσεις (the harmonic proportions of the soul, see p. 349 sq.), ἐπειδὴ παντελῶς λυταὶ οὐκ ἦσαν πλὴν ὑπὸ τοῦ ξυνδήσαντος, πάσας μὲν στρέψαι στροφάς, &c. But, as we have seen, the Phædo itself suggests a similar restriction. If then we are to press the words as Ueberweg does, we must assert not only of the Timæus but of the Phædo that it does not assume a natural imperishability of the soul. And in the Timæus natural immortality

must be denied both to the human and to the World-soul. But this would be going beyond Plato's real meaning. The principle that everything composite is dissoluble is with Plato a fundamental metaphysical principle which occurs equally in the Phædo, the Republic, and the Timæus The soul in spite of this has no dissolution to fear; and this can be substantiated in two ways. We can either deny that the soul is composite, or we can say that, so far as in a certain sense the soul is composite, it is in itself dissoluble, but this possibility for other reasons is never realised. We can derive its immortality either from a metaphysical or a moral necessity. The former is the method pursued in the Republic and Phædo; the latter is hinted at in the Timæus, where the psychogony does not permit simplicity to be attributed to the soul in the same strict sense as in the other dialogues. Cf the Republic, 611 B: οὐ ῥᾴδιον ἀΐδιον εἶναι σύνθετόν τε ἐκ πολλῶν καὶ μὴ τῇ καλλίστῃ κεχρημένοι συνθέσει, as is the case with the soul in its present condition, though not according to its original Being. The possibility is suggested of the soul's being indeed a σύνθετον, but one so beautifully combined that it may last for ever. So far as there is any actual difference on this point between the Timæus and the Phædo, it proves the Timæus to be not the earlier, but the later work The simplicity of the soul is modified in the Timæus (and not before) by the doctrines of its composition out of its elements. The same holds good against Ueber-

D D

cease, so it is impossible that the soul should either have had a beginning or be subject to destruction.[34] Plato cannot mean that this holds good only of the World-soul, and not of individual souls. In his view these are not emanations of the World-soul, coming forth from it for a certain time, and returning into it; but as particular Ideas stand side by side with the highest Idea, so particular souls stand beside the universal soul in self-dependent individuality. Both are of like nature: both must be equally imperishable. The soul, as such, is the principle of motion, and is inseparably combined with the Idea of Life: therefore each particular soul must be so. This argument is not altogether valid.[35] It certainly follows from the premises that there must always be souls, but not that these souls must be for ever the same.[36] It is question-

weg's assertion (loc. cit. 292) that the Politicus also must be later than the Timæus, because the higher part of the soul is called (309 C) τὸ ἀειγενὲς ὂν τῆς ψυχῆς μέρος. If any conclusion at all can be drawn from these words it is that the Politicus is earlier than the Timæus. It is not till we come to the Timæus that we find any mention of the origin of the soul in all the preceding dialogues, Phædrus, Meno (86 A), Phædo and Republic (611 A, B), it is regarded as without beginning — ἀεὶ ὄν. Considering the mythical character of the psychogony and cosmogony in the Timæus, I should be inclined to attach little importance to these deviations

[31] Phædr. 245 D: τοῦτο δὲ [τὸ αὐτὸ αὑτὸ κινοῦν] οὔτ' ἀπόλλυσθαι οὔτε γίγνεσθαι δυνατόν, ἢ πάντα τε οὐρανὸν πᾶσάν τε γένεσιν συμπεσοῦσαν στῆναι καὶ μήποτε αὖθις ἔχειν ὅθεν κινηθέντα γενήσεται.

[35] Phædo, 107 B sq., 114 C; Rep x. 610 D, 613 E sq., 621 B; Gorg. 522 E, 526 D sq.; Theæt. 177 A; Laws, xii. 959 A sq.

[36] It does not follow that Plato considered his proofs invalid. Teichmuller tries to prove in his Studien zur Gesch. d. Begriffe, p. 110-222, that Plato did not believe in an individual immortality, but considered the individual in the soul to be mortal, disappearing at death. (Teichmüller is, as far as I remember, the first to promulgate this theory.) His view not only wants foundation, but contradicts every result of Plato's most unequivocal explanations.

able whether Plato would have attained his firm conviction of immortality had it not commended itself to

Teichmüller thinks that if the individual soul is not an Idea, it cannot be imperishable, and convicts me of 'a clear contradiction' (p. 210) in having represented the individual souls with an independent existence by the side of the World-soul, while (p. 554) I deny that the individual is an Idea. I have not, however, yet discovered where the contradiction lies. Are there according to Plato no individual Beings by the side of the Ideas? or must they be perishable because they are not Ideas? Does not Plato expressly say (Phædo, 104 B, 105 D, 106 D sq), that, besides the Ideas themselves, all things with which an Idea is at any time connected exclude the opposite of that Idea? Hence, not only the Idea of life, but the soul which participates in that Idea, excludes death. Teichmüller further remarks (p. 111) that, as the soul is a becoming or actually existing thing, it must, like all else which actually exists, be a mixed thing composed of an Ideal and a principle of Becoming, of which one part (the individual) passes away, while the eternal factor returns into its eternal nature. But he neither has brought, nor could bring proofs to show that Plato thought this to be the case with all actually existing things. Are not the world and World-soul, the stars and the star-spirits, actually existing things? Do they not belong to the category of Becoming just as much as, and in the same sense as, the human soul? Yet we cannot infer that one part of their Being passes away, while the other returns to its eternal nature. Even if it were correct to say that the individual is to be found neither in the Ideas nor in the principle of Becoming, but only in the actual mixture of the two (p. 114), it would not necessarily in Plato's view 'belong only to things which originate and pass away.' There would remain the possibility that he supposed an enduring and indissoluble connection of the Idea with the principle of Becoming as well as the transient connection. This is undoubtedly the case in the frequently quoted passage of the Phædo, 103 C sqq. We cannot, however, say absolutely that individuality according to Plato arises from the mixture of the Ideas with the principle of Becoming;—at least, if we understand by the latter term what he himself explicitly calls it, the τιθήνη γενέσεως (Tim 52 D)—Matter —for this is not in the soul. Individual corporeal Beings do so originate, but how the spiritual individuality arises Plato gives us no explanation beyond the mythical partition of the soul-substance into the individual souls, Tim 41 D, and it is more than uncertain that he could account for it to himself. How can the assertion be justified that the eternity of individual souls most distinctly affirmed by Plato 'must have been inconceivable from the nature of their origin?' We may see that Plato's evidences for the personal duration of the soul after death have no actual cogency, or (which, however, would be difficult to prove) that such a belief is not in harmony

404 PLATO AND THE OLDER ACADEMY.

him on other grounds. We must remember the strong moral interest attaching to a belief in future retribution which is so prominent in his writings,[37] and the agreement of the doctrine of immortality with his high idea of the worth and destiny of the spirit;[38] together with the support it gave to his theory of knowledge, by means of the principle of Recollection. As far as the scientific establishment of this doctrine is concerned, Plato comprehends everything in the single demand that we should recognise the essential nature of the soul, which excludes the possibility of its destruction.

This argument shows the close interconnection between the doctrine of immortality and that of pre-existence. If it be impossible to imagine the

---

with the general suppositions of his system. But our next question must simply be whether he held this belief himself or not; and to undertake to prove this expressly to a reader of Plato by single passages, e g. Phædo, 63 E, 67 B sq., 72, A 80 B, 107 B sq ; Rep. x. 611 A—where the constant number of the souls is by no means to be set aside with Teichmuller as a mere metaphor (Tim. 42 B)—is simply 'bringing owls to Athens' With this belief stands and falls the theory of future retribution and of ἀνάμνησις, which, as will be presently shown, Plato seriously thought it impossible to renounce Teichmüller endeavours (p 143) to extract from the words (Phædo, 107 D), οὐδὲν γὰρ ἄλλο ἔχουσα εἰς Ἅιδου ἡ ψυχὴ ἔρχεται πλὴν τῆς παιδείας τε καὶ τροφῆς, the following sense· 'What do we take with us into Hades?' Answer: 'Our general nature.' Such an obvious artifice will hardly serve to recommend his explanation. In his citation of proofs for immortality (p. 115 sqq.), he considers it 'obvious' and 'a matter of course' that the question is not about any individual immortality. Throughout he has omitted to substantiate these assertions by any accurate analysis of Plato's text.

[37] Phædo, 107 B sqq., 114 C; Rep. x 610 D, 613 E sqq., 621 B; Gorg 522 E, 526 D sqq ; Theæt. 177 A; Laws, xii 569 A sq.

[38] Cf Phædo, 64 A sqq ; Rep. x. 611 B sqq ; Apol 40 E sqq. He who sees the true nature of the spirit exclusively in its intellectual nature, and its true determination exclusively in the activity of the intellect, and in sense merely a hindering clog, can hardly fail to suppose that when man is once free from sense, he will be free from this clog.

soul as not living, this must equally hold good of the future and of the past; its existence can as little begin with this life as end with it. Strictly speaking, it can never have begun at all; for the soul being itself the source of all motion, from what could its motion have proceeded? Accordingly, Plato hardly ever mentions immortality without alluding to pre-existence, and his expressions are as explicit and decided about the one as the other. In his opinion, they stand or fall together, and he uses them alike to explain the facts of our spiritual life. We therefore cannot doubt that he was thoroughly in earnest in his assumption of a pre-existence. And that this pre-existence had no beginning is so often asserted by him [39] that a mythical representation like that of the Timæus can hardly be allowed any weight to the contrary.[40] We must nevertheless admit the possibility

---

[39] This is explained most distinctly in the Phædrus; cf supra notes 30 and 34. The Meno is less definite, 86 A: εἰ οὖν ὃν ἂν ᾖ χρόνον καὶ ὃν ἂν μὴ ᾖ ἄνθρωπος, ἐνέσονται αὐτῷ ἀληθεῖς δόξαι . . . ἆρ' οὖν τὸν ἀεὶ χρόνον μεμαθηκυῖα ἔσται ἡ ψυχὴ αὐτοῦ; δῆλον γὰρ ὅτι τὸν πάντα χρόνον ἔστιν ἢ οὐκ ἔστιν ἄνθρωπος. It might be objected that this refers only to the time since the soul existed at all. This, however, is clearly not Plato's meaning here, or he would have said so. The same holds good of the explanation in the Phædo, 70 C–72 D—that every living thing springs from the dead, and vice versâ, and that it must be so unless life is to cease altogether. So too in the corresponding passage, Rep. x. 611 A: the same souls must always exist: for that which is immortal cannot pass away; but their number is not increased, otherwise the mortal element would in the end be consumed. Phædo, 106 D, the soul is designated as ἀίδιον ὄν, Rep. loc. cit. as ἀεὶ ὄν, which of course refers to endless duration. These expressions show how to Plato's mind the absence of a beginning and the absence of an end coincide.

[40] It has been already shown, p 369 sqq., in what contradictions Plato became involved by the supposition of a beginning of the world. In the present case there is the contradiction that the soul was fashioned in a determinate moment by the Demiurgus, whereas

that in his later years he did not strictly abide by the consequences of his system, nor definitely propound to himself the question whether the soul had any historical beginning, or only sprang, to its essential nature, from some higher principle.

If the two poles of this ideal circle, Pre-existence and Immortality, be once established, there is no evading the doctrine of Recollection which lies between them; and the notions of Transmigration and of future rewards and punishments appear, the more we consider them, to be seriously meant. With regard to Recollection, Plato speaks in the above-cited passages so dogmatically and definitely, and the theory is so bound up with his whole system, that we must unconditionally reckon it among the doctrinal constituents of that system. The doctrine is an inference which could not well be escaped if once the pre-existence of the soul were admitted; for an existence of infinite duration must have left in the soul some traces which, though temporarily obscured in our consciousness, could not be for ever obliterated. But it is also in Plato's opinion the only solution of a most important scientific question: the question as to the possibility of independent enquiry—of thought transcending the sensuous perception. Our thought could not get beyond the Immediate and the Actual; we could not seek for what is as yet unknown to us; nor recognise in what we find, the thing that we sought for; if we had not unconsciously possessed it before we recog-

the Demiurgus himself could not be imagined without soul. It cannot be supposed that his soul is eternal and all the rest created; Tim. 34 B sqq. certainly looks as if it were the primal origin of the soul that is meant.

nised and were conscious of it.[41] We could form no conception of Ideas, of the eternal essence of things which is hidden from our perception, if we had not attained to the intuition of these in a former existence.[42] The attempt of a modern work to exclude the theory of Recollection from the essential doctrines of the Platonic system,[43] is therefore entirely opposed to the teaching of Plato. The arguments for the truth and necessity of this doctrine are not, indeed, from our point of view, difficult to refute; but it is obvious that from Plato's they are seriously meant.[44]

As Recollection commended itself to him on scientific grounds, the belief in retribution after death was necessitated by his moral and religious view of the world. However firm his conviction that the uncondi-

[41] Meno, 80 D sqq. See p. 396, where the question: τίνα τρόπον ζητήσεις τοῦτο, ὃ μὴ οἶδας τοπαράπαν ὅτι ἔστι... ἢ εἰ καὶ ὅτι μάλιστα ἐντύχοις αὐτῷ, πῶς εἴσει ὅτι τοῦτό ἐστιν ὃ σὺ οὐκ ᾔδησθα; is answered by the doctrine of ἀνάμνησις: τὸ γὰρ ζητεῖν ἄρα καὶ τὸ μανθάνειν ἀνάμνησις ὅλον ἐστίν.

[42] Phædo, 73 C sqq., where special weight is attributed to the fact that things always remain behind the Ideas of which they remind us; the Ideas, therefore, must have been known previously, because otherwise we could not compare them with things and remark the deviations of things from them. Plato therefore pronounces the pre-existence of the soul to be the indispensable condition of the knowledge and assumption of the Ideas; Phædo, 76 D: εἰ μέν ἐστι ἃ θρυλλοῦμεν ἀεί, καλόν τε καὶ ἀγαθὸν καὶ πᾶσα ἡ τοιαύτη οὐσία, καὶ ἐπὶ ταύτην τὰ ἐκ τῶν αἰσθήσεων πάντα ἀναφέρομεν . . καὶ ταῦτα ἐκείνῃ ἀπεικάζομεν, ἀναγκαῖον, οὕτως ὥσπερ καὶ ταῦτα ἔστιν, οὕτως καὶ τὴν ἡμετέραν ψυχὴν εἶναι καὶ πρὶν γεγονέναι ἡμᾶς. Cf. supra, note 24.

[43] Teichmuller, loc cit 208 sq., whose refutation of my view is here limited to the question: 'Is it meant that the souls saw the Ideas, before birth, with the eyes of sense?' No one has ever attributed such an absurdity to Plato, nor has Plato anywhere spoken of a sensible appearance of the Ideas in the previous life. In fact, he guards against such an assumption even in his myths (Phædr. 247 C).

[44] The apparent deviation of the Meno from the rest of the dialogues in its account of the doctrine of ἀνάμνησις has been already noticed. Supra, p. 126, 82.

tional worth of morality could be shown without reference to a hereafter, he held that there would be a discord in the universal order, and that Divine justice would be at fault if, after death, good was not invariably rewarded and evil punished, whatever might have been the case in this world.[45] He, therefore, insists on the doctrine of future retribution not only in passages where some concession to popular notions might naturally be expected for didactic or political reasons,[46] but also in the strictest scientific enquiries, in a manner which clearly testifies to his personal belief in it;[47] and he rightly regards it as so necessary a consequence of immortality, that the one doctrine is involved in the other.[48] The precise kind and manner of retribution, however, he thought it impossible to determine; and in reference to this, he was obliged to content himself either with consciously mythical representations, or, as in the physics of the Timæus, with probability.[49]

With regard to Transmigration, too, Plato is on the

[45] Rep. x. 612 A sqq. (cf. ii. 357 A-369 B); Laws, x. 903 B-905 C.
[46] E.g. Laws, loc. cit.; Gorg. 523 A sqq.
[47] E g. Rep. loc. cit ; Phædo, 63 C, 95 B sq., 114 D , Phædr. 248 E.
[48] Phædo, 107 B sq., 114 D.
[49] As has been already shown We cannot, however, say that 'it is a contradiction to acknowledge the poetical play of imagination in all the particulars of a theory,' and yet 'to consider it on the whole as an essential and doctrinal element of the system' (Teichmüller, loc. cit. 209). At any rate this is not Plato's opinion. τὸ μὲν οὖν ταῦτα διισχυρίσασθαι οὕτως ἔχειν ὡς ἐγὼ διελήλυθα, he says at the end of the eschatologic myth in the Phædo, 114 D, οὐ πρέπει νοῦν ἔχοντι ἀνδρί· ὅτι μέντοι ἢ ταῦτ' ἐστὶν ἢ τοιαῦτ' ἄττα περὶ τὰς ψυχὰς ἡμῶν καὶ τὰς οἰκήσεις, ἐπείπερ ἀθάνατόν γε ἡ ψυχὴ φαίνεται οὖσα, τοῦτο καὶ πρέπειν ἐμοὶ δοκεῖ καὶ ἄξιον κινδυνεῦσαι οἰομένῳ οὕτως ἔχειν. And why should not a philosopher say: 'I think it can be proved that a future retribution will take place, although I admit the uncertainty of all detailed determinations as to the manner of its fulfilment?'

whole in earnest. He himself shows us how it is connected with his whole system. As the living can only arise out of the dead, and the dead out of the living, souls must necessarily be at times without bodies, in order that they may return into new bodies.[50] This vicissitude is, therefore, only a consequence of the circle in which all created things are constantly moving and vibrating between opposite poles. The notion of justice, too, requires such an alternation; for if life apart from the body be higher than life in the body, it would be unjust that all souls should not alike be obliged to descend into the lower kind of existence, and that all should not be given a chance of ascending to the higher.[51] This argument seems, in Plato's opinion, to involve that the body and habitation allotted to one rational soul shall not be less perfect than that of another, unless through the soul's own fault.[52] Yet, on the other hand, he considers it quite according to nature that each soul should be removed into a place corresponding with its internal constitution[53]

[50] Phædo, 70 C sqq., 83 D, Rep. x. 611 A: cf. note 39.

[51] Tim 41 E sq. The account of the Phædrus is, as we have said, somewhat different. Perhaps Plato had not yet advanced to his later determinations, or it may have best suited his exposition to treat the degradation of the souls as a matter of will. Cf Deuschle, Plat Mythen, p. 21 sq, with whose remarks, however, I cannot entirely agree.

[52] Tim. loc. cit , cf. Phædr. 248 D.

[53] Laws, x. 903 D, 904 B: God willed that everything should take such a position in the universe that the victory of virtue and the defeat of evil in the world might be assured. μεμηχάναται δὴ πρὸς πᾶν τοῦτο τὸ ποῖόν τι γενόμενον ἀεὶ ποίαν ἕδραν δεῖ μεταλαμβάνον οἰκίζεσθαι καὶ τίνας ποτὲ τόπους· τῆς δὲ γενέσεως τὸ [τοῦ] ποῖον τινὸς ἀφῆκε ταῖς βουλήσεσιν ἑκάστων ἡμῶν τὰς αἰτίας. ὅπῃ γὰρ ἂν ἐπιθυμῇ καὶ ὁποῖός τις ὢκ τὴν ψυχὴν, ταύτῃ σχεδὸν ἑκάστοτε καὶ τοιοῦτος γίγνεται ἅπας ἡμῶν ὡς τὸ πολύ. Everything which possesses a soul changes constantly, ἐν ἑαυτοῖς κεκτημένα τὴν τῆς μεταβολῆς αἰτίαν, and according to the direction and degree of this change it moves this way or that, to the surface of the

and seek out a body that suits it.[54] The notion of the soul adopting for its dwelling an animal body, is not only very repugnant to ourselves, but even from the Platonic point of view is involved in so many difficulties,[55] and is treated by Plato with so much freedom,[56] that it is easy to see how ancient and modern commentators have come to regard it as a merely allegorical rendering of the thought that man when he loses himself in a life of sensuality is degraded into a brute.[57] Had the question been definitely proposed to Plato, it is probable that he would not have claimed for this notion the dignity of a scientific doctrine.[58] Nevertheless, we are clearly not justified in explaining a trait which so persistently

earth, into Hades, into a higher and purer or into the opposite place. Theæt. 177 A: the just are like the divine, the unjust like the non-divine; if the unjust do not amend, καὶ τελευτήσαντας αὐτοὺς ἐκεῖνος μὲν ὁ τῶν κακῶν καθαρὸς τόπος οὐ δέξεται, ἐνθάδε δὲ τῶν αὑτοῖς ὁμοιότητα τῆς διαγωγῆς ἀεὶ ἔξουσι κακοὶ κακοῖς συνόντες.

[54] Phædo, 80 E sqq. (see p. 395): if a soul leaves the body pure, εἰς τὸ ὅμοιον αὐτῇ τὸ ἀειδὲς ἀπέρχεται· otherwise, ἅτε τῷ σώματι ἀεὶ ξυνοῦσα ... καὶ γεγοητευμένη ὑπ' αὐτοῦ, ... βαρύνεταί τε καὶ ἕλκεται πάλιν εἰς τὸν ὁρατὸν τόπον Such souls wander about the earth, ἕως ἂν τῇ τοῦ ξυνεπακολουθοῦντος τοῦ σωματοειδοῦς ἐπιθυμίᾳ πάλιν ἐνδεθῶσιν εἰς σῶμα.

[55] The question is obvious, How can man, to whose nature the capability of forming concepts, according to Phædr. 249 B, essentially belongs, become a beast? How can the dull and purely sensual life of the beast serve to purify the soul? Are the souls of the beasts (acc. to Tim 90 E sq) all descended from former human souls, and so all intelligent and immortal according to their original Being, or (Phædr loc. cit.) only some of them?

[56] Cf. p. 397.

[57] E.g. among Greek Platonists, the Pseudo-Timæus, Plutarch apparently, Porphyry, Iamblichus, and Hierocles (see vol iii. b 121, 165, 590, 641, 684, 2nd edit.); among modern scholars, Susemihl, Genet. Entw. i. 243, ii. 392, 465; Philologus, xv. 430 sqq.

[58] We cannot quote Rep. iv. 441 B here. It is said there that beasts have no reason (λογισμὸς); but the same was said immediately before of children. Plato might deny the *use* of reason to children, from his point of view, but not its possession.

recurs in all Plato's eschatology, as the conscious allegorisation of a moral theorem not essentially belonging to the representation of the future life. Plato seems to have seen in this theory—originally borrowed from the Pythagoreans—one of those pregnant myths which he was convinced contained a fundamental truth, though he did not trust himself to determine (and being still a poet as well as a philosopher, perhaps felt no necessity for determining) exactly where this truth began and how far it extended. The souls in their original state, and when sufficiently perfected to return to that state, are represented as entirely free from the body,[59] and this doctrine is too closely interwoven with his whole philosophy to justify our limiting it to mean [60] that perfect incorporeality is merely an unattainable ideal, and that in reality man even after this present life will possess a body—a nobler body, however, and more obedient to the soul. A philosopher who in his whole procedure consciously and exclusively strives after a release from the body, who so long as the soul carries about with it this evil despairs of attaining his end; who yearns to be free from corporeal bonds, and sees in that freedom the highest reward of the philosophic life; who recognises in the soul an invisible principle, which only in the invisible can reach its natural state;[61] such a

---

[59] Phædr. 246 B sq., 250 C; Phædo, 66 E sq., 80 D sq, 114 C; cf. 81 D, 83 D, 84 D, Tim 42 A, D.

[60] With many of the earlier Neoplatonists, on whom compare vol. iii. b. 641, 684, 698, 736 (it is obvious that they all found this view of theirs in Plato); likewise Ritter, ii 427 sqq., Steinhart, iv. 51; Susemihl, Genet. Entw. i. 461, Philol. xv. 417 sqq.

[61] Phædo, 64 A-68 B, 79 C sq., 80 D-81 D, 82 D-84 B; cf. also

philosopher, if any one at all, must have been convinced that it was possible for the disciple of true wisdom to attain in the life to come full release from the material element. Since this is just what he does assert, without a word to the contrary, we have not the slightest reason for mistrusting such explanations.[62] In these main features, therefore, of the Platonic eschatology, we have to do with Plato's own opinions.[63] Other points may have had in his eyes at any rate an approximate probability; for example, the cosmic revolutions of ten thousand years,[64] the duration of future intermediate states, the distinction between curable and incurable transgressions.[65] But the further

Tim. 81 D, 85 E, and subter, note 66.

[62] The original appearance of the Ideas presupposes the non-corporeity of the soul; it is at our entry into the body that we forget them, Phædo, 76 D; Rep x 621 A; cf supra, note 13.

[63] Hegel, Gesch d. Phil. ii. 181, 184, 186, is therefore incorrect in pronouncing the conceptions of the pre-existence, the fall of the soul and ἀνάμνησις, to be doctrines not reckoned essential to his philosophy by Plato himself.

[64] V. p. 383. The whole calculation is of course purely dogmatic. The world-year is a century (the longest time of a man's life) multiplied by itself; its parts are ten periods of a thousand years, of which each one allows space for a single return to life and the possibility of retribution of tenfold duration.

[65] This distinction was the result of Plato's general view as to the object of punishment (see next chapter). The consideration that the equilibrium between the numbers of the dying and of those returning into life (Phædo, 72 A sq.; Rep. x. 611 A) might be disturbed, and in the end quite destroyed, if in each period of the world even a small number only of incurable criminals withdrew from the ranks of those set apart to return to life, could be met by the supposition that the punishment (Gorg. 525 C; Rep. 615 C sqq., denoted as endless) of such persons extended only to the end of each great year of the world. This of course would not be an eternity of punishment, but still such as would extend over the whole period of time comprehended by Plato's eschatologic myths. It is, however, open to question whether Plato himself rose to this consideration. I see, therefore, no sufficient reasons for the assertion (Susemihl, Philol. xv. 433 sqq.)

details concerning the other world and the soul's migrations are so fanciful in themselves, and are sometimes so playfully treated by Plato, that his doctrine, in proportion as it descends into particulars, passes into the region of the Myth.

In connection with these notions, by which alone it can be fully understood, we have now to consider the Platonic theory of the parts of the soul and its relation to the body. As the soul entered the body out of a purer life, as it stands related to the body in no original or essential manner, the sensuous side of the soul's life cannot belong to its specific essence. Plato therefore compares the soul [66] in its present condition to the sea-god Glaucus, to whom so many shells and sea-weeds have attached themselves that he is disfigured past recognition. He says that when the soul is planted in the body, sensuality and passion [67] grow up with it; and he accordingly distinguishes a mortal and an immortal, a rational and an irrational division of the soul.[68] Of these, only the rational part is simple; the irrational is again divided into a noble and an

---

that this point 'cannot be seriously meant' in Plato.

[66] Rep. x. 611 C sqq. Another similar image occurs, ix. 588 B sqq. Cf. Phædr. 250 C.

[67] Tim. 42 A sqq.; 69 C.

[68] Tim. 69 C sqq., 72 D: cf. 41 C, 42 D; Polit. 309 C, cf Laws, xii. 961 D sq, Arist. De An. iii. 9; 433 a. 26; Magna Moral. i. 1, 1182 a. 23 sqq. This theory is much less developed in the Phædrus, 246, where the θυμὸς and ἐπιθυμία (see p 393) are reckoned under the immortal soul, and the body only is designated as mortal. This exposition must not, owing to its mythical character, prevent us from seeking Plato's real opinions in the explicit theories of the Timæus, propounded as they are with all dogmatic determination, however much the views of later Greek Platonists may be at variance on this point (cf. Hermann. De part. an. immort. sec. Plat. p. 4 sq.).

ignoble half.[69] The former, the noble soul-steed of the Phædrus, is Courage or vehement Will (ὁ θυμὸς—τὸ θυμοειδὲς), in which anger, ambition, love of glory, and in general, the better and more powerful passions have their seat. In itself without rational insight, it is disposed to be subordinate to Reason as its natural ally. It has an affinity with Reason, an instinct for the great and good;[70] though when deteriorated by evil habits it may often give Reason trouble enough.[71] The ignoble part of the mortal soul includes the sum total of sensuous appetites and passions; those faculties under the dominion of sensible likes and dislikes, which Plato usually calls the ἐπιθυμητικὸν, or so far as property is desired as a means of sensuous enjoyment, the φιλοχρήματον.[72] The reasonable part is Thought.[73] Thought has its dwelling in the head; Courage in the breast, especially in the heart; Desire in the lower regions.[74] The two inferior divisions are not possessed by man alone: the appetitive soul belongs to plants,[75] the soul of Courage to animals.[76] Even in man the three faculties are not equally distributed, neither in individuals nor in whole nations. Plato assigns Reason pre-eminently to the Greeks, Courage to the northern barbarians, love of

[69] Rep iv. 438 D sqq, ix. 580 D sqq.; Phædr. 246 A sq., 253 C sqq.; Tim. 69 C sqq., 89 E.
[70] Rep loc. cit; Phædr. 246 B, 253 D sqq.
[71] Rep. iv. 441 A, Tim. 69 D: θυμὸν δυσπαραμύθητον.
[72] Rep. iv. 436 A, 439 D, ix 580 D sqq.; Phædo, 253 E sqq.; Tim. 69 D.

[73] Usually called λογιστικὸν, or λόγος; also φιλόσοφον, φιλομαθὲς, ᾧ μανθάνει ἄνθρωπος, Phædr 247 C; cf Laws, loc. cit. and supra, p. 288, 172; also νοῦς.
[74] Tim 69 D sqq., 90 A.
[75] Tim. 77 B.
[76] Rep. iv. 441 B, Rep. ix. 588 C sqq, can prove nothing in favour of this

PARTS OF THE SOUL. 415

gain to the Phœnicians and Egyptians.[77] Here, however, the determination universally applies that where the higher part exists, the lower must be presupposed, but not conversely.[78]

Plato then considers these three faculties not merely as separate forms of activity, but as separate parts of the soul;[79] and he proves this from the experimental fact that not only is Reason in man in many ways at strife with Desire, but that Courage, on the one hand, acts blindly without rational intelligence, and on the other, when in the service of Reason, combats Desire. As the same principle in the same relation can only have the same effect, there must be a particular cause underlying each of the three activities of soul.[80] The general ground of this theory is to be found in the whole Platonic system. As the Idea stands abruptly in opposition to the Phenomenon, the soul, as most nearly related to the Idea, cannot have the sensible principle originally in itself. Hence the discrimination of the mortal and immortal part of the soul. If, however, the soul has at any time received into itself this sensuality (as is certainly the case), a

---

[77] Rep. iv. 435 E.
[78] Rep. ix. 582 A sqq.
[79] He also uses the expression μέρη, Rep. iv. 442 C, 444 B; and ibid. 436 A, he puts the question· εἰ τῷ αὐτῷ τούτῳ ἕκαστα πράττομεν ἢ ἄλλο ἄλλῳ· μανθάνομεν μὲν ἑτέρῳ, θυμούμεθα δὲ ἄλλῳ τῶν ἐν ἡμῖν ἐπιθυμοῦμεν δ' αὖ τρίτῳ τινὶ ... ἢ ὅλῃ τῇ ψυχῇ καθ' ἕκαστον αὐτῶν πράττομεν. But he more frequently speaks of εἴδη or γένη, Phædr. 253 C; Rep. 435 C, 439 E, 441 C, 443 D, 444 B, 504 A; Tim. 69 C, E, 77 B. cf. Wildauer, Philos. Monatschr. 1873, p. 241.

[80] Thus poets like Epicharmus, Theognis, and others oppose θυμός and νοῦς, and speak of a battle of θυμός and νοῦς (Theogn. v. 1053, where, however, Bergk reads not μάχεται, but πέτεται θυμός τε νόος τε), and a νόος θυμοῦ κρέσσων (ibid. 631). From this it is an easy step to suppose that both are really distinct parts of the soul.

mediatizing principle must for a similar reason be sought between the two. Hence, within the mortal soul, the second division of the noble part and the ignoble. In accordance with this theory, the threefold partition should be still further carried out and extended not only to the faculty of Desire, but to Opinion and Knowledge; so that Sensation might belong to the Desiring soul, Opinion to Courage, Knowledge to Reason. These three forms of presentation are definitely distinguished,[81] and even assigned to different parts of the soul.[82] Plato seems to have been deterred from this combination by the circumstance that he ascribes even to knowledge derived from the senses and from envisagement, as preparatory to reasoned knowledge, a greater worth than to Courage and Desire. He attributes Perception,[83] indeed, to the appetitive part of the soul, excluding Reason and Opinion. But he means by this, not so much sensuous perception as the feeling of pleasure and pain. He further contrasts Opinion, even right Opinion, with Reason, and says of the virtue that is entirely founded on Opinion, that it is without intelligence, a mere affair of custom.[84] So that Opinion bears the same analogy to Reason that Courage does.

[81] See pp. 170, 174, 14.
[82] Rep x. 602 C sqq.; vii. 524 A sq. The αἴσθησις which leads us to form wrong judgments must be different from the λογισμὸς which forms right judgments. Tim. 43 A sqq. (cf 37 B sq.): the two circles of the soul, the κύκλος (or περίοδος) ταὐτοῦ and θατέρου, the former the source of νοῦς and ἐπιστήμη, the latter of δόξαι and πίστεις: cf. pp. 218, 358 sq.
[83] Tim 77 B, on the vegetative soul · τοῦ τρίτου ψυχῆς εἴδους... ᾧ δόξης μὲν λογισμοῦ τε καὶ νοῦ μέτεστι τὸ μηδὲν, αἰσθήσεως δὲ ἡδείας καὶ ἀλγεινῆς μετὰ ἐπιθυμιῶν, ibid. 69 D: to the mortal soul belong ἡδονὴ, λύπη, θάρρος, φόβος, θυμὸς, ἐλπὶς, αἴσθησις ἄλογος and ἔρως, ibid. 65 A, 71 A.
[84] See p. 175.

PARTS OF THE SOUL. 417

In their general relation to moral action they appear to be the same. In the Republic, the guardians of the State first undergo a complete training as warriors, and then [85] only a part of them are admitted to the scientific training of rulers. All that belongs to the first educational stage represents the finished development of the courageous part (θυμοειδές), to which the grade of warrior corresponds in the State, and to this stage is also ascribed the virtue founded on habit and opinion.[86] But however necessary such a connection may seem to the completion of the Platonic theory, Plato himself, as far as we know, has never expressly enunciated it; and as he elsewhere ascribes Right Opinion and even Perception to the rational part of the soul,[87] we should, in pressing the point, be attributing to him what is alien to his system.[88]

How the unity of the soul is consistent with this threefold partition is a question which Plato doubtless never definitely proposed to himself, and certainly did not attempt to answer. The seat of personality and self-consciousness could of course only lie in the Reason, which originally exists without the other powers, and even after its combination with

---

[85] v. 471 B sqq.; vi. 503 B sqq.

[86] See p. 215, cf. Rep iv. 430 B, where the peculiar virtue of the θυμοειδές in the state—courage—is defined as the δύναμις καὶ σωτηρία διὰ παντὸς δόξης ὀρθῆς τε καὶ νομίμου δεινῶν περὶ καὶ μή.

[87] Both belong (see note 82) to the two circles of the soul (which attach originally to the human soul as well as to the World-soul, v. p. 358; p. 359, 166), to the θεῖαι περίοδοι (Tim 44 D, 90 D), which are united in the rational part of the soul, and have their seat in the head According to Tim. 45 A the organs of sense are also situated in the head, because they are the instruments of this part of the soul; the sensible is perceived by reason · Tim. 64 B, 67 B

[88] Cf, Brandis, p. 401 sq.

E E

418 *PLATO AND THE OLDER ACADEMY.*

them remains the ruling part.[89] But how the Reason can become one with these powers when, according to its own essential nature, it cannot belong to them, it is hard to see. Plato does not show us how Reason can be affected by the inferior parts of the soul and fall under their dominion:[90] nor does he explain why Courage is in its very nature subject to Reason: and when he tells us[91] that the covetous part is governed by Reason, by means of the liver, through dreams and prophetic intimations, we are not much assisted by so fanciful an idea. We have here three essences combined with one another; not one essence operating in different directions. This deficiency becomes most apparent in Plato's conceptions of the future life. How can the bodiless soul still cling to the things of sense—how by its attachment to earth, and its false estimate of external advantages, can it be led into the most grievous mistakes[92] in the choice of its allotted life,—how can it be punished in the other world for its conduct in this,—if in laying aside the body it also lays aside its own mortal part, the seat of desire, of pleasure, and of pain? Yet we cannot suppose that the mortal part of the soul survives death, and that that which first belonged to it at its union with the body and in consequence of this union remains when the union is dissolved. There is a manifest lacuna here, or rather series of contradictions: nor can we

---

[89] ἡγεμονοῦν, Tim. 41 C, 70 B; cf. the Stoic ἡγεμονικόν.

[90] To say that the perceptions of sense hinder the revolution of the circle of the ταὐτὸν in the soul by their counter-current is merely an allegorical method of expression, not an explanation.

[91] Tim. 71

[92] Rep. x. 618 B sqq.

wonder at it; it would have been much more remarkable had Plato succeeded in developing such strange notions quite consistently.

The case is somewhat similar with regard to another question, which has given much trouble to modern Philosophy,—the freedom of the will. There is no doubt that Plato presupposes this in the sense of freedom of choice. He often speaks of voluntariness and involuntariness in our actions, without a word to imply any other than the ordinary meaning[93] of the terms. He distinctly asserts that the will is free;[94] and he makes even the external lot of man, the shape under which the soul enters upon earthly existence, the kind of life which each individual adopts, and the events which happened to him, expressly dependent on free choice in a previous state of being.[95] Should this

[93] E.g. Rep. vii. 535 E (ἑκούσιον and ἀκούσιον ψεῦδος, and Laws, v. 730 C), Polit. 293 A; Laws, ix. 861 E.

[94] Rep x. 617 E· each chooses a life, ᾧ συνέσται ἐξ ἀνάγκης (i.e. when once chosen) ἀρετὴ δὲ ἀδέσποτον ἣν τιμῶν καὶ ἀτιμάζων πλέον καὶ ἔλαττον αὐτῆς ἕκαστος ἕξει. αἰτία ἑλομένου· θεὸς ἀναίτιος. 619 B: καὶ τελευταίῳ ἐπιόντι, ξὺν νῷ ἑλομένῳ, συντόνως ζῶντι, κεῖται βίος ἀγαπητὸς, οὐ κακός. Similarly Tim. 42 B sq., where the Creator previously makes known to the souls the ordinance that each by its own behaviour will determine its future destiny, ἵνα τῆς ἔπειτα εἴη κακίας ἑκάστων ἀναίτιος, and with especial stress on the freedom of the will; Laws, x. 904 B sq. (supra, note 53).

[95] See p. 390 sqq., and specially the quotations, pp. 392, 394: all souls at their first birth come into the world as men, ἵνα μή τις ἐλαττοῖτο ὑπ' αὐτοῦ [τοῦ θεοῦ] This would have no meaning in the mouth of a necessitarian if the behaviour of men is determined exclusively by divine causality, the same obviously holds good of their destiny, which is conditioned by their behaviour Hence no necessitarian system has ever asserted that the divinity could not put any men behind others without their being guilty of wrong These systems appeal to the impossibility of God's placing individuals on a level in their mortal and spiritual beginnings any more than in their corporeal qualities and their destinies; because the completeness of the world requires infinitely many different kinds and grades of being.

seem to indicate the doctrine of so-called Predestination, a closer examination of passages will contradict any such notion. It is only the outward destiny that is decided by the previous choice; virtue is absolutely free, and no state of life is so evil that it does not lie in a man's own power to be happy or unhappy in it.[96] Plato indeed maintains with Socrates that no one is voluntarily bad.[97] But this maxim only asserts that no one does evil with the consciousness that it is evil for him: and in Plato's opinion, ignorance concerning what is truly good, is still the man's own fault and the result of cleaving to the things of sense.[98] And though

[98] The difficulties which here arise are to some extent explained, but not removed; the external circumstances of life are not so independent of particular behaviour that the former could be determined beforehand, and the latter free at each moment. How, for instance, could he who chose the life of Archelaus or of any great criminal be at the same time an honest man? Plato himself admits, 618 B: ἀναγκαίως ἔχειν ἄλλον ἑλομένην βίον ἀλλοίαν γίγνεσθαι [τὴν ψυχήν]; but according to what has just been quoted, this cannot refer to virtue and vice.

[97] Tim 86 D σχεδὸν δὴ πάντα, ὁπόσα ἡδονῶν ἀκράτεια καὶ [? κατ'] ὄνειδος ὡς ἑκόντων λέγεται τῶν κακῶν οὐκ ὀρθῶς ὀνειδίζεται· κακὸς μὲν γὰρ ἑκὼν οὐδείς, διὰ δὲ πονηρὰν ἕξιν τινὰ τοῦ σώματος καὶ ἀπαίδευτον τροφὴν ὁ κακὸς γίγνεται κακός 87 A πρὸς δὲ τούτοις, ὅταν οὕτω κακῶς παγέντων πολιτείαι κακαὶ καὶ λόγοι κατὰ πόλεις ἰδίᾳ καὶ δημοσίᾳ λεχθῶσιν, ἔτι δὲ μαθήματα μηδαμῇ τούτων ἰατικὰ ἐκ νέων μανθάνηται, ταύτῃ κακοὶ πάντες οἱ κακοὶ διὰ δύο ἀκουσιώτατα γιγνόμεθα. (Cf. Rep. vi. 489 D sqq.; especially 492 E.) ὧν αἰτιατέον μὲν τοὺς φυτεύοντας ἀεὶ τῶν φυτευομένων μᾶλλον καὶ τοὺς τρέφοντας τῶν τρεφομένων, προθυμητέον μὴν, . . . φυγεῖν μὲν κακίαν. τοὐναντίον δὲ ἑλεῖν Cf. Apol 25 E sq., Prot. 345 D, 358 B sq.; Meno, 77 B sqq.; Soph. 228 C, 230 A; Rep. ii. 382 A, iii. 413 A, ix. 589 C; Laws, v. 731 C, 734 B, ix. 860 D sqq. (where Plato rejects the distinction of ἑκούσια and ἀκούσια ἀδικήματα, because all wrong is involuntary, and would substitute the terms ἀκούσιοι and ἑκούσιοι βλάβαι), and the quotations, Pt. i 123, 1, and supra, p. 179.

[98] Cf Phædo, 80 E sqq.: it all amounts to whether the soul leaves the body pure, ἅτε οὐδὲν κοινωνοῦσα αὐτῷ ἐν τῷ βίῳ ἑκοῦσα εἶναι, &c. Rep. vi. 485 C: the primary requirement in the philosophic disposition is, τὸ ἑκόντας ειναι μηδαμῇ προσδέχεσθαι τὸ ψεῦδος. Laws, x. 904 D: μείζω δὲ δὴ ψυχὴ κακίας ἢ

he says that in most cases of moral degeneracy a sickly constitution or a bad education should chiefly bear the blame, yet we are clearly given to understand that those in such a situation are by no means to be entirely excused, or shut out from the possibility of virtue. Whether these theories are throughout consistent with each other, whether it is logical to declare all ignorance and wickedness involuntary, and yet to assert that man's will is free and to make him responsible for his moral condition, may be doubtful; but this does not justify us in disregarding the distinct enunciations on free-will that we find in Plato.[99] He was probably unconscious of the dilemma in which he was involved. The more general question,—whether we can conceive a free self-determination, and whether such a determination is compatible with the Divine government of the world, and the whole scheme of nature,—appears never to have been raised by him.

The relation of the soul to the body is likewise beset with considerable difficulties. On the one hand, the soul is in its essence so entirely distinct, and in its existence so independent, that it has even existed, and is destined again to exist, without the body; and will only attain a perfect life, corresponding with

ἀρετῆς ὁπόταν μεταβάλῃ διὰ τὴν αὐτῆς βούλησιν. Tim. 44 C. if man arrives at reason and secures a right education for his reason, he becomes mature and sound, καταμελήσας δὲ ... ἀτελὴς καὶ ἀνόητος εἰς "Αιδου πάλιν ἔρχεται. The blame therefore lies with his own neglect of the means of moral education.—The Platonic schools always regarded the freedom of the will as their characteristic doctrine.

[99] E.g. Martin, ii. 361 sqq.; Steger, Plat. Stud. ii. 21, 47, iii. 38 sq., Teichmuller, Stud. z Gesch. d. Begr. 146 sq., 369 sq.

its true nature, when it is freed from corporeal fetters.[100] On the other hand, this alien body exerts on the soul so disturbing an influence, that the soul is dragged down into the stream of Becoming, overwhelmed in error, filled with unrest and confusion, intoxicated by passions and desires, by imaginations, cares and fears.[101] The stormy waves of corporeal life disturb and hinder its eternal courses.[102] At its entrance into the body it drinks the draught of forgetfulness,[103] the visions of its past existence are blotted out beyond recognition. From its union with the body arises that entire disfigurement of its nature which Plato paints in such strong colours.[104] Moral faults and spiritual sicknesses are caused by a bodily constitution disordered or diseased; rational care of the body and judicious exercise are most important as a means of spiritual health, and indispensable as preliminary moral training for individuals and for the commonwealth at large.[105] Descent and parentage are of the greatest moment; the dispositions and qualities of parents are, in the natural course of things, entailed upon their children. The better the former, the nobler the latter, as a general rule.[106] From fiery ancestors spring fiery descendants; from calm ones, calm. Both qualities, if exclusively transmitted in a race, develop themselves unduly:[107]

[100] See p. 412 sq., and Phædo, 79 A sq.
[101] Phædo, 79 C sq, 66 B sqq., and elsewhere
[102] Tim. 43 B sqq.
[103] Rep. x. 621 A; Phædo, 76 C sq
[104] See p 414. Further in the Ethics.
[105] Tim. 86 B–90 D; Rep. iii. 410 B sqq. Details on this subject will be given later on.
[106] Rep. v 459 A sq.; cf. iii 415 A, Crat. 394 A. It is remarked, Rep. 415 A sq, cf. Tim. 19 A, that the rule admits of exceptions.
[107] Polit 310 D sq., cf. Laws, vi. 773 A sq.

whole nations are often essentially distinguished from one another by some natural characteristic.[108] The circumstances under which marriage takes place are therefore an important matter of consideration; not only the bodily and spiritual condition of the individuals,[109] but also the general state of the world must be taken into account. As the universe changes in great periods of time, so for plants, beasts, and men there are varying seasons of fruitfulness and unfruitfulness for soul and body; consequently, if marriages are consummated at unfavourable times, the race deteriorates.[110] Thus we see that corporeal life in

[108] See note 77.

[109] Laws, vi. 775 B sqq : married people, so long as they continue to have offspring, must keep themselves from everything unhealthy, from all wrong-doing, and all passion, but particularly from drunkenness, because all such things transfer their results to the bodies and souls of the children.

[110] Rep. viii. 546. Plato says that for all living beings as for plants, after the times of their bodily and spiritual fruitfulness, there come periods of unfruitfulness, if they are caused to return to their former path owing to some revolution of the spheres, &c. This is further developed by a comparison between the periods of the universe and those of the human race. But instead of saying generally: 'even the universe is subjected to a change, only in longer periods of times, while mankind changes in shorter periods,' Plato marks the duration of the two periods in definite numbers. These he states indirectly, giving us a numerical enigma, in the manner of the Pythagoreans. ἔστι δὲ, he says, θείῳ μὲν γεννητῷ περίοδος, ἣν ἀριθμὸς περιλαμβάνει τέλειος, ἀνθρωπείῳ δὲ [sc περίοδός ἐστιν, ἣν ἀριθμὸς περιλαμβάνει] ἐν ᾧ πρώτῳ αὐξήσεις δυνάμεναί τε καὶ δυναστευόμεναι, τρεῖς ἀποστάσεις τέτταρας δὲ ὅρους λαβοῦσαι ὁμοιούντων τε καὶ ἀνομοιούντων καὶ αὐξόντων καὶ φθινόντων, πάντα προσήγορα καὶ ῥητὰ πρὸς ἄλληλα ἀπέφηναν· ὧν ἐπίτριτος πυθμὴν πεμπάδι συζυγεὶς δύο ἁρμονίας παρέχεται τρὶς αὐξηθείς, τὴν μὲν ἴσην ἰσάκις, ἑκατὸν τοσαυτάκις, τὴν δὲ ἰσομήκη μὲν τῇ, προμήκη δὲ [so Hermann and most moderns, with a few good MSS.; Weber's proposal, De num. Plat. 13 to read ἰσομ. τῇ μὲν, gives the same sense, but does not commend itself] ἑκατὸν μὲν ἀριθμῶν ἀπὸ διαμέτρων ῥητῶν πεμπάδος, δεομένων ἑνὸς ἑκάστων, ἀρρήτων δὲ δυεῖν, ἑκατὸν δὲ κύβων τριάδος. ξύμπας δὲ οὗτος ἀριθμὸς γεωμετρικὸς, τοιούτου (what follows, γένεσις) κύριος, ἀμεινόνων καὶ χειρόνων γενέσεων. This riddle, the key to which was evidently possessed by Aristotle (Polit. v. 12, 131 b. a. 4 sqq.), had by Cicero's

its commencement and throughout its course has an important bearing upon the spirit. How this is

time become proverbially unintelligible (ad Att 7, 13), and in our own day has variously exercised the ingenuity of scholars, see the references ap. Schneider, Plat. Opp. iii. Præf. 1–92; Susemihl, Genet. Entw ii. 216 sqq.; Weber, De numero Platonis (Cassel,1862; Gymn. progr. added to the second edition). Hermann, Susemihl, and Weber seem to have come nearest to the truth. Meanwhile, availing myself of their work, and referring to them for particulars (the discussion of which in the present place is as impossible as a detailed account including all differences of view), I may give the following as my own view. God's product, i e. the world, Plato says, moves in longer periods, and undergoes a slighter change, than the races of mankind, who change more quickly and decidedly. In Pythagorean language: the former has for its circuit a larger number, the latter a smaller; the former a complete, the latter an incomplete; the former a square, the latter an oblong number. (Oblong numbers are those composed of two unequal factors, the rectangle, however, compared with the square, stands on the side of the incomplete; see vol. i. 3rd edit., p 341, 3, 4, 302, 3) These numbers are now to be described more in detail. The circuit of the world is contained by a complete number, for the duration of the year of the world, at the expiration of which everything returns to the position which it had at the beginning, consists of 10,000 years (see p 344) The number 10,000 is a complete number as being a square, but even more so as arising from the number ten, the $\tau\acute{\epsilon}\lambda\epsilon\iota\circ\varsigma\ \mathring{a}\rho\iota\theta\mu\grave{o}\varsigma$ (see vol. i. 342). The number ten raised to the fourth power, is multiplied by itself four times (according to the scheme of the potential decad, the sacred tetractys) To this number of the world's circuit is opposed the number which contains the revolution of human kind, i.e. which gives the numbers of years, at the expiration of which a change to worse or better comes about in the production of new races of mankind—a change to $\epsilon\mathring{v}\gamma\text{ον}\acute{\iota}a$ or $\mathring{a}\phi\text{ορ}\acute{\iota}a$ (cf. 546 A C) We are told firstly, that it is the first number in which $a\mathring{v}\xi\acute{\eta}\sigma\epsilon\iota\varsigma\ \delta\upsilon\nu\acute{a}\mu\epsilon\nu a\iota$, &c., occur, pure rational proportions which can be expressed in whole numbers ($\pi\acute{a}\nu\tau a\ \pi\rho\text{οσ}\acute{\eta}\gamma\text{ορα}\ \kappa a\grave{\iota}\ \acute{\rho}\eta\tau\grave{a}\ldots\ \mathring{a}\pi\acute{\epsilon}\phi\eta\nu a\nu$) Secondly, the $\acute{\epsilon}\pi\acute{\iota}\tau\rho\iota\tau\text{ος}\ \pi\upsilon\theta\mu\grave{\eta}\nu$ of the series so obtained (for this must be the meaning, whether the $\mathring{\omega}\nu$ before $\acute{\epsilon}\pi\iota\tau$. be referred to $a\mathring{v}\xi\acute{\eta}\sigma\epsilon\iota\varsigma$, or, as seems preferable, to $\pi\acute{a}\nu\tau a$), joined with the number five, and three times increased, gives two $\mathring{a}\rho\mu\text{ον}\acute{\iota}a\iota$, which are described at length. We learn further that the whole combination of numbers here described is 'geometric,' i e. all the numbers out of which it is composed can be exhibited in a geometrical construction. In the first part of this description, the $a\mathring{v}\xi\acute{\eta}\sigma\epsilon\iota\varsigma\ \delta\upsilon\nu\acute{a}\mu\epsilon\nu a\acute{\iota}\ \tau\epsilon\ \kappa a\grave{\iota}\ \delta\upsilon\nu a\sigma\tau\epsilon\upsilon\acute{o}\mu\epsilon\nu a\iota$ refer to the fact that we are dealing with equations, the roots of which are the numbers of the Pythagorean triangle, 3, 4, 5. The Pythagoreans call three and four $\delta\upsilon\nu a\sigma\tau\epsilon\upsilon\acute{o}\mu\epsilon\nu a\iota$, five $\delta\upsilon\nu a\mu\acute{\epsilon}\nu\eta$, because $5^2 = 3^2 + 4^2$ (see details in

to be reconciled with other theories of Plato does not appear.

vol i. 344, 2, 3rd edit.). To start from these numbers was all the more suitable because the law of the combination of kind, the law of γάμυς, was to be here determined, and the number five, in which three and four are potentially contained, is called γάμος by the Pythagoreans, as the first combination of a male and female number (vol i 343, 4; 335, 3). The old commentators recognise the Pythagorean triangle in this passage; cf. Plut De Is. 56, p. 373, who says of this triangle ᾧ καὶ Πλάτων ἐν τῇ πολιτείᾳ δοκεῖ τούτῳ (?) προσκεχρῆσθαι τὸ γαμήλιον διάγραμμα συντάττων. From these elements, then, by repeated augmentation (αὐξήσεις) a proportion, or even several proportions (for the expression αὐξήσεις leaves this indefinite), are to be found with four terms (ὅροι, which is here used in the same sense as iv. 443 D), and three determinations as to the distance (the arithmetical ratio) of these terms, i.e. one or more proportions of the form: A : B = B : C = C . D (the words ῥητὰ πρὸς ἄλληλα show that we have to deal with proportions). The numbers of these ὅροι are to be partly ὁμοιοῦντες, partly ἀνομοιοῦντες, and partly αὔξοντες, partly φθίνοντες. (The genitives, ὁμοιούντων, &c., must, of course, be made to depend on ὅροι, ἀριθμῶν is to be supplied, and ὅροι ὁμοιούντων, &c., to be explained : ὅροι which consist in ἀριθμοὶ ὁμοιοῦντες, &c.) What this means is a question. As the square numbers are called ὅμοιοι and the oblong ἀνόμοιοι (Jambl. in Nicom. p. 115 Tennul.), Hermann,

p. ix is quite right in referring ὁμοιοῦν to the formation of square numbers, ἀνομοιοῦν to the formation of oblong numbers. Αὐξόντων and φθινόντων are obscure. I do not think it probable that the former is equivalent to ὁμοιοῦν, and the latter to ἀνομοιοῦν (Weber, p. 22, following Rettig). It seems unlikely that in a description otherwise so extraordinarily concise, Plato should have used such a pleonasm ; and the meaning in question cannot be extracted from the original signification of 'increasing and diminishing' without straining the words The καί, too, before αὐξόντων leads us to expect something new, and not a mere repetition of what we have already been told by ὁμοιούντων and ἀνομοιούντων Weber believes that the proportion intended by Plato (and the only one as he thinks) in the words ἐν ᾧ πρώτῳ ... ἀπέφηναν must have been formed out of certain powers of five, four, and three, in such a way that the first and third term are square numbers, the second and fourth oblong numbers, and that the terms (an account of the ἐπίτριτος πυθμὴν to be mentioned immediately) stand in the proportion of 4 : 3. Hence he gets the following proportion: $5^2 \times 4^2 \times 4^2 : 4^3 \times 5^2 \times 3^2 : 5^2 \times 4^2 \times 3^2 : 3^3 \times 5^2 \times 4$ = 6400 : 4800 : 3600 : 2700. Here the sum of the first and third term give the complete number 10,000 ; that of the second and fourth term the incomplete number 7500. But, in the first place, the suppositions from which he starts are very uncertain. The tone of the passage itself leaves it undecided whether

Plato connects his doctrine of the soul with his physiological theories by means of a teleology, which,

we have to do with one or several proportions of four terms. It is not said that in this or these proportion or proportions the first and third term must be square, and the second and fourth oblong, but merely that, generally speaking, square and oblong numbers do occur in those places And we cannot infer from the ἐπίτριτος πυθμὴν that the proportion (if it is only one) advances in the ratio of 4 : 3, because in every equation proceeding from the elements 3, 4, 5, there is an ἐπίτριτος πυθμὴν together with the number five Secondly (and this is the main point), Weber gets two numbers by his proportion, these occur in what follows as the sums of the two ἁρμονίαι the number of the year of the world, 10,000, and the number 7500. But in the words ἐν ᾧ πρώτῳ . . . ἀπέφηναν Plato means to describe only one number, that of the period of the ἀνθρώπειον γεννετόν. What this is, and how it is to be found, is not sufficiently stated in these words, so long as their meaning is not more clearly explained. From the three elements, 3, 4, 5, which Plato makes the basis of his calculation, we could derive proportions of four terms in such a way that, raised to the third power, they could be connected, by proportional means (on the system described p. 671, 3), two and two. Then we get the three equations: 1) $3^3 : 3^2 \times 4 : 3 \times 4^2 : 4^3 = 27 : 36 : 48 : 64$; 2) $3^3 : 3^2 \times 5 : 3 \times 5^2 : 5^3 = 27 : 45 : 75 : 125$, 3) $4^3 : 4^2 \times 5 : 4 \times 5^2 : 5^3 = 64 : 80 : 100 : 125$. From these the number required, the ἀριθμὸς κύριος γενέσεων, can be obtained by forming a series of their collective terms (27, 36, 45, 48, 64, 75, 80, 100. 125), and summing the numbers of this series (just as the numbers of the harmonic series are summed in Tim. Locr. 96 B). This would give 600 as the result, and the notion would then be that εὐγονίαι and ἀφορία of mankind change in periods of 600 years. We might further observe that 600 is ten times 60, and 60 $= 3 \times 4 \times 5$; and if at the same time we could assume that Plato determined the γενεὰ in the present case at 60 years (say, as the longest period of procreative power in man) we should get this result: As a new circuit begins for the individual souls after 10 hundred years, and for the universe after 10 thousand years (see above), so the race undergoes a revolution after 10 generations. Hitherto, however, we have too little ground to explain Plato's meaning with any certainty. In the second part of the description, the numbers meant by the words ὧν ἐπίτριτος πιθμὴν . . . ἑκατὸν δὲ κύβων τριάδος can be more definitely specified. Of the two ἁρμονίαι here mentioned, one must give the number $100 \times 100 = 10,000$. The other (as Hermann rightly explains) must give a number consisting of 100 cubes of the number 3, and a hundred numbers obtained from the rational diagonale of the number 5 after the deduction of 1, and from its irrational diagonals after the deduction of 2. This number is 7500; obtained from $100 \times 3^3 = 2700$ and 100×48. 48 is one less t an the square of the rational diagonals,

though sometimes graceful and ingenious, is poor in scientific results. The details of his physiology are

and two less than that of the irrational diagonals of 5; the diagonal of $5 = \sqrt{(2 \times 5^2)} = \sqrt{50}$, its rational diagonal $= \sqrt{49} = 7$; the square of the former is therefore 50; of the latter 49. Any further steps are uncertain. The two numbers mentioned are to proceed from two harmonies, i.e. two series of numbers progressing in a definite arithmetical ratio (ἁρμονία is to be taken in a mathematical, and not in a musical or metaphysico-ethical sense), by multiplying the ἐπίτριτος πυθμήν of the series previously arrived at (see p 421) in combination with the number 5 three times (τρὶς αὐξηθείς). The ἐπίτριτος πυθμήν can only be the numbers 3 and 4 themselves, for πυθμένες means (Theo Math 125 sq., Bull) for any arithmetical relation οἱ ἐν ἐλαχίστοις καὶ πρώτοις πρὸς ἀλλήλους λόγοις ὄντες (ἀριθμοί)... ἐπιτρίτων δὲ ὁ τῶν δ' πρὸς γ'. The τρὶς αὐξηθεὶς means, as Aristotle explains, Polit. v. 12, 1316 a. 7: ὅταν ὁ τοῦ διαγράμματος ἀριθμὸς τούτου (the number of the Pythagorean triangle: 3, 4, 5) στερεὸς γένηται. Those two series of numbers are to be obtained by a combination of the three, four, and five cubes, which give the above sums. Weber's proposal (p 27 sq) is worth consideration He combines 3 and 4 singly at first by multiplication with 5, and then again multiplies both multiples 3×5 and 4×5 with the numbers of the Pythagorean triangle. He thus gets two series of three terms progressing in the ratio of 3, 4, 5 (and at the same time in arithmetical proportion), which can also be exhibited in a geometrical construction, as he shows: 1) $3 \times 3 \times 5 = 45$; $4 \times 3 \times 5 = 60$; $5 \times 3 \times 5 = 75$, 2) $3 \times 4 \times 5 = 60$; $4 \times 4 \times 5 = 80$; $5 \times 4 \times 5 = 100$. Multiply the first term of the first series with the first term of the second, &c., and we arrive at the oblong numbers $45 \times 60 = 2700$, $60 \times 80 = 4800$, $75 \times 100 = 7500$. Multiply each of the three terms of the second series into itself, and we get the square numbers $60 \times 60 = 3600$; $80 \times 80 = 6400$, and as a third the sum of both: $100 \times 100 = 10,000$. Symmetry would perhaps require that the three terms of the first series should also be multiplied into themselves, which does not fit into the Platonic construction. But, however we are to understand Plato's exposition, and however we are to fill up its deficiencies, we must not expect from the present passage any serious information as to the law governing the change of the races of mankind Plato himself indicates as much when he says, 546 A sq.. however wise the rulers of the state may be, it is impossible for them to know the times of εὐγονία and ἀφορία for our race, and to avoid fatal mistakes in managing the union of parents Plato's object is rather to show the mysterious importance of that law by giving an interpretation of it in enigmatical formulæ, but the law itself becomes no clearer (as Aristotle, loc. cit. objects), even if we could interpret the formulæ mathematically. The mystic element here, as the mythical elsewhere, is

interesting, as showing the then state of that science and his acuteness in explaining the complicated phenomena of life from such inadequate experimental data; but in reference to his philosophic system their importance is very small.

That the three parts of the soul may be undisturbed in their specific nature and proper relation, a separate dwelling, says Plato, is allotted to each.[111] The two circles of the rational soul are placed in the head, which is round, that thence as from a citadel, the whole may be ruled.[112] The senses are appointed to be its organs.[113] Sensible perception, however, does not belong exclusively to the rational soul, but extends to the

---

intended to conceal a deficiency of scientific knowledge under apparent explanations.

[111] ψυχῆς περίοδοι, p. 43 D sqq., 44 B D, 47 D, 85 A, 90 D, cf supra, p 358; p. 359, 166. The sutures of the skull are (76 A) derived from the revolution of this circle of the soul, and its interruption by the afflux of nourishment (cf. 43 D sqq.).

[112] 44 D sq.

[113] Tim 45 A. Of the particular senses Plato explains sight by the supposition that there is an interior fire (or light) in the eye, which passing out from the eye unites with the kindred fire which comes out of luminous bodies, and transmits the motion through the whole body to the soul. (Tim 45 B–D, cf. Soph. 266 C; Theæt. 156 D, Rep vi. 508 A.) This light dwelling in the eye Plato calls ὄψις. The phenomena of reflected light, and reflections in mirrors, are discussed, Tim. 46 A–C; the colours of lights, 67 C sqq Cf Martin, ii. 157–171, 291–294 ad h. loc. Sleep also is derived from the interior fire of the eyes: if the eyelids close, the inner movements of the body must be relaxed and at rest, Tim. 45 D sq. The sensations of hearing are caused by the tones moving the air in the inside of the ear, and this motion is transmitted through the blood into the brain, and to the soul. The soul is thus induced to a motion extending from the head to the region of the liver, to the seat of desire, and this motion proceeding from the soul is ἀκοή (Tim. 67 A sq.). Taste consists in a contraction or dilatation of the vessels (φλέβες) of the tongue (Tim. 65 C sq.). Smell depends on the penetration of vapours (καπνὸς and ὀμίχλη, see p. 378) into the vessels between the head and the navel, and the roughness or smoothness of their contact (66 D sqq.).

inferior parts.[114] With it is connected the feeling of pleasure and pain,[115] of which the mortal soul only is

[114] Cf supra, note 81, and what has just been quoted as to hearing and smell; p 65 C we are told that the blood-vessels of the tongue, the organs of taste, run into the heart.

[115] Αἴσθησις, according to Tim. 64 sqq, takes place when an external shock brings about a movement in the body, which is transmitted to the soul. Hence it occurs only to the parts of the body which are mobile, while those which are immobile, such as bones and hair, are insensible. The most important medium for the dissemination of sensations in the body, Plato considered to be the blood, on account of its superior mobility (Tim. 70 A sq., 77 E, 65 C, 67 B). (The nerves were quite unknown in his day, and remained so for a considerable time afterwards.) If the motion only takes place in the body very gradually, it is not noticed at all, and is not a sensation. If it passes quickly, easily, and unrestrained by any obstacles, as the motion of light in seeing, it creates a very distinct sensation, but one neither pleasurable nor painful. If it is combined with a noticeable interruption, or a noticeable re-establishment of the natural condition, there arises in the former case pain, in the latter pleasure (Tim. 64 A sqq.; with regard to pleasure and the absence of pleasure cf. Phileb. 31 D sqq., 42 C sqq ; Gorg. 496 C sqq.; Rep. ix. 583 C sqq). But pain and pleasure are not always conditioned by one another. It may happen (Tim. loc. cit.) that only the interruption of the natural condition takes place quick enough to be remarked, while its re-establishment passes unnoticed; or the case may be exactly reversed. Then, in the former instance, we have pain without pleasure; in the latter that purely sensuous pleasure which is spoken of, Phileb 51 A sqq, 62 E, 63 D, 66 C. To say that the latter is 'no longer merely sensuous, but has become intellectual, mathematical' (Susemihl, ii 429), does not seem to correspond with Plato's meaning As he says, Tim 65 A, that a pleasure without pain affords ὅσα κατὰ σμικρὸν τὰς ....
κενώσεις εἴληφε, τὰς δὲ πληρώσεις ἀθρόας καὶ κατὰ μεγάλα. e.g. pleasant smells, so Phileb. 51 B, he mentions, as examples of pure ἡδοναί, τὰς περί τε τὰ καλὰ λεγόμενα χρώματα, καὶ περὶ τὰ σχήματα, καὶ τῶν ὀσμῶν τὰς πλείστας, καὶ τὰς τῶν φθόγγων, καὶ ὅσα (and generally everything which) τὰς ἐνδείας ἀναισθήτους ἔχοντα ... τὰς πληρώσεις αἰσθητὰς .. παραδιδῶσιν. Of these sensations of pleasure, however (among which those of smell are of course less noble than those of sight and hearing), 52 A, αἱ περὶ τὰ μαθήματα ἡδοναί are expressly distinguished. In Phileb. 66 C (ἃς ἡδονὰς ἔθεμεν ἀλύπους ὁρισάμενοι, καθαρὰς ἐπονομάσαντες τῆς ψυχῆς αὐτῆς ἐπιστήμαις, ταῖς δὲ αἰσθήσεσιν ἐπομένας), where the received reading certainly agrees with the above remarks, but in itself is liable to verbal and logical difficulties, I would therefore propose: τὰς μὲν τ ψ αὐτ ἐπιστήμαις (as one MS. reads), τὰς δ' αἰσθ. ἐπ.

430   *PLATO AND THE OLDER ACADEMY.*

capable.[116] This soul inhabits the trunk of the body, but being itself divided into a noble and ignoble part, its dwelling has likewise two divisions, as the chambers of women in houses are partitioned from those of men. Courage has its place in the breast, nearest the sovereign Reason; Desire in the lower parts.[117] In the breast is the heart, the chief organ of Courage; thence, throughout the whole body spread the channels of the blood, which is quick to proclaim in every direction the mandates and threatenings of Courage.[118] These channels further serve to convey in the blood continual restitution of decaying particles;[119] in them the air circulates,[120] entering and leaving the body partly through the breathing passages,[121] partly through the flesh and the skin.[122] The lungs are placed about the

---

[116] Cf. supra, note 82 This, however, can only hold good of sensible pleasure and its opposite Plato recognises a spiritual pleasure besides, Rep. ix. 582 B, 583 B, 586 E sqq., vi. 485 D; Phileb. 52 A; see p. 187.

[117] Tim 69 E sq, 70 D, 77 B

[118] 70 A sq. It has already been noticed, note 115, that the blood is the transmitting medium of sensation. Tim 77 C eqq. (cf. Martin, ii. 301 sqq, 323 sqq) is an attempt to describe the system of the blood-vessels; there is no mention here of the distinction between veins and arteries, still less of the circulation of the blood, which was entirely unknown to the ancients.

[119] Plato's theory in detail is as follows (Tim. 80 C sqq., 78 E sq.): Every element tends towards what is homogeneous to it: parts are constantly disappearing from the human body; but, according to the same principle, these are continually repaired out of the blood, into which the nourishment spread by means of the fire (the inner warmth) in the body, is brought by the air which enters in the act of breathing (cf note 122). In youth, so long as the elements of the body are fresh, they hold together faster and digest nourishment more easily, more goes into than out of the body—it grows; in age, after it is worn out, it diminishes, and finally breaks up altogether.

[120] 78 E sq, 80 D. Plato here follows Diogenes; see vol. i. 227, 7, 3rd edit.

[121] The obscure description, 77 E sqq, is elucidated by Martin, ii. 334 sqq, Susemihl, ii. 453 sqq.

[122] Plato supposes with Empedocles (see vol. i. 647), not only a respiration but a perspiration. The

heart to cool it, and to make a soft cushion for its violent beating.[123] The connection of Desire with Reason is accomplished by means of the liver; as Desire, pursuant to its nature, neither understands nor inclines to follow rational arguments, it must be ruled by imaginations; and this is the purpose of the liver The Reason causes to appear on its smooth surface, as on a mirror, pleasant or terrible images: it changes the natural sweetness and colour of the liver by the infusion of bile, or else restores it: thus alarming or quieting the part of the soul which has its dwelling there. The liver is, in a word, the organ of presentiments and of prophetic dreams;[124] in the same way, divination in general belongs only to the irrational man.[125] Plato ascribes no great importance to the

air, he thinks (78 D–79 E), enters into the body alternately through the windpipe and throat, and through the skin; here it becomes warmed by the inner fire, and then seeks its kindred element outside the body by one or the other of the ways just mentioned. There is no void space, and, accordingly, other air is pressed into the body by the air passing out; through the skin if the one current is coming out through the mouth and nose, through the mouth and nose if the current is passing out through the skin.

[123] 70 C sqq, not only air but drink is supposed to pass into the lungs.

[124] Tim. 71 A–72 D Even after death traces of prophetic pictures remain in the liver. Plato, however, observes that they are too dull and obscure for any definite conclusions to be drawn from them. He also rejects vaticination from victims —The spleen is intended to keep the liver pure.

[125] 71 E: μαντικὴν ἀφροσύνῃ θεὸς ἀνθρωπίνῃ δέδωκεν· οὐδεὶς ἔννους γὰρ ἐφάπτεται μαντικῆς ἐνθέου καὶ ἀληθοῦς ἀλλ' ἢ καθ' ὕπνον τὴν τῆς φρονήσεως πεδηθεὶς δύναμιν ἢ διὰ νόσον ἢ διά τινα ἐθουσιασμὸν παραλλάξας. Only the interpretation of prophecy is matter of reason and reflection Cf Laws, 719 C, and supra, p 176 sq, and, on the other side, p 191. Prophetic and significant dreams occur, as is well known, in the Phædr. 60 D sq, and Crito, 44 A, and in the Eudemus (Cic Dio. 1. 25, 53) composed by Aristotle as Plato's scholar; and the belief in presentiments, expressing themselves sometimes in sleep, sometimes in waking, may have been seriously held by Plato, on the

other organs: those of digestion he especially regards as a place of reserve for food, the decomposition of which he derives from the natural warmth of the body.[126] Some other physiological theories of his can in this place be only shortly indicated.[127]

Plants[128] and animals,[129] he says, are formed for the sake of man; plants to be his food, animals to serve as an abode for those human souls which have rendered themselves unworthy of a higher life. Plants too are living beings, but their soul is of the lowest kind, capable neither of reason nor opinion, but only of desire and sensation; a soul only moved from without, to which has been denied the motion that proceeds from and returns into itself[130]—self-consciousness; therefore, plants can never change their place. The Timæus represents animals as having been all originally

precedent of the Socratic Dæmon. On the other hand, he certainly remarks (and this is the more correct consequence from his point of view) that the animal desires assert themselves more unrestrainedly in dreams, because in sleep the rational life recedes into the background. (Rep. ix 571 C, where Schleiermacher, Pl. WW. III. 1. 601 tries to find too much; the example which Plato quotes is taken from Sophocl. Œdip. Rex, 981)

[126] 71 E sq.; cf. 80 D sq.

[127] Cf. 44 E sq. on the limbs; 73 A sqq. on the formation of marrow, brain, flesh, and bones; 75 D on the mouth; 75 E sqq. on the skin, hair, and nails.

[128] 77 A–C, see p 416, 83.

[129] 90 E, 91 D sqq., with which further cf the quotation on 392 sqq.

[130] 77 B: πάσχον γὰρ διατελεῖ πάντα, στραφέντι δ' αὐτῷ ἐν ἑαυτῷ περὶ ἑαυτὸ τὴν μὲν ἔξωθεν ἀπωσαμένῳ κίνησιν τῇ δ' οἰκείᾳ χρησαμένῳ τῶν αὑτοῦ τι λογίσασθαι κατιδόντι φύσιν οὐ παραδέδωκεν ἡ γένεσις. These words have generally been wrongly construed, e g. by Stallbaum, Martin (i. 207, ii 322), and by H Muller. The translation is· 'Its γένεσις has not conferred upon it such a nature as to repel movements coming from without, while it moves in and round itself' (or joining φύσιν with κατιδόντι, 'has not granted it to repel, &c.'),'but to avail itself of its own motion, and so to perceive somewhat of its own conditions, and to reflect on them.'

men; the Phædrus,[131] on the contrary, discriminates between animal souls proper, and souls which have descended out of human into animal forms; at the same time intimating that the soul of man as such can never become that of a beast. According to the measure and the nature of the soul's unfaithfulness to its human vocation is regulated the animal body it is to occupy.[132] So that in this theory the generic differences in the animal world are a consequence of human conduct. Elsewhere, however, these are more truly regarded as necessary for the general completeness of the universe.[133]

Even the distinctions of sex and the propagation of mankind are made to result from the misdeeds through which some human souls were degraded into lower forms:[134] though this is hardly consistent either with the unconditional necessity of propagation,[135] or with the essential equality of the two sexes,[136] which Plato elsewhere asserts.

The Timæus, in its last section, treats at considerable length of diseases; not only diseases of the body,[137] but such maladies of mind as result from bodily

---

[131] 249 B, see p. 411. 55.
[132] Tim. 91 D sqq., Phædo, 82 A, cf. supra, pp. 178, 394, 411, 499 sq.
[133] See p 388
[134] Tim 90 E sqq, 41 E sqq. (see p. 392). In the first of these passages sexual impulse is thus explained The male semen (an efflux of the spinal marrow) is like the corresponding matter in the female, a ζῷον ἔμψυχον. In the one there dwells a desire for ἐκροή, in the other for παιδοποιΐα, cf. the quotations from Hippo and Empedocles, vol. i. 216, 1; 645, 4, 3rd edit.
[135] Symp 206 B sqq.; Laws, iv. 721 B sq, vi. 773 E: see p. 193.
[136] Rep. v. 452 E sqq. I shall return to this point later on.
[137] 81 E–86 A Three causes of disease are mentioned: 1. The condition of the elementary materials. Some may be too abundant or too scanty, or not rightly apportioned, or some one organ may be acted

causes.[138] These are all placed in two classes: madness and ignorance. In comprehending under these two classes every species of immorality; in making State neglect and defective education, as well as bodily constitution, answerable for their existence; in laying greater stress, for the cure of even bodily diseases,[139] on rational care of the body than on medicine;[140] and above all, in insisting on the harmonious training at the whole man, the even balance of physical and mental education, and the perfecting of reason by means of science—in all this Plato points out the boundary of Physics, and leads us on to Ethics, which from the outset has been the proper goal of his physical investigations.[141]

upon by other kinds of fire, water, &c., than are proper for it (82 A sq., 86 A). 2. A second source of disease consists in the same deficiencies with respect to the organic elements (marrow, bones, flesh, sinews, blood). The perversion of the natural order in the production of these organic materials out of one another is especially dangerous. Naturally, the flesh together with the sinews is formed out of the blood, the bones out of flesh and sinews, the marrow out of the bones. If instead of this a counter-formation in the opposite way sets in, the most grievous sufferings result (82 B sqq.). 3. A third class of diseases spring from irregularity in the apportionment and the condition of the πνεύματα, the mucus, and the bile (84 C sqq.). Further details are given in Martin, ii. 347-359; Susemihl, ii. 460 sqq.

[138] 86 B-87 B.
[139] 87 C-90 D.
[140] Cf. Rep. iii. 405 C sqq., and Schleiermacher, Werke z Philosophie, iii. 273 sqq.
[141] 27 A. It is proposed that Timæus should begin with the origin of the world and end with mankind, whose education Socrates had described the day before in the dialogue on the State.

CHAPTER X.

ETHICS.

THE philosophy of Plato is primarily Ethical. He starts from the Socratic enquiries on virtue, which furnished the material for the earliest development of his dialectic method, and for those conceptual determinations from which the doctrine of Ideas eventually sprang. His own procedure is essentially directed not only to theoretic science, but to moral training and the Socratic knowledge-of-self.[1] He would have been untrue to himself and to the spirit of the Socratic teaching had he not constantly paid special attention to such questions. But the later development of his system required that the ethical views acquired during his intercourse with Socrates should be essentially enlarged, more precisely defined, recast, and applied to actual conditions. Therefore, although his own speculation was from the commencement under the influence of the Socratic Ethics, the form which he gave to ethical theories was conditioned by his Metaphysics and Anthropology, and also more remotely by his Physics; and apart from these it cannot be fully explained. That which is the starting-

[1] See p. 216 sq., and Phædr. 229 E sq.

point in the historical beginning of his system appears in the perfected system at the end also. The purity, fervour, and decisiveness of his moral endeavour, his conviction of the necessity of moral knowledge, the fundamental conceptions of his Ethics, Plato brought with him from the Socratic school. But the lofty Idealism by which his Ethics so greatly transcended those of Socrates—the accurate determination which they received in the concept of the virtues and of the State—would never have been attained but for the doctrine of Ideas and the Anthropological part of the system. As to their particular contents, the Platonic Ethics fall under three divisions of enquiry:—

I. The ultimate aim of moral activity, or the highest Good.
II. The realisation of the Good in individuals; or Virtue.
III. Its realisation in the Commonwealth; or the State.[2]

I. *The Highest Good.* Socrates had designated the Good as the supreme and ultimate object of all human endeavour; and the concept of the Good was the primary ethical idea of all the minor Socratic schools.[3] By the Good, however, Socrates had only understood that which is a good for man and conduces to happiness. This, indeed, naturally resulted from the Greek view of Ethics, and so far Plato and Socrates are agreed. The question of the highest moral problem

[2] Cf. Ritter, ii. 445.
[3] See Pt. i. 124 sqq., 221, 257, 297 sq., 304.

coincides with that of the highest Good, and this with the enquiry for happiness. Happiness is the possession of the Good, and the Good is that which all desire.[4] But wherein does the Good or happiness consist? A twofold answer to this question may be deduced from the presuppositions of the Platonic system. The Idea is that which alone is real; Matter is not merely Non-being, but the opposite of the Idea, hindering its pure manifestation.[5] The soul, in its true essence, is declared to be an incorporeal spirit destined for the intuition of the Idea. Hence morality might be regarded negatively; the highest end and Good might be sought in withdrawing from the life of sense and retiring into pure contemplation. But the Idea is the underlying ground of all

[4] Symp. 204 E sqq : κτήσει γὰρ ἀγαθῶν οἱ εὐδαίμονες εὐδαίμονες καὶ οὐκέτι προσδεῖ ἐρέσθαι, ἵνα τί δὲ βούλεται εὐδαίμων εἶναι ὁ βουλόμενος, &c. All strive after an enduring possession of the good: ἔστιν ἄρα ξυλλήβδην ὁ ἔρως τοῦ τὸ ἀγαθὸν αὑτῷ εἶναι ἀεί. Euthyd. 288 E sqq.: no knowledge is valuable unless it is useful to us, i.e. (289 C sq., 290 B, D, 291 B, 292 B, E) unless it makes us happy. Phileb. 11 B sq.: see p. 280, 148, cf. Gorg. 470 D sq., 492 D sqq.; Rep. i. 354 A, et alibi; Arist. Eth. Nicom i. 2, beginn. ὀνόματι μὲν οὖν σχεδὸν ὑπὸ τῶν πλείστων ὁμολογεῖται (τί τὸ ἀγαθόν). τὴν γὰρ εὐδαιμονίαν καὶ οἱ πολλοὶ καὶ οἱ χαρίεντες λέγουσιν, τὸ δ' εὖ ζῆν καὶ τὸ εὖ πράττειν ταὐτὸν ὑπολαμβάνουσι τῷ εὐδαιμονεῖν. The fact that Plato censures the confusion of the good with the pleasant, or the foundation of morality on pleasure and external advantage (see pp. 182,185, 186 sq.), proves nothing against this, for happiness is not identical with pleasure or advantage; nor is there any real contradiction involved when, in Rep iv. beginn. vii. 519 E, he explains that the enquiry into the State must be conducted without regard to the happiness of the individual members, for this only refers to the good of the whole being prior to that of the individuals. Indeed (loc. cit. 420 B), happiness is pronounced to be the highest aim for the State, just as afterwards, 444 E, ix. 576 C-592 B. the advantage of justice, the happiness or unhappiness involved in every constitution, whether of state or soul, is made the basis of their different values.

[5] Cf. pp. 315, 340 sq.

form, and the cause of all that is good in the world of Sense. This aspect might be more prominently brought forward for its representation in human life; and thus among the constituents of the highest Good might be reckoned, side by side with the knowledge of the pure Idea, the harmonious introduction of the Idea into sensible existence, and the satisfaction of which this is the source. Both of these enunciations are to be found in Plato, though they are not so entirely separated as to be mutually exclusive. The first occurs in passages where the highest problem of life is sought in flight from sensuality; the second, in places where even sensuous beauty is described as worthy of love; and external activity, sensible pleasure, is included among the component parts of the highest Good.

We meet with the former view as early as the Theætetus.[6] As earthly existence, says Plato in that dialogue, can never be free from evil, we must flee away as quickly as possible from this world to God, by making ourselves like to Him through virtue and wisdom. This thought is still further expanded in the Phædo,[7] where the deliverance of the soul from the

[6] 176 A: ἀλλ' οὔτ' ἀπολέσθαι τὰ κακὰ δυνατόν· ὑπεναντίον γάρ τι τῷ ἀγαθῷ ἀεὶ εἶναι ἀνάγκη· οὔτ' ἐν θεοῖς αὐτὰ ἱδρύσθαι, τὴν δὲ θνητὴν φύσιν καὶ τόνδε τὸν τόπον περιπολεῖ ἐξ ἀνάγκης· διὸ καὶ πειρᾶσθαι χρὴ ἐνθένδε ἐκεῖσε φεύγειν ὅτι τάχιστα· φυγὴ δὲ ὁμοίωσις τῷ θεῷ κατὰ τὸ δυνατόν. ὁμοίωσις δὲ δίκαιον καὶ ὅσιον μετὰ φρονήσεως γενέσθαι. On the latter principle cf Rep. vi. 500 B; Tim. 47 B, where it is found as a natural consequence that he who contemplates God and His eternal ordinance does himself become well ordered in soul.

[7] E g 64 sqq., 64 E: οὐκοῦν ὅλως δοκεῖ σοι ἡ τοῦ τοιούτου (τοῦ φιλοσόφου) πραγματεία οὐ περὶ τὸ σῶμα εἶναι, ἀλλὰ καθ' ὅσον δύναται ἀφεστάναι αὐτοῦ πρὸς δὲ τὴν ψυχὴν τετράφθαι; 67 A: ἐν ᾧ ἂν ζῶμεν οὕτως, ὡς ἔοικεν, ἐγγυτάτω ἐσόμεθα τοῦ εἰδέναι, ἐὰν ὅτι μάλιστα μηδὲν ὁμιλῶμεν τῷ σώματι,

body is considered the most necessary and beneficial of all things, and the philosopher's special aim and concern. To the same effect is the celebrated passage of the Republic,[8] which represents us as living here like prisoners in a dark cave, who are accustomed to see nothing but dim shadows, and are with difficulty brought to the vision of the Real, in the daylight of the Idea. In connection with this, there is the reiterated assurance[9] that the true philosopher would never voluntarily descend from the heights of scientific contemplation to mind the affairs of the State, but only when compelled to do so. Souls, so far as they are faithful to their destiny, are only prevailed on by Necessity to enter this earthly existence; and those who have entered it, and recognise their true vocation, trouble themselves as little as they can with the body and its concerns. Here the body appears as a fetter, a dungeon of the soul: the grave of its higher life.[10] It is an evil to which the soul is chained, and from which it longs to be free as soon as possible.[11] The body is, indeed, the cause of all evil; for though unrighteous-

μηδὲ κοινωνῶμεν, ὅ τι μὴ πᾶσα ἀνάγκη, μηδὲ ἀναπιμπλώμεθα τῆς τούτου φύσεως, ἀλλὰ καθαρεύωμεν ἀπ' αὐτοῦ, ἕως ἂν ὁ θεὸς αὐτὸς ἀπολύσῃ ἡμᾶς. Cf 83.

[8] vii 514 sqq

[9] Rep. vii 519 C sqq.; cf 1. 345 E sqq., 347 B sq.; Theæt. 172 C sqq, especially 173 E. It is not correct to say that the discussion in these passages is throughout only concerned with the immoral and incomplete states (Brandis, Gr -röm Phil. 11. a 516)· Rep vii 519 treats of the Platonic state

[10] Phædo, 62 B; Crat. 400 B. In the former the doctrine of the Mysteries, ὡς ἔν τινι φρουρᾷ ἐσμεν οἱ ἄνθρωποι, in the latter the Orphic comparison of the σῶμα to a σῆμα and a prison, are quoted; but only in the first passage with an expression of assent. Cf. vol. 1. 388 sq

[11] Phædo, 66 B: ὅτι, ἕως ἂν τὸ σῶμα ἔχωμεν καὶ ξυμπεφυρμένη ᾖ ἡμῶν ἡ ψυχὴ μετὰ τοῦ τοιούτου κακοῦ, οὐ μήποτε κτησώμεθα ἱκανῶς οὗ ἐπιθυμοῦμεν φαμὲν δὲ τοῦτο εἶναι τὸ ἀληθές.

ness has place at first in the soul, and is its own deed—though, consequently, it is the soul itself that in the world beyond will be cleansed from it and punished for it; yet the soul would have no motive or inducement to evil if it were not in the body. When it entered the body it first acquired those lower elements by which its proper nature is hidden and defaced.[12] From thence proceed all disturbances to spiritual activity—all the appetites and passions which seduce us from our true destiny.[13] Philosophy is therefore essentially a purification.[14] As perfect deliverance from all evils is to be found only in the separation of the soul from the body,—so the nearest earthly approach to such a deliverance is that philosophic dying, by which alone the soul even after the body's death is fitted for incorporeal existence.[15]

---

[12] See p. 414.

[13] Phædo, loc cit.· μυρίας μὲν γὰρ ἡμῖν ἀσχολίας παρέχει τὸ σῶμα διὰ τὴν ἀναγκαίαν τροφήν· ἔτι δὲ ἄν τινες νόσοι προσπέσωσιν, ἐμποδίζουσιν ἡμῶν τὴν τοῦ ὄντος θήραν, ἐρώτων δὲ καὶ ἐπιθυμιῶν καὶ φόβων καὶ εἰδώλων παντοδαπῶν καὶ φλυαρίας ἐμπίπλησιν ἡμᾶς πολλῆς, ὥστε τὸ λεγόμενον ὡς ἀληθῶς τῷ ὄντι ὑπ' αὐτοῦ οὐδὲ φρονῆσαι ἡμῖν ἐγγίνεται οὐδέποτε οὐδέν. καὶ γὰρ πολέμους καὶ στάσεις καὶ μάχας οὐδὲν ἄλλο παρέχει ἢ τὸ σῶμα καὶ αἱ τούτου ἐπιθυμίαι, seeing that it is always a question of possession, and possession is coveted for the body's sake. The worst point is that the soul in its thinking activities is continually hindered by the body, so that it can only arrive at the intuition of truth by withdrawing from the body. Cf. 82 E sq., 64 D sqq.; Rep. ix. 588 B sqq. is quite in accordance with this exposition, in showing all kinds of immorality to depend merely on the triumph of the animal over the human element of lust and savage, irrational courage over reason, for these lower elements of the soul arise from its connection with the body.

[14] Phædo, 67 C· κάθαρσις δὲ εἶναι οὐ τοῦτο ξυμβαίνει, ὅπερ πάλαι ἐν τῷ λόγῳ λέγεται, τὸ χωρίζειν ὅτι μάλιστα ἀπὸ τοῦ σώματος τὴν ψυχήν, &c., ibid. 69 B; cf. also Soph. 230 D.

[15] Phædo, loc. cit. Cf. the quotations p 393, 13; pp. 412, 413 and Crat. 403 E: it is wise of Pluto not to have any intercourse with mankind except ἐπειδὰν ἡ ψυχὴ καθαρὰ ᾖ πάντων τῶν περὶ τὸ σῶμα κακῶν καὶ ἐπιθυμιῶν, for it is then

If Plato had stopped short at this view of morality, the result would have been a negative theory, at variance not only with the spirit of Greek antiquity, but also with many essential elements of his own philosophy. He proceeds, however, to complete it with other representations, in which a more positive importance is ascribed to sensible things and our concern with them. A series of these representations we have already noticed in his doctrine of Love. The proper object of this Love is that which is desirable in and for itself, namely the Idea; but the sensible Phenomenon is here treated not merely in the manner of the Phædo, as that which conceals the Idea, but also as that which reveals it. The enquiry of the Philebus concerning the highest Good has the same tendency. How this dialogue refutes the doctrine of pleasure has been already shown: it is further to be noted that the argument does not side unconditionally even with the opposite view (the Cynic-Megarian identification of the Good and intellectual wisdom [16]), but describes the highest Good as compounded of various constituents. Intelligence and reason, we are told, are certainly far above pleasure, inasmuch as the latter is related to the Unlimited or Indefinite, and the former in the closest manner to the First Cause of all.[17] But yet a life without any sensation of pleasure or pain would be pure apathy, not worth wishing for.[18] And within the sphere of intellect,

only that any moral influence can be successfully exercised upon it.

[16] We have already seen, Pt. i. p. 261, 5, that it is probably against these persons, and next to them, against the Cynics, that the polemic of the Philebus is directed.

[17] Phil. 28 A sqq., 64 C sqq; cf. p. 185.

[18] 21 D sq., 60 E sq, 63 E: we

pure Ideal knowledge (though far higher than aught besides) cannot in itself suffice: Right Opinion must be added to it, otherwise man could never find his way upon earth. Further, Art (the Philebus especially mentions music) is indispensable to the adornment of life; in fact, all knowledge is so, and every kind of knowledge; for each in some way participates in truth.[19] Pleasure cannot be quite so unconditionally reckoned a part of the highest Good. We must here discriminate true and pure sensations of delight,[20] and necessary, harmless, and passionless pleasures (above all, those that are consistent with reason and health of mind), from deceptive, impure, and sickly pleasures. The former alone can be included in the good.[21] On the whole we get this result.[22] The first and chief constituent of the supreme Good is participation in the Eternal nature of proportion (in the Idea).[23] The

may observe how briefly this point is always settled—doubtless because Plato, after expressing himself elsewhere so strongly against pleasure, is at a loss how to assign it a place and value scientifically. Plato's own explanations, Phil. ii. B, Rep. vi 505 B, and the Megaric and Cynic doctrines on the point (see Pt. i. pp. 221 sq., 257 sqq.) do not allow us to suppose that it was ' because he did not feel the necessity of refuting those who estimate φρόνησις too high' (more precisely, who consider φρόνησις alone to be the highest good, entirely excluding pleasure), Ribbing, Plat. Ideenl. i. 107 sq.

[19] 62 B sqq.

[20] Those which do not depend on an illusion, and are not conditioned by the opposite of pleasure, as is generally the case (see p. 185 sq.) in the pleasures of sense. The pleasure connected with virtue and knowledge is not specially represented (see p. 186; Laws, ii 662 B sqq, 667 C; Rep i. 328 D, vi 485 D; Phileb. 40 B sq.; Phædr. 276 D; Tim. 59 C).

[21] 62 D sqq, cf. 36 C–53 C.

[22] 64 C sq, 66 sq.

[23] 66 A. ὡς ἡδονὴ κτῆμα οὐκ ἔστι πρῶτον οὐδ' αὖ δεύτερον, ἀλλὰ πρῶτον μέν πῃ περὶ μέτρον καὶ τὸ μέτριον καὶ καίριον, καὶ πάντα ὁπόσα χρὴ τοιαῦτα νομίζειν τὴν ἀΐδιον ᾑρῆσθαι [Herm. εἰρῆσθαι, which, however, does not give a suitable sense] φύσιν . . . δεύτερον μὴν περὶ τὸ σύμμετρον καὶ καλὸν καὶ τὸ τέλεον καὶ ἱκανὸν καὶ πάνθ' ὁπόσα

THE HIGHEST GOOD.

second is the realisation of this Idea in actuality; the formation of that which is harmonious, beautiful, and

τῆς γενεᾶς αὖ ταύτης ἐστίν. This passage, however, gives rise to a difficulty. As the μέτρον and σύμμετρον are mentioned here quite generally, and both are separated from νοῦς, it might appear as if something not belonging to man but existing externally were intended, by the μέτρον, &c., the Idea of the Good (Hermann, Ind. lect Marb. 183⅔, Plat. 690 sq A 648, 656; Trendelenburg, de Philebi Consil 16, Steger, Plat Stud. ii. 59) or even the Ideas in general (Brandis, ii. a. 490), by the σύμμετρον, &c., everything beautiful in the world. On the other hand, the Philebus generally has not only aimed at giving a definition of the highest Good for mankind (see p. 280), but in the passage before us it treats expressly of the κτῆμα πρῶτον, δεύτερον, &c. The Good, therefore, is here considered not in its essence, but in reference to the subject in which it occurs (so Stallbaum in Phileb Prolegg. 2 A p. 74 sq.; Ritter, ii. 463; Wehrmann, Plat de s. bono doctr. 90 sq.; Steinhart, Pl. WW. iv. 659 sq.; Susemihl, genet. Entw. ii. 52, Philologus Supplementhl. ii. 1, 77 sqq.; Strümpell, Gesch. d pr. Phil. d. Gr. i. 263 sqq.). Plato says of the first and second term of his classification that they are περὶ μέτρον, περὶ τὸ σύμμετρον, &c., of the following simply : τὸ τοίνυν τρίτον νοῦν καὶ φρόνησιν τιθείς, &c. As the first element of the highest Good, participation in the μέτρον is specified (i e. immutable laws form the measure of all living activities); as the second element, the beauty and completeness proceeding thence. The first of these points was previously described (64 D sqq.) more definitely as the unity of κάλλος, συμμετρία and ἀλήθεια; it must then be intended to stand generally for the Ideal in human nature, from which springs all that is precious and really true in life, while the second point comprehends the effects proceeding from the former But we have still to explain how it is that both these are brought prominently forward, and that νοῦς gets only the third place (cf. Schleiermacher, Platon's WW. ii. 3, 133 sq.; Ribbing, Plat. Ideenl i. 287 sq.); and the answer is, that as the highest Good, according to Plato, does not consist in an individual activity, but in the whole of all activities which are agreeable to nature, the first condition of it (the αἰτία ξυμπάσης μίξεως, the τιμιώτατον ἅμα καὶ μάλιστ' αἴτιον therein, 64 C sq., 65 A) is the harmony of human existence. By virtue of this the production of such a whole is to be aimed at; this harmony we have displayed in our two first determinations, and then come the individual Goods. Still there remains a certain obscurity in the exposition of the Philebus, even if it be recollected that one and the same concept, that of the Good, is intended to denote that which is highest in man and in the universe. This inconvenience makes itself felt much more strongly in the Republic, vi. 505 B sqq, than in the Philebus (and

perfect. The third, reason and intelligence. The fourth, special sciences, the arts, and right opinions. The fifth and last, pure and painless pleasures of the senses.[24] We cannot fail to perceive the moderation, the respect for all that is in human nature, the striving for the harmonious culture of the whole man by which the Platonic Ethics prove themselves such genuine fruits of the Greek national mind. Plato is far removed from the apathy of the Cynics, as may be seen in his remark[25] that it is impossible not to sorrow under heavy trials (for instance, the death of a son); all that can then be expected of a man is moderation and control of his grief. That life according to nature, which the older Academy adopted as its watchword—that Metriopathy, which perhaps descended to the later Sceptics from the New Academy—is entirely in harmony with the spirit of Plato.

II. *Virtue.* The essential and sole means of happiness is virtue. As each nature can only attain its destined end by the virtue befitting it, so it is with the soul. Only in attaining that end can the soul live well; if it misses this, its life must be evil. In the one case it will be happy; in the other, miserable.

---

therefore cannot be turned into a proof of the spuriousness of the latter, with Schaarschmidt Samml. plat. Schr. 305 sq.). We must not attribute too much importance to such classifications in Plato, nor make the distance between their particular terms absolutely the same, they belong to a mannerism of style in which he allows himself every freedom: cf. Phædr. 248 D, Soph. 231 D sqq.; Rep. ix. 587 B sqq., and supra, p. 219, 147; Plat. Stud. p. 228.

[24] With the argument of the Philebus may be compared the discussion of the Laws, v. 728 C sqq.: cf. iv. 717 A sqq., on the relative values of the different goods; which, however, is too unscientific to be noticed here.

[25] Rep. x. 603 E sq.

Virtue is therefore the cause of happiness, vice of misery.[26] Virtue is the right constitution, the internal order, harmony, and health of the soul: vice is the contrary condition. To enquire whether justice or injustice is the more advantageous for man, is no wiser than to question whether it is better to be sick or well; to have a marred and useless soul, or a soul that is capable and strong;[27] to subject the human and divine element in our nature to the animal, or the animal to the divine.[28] The virtuous man alone is free, and follows his own will; for in his soul it is Reason that bears rule—the part to which rule belongs. He only is rich in himself, cheerful and at rest. Wherever passion occupies the throne, the soul is essentially poor and enslaved: fear and sorrow and disquietude run riot through it.[29] Only he who takes hold on the Eternal and fills himself therewith can be truly satisfied. All other delights are alloyed and delusive, in propor-

---

[26] Rep. i. 353 A sqq, e.g.: ἆρ' οὖν ποτε ψυχὴ τὰ αὑτῆς ἔργα εὖ ἀπεργάσεται στρεφομένη τῆς οἰκείας ἀρετῆς, ἢ ἀδύνατοι; 'Αδύνατον. 'Ανάγκη ἄρα κακῇ ψυχῇ κακῶς ἄρχειν καὶ ἐπιμελεῖσθαι, τῇ δὲ ἀγαθῇ πάντα ταῦτα εὖ πράττειν ... Ἡ μὲν ἄρα δικαία ψυχὴ καὶ ὁ δίκαιος ἀνὴρ εὖ βιώσεται, κακῶς δὲ ὁ ἄδικος ... 'Αλλὰ μὴν ὅ γε εὖ ζῶν μακάριός τε καὶ εὐδαίμων, ὁ δὲ μὴ τἀναντία ... Ὁ μὲν δίκαιος ἄρα εὐδαίμων, ὁ δ' ἄδικος ἄθλιος. Similarly Gorg. 506 D sqq. cf. Laws, ii. 662 B sqq., v. 733 D sqq.

[27] Gorg. 504 A sqq., Rep iv. 443 C–445 B cf. viii 554 E, x. 609 B sq ; Phædo, 93 B sq.; Tim. 87 C cf. Laws, x. 906 C, and supra, p 187. Hence, Rep. iii. 392 A, Laws, ii 660 E sqq., to portray injustice as profitable, the bad as happy, the just as unhappy, is a heresy, radically pernicious, and not to be tolerated by the State.

[28] From this point of view the contrast of morality and immorality is exhibited in the detailed discussion, Rep ix 588 B–592 B : cf. Phædr. 230 A.

[29] Rep ix. 577 D sq , with the addition that this holds good in the highest degree of those who externally have the very highest power, viz tyrants Phædr. 279 C: πλούσιον δὲ νομίζοιμι τὸν σοφόν.

tion as they deviate from the only true pleasure—that of the Philosopher. And true philosophy and perfect morality are the same.[30] Virtue can therefore dispense with those impure motives by which it is generally recommended.[31] It carries in itself its own reward, as vice does its own punishment. Nothing better can befal a man than that he should grow like the Good and the Divine: nothing worse than that he should become like the evil and the Non-divine.[32] Even if we put aside all the advantages which virtue ensures —if we suppose the impossible case of a righteous man mistaken by gods and men, or an evil-doer concealing his wickedness from both—still the former would be the happy person, the latter the unhappy.[33] That this, however, is quite inconceivable—that right and wrong, as a rule even in this life, but certainly in the life to come, are duly recompensed, Plato constantly affirms as his settled conviction.[34] This seems to him necessary, on every account; as little can the righteous man be deserted by God,[35] as the wicked escape His punishment: he must either be cured by it of his ungodliness;

---

[30] Rep. ix 583 B–588 A, where finally this thought is, strangely enough, and of course by a very arbitrary calculation, reduced to the formula that the philosopher is 729 times happier than the tyrant. (On this number cf. vol. i. 368, 4, 3rd edit.) The same result was previously (580 D sqq., cf. Laws, ii. 663 C) obtained from the consideration that only the philosopher knows how to judge of the worth of different lives, and consequently that which he prefers must be the best. Cf. the quotation, p 187.

[31] See p. 182; Theæt. 176 B.

[32] Theæt. 177 B sqq.; Laws, iv. 716 C sq, v. 728 B.

[33] Rep iv. 444 E sq.; cf. with ii. 360 E–367 E, x. 612 A sq.

[34] Rep. x. 612 B sqq. et passim; see supra, p. 207 sq. 215, 134, 218.

[35] Rep. x 612 E.; Theæt 176 C sqq., Apol. 41 C sq.: Laws, iv. 716 C sq.

VIRTUE.

or, if he be incurable, must serve as a warning to others.[36] But as Plato holds moral obligation and the unconditional worth of virtue independently of future retribution, this view does not affect the purity of his principles.[37] The Socratic doctrine of expediency[38] is immeasurably transcended by Plato; it has become purified and deepened in the spirit of the Socratic life.

[36] Plato considers punishment in general as a moral necessity. For its particular justification he combines the two points of view, of improvement and deterrence. Prot 324 B: ὁ μετὰ λόγου ἐπιχειρῶν κολάζειν οὐ τοῦ παρεληλυθότος ἕνεκα ἀδικήματος τιμωρεῖται—οὐ γὰρ ἂν τό γε πραχθὲν ἀγένητον θείη—ἀλλὰ τοῦ μέλλοντος χάριν, ἵνα μὴ αὖθις ἀδικήσῃ μήτε αὐτὸς οὗτος μήτε ἄλλος ὁ τοῦτον ἰδὼν κολασθέντα. Punishment is a means of purifying the soul from wickedness (Gorg. 478 E sqq., 480 A sq , 505 B, 525 B sq.; see p. 379 sq ; Rep. ii. 380 A, ix. 591 A sqq.; Laws, v. 728 C, ix 862 D; ibid. xi. 934 A, where retaliation as the object of punishment is expressly rejected, as in Prot. loc. cit.), indeed, Plato thinks it quite indispensable for this purpose: Gorg. loc. cit., Rep. ix. 591 A sq., he goes so far as to declare that everyone must wish to be punished for his transgressions because it is better to be healed than to remain sick, and Rep. x. 613 A, he would consider many evils which befall the just as an inevitable punishment of previous sins. The theory of the future expiation of curable injustice is based on the same view (see p. 390 sq.) But, on the other hand, there are absolute punishments, for the justification of which this definition does not suffice, such, for instance, as the punishment of death in civil administration, and of eternal damnation in divine justice. Some further end in punishment must be therefore supposed the criminal who is beyond reformation is at least made useful for the general good, by being made to contribute to the maintenance of moral order as a deterrent example (Gorg. 525 B sq.; Laws, v. 728 C, ix 854 E, 862 E) With this is connected, as regards the future, the conception of a natural distribution of individuals in the universe (see supra, p 409, 53), with reference to the State, the idea (in which can be traced the germ of a theory of elimination) that it must be purified of irreclaimable criminals by putting them to death or banishing them (Polit 293 D, 308 E; Laws, ix. 862 E. The latter passage adds that it is really better for themselves that such men should live no longer).

[37] After having first proved the superiority of justice as such, and apart from its results, he turns to the latter with the words, Rep. x. 612 B· νῦν ἤδη ἀνεπίφθονόν ἐστι πρὸς ἐκείνοις καὶ τοὺς μισθοὺς τῇ δικαιοσύνῃ καὶ τῇ ἄλλῃ ἀρετῇ ἀποδοῦναι.

[36] See Pt. i. p. 125 sqq.

Socrates had made virtue to consist entirely in knowledge. He had consequently maintained that there could in reality be but One Virtue, and that the disposition to virtue must be similar in all. He had assumed that virtue, like knowledge, could be taught.[39] In all these respects Plato at first followed him; as against the ordinary notions of virtue he would indeed always have acknowledged the view of Socrates to be substantially correct.[40] But riper reflection led him in after-life to modify the Socratic doctrines and to determine them more accurately. He became convinced that side by side with perfect virtue, which is, no doubt, founded on knowledge, the unscientific virtue of ordinary men has also its value; that though the former is based on instruction, and the latter only on custom, yet that this virtue of custom precedes the higher kind as an indispensable preparatory stage. He observed the variety of moral dispositions, and could not deny its influence on the forming of morality in individuals. Lastly, he learned to combine the distinction of many virtues with the Socratic doctrine of the Unity of all virtue; for he looked on the particular virtues as so many different sides of a proportion, which considered as a whole is virtue. These determinations we have now to examine in detail.

All virtue presupposes a natural disposition for virtue, which is not merely bestowed on human nature in general, but varies according to temperaments and individuals. Plato instances the contrast of σωφροσύνη

[39] See Pt i. p. 117 sqq   [40] Cf. p. 175 sqq.

and ἀνδρεία, of fiery temperaments and calm, as a difference in natural disposition.[41] He also speaks of a special gift for philosophy,[42] and in the Republic[43] indicates a threefold gradation of capacity. On the lowest stage he places those who by nature are limited to the virtues indispensable for all classes,—justice and self-control,—and even in the exercise of these require external guidance; on the second stage, those who, in addition, are capable of valour; on the third and highest, such as are endowed with philosophy. If this series of dispositions be combined with the above-stated theory of the divisions of the soul, and with that of the virtues, on which we are just entering, it would seem that the disposition to virtue varies according as the moral impulse is chiefly manifested in the appetitive, courageous, or rational part of the soul. It is quite consistent with this that the different grades of moral disposition should be related to each other, as the diffcrent parts of the soul, that the higher should include the lower. The disposition to philosophy at any rate (Rep. vi. 487 A) seems to comprehend all other capacity for virtue; and similarly the superior ranks in the State are, in addition to their own virtues, to possess the virtues of the lower. Plato, however, has nowhere expressly drawn out this parallel, and the exposition of the Politicus would not fall in with it.

[41] Polit. 306 A sqq , cf. Rep. iii. 410 D. The statement of the Laws, xii. 963 E, that courage dwells even in children and beasts, is not applicable here · it is not the mere disposition to courage that is referred to in that passage, and in Rep. iv. 441 A we certainly find the statement made with regard to θυμός.

[42] Rep. v. 474 C, vi. 487 A

[43] iii. 415, in the myth about the different mixture of the souls in the three ranks.

Self-control is there not subordinated to valour; they are co-ordinated in relative opposition.

In directly identifying virtue with knowledge Socrates left only one way open for the cultivation of the moral disposition, the way of intellectual instruction. Plato in his earliest dialogues expresses himself in a similar manner, but even in the Meno he has discovered that there are two guides to virtue, Right Opinion and scientific Knowledge; and though the one rests on cognition, and the other is uncertain and blind, still he allows that this traditional goodness has produced brave men and noble deeds.[44] In the Republic he goes a step farther, plainly saying that ordinary virtue, founded on habit, custom, and Right Opinion, must precede philosophy and philosophic morality; for the rulers of his State are first to be educated by music and gymnastic to the lower kind of virtue, and subsequently only, by scientific instruction, to the higher.[45] Thus the opposition of philosophic and ordinary virtue with which Plato, as a disciple of Socrates, began, transforms itself more and more into their close interdependence. Philosophic virtue presupposes the virtue of custom, and this again must perfect itself in the virtue of philosophy.

[44] See p. 175 sq.
[45] See p. 214 sq.: cf. Rep. vii. 518 D: αἱ μὲν τοίνυν ἄλλαι ἀρεταὶ καλούμεναι ψυχῆς κινδυνεύουσιν ἐγγύς τι εἶναι τῶν τοῦ σώματος· τῷ ὄντι γὰρ οὐκ ἐνοῦσαι πρότερον ὕστερον ἐμποιεῖσθαι ἔθεσί τε καὶ ἀσκήσεσιν· ἡ δὲ τοῦ φρονῆσαι παντὸς μᾶλλον θειοτέρου τινὸς τυγχάνει, ὡς ἔοικεν, οὖσα, ὃ τὴν μὲν δύναμιν οὐδέποτε ἀπόλλυσιν, ὑπὸ δὲ τῆς περιαγωγῆς (sc. πρὸς τὸ ὄν) χρήσιμόν τε καὶ ὠφέλιμον καὶ ἄχρηστον αὖ καὶ βλαβερὸν γίγνεται. Accordingly, we read, in what precedes, that a peculiar methodical and scientific education is necessary.

PRIMARY VIRTUES. 451

Plato's theories on the unity of virtue were also essentially rectified in his later years. He continued, indeed, to maintain that all particular virtues are only the realisation of the One Virtue, and that knowledge or wisdom could not be conceived without them; that justice must comprehend all virtues, and that in the perfect philosophic virtue all moral aims and endeavours unite; but, instead of stopping short at this point, he afterwards admitted that this unity of virtue did not exclude a plurality of virtues, and that some part of these (the rest being rejected) might be preparatory stages of moral training, without ceasing on that account to be real virtue.[46] The cause of this plurality is sought by Plato—and this is the peculiarity of his theory—not in the diversity of the objects to which moral activity refers, but in the diversity of mental powers at work in it (or, according to his view, the parts of the soul). In this way he arrives at the four primary virtues, which had indeed already appeared in the sophistic and Socratic enquiries, but seem first to have been definitively established by Plato, and only in his more advanced age.[47] If the virtue

[46] Cf Rep. iii. 410 B sq., where the warriors are trained to σωφροσύνη and ἀνδρεία by means of music and gymnastic, while knowledge, and consequently σοφία, are still absent, and Polit. 309 D sqq., where Plato calls these two virtues ἀρετῆς μέρη ἀνόμοια καὶ ἐπὶ τἀναντία φερόμενα. The contrast is put in a still stronger light in the Laws (i. 630 E sq., ii. 661 E sq., iii. 696 B, xii. 963 E and passim). Perhaps Plato intends this to refer only to the ordinary form of these virtues. Still, even then there is something strange in these expressions: in his earlier period Plato would scarcely have so expressed himself without at the same time intimating that a valour, e.g. which takes away all self-control, cannot be true valour.

[47] The Protagoras, 330 B sqq., mentions, as a fifth, piety (ὁσιότης), which is specially discussed in the Euthyphro (likewise in the Laches,

of the soul—the right constitution and proper relation of its parts—consists in the efficient performance of the special work of each and the harmony of all one with another. Reason, with clear discernment of that which is good for the soul, must be the ruler of the soul's life: and this is Wisdom. Secondly, Courage must defend the award of Reason concerning things to be feared and not to be feared, as against Pleasure and Pain: this is Valour, which thus appears in the Platonic theory as primarily directed by man against himself, and secondarily against external danger. In the third place, the inferior parts of the soul, Courage and Desire, must submit themselves to Reason, and come to an agreement with it, as to which is to obey and which to rule: this is Self-control or Temperance (σωφροσύνη). Fourthly and lastly, that there may be this harmony of the whole, each part of the soul must fulfil the task allotted to it, and not meddle with anything else. This is Justice,[48] which is thus primarily concerned with the

199 D, and Gorg. 507; the latter dialogue, however, seems to embrace wisdom in σωφροσύνη, which it proves to include all virtues). Similarly Xen. Mem. iv. 6, piety, justice, valour, and wisdom are mentioned, the latter in Mem. iii. 9, 4, is identified with σωφροσύνη. Rep. ii. 402 C does not give a complete classification of highest goods any more than Theæt. 176 B.

[48] The above account follows Rep. iv. 441 C-443 B. But a difficulty arises here owing to what is said about σωφροσύνη and its relation to δικαιοσύνη. Plato himself remarks before, in the discussion on the virtues of the state (see chap. xi.), 430 E, 431 E, that its σωφροσύνη, unlike its wisdom and valour, has its seat not merely in a part of the people, ἀλλὰ δι' ὅλης [τῆς πόλεως] ἀτεχνῶς τέταται, διὰ πασῶν παρεχομένη ξυνᾴδοντας, that it resembles a symphony and harmony; and he likewise says that the individual soul, 442 C, becomes σώφρων through the φιλία and ξυμφωνία of its parts. R. Hirzel is so far not incorrect when in his thorough

internal condition of the soul, the arrangement of its activities, and only indirectly with duties to fellow-creatures.[43]

examination of the present question ('über den Unterschied der δικαιοσύνη and σωφροσύνη,' &c., Hermes, viii. 379 sqq.) he insists on σωφροσύνη being not merely a virtue of the ἐπιθυμητικὸν, but of the entire soul. Still, however, it is not *the* virtue of it without any limitation, but only that virtue which consists in τό τε ἄρχον καὶ τὼ ἀρχομένω τὸ λογιστικὸν ὁμοδοξῶσι δεῖν ἄρχειν καὶ μὴ στασιάζωσιν αὐτῷ (442 D), in the right of reason to control courage and desire being unanimously acquiesced in by all parts of the soul. But for this it is necessary in the first place that the two inferior parts submit to the sway of reason (the μὴ στασιάζειν required of them). Reason has the consciousness of its right to rule over the others given to it in its σοφία, just as immediately as it has right opinions as to what is to be feared and what is not to be feared, in the observance of which by the spirited element true valour consists. And as in the latter there is no need of any further distinct activity on the part of reason beyond knowing, so also in the case of σωφροσύνη. Hence, if σωφροσύνη consists in a definite condition of the whole soul, in the acquiescence of its three parts in the rightful domination of reason, the condition for the existence of this state is in the subordination of the mortal to the immortal parts of the soul. And as σωφροσύνη cannot be called so exclusively the virtue of the ἐπιθυμητικὸν as valour that of the θυμὸς (which according to Hirzel's account, loc. cit., is done not only by the pseudo-Aristotle, De virt. et vit. 1249 a. 30 sqq., 1250 a. 7, but also by the genuine, Top. v 1, 7, 8, 129 a. 10, 136 b. 10, 138 b 1), the determination given in our text does not contradict Plato's meaning. For δικαιοσύνη Plato demands all three parts of the soul. It consists, according to 441 D sq. (cf. 433 A, and Hirzel, loc. cit. 396 sq.), in the fact that each part of the soul τὰ αὑτοῦ πράττει, which means that each part performs its own allotted task and at the same time does not hinder the others in the performance of theirs (the former is τὰ αὑτοῦ πράττειν, the latter μὴ πολυπραγμονεῖν, 433 A: cf. 434 B sq.). According to Plato this is the fundamental condition for the health and order of the life of the soul, just as τὰ αὑτοῦ πράττειν in the different ranks is the fundamental condition of the health and success of the life of the state. Justice is (as Hirzel, loc cit. rightly recognises) the root of all virtues, that ὃ πᾶσιν ἐκείνοις τὴν δύναμιν παρέσχεν ὥστε ἐγγενέσθαι, καὶ ἐγγενομένοις γε σωτηρίαν παρέχειν [-έχει], as is said in 433 B, with reference primarily to the virtues of the state. In the individual soul, by preventing its parts from ἀλλότρια πράττειν and πολυπραγμονεῖν, it makes a man at one with himself, σώφρων and ἡρμοσμένος (443 D), and therefore it can be identified with the health of the soul, ἀρετή in general (444 A sqq, 445 B).

[40] Cf. on this passage Rep. iv.

If, then, we imagine this theory of virtue farther extended so as to show, in the case of individuals, what activities proceed from each of the four virtues, and how each should manifest itself in the various relations of life, the result would be a representation of subjective morality from the Platonic point of view. Plato, however, as far as we can judge from his writings, never proposed to himself such a task; it would therefore be unwarrantable to attempt to construct from his scattered utterances a detailed system of duties or virtues.[50] We may, however, without any impropriety, omitting all the less distinctive characteristics, set forth his moral view of the world on certain points which deserve our attention, either in regard to their general acceptation among the Greeks, or their changed aspects among the moderns.

Some instances of this kind have already come before us. We have seen that Plato, in enunciating the principle that the just man should do only good, even to his enemies, greatly transcended the limits of ordinary Greek morality.[51] We have considered those singular views of truth and falsehood [52] which make the real lie to consist only in self-deception and to be under all circumstances and conditions reprehensible; whereas the deception of others is to be allowed in all cases, for their good: Plato in his Republic forbidding, on these grounds, all untruth to individuals, but permitting it with dangerous

---

443 C sqq., where I agree with Hirzel's view.

[50] As Tennemann does, Plat. Phil. iv. 115 sqq.

[51] P. 182, 32.

[52] P. 179, 24, 25; and further, cf. Rep. iii. 389 B sqq., 414 B, v. 459 C sqq., vi. 485 C; Laws, ii. 663 D.

MORALITY. 455

freedom to the State, as a means of education and government.[53] We have also spoken of [54] the peculiar form of friendship which was so closely bound up with the social life of Greece. It is here only necessary to observe that, in the moral treatment of this connection, Plato throughout follows Socrates.[55] On the one hand, he allies himself with the custom of his nation, and its sensuous æsthetic side is in no way alien to him. Friendship thus becomes Eros, a passionate excitement, the workings of which among men are portrayed in glowing colours;[56] and he not only approves of this passion in regard to innocent concessions, which, however, always betray the element in question,[57]—but he expresses himself as to its greatest excesses with a leniency [58] that would be surprising if we did not bear in mind that Plato was a Greek. On the other hand, he does not conceal his own decided disapprobation of these excesses. The Phædrus [59] describes them as a degradation of the Divine to which love properly belongs,—as an animal and unnatural pleasure, to which man is hurried away by the 'vicious steed' of the soul. The Republic declares that the

[53] The former, as we shall find later on, in the primary education of youth by means of myths; the latter, when, in the distribution of the women and the classification of the citizens into the three ranks, all kinds of fictions and even false lots—in elections—are brought into use.

[54] P. 191 sqq.

[55] See Pt. i p. 138.

[56] Phædr. 251 A sqq.; Symp. 215 D sqq, 218 A; cf. 192 B sqq.

[57] Rep. iii. 403 B, v. 468 B sq.

[58] Phædr 256 B sq.: if the lovers in unguarded moments are carried too far by their passion, provided this does not occur too often, and they remain true to each other all their life long, although they do not attain to the highest destiny, still they have a happy lot after death.

[59] 250 E sq., 253 E sqq, 256 B sq.

excitement and disorderliness of sensuous delight are incompatible with the pure and fair harmony of true love.[60] And in the Laws[61] they are treated as altogether contrary to nature, and corrupting to manners, to be tolerated in no well-ordered State. In this dialogue, simple unchastity is not quite so severely dealt with; but it is to be banished, or at any rate repressed and concealed to the uttermost:[62] whereas the Republic[63] puts no restraint on those who have had children, and thus fulfilled their duty to the commonwealth. But Plato has certainly not as yet discovered the right point of view for the general relation of the sexes. As he limits their specific differences to physical organic distinctions, and considers all other differences to be merely questions of greater or lesser strength,[64] he can only regard marriage physiologically; and as this aspect can have no independent importance in his eyes, it is the more natural that he should have adhered to the Greek view, which makes the aim of marriage entirely objective—to furnish children to the State.[65] In the Republic, indeed, this view so entirely predominates that the moral character of marriage is altogether lost sight of. Plato seeks, however, to exalt the female sex both mentally and morally,[66] thus reprobating

[60] iii. 402 E. The same truth is set forth historically in the Symposium, 216 C sqq., in the example of the true lover, Socrates.

[61] i 636 C, 836 B sqq., 838 E, 841 D.

[62] viii. 839 A, 840 D, 841 D.

[63] v. 461 B.

[64] Rep. v. 451 D sqq, 454 D sqq., with which the quotations from the Timæus and Phædrus, pp. 392, 394, do not entirely agree: cf. p. 434. In Repub. iv. 431 C, v. 469 D; Laws, vi. 781 A sq., the weakness and imperfection of the female sex is still more strongly emphasised.

[65] Laws, iv. 721 B sq.: cf. vi. 773 B, E, 783 D.

[66] Cf. with respect to this pro-

the entire neglect of women among the Greeks. But he has too mean an opinion of its special vocation; he shares too entirely the prejudice of his countrymen (who only saw merit in the activity of men) to imagine such an exaltation possible through the ennobling of woman's sphere of action. What he seeks is the entire abolition of that sphere. He would have women share in the training and pursuits of men to an extent that is quite incompatible with the peculiarities and social requirements of their nature.[67] In this, as in so many other cases, his suggestions are striking, as showing how he strove to get beyond the Greek morality and view of life, without being able to free himself altogether from their defects, or to attain the result which was subsequently accomplished on another soil.

He was still less successful with regard to two other points which must now be mentioned. The contempt of the Greeks for handicraft arts he not only upheld, but intensified; and he makes no objection to slavery, the cancer of antiquity, though he tries to mitigate its practical evils by judicious management. Those occupations which among the Greeks were so scornfully branded as vulgar and paltry must inevitably have appeared to Plato degrading and unworthy of free men, if only for the reason that they fetter the mind to the corporeal instead of leading it away to something higher.[68] In his opinion, they all relate to the satis-

visionally the remarks in Laws, vii. 804 D–806 C on the neglect of the education of women.

[67] This point is treated in detail in the discussion on the state of the Republic and the Laws.

[68] Socrates held a different opinion, as was shown, Pt. 1. p. 142.

faction of merely bodily wants: it is the sensuous, appetitive part of the soul, not reason, nor courage, from which they proceed, and which they call into action.[69] He can therefore only imagine that, in a man who devotes himself to them, the nobler faculties must become weak, and the lower attain the mastery; that such a man wears out his soul and body and acquires no kind of personal efficiency.[70] On this account, in his two political works, he prohibits to the perfect citizens not only trade and commerce, but even agriculture, which was everywhere except in Sparta held to be a free and noble occupation. Tradesmen and agriculturists are in the Republic condemned to complete political nonage. Plato thinks it hardly worth the trouble to provide even for their education, since the State is very little concerned with them.[71] On similar grounds he seems to defend slavery, when he says that the ignorant and base-minded are to be thrust by the statesman into the class of slaves.[72] There is here an indication of the thought which was afterwards turned

[69] Cf. p. 414 sq.
[70] Rep ix. 590 C· βαναυσία δὲ καὶ χειροτεχνία διὰ τί, οἴει, ὄνειδος φέρει; ἢ δι' ἄλλο τι φήσομεν, ἢ ὅταν τις ἀσθενὲς φύσει ἔχῃ τὸ τοῦ βελτίστου εἶδος, ὥστε μὴ ἂν δύνασθαι ἄρχειν τῶν ἐν αὑτῷ θρεμμάτων [=τῶν ἐπιθυμιῶν], ἀλλὰ θεραπεύειν ἐκεῖνα, &c , vi. 495 D· the want of true philosophers results in unworthy persons of any profession throwing themselves into philosophy, ὑπὸ τῶν τεχνῶν τε καὶ δημιουργιῶν, ὥσπερ τὰ σώματα λελώβηνται, οὕτω καὶ τὰς ψυχὰς ξυγκεκλασμένοι τε καὶ ἀποτεθρυμμένοι διὰ τὰς βαναυσίας . . . ἢ οὐκ ἀνάγκη;
[71] Rep. iv. 421 A.
[72] Polit. 309 A: τοὺς δ' ἐν ἀμαθίᾳ τ' αὖ καὶ ταπεινότητι πολλῇ κυλινδουμένους εἰς τὸ δουλικὸν ὑποζεύγνυσι γένος. Rep. ix. 590 C: if anyone is not in a position to control his desires himself, ἵνα καὶ ὁ τοιοῦτος ὑπὸ ὁμοίου ἄρχηται οἷάπερ ὁ βέλτιστος, δοῦλον αὐτόν φαμεν δεῖν εἶναι ἐκείνου τοῦ βελτίστου, &c., which, however, does not here refer to slavery, but to the rule of the higher classes over the uneducated masses.

to account by Aristotle—viz. that those who are incapable of mental activity and moral freedom have to obey the will of another in rendering bodily service. Plato, however, does not in his writings pursue the subject. He presupposes slavery as a necessity;[73] and even the remembrance of the danger which once threatened him in Ægina did not disturb him in this conclusion. Any express justification of the practice he appears to think superfluous, especially if it be acknowledged that slaves are often distinguished for their virtues.[74] On the other hand, he gives directions as to the relations between master and slave which do honour to his intelligence and feelings. He forbids Hellenes to enslave Hellenes, or to hold their countrymen in possession[75] when enslaved. He speaks, in reference to servile revolts, of the risk incurred by accumulating slaves of the same race and language. Above all, he insists on a just and humane, yet withal a strict and well-regulated, management of slaves, so as not to spoil them by familiarity and unsuitable indulgence.[76] That a time might and must come when there should be slaves no longer, was a thought beyond the imagination even of a Plato.

Finally, as to the moral permissibility of suicide—a question on which even the opinion of antiquity was divided—Plato, like the Pythagoreans, decides in the

[73] E.g. Rep. v. 469 B sq., 431 C; Laws, vi. 776 B sqq.

[74] Laws, vi. 776 D: πολλοὶ γὰρ ἀδελφῶν ἤδη δοῦλοι καὶ υἱέων τισὶ κρείττους πρὸς ἀρετὴν πᾶσαν γενόμενοι σεσώκασι δεσπότας καὶ κτήματα τάς τε οἰκήσεις αὐτῶν ὅλας.

[75] Rep. v. 469 B sq. Elsewhere Plato censures the opposition of Hellenes and barbarians (see 297, 93), but his own tone of thought is nevertheless entirely pervaded by it· cf. p. 416.

[76] Laws, vi. 776 B–778 A.

negative;[77] for the reason that man, the property of God, ought not wilfully to quit the place assigned to him. The Stoics, as is well known, afterwards took a different view. All this, however, and whatever besides might be quoted from the Platonic writings as to particular points of so-called practical morality, is entirely disconnected. Plato attempted no systematic application of his moral principles except in politics.

[77] Phædo, 61 D sqq.

CHAPTER XI.

THE STATE.

Virtue is the highest good for individuals, and the highest aim of the State; the right constitution of particular souls depends upon the proper and natural relation of their parts, and the same is true of the community. Of the two comprehensive works which Plato has devoted to the State, the Republic, with its precursor the Politicus, will first engage our attention, the Laws being reserved for a later place.

a. *End and Problem of the State.*

It has just been asserted that virtue is the end and aim of the existence of the State. Plato seems at first to contradict this by a much more external derivation of it. The State, he says,[1] arose because the strength of individuals is not sufficient to supply their material wants; they therefore combine and form a society. The primitive State, therefore, consists entirely of handicraftsmen, who are without artificial wants and higher culture, and lead the simplest lives. Luxury alone necessitates the class of warriors and rulers, and with them the whole state-organism. The same is

[1] Rep. ii. 369 B sqq.

mythically expressed in the Politicus.² In the Golden Age, we are told, mankind living under the protection of the gods, in material abundance, formed no states, but only accumulated flocks and herds. States and laws became necessary on account of the deterioration of the world. Plato, however, clearly shows that he was not in earnest when so speaking, for in the Republic³ he describes the so-called healthy 'natural State' as a city of swine; and in the Politicus (272 B) he only admits the Golden Age to have been happier than ours, on the supposition that the men of that time improved their external advantages to the acquisition of higher knowledge. Such descriptions seem intended to disabuse us of the false ideal of a natural State⁴ rather than to instruct us as to the origin of communities.⁵ These, in Plato's opinion, are founded on moral necessity.⁶ His philosophy had led him far beyond the one-sided political theories of his countrymen; for him the State could not possess the unconditional importance that it did for the ancient Greeks. In their view, the State was the first object of all moral activity; the virtue of a man was wholly identical with political efficiency. Plato, like his master, regards the work of man in himself as his first duty; and participation in govern-

---

² 269 C sqq.; cf. especially 271 E sqq., 274 B sqq.

³ ii. 372 D.

⁴ As Antisthenes had maintained; cf. Pt. i. p. 278 sq.

⁵ Steinhart's objection, iii. 710 sq., that Plato seriously commends those states in which a natural virtue rules, is not to the point: a state in which, 'instead of law a natural, innate, and educated virtue rules,' is found in the Platonic Republic; and there is no need of the state of the Golden Age, or that sketched Rep. ii.

⁶ Cf. Susemihl, ii. 112 sqq.: his deviations from my view are unimportant.

ment only as a relative and conditional duty.[7] The Greeks in general knew of no higher problem than work in and for the State. Plato sees in the calm life of the philosopher, in the contemplation of what is essential and eternal, a far more glorious and attractive end. In comparison with this, the aims of ordinary politicians appear to him worthless, and their arts and endeavours slavish. He says, in regard to States as they are usually constituted, that the philosopher dwells in them with his body alone, his soul being a stranger, ignorant of their standards, unmoved by their ambitions;[8] and that everyone who desires to do the right must keep clear of public concerns, or he will speedily perish.[9] And in his city of philosophers [10] the best of the inhabitants will only descend upon compulsion from the blessed heights of intellectual contemplation to the common affairs of life in the dark prison of this present world. But though this abolishes the absolute and unconditional value of public life, which made it impossible for the earlier Greek to conceive a noble human existence apart from political activity, public life is still, according to Plato, morally necessary. The necessity, however, is indirect, and not immediate. The State is neither the first nor the highest object of man's energy, but it is the indispensable condition for knowledge and virtue, the sole means of producing and continuing them, of establishing their dominion in

---

[7] Symp. 216 A : cf. Pt. i. p. 55.
[8] Theæt. 172 C–177 B : cf. Rep. vii. 316 C sqq ; Gorg. 464 B sqq. 518 E sq.
[9] Apol. 31 E ; Gorg. 521 D sqq. ; Polit. 297 E sqq.; Rep. vi. 488 A sqq., 496 C (see p. 29, 62).
[10] Rep. vii. 519 C sqq.. cf. i. 347 B sqq., vi. 500 B.

464   *PLATO AND THE OLDER ACADEMY.*

the world. If education and instruction be wanting, virtue is a matter of chance. Natural disposition is so little able to engender it, that the most gifted, under the influence of wrong treatment, usually take to the worst courses, unless protected by exceptionally favourable circumstances. Education is only possible in the State; and conversely, bad government is the source of the most fatal and irresistible of those evil influences, to which the most brilliant talents as a rule most surely succumb. So long therefore as the life of the State is diseased, and public institutions are defective, no thorough improvement in moral conditions is to be hoped for. Some few individuals may perhaps be saved, by a special aptitude for knowledge and virtue: but these cannot attain the best of which they are capable, even for themselves. Still less can they assist others; it is much if they can make their own way, and neither become contaminated with the wrong that is around them, nor fall in battle with it before their time. Nothing can rectify this but an entire reformation of the commonwealth. The State alone can secure the general victory of good over evil.[11] The proper end of Government is the virtue of the citizens,[12] the hap-

---

[11] Rep. 490 E–495 A, 496 A sqq. (see p. 13, 23, and p. 29); Tim. 87 A, Gorg. 521 D sqq.; cf. quotation on p. 176 sqq. as to the casualness of customary virtue.

[12] Gorg. 464 B sq.: the problem of state-craft is the θεραπεία ψυχῆς. Ibid. 515 B: ἢ ἄλλου του ἄρα ἐπιμελήσει ἡμῖν ἐλθὼν ἐπὶ τὰ τῆς πόλεως πράγματα, ἢ ὅπως ὅτι βέλ- τιστοι οἱ πολῖται ὦμεν; ἢ οὐ πολλάκις ἤδη ὡμολογήκαμεν τοῦτο δεῖν πράττειν τὸν πολιτικὸν ἄνδρα; Ibid. 504 D, 513 D sqq., 517 B, 518 E; Rep. vi. 500 D. The Laws in particular speak continually of this, e.g. i. 631 B sqq., iii. 688 A sq , iv. 705 D, 707 C sq., 718 C, v. 742 D sqq., vi 770 E, xii. 963 A.

piness of the people as a whole :[13] for virtue and happiness are the same thing. The State in its highest acceptation is an educational institution :[14] its special and primary function is the care of Morality and Science; in a word, of Philosophy. The ends which ordinary State-craft has in view are utterly worthless, and, so far as they interfere with that higher end, are absolutely pernicious.[15] The true State should be a pattern of true virtue. Plato's first purpose in designing his Republic is to seek the concept of Justice, where it is written in large letters;[16] and in the first pause of his description, he refers to it as the seat of all virtues.[17] This entirely corresponds with his determinations on the problem of the State. The complete realisation in the commonwealth of the moral idea constitutes that happiness of the whole which is the State's ultimate end.

[13] Rep. iv. 420 B, 421 B sq., vi. 500 D sq., vii. 519 E, where it is particularly insisted on that State-management is concerned with the happiness of the whole and not of a part; cf. Laws, iv. 715 B, viii. 828 E.

[14] Polit. 309 C: the statesman is to unite the citizens by ties human and divine. By divine ties are meant τὴν τῶν δικαίων περὶ καὶ ἀγαθῶν καὶ τῶν τούτοις ἐναντίων οὖσαν ἀληθῆ δόξαν μετὰ βεβαιώσεως ... τὸν δὴ πολιτικὸν καὶ τὸν ἀγαθὸν νομοθέτην ἆρ' ἴσμεν ὅτι προσήκει μόνον δυνατὸν εἶναι τῇ τῆς βασιλικῆς μούσῃ τοῦτο αὐτὸ ἐμποιεῖν τοῖς ὀρθῶς μεταλαβοῦσι παιδείας ; This is the leading point of view in the Platonic State; and its result is rightly summed up in the words (Tim. 27 A). δεδεγμένον ἀνθρώπους παρὰ σοῦ πεπαιδευμένους διαφερόντως.

[15] Theæt. 174 D sqq. ; Euthyd. 292 B: freedom, peace, riches are in themselves neither good nor evil, if State-craft is to make the citizens happy, it must give them wisdom and knowledge. Gorg. 518 E: we praise the old statesmen because they satisfied the desire of the people and increased the State : ὅτι δὲ οἰδεῖ καὶ ὕπουλός ἐστι δι' ἐκείνους τοὺς παλαιούς, οὐκ αἰσθάνονται. ἄνευ γὰρ σωφροσύνης καὶ δικαιοσύνης λιμένων καὶ νεωρίων καὶ τειχῶν καὶ φόρων καὶ τοιούτων φλναριῶν ἐμπεπλήκασι τὴν πόλιν.

[16] Rep. ii. 368 E sqq.

[17] iv. 427 D sq., 443 B. Further details presently.

H H

If such be the purpose of social community, it is evident that a State deserving the name can only arise under the same conditions and by the same forces that produce morality in general. The only power that can place morality on a firm foundation, that can purify its content and motives, free it from the contingent character of ordinary virtue, and guarantee its existence and continuance,—is, according to Plato, Philosophy.[18] The highest problem of political life can therefore only be solved by founding it upon Philosophy. When everything in the State—every law and regulation—springs from scientific knowledge, then alone will it be possible for all to subserve the one end of the State and to be regulated in reference to it. In proportion as any part withdraws itself from this guidance, the perfection of the Commonwealth and the fulfilment of its vocation must suffer. The main principle of the true State is the absolute dominion of Philosophy, and consequently the dominion of philosophers.[19] 'Unless philosophers become rulers, or rulers truly and thoroughly study Philosophy; unless political power and Philosophy are united in the same hands, there will be no period to the troubles of States and of humanity.'[20] These words are the key to Plato's whole theory of Politics.

[18] See p. 176 sqq.

[19] According to Plato, knowledge can in nowise be separated from the knowing subject. It cannot be possessed as a dogma, but only put into practice as an art, and every special knowledge can only be rightly applied by the philosopher (see p. 198, 75). Hence (Polit. 294 A; see p. 467 sq.) not the law, but the ἀνὴρ μετὰ φρονήσεως βασιλικὸς is to have the highest power in the State.

[20] Rep. v 473 C. cf Polit. 293 C: πολιτείαν . . . ταύτην ὀρθὴν διαφερόντως εἶναι καὶ μόνην πολιτείαν, ἐν ᾗ τις ἂν εὑρίσκοι τοὺς ἄρχοντας ἀληθῶς ἐπιστήμονας, &c.

b. *The Constitution of the State.*

The most essential element in the State is the absolute rule of true State-craft,—of Philosophy. At the outset of the enquiry it seems indifferent in what manner and under what forms this consummation shall be brought about. It is of little consequence whether one or more, few or many, rich or poor, wield the power; whether they do so by the will of the people or against it, rule by fixed laws or without laws, use gentle means or harsh. If only the government is good and statesmanlike, is based on true knowledge, and tends to the common weal, all else is of secondary importance.[21] But this is merely a preliminary explanation, to keep us from confusing what is accidental with what is essential. On closer deliberation, Plato finds that these determinations are not so immaterial as they at first appear. With regard to the question whether a government shall rule by consent of the people or by force, it is not to be expected, he thinks, that reasonable laws will ever be tolerated by the mass of the people, without coercion. It is no pleasant treatment to which the true statesman subjects those committed to his care: he orders them bitter medicine. He will have nothing to do with the flattery of their inclinations, or the satisfaction of their desires: he educates them in a strict school to virtue and wisdom. How could such a discipline be at its commencement agreeable to those who are first trained by its means to morality?[22] Plato acknowledges that a State like the one he intends,

---

[21] Polit. 292 A–297 B. [22] Cf. Gorg. 521 D sqq.

could scarcely be established without great and effectual external helps.[23] Once established, it would be impossible, he conceives, to find in any other so great unanimity and general contentment.[24] Again, after declaring it a matter of small consequence whether the ruler is or is not bound by existing laws, he goes on to show that it would be wrong to limit the really discerning statesman by the law, which, being a universal, can never fully adapt itself to the individuality of particular persons and cases; and being unchangeable, cannot keep pace with changing circumstances.[25] In the absence of true State-craft, however, it would certainly be better to be bound by laws that have the warranty of experience, than to follow senseless or self-interested fancies.[26] As respects the distinction of rich and poor, Plato knows too well the political dangers with which this contrast is fraught[27] not to take precautions against them. We shall presently see that in one of his political works, he seeks to eradicate this distinction, by a universal community of goods, and in the other to render it innocuous. Lastly, though it may in itself be immaterial how many

---

[23] Rep. vii. 540 D sqq.: the philosophical ruler must remove all the inhabitants of the State over ten years old in order to educate the rest according to his principles. Polit. 293 D, 308 D sqq.; the true statesman will admit no bad material into his State, those who cannot be educated to virtue may be put to death or banished; those who cannot be raised out of ignorance may be degraded into the condition of slaves.

[24] Cf. Rep. v. 462 A-464 B, 465 D sqq.

[25] Polit. 294 A-295 B, 297 A-299 E. The objection here to laws is virtually the objection of the Phædrus (cf. p. 156) to all written statements. Like books, laws will answer no questions and take no information. The Phædrus, 257 E, 277 D, from its fundamental principles, does actually make this objection to laws.

[26] Polit. 295 B, 297 B sqq., 300 A sqq.

[27] Rep. iv. 422 E sq.

shall hold the supreme power, yet we can at once understand that a philosopher who was convinced that the true art of government is never possessed, nor the possessor of it endured, by the majority,—that out of a thousand men, there would hardly be found fifty statesmen,[28]—such a philosopher would be certain to limit the rulers to one, or, at any rate, to a very small number.[29] The Platonic State can only be an aristocracy,[30] a government of virtue and intelligence exercised by one or a few. As in the soul the simplest, and, with regard to its extent, the smallest part is to rule, so in the State the sceptre is to be wielded by the minority who in knowledge and character excel all the rest.[31]

This idea is more particularly developed as follows. As every kind of occupation is better attended to if a man entirely devotes himself to it, than if he is busy in many directions, so there must be a division of labour in the work of the State. Each person must do for the community the service for which training and disposition have especially adapted him, and none shall

---

[28] Polit. 292 E sq., 297 E sqq.; Gorg. 521 D sqq.; Apol. 31 E; Rep. vi. 488 A sqq.

[29] Polit. 293 A: ἑπόμενον δὲ οἶμαι τούτῳ τὴν μὲν ὀρθὴν ἀρχὴν περὶ ἕνα τινὰ καὶ δύο καὶ παντάπασιν ὀλίγους δεῖν ζητεῖν In the Republic the ruling class appears certainly somewhat more numerous, although it is still meant to form only a small part of the population (see iv. 428 E). This is rendered possible only because care is taken for a methodical education towards the art of government. Plato's political ideal itself has not changed in the Republic (as Steinhart believes, Pl. W. iii. 611).

[30] So he calls his ideal constitution, Rep. iv. 445 D, viii. 544 E, 545 C. ix. 587 D: cf. iii. 412 C sqq., viii. 543 A. In the Politicus (see below) he applies this name to the constitutional rule of a small number. In the Laws, iii. 681 D, iv. 712 C sq., it is used in the ordinary sense, but in iii. 701 A it apparently means a rule of the best, in a favourable sense.

[31] Rep. iv. 428 E: cf. ix. 588 C sq.

exceed the limits of this his specific task. The government of the state and its protection against external and internal enemies must be confided to other persons than those concerned with the arts which supply the necessaries of life; and accordingly the first division is between the 'guardians' of the State, to whom is entrusted the care of public affairs, and the handicraftsmen. The former are further divided into those who rule and those who obey—the rulers proper, and their assistants.[32] Thus we obtain three grades. First, the people, that is, agriculturists and traders, the industrial class[33] (Nährstand). Secondly, the guardians or warriors, the military order[34] (Wehrstand). Thirdly, the rulers or official order,[35] which, however, we shall find to be at the same time the teaching order (Lehrstand). Nature herself has laid the foundation for this division, by her various allotment of dispositions; some are raised above the mass of men by their courage, others by their powers of thought.[36] The art of government is concerned with the right and proportionate arrangement of

---

[32] Rep. iii. 374 A sqq.: cf. 369 E sqq., iii. 412 B, 413 C sqq.

[33] γεωργοὶ καὶ δημιουργοί, iii. 415 A; δῆμος, v. 463 A; μισθοδόται καὶ τροφεῖς, ibid.; ἀρχόμενοι, iv. 431 D.

[34] Usually called φύλακες or ἐπίκουροι, also προπολεμοῦντες (iv. 423 A, 429 B, 442 B, viii. 547 D; Tim. 17 C) or (iii. 398 B, iv. 429 E, v. 470 A) στρατιῶται.

[35] As a rule, ἄρχοντες or τὸ προεστὸς (iv. 428 E), together with the warriors (e.g. v. 463 B sq.), φύλακες, in distinction from them, iii. 414 B, iv. 428 D : cf. 415 C, φύλακες παντελεῖς or τέλειοι, the guardians, properly speaking, by whose side the warriors stand only as ἐπίκουροι.

[36] Rep. iii. 415 A sqq : this is mythically expressed by saying that those who are qualified for rulers have gold in the composition of their souls, while the warriors have silver, and the artisan class copper and iron. As a rule, the children are like their parents, but it may also happen that a son of a man in a higher rank may have a nature qualified only for an interior rank : cf. p. 423 sq.

the three grades. And such an arrangement cannot be attained unless each grade devotes itself to the business incumbent upon it, paying no attention to other spheres. Nothing is more dangerous to a State than a confusion of these boundaries; when public matters are entrusted to one who is naturally unfit for them, when artisans would be warriors, and warriors rulers, or the same person lays claim to all these functions at once.[37] All that belongs to the business of government must exclusively devolve upon the class of rulers: their power is unbounded and unshared. The protection of the State, both within and without, is restricted as exclusively to the second class. The mass of the people is not to meddle with weapons; for they are not in a position to learn the proper management of them. All industrial activity is, for the same reason, prohibited to the higher ranks. Trade and agriculture are only permissible in the third class: the other classes are not merely debarred from these common pursuits, but are forbidden to possess private property, the first condition of such pursuits: they must devote themselves entirely to the community, and derive their subsistence from the labour of the third class.[38] The virtue of the State depends upon the maintenance, and perfect carrying out of this order. The State is wise, when the rulers possess true knowledge. It is courageous when the warriors hold fast a true opinion of what is and is not to be feared, about pains and dangers, as well as plea-

[37] Rep. iv. 433 A sqq., 435 B, D sqq.: cf. subsequent quotation iii. 415 B sq. as to the life of the φύλακες.
[38] Loc. cit. ii. 374 A–E, iii. 415

sure and desire. Its temperance, σωφροσύνη, is the agreement of governors and governed as to who is to rule, and who to obey: for then the sensual passions of the multitude will be bridled by reason and the noble impulses of the good. Its justice is to be found in the maintenance of this proportion as a whole, —in the fulfilment by everyone of his appointed duty without overstepping its bounds (the οἰκειοπραγία of the three classes).[39] Special constitutional laws, like all particular legislation, Plato, as already observed,[40] considers superfluous, and even injurious, in a well-ordered State. He only decrees that the rulers should devote the greater portion of their time to philosophic meditation,[41] and a smaller portion, periodically, to affairs of State: so that State affairs will thus be managed by a selected number of the ruling class, in rotation.

The constitution is but partially founded on the principle of division of labour. This principle is itself externally derived from teleological considerations; and even if established, it would not involve that work for the commonwealth must be distributed precisely in this way, and that the grade corresponding to each kind of work is to become a permanent caste. The distinction of classes and the constitution of the State are manifestly based upon wider grounds; and the theory of the division of labour was subsequently applied to their scientific justification. The sole dominion of Philosophy followed directly from Plato's views on the political

---

[39] iv. 427 D sqq., and supra, p. 453, 48.
[40] See p. 468 sq.: cf. Rep. iv. 425 A sqq.
[41] vii. 519 D sqq., 540 A sq.

problem and the conditions of true morality; it was indeed included in the Socratic principle that the wise alone are entitled to rule. But it was impossible for the philosopher who so lightly esteemed the intelligence and moral status of the multitude, to assume that the majority would voluntarily conform to that sway. He must therefore arm the philosophic regents with power to compel obedience to their ordinances. He must place at their side a sufficient number of able and willing instruments; for they themselves, as we have seen, would be too few to fulfil the task. A special class of warriors was thus required, more for the purposes of internal administration than for external protection: and Plato has neither entirely overlooked nor satisfactorily removed the difficulties with which his arrangement is ultimately beset.[42] Lastly, there were other reasons, apart from division of labour, why Plato should forbid industrial occupations to the higher classes. As a true aristocrat, he too greatly despised material work, and ascribed to it too evil an influence on character, to expect from those engaged in it the political and military ability necessary for his ' guardians.'[43] The distinction of classes and the unconditional subordination of the lower to the higher were therefore inevitably required by his political views. There was also this advantage in it: that the State was thus divided similarly to the Cosmos and the human soul; that it represented an enlarged picture of man, and a miniature copy of the world. As the three estates correspond to the three

[42] Cf. Rep. iv. 422 A sqq.   [43] V. quotations, p. 459, and p. 472, 37.

parts of the soul,[44] so they may be compared with the three divisions of the universe; the dominion of the Idea (or what is the same thing, of Reason) over the material world by means of the soul, is brought about in the same manner as that of the first class over the third by means of the second.[45] It was only through this determination that Plato could apply his concept of justice to the State, or make the State sufficiently a work of art, to correspond with his view of morality. Virtue for him, according to Greek, and especially to Pythagorean notions, consists in harmony, in the agreement of all the parts, and their subordination to the purpose of the whole.[46] This does not necessarily ex-

---

[44] Cf. Rep. ii. 368 E, iv. 434 C sqq., and supra p 470, 31.

[45] Neither of the comparisons, of course, can be strictly carried out between such dissimilar things as the State and the soul, the State and the universe. The rulers of the Platonic State are (as Strumpell, Gesch. d. prakt. Phil. d. Gr. i. 456, rightly observes) merely a committee chosen out of the second rank, in the manner of life and education of which they partake, except that the education of the rulers is completed by scientific instruction. They are the ἄριστοι φυλάκων, the τέλειοι φύλακες, the ἀριστεύσαντες who are chosen out of the collective number (iii. 412 C, 413 E sqq.; iv. 428 D; vii. 540 A, &c.). As such they stand far nearer to the warriors than reason, the immortal part of the soul, does to θυμός, which is only the more noble of the mortal parts. The position of the soul in the universe corresponds more accurately to that of the second rank in the State. But even in this parallel (not expressly drawn out by Plato) there is this distinction to be noticed, that the soul proceeds from the Ideal world in its connection with the corporeal world (see p. 346 sq.), whereas the warrior class inversely produces the ruling class out of itself. Susemihl's objection against the comparison of the three ranks with the triad of Ideal world, soul, and corporeal world seems to me unimportant. He gives, instead of this, the division of the universe into fixed stars, planets, and earth. I fail to see here a sufficiently strong point of comparison; the planets are not the instrument by means of which the earth is ruled from the sphere of the fixed stars.

[46] See pp. 445, 458.

clude a freer movement of political life, in which the separate activities are exercised by the same persons, sometimes in turn, sometimes together; but irrespective even of Plato's philosophic absolutism this latter view is not the most agreeable to him. He likes to keep that which is Ideally distinct externally separate;—to realise the moments of the Idea in clear and well-defined presentations. It is quite in accordance with this plastic genius that the different political activities should divide into as many grades, distinct and separate, each existing for its specified task, and representing only this one particular concept. As the Idea belongs to a special world, outside the world of phenomena, so the reason of the State is assigned to a special class over and above that of the people, and as the Soul, or motive power, comes in as a particular essence between the Idea and the phenomenon, so does the warrior class which carries out the resolutions of the ruling philosophers interpose between these and the people. Everything is fixed and determined, bound together by unchangeable relations. It is a work of art in the severest style—transparent, harmonious, well-proportioned, plastic. But it is a work of art only. The Platonic State rests wholly upon abstractions: it cannot endure the multiplicity and elasticity of actual life.

The first condition of the State, and at the same time its ultimate aim, is the virtue of the citizens. In order to secure this, stringent regulations concerning their education, manner of life and even of birth, must be enforced. Where men are not as they should be, the best laws are worthless; but where men are of the right kind, good laws will always be forthcoming.[47] All therefore that tends to improve men must be of the highest importance. In discussing this subject, however, Plato has entirely confined himself to the two higher ranks; for the mass of the people he presupposes the ordinary way of life,[48] and then seems to leave them altogether to themselves.[49] How they are to attain even that kind of virtue which he requires in them, without proper guidance, it does not appear; but from his aristocratic point of view, their condition seems a matter of indifference to the commonwealth.[50] In political affairs they have no voice: the separation of caste withdraws the higher ranks from their moral influence; and as to their economical importance, Plato, despising as he did every kind of industrial activity, could never entertain the question at all.

---

[47] iv. 423 E, 424 D sqq.

[48] E.g. iii. 417 A, iv. beginn. Still (iv. 423 D), even their employment is to be determined by authority.

[49] As Aristotle rightly objects, Polit. ii. 5, 1264 a. 11 sqq. In his own state, iv. 431 B sq., he supposes that the masses merely follow sense, and that their desires are ruled only by the reason which resides in the few.

[50] Cf. iv. 421 A: ἀλλὰ τῶν μὲν ἄλλων ἐλαττόνων λόγος· νευρορράφοι γὰρ φαῦλοι γενόμενοι καὶ διαφθαρέντες καὶ προσποιησάμενοι εἶναι μὴ ὄντες πόλει οὐδὲν δεινόν· φύλακες δὲ νόμων τε καὶ πόλεως μὴ ὄντες ἀλλὰ δοκοῦντες ὁρᾷς δὴ ὅτι πᾶσαν ἄρδην πόλιν ἀπολλύασι, καὶ αὖ τοῦ εὖ εἶναι καὶ εὐδαιμονεῖν μόνοι τὸν καιρὸν ἔχουσιν. This definite statement, and the fact that Plato nowhere mentions the necessity of any provision for the education of the lower classes or the means adapted to that purpose, seem to forbid Strumpell's supposition (Gesch. d. pr. Phil. d. Gr. i. 387 sq.) that 'Plato intended his reform of moral and religious instruction to apply to the third class also (see p. 479 sq.), but omitted' (for reasons which are, to me, far from satisfactory) 'to say so.' This class would of course have been influenced by the banishment of Homer and by the rest of Plato's scheme. But it does not follow that in forming his scheme Plato had this third class or its needs in view.

c. *The Social Regulations of the Platonic State.*

1. To make a political life such as Plato desires, possible, two things are necessary; first, all disturbing elements must be banished from the community, and secondly, an aftergrowth of well-disposed citizens must be secured. For it is obvious that out of worthless materials nothing good can arise.[51] Plato expects to accomplish the first end by those vigorous measures which are to clear the way for the rule of reason.[52] For the attainment of the second, he would place the parentage of the citizens entirely under State control. So great an importance does he attach to the circumstances of a man's birth, that the only possible cause he can foresee for the future degeneracy of his pattern State is some mismanagement in this direction.[53] Hence those expedients which to us sound so strange. The public authorities are not only to decide upon the number of children required, and the ages within which the citizens may become parents,—but they are to superintend each individual case, and take away the children immediately after birth. All kinds of artificial means are to be used in order that the children of the good may be more numerous than those of the bad.[54] Plato indeed recommends that the latter, as well as all sickly children, shall

---

[51] Polit. 308 C sq.

[52] See p. 468, 23 and Rep vi. 501 A: the philosophic statesmen λαβόντες ὥσπερ πίνακα πόλιν τε καὶ ἤθη ἀνθρώπων πρῶτον μὲν καθαρὰν ποιήσειαν ἄν, for they will not attempt any legislation πρὶν ἢ παραλαβεῖν καθαρὰν ἢ αὐτοὶ ποιῆσαι.

[53] See p. 424 sq.

[54] Rep. v. 457 C–461 E. The Politicus, which cannot presuppose the constitution as given by the Republic, demands less definitely (310 A sqq.) that in marriages care should be taken to combine peaceful and fiery natures.

be got rid of; and that the offspring of marriages unsanctioned by the authorities shall be destroyed or exposed.[55] He cannot quite conceal from himself that these regulations would be difficult to carry out;[56] but the inhumanity of many of them, and the degrading view of marriage as the merely economic supply of population, do not disturb him in his political ideal.

2. The State being thus provided with material for worthy citizens, the next and most important thing is to see that the children born at its behest shall be exclusively trained for its service and purposes. This can only be achieved by State Education. From the first moment of their existence, they belong to the State alone. The newly-born infants are at once to be conveyed to public nurseries, and care is to be taken that neither parents nor children shall ever know one another.[57] They are to be brought up publicly.[58] No individual can choose his station, nor can the parents determine it; the magistrates are to place every one in the class for which his disposition and character have fitted him.[59] Nothing is so important for the well-being of the State as that its affairs should be given into right hands.[60] The part that individuals will take in the

---

[55] Rep v. 460 D, 461 C admits no other explanation. In the Timæus, 19 A, this is repeated, with the alteration that the children of the bad are to be degraded into the third rank.

[56] Cf. 459 C.

[57] v 460 B sqq.

[58] As appears from the whole exposition of ii. 375 E, vi. 502 C.

[59] iii. 413 C sqq., 415 B sq. (cf. p. 470, 36): as a rule children will take after their parents, but exceptions may occur.

[60] 415 B (with reference to the myth mentioned loc. cit.): τοῖς οὖν ἄρχουσι καὶ πρῶτον καὶ μάλιστα παραγγέλλει ὁ θεὸς, ὅπως μηδενὸς οὕτω φύλακες ἀγαθοὶ ἔσονται μηδ᾿ οὕτω σφόδρα φυλάξουσι μηδὲν ὡς τοὺς ἐκγόνους, κ.τ.λ. Even their own sons are to be inexorably degraded into the artisan class if they are unfit for anything higher;

direction of those affairs cannot then be left to their own discretion. As to the more particular training of the higher classes, Plato considers the ordinary education of his countrymen, in music and gymnastic, as essentially proper and sufficient[61] for the warriors. Only he requires that both arts shall be pursued differently from what they usually are. In gymnastic, the body should be far less considered than the soul and the whole man. Gymnastic and music, in natural combination, will produce the fairest of all results,—the harmony of the individual with himself: they cause bodily and mental development to keep equal pace; and even within the soul itself they effect a union of force and gentleness, of courage and morality.[62] Gymnastic should be directed to the hardening and simplifying of life;[63] music is to produce the love of the beautiful, the moral discipline and healthfulness, which before a man attains scientific knowledge, keeps him steadfast in the right way.[64] Music is by far the more important of the two. Plato thinks so highly of its influence that he calls it the fortress of the State, in which nothing can be shaken without involving the entire ruin of the existing customs and laws.[65] Intelli-

---

and, conversely, the sons of the people, if fit, are to be raised to the warrior or the ruling class, ὡς χρησμοῦ ὄντος τότε τὴν πόλιν διαφθαρῆναι, ὅταν αὐτὴν ὁ σίδηρος ἢ ὁ χαλκὸς φυλάξῃ. Cf. iv. 423 C, 434 A, and supra p. 471.

[61] ii. 376 E sqq.; cf. supra 214 sq.

[62] Rep. iii. 410 B sqq, ix. 591 B sq.; Tim. 87 C sqq. To this belongs the account of the Politicus, 306 A–310 A as to the combination of σωφροσύνη with ἀνδρεία. This combination is the ultimate end of the education of the warriors in the Republic.

[63] Rep. iii. 403 C sqq.

[64] See p 214.

[65] iv. 423 E sqq.; cf. Laws, vii. 797 A sqq. These expressions are not to be referred to melodies only, as has been so often done from Cic. Legg. iii. 14, 32 downwards. The subject discussed is music (in-

gent rulers will therefore pay great attention to music; —neither suffering an immoral and effeminate character to creep into its harmonies, nor allowing to poetry forms which might alienate the citizens from simplicity and love of truth. In the sphere of the plastic arts, they will only tolerate that which is noble and seemly: but especially they must supervise the contents of poetical compositions, and forbid all that is immoral and derogatory to the gods.[66] Art, in a word, is to be strictly subordinated to ethics: it is to be a means of moral education, and nothing else. The Platonic State will not suffer any art that does not conform to this standard. Homer and all poetry imitated from him are denied an entrance there.[67] After this preparatory discipline, the first rank is to recieve intellectual training, the nature and stages of which we have already examined.[68] This course of instruction, however, is not intended only for youths; it extends far into manhood: nor may the pupils enter the guild of rulers, until they have been tested by many years' practical activity.[69]

3. In order that no one may belong to himself or his family even in advanced age, but all to the State,—Plato, in a series of remarkable ordinances, lays down for the two higher ranks a rule of life which goes far beyond anything hitherto proposed or attempted in

cluding poetry) and moral culture in general, παιδεία καὶ τροφή.

[66] ii. 376 E–iii. 403 C. Further particulars, pp. 510 sq., 498 sq., p. 501 sq.

[67] Rep. x. 595–608 B.

[68] See p. 215 sq.

[69] vii. 536 D sqq.: as boys, they are to be educated rather in play; from their 20th year, more scientifically (in the mathematical branches); from their 30th year in dialectic; at 35 they are to be employed in positions of command, and other offices; and they are not admitted among the rulers until their 50th year.

Greece.[70] Nothing is more beneficial to the State than that which unites it, nothing more baleful than that which divides and splits it up. Nothing is so uniting as an identity of interests, nothing so sundering as a division of interests. The more absolutely the citizens call one and the same thing their own, or not their own, the more perfect will be their concord, and the better it will be for the State.[71] Thus the main point of view for the social economy of the Platonic State is the abolition, as far as possible, of private interests. This, in Plato's opinion, can only be attained by the abolition of private possessions. He therefore forbids private property to his warriors and rulers, beyond what is absolutely necessary; they are to have common dwellings and common meals, to possess neither gold nor silver, and to have a certain prescribed maintenance which is to be provided by the third class, and must not exceed moderate requirements.[72] He substitutes for family life, a community of wives and children, the chief characteristics of which have been already noticed.[73] Since such a mode of life would put an end to the household sphere of women, he demands (conformably with the Socratic theory of the similarity of moral disposition in both sexes [74]) that they should share the education of men, in war and in political affairs.[75] Further regulations for the lives of his guar-

---

[70] Cf. Aristotle, Polit. ii. 7 beginn.: οὐδεὶς γὰρ οὔτε τὴν περὶ τὰ τέκνα κοινότητα καὶ τὰς γυναῖκας ἄλλος κεκαινοτόμηκεν, οὔτε περὶ τὰ συσσίτια τῶν γυναικῶν.

[71] v. 462 A sq.

[72] iii. 416 C sqq., iv. beginn.

[73] iv. 423 E, v. 457 C–461 E; cf supra, p. 478 sq.

[74] See supra, Pt. i. p. 121.

[75] v. 451 C–457 B (an amusing limitation, however, with regard to fighting occurs, v. 471 D). The way in which the participation of

dians Plato holds to be unnecessary, for the reason quoted above;—that persons properly educated will themselves find out what is right; while those who are deficient in this main qualification are beyond the help of laws. All attempts to support a State by particular legislation are merely makeshifts.[76] He also thinks that lawyers and doctors will have little occupation in his State;—for the strictness of manners and the virtue of the citizens will allow of no lawsuits, and their healthy mode of life will diminish diseases. He who cannot be cured quickly and by simple means had better be suffered to die: it is not worth while to live for the care of a sickly body.[77] Another department of legislation, the arrangement of public religious worship, he leaves entirely to the Delphic God;[78] but he enlarges on the conduct of war, with a view to the introduction of a more humane martial law, especially among the States of Greece.[79]

Since Hegel's excellent observations on the subject[80] it has been generally acknowledged[81] that Plato, in this

the women in gymnastic exercises is here described is very significant from the Greek point of view. We are offended by the demand that they should display themselves naked, and by the loss of the feeling of shame. Plato's only fear (452 A) is that people might think it ridiculous; and his answer is given in the beautiful words (457 A): ἀποδυτέον δὴ ταῖς τῶν φυλάκων γυναιξίν, ἐπεί περ ἀρετὴν ἀντὶ ἱματίων ἀμφιέσονται.

[76] iv. 423 E, 425 A–427 A.
[77] iii. 405 A–410 B, and cf. p. 435, 140.

[78] iv. 427 B sq.; cf. 469 A, vii. 540 C, v. 461 E.

[79] v. 469 B sqq.: Greeks are not to be made slaves, nor their cities destroyed, nor their lands devastated, nor the dead plundered, nor are the weapons of the slain to be hung up as trophies in the temples. Strife among the Greeks will not be regarded as war, but as civil discord.

[80] Gesch. d. Phil. ii. 240 sqq.
[81] Strumpell, Gesch. d. prakt. Phil. d. Gr. i. 353 sqq., expresses himself to this effect at consider-

State of his, could not have intended to portray a mere ideal in the modern sense, that is, a fancy picture impossible to reduce to practice.[82] Everything is against such a supposition. The principle of the Platonic commonwealth is thoroughly Greek; it is expressly said to be an Hellenic State,[83] and its legislation takes account only of Greek conditions.[84] The fifth, sixth, and seventh books of the Republic are entirely devoted to the means of its realisation. Plato distinctly declares that he considers such a State not merely possible, but absolutely necessary; and no other to be deserving of the name. In it alone public affairs are duly shared and divided; from it alone he expects the welfare of mankind;[85] all other forms of government he regards as evil and mistaken.[86] The whole character of his philosophy contradicts the notion that that which was definite in its Idea could be unreal and impracticable. We cannot doubt, therefore, that his propositions are seriously meant. In the enquiry as to how Plato arrived at so peculiar a theory, we must bear in mind

able length. But he decidedly goes beyond Plato's own statements (see nt. 6) in asserting (p. 367 sq.) that 'Plato does not construct from the Idea, and, consequently, does not construct an ideal state, which would always and everywhere be the best and the only true one. He is merely making proposals for the reform of the Athenian state.'

[82] As previous writers generally suppose, e.g. Morgenstern, De Plat. Rep. 179 sqq. Further details apud Susemihl, ii. 176.

[83] v. 470 E: τί δὲ δή; ἔφην, ἦν σὺ πόλιν οἰκίζεις οὐχ Ἑλληνὶς ἔσται; Δεῖ γ' αὐτὴν, ἔφη.

[84] See notes 78 and 79.

[85] Rep. vi. 499 B–502 C, 497 A sq., iv. 422 E, v. 473 C, ix. 592 A sq.; Polit. 293 C, 300 E, 301 D; cf. supra, p. 467 and p. 464, 9. It has already been shown in my Plat Stud. p. 19 sq., to which I here give a general reference, that passages such as Rep. v. 471 C sqq, ix. 592 A sq. prove nothing against this.

[86] Rep. v. 449 A, viii. 544 A; Polit 292 A, 301 E sqq.

his well-known political principles and those of his family; his aristocratic modes of thought, and that predilection for Doric forms and customs [87] which had early exposed him to censure.[88] The traces of such influence are very evident in the Republic. The principle he so prominently upheld,—that the individual belongs to the Whole, and exists entirely for the sake of the Whole, was carried out in no Grecian State so uncompromisingly as in Sparta: in none do we find such strict subordination of the citizens to law and authority, such perfect control of education and of the entire life, exercised by the State for its own ends. Plato forbids agriculture and trade to his guardians; in Sparta they were given over to the Periœci and Helots. He requires them to dispense with domestic habits and to live in public like a garrison; the Spartan State even in peace was a camp;[89] meals, exercises, recreations, even sleeping-places were in common for the male population, as for the army in the field. Plato requires the utmost simplicity and austerity, and this is truly Spartan. His refusal to allow the possession of gold and silver recalls a similar prohibition of Lycurgus, with his iron coinage. The community of goods has a precedent not only in the equality and invariability of inheritances, but also in the use of others' tools, stores, domestic animals, and slaves, which was sanctioned by Lacedæmonian custom. The community

---

[87] See Morgenstern, De Plat. Rep. p. 305 sqq.: Hermann, Plat. i. 541 sq., and Hermann, 'Die historischen Elemente des plat. Staatsideals, Ges. Abhandl.' pp. 132–159.

[88] Cf Gorg. 515 E.

[89] στρατοπέδου πολιτείαν ἔχετ·, says Plato to the Spartans, Law-, ii. 666 E.

of wives finds its counterpart in the enactment that an elderly man might pass on his consort to another, and that an unmarried man might borrow the wife of his friend. The Spartan law, like that of Plato, fixed a definite age for marriage. In the Platonic state all parents are to be universally honoured as fathers; in Sparta, similarly, they had a general claim on the reverence of the young, and each might chastise the children of others. Comradeship was allowed by Plato, and also by the Spartans, but its excesses were strictly prohibited. In both States, gymnastic exercises are principally directed to efficiency in war; Plato throws them open to women, and in Sparta the maidens at any rate were accustomed to take their part. There, too, music and poetry were carefully supervised as a means of moral education: we often hear of State interference against a too ornate style of music, and of the banishment of poets. Sickly children also were exposed. Plato forbids the dedication of captured arms to the gods; so did the Spartans.[90] Besides all this, his preference for the Doric aristocracy is well known. The Platonic State thus offers numerous characteristics which may be regarded partly as a repetition, partly as a development and enforcement of Spartan regulations, and Plato is himself careful to draw our attention to the points of similarity.[91] But the most distinctive element of his political theory cannot be derived from this source. Not to speak of the community of wives and goods, the

---

[90] For detailed evidences of the above (to be found mainly in Xenophon, De Rep. Laced.) cf. Hermann's Staatsalterth. § 26 sqq.
[91] Rep. viii. 547 D.

germs of which were only just discernible in Sparta,—not to dwell on Plato's severe censure of the Lacedæmonian constitution,[92]—it is plain that his main political point, the philosophic education of the rulers, is entirely alien and contradictory to the Lacedæmonian spirit. Between the Spartan legislation, founded on ancient usage and unchallenged tradition,—directed only to the military greatness of the State and the manly energy of its citizens,—and the Platonic constitution, originating from the Idea, consisting wholly in the service of Philosophy, there is such a radical difference, that to regard the Republic as an improved edition of the State of Lycurgus, is to overlook its most essential determinations. We might rather perhaps find in it a reminiscence of the political tendency of the Pythagorean society, which also aimed at a reform of the State through philosophy, and doubtless was not without some influence on Plato. But this precedent is no adequate explanation of his political system. So far as we know, the Pythagoreans sought only to maintain the existing aristocratic governments, and somewhat to improve them on minor points; not to realise in the State theories that were essentially new. Hegel's remarks,[93] striking as they are, on the interconnection of the Platonic policy with the principle of Greek morality and the then state of Greece, only help us in part. The Platonic Republic exhibits indeed very strikingly the specific peculiarity which distinguishes the Greek from the modern spirit—the subordination

[92] Rep. viii. 547 E; Laws, i. 625 C–631 A, ii. 666 E sq., vii. 805 E sqq., &c. [93] Gesch. d. Phil. ii. 244 sq.

of the particular to the Whole, the limitation of individual freedom by the State, the substantiality, in short, of Greek morality. It is also true that Plato must have had a strong motive, in the political experiences through which his country had only just passed, for unduly emphasizing this view. It was the unbridled self-will of individuals which, in the Peloponnesian war,[94] had been the ruin of Athens and of Greece. We have here therefore this phenomenon —that the Greek spirit at the same instant that it withdraws from actuality into its Ideality, recognises this severance of the subject from the State as his destruction, and demands his enforced subordination to the State. One of the most essential constituents of the Platonic State, the formation of a distinct military class, was supported not only by the precedent of Sparta, but by the transmutation (brought about by the great increase of mercenaries) of the old national militia into the standing armies with which Philip and Alexander soon afterwards conquered the world. Plato founds this institution upon the theory that the art of war, in order to be perfected, must be made a life's calling, like any other art;[95] a theory which must have been greatly elucidated by the successes of Iphicrates and Chabrias with their companies. All this, however, does not show the connection between Plato's politics and his philosophic principles. It lies, as already indicated, in that dualism which is meta-

---

[94] Cf. the quotations, pp. 464, 481; and p. 470, 29, and Rep. viii. 557 A sqq., 562 B sqq.

[95] Rep. ii. 374 A : τί οὖν; ... ἡ περὶ τὸν πόλεμον ἀγωνία οὐ τεχνικὴ δοκεῖ εἶναι, &c ; cf. p. 470.

physically expressed in the transcendency of Ideas; anthropologically, in the theory of the parts of the soul; ethically, in the postulate of the philosophic death. The Idea is here too abruptly contrasted with the phenomenon, and Reason with Sense, to allow of a satisfactory result from the natural growth and development of individuals and of Society. Only the few who have attained to the contemplation of pure Ideas, and who are able to behold the Idea of the Good, live in the light—all others lead a shadowy existence, and can at best produce but a mimicry of true virtue.[96] How then is it possible that a commonwealth corresponding to the Idea can be established except through the unconditional dominion of these few? How can we hope that the generality of mankind will voluntarily submit themselves to a government, the necessity and reasonableness of which they are not in a position to comprehend, and the severity of which they can only regard as an unbearable restraint upon their sensuous nature? How could even the philosophers become fit for their task, if they did not renounce those inferior occupations and pleasures, by which man is disturbed in his intercourse with what is higher, estranged from his true vocation, and rendered incapable of virtue;— if they too were immersed in the small particular interests which divide the commonwealth, and never arrived at full self-devotion to the State?[97] From this point of view we must interpret the severities of the Platonic theory—the unnatural and violent suppression

---

[96] Rep. vii. 514 sqq.; Meno, 100 A; Symp. 212 A; cf. p. 175 sqq., 215 sq., 436.
[97] Cf. p. 438 sq., 443, 459 sq.

of the individual, the reckless disregard of personal and political freedom. Plato was compelled to this course, because his system left no other open to him. The realisation of the moral Idea cannot be brought about by the free activity of individuals, by the recognition of their personal interests as justifiable in themselves,—it must develop itself by conflict with these; because the Idea stands over against man as something opposite, to which he can only raise himself by flight from the world of sense. As in his physics Plato required a universal architect, in order to subdue Matter by force to the Idea, so in his politics, absolute sovereignty is necessary in order to control individual egoism. He is not content with the community of spirit arising from the free action of each separate member; the Idea of the State must exist as a particular rank. And it can only be realised in individuals, when they have been denuded of everything in which individual interest finds satisfaction. In all this there is a union of the speculative element with the practical, like that in the mediæval church, which has been aptly compared with the Platonic State.[98] In that church the presupposed transcendency of the Divine gave rise to a separation of the kingdom of God from the world; to an external government of the community by means of a faith distant and inaccessible to it, and deposited in a special order, pledged to the renunciation of essentially individual aims in priestly and monastic vows.

[98] Baur, Das Christliche d. Plat. Tub. Zeitschr. 1837, 3, 36.

In the Republic similar presuppositions produced very similar results.

This parallel may also serve to throw light on Plato's political ideas from another side. His ideal state appears to us strange and impossible to carry out; but its affinity with our modes of thought and with the subsequent historical reality is all the more remarkable. We might even say that it is unpractical only because Plato attempts to accomplish on Greek soil and in Greek fashion that which was destined to be realised under entirely different circumstances and conditions; because he boldly anticipates the laws and endeavours of the future. His error did not consist in setting up new aims invented by his own caprice or fancy, but in seeking prematurely, and therefore with insufficient means,[99] to solve the problems of after-history, which his prophetic vision anticipated. The discord in his work between two principles,—the political Absolutism which sacrifices all the rights of the individual to the State, and the philosophic Idealism which leads man away from public life into himself, to give him higher aims in another world,—may be a disturbing feature, but it is the very struggle which was afterwards repeated in the conflict of Hellenism with Christianity. Though his verdicts may sometimes be unjust on the States and statesmen of his country, history has ratified his conviction that the existing kind of government was past help, and must be superseded by another essentially new. In declaring the philosophic discernment of the

---

[99] Cf. Hermann, Ges. Abhandl., 141; Steinhart, Pl. W. v. 16 sqq.; Susemihl, ii. 286 sqq.

rulers to be the indispensable means of this reform, and in constituting his State out of the well-known three orders, he has not only set a pattern,—among the Greeks the first and only pattern,—for the mediæval distinction of teaching, fighting, and producing classes (Lehr,—Wehr,—Nährstand), but for the modern institutions resulting from these. Though Plato would scarcely have recognised his guardians in our standing armies, or his ruling philosophers in our civil functionaries,—the separation of a special class educated for war, as opposed to the old national armies, and the demand for the scientific training of those holding office, are in principle coincident with his ideas. We are justly startled at his projects for the community of wives and children, and for the education and pursuits of women, but the general idea of equality between the sexes, and of extending the same attention to female as to male education, is in perfect harmony with the requirements of Christianity and of modern times.[100] Lastly, although his severity in regard to the great poets of his country was displeasing to antiquity and surprises us not a little, its underlying cause is the well-founded conviction that religion stood in need of a thorough reformation from the moral point of view. Plato is an Idealist, not in the ends for which he strove, but in the means by which he hoped to attain them.[101]

Side by side with the perfect form of government,

---

[100] Cf. Laws, vii. 806 C; see p. 457, 66.

[101] Cf. with the above the pamphlet. 'Der plat. Staat in seiner Bedeutung für die Folgezeit' in my 'Vorträgen und Abhandlungen,' p. 62 sqq. (2nd edit. p. 68 sqq).

Plato treats somewhat minutely of the defective forms known to actual experience, and of their nature and institutions.[102] Though these discussions are in themselves very interesting, and prove that the Philosopher in his estimate of political conditions was deficient neither in experimental knowledge nor in keenness of perception, we cannot at present examine them in detail, as they only serve to elucidate his views on minor points. It should be mentioned, however, that there is a slight difference, in regard to them, between the Republic and the Politicus. The Politicus enumerates, over and above the perfect constitution, six which are imperfect; distinguished from each other partly in the number and rank of the rulers, partly in the legitimacy or arbitrariness of their rule. In order of merit, they follow one another thus:—Monarchy, Aristocracy, Democracy that conforms to law, and Democracy that dispenses with law, Oligarchy, and Tyranny. The Republic names only four defective constitutions, and estimates them somewhat differently, so that Timocracy comes first, then Oligarchy, next Democracy, and lastly, as before, Tyranny. This variation is, doubtless, to be explained by Plato's having only subsequently arrived at the more precise definitions of the Republic; while in the Politicus, being chiefly concerned with the difference between false statecraft and true, he describes the former, in reference to the ordinary classifications,[103]

[102] Rep. viii. and ix. B; cf. iv. 445 C sq., v. 449 A; Polit. 300 A sqq.

[103] The arguments of Deuschle, Plat. Polit. 36, and of Susemihl, genet. Entw. ii. 307 sq., who follows D., to explain the order of the constitutions in the Politicus in a different way, do not seem to me convincing, nor can I give

which he admits to be inadequate.[104] As to the form of this representation, it has been elsewhere observed [105] that the derivation of the different governments from one another is evidently intended to mark their relative proportion of truth and merit, and not their historical order.[106]

more than a partial assent to the remarks of Hildebrand on the subject (Gesch. und Syst d. Rechts- und Staatsphilosophie, i. 146 sq.).

[104] See Polit. 292 A, and supra 467 sq.

[105] Plat. Stud. 206 sq, with which Hildebrand agrees, loc. cit. 147 sq.

[106] This is clear, as Hildebrand rightly remarks, from the fact that the ideal constitution, from which all others are to arise by a process of deterioration, is not posited by Plato himself as historical (beyond the myths in the introduction to the Timæus and Critias). It is expressly acknowledged (ix. 592 A sq.) that even if such a constitution were not in itself impossible, it is nowhere to be found as a matter of fact. And Plato could not possibly fail to see that the historical succession of the different forms of constitution by no means agrees throughout with his scheme. But, apart from this, the parallel with the development of the individual soul, which regulates his exposition throughout, and the form of genealogical succession which this necessitates (viii. 549 C, 553 A, 558 C, ix 572 D), show that the development of the state is ideal, not historical. Aristotle, in his critique (Polit. v. 12), fully recognises this.

CHAPTER XII.

PLATO'S VIEWS ON RELIGION AND ART.

PLATO has frequently discussed both these subjects, but only incidentally. Neither the philosophy of religion nor æsthetics proper are so included in his scheme of doctrine that they might be co-ordinated with Dialectics, Physics, and Ethics as parts of his system, or classified under either of these sciences. In the evolution of his theories, however, he must too often have encountered Art and Religion, either as enemies or as allies, to escape the task of determining for himself and for his readers their relation to philosophy. Therefore, although we could not assign a place to such discussions in the foregoing exposition, we can as little venture to pass them entirely over, and they are here treated of supplementarily.

1. *Religion.* We have already seen that Plato makes true religion absolutely identical with philosophy, and the truly divine with the highest objects of philosophic contemplation. To him, philosophy is not merely theoretic speculation, but moral conduct;—it is Love and Life, the filling of the whole man with the truly Existent and the Infinite.[1] What special field then

[1] See p. 214 sqq.

is left side by side with philosophy for religion? The philosopher alone is the truly pious man, well-pleasing to God; all things must work together for his good; death itself is for him only a reunion with God, for he lives wholly in the Divine, and moulds himself according to it, holding all else as contemptible,[2] in comparison with this one end. The eternal essence of things, with which philosophy is concerned, is the highest that exists. Ideas are those eternal gods from whom the world and all things in the world were copied;[3] and the Deity, in an absolute sense, is not distinct from the highest of the Ideas.[4] Even when Plato is speaking in an unscientific manner of God or the gods, it is easy to perceive that such is his real opinion. He proves the existence of gods as against materialistic Atheism,[5] by the same arguments that he elsewhere uses to refute the Materialism of Philosophy. He maintains the causality of Ideas and the rule of reason in the world,[6] on the ground of its being impossible to explain the Derived, except from an Underived; movement, except by the soul; the orderly adaptation of means to ends in the economy of the universe, except as the work of reason. And in all that he says about God, the Idea of the Good, of the highest metaphysical and ethical perfection, is the leading point of view. His highest

[2] Cf. Symp 211 E sq.; Theæt. 176 B sq.: Rep. x. 613 A; Phædo, 63 B-69 E, 79 E-81 A, 82 B sq., 83 D sq., 84 B, &c. Hence (v. p. 394 sq., 398 sq) philosophy is the only way to the highest happiness after death.

[3] See p. 283, 160 end.

[4] See p. 279 sq.

[5] Laws, x. 889 E-898 C (v. p. 342), xii. 966 D, 967 D, cf. Soph. 265 C sq; Tim. 27 E sq. Socrates had done the same (v. Pt. i. p. 144 sqq.), only more from the outside.

[6] Soph. 246 E sqq.; Phædo, 96 A sqq., Phileb. 28 D, 30 A sqq.; see p. 228 sq, 261 sq

Idea stands above all other Ideas, as the First Cause of all Being and Knowledge; so, above all other gods, equally difficult to find and to describe, is the One Everlasting, Invisible God, the Fashioner and Father of all things.[7] As the highest Idea is denoted by the concept of the Good, so the most essential attribute of God is goodness;[8] Plato therefore combats the ancient notion of the envy of the Divine Being, and the opinion that evil originates with Him, by the principle that being altogether good and just He can only produce absolute goodness and justice.[9] In opposition to the mythical stories of the gods appearing in visible form to men, he deduces from the goodness of God His unchangeableness: for that which is perfect can neither be changed by another, nor alter in itself, and thereby become deteriorated. He further says that God will never show Himself to man otherwise than as He is: for all lying is alien to Him. He is not subject to

---

[7] Vide the Timæus, particularly 28 C, 29 E, 34 A, 37 C, 41 A, 92 B, and supra p. 283, 160. In Polit. 269 E it is said that there can be only one God, and not two antagonistic divinities.

[8] See following note and Rep. ii. 379 A, where the discussion on the rules to be observed in theological exposition opens with the words: οἷος τυγχάνει ὁ θεὸς ὢν ἀεὶ δήπου ἀποδοτέον . . . οὐκοῦν ἀγαθὸς ὅ γε θεὸς τῷ ὄντι καὶ λεκτέον οὕτως; so that this concept forms the highest standard for all statements about the gods

[9] Tim. 29 D (see p. 291, 182); cf. Phædr. 247 A: φθόνος γὰρ ἔξω θείου χοροῦ ἵσταται. Tim. 37 A; see p. 283, 160; Rep. ii 379 B: οὐκ ἄρα πάντων γε αἴτιον τὸ ἀγαθὸν, ἀλλὰ τῶν μὲν εὖ ἐχόντων αἴτιον, τῶν δὲ κακῶν ἀναίτιον . . . οὐδ' ἄρα . . . ὁ θεὸς, ἐπειδὴ ἀγαθὸς, πάντων ἂν εἴη αἴτιος, κ.τ λ.; when, therefore, evil befalls men ἢ οὐ θεοῦ ἔργα ἐατέον αὐτὰ λέγειν, ἢ εἰ θεοῦ . . . λεκτέον, ὡς ὁ μὲν θεὸς δίκαιά τε καὶ ἀγαθὰ εἰργάζετο, οἱ δὲ ὠνίναντο κολαζόμενοι . . . κακῶν δὲ αἴτιον φάναι θεόν τινι γίγνεσθαι ἀγαθὸν ὄντα, διαμαχετέον παντὶ τρόπῳ μήτε τινὰ λέγειν, κ.τ.λ. Theæt. 176 C: θεὸς οὐδαμῇ οὐδαμῶς ἄδικος, ἀλλ' ὡς οἷόν τε δικαιότατος, καὶ οὐκ ἔστιν αὐτῷ ὁμοιότερον οὐδὲν, ἢ ὃς ἂν ἡμῶν αὖ γένηται ὅ τι δικαιότατος. See also supra, p. 419, 94.

THE DEITY. 497

ignorance and self-deception, which are the veriest lies of all; and with Him there can be no necessity for deceiving others.[10] Plato also extols the Divine completeness, wanting in nothing that is fair and excellent;[11] the Divine power, all embracing, and able to do whatever can be done at all;[12] the wisdom, which has everywhere so perfectly adapted means to ends;[13] the omniscience, which nothing escapes;[14] the justice, which leaves no crime without its punishment, and no virtue without its reward;[15] the goodness, which cares for all in the best possible manner.[16] He repudiates not only the anthropomorphism of conceiving that God could have a body,[17] but also those tales which ascribe passions, quarrels, and crimes of all sorts to the gods.[18] He declares the gods to be above pleasure and pain,[19] and untouched by evils.[20] He indignantly denies that they allow themselves to be propitiated, or rather bribed, by prayers and offerings.[21] He further shows that all

[10] Rep. ii. 380 D sqq.; cf. Symp. 208 B.
[11] Rep. ii. 381 B sq.; Laws, 900 C sq.
[12] Laws, iv. 715 E, x. 901 C, 902 E, Tim. 41 A, 68 D. The bounds of omnipotence, which Plato himself intimates, relate partly to that which is morally, and partly to that which is metaphysically impossible. It is impossible for God to wish to change (Rep. ii. 381 C), it is impossible for evil to cease (Theæt. 176 A), and from the doctrines of the formation of the world of matter it is clear that the divine creative activity is limited by the nature of the finite. Cf. p. 337 sqq., and Theophr. Metaph. p. 322, Brand. (Fragm. 12, 33 Wimm.)
[13] Laws, x 902 E; Phædo, 97 C; Phileb. 28 D sqq., and the whole of the Timæus.
[14] Laws, x. 901 D.
[15] Laws, iv. 716 A, x. 904 A sqq., 907 A; Theæt. 176 C sqq.; Rep. x 613 A; cf. ii. 364 B, and other passages.
[16] Laws, x. 902 B sq.; Rep x. 613 A; Phædo, 62 B, D, 63 B.
[17] Phædr. 246 C.
[18] Rep. ii. 277 E sq.; Crit. 109 B; Euthyphro, 6 B, 7 B sqq.; Laws, xii. 941 B
[19] Phileb. 33 B.
[20] Theæt. 176 A.
[21] Laws, x. 905 D sqq.; cf. Rep. ii. 364 B.

K K

things are ordered and governed by the Divine Providence, and that this Providence extends to the small no less than to the great:[22] he is convinced that men are the cherished property of God,[23] and that all things must conduce to the welfare of those who by their virtue have gained the Divine favour.[24] If it be objected that the distribution of human lots is unjust and unequal, Plato replies that virtue bears within itself its own immediate reward, and vice its own punishment; and that perfect retribution is certain to both hereafter. Even in this life, however, as a rule, recognition and gratitude are sooner or later the portion of the righteous man, and hate and aversion of the sinner.[25] The

---

[22] Tim. 30 B, 44 C, Soph. 265 C sq.; Phileb. 28 D sqq.; Laws, iv. 709 B, x 899 D sqq.; not to mention the teleological explanations of nature in the Timæus. Cf. Laws, iv. 716 C: God is the measure of all things. The expression πρόνοια (calculating care) seems to have become current, chiefly through the Socratic schools, as applied to the activity of the divinity both as creating and ruling the world, and corresponds with the Socratic teleology. Neither in Plato (who, acc. to Favorinus ap. Diog. iii 24, introduced the expression θεοῦ πρόνοια), nor in Xenophon does the word stand by itself to signify the divine providence. In Mem. i. 4, 6 (where Krohn, Sokr. und Xenophon, 5 sq, objects that it is so used), the words προνοίας ἔργον mean not 'work of the divine providence,' but (as the προνοητικὸν in iv. 3, 6) 'something produced by provident consideration,' work of a πρόνοια, not the πρόνοια.

[23] Phædo, 62 B sqq.; Laws, x. 902 B sq., 906 A; cf. Polit. 271 D; Crit. 109 B.

[24] Rep. x 612 E: only the just man is pleasing to God: τῷ δὲ θεοφιλεῖ οὐχ ὁμολογήσομεν, ὅσα γε ἀπὸ θεῶν γίγνεται πάντα γίγνεσθαι ὡς οἷόν τε ἄριστα, εἰ μή τι ἀναγκαῖον αὐτῷ κακὸν ἐκ προτέρας ἁμαρτίας ὑπῆρχεν; Apparent evils may befall him, but τούτῳ ταῦτα εἰς ἀγαθόν τι τελευτήσει ζῶντι ἢ καὶ ἀποθανόντι, οὐ γὰρ δὴ ὑπό γε θεῶν ποτε ἀμελεῖται ὃς ἂν προθυμεῖσθαι ἐθέλῃ δίκαιος γίγνεσθαι καὶ ἐπιτηδεύων ἀρετὴν εἰς ὅσον δυνατὸν ἀνθρώπῳ ὁμοιοῦσθαι θεῷ.—Εἰκός γ', ἔφη, τὸν τοιοῦτον μὴ ἀμελεῖσθαι ὑπὸ τοῦ ὁμοίου. Theæt. 176 A sqq.; Laws, iv. 716 C sq.; Apol. 41 C sq

[25] See particularly the exhaustive discussions of Rep. ix. 576 C-592 B, x. 612 A sqq., iv. 444 E sq.; cf. ii. 358 A-367 E. The whole Republic thus acquires the

existence of Evil in the world seemed to him too inevitable to require any express justification of the ways of God.[26] All these discussions ultimately lead to one and the same result. It is the Idea of the Good, from the application of which Plato derives the sublime doctrine of God, the purification of the popular faith, which makes his place so important in the history of religion. He declares that the worship of God consists solely and entirely in a disposition to morality. He only can please. God who is like Him; and he only is like Him who is wise, pious, and just. It is impossible that the gods can accept the gifts of the wicked. The virtuous man alone has the right to invoke them.[27] God is the Good: he who does not carry in himself the image of God's goodness cannot hold communion with God.

Besides the Eternal and Invisible God, Plato, as we have seen, recognises visible and created gods: the universe and the heavenly bodies.[28] In the Timæus, these visible gods are represented as fashioning the mortal part of man;[29] which seems to express the thought that the human race arose under the influence of the sun and the stars. But their significance is afterwards limited to their natural connection with our globe, and to the setting forth of the eternal laws; the knowledge of which Plato declares to be the best thing we

character of a magnificent Theodicee; cf. Laws, iv. 715 E sq., x. 903 B–905 C; cf. 899 D sq., and the quotation on p. 404, 37, and p. 444 sqq.

[26] On the origin and inevitableness of evil and wickedness cf. p. 337 sqq. pp. 423, 438 sq. p. 419 sq. p. 498, 12.

[27] Theæt. 176 B sqq.; Rep. x, 613 A (see p. 409, 6; 499, 24); Laws iv 716 C sqq.

[28] See p. 367 sq. The earth is also called a θεὸς, Tim. 40 B sq.; cf. Phædr. 247 A.

[29] 41 A sqq.

can gain from the contemplation of the heavens.[30] The theory which pretends to discover prognostications of future events in the position of the stars, he clearly designates[31] as a superstition arising from ignorance.

Through this doctrine of the divinity of the stars, Plato comes in contact with the popular religion, which likewise deified the brightest of the heavenly bodies: and he does not hesitate to profit by this circumstance when his object is to prove the existence of the gods from the ordinary point of view.[32] This, however, is the extent of his agreement with the national faith. He calls the soul of the universe by the name of Zeus;[33] he repeatedly speaks of the gods when he means only the Deity; he introduces Zeus, Apollo, and the rest into mythical representations; but the existence of these divinities as held by the Greeks he has never believed, nor does he in the least conceal it. Even in passages which apparently acknowledge them, his expressions clearly show that he only regards them as mythical imagery. He attacks the prevailing notions about them in all aspects,[34] making use of these notions, and intermingling them in his myths with the freedom of an Aristophanes.[35] In the Timæus[36] he

---

[30] Tim. 47 A sqq.

[31] Tim. 40 A sq. Here we ought to read (as Susemihl, II. 218, rightly observes) τοῖς ο ὐ δυναμένοις ταῦτα λογίζεσθαι. Rep. viii 546 A proves nothing on the other side. Plato passes the same judgment on augury from sacrifices (v. p. 432, 124).

[32] Laws, x. 893 B sqq, where the conclusion is (898 C sqq.) that not only the universe but the individual stars must be animated.

[33] Phileb. 30 C; see p. 266, 112, and p. 288, 172.

[34] See p. 498. It is obvious that this polemic, though nominally applied to the poets only, holds good of the popular religion as well.

[35] E.g. Symp. 190 B sqq.; Polit. 272 B; Phædr. 252 C sqq.; Tim. 42 E sq.

[36] 40 D, and the Laws, xi. 948 B, speak in the same sense.

says that to tell of their origin is beyond his power: the customary belief, however, should be accorded to the men of old time who have spoken on such subjects: for they asserted themselves to be the offspring of the gods, and must certainly have known best about their own ancestors. Such an explanation spares us all further enquiry.[37]

The same course is pursued with regard to the Dæmons. Often as Plato mentions these intermediate beings,[38] and much as has been borrowed from him by later dæmonology, he nowhere says a word to imply that he really believes in them. On the contrary, while in some passages he speaks in the traditional manner of guardian spirits, he declares (Tim. 90 A, C) Reason to be the true guardian spirit of mankind; and in the Republic[39] he ordains that distinguished men shall, after their death, be reverenced as dæmons. The dæmon is, after all, only the truly human element. The popular faith and time-honoured religious worship he desires to be maintained,[40] for the State and the

[37] Grote certainly (Plato, iii. 258 sqq., 189) has no eye for Plato's deep irony, approaching almost to scorn. Grote says that Plato here declares himself incompetent (' Here then Plato formally abnegates his own self-judging power, and subjects himself to orthodox authority '); and would at least leave the question undecided whether Plato is in earnest, or whether Martin is right in seeing an instance of irony here (Etudes, ii. 146).

[38] The main passages are. Symp. 202 E sqq.; Phædo, 107 D. 108 B; Rep. iii. 392 A, x. 617 E, 620 D; Polit. 271 D; Apol. 27 C sq.; Phædr. 246 E, Laws, iv. 713 C, 717 B, v. 738 D; Crat. 397 D.

[39] vii. 540 B sq.

[40] According to Rep. ii. 369 E even the guardians are to be educated by the mythe, which are replaced later by scientific knowledge, in the case of the smaller portion of them only. The public culture is therefore intended to conform to Greek custom (see 473, 78). The Laws, in which the philosophic rulers of the Republic do not occur, consider the popular

great majority of the citizens: both faith and worship, however, are to undergo a moral purification,[41] and the excessive pretensions to which their leaders were even then inclined are to be checked.[42] In the Laws,[43] not only atheism and other offences against religion, but private worship and its attendant abuses, are visited with severe penalties, and even with death. Though the popular faith might be very imperfect, and not much bettered by the allegorical interpretations then so much in fashion,[44] Plato still thought that such a faith was indispensably necessary for all without intellectual culture. Men are first to be educated by falsehoods and afterwards by the truth. Wholesome convictions are to be imparted to them under the disguise of stories.[45] Only a very small proportion of mankind ever become fit for the reception of a purer knowledge. Myths, and a religious worship founded on myths, are therefore the primary form of religion for all; and the

---

religion throughout as the moral basis of the State's existence, as we shall see later on.

[41] See pp. 480, 498.

[42] Polit. 290 C sqq.. however much priests and soothsayers may pride themselves, they are, after all, merely servants of the State. In order to keep them in this position, the Laws, vi. 759 D, limit the duration of the priest's office to one year.

[43] x. 907 D sqq.

[44] Vide besides the passages quoted p. 283, 2, Ed. Muller, Gesch. d. Theorie d. Kunst b. d. Alten, i. 242. Plato (Phædr. 229 C sq.; Rep. iii. 378 D) thinks these interpretations unprofitable and uncertain, and remarks with truth that the young take the myths not in their hidden meaning but literally.

[45] Rep. ii 376 E. the first means of education is music, i e. speech: λόγων δὲ διττὸν εἶδος, τὸ μὲν ἀληθές, ψεῦδος δ' ἕτερον; Ναί. Παιδευτέον δ' ἐν ἀμφοτέροις, πρότερον δ' ἐν τοῖς ψευδέσιν; Οὐ μανθάνω, ἔφη, πῶς λέγεις. Οὐ μανθάνεις, ἦν δ' ἐγώ, ὅτι πρῶτον τοῖς παιδίοις μύθους λέγομεν; τοῦτο δέ που ὡς τὸ ὅλον εἰπεῖν ψεῦδος, ἔνι δὲ καὶ ἀληθῆ. The greater myths (377 D) are those about gods and heroes, μῦθοι ψευδεῖς, which are to be censured above all.

sole form for the great majority.[46] Plato's own opinion cannot of course be deduced from this conditional acknowledgment of the popular belief; but he lets us see pretty clearly in what relation he stood to it.

It appears then, from the foregoing observations, that the religious character, for which the Platonic philosophy is so justly celebrated, is to be sought far less on its scientific than on its practical side. Plato's scientific convictions placed him, with regard to the Greek religion, in an antagonism, only very partially counterbalanced by the acknowledgment of visible gods; and these convictions, if logically developed, must have made impossible to him more than one of the determinations which connect him with ordinary monotheism. If the Universal be the only primary and absolute reality, it is not easy to understand how God can be conceived otherwise than as impersonal. And, though the disposition and governance of the All by the Idea of the Good brings the assumption of a moral order in the world quite within the scope of the Platonic system, no place is left for a Providence superintending that order in every particular, which Plato so warmly maintains. Nay, more; however perfect the general scheme of the world, it would seem, with regard to particulars, as though God Himself could not avert the evils which result from the nature of the corporeal; and, at any rate, that man (whose free will, however, is decidedly affirmed) must, by means of that nature, necessarily

[46] This supposition underlies Plato's whole treatment of these subjects; cf. p. 502, 40. It is his decided conviction that philosophic knowledge must always be limited to a small minority; cf. pp. 469, 470 and Rep. iv. 428 E, vi. 496 A sqq.

introduce much that is wrong. That which prevented these considerations from occurring to Plato, and gave to his philosophy a warmth and a practical bent transcending even his scientific principles,—that which compels him to the closest alliance possible under his circumstances, with the popular faith, is the moral religious interest which in him, as a genuine Socratic, is so intimately connected with the scientific interest. Philosophy, as he regards it, is not merely knowledge, but a higher life, penetrating the whole man; and though it is presupposed that this life in its highest perfection shall throughout be grounded on knowledge, Plato freely acknowledges that its essential contents may be present in another form. He points to the enthusiastic love of Beauty, as the common root of Morality and Philosophy, antecedent to all Knowledge. He bids us recognise in unphilosophic virtue a preliminary stage of philosophic virtue; in religious faith, an analogue to intelligent discernment, replacing the latter in the majority of men. Can we wonder that he feared to violate unnecessarily these imperfect, but, from his own point of view, well-directed forms of education? or used them to fill up gaps in his system, and to enunciate principles which that system was unable to establish, but of which personally he entertained no doubt? We must not, however, over-estimate the value of such utterances. The religious importance of Platonism lies chiefly in the blending of the speculative and practical elements, in the ethical tone given to it by the Socratic teaching, by virtue of which philosophy was no longer restricted to knowledge, but was applied directly to the personal life of men. The particular notions which bring Plato in contact with positive religion are, for the most part, mere outworks of his system, or else an inconsistent relapse into the language of ordinary opinion.[47]

2. *Art.*[48] Plato has instituted no independent enquiries[49] into the essential nature of Art and of the

[47] An enquiry might perhaps be expected here into the relation of Platonism to Christianity. It is a subject much discussed both in ancient and modern times. There are the old fancies about Plato's doctrine of the Trinity, a particular account of which is given by Martin, Etudes, ii. 50 sqq., and Brandis, ii. a. 330. The most important modern treatises are: Ackermann's Das Christliche im Plato, &c., 1835, which does not go very deeply into the matter; Baur's Das Christliche des Platonismus oder Sokrates und Christus Tub. Zeitschr. f Theol. 1837, 3; Michaelis, Die Philosophie Platons in ihrer inneren Beziehung zur geoffenbarten Wahrheit, 1859 sq. Other authorities are given in Ueberweg, Gesch. d. Phil. i. 127, 4 A. I do not regard this as the place to enter upon such a subject. If we listen to theologians, it often seems as if the Platonic philosophy could be only understood in the light of Christianity. They proceed to enquire about the Christian element in Platonism as if Christianity were one of the presuppositions of that Philosophy, not Platonism one of the presuppositions and sources of Christianity. And this was actually the idea of those Alexandrine fathers of the Church who first introduced the great conception of Plato's agreement with Christianity. As the Hebrew prophets were made out to have spoken not in the spirit and from the history of their own times, but from Christian history and dogma miraculously imparted to them, so Plato was represented as having drawn on the sources of Christian revelation, partly the internal (the Logos), partly the external (the Old Testament). A strict historical consideration will reverse this relation, and enquire not as to the Christian element in Platonism, but the Platonic element in Christianity. These questions, however, concern the history not of Greek philosophy but of the Christian religion.

[46] Ruge, Platonische Æsthetik; E. Muller, Gesch. d. Theorie d. Kunst bei den Alten, 1. 27–129, 228–251; Vischer, Æsthetik, i. 90 sqq., 98 sq., 11. 60, 359 sq.; Stræter, Stud z. Gesch. d. Æsth. i. H; die Idee des Schönen in d. Plat. Phil. Further details in Ueberweg, Grundr. i. 141, H A.

[48] I have said, p. 418, that I do not consider the Hippias Major or the Ion genuine. They would but slightly modify the above position; the Hippias aims at no positive result, and the Ion merely mentions poetic inspiration without any minute enquiry into it.

Beautiful any more than into that of the philosophy of religion. He often alludes to both, but always in connection with some other discussion; and what he says does not give us a very clear idea of their distinguishing characteristics. Because Plato is himself an artist, though a philosophic artist, he cannot be just to pure art. Because his scientific view of the world is at the same time æsthetical, he cannot discriminate sharply enough the object of art from that of philosophy,—the Beautiful from the True and Good. It is quite otherwise with Aristotle. He renounces all artistic treatment, excludes from the contents of his system all æsthetic motives (so far as this was possible to a Greek), that the scientific motives may alone prevail: but, for that very reason, he gains, with respect to art, freedom to understand and maintain it in its specific essence.

This is shown in the primary concept of æsthetics —the concept of Beauty. The two elements which intermingle with each other in all beauty are the sensible phenomenon and the Idea — the concrete individuality and the universal import. Plato ascribes no specific value to the former; the immaterial Universal is alone, in his opinion, true and essential. The material and the particular can, indeed, lead up to this, but only in such a manner that we then immediately turn away from the particular and leave it behind us. Plato must therefore seek for the essence of the beautiful in the contents, not in the form; he must ignore his discrimination of it from the true and the good, he must degrade the beautiful phenomenon over against the shapeless concept as a subordinate and unimportant, even disturbing accessory. Plato maintains the Greek idiom, so significant of Greek thought, by which 'beautiful' and 'good' are made nearly equivalent, but he inverts it. Whereas the prevalent acceptation tends to reduce the good to the beautiful, he, following the example of Socrates,[50] though more ideally, reduces the beautiful to the good. There is only a faint indication of a difference between them in the remark [51] that Beauty produces such an extraordinarily powerful impression, because in the heavenly world it has outshone all other Ideas, and, even in this world, differs from wisdom and virtue in revealing itself to the bodily eye with shining clearness. But, with this exception, the concept of the Beautiful always resolves itself into that of the Good. The primeval beauty is bodiless and colourless, to be likened with no particular, either material or spiritual. It belongs to no other as a quality.[52] Corporeal beauty is only the lowest rung in the ladder of the beautiful: fair souls are higher; higher yet, fair virtues and sciences; but highest of all is that pure Idea of the Beautiful to which nothing akin to the phenomenon any longer cleaves.[53] Though measure and harmony,[54] purity [55] and completeness [56] are also set forth as characteristics of the Beautiful, these

[50] V. Pt. i. p 125.
[51] Phædr. 250 B, D
[52] Symp. 211 A E; cf. Rep. v. 476 A sqq., 479 A, and supra, p. 240.
[53] Symp. 208 E sqq. (v. supra, p. 193 sq.); cf. Rep. iii. 402 D.
[54] Phileb. 66 E sqq., 66 B; Tim 87 C; cf. 31 B, Soph. 228 A; Polit. 284 A.
[55] Phileb. 53 A; cf. 51 B, 63 B, 66 C.
[56] Tim. 30 C; Phil. 66 B.

are not peculiar to it; they themselves, and beauty itself, belong likewise to the Good.[57] Virtue, too, is beauty and harmony:[58] to Truth and Wisdom, also, the criterion of purity is to be applied.[59] All that is Good is beautiful;[60] the primeval Good is of unutterable beauty;[61] the specific concept of beauty, however, is not what is here meant.

Besides the object with which Art is concerned, the mental activity from which it proceeds must also be considered. Plato has not overlooked this point, but what he says about it is still far removed from an exact investigation and precise definition of the nature of fancy. The source of all artistic and poetic creation is, according to his theory, a higher inspiration, and, thus far, art has the same origin as philosophy. But, while in the philosopher the enthusiastic fervour is purified by the discipline of Dialectic and developed into knowledge, the artist remains among misty envisagements and shadowy imaginations, destitute of any clear consciousness of his actions,[62] and having no right concept of the objects which he presents.[63] He allows himself to be guided even in his creations, not by regular and scientific methods, but by an uncertain and tentative empiricism.[64] The consequence of this

[57] Phileb. 64 E sqq., 66 B, 60 B sq.
[58] See p 445; Rep. ix. 591 D.
[59] Phileb 53 A sq., 62 C.
[60] Tim. 87 C, cf. Laws, ix. 859 D; Gorg. 474 C sqq., not to mention innumerable places in which καλὸς and ἀγαθὸς are synonymous.
[61] Rep. vi. 509 A.
[62] Phædr. 245 A; Apol. 22 B; Meno, 99 D; Laws, iv. 719 C (Ion, 533 D sqq); cf. p. 191 sq., 176 sq.
[63] Rep. x. 598 B–602 B; Laws, vii. 801 B; Symp. 209 D, where he expresses himself more favourably as to Homer and Hesiod. Plato is speaking according to popular opinion.
[64] Phileb. 55 E sq, 62 B.

unscientific procedure is the disjoining of kindred branches of art, which corresponds to the separation of the virtues,[65] censured elsewhere, and arising from a similar cause. This seemed to Plato universally true of art, as he saw it in actual existence: in at least one passage, however, he hints that there might be a higher and more uniform art, based on clearer knowledge.[66] But this perfect art would simply be applied philosophy; Plato derives ordinary art from unregulated enthusiasm, and thus he only states what it has in common with every other unphilosophic mental activity: he does not tell us wherein the specific essence of the artistic phantasy consists.

The distinguishing characteristic of art lies, according to Plato, in imitation[67] or, since all human actions are in a higher sense an imitation of the Idea, the activity of the artist is distinguished from all

[65] Rep. iii. 395 A; cf. Symp. 223 D; this is said of tragic and comic poetry; the Ion follows it out, 532 B sq., 534 B sq, with some exaggeration. Cf. quotation on p. 180.

[66] Symp. loc. cit. the narrator of the dialogue remembers that Socrates extorted from Agathon and Aristophanes the confession that τοῦ αὐτοῦ ἀνδρὸς εἶναι κωμῳδίαν καὶ τραγῳδίαν ἐπίστασθαι ποιεῖν, καὶ τὸν τέχνῃ (this is to be emphasized in opposition to τριβῇ ἄτεχνος) τραγῳδιοποιὸν ὄντα κωμῳδιοποιὸν εἶναι. The knowledge of what is wrong is given with the knowledge of what is good and right, and the latter would be incomplete without the former (Rep. iii. 409 D, vii. 520 C; Phædo, 97 D; Laws, vii. 816 D; Hipp. Min. 366 E): so he who can, as a tragic writer, depict men in their greatness, must also be able, as a comic writer, to depict their follies (for these are the subjects of comedy acc. to Phileb. 48 A sqq.). The object of each kind of representation is to influence men's hearts; tragic as well as comic effect, if it is to be attained artistically, will therefore presuppose a scientific knowledge of mankind (cf. Phædr. 270 E sqq.), and this knowledge will fit its possessor equally for either capacity. Cf. Müller, loc cit. 232 sqq

[67] Rep. ii. 373 B; Laws, ii. 668 A sqq, iv. 719 C; Phædr. 248 E; Polit. 306 D; cf. following note.

others in that it does not imitate the immaterial essence of things in the material reality, but only makes images of their phenomena.[68] But what value can we attach to such imitation? In itself it is but a pastime intended to afford us pleasure and recreation, not advantage or instruction;[69] and this pastime, as it is generally treated, is far from being safe. Art, in order to please, flatters the tastes of mankind; more particularly those of the populace:[70] that which it represents is in great part wrong and immoral. Poets and artists, being unscientific and restricted to the reproduction of contemporary opinion and thought,[71] disseminate most unworthy notions of the gods, and principles and precedents most dangerous to morals.[72] The sensuous multifariousness and wantonness by which they seek to please, enervate and corrupt men;[73] the imitation of what is bad and unworthy, which in music and poetry, but especially in the drama, plays so prominent a part, will imperceptibly accustom both artists and the public to reprehensible practices and thoughts:[74] and the imita-

[68] Soph. 266 B sqq. (cf. 233 D sq.), where all imitative arts are comprehended under the name εἰδωλοποιική; but especially Rep. x 395 C–598 D. The productive arts (e.g carpentry) copy the Ideas; the imitative arts in a stricter sense, such as painting and dramatic poetry, are φαντάσματος μίμησις; they do not produce anything real, but τοιοῦτον οἷον τὸ ὄν, ὂν δὲ οὔ, merely an εἴδωλον of the thing. Hence they are πόρρω τοῦ ἀληθοῦς, τρίται ἀπὸ τῆς ἀληθείας, &c.; the poets are (600 E) μιμηταὶ εἰδώλων ἀρετῆς καὶ τῶν ἄλλων, but do not grasp the ἀλήθεια of them.

See further Crat. 423 C sq.; Laws, x. 889 C sq.

[69] Polit. 288 C; Rep. x. 602 B, ii. 373 B; Laws, ii. 653 C, 655 D, 656 C; cf. Gorg. 462 C.

[70] Gorg. 501 D sqq.; Laws, ii. 659 A sqq.; Rep. x. 603 A sq.

[71] See above and Tim. 19 D.

[72] Rep. ii. 377 E–iii. 392 C; Euthyphro, 6 B, and supra, pp. 480, 498

[73] Gorg. loc. cit.; Laws, ii. 669 A sqq.; cf. vii. 812 D; Rep. iii. 399 C sq.

[74] Rep. iii. 395 C sqq., 398 D sq., 401 B; Laws, vii. 816 D.

tion of various characters will in itself be prejudicial to the purity and simplicity of the actor.[75] Lastly, the effect of Tragedy depends on the excitement of our compassion and grief; that of Comedy on the excitement of laughter, and, ultimately, of joy at the misfortunes of others. The poets claim our sympathy for love, anger, fear, jealousy, &c. But all these are unworthy passions, which we do not approve in ourselves, and the representation of which ought not to afford us pleasure.[76] To avoid these evils, artists must be subjected to a strict supervision; and, that art may be kept pure in its content, it must be treated as a means of education. Accordingly Plato demands that the verdict of competent judges, thoroughly versed in the subject, shall be obtained concerning all artistic representations.[77] He will have the framing of myths and the exercise of art in general placed under the guidance of public authorities,—and all that is not in accordance with the moral aims of the State ejected.[78] He forbids in the Republic all myths which relate

[75] Rep iii. 394 E sqq., 396 A sqq.
[76] Rep. x. 603 C-607 A, iii. 387 C sqq., Phileb. 47 D sqq.; Laws, vii. 800 C sq.
[77] Laws, ii. 668 C sqq., cf. Rep. x. 601 C sqq.; there are three arts, the χρησομένη, the ποιήσουσα, the μιμησομένη. The man who uses a tool must know how it ought to be made, and the maker of the tool, to whom the commission is given, thereby gains a correct opinion about the tool, while the mere imitator who paints, e.g. a flute or a bridle, has neither of these kinds of knowledge. From this passage is easily derived the result (stated elsewhere more definitely) that imitation, so far as it is not mere amusement, but a means of education, has to follow the directions of the competent judge, i.e. the philosopher.
[78] Rep. ii 376 E sqq. (see p. 479), and in the Laws (see nt. 84). Rep. ii. 377 B is a representative passage: πρῶτον δὴ ἡμῖν, ὡς ἔοικεν, ἐπιστατητέον τοῖς μυθοποιοῖς, καὶ ὃν μὲν ἂν καλὸν ποιήσωσιν, ἐγκριτέον, ὃν δ' ἂν μή, ἀποκριτέον· Myths of the first kind are then to be introduced generally.

dishonourable things concerning the gods and heroes.[79] He wholly banishes from the State dramatic poetry, and though he permits to Epic the imitation of the speeches of other persons as well as simple narration, it is only in cases where these speeches would serve as a moral exemplar.[80] So that, as he says,[81] nothing would remain of the whole Art of Poetry but hymns to the gods and praises of famous men. He will, moreover, permit only such music and metres as express a manly temper of mind in the various circumstances of life.[82] Lastly, he asserts that the same principles hold good with regard to the plastic arts.[83] He speaks in a similar manner in the Laws, where special attention is likewise paid to music. All poems, songs, melodies, and dances are to represent moral dispositions, and to aim at strengthening the conviction that the virtuous man alone is happy, the wicked man always miserable.[84] For this reason the productions of all these arts are to be strictly watched over by the State,[85] and all innovations prohibited.[86] The merit of artistic representations is to be decided, not by the taste of the multitude, but by that of the best and most virtuous persons,[87]—not by the masses who fill the seats in the theatre, but by selected

[79] ii. 376 E–iii. 392 E.
[80] iii. 392 C–398 B, x. 595 A–608 B. In these discussions Plato has to do principally with Homer, and opens the controversy, x. 595 B, with words similar to Aristotle's Eth. N. i. 4 in beginning his polemic against Plato himself: φιλία γέ τίς με καὶ αἰδὼς ἐκ παιδὸς ἔχουσα περὶ Ὁμήρου ἀποκωλύει λέγειν ... ἀλλ' οὐ γὰρ πρό γε τῆς ἀληθείας τιμητέος ἀνήρ, &c.
[81] x. 607 A.
[82] iii. 398 C–401 A, where particulars are given about the respective harmonies and metres.
[83] Loc cit. 401 B.
[84] ii. 653 A sqq., 660 E sqq., vii. 800 B sqq., 814 D sqq.
[85] ii. 656 C, 671 D, vii. 800 A, 801 C sq., 813 A.
[86] ii. 656 D sqq , vii. 797 A–800 B.
[87] ii. 658 E sqq.

judges. The whole community is to be divided, according to age, into choirs, and theoretical instruction in the elements of music is to be combined with the practice of the art, in order that suitable metres and melodies may be chosen in each case.[88] All artistic conceits are to be banished from musical teaching;[89] no poem, dance, or measure is to be put forth without the consent of the authorities: and a selection of approved songs, melodies, and dances, some adapted for men and some for women, is to be compiled.[90] Dramatic poetry is allowed as a means of education; comedy is to instruct us about evil things, what we should avoid; tragedy about fair things, what we should strive after. Still, there must be public surveillance in the matter: none but slaves and foreigners may be introduced into comedy, and no ridicule of the citizens is to be allowed.[91]

Plato has made no classification of the arts which in any way aspires to completeness. In treating of music, he distinguishes airs and melodies with rhythm[92] from discourses and myths: then, with regard to the latter, he separates the contents from the form;[93] and again he divides the form into narrative, imitative, and mixed.[94] He elsewhere designates singing and dancing

---

[88] ii. 664 B sqq., 667 B-671 A, vii. 812 B.
[89] vii. 812 D sq.
[90] vii. 800 A, 801 D, 802 A sqq., cf. 811 D sqq.
[91] vii. 816 D sqq., xi. 935 D sqq.
[92] Rep. ii. 398 B sq., 399 E.
[93] λόγοι and λέξις loc. cit. 392 C.
[94] Ibid. 392 D-394 C; cf. x. 595 A. Imitative postry is divided into comedy and tragedy, and under the latter epos is included (Symp. 223 D, Rep. iii 394 C, x. 595 B, 607 A; Laws, vii. 816 D sqq.). A kind of definition of tragedy is given in Phædr. 268 D.

as the two divisions of music, without farther pursuing the classification.[95] The plastic arts are always dismissed with a passing mention.[96] It is evident, therefore, that a theory of art did not lie within the scope of Plato's design.

He places Rhetoric or Discourse among the arts,[97] as it is practised with a view to please rather than to benefit or instruct. We have already seen [98] how low his estimation was of ordinary rhetoricians and their devices; and what reproaches he therefore casts upon their art. He, however, proposes to give Rhetoric a higher aim. He requires from the orator dialectical training and scientific knowledge of the things on which he discourses, and of the human souls which he desires to influence: that so he may be able to guide the wills and opinions of his hearers with skill and design.[99] He should place himself and his art in the service of God, and assist the true statesman in establishing the rule of right and morality.[100] Rhetoric, as defined by Plato, is thus made an offshoot of Philosophy,[101] pursuing the same moral ends. Yet they do not absolutely coincide.

[95] Laws, ii. 654 B, 672 E sqq.
[96] As Rep. ii. 373 B, iii 401 B, x. 596 B sqq., 601 C, 603 A, v. 472 D; Polit. 288 C and elsewhere.
[97] Gorg. 501 D sqq.; cf. Phædr. 259 E sqq.
[98] P. 189 sq., with which further cf. Phædr. 266 D sqq., 272 D sqq.
[99] Phædr. 259 E–266 C, 269 E–274 B. Rhetoric is here treated from the point of view of its psychical influence; it is (261 A, 271 B) ψυχαγωγία τις διὰ λόγων.
[100] Phædr. 273 E sq.; Gorg. 480 B sq, 504 D sq, 527 C; Polit. 304 A sqq.
[101] For only he who knows the φύσις τοῦ ὅλου is able to judge of and treat that of the soul rightly, and it is only from philosophy that the orator can create the ὑψηλόνουν καὶ πάντῃ τελεσιουργὸν, which he requires, Phædr. 269 E sqq.

The philosopher instructs his hearers by imparting truth, and guides them methodically to discover it; the rhetorician seeks only to persuade, and to work upon their wills and inclinations:[102] and, as the majority of mankind is incapable of scientific knowledge, he can only rely on probabilities, and must not hesitate to deceive those whom he wishes to convince.[103] Plato himself, in his dialogues, thus intermingles popular rhetorical discourses with scientific enquiries, and introduces myths in this manner with great effect.[104] But the philosopher alone is in a position to employ Rhetoric rightly; he alone, or (what to Plato is the same thing) the true statesman, can decide on the application of this art. Rhetoric can only be regarded as an instrument by means of which the philosopher brings his principles to bear on the unphilosophic many. Little value attaches to its specific task,[105] and when it loses sight of its connection

---

[102] Its province is (Polit. 304 C) τὸ πειστικὸν πλήθους τε καὶ ὄχλου διὰ μυθολογίας ἀλλὰ μὴ διὰ διδαχῆς, —it is (nt. 4) a leading of souls: πειθὼ γὰρ ἐν τούτῳ (the soul) ποιεῖν ἐπιχειρεῖ (Phædr. 271 A).

[103] This is assumed in the Phædrus, in 261 D sqq, 273 D, the necessity of dialectic for the orator is pointed out by the remark that he who is μέλλων ἀπατήσειν μὲν ἄλλον, αὐτὸς δὲ μὴ ἀπατήσεσθαι must know in what things are like and unlike. This no one can know unless he knows ὃ ἔστιν ἕκαστον τῶν ὄντων. The εἰκὸς τοῖς πολλοῖς arises δι' ὁμοιότητα τοῦ ἀληθοῦς, but he who knows the truth can most easily find what is like the truth.

This in itself might be said from the hostile point of view; but the Politicus, loc. cit., assumes that the true art of statesmanship makes use of rhetoric (the art of unscientific persuasion) under certain circumstances, and in the Republic (see p. 503) Plato declares the 'lies,' i e. the myths, to be an indispensable means of education, especially for youth.

[104] Cf Hirzel, Ueber das Rhetorische und seine Bedeutung bei Plato (Lpz. 1871), who, however, goes rather too far in identifying the rhetorical and mythical element.

[105] As intimated by the Phædrus, 273 E sq.

with Philosophy it sinks into a flattering, dilettante art.[106]

Plato institutes no particular enquiry into the rules of Rhetoric, nor is this to be expected, considering the subordinate place he assigns to it.

[106] See p. 189 sq. and Phædr. 260 E.

CHAPTER XIII.

THE LATER FORM OF PLATONIC DOCTRINE.—THE LAWS.

WE have hitherto confined ourselves to those sources which most clearly show us the Platonic system in its original purity. Is this, however, its one and only form, or did it undergo a later remodelling at the hands of its author? In support of the second of these theories two testimonies may be cited: the statements of Aristotle with regard to Plato's doctrine, and the treatise called the Laws. We are told by Aristotle that Plato, in the discourses which Aristotle heard from him, took a very different view of the main tenets of his system from that contained in his works. He had at first extended the sphere of Ideas to all that is an object of thought; he subsequently restricted it to natural objects.[1] In order to express the combination in Ideas of Unity and Plurality, he designated Ideas as numbers, and he made the distinction between these Ideal numbers and mathematical numbers to consist in this: that the former differ from one another in kind, and, therefore, cannot be reckoned together; while the latter are alike in kind and therefore there is no difficulty in so

---

[1] See p. 275, 128.

reckoning them. Among Ideal numbers there exists a definite logical succession, but among mathematical numbers there is none.[2] He also taught that Ideas arise out of two elements,[3] the One and the Unlimited. The Unlimited he more precisely described as the Great-and-Small; and, so far as numbers result from it, as indefinite duality.[4] The One he identified with the Good,

---

[2] See p. 254 sqq; 279, 146. The assertion of Philoponus, De An. C, 2 m. that all Ideas are decads, is rightly rejected by Brandis, ii. a. 318.

[3] Aristotle says that he used the word στοιχεῖα to signify these, Metaph. xiv. 1, 1087 b. 12: τὰς ἀρχὰς ἃς στοιχεῖα καλοῦσιν οὐ καλῶς ἀποδιδόασιν. See also De An. i. 2, 404 b. 25 (see 331, 103) and the quotation, p. 369, 14.

[4] Cf. besides the evidences given, p. 300, 16; pp. 306, 321, 327 sq, p. 279,145, my Plat Stud. 217 sqq. and Susemihl, Genet. Entw. ii. 509 sqq., 532 sqq. I cannot however agree with Susemihl in his rejection, p. 533 sq., of the statements about the indefinite dyad, which Alexander derived from the Aristotelian treatise on the Good (Alex. ad Metaph. i. 6, 987 b. 33 and i. 9, 990 b. 17; Schol. 551 a. 31 sqq.; 567 b. 31 sqq. Cf. Simpl. Phys. 104 b.; Schol 362 a. 7). (This treatise Susemihl with Rose declares to be spurious.) Alexander says that, as the Ideas are numbers, the principles of numbers are also the principles of the Ideas. These principles are the monad and the dyad; the latter because it is the first non-unit (πρώτη παρὰ τὸ ἕν), and contains in itself the Many-and-Few. Plato further assigned the ἴσον to unity, and the ἄνισον to ὑπεροχὴ and ἔλλειψις, because all inequality exists between two terms, a great and a small, a ὑπερέχον and an ἐλλεῖπον. Hence he called the dyad indefinite, because neither the ὑπερέχον nor the ὑπερεχόμενον as such is definite (ὡρισμένον), but indefinite and unlimited. But if this indefinite dyad is limited by the unit, it becomes the number two. This is the first in which the double and the half occur. The double and the half are definite kinds of the ὑπερέχον and ὑπερεχόμενον, which can only spring from these latter by being limited by the unit, the principle of all determination and limitation. The number two (ἡ δυὰς ἡ ἐν τοῖς ἀριθμοῖς) has therefore the unit and the Great-and-Small for its principles. Susemihl objects to this exposition on the ground that the mathematical number two is thus derived immediately from the unit and the definite dyad; and that mathematical numbers (the Ideas being left out of consideration) are explained to be the first elements of things, next to the unit and the infinite I cannot, however, find this in Alexander. He says, indeed, that Plato, according to Aristotle, ἐν τοῖς περὶ τ' Ἀγαθοῦ made the

or the highest Idea.[5] Intermediate between the Ideas and material things he placed the sphere of mathematics.[6] From numbers, in their combination with the Great-and-Small, he derived magnitudes;[7] the line from the number two, the plane from the number three, the solid from the number four;[8] and here again he

---

unit and the dyad ἀρχὰς τῶν τε ἀριθμῶν καὶ τῶν ὄντων ἀπάντων. But he does not say that these numbers are meant to be mathematical numbers, on the contrary, if their principles are intended to be the principles of all things, we should rather have to understand the numbers which are identical with the Ideas, viz. the Ideal numbers. Of these Aristotle says, Metaph. i. 6, 987 b. 18, 37: 'because the Ideas are the causes of everything else, Plato considered their elements to be the elements of things,' and 'Plato made the material principle a dyad, because numbers' (in our text the reading is ἔξω τῶν πρώτων, which however is a gloss, cf. p. 329, 98) 'can conveniently be derived from this.' This view removes the scruples in my Plat. Stud p. 222.

[5] See p. 284 sq.; cf. also Arist. Metaph. xii. 10, 1075 a. 34 and Eth. Eud. i. 8, 1218 a. 24, where the Platonic doctrine of the Idea of the Good is met by the objection: παράβολος δὲ καὶ ἡ ἀπόδειξις ὅτι τὸ ἓν αὐτὸ τὸ ἀγαθόν (the argument, however, which is cited for the position that the unit καθ' αὑτό is the Good, is doubtful), ὅτι οἱ ἀριθμοὶ ἐφίενται (sc. τοῦ ἑνός).

[6] See the quotation, p. 256, 100 and Metaph. i. 8, end; i. 9, 991 b. 27; Plat. Stud. 225 sq.

[7] Cf. also note 10.

[8] Arist. De An. i. 2, see 331, 103; Metaph. xiv. 3, 1090 b. 21 (cf. Plat. Stud. 237 sq.): ποιοῦσι γὰρ [οἱ τὰς ἰδέας τιθέμενοι] τὰ μεγέθη ἐκ τῆς ὕλης καὶ ἀριθμοῦ, ἐκ μὲν τῆς δυάδος τὰ μήκη, ἐκ τριάδος δ' ἴσως τὰ ἐπίπεδα, ἐκ δὲ τῆς τετράδος τὰ στερεὰ ἢ καὶ ἐξ ἄλλων ἀριθμῶν· διαφέρει γὰρ οὐδέν. vii. 11, 1036 b. 12: (τινὲς, the Pythagoreans) ἀνάγουσι πάντα εἰς τοὺς ἀριθμοὺς καὶ γραμμῆς τὸν λόγον τὸν τῶν δύο εἶναί φασιν. καὶ τῶν τὰς ἰδέας λεγόντων οἱ μὲν αὐτογραμμὴν τὴν δυάδα, οἱ δὲ τὸ εἶδος τῆς γραμμῆς. Alex. ad Metaph. i. 6 (see vol. i. 325, 2); Pseudo-Alex. ad xiii. 9 (ibid. 349, 4). Beside this derivation of spatial magnitude, is a second, according to which the line was reduced to the Long-and-Short, the superficies to the Broad-and-Narrow, the solid to the Deep-and-Shallow (or the High-and-Low βαθὺ καὶ ταπεινόν), as kinds of the Great-and-Small (Arist. Metaph. i. 9, 992 a. 10, and likewise acc. to Alex. ad loc. in the treatise περὶ φιλοσοφίας. Metaph xiii. 9, 1085 a. 7, xiv. 2, 1089 b. 11. De An. loc. cit). But how these two explanations stand in detail, whether the Long-and-Short is meant to arise from the combination of the Great-and-Small with the dyad, the Broad-and-Narrow from its combination with the triad, the Deep-and-Shallow from its combi-

distinguished Ideal from mathematical magnitudes, in making the former arise out of Ideal, and the latter out of mathematical numbers.[9] But, in the discourses which Aristotle heard, Plato does not seem to have entered much into Physics,[10] though he constantly reduces particular phenomena either to the One and numbers, or to the Unlimited, or to both.[11] Nor does

nation with the quadruple, and then out of these the line, superficies, and solid, or whether, inversely, the line was derived from the combination of the dyad with the Long-and-Short, the superficies from the combination of the triad with the Broad-and-Narrow, &c., cannot be determined either from Aristotle or from his interpreters. Susemihl's conjectures (ii. 544) on Plato's construction of spatial magnitude are doubtful. Aristotle says, Metaph. i. 9, 992 a. 20, that Plato did not admit the point in his deduction, because he asserted that the point was only a geometrical hypothesis. Instead of the point he said 'beginning of the line;' and this led him to the assertion of indivisible lines. I must concede to Schwegler and Bonitz ad loc., and Brandis, ii. a. 313, that this assertion is actually attributed to him; it is not clearly more strange than the supposition of smallest superficies in the elementary theories of the Timæus. Alex. ad loc., knew it in Plato from the present passage only.

[9] Metaph. i. 9, 992 b. 13 sqq.; xiii. 6, 1080 b. 23 sq.

[10] See pp. 74, 329; Plat. Stud. 266 sq., and cf. Theophrastus' argument, Metaph. p. 312, Brand (Fragm. xii. 12, Wimm.) against those who suppose the $\ell\nu$ and the $\delta\nu\dot{\alpha}s$ $\dot{\alpha}\acute{o}\rho\iota\sigma\tau os$· $\tau o\grave{\upsilon}s$ $\gamma\grave{\alpha}\rho$ $\dot{\alpha}\rho\iota\theta\mu o\grave{\upsilon}s$ $\gamma\epsilon\nu\nu\dot{\eta}\sigma a\nu\tau\epsilon s$ $\kappa a\grave{\iota}$ $\tau\grave{\alpha}$ $\dot{\epsilon}\pi\acute{\iota}\pi\epsilon\delta a$ $\kappa a\grave{\iota}$ $\tau\grave{\alpha}$ $\sigma\acute{\omega}\mu a\tau a$ $\sigma\chi\epsilon\delta\grave{o}\nu$ $\tau\ddot{a}\lambda\lambda a$ $\pi a\rho a\lambda\epsilon\acute{\iota}\pi o\upsilon\sigma\iota$ $\pi\lambda\grave{\eta}\nu$ $\ddot{o}\sigma o\nu$ $\dot{\epsilon}\phi a\pi\tau\acute{o}\mu\epsilon\nu o\iota$ $\kappa a\grave{\iota}$ $\tau o\sigma o\hat{\upsilon}\tau o$ $\mu\acute{o}\nu o\nu$ $\delta\eta\lambda o\hat{\upsilon}\nu\tau\epsilon s$ $\ddot{o}\tau\iota$ $\tau\grave{\alpha}$ $\mu\grave{\epsilon}\nu$ $\dot{\alpha}\pi\grave{o}$ $\tau\hat{\eta}s$ $\dot{\alpha}o\rho\acute{\iota}\sigma\tau o\upsilon$ $\delta\upsilon\acute{\alpha}\delta os$, $o\hat{\iota}o\nu$ $\tau\acute{o}\pi os$ $\kappa a\grave{\iota}$ $\kappa\epsilon\nu\grave{o}\nu$ $\kappa a\grave{\iota}$ $\ddot{a}\pi\epsilon\iota\rho o\nu$ (cf. the Pythagorean theory, Pt. i. 376 sq.; 3 A), $\tau\grave{\alpha}$ δ' $\dot{\alpha}\pi\grave{o}$ $\tau\hat{\omega}\nu$ $\dot{\alpha}\rho\iota\theta\mu\hat{\omega}\nu$ $\kappa a\grave{\iota}$ $\tau o\hat{\upsilon}$ $\dot{\epsilon}\nu\grave{o}s$ $o\hat{\iota}o\nu$ $\psi\upsilon\chi\grave{\eta}$ $\kappa a\grave{\iota}$ $\ddot{a}\lambda\lambda'$ $\ddot{a}\tau\tau a$, $\chi\rho\acute{o}\nu o\nu$ δ' $\ddot{a}\mu a$ (time, however, originates from both at once, from the indefinite dyad and the unit), $\kappa a\grave{\iota}$ $o\dot{\upsilon}\rho a\nu\grave{o}\nu$ $\kappa a\grave{\iota}$ $\ddot{\epsilon}\tau\epsilon\rho a$ $\delta\grave{\eta}$ $\pi\lambda\epsilon\acute{\iota}\omega$· $\tau o\hat{\upsilon}$ δ' $o\dot{\upsilon}\rho a\nu o\hat{\upsilon}$ $\pi\epsilon\rho\grave{\iota}$ $\kappa a\grave{\iota}$ $\tau\hat{\omega}\nu$ $\lambda o\iota\pi\hat{\omega}\nu$ $o\dot{\upsilon}\delta\epsilon\mu\acute{\iota}a\nu$ $\ddot{\epsilon}\tau\iota$ $\pi o\iota o\hat{\upsilon}\nu\tau a\iota$ $\mu\nu\epsilon\acute{\iota}a\nu$. These expressions can only refer to Plato: for Theophrastus continues, 'Speusippus and the rest, with the exception of Xenocrates and perhaps Histiæus, give the same account. Plato, however, takes the derived $\mu\acute{\epsilon}\chi\rho\iota$ $\tau\hat{\omega}\nu$ $\epsilon\dot{\iota}\rho\eta\mu\acute{\epsilon}\nu\omega\nu$, $o\dot{\iota}$ $\delta\grave{\epsilon}$ (Speusippus and the rest) $\tau\hat{\omega}\nu$ $a\rho\chi\hat{\omega}\nu$ $\mu\acute{o}\nu o\nu$.'

[11] Cf. preceding note, and Eudemus apud Simpl. Phys. 98 b. m. (Schol. 360 a. 8; Eud. Fragm. Ed. Sp. Nr. 27)· Πλάτων δὲ τὸ μέγα καὶ μικρὸν καὶ τὸ μὴ ὂν καὶ τὸ ἀνώμαλον καὶ ὅσα τούτοις ἐπὶ ταυτὸ φέρει τὴν κίνησιν λέγει ... τὸ δ' ἀόριστον καλῶς ἐπὶ τὴν κίνησιν οἱ Πυθαγόρειοι καὶ ὁ Πλάτων ἐπιφέρουσιν. We may compare the mention made by Aristotle himself, in the passage here para-

he exactly explain how this Unlimited, or Great-and-Small,—which is in the Ideas as in all things,—is related to corporeal Matter. Aristotle remarks on the omission, and it is easy to see from this how he himself arrived at the actual identification of the Unlimited and Matter, which cannot with justice be ascribed to Plato, even in his later life.[12] The few further particulars that have been handed down to us respecting these oral discourses are of little importance;[13] but the statement that he added to the four elements Ether, as the first of the five bodies,[14]

phrased by Eudemus, Phys. iii. 2, 201 b. 20, of the assertion (ἔνιοι φάσκονες): ἑτερότητα καὶ ἀνισότητα καὶ τὸ μὴ ὂν εἶναι τὴν κίνησιν, and the objection to the Platonic doctrine of Ideas in Metaph 1. 9, 992 b. 7 εἰ μὲν ἔσται ταῦτα κίνησις (if this—the Great-and-Small—is to be motion), δῆλον ὅτι κινήσεται τὰ εἴδη. Cf. the unregulated motion of the so-called matter in the Timæus (see pp. 301; 303, 20), and particularly Tim. 57 E (supra, 379, 35). The derivation of the soul from the unlimited can only be brought into harmony with the principle that the soul is the cause of all motion (see p. 344) if, by the motion which originates from the unlimited, is meant merely the mutability peculiar to sensible things, the change of Becoming and perishing. This is found elsewhere; cf. p. 352, 143.

[12] See p. 321 sqq.

[13] Besides the instances adduced, p. 331, 103; p. 397, 23, we find as belonging to these discourses a definition of man in Aristotle, Anal. Post. ii. 5, 92 a. 1 (cf. Top. vi. 10, 148 a. 15), similar to that in the Politicus, 266 A sqq.; Part. Anim i. 2, 642 b. 10 sqq., a classification of birds from the διαιρέσεις (see 46, 5); Gen. et corr. ii. 3, 330, b. 15 (see supra, loc. cit.), a classification of the elements from the same treatise; Top vi. 2, 140 a. 3, some Platonic expressions. Diogenes, III. 80, avowedly after Aristotle, probably also out of the 'classifications' (cf. v 23), gives the classification of Goods into spiritual, bodily, and external, quoted by Arist. Eth. N. 1. 8, 1098 b. 12; cf. Plat. Rep ix. 591 B sqq; Laws, v. 728 C sqq.; but especially Laws, v. 743 E.

[14] To prove that Plato assumed five ἁπλᾶ σώματα corresponding to the five regular solids, Simplicius, in three passages (Phys. 268 A. n.; Schol. 427 a. 15; De Cœlo, 8 b.' 16; 41 a. 1; Karst. Schol. 470 a. 26, 474 a. 11), quotes from Xenocrates' treatise, περὶ τοῦ Πλάτωνος βίου, the words: 'τὰ μὲν οὖν ζῷα οὕτω πάλιν διῃρεῖτο, εἰς

deserves attention, since, if true, it shows a departure from his original doctrine, and an approximation to the Pythagoreans.

The practical tendency of the Laws contrasts at first sight very strikingly with the abstract character of the enquiries we have just been considering. Yet there are certain common traits by which we can discover in both Plato's advanced age. We find in each, for example, a greater amount of dogmatism, a decline of dialectical power and versatility, a leaning to the Pythagorean doctrines, a predilection for mathematical symbols. The Republic makes Philosophy the groundwork of rational political life, and, presupposing philosophic rulers, plans the State purely from the Idea; the Laws seek to show us how far, and through what means, the State may be adequate to its task without this presupposition. It is not denied that the institutions of the Republic are greatly superior; but, while Plato at first never doubted the practicability of these institutions, and placed in them all his hopes for the welfare of mankind; while in his pattern State the philosopher alone was allowed to take part in the government,[15] in the Laws we are told[16] that among gods or the sons of gods such a State might indeed

---

ἰδέας τε καὶ μέρη, πάντα τρόπον διαιρῶν, ἕως εἰς τὰ πάντων στοιχεῖα ἀφίκετο τῶν ζώων. ἃ δὴ πέντε σχήματα καὶ σώματα ὠνόμαζεν, εἰς αἰθέρα καὶ πῦρ καὶ ὕδωρ καὶ γῆν καὶ ἀέρα.' The evidence is so definite, particularly in the statement that Plato called the five elements πέντε σχήματα καὶ σώματα, that we are forced to attribute this deviation from his earlier doctrine (mentioned p. 371 sq.) to Plato himself, and not to his scholars, on whom see chapters xv. and xvi. (Xenocrates, Epinomis).

[15] See p. 483, 85.

[16] V. 739 D sq., with which cf. Rep. ix. 592 B, vii. 807 B.

exist, and that in no other could the ideal of the State be represented, but that in this dialogue we must be satisfied with the second best.[17] The author has convinced himself that laws must be adapted to the nature of the country and people:[18] he only wishes to propound such as might possibly be brought into operation by his countrymen and contemporaries. Accordingly we find in this work little or no mention of the fundamental doctrines of the Platonic system, or of the philosophic training of the rulers. God or Reason is, indeed, still to reign in the State; Law (νόμος) is expressly defined as the distribution of mind or Reason (νοῦ διανομή);[19] the supreme end of the State is still Virtue, and that happiness of the citizens which is conditional on virtue.[20] But this rule of reason and of virtue is not now apprehended as the rule of philosophers; the wisdom which is to guide the State is not conceived as scientific knowledge. The theory of Ideas, with which all the institutions of the Republic are ultimately connected, is only once mentioned in the Laws; and even then it is left doubtful whether the Platonic Ideas, as distinguished from the Socratic concepts, are meant. The dialectical knowledge of Ideas, which in the Republic is the goal of all intellectual training, and the indispensable condition of

[17] Against Steinhart's attempt to invalidate this explanation, and represent the change in Plato's political point of view as less than it really is, cf. Susemihl, ii. 619 sqq.
[18] V. 747 D. sq.
[19] IV. 713 A, E (cf. 715 E sqq.):
ὅσων ἂν πόλεων μὴ θεὸς ἀλλά τις ἄρχῃ θνητὸς οὐκ ἔστι κακῶν αὐτοῖς οὐδὲ πόνων ἀνάφυξις: a remodelling of the celebrated expression of the Republic (see note 22).
[20] See p. 465, 12.

participation in the government, is now reduced to the first elements of the scientific method:[21] there is no longer question of a life-long education to Philosophy, such as the earlier dialogue demands. The Republic hopes for the realization of its State when rulers become philosophers; the Laws, when they become upright and prudent. Where the former speaks of Philosophy, the latter substitutes morality and practical wisdom:[22] as

[21] The only reminiscence in the Laws of the scientific demands of the Republic is in the magistracy conspicuous above the general mass of the people for its higher knowledge, which is to form the depository of the wisdom of the state, xii. 961 A sqq; xi. 951 C sqq (see p. 538 sq.). From the members of this magistracy it is required that they should be able to give an account of the object of the state and the foundations of the Laws (962 A sq; 966 B; cf. 951 B sq.) to πρὸς μίαν ἰδέαν ἐκ τῶν πολλῶν καὶ ἀνομοίων βλέπειν (965 C); that they should know not only the individual virtues, but the common essence of virtue, that they should generally be able to understand and to teach the true nature of the good and the beautiful. But unmistakeable as is the reference to philosophy as the necessary completion of the political praxis, the treatise before us does not go beyond these elementary indications. Its object is not to describe the actual State of philosophers; and though from our general knowledge of Platonic doctrine we cannot doubt that Plato, as the author of the Laws, meant by the μία ἰδέα what he otherwise calls the εἶδος, or Idea, the reader is not obliged, either by this expression or by the connection in which it occurs, to understand more than the simple concept. The Ideas are here touched upon only on their logical side, so far as they coincide with the Socratic concepts; there is not a word in reference to their distinctive metaphysical determination, nor to their self-existence, their objective reality. I, therefore, maintain the correctness of my assertion (in the second edition of the present work), as against Susemihl and others (Susemihl, ii. 576 sqq.; cf. Steinhart, vii. 359), that there is no mention of the theory of Ideas in the Laws. The theory of Ideas as such is not mentioned there. To avoid any misunderstanding, however, I have altered the wording of the above.

[22] With the passage in the Laws, iv. 712 C sqq., compare Rep. v. 473 C sqq., e.g. in the Laws: ὅταν εἰς ταὐτὸν τῷ φρονεῖν τε καὶ σωφρονεῖν ἡ μεγίστη δύναμις ἐν ἀνθρώπῳ ξυμπέσῃ, τότε πολιτείας τῆς ἀρίστης καὶ νόμων τῶν τοιούτων φύεται γένεσις, ἄλλως δὲ οὐ μή ποτε γένηται; in the Republic: ἐὰν μὴ οἱ φιλόσοφοι

to morality and wisdom being only attainable through Philosophy, nothing definite is said.[23] But in proportion as the philosophic basis of political life disappears, the religious basis becomes more prominent. There is a solemnity and devoutness in the very style and tone of the Laws; and throughout, the gods play a most important part.[24] This trait has a still greater influence on the contents of the dialogue. The whole constitution is made to depend on religion. Even in the choice of a site for the new city the first thing is to make sure that oracles and dæmons do not inhabit it. The work of legislation is to be begun by the invocation of the gods: the direction of it, both general and particular, is to be confided to them. All good that is to be found in political life is their gift: the highest end of all endeavour is to become like them, the best means of happiness is to honour them. Every part of the country is to be consecrated to some god, hero, or dæmon: tutelary deities are to preside over the different classes of the citizens. Sacrifices, feasts and sacred choruses are to be the most important business of the citizens all their life long. The transgressor of the laws, whether of petty laws or great, sins directly against the gods. The settlement of religious institutions is a weighty and difficult matter: the violation of these institutions the most dreadful of all.

βασιλεύσωσιν ... καὶ τοῦτο εἰς ταὐτὸν ξυμπέσῃ, δύναμίς τε πολιτικὴ καὶ φιλοσοφία, ... οὐκ ἔστι κακῶν παῦλα ταῖς πόλεσιν, κ.τ.λ.; cf. p. 467.

[23] Even from the passage already quoted, xii. 965 A sqq., we can only get, with the help of the Republic, a very indefinite conclusion.

[24] Cf. Plat. Stud. 71 sqq.

crimes.[25] Considerable importance is ascribed to the dæmons and heroes; the former especially are reverenced next to the gods, as the lords and masters of men and their helpers amidst the ills of life.[26] In the Laws as in the Republic there is a demand for a purification, if a less thorough one,[27] of the popular faith from all that is unworthy in it and dangerous to morals;[28] and while religious belief is grounded on law and tradition,[29] and blasphemous doctrines are threatened with heavy penalties,[30] there is yet to be added to this belief a conviction based upon intelligence. To this end, the existence of the gods, their care for men, and their incorruptible justice, are demonstrated in detail.[31] Mathematics are then brought into connection with theology, in a way very characteristic of the Laws, and of its intermediate position between the ordinary and the philosophic stand-point. In the scientific

---

[25] Cf. Plat. Stud. p 46, Laws, v. 747 E; iv. 712 B; xi. 934 C; ii 653 C, 665 A, iii. 691 D sqq.; iv. 715 E sqq.; xii 941 A sq ; vii. 799 A sqq.; viii. 835 E, 848 D; v. 729 E sq.; 738 D; xii. 946 B sqq.; 953 E; viii 842 E sq.; xi. 917 D; 920 D sqq ; x. 909 E; ix. 854 A; x. 884 A. Further references, p. 473.

[26] See iv. 717 B; v. 738 D; 747 E; vi 771 D; vii. 801 E; 818 C; viii. 848 D; ix 853 C; 877 A; x. 906 A; xi 914 B.

[27] See p. 463 eq. I cannot attribute any weight to the distinction between the visible gods (the stars) and those who are worshipped in images, xi. 930 E sq. The words καθάπερ οἱ κατὰ νόμον ὄντες θεοί, x. 904 A, in the connection in which they stand, give no suitable meaning, and appear to be a gloss. We cannot appeal to this passage to prove that Plato in the Laws treats the popular gods merely as symbols of the real gods.

[28] Susemihl, ii. 588, with reference to vii. 804 A sq.; xi. 930 E sq ; ix. 870 D sq.; 872 D sqq., and elsewhere.

[29] As ix. 927 A with regard to the belief in immortality.

[30] x. 907 D sqq ; see p. 473.

[31] x. 885 B–907 D; see p. 463 sqq.

exposition of his metaphysics, Plato had approximated considerably to the Pythagoreans; but in the Laws, Mathematics altogether take the place of Philosophy. He is not satisfied, even now, with the ordinary education by means of music and gymnastic; the higher dialectical education he purposely sets aside; nothing, therefore, remains but to close with that which ought properly to be a preparatory stage of Philosophy,— a mediatising between Opinion and dialectical Thought, —viz. mathematical science. In this we must now seek for that perfecting of ordinary morality which in the original Platonic State had been effected by Philosophy.

There are two things, according to the Laws,[32] which afford a firm foundation for the fear of God, and alone make a man capable of filling a public office, and of entering into the guild of the more highly cultivated. The one is that he should be convinced of the superiority of the soul over the body. The other, that he should recognise the reason that directs the heavenly bodies, should acquire the necessary musical and mathematical knowledge, and should apply it to the harmonious formation of his character. Instead of pure Philosophy, we have here the mathematics which, in their combination with religion, music, and ethics, are peculiar to the Pythagoreans. Mathematics, we are assured, are not only of the greatest use in life and in all the arts, but they also arouse the understanding, make the unteachable

[32] xii. 967 D sq.

528 PLATO AND THE OLDER ACADEMY.

docile, and the dull inventive.[33] They are especially valuable to religion, for they teach us to recognise the Divine wisdom in the ordering of the stars, and prevent our blaspheming the heavenly gods by false assertions concerning their courses.[34] Hence arises the principle [35] that the whole economy of our lives, even to the smallest particulars, must be precisely and symmetrically determined by number and measure. Hence the emphasis with which citizens of the State are enjoined to honour similarity and equality, and sameness and agreement, in number and in all that is fair and good.[36] Hence the value that is set on a classification of the citizens as perfect and accurate as it can be made.[37] Hence, too, the preference for arithmetical enumerations, by which this work is distinguished above all Plato's other works.[38] There can be no doubt that we are now on a different level from that of the Republic;[39] the only question is

---

[33] v. 747 A sq.

[34] vii. 821 A sqq.; xii. 967 D sq. It is a mistake to suppose that an enquiry into the Being of God is forbidden in the first of these passages (Cic. N. D. i. 12, 30; Clemens, Strom. v. 585 B, &c.; cf. Ast ad loc.). Plato is finding fault with the prevalent prejudice against Meteorosophy; cf. Krische, Forschungen, i. 187 sq.

[35] v. 746 D sq.

[36] v. 741 A.

[37] v. 737 E sq.; cf. 745 B; vi. 756 B; 771 A sqq.

[38] For proofs, cf. Plat. Stud. 48.

[39] Susemihl, ii. 591 sqq., is quite right in referring to kindred expressions in other writings; but the quantitative relation in which the mathematical element stands to the other elements is different in this place. Philosophy proper, Dialectics (to which Mathematics is elsewhere subordinated), receives a not very definite consideration at the end of the whole treatise: v. p 811, 1. In the rest of the exposition it withdraws, and mathematics takes its place. If, on the other hand, the accurate classification of the citizen society, the pedantry (σμικρολογία, v. 746 E) noticed by Plato himself, of determining everything according to number and proportion, be intended to serve practical ends, it cannot be mis-

whether Plato had himself abandoned his earlier point of view, or had merely exchanged it, in regard to his readers, for another that was more generally comprehensible.

As the ethics of the Laws are no longer, like those of the Republic, founded on Philosophy, they must necessarily assume an altered form. The Laws, indeed, still recognise four chief virtues,[40] but the concept and mutual relation of these virtues is by no means the same. The requirement of a strictly philosophic education being now abandoned, there appears in the place of scientific cognition, practical good sense or understanding, which, in itself, presupposes no higher knowledge. Instead of intellectual wisdom, the Laws speak more vaguely, and rather with reference to action, of prudential wisdom, or sagacity ($\phi\rho\acute{o}\nu\eta\sigma\iota\varsigma$); and in this we can only recognise ordinary virtue. Prudence or sagacity consists in harmonising all inclinations and aversions with reason.[41] This, according to Plato, is also the essence of temperance or self-control ($\sigma\omega\phi\rho\sigma\sigma\acute{u}\nu\eta$); which here so entirely coincides with wisdom, that it is even said to include it in itself,—

taken that, as opposed to the quantitative equality to be obtained in this way, the qualitative differences of men and their relations are inadequate.

[40] i. 631 C: of divine Goods, the first is φρόνησις, the second the σώφρων ψυχῆς ἕξις, ἐκ δὲ τούτων μετ' ἀνδρείας κραθέντων τρίτον ἂν εἴη δικαιοσύνη, τέταρτον δὲ ἀνδρεία. Cf. 632 E, xii. 963 C; cf. x. 906 B.

[41] iii. 689 A sqq. The greatest ignorance is the διαφωνία λύπης τε καὶ ἡδονῆς πρὸς τὴν κατὰ λόγον δόξαν; the main point in φρόνησις is the συμφωνία in this respect. The man in whom this is found, is to be called wise (σοφὸς, σοφία), however wanting he may be in other knowledge. Cf. 688 A· the highest virtue is φρόνησις καὶ νοῦς καὶ δόξα μετ' ἔρωτός τε καὶ ἐπιθυμίας τούτοις ἑπομένης.

530   *PLATO AND THE OLDER ACADEMY.*

to be that which makes us like God, and from which all other excellences derive their value.[42] Courage, on the contrary, is decidedly depreciated in the Laws. It is represented as the least and worst part of virtue, a merely natural quality which is not necessarily combined with wisdom, and is shared with children and with animals:[43] legislation must, therefore, be directed to the education of the citizens in temperance rather than courage.[44] In all these details it is clear that the ordinary notion of virtue is alone presupposed.[45] That deeper conception which makes virtue to consist in an internal relation between the parts of the soul is wanting, and must be wanting, because the tripartite division of the soul is itself passed over in silence.[46] Justice, the essence of which the Republic had sought in the harmony of the parts of the soul, is here more popularly designated as a mixture of the other virtues;[47] this

[42] iv. 710 A, 716 C; iii. 696 B sqq.

[43] i. 630 E sq.; xii. 963 E; cf. i. 630 C, D; 631 C; 667 A and supra, p. 451, 46. We find a similar statement (iv. 710 A) as to σωφροσύνη, but only in so far as it is treated as a mere natural disposition; from this δημώδης σωφροσύνη, the inclination to temperance innate even in children and animals, σωφροσύνη in a higher sense, including in itself knowledge, is distinguished. The expressions as to courage are not thus modified: they mostly relate to courage as one of the four cardinal virtues, which it is not when regarded as a mere natural disposition. In spite of Susemihl's opposition (ii. 615 sq.), I cannot withdraw the view expressed here, however strange it may seem to him.

[44] See the first two books, from 633 C onwards.

[45] Cf. also v. 733 E sq. and Plat. Stud. 35.

[46] Even in iii 689 A, ix. 863 B, E, this is hardly intimated. The dull argumentation, i. 626 D sqq., seems to be directed not against that doctrine itself, but only against the conclusion that there must be an internal strife in the soul if a man is to speak of a victory over himself.

[47] See note 40, and p. 476 sq.

only conveys an uncertain hint that it is *the* virtue which comprehends them all. This dialogue treats solely of the virtue which is possible without philosophic culture, and apprehends that virtue simply as it presents itself to common observation.

The same holds good of the main content of the Laws, the outline of the constitution. The philosophic absolutism of the Republic is in principle given up; its very first condition, a special class of philosophers, trained and perpetuated by regular scientific instruction, is absent. Of the three ranks in the Republic, the Laws in fact recognise only the second.[48] The first, as before remarked, does not exist; the third is excluded from the community of citizens, for trade and agriculture are to be carried on by means of foreigners and slaves. But, as we shall presently find, the citizens are to receive essentially the same education, and are in the same stage of culture, as that assigned in the Republic to the warriors. The problem of the Laws, therefore, is to make the best of this element, to discover what constitution and manner of life are most adapted to it. It is clear that this constitution must differ considerably from that of the Republic, even though the latter may still remain the ideal which is constantly to be kept in view, and is to be imitated as nearly as possible.

Among these inevitable alterations we find, in the first place, that particular legislation which Plato had

[48] Cf. Hermann De vestigiis institutorum veterum, imprimis Atticorum, per Platonis de Legibus libros indagandis, Marb. 1836, p. 9.

before repudiated[49] becomes a necessity in such a state as we are now considering. The perfect statesman, indeed (this is reiterated in the Laws[50]), should have no law set over him; for knowledge can never be the servant of another, but must everywhere take the command. This perfect statesman, however, is nowhere to be found; hence the attempt of the Laws to seek out the best possible substitute in the State which is without him. Here, then, we have the very contingency which Plato had foreseen in the Politicus: we must choose the second best alternative, law and order, which cannot, indeed, provide for all cases, though they can for the greater number.[51] The law must fill the place of the true ruler. While, therefore, in the Republic, Plato had entered very slightly into the details of legislation, he now enlarges greatly upon them. All the circumstances of life, down to the most trivial, are regulated by definite enactments.[52] Nothing is more urgently insisted on than obedience to the laws, of which the magistrates are merely the ministers or servants;[53] against nothing are we more earnestly warned than innovations in the existing institutions.[54] Where true knowledge exists, laws are troublesome and superfluous; where true knowledge is wanting, it becomes necessary that the legislation should be as precise and rigid as possible. Yet, even upon this sup-

---

[49] See p. 468, 25 and p. 472, 40.
[50] ix. 875 C sq.
[51] Laws, loc. cit; cf. Polit. 297 D; 300 A sqq.; supra, p. 468, 25, 26.
[52] Some particular points are necessarily passed over even by the Laws, viii. 843 E; 846 B.
[53] E.g. iv. 715 B sqq.; v. 729 D; vi. 762 E.
[54] Cf. vii. 797 A sqq.; ii. 656 C sqq.; xii. 949 E; vi. 772 C.

position, the principle of knowledge is to be so far recognised that the citizens are not to obey the laws mechanically, but from a consciousness of their necessity.[55] If men are destitute of philosophic knowledge, they can at least act from right opinion. Hence those special preambles to the laws,[56] which would be unsuitable for actual legislation,[57] but may easily be accounted for in this work, from its intermediate position between the ordinary and the ideal State, the problem it sets itself, and the stage of culture it presupposes in its citizens.

If we enquire further into the constitution of the State, we shall see that an aristocracy of the wise, such as Plato at first demanded, is here impossible, for the reason already given. A class of philosophers, able, by their superior knowledge, to direct the commonwealth from a higher point of view, does not exist in the State of the Laws. This State is restricted to ordinary virtue, and right opinion the basis of that virtue. Ordinary virtue consists in a plurality of particular activities, and has no clear conscious-

---

[55] Cf. also xii. 951 B.

[56] See iv 719 A–723 D, where they are defended as the only suitable way of introducing laws to free men. Plato expressly remarks (722 B, E) that no lawgiver has published such introductions to his laws, and, indeed, to do so would not be at all in the spirit of ancient legislation. That spirit is quite foreign to the Socratico-Platonic principle, of action being only valuable when it proceeds from free personal conviction. Hence, Hermann (loc. cit. p. 21; Plat. 706, following Bentley and Heyne) rightly rejects later procemia to the Laws of Zaleukus and Charondas (Cic. Legg. ii. 6, 14 sq.; Stob Floril. 44, 20, 40), however genuine in appearance.

[57] Posidonius, ap. Seneca ep. 94, 38, censures them.

ness of the internal unity and interdependence of these.[58] The highest that it can attain is a just mean, which results from the harmonious combination of all the moral qualities.[59] The state which is limited to this kind of virtue, instead of the uniform guidance of all its elements by sovereign knowledge, must be content with such a mingling and blending of those elements as will guard against transgression on the right hand or on the left. In the Laws the ultimate goal of ethics is the union of courage and temperance; and the highest problem of politics is the union of order and freedom. In both cases, however, the end is attained, not by conceptual knowledge, but by the practical skill or tact which supplements and controls tendencies that are opposite, and in themselves one-sided, by means of each other. The main point of view in the constitution of the Laws is the right apportionment of political power, the limitation of the different authorities each by each.[60] It is, in fact, a mixed constitution, and may be set out in detail as follows.[61] The essential conditions of all sound political life are Unity and Freedom.[62] Unity is brought about by monarchical, Freedom by democratic, institutions. Monarchy and democracy are therefore the fundamental political forms: the perfection of a commonwealth[63] consists

---

[58] See p. 180.
[59] See p. 214.
[60] Cf. iii. 691 C sqq., where (693 B) it is expressly observed that this demand coincides with the one elsewhere mentioned, viz. that legislation should aspire to virtue and knowledge (see p. 465 sq.).
[61] iii. 693 D sqq., 701 D sq.
[62] ἐλευθερία τε καὶ φιλία μετὰ φρονήσεως.
[63] As in Sparta, where they succeed best, but still not sufficiently.

in their being properly blended.[64] If either of these elements gains absolute ascendancy (as monarchy among the Persians, or democracy among the Athenians), if one part of the nation has unlimited power, then, instead of the common weal, the advantage of the rulers will be sought as the highest end, freedom and unity will perish; the state will be unworthy of its name.[65] In reality, however, as Aristotle observes,[66] the institutions which the Laws combine with democracy are not so much monarchical as oligarchical. For example, the character of a government is made to depend principally on its laws concerning the education and appointment of magistrates. We are told that in such appointments the aristocratic form of election must be combined with the democratic form of the lot. This, however, is avowedly only a concession required by the obvious necessities of the case. The higher equality, political justice proper, consists in assigning the greatest share of honour and power to the wisest and best. But as to carry out this principle uncompromisingly would be very irritating to the mass of the people, the legislators are compelled to unite with the higher equality, common equality, by which all share alike. The lot must therefore be superadded to election; for here everyone is on a par, and the result is left to chance; yet for this very reason, the use of the lot is to be limited as much as

---

[64] Cf. vi. 756 E: μοναρχικῆς καὶ δημοκρατικῆς πολιτείας, ἧς ἀεὶ δεῖ μεσεύειν τὴν πολιτείαν.
[65] iv. 712 E; 714 B; 715 B; 701 E; 697 D; 693 A sq.; viii. 832 B sq.
[66] Polit ii. 6, 1266 a. 1 sqq.

536 PLATO AND THE OLDER ACADEMY.

possible.[67] The criterion of wealth [68] too is brought to bear upon the matter; class elections [69] are to be combined with the general election, and in these the higher and richer ranks are allowed several unmistakeable advantages.[70] Thus there are three essentially different political principles which this work attempts to reconcile: the preference of merit, the privilege of property, the equal rights of all. Aristocracy, oligarchy, and democracy are to be united to form a mixed government.[71]

With regard to the exercise and distribution of public authority, all legislation, except that which concerns the alteration of existing laws, is placed in the hands of thirty-seven guardians of the law, whose

[67] vi. 756 E–758 A; 759 B; 768 B; cf. iii. 690 B sq.
[68] v. 744 B.
[69] According to four property-classes; see v. 744 C sq.; vi. 754 D sq., and Hermann, loc. cit. 36.
[70] Equally many are to be chosen out of all the property-classes, while the higher classes will, as a rule, be smaller; again, the higher classes are to be obliged to participate in the whole election, whereas among the lower classes this is only the case with a part. See next note and Aristotle loc. cit.
[71] Cf. the directions as to the election of the different magistrates, vi. 753 A–768 E. We may take as example the rules about the βουλή, 756 B sqq. This magistracy is to consist of 360 members, a fourth part of whom belongs to each of the four property classes. In order to determine these, a list of candidates out of each of the four classes is obtained by a general election of the people. In this election, however, only the members of the first two classes are absolutely bound to participate, while the members of the third class are obliged to choose only the candidates out of the three first, and those of the fourth only out of the two first. From each list of candidates thus 180 men for each class are marked out by a general election, in which every one is obliged to take part under penalty. Half of these are chosen by lot for actual entrance into the βουλή, after a preliminary examination in the legal qualifications. These are then divided into twelve sections (called Prytanies, vi. 755 E; 760 A; 766 B; xii. 953 C), each of which has to attend to the business of government for one month.

THE LAWS. CONSTITUTION OF THE STATE. 537

further duty it is to classify the citizens according to their amount of property.[72] When the laws require to be changed, there must be a unanimous agreement of the magistrates, the people, and the oracle.[73] Civil causes that cannot be settled by arbitration are to be decided in the lower courts by tribunals formed of neighbours, and popular tribunals elected by lot; and in the higher courts, by a supreme tribunal chosen with public observances by a collective body of official persons. All graver offences are to be referred to this tribunal; but crimes against the State are to be brought before the whole people.[74] The supreme authority in the government is the council,[75] which has a number of civil functionaries [76] under and

[72] vi. 770 A sqq; 754 D. These guardians are chosen by 100 electors being appointed by a double general voting, and these latter choosing the 37 out of themselves. The guardians may not be less than 50 nor more than 70 years old; vi. 753 B; 755 A.

[73] vi. 772 C.

[74] vi. 766 D sqq.; ix. 855 C; 856 E; 871 D, 877 B. Of the further determinations concerning administrative and penal justice, three are especially to be noticed: the abolition of the αὐτωμοσία (i.e. the affidavits of the two parties as to their evidence), because it necessarily leads to false oaths and to the depreciation of the oath (xii. 948 B sqq.); the division of wrongs into such as are done designedly, such as are done undesignedly, and such as are done under the influence of passion (ix. 860 C–862 C; 866 D sqq.); the abolition of the confiscation of property, of complete ἀτιμία and of all other penalties which extend to posterity (ix. 855 A, C; 856 C).

[75] See note 71.

[76] Priests, temple-keepers, and interpreters, the first chosen from the elder citizens by lot, but only for a period of one year, vi. 759 A sqq.; Agronomi, 60 in number, who form the country police, and employ a part of the young men in maintaining order, fortification, road-making, and other generally useful works, and at the same time exercise them for the defence of the country (760 A sqq.); Astynomi and Agoranomi, who are occupied with the city police, public works, etc., 763 C sqq., Strategi, Hipparchs, Taxiarchs, Pylarchs, chosen out of those who are capable of bearing arms; the lower places are occupied by the Strategi, 755 B sqq.

beside it. The popular assembly, which in Athens finally appropriated all the power to itself, is scarcely mentioned; its whole activity is confined to elections, and judgments on state-crimes. This is an important limitation of the democratic element; but, on the other hand, this element reappears strongly in the principle that all civil officers, before entering on their duties, are to have their legal qualifications tested,[77] and on leaving office are to give an account of their administration; a special court is appointed to receive these statements, the members being chosen by the people in repeated general elections.[78] Plato in this follows the customs of his country: indeed, the pattern of the existing states of Greece throughout underlies the whole political organism of his constitution. There is, however, as close an approach to the type of the Republic as the difference of presuppositions allows, in two other ordinances of a more specific kind. A functionary, declared to be the highest officer in the State, and therefore selected with the greatest care,[79] is appointed to preside over instruction and education, and to supervise all music and poetry, in which duties he is to be allowed the assistance of subordinates.[80] And while education is thus provided for, express means are devised for the maintenance of a high standard of public opinion, first among the rulers, and through them among the

---

[77] See on this δοκιμασία, vi. 753 E; 754 D; 755 D; 756 E; 759 D; 760 A; 767 D, &c.

[78] xii. 945 B sqq.; cf. vi. 761 E; 774 B; xi. 881 E.

[79] vi. 765 D sqq.; cf. vii. 801 B; 808 E; 813 B; xi. 936 A.

[80] vi. 764 C sqq.; vii. 813 C sqq.

community at large. A council [81] is to be formed, consisting of the most tried and proved guardians, to be the anchor of the State,[82] and, like the Synhedria among the Pythagoreans,[83] to be the supreme authority in the ordering of the commonwealth. The members of this council must be distinguished above all the other citizens for that higher culture which has already been mentioned;[84] they are to possess not merely true opinions, but real intelligence.[85] Here we see plainly a substitute for the philosophic rulers of the Republic.[86] We are also told[87] that it can only be determined in the course of their education what these elected ones are to learn, and how much time they are to devote to each subject. This would seem to imply that after all they cannot attain to ethical and political wisdom without a more comprehensive scientific training, and consequently that the State of the Laws, should its actualization be attempted, must again tend towards the philosophic State of the Republic. There are other indications of a similar nature.[88] But as the rest of the govern-

---

[81] xii. 960 B–968 E; 951 C sqq.
[82] ἄγκυρα πάσης τῆς πόλεως, 961 C.
[83] See vol. i. 275.
[84] See note 21; and pp. 526, 527.
[85] i. 632 C.
[86] Cf. too the ordinance requiring that a man shall be 50 years old to participate in the council, and that, together with the members proper, younger men are to be chosen as their assistants (xii. 951 C; 961 A; 964 D sq.; 946 A; vi. 755 A; cf. 765 D and supra, p. 480, 69), besides the name φύλακες, and the remark that they correspond to the element of reason in man, xii. 962 C; 964 B sqq.; cf. supra, 474, 44.
[87] 968 C sq.
[88] Especially xii. 951 B sq.: all laws are incomplete and of uncertain stability so long as they appeal only to custom and not to judgment (γνώμη). They, therefore, who are led to this judgment by a nobler nature ought to be

540   *PLATO AND THE OLDER ACADEMY.*

ment is in no way based upon this council of the wise, and as the council itself is not incorporated into the organism of the State by any definite official sphere of action, there is a certain ambiguity and uncertainty about the whole scheme.

As in the constitution, so in social regulations, the Laws seek to mediate between the theories of the Republic and ordinary conditions. Community of goods is abandoned as impracticable;[89] but in order to approach it as nearly as possible, and to guard on the one hand against poverty, and on the other against inordinate wealth, both being generally incompatible with virtue,[90] complete equality of landed property on the Spartan model is introduced. The number of citizens is fixed at 5,040: should there be any danger of exceeding this number, the increase of children is to be restricted; otherwise it is to be encouraged. The emigration of colonists and the admission of foreigners are to serve the same end.[91] Among these 5,040 citizens, the land is to be divided into equal parts, which are to descend inalienably from father to sons; in case of a man having no sons, he must adopt some.[92] A fixed proportion, never to be exceeded, is established in the case of moveable property. According to the amount which they possess of such property, the citizens are divided into four classes.[93] Lastly, with a

sought out everywhere, even from without; for such contemplative study ($\theta\epsilon\omega\rho\iota\alpha$) is quite indispensable.
[89] v. 739 D sq., see note 16.
[90] v. 742 D sqq.
[91] v. 737 C sqq.; 740 C sq
[92] Ibid. 789 E–741 D; xi. 923 C

In 745 C sq., we find scrupulous care for the equal value of the portions of land; hence the division of each estate into a nearer and a more remote half.
[93] 744 B sqq.; cf. supra, note 69.

view to nullifying some of the chief inducements to the amassing of riches and to covetousness, the law of Lycurgus prohibiting marriage dowries is resorted to;[94] all lending money upon usury is forbidden; as in Sparta, the citizens are to possess neither gold nor silver, but money peculiar to the country, which will not pass current elsewhere. Trade and commerce are to be exclusively carried on by metics or freedmen, who are allowed only a temporary settlement in the State.[95] Marriage is not abolished by the Laws, any more than private property; but its strict supervision by the State is represented as altogether indispensable. The age during which marriages may take place is accurately fixed; celibacy is threatened with fines and disgrace; in marriage compacts, care is to be taken that the two characters supplement each other. With regard to the conduct of married people, especially in the matter of children, there are not only detailed prescripts, but a special magistrate to see that they are obeyed. Divorce is to be reserved by the authorities for cases of childlessness, incurable discord, or grave offences against children. Second marriage is discouraged, if there are children by the first; otherwise it is enjoined:[96] unchastity is strictly prohibited.[97] As in the Republic, the greatest attention is bestowed upon education. The care of the State for the training

---

[94] v. 742 C; vi. 774 C sq. (where there is only a slight modification). Somewhat similar is xi. 944 D.

[95] v. 741 E sqq.; vii. 806 D; viii. 846 D–850 D; 842 D; xi. 915 B; 919 D sqq.; 921 C.

[96] vi. 771 E; 772 D–776 B; 779 D; 783 D–785 B; iv. 721 A sqq.; xi. 930 B; ix. 868 C.

[97] See p. 456, 62 and xi. 930 D.

of its citizens begins at their entrance into life, or even before. As soon as the age of the children will permit, they are to be received, as in Sparta, into educational establishments,[98] The principle of public education is to be so rigidly carried out, that parents are not even to be allowed to devote their child to a particular branch of study for a longer or shorter time than the school arrangements prescribe.[99] The subjects for instruction are the usual music and gymnastic, to which, however, a certain amount of arithmetic, geometry, and astronomy is superadded. The main principles of education are essentially the same as in the Republic.[100] There is the same demand that women shall receive an education identical with that of men, even in warlike exercises.[101] The regulations as to the ordinary life of the citizens are as nearly as possible alike. Though the family and private property are maintained, domestic life is in great part done away with by the publicity of education, and by the common meals, which are a universal institution for both sexes.[102] The women are still to take part in public employments and in war.[103] Excluded from all commercial activity, and leaving even agriculture to their slaves, the citizens are to devote themselves

---

[98] From the age of four onwarde the children are to be kept under inspection in infant schools, vii. 793 E sq.

[99] vii. 810 A; cf. 804 D.

[100] The whole seventh book comes under this head. The mathematical sciences are treated, 809 C sq., 817 E sqq. Hunting is discussed by way of appendix, 822 D sqq.; cf. p. 479, 497 sq., 511 sq.

[101] vii. 793 D sqq.; 804 D–806 D.

[102] vi 780 D sqq.; vii. 806 E; cf. viii. 842 B; 847 E sq.; Hermann, loc. cit. 28 sq.

[103] vi. 785 B; 784 A sq., vii. 805 C sqq.; 806 E; 794 A sq., &c.

THE LAWS. SOCIAL REGULATIONS. 543

entirely to the State and to their own improvement.[104] Simplicity, temperance, and hardiness are to be insured not only by education, but by strict rules of life,[105] and laws against luxury.[106] Trade and commerce are carefully supervised : precautions are taken by means of heavy penalties and thorough public surveillance [107] against fraud and overreaching. Beggars are not tolerated.[108] That no disturbing elements may intrude into the State, from its very foundation, its purity is jealously to be guarded.[109] That no foreign admixture may afterwards alter its peculiar character, all kinds of restrictions are imposed upon the intercourse of strangers with the inhabitants; travels into other countries are only permitted to men of mature age for public or educational purposes, and returned travellers are to be prevented from introducing injurious customs and principles.[110] Similarly the citizens are to be preserved from moral infection by supervision of the arts, as has already been shown.[111]

If, then, we take into account all the features that distinguish the State of the Republic from that of the Laws, we cannot help seeing that there is not merely here and there a difference, but that the two States are drawn from wholly distinct points of view. The difference is not, indeed, of a kind to imply any radical alteration in philosophic principles. It is avowed in

[104] vii. 806 D–807 D; viii. 842 D; 846 D; 847 A; xi. 919 D sq.
[105] E.g. vii. 806 D; 807 D sqq.; ii. 666 A sq.; 674 A sq.
[106] Cf. viii. 847 B; vi. 775 A sq.; xii. 955 E sq.; 958 D sqq.
[107] xi. 915 D–918 A; 920 B sq.; 921 A–D.
[108] xi. 936 B sq.
[109] v. 735 C sqq.; cf. supra, p. 468, 23.
[110] xi. 949 A–953 E.
[111] 571 sqq.

the Laws, sometimes by slight indications, sometimes more directly, that the institutions of the Republic are the best; that the perfect polity must be founded on Philosophy, and that even the State of the Laws can only exist by virtue of scientific intelligence in the ruling authorities. But the author's faith in the practical realization of his ideal, or, rather, his faith in mankind, on whose virtue and wisdom this realization depends, is deeply shaken. Not men, he says, but only gods and sons of gods, would conform themselves to such institutions.[112] Only they would be able to endure the unlimited power which the Republic and the Politicus place in the rulers. Human nature is much too weak to recognise what is best and remain true in practice to this recognition.[113] Wherever Plato turns his gaze, he finds so much wrong and perversity that he is inclined to pass the bitterest judgments on mankind.[114] Human things appear[115] to him poor and worthless, and man himself scarcely more than a plaything of the gods.[116] He sees, indeed, so great an amount of imperfection and evil in the world, that (unless there is some error in the original text of this passage of the Laws), departing from his earlier expositions and contradicting the spirit of his

---

[112] v. 739 D sq.; see p. 522.
[113] ix. 874 E sqq.; see p. 531.
[114] E.g. v. 727 A; 728 B; 731 D sqq.; vi. 773 D; vii. 797 A; cf. Plat. Stud p. 75.
[115] vii. 803 B: ἔστι δὴ τοίνυν τὰ τῶν ἀνθρώπων πράγματα μεγάλης μὲν σπουδῆς οὐκ ἄξια, κ.τ.λ.; cf. also v. 728 D sq.

[116] i. 644 D, vii. 803 C; 804 B; x. 903 D, with which compare the quotation from Heraclitus, vol. i. 536; i. 587, 6, 3rd edit. In the Laws he even does not hesitate to call his own inquiries mere play: i. 636 C; iii. 685 A; 688 B; 690 D; x. 885 C; Plat. Stud. 73.

whole theory,[117] he can only explain it on the assumption that there is at work, beside the good and the divine soul, a soul that is evil and opposed to the divine. As all activity results from the soul, wrong and perverted activities must be traced to an evil and perverse soul;[118] and, because evil is so much more

[117] The earlier writings and the Timæus know nothing of an evil World-soul, but derive everything bad and incomplete exclusively from the nature of the corporeal element (see 338, 115). In Polit. 269 E the opinion, which does not differ from the supposition of the Laws, viz. that there are two antagonistic divinities which move the world, is expressly contradicted. It is hard to see how an evil World-soul could be brought into harmony with such a system as Plato's. Is it to spring from the Idea, from the combination of which with space the Timæus derives its World-soul? But in that case it could not possibly be evil, nor at strife with the divine soul of the universe. Or again, is it meant to be originally innate in matter (as Martin and Ueberweg maintain, following Tennemann. Plato, iii. 175 sqq.)? But matter as such is without motive power (see p. 345), or rather it is not at all. Only the Idea is real. Or finally, is it meant that the World-soul, good in itself, afterwards becomes evil (Stallbaum, see p. 338 sq)? Plato's conception is clearly not this, for in the Laws he speaks of two juxtaposed souls, a good and an evil, and not of two successive conditions of one and the same soul. How could the soul of the universe, the most divine of all become things, the source of all reason and order, prove untrue to its nature and determination?

[118] x. 896 C sqq ; 898 C; 904 A sq. As to the attempt to remove these theories from the Laws, cf my Plat. Stud. p 43. These attempts may be made in two ways: either (1) by admitting that the Laws do actually suppose an evil as well as a good soul, but referring this evil soul not to the whole world, but merely to the evil that is in mankind, or (2) by acknowledging that an evil World-soul is spoken of here, but denying that the author of the Laws meant actually to assert the existence of such a soul. His statements are then explained as something posited merely provisionally and by way of hypothesis, and vanishing in the process of development. Fries, Gesch. der Phil. i. 336, as well as Thiersch and Dilthey, adopt the first supposition, and Ritter (Gött. Anz. 1840, 177), Brandis (Gr.-rom Phil. ii. a. 566). Stallbaum (Plat. Opp. x a. CLVIII. sq.), Suckow (Form der Plat. Schr 139 sq), and (virtually) Steinhart agree with the second, which was introduced by Bockh (Steinhart, Pl. WW. vii a. 315, where the two souls are referred to the double motion

common in the world than good, he regards the assistance of the gods indispensable for conflict with it.[119] A philosopher who held such an opinion of the world and of men might well become perplexed as to the practicability of his ideal, and even give up the hope that a whole people would ever submit to the rule of Philosophy: it cannot therefore surprise us that he should attempt to save by a compromise, at least a portion of the former design, with a view to its

of the soul, the regulated and unregulated, in the life of nature); still I cannot consider either of them admissible as long as passages such as the following are not accounted for—x. 896 D. sq.. ψυχὴν δὴ διοικοῦσαν καὶ ἐνοικοῦσαν ἐν ἅπασι τοῖς πάντῃ κινουμένοις μῶν οὐ καὶ τὸν οὐρανὸν ἀνάγκη διοικεῖν φάναι; Τί μήν; Μίαν ἢ πλείους; Πλείους· ἐγὼ ὑπὲρ σφῶν ἀποκρινοῦμαι. Δυοῖν μέν γέ που ἔλαττον μηδὲν τιθῶμεν, τῆς τε εὐεργέτιδος καὶ τῆς τἀναντία δυναμένης ἐξεργάζεσθαι. 898 C: τὴν οὐρανοῦ περιφορὰν ἐξ ἀνάγκης περιάγειν φατέον ἐπιμελουμένην καὶ κοσμοῦσαν ἤτοι τὴν ἀρίστην ψυχὴν ἢ τὴν ἐναντίαν. The author himself does, it is true, decide for the first horn of this dilemma (897 B sq.); but it does not follow that he considers the evil World-soul as nothing actual. It certainly exists; but on account of the superiority of the good it cannot rule the universe. That this doctrine is actually propounded in the Laws is acknowledged by Hermann (Plat. 552), Michelet (Jahrbb. fur Wissensch. Kritik, 1839, Dzbr. p. 862), Vögeli (Uebers. der Gess. Zür.

1842, Pt. ii. p. xiii.), Susemihl (Genet. Entw. ii. 598 sq.). If it once be admitted that evil just as much as good must be caused by the soul (896 D), that the universe (οὐρανὸς) is full of evil and perversion (906 A), and (as is incontestably Plato's opinion, see p. 358 sq.; 385 sq.; Laws, 898 C), that reason only and divine completeness can be ascribed to the soul, which moves the structure of the universe—the conclusion at once presents itself, that the evil and incomplete must spring from another soul, which rules in the world together with the former. The Laws thus only advance a step further than Plato's original doctrine. This doctrine derived the bad and evil from matter (see 338 sqq., 422 sq.; 440): now it is observed that every motion, even faulty motion, must be occasioned by the soul. We could accept the supposition of an evil World-soul as quite consistent, if it did not stand in contradiction with other determinations of Plato's system.

[119] x. 906 A.

realization. Considered in this aspect, the value of the Laws is not to be lightly estimated. They not only display in their details comprehensive knowledge, thorough acquaintance with political questions, reflection, and ripeness of judgment, but in their main outlines are carried out with consistency and ability. Their purpose is to mediate between the ideal State of the Republic and actual conditions: to show what might be attained, even without the rule of Philosophy and of philosophers, on the presupposition of ordinary morality and education, if only there existed practical wisdom and goodwill. For this reason they keep as much as possible to given circumstances, employing for the constitution and social regulations sometimes Athenian, but principally Spartan, models, and for jurisprudence chiefly the Attic laws.[120] At the same time they seek to maintain the ideal of the State of philosophers in such a manner that the merit of the new designs shall be measured by its standards. to make the actual approximate to the perfect State as nearly as men and circumstances will allow, and at least to prepare the way for a still closer approximation.[121] This design is the key, as we have already pointed out, to the most prominent peculiarities of the

[120] The detailed account of this, so far as is possible at the present day, is given by Hermann in the above-mentioned dissertation and its contemporary supplement 'Juris domestici et familiaris apud Platonem in Legibus cum veteris Græciæ inque primis Athenarum institutis comparatio.'

[121] Cf. especially p. 539, and in general Arist. Polit. ii. 6, 1265 a. 1 · τῶν δὲ νόμων τὸ μὲν πλεῖστον μέρος νόμοι τυγχάνουσιν ὄντες, ὀλίγα δὲ περὶ τῆς πολιτείας εἴρηκεν. καὶ ταύτην βουλόμενος κοινοτέραν ποιεῖν ταῖς πόλεσι, κατὰ μικρὸν περιάγει πάλιν πρὸς τὴν ἑτέραν πολιτείαν (that of the Republic).

548   *PLATO AND THE OLDER ACADEMY.*

Laws. Our judgment as to the genuineness of the work [122] will, therefore, mainly depend on our being able to ascribe to Plato in the last decade of his life [123] an overclouding of his original idealism, a doubt of the possibility of his State of philosophers, a bitterness in his view of the world and of human nature,—such as the Laws presuppose. As to particular defects which are to be found in the dialogue,[124] some of them are readily accounted for,[125] others [126] may be explained by the

---

[122] With reference to the discussions as to the genuineness of the Laws, occasioned by Ast's attacks and my Platonic Studies, compare, together with the remarks, p. 100 sqq., Steinhart, Plat. WW. vii. a. 90 sqq.; Susemihl, Genet. Entw. 562 sq. The believers in their spuriousness have been, besides Suckow (see p. 50, 13; p 108, 44), Strumpell, Gesch. der Prakt. Phil. d Gr. i. 457, and Ribbing, Plat. Ideenl. ii. 150 sqq. Ueberweg (see 109, 45) and Schaarschmidt (Samml. d. plat. Schr 94, 148, 1, etc.) do not extend their doubts to this treatise, and Steinhart and Susemihl (who often corrects the former in certain points), prove its original Platonic source in a detailed discussion. I withdrew my earlier doubts in the first edition of the present work.

[123] That the Laws cannot belong to any earlier period is rendered probable (besides the quotations on pp. 141, 142; p. 32, 68) by the passage, i. 638 A. The subjugation of the Locrians by the Syracusans mentioned here can scarcely (as Bockh remarks, following Bentley, Plat. Min 73) refer to anything but the despotism of Dionysius the younger, in Locri, after his first banishment from Syracuse, which is recorded in Strabo, I i. 8, p. 259; Plut. præc. ger. reip. 28, 7, p. 821; Athenæus, xii 541 C. Not much is proved against this by ii. 659 B.

[124] Plat. Stud 32 sq., 38. 108 sq

[125] As the θείᾳ μοίρᾳ, i 642, on which cf. p. 176, and the expressions as to παιδεραστία, cf. p 456. The frequent praise of the Spartan constitution, which, however, is counterbalanced by open censure of its one-sidedness, finds its justification in the supposed situation; the remarkable determination, ix. 873 E, corresponds to an old Attic regulation (a similar thing exists at the present day in England); the contradiction between iii. 682 E and 685 E can be removed by a correct explanation of the former passage. Ix. 855 C, according to the correct reading, and in order to avoid a contradiction with 877 C, 868 A, must be interpreted as follows: 'No one, not even the exile, shall be entirely deprived of his rank as a citizen.' This determination has its value,

infirmities of age, and by the circumstance that the author did not himself put the final touches to his work. Editors[127] and even transcribers[128] may well be held responsible here and there.[129] We may, on similar

because the Laws are acquainted with banishment for a short period (ix. 865 E sq.; 867 C sq.; 868 C sqq.), and because complete ἀτιμία brought its consequences on the children. Finally, although the case supposed (iv. 709 E sqq) and expressly desired might strike us as strange, viz. that a tyrant endowed with all possible good qualities should undertake the realization of the Platonic proposals, still in its connection this is not without congruity. The meaning is, not that the tyrant as such could be the true ruler, but that a tyranny can be most quickly and easily changed into a good constitution, if a chief, as Plato might have imagined to himself the younger Dionysius (cf. 368, 2), endowed with good natural talents, young, and hence an uncorrupted heir to such a single rulership, submitted himself to the guidance of a wise lawgiver. Such a case was supposed in Rep. vi. 499 B, cf. v. 473 D. Even the τυραννουμένη ψυχή (710 A) can be justified from this point of view: the soul of the tyrant is a τυραννουμένη, in so far as it is itself bound by its position, but, just as the πόλις τυραννουμένη, it is to be set free through the influence of the lawgiver.

[126] To these belongs the much boasted invention that drunkenness (for it is this that is being discussed, and not mere drinking banquets. i. 637 D; 638 C; 640 D, 645 D; 646 B; ii. 671 D sq.) is to be applied as a means of education and training (i 635 B–650; ii. 671 A sqq). This is subsequently falsified (ii. 666 A sq.), when it is said that this means is only admissible in the case of mature men. There is also a contradiction between vi. 772 D, where the 25th year is given as the earliest period for marriage in men, and iv 721 B, vi. 785 B, where the 30th year is given. On the other hand it is not correct that (vii. 818 A, xii. 957 A) unfulfilled promises occur, which point to an incomplete form of the work (Hermann, Plat. 708); the first passage refers to xii. 967 D sqq., the second to 962 D sq.

[127] See p. 142, 122. Proclus (as Suckow, p. 152, points out from the Προλεγόμενα τ. Πλάτωνος φιλοσ. c 25) believed that the Laws were not quite finished by Plato.

[128] The present text of the Laws is not good. In many places Hermann, Susemihl (Jahrb. f. Phil. lxxxiii. 135 sqq., 693 sqq), and Peipers (Quæst. crit. de Plat. leg. Berl. 1863) have endeavoured to improve it, partly by conjecture and partly by MSS.

[129] In this way, as I have remarked in my treatise on Platonic anachronisms (Abh. d. Berl. Akad. 1873; Philes.-hist. Kl p. 97), the two offending passages may be easily got rid of, as also the striking and purposeless anachronism with regard to Epimenides (details about which are given, loc. cit. 95 sq.; Plat. Stud.

grounds, in some instances excuse, and in others explain, the defects of form in the Laws: the awkward, and occasionally obscure and overcharged expressions, the want of dialectical versatility and conversational movement, the solemnity of the tone, the various small exaggerations, the many reminiscences of earlier works. If we conceive the Laws as written by Plato in his old age, when he could no longer give artistic completeness to the work, and suppose that one of his disciples in editing it may have passed over much crudity, carelessness, and repetition,—may have ventured upon certain additions, and unskilfully supplied certain gaps,—these peculiarities are at once accounted for. The chief question to determine is whether or not the general standpoint of the Laws is

iii.), and the expressions about the evil World-soul, mentioned p. 544 sq. The first would be removed without changing a single word and merely by omissions, if we read i 642 D sq: τῇδε γὰρ ἴσως ἀκήκοας ὡς Ἐπιμενίδης γέγονεν ἀνὴρ θεῖος, ὃς ἦν ἡμῖν οἰκεῖος, ἐλθὼν δὲ παρ' ὑμᾶς κατὰ τὴν τοῦ θεοῦ μαντείαν θυσίας ἐθύσατό τινας, ἃς ὁ θεὸς ἀνεῖλεν· τοτ' οὖν ἐξενώθησαν ὑμῖν οἱ πρόγονοι ἡμῶν, κ.τ.λ. The explanation about the evil World-soul might by an inconsiderable change of the words be taken out of the paragraph in which it stands, and the connection would distinctly gain. If, after the words τί μήν (896 E), we were to continue (898 D): ἥλιον δὲ καὶ σελήνην, κ.τ.λ., no one would notice the slightest loss; neither in what follows is there any reference to the supposition of a double soul, nor is there anything pointing to it in what precedes. Plato does not say one word to signify that the κίνησις ἐν πολλοῖς, mentioned 893 C sq., is the irregular motion proceeding from the bad soul (Steinhart, loc. cit. 315 sq.), nor do we need to derive (with Susemihl, ii. 600) the whole of the corporeal motions besides the circular motion from it. In the Timæus he is acquainted with many other motions as well as the circular one of reason, without assuming a double soul (p. 360, 166, where the passage from the Laws is of doubtful cogency by the side of those just quoted). To reject the section 896 E (μίαν-) to 898 D (ποῖον;) would distinctly strengthen the cogency of the argument for the divinity of the world and stars. Possibly the whole discussion is due to an editors's insertion.

consistent with the theory of its Platonic origin? and this may well be answered in the affirmative, if we take into consideration the influence which years and the experiences of a long life usually have, even on the most powerful minds;—and also the extent to which Plato's confidence in the realization of his ideal State must have been shaken by the then condition of Greece, and especially by the failure of his Sicilian enterprise. The Laws are, after all, no farther removed from the Republic than the second part of Goethe's 'Faust' is from the first; scarcely farther indeed than the 'Wanderjahre' from the 'Lehrjahre' of the Wilhelm Meister; and if, in the one case, we can follow the transition from the earlier to the later period, and the gradual advance of the poet's age, more perfectly than in the case of Plato,—for, with the exception of the Laws, there is no probability that we possess any work of his last twenty years,—in the other we have the statements of Aristotle to prove that considerable changes did take place during those years in Plato's manner of teaching, and that in his Metaphysics especially he made very important concessions to Pythagoreanism, to which the Laws approximate much more closely than the Republic. Since then the contents of this book are too important and betray too much of the Platonic spirit to be ascribed to any disciple of Plato that we know of; since such matured political wisdom, such accurate knowledge of Greek laws and institutions as we there find are quite worthy of the philosopher in his old age; since, finally, the express testimony of Aristotle can hardly be set aside; we have every ground for believing that this treatise was composed by Plato, but published by another—Philippus of Opus—after Plato's death; and this origin explains many defects which the author would have removed had he himself completed his work. But its contents must in all essential points be considered as genuine, and it thus forms the only direct source of information as to the Platonic Philosophy in its latest period. We learn, indeed, nothing from the Laws respecting the speculative bases of that philosophy, but the whole tenor of the work is in harmony with what Aristotle tells us of Plato's oral discourses, and with all that is distinctive in the thought of the Older Academy.

THE PLATONIC SCHOOL.

CHAPTER XIV.

THE OLDER ACADEMY. SPEUSIPPUS.

PLATO's long continued instructions had assembled in the Academy a numerous circle of hearers, men of various ages, who were attracted by his fame, often from distant countries; and so far as an individual may be said to have contributed to that result, Athens owes it to him, more than to any one, that even after the loss of her political ascendancy, she still remained the centre of all the philosophic aspirations of Greece. Among the disciples of Plato that are known to us,[1]

---

[1] The wide propagation of the Platonic school is attested, amongst other evidences, by the large number of those who are called personal pupils of Plato. I give in what follows an alphabetical list of them, in which those who have been already cited, p. 30, 64, or who are to be cited with more detail immediately, are only named, about the rest I add more particulars. The register of Academics in Fabricius, Bibl. Gr. iii. 159 sqq, Harl. has many deficiencies, and makes the mistake of representing as Platonists all who have any connection whatever with Plato, even to his slaves. (1) Amyntas of Heraclea, as he is called in the catalogue of Academic philosophers ('Ind. Hercul.'), edited by Spengel, Philol. Supplement-bl. ii. 535 sqq and Bucheler, in the Griefswalder Ind. Schol. for 1869–70, from the second collection of the Volumina Herculanensia, i. 162 sqq ; Diog iii. 46, calls him Amyclus, Ælian, V H iii. 19 and Procl. in Eucl. 19 (p. 67, Fried.) Amyclas. The former reckons him among the more eminent Platonists, the latter among the mathematicians of merit. (2) The Locrian, Aristides, who is called Plato's ἑταῖρος by Plut. Timol. 6 (3) Aristonymus, see above. (4) Aristotle. (5) Athenæus of Cyzicus (apud Procl. loc. cit. according to the corrected reading). (6) Bryso, if the contemporary comedian, Ephippus, is right.

we find many more foreigners than Athenians: the greater number belong to that Eastern portion of the

in assigning him to the Academy, apud Athen. xi. 509 C; it is not clear how this Bryso is related to Bryso the Heracleote (see Pt. i. 206, 4), to Bryso the mathematician (Ep. Plat. xiii. 360 C), whose failure to square the circle is frequently mentioned by Aristotle (Anal. post. i. 9, beginn.; Soph. Elench. ii. 171 b. 16, 172 a. 3; cf the commentators, Schol in Arist. 211 b. sq.; 306 b. 24 sqq.; 45 sqq.; Waitz Arist. Org. ii. 324), and, finally, to the Sophist of the same name mentioned by Aristotle, Hist. Anim. vi. 5; 563 a. 7; ix. 11; 615 a 9; Rhet. iii 2; 1405 b. 9. (7) Chæro of Pellene; see p. 31 and Ind. Herc. ii. 7, where, as in Athenæus, probably on the authority of Hermippus, it is stated that he set himself up for a tyrant. (8) Chio and (9) Leonides (loc. cit. and Ind. Herc. 6, 13). (10) Delius, see above (11) Demetrius of Amphipolis (Diog. 46). (12) The mathematician Dinostratus, brother of Menæchmus (Procl. in Eucl. loc. cit.). (13) Dion, see above. (14) Erastus and (15) Coriscus of Scepsis (Diog 46; Stob. Floril. vii 53; Ep Plat vi.; Strabo, xiii. 1, 54; p 603). The latter calls them both Socratics; but as he at the same time adds that Coriscus was the father of Neleus, who inherited the library of Theophrastus, they can only have been so called as having been pupils of some Socratic. (Cf. Böckh, Abhandl. d. Berl. Akad. 1853; Hist.-phil. Kl. p. 139.) (16) Evæon of Lampsacus; v. supra. (17) Eudemus of Cyprus, the friend of Aristotle; cf. vol. ii b. 9; i 45 sq. 2nd edit. (18) Eudoxus, see infra. (19) Euphræus, see above. (20)

Helicon, the astronomer, of Cyzicus (Plut. Dio, 19, gen.; Socr. 7, p. 579; Epist. Plat. xiii. 360 C; Philostr. v. Apoll. i. 35, 1). (21) Heraclides Ponticus, see infra. (22) Heraclides of Ænos; see above and Ind. Herc. 6, 15 sq. (23) Hermias, Prince of Atarneus; see above and Pt. ii. b. 16 sq. 2nd edit. (24) Hermodorus of Syracuse, well known as a mathematician, a biographer of Plato, and a buyer of Platonic writings; Diog. Procem. 2, 6; ii. 106; iii. 6; Ind. Herc. 6, 6 sq.; Cic. ad Att. xiii. 21. Suidas, Λόγοισιν, ii. a. 601, Bernh. Simpl. Phys. 54 b. o.; 56 b. o.; Ps. Plut. De nobil. p. 627; cf. my treatise De Hermodoro, 17 sqq. and supra, p. 14, 26; p. 242, 47; p. 277, 138. (25) Hestiæus, see below. (26) Hippothales of Athens (Diog. 46). (27) Leo of Syzantium, see supra and Müller, Fragm. Hist. gr. ii. 328. (28) The mathematician Menæchmus, the pupil of Eudoxus and Plato: Theo Astron. c. 41, p. 27, a (on the authority of Dercyllides): Procl. in Euclid. 19 w.; 21, o.; 22 m.; 31 o.; 68 w. (p. 67, 72, 78, 111, Friedl.) in Plat. Tim. 149 C, Eratosth. ap. Eutoc. in Archimed. de sph. et Cyl. p. 21 sq., Martin, on Theo's Astron. p. 58 sqq., who is quite right in identifying him with the Platonist Μάναιχμος of Suidas and Eudocia. (29) Menedemus, the Pyrrhæan, see supra and Ind. Herc. 6, 2; 7, 2; according to the latter passage Menedemus was held in such respect by his fellow-scholars, that in the election of a successor to Speusippus he, together with Heraclides, was only a few votes behind Xenocrates. (30) The soothsayer Miltas of

Greek world which since the Persian War had fallen chiefly under the influence of Athens. In the Western regions, so far as these were at all ripe for philosophy, Pythagoreanism, then in its first and most flourish-

Thessaly (Plut. Dio, 22). (31) Pamphilus, perhaps of Samos, where he heard Epicurus; Cic. N. D. i. 26, 72. (32) Philippus of Opus, see infra, probably the same person as Philippus the Medmæan. (33) Phormio, see above. (34) Python of Ænos, see above, and Ind. Herc. 6, 15 sq. (35) Speusippus, see below. (36) Theætetus the Athenian: Plato, Theæt Soph. Polit., cf. Pt. i. 198; and supra 18, 31; Procl. in Eucl. 19 w.; 20 o. (p. 66 sq Fr). Suidas, Θεαίτ. distinguishes from him a philosopher of the same name of Heraclea in Pontus, calling the former a pupil of Socrates, the latter an ἀκροατὴς Πλάτωνος. But at the same time he asserts that the Socratic taught in Heraclea; he calls him an astronomer, and says that he was the first to write on the five regular solids, whereas, according to Proclus, the mathematician (in which character Plato depicts his Theætetus) is not distinct from the Platonist. The Theætetus of Plato becomes acquainted with Socrates only a few weeks before his death, and so far, even if this trait is meant to be historical, could scarcely have been called a scholar of Socrates. Everything, therefore, seems to support the supposition that Suidas made the one Theætetus into two, by referring two notices, of which the one called him a Socratic and the other a Platonist, to two distinct persons. Still the question might be raised whether Theætetus did actually come into connection with Socrates, or whether he was only represented in that connection by Plato in order that a part might be given to him in the dialogues mentioned. The same may be the case with (37) the younger Socrates (Pt. i. p. 198): he seems to have been a pupil of Plato's; whether he was known to Socrates must remain undecided. (38) Theodectes of Phaselis, the well-known rhetorician and tragic poet, who, acc. to Suid. Θεοδ., together with Isocrates, heard both Plato and Aristotle, and was often quoted by the latter (see the index). More particulars about him are to be found in the passages pointed out by Bernhardy ad Suid. sub voce; cf. also Plut. Alex. 17, end. (39) The mathematician Theudius of Magnesia (Procl. 19 u.) (40) Timolaus of Cyzicus · see above, p. 366. (41) Timonides the Leucadian (Plut. Dio, 22, 30, 31, 35; Diog. iv 5, cf. p. 840), the companion and historian of Dio, seems, like Eudemus, to have belonged to the Platonic school. (42) Xenocrates will be spoken of later on Several persons whose connection with Plato is uncertain, or who, at any rate, could not be considered his scholars, were mentioned, p 30 e.g. Calippus, Clearchus, Chabrias. Timotheus, Phocion, the orators Hyperides, Lycurgus, Æschines, Demosthenes. Two women, Axiothea of Phlius and Lasthenia of Mantinea, are said to have frequented Plato's discourses. Diog. iii. 46, iv 2; Athen.

ing period, most probably hindered the spread of Platonism, despite the close relation between the two systems. The external gathering point of the Platonists was that garden near the Academy [2] which descended by inheritance from Plato to Speusippus,[3] and afterwards in regular order to each successive head of the School: the spirit of community was maintained by the social meals instituted by Plato.[4] The direction of the Society was, as a general rule, passed on by the dying or retiring leader to one of his disciples; but though this recommendation was almost always respected, the community appears to have reserved to itself the right of final election.[5]

---

vii. 279 e. xii. 546 d. Clemens Strom. iv. 523 A; Themist. Orat. xxiii. 295 c.

[2] See above, p 25, 49, p. 24, 48.

[3] This is clear, not so much from express information (for even in Plato's will, apud Diog. iii. 42, the garden is not disposed of), as from the indubitable fact that it was in the possession of Xenocrates, Polemo, and their successors downwards up to the sixth century of the Christian era, cf. Plut. De Exil c. 10, p. 603, where by the 'Academy' in which Plato, Xenocrates, and Polemo dwelt, we can only understand Plato's garden. Diog. iv 6, 19, 39, Xenocrates, Polemo, Arcesilaus lived in the garden. Damasc v. Isid. 158 (more at length ap. Suid. Πλάτων, ii. b. 297 B): the produce of the garden in his time formed only the smallest portion of the revenues of Plato's successors. The Museum, also erected by Plato, in which Speusippus exhibited pictures of the Graces (Diog. iv. 1, 19), perhaps stood in the garden. Speusippus himself, however, does not seem to have lived there: cf. Plut. loc. cit. with Diog. iv. 3. Together with the Museum, seats for the lectures are mentioned (ἐξέδρα) (Diog. 19), which, however, acc. to Cic Fin. v. 1, 2, Diog. iv. 63, were in the Academic Gymnasium. The analogy of the Peripatetic and Epicurean school, to be mentioned later on, confirms the above. More details are given apud Zumpt 'On the continuance of the philosophical schools in Athens,' Abh. der Berl Akademie, 1842, phil. hist Kl. p. 32 [8] sqq.

[4] See p. 28, 59. Acc to Athen. i. 3 sq v. 186, b. Speusippus and Xenocrates, and then Aristotle, composed special table laws for these meetings. They had a school discipline (Diog. v. 4), to which, among other things, belonged the regulation that every ten days one of the scholars should be appointed ἄρχων.

[5] The usual course, doubtless,

EXTERNAL HISTORY. 557

Plato's immediate successor was his sister's son, Speusippus.[6] He was followed after eight years by

was for the scholarch, before his death, to appoint his successor; this was done e. g. by Speusippus apud Diog. iv. 3, and ibid. 60 we read that Lacydes was the first who resigned the school to another during his lifetime. Arcesilaus received it (ibid. 32) after the death of Crates ἐκχωρήσαντος αὐτῷ Σωκρατίδου τινός. Still, this supposes an election or, at least, the consent of the whole body, even if this retirement was voluntary. If the outgoing scholarch appointed his successor, this appointment required the consent of those who were to be under him. The Herculanean catalogue, at least, asserts (cf. note 1, 'Menedemus') that after the death of Speusippus Xenocrates was carried by only a few votes against Heraclides and Menedemus. Among the Peripatetics we find, as well as the ordinary succession by bequest (as Theophrastus according to A. Gell. xiii 5, and doubtless also the later heads), an election of his successor ordered by Lyco (Diog. v. 70). Zumpt, loc. cit. 30 sq

[6] Fischer. De Speusippi Vita, Rast. 1845 Speusippus, the nephew of Plato, son of Eurymedon (who is, doubtless, not the same as the Eurymedon mentioned in Plato's will, ap. Diog. iii. 43, and next after Speusippus amongst the executors), and Potone (Diog. iii. 4, iv. 1, Cic. N. D. i. 13, 32, etc.), seems to have been some 20 years younger than Plato We can hardly assume less difference in their ages, it Plato was the eldest child of his parents. Speusippus' mother would thus be younger than Plato, which, however, is uncertain (cf. p. 3, 3, end, 44, 111). Again, the difference cannot be much greater, because Speusippus (acc. to Diog. iv. 14, 3, 1; Ind. Hercul vi. 5, v a.), died Ol. 110, 2 (339 B.C. acc. to Eus. Chron. Ol. 110, 3), after attaining a considerable age (γηραιός). Ammonius also, V. Arist. p. 11, West; cf. Hermipp. apud Diog. V. 2, says that in 335, when Aristotle came to Athens, he was no longer alive. His reported poverty is not proved by the pseudo-Chio Epist. 10. Educated under the influence of Plato (Plut. adul. et am. c. 32, p. 71, similarly frat. am c 21, p 491), he gave himself up to his philosophical instruction; according to Diog iv. 2 he also availed himself of that of Isocrates. When Dion came to Athens a very close connection was formed between him and Speusippus, who supported Dion's plans both in Sicily, whither he had accompanied Plato in his last journey, and also later on (Plut. Dio, 17, 22 —see above, p. 34, 73, 75; cf c. 35, and Diog. iv 5, where Fischer p. 16, and Müller fragm. hist gr ii. 33 correctly read Τιμωνίδης instead of Σιμωνίδης. Epist. Socrat. 36, p. 44. It is, however, incredible that the letter was genuine out of which Plut De Adul c. 29, p. 70, quotes a passage. Speusippus held the office of teacher in the Academy only eight years (Diog. iv. 1, Ind. Herc. loc. cit.); having become paralysed by illness, he appointed Xenocrates to be his successor, and, as it is reported, voluntarily put an end to his life (Diog. iv. 3,

Xenocrates,[7] a man who from his attachment to Plato[8] might have been expected to be a faithful interpreter

Galen, hist. phil. c. 2, p. 226; Themist. or xxi 255, B; also Stob. Floril. 119, 17, which, however, is not consistent with his self-murder). The mention by Diog. iv. 4 (professedly from Plutarch's Sulla and Lysander, where, however, it does not occur), of the unavoidable φθειρίασις, depends entirely upon a confusion. In his younger years Speusippus is said to have lived somewhat licentiously; but Plato, without much exhortation, merely by the force of example, brought him to better courses (Plut. adul. et am. c. 32, p. 71, frat. am. c. 21, p. 491). The reproaches heaped upon him in later times (apud Diog. iv. 1 sq ; Athen. vii. 279 e. xii. 546; d. Philostr. V. Apollon. c. 35, p. 43 ; Suidas, Αἰσχίνης, in. b. 64, Bernh. Epist. Socrat. 36, p. 44; Tertull. Apeleget. 46) spring from such impure sources that no stain can thus accrue to his character. The calumny, e g., of his deadly enemy Dionysius (ap. Diog. and Athen.) seems to have no other foundation than the fact that he was an intimate friend of Lasthenia, and that he started a collection to pay off the debts of a friend (there is nothing about paying for his tuition). The inordinate love of pleasure, with which he is charged, would hardly agree with his ethical principles. On other points see Fischer, p. 29 sq. Plut. Dio, 17 praises his amiability, Antigonus (see 363, 3) the temperance of his meals in the Academy. His reported marriage we must leave undecided. His writings (to be mentioned later on) are said to have been bought by Aristotle for three talents; Diog. iv. 5, Gell. N. A. iii. 17, 3.

[7] Van de Wynpersse, De Xenocrate Chalcedonio, Leyd. 1823. The mother city of Xenocrates is Chalcedon (Cic. Acad. i. 4, 17; Diog. iv. 6 ; Strabo, xii. 4, 9, p. 566; Stob. Ecl. i. 62; Athen. xii. 530, d. &c ; Καρχηδόνιος in Clem. cohort. 44, A ; Strom. v. 590, C. Euseb. pr ev. xiii 13, 53, and in the MSS. of Diogenes and Ælian, V. H. ii. 41, xiii. 31, is a mistake; cf. Krische Forsch. 318, 2, Wynpersse, p. 5; ibid. 9 on the name of his father; Agathenor). He received the headship of the school Ol. 110, 2; he died, acc to Diog. iv. 14, 16, after holding it for 25 years, consequently in Ol. 116, 3 (B.C 31⅔) at the age of 82 years (Lucian, Macrob 20, puts it at 84, Censorin. Di nat. 15, 2, at 81); so that he was born Ol. 96, 1 (39⅔ B.C.). As a young man, he came to Athens, where he is said to have been at first the pupil of Æschines (Hegesander apud Athen. xi. 507, c.: cf. however the remarks Pt. i. 204. 3 ; supra, 36, 85), but soon passed over to Plato. Henceforward he remained the constant and absolute follower of his teacher, and accompanied him in his last Sicilian voyage (Diog. iv. 6, 11; Ælian xiv. 9 ; cf. Valer. Max. iv. 1, ext. 2; Ælian iii. 19 would bear upon the subject if the fact were true). After Plato's death he went with Aristotle to Atarneus, at the invitation of Hermias (Strabo, xiii. 1, 57, p. 610); we do not know whether he passed from here to Athens or to his native town. It is perhaps a misunderstanding

of the traditions of the School, whose earnestness, strength, and purity of character [9] won for him universal veneration,[10] but whose melancholy cast of mind and acrimonious nature [11] qualified him far more for the dogmatic establishment and mystical obscuration of Plato's doctrine than for its dialectical development.

to suppose (Themist. or. xxi. 255, B) that Speusippus caused him to come from Chalcedon in order that he might hand over the school to him; cf. Diog. iv. 3. While he was at the head of the Academy the Athenian magistrates once had him sold as a slave because he could not pay the protection-tax levied on metics, but he was released by Demetrius Phalereus (Diog. iv. 14, cf. Plut. Flamin. 12, vit. x. orat. vii. 16, p. 842). He is said to have rejected the offer of full Athenian citizenship from repugnance to the prevailing state of affairs (Plut. Phoc. c. 29, Ind. Herc. 8). He died of an accidental wound (Diog. 14). On his pictures see Wynpersse, 53 sqq.

[8] See preceding note.

[9] We have many traits recorded of Xenocrates' earnestness, austerity, contentedness, integrity, love of truth, and conscientiousness, see Diog iv 7–9, ii. 19, Cic. ad Att. i. 16; Pro Balbo, 5, 12, Tusc. v. 32, 91; Off. i. 30, 109; Valer. Max. ii. 10, ext. 2; iv. 3, ext. 3; vii. 2, ext. 6 (where, however, others mention Simonides; Wynpersse 44); Plut. Alex. virt. c. 12, p. 333, Sto. rep. 20, 6, p. 1043; Stob. Floril. 5, 118, 17, 25; Themist. or. ii. 26 A; xxi. 252 A; Athen. xii. 530 d.; Hesych. and Suidas, Ξενοκράτης. His mildness even towards animals is noticed, Diog. 10, Æl. V. H. xiii. 31. The story (Diog. 8; Athen. x. 437, b.; Æl. V. H. ii. 41; Ind. Herc. 8, 9, v. u., Wynpersse, 16, sqq.) about Xenocrates winning a drinking prize is, according to Greek notions, not at all at variance with his moderation, but is to be judged according to the well-known Socratic precedent (see Pt. i. p 63 sq.). The golden chaplet which he won on this occasion he gave away.

[10] See on the recognition which Xenocrates found in Athens, and the consideration which was shown him by Alexander and other princes, Diog. 7, 8, 9, ii.; Plut. Phocion, c. 27, vit. pud. c. ii. p. 533; adv. Col. 32, 9, p. 1126; Ind. Herc. 7, 10 sqq., and other passages quoted in the previous note. The narrative about Polemo (see below) corroborates the impression produced by his personality, Diog. 6.

[11] Cf. Cic Off. i. 30, 109; Plut. De Audiendo, c. 18, p. 47; conjug. præc. c. 28, p. 141; vit. pud. c. ii p. 533, Amator. 23, 13, p. 769; Diog. 6, where are the well-known expressions of Plato: Ξενόκρατες θῦε ταῖς χάρισιν, and about Xenocrates and Aristotle: ἐφ' οἷον ἵππον οἷον ὄνον ἀλείφω, and τῷ μὲν μύωπος δεῖ τῷ δὲ χαλινοῦ. The latter, however, is told of others; see Diog. v. 39, Cic. De Orat. iii. 9, 36; Wynpersse, p. 13.

Besides these two, there are mentioned among Plato's personal disciples Heraclides of Pontus,[12] who, however, seems to have been more of a learned man than a philosopher,[13] and is often claimed for other schools;[14]

[12] On the life and writings of Heraclides cf. Diog. v. 86 sqq.; Roulez, De vitâ et scriptis Heraclidæ P. in the Annales Acad. Lovan. viii 1824; Deswert, De Heraclide P., Löwen, 1830, Müller, Fragm. hist. gr. ii 197 sqq.; Krische Forsch. 325 sq. Born at Heraclea in Pontus (Strabo, xii. 3, 1, p. 541; Diog. 86, Suid. Ἡρακλείδ.), wealthy, and of an illustrious house (Diog. Suid. loc. cit.), he came to Athens, where he seems to have been introduced into the Platonic school by Speusippus (Diog. 86). If it is true that on his last Sicilian voyage (361 B.C) Plato transferred to him the headship of the school (Suid. see p. 34, 73), he can scarcely have been younger than Xenocrates; and as he could speak of the founding of Alexandria (Plut Alex c. 26), he must have lived beyond Ol. 112, 2 (B.C. 330). According to Demetrius, apud Diog. 89, he liberated his native city by killing a tyrant. This, however, scarcely fits in with the history of Heraclea; for it cannot refer to the murder of Clearchus (Roulez, p. 11, sq) Perhaps Demetrius confused him with the Thracian of the same name (supra, 30, 64). Acc. to the Ind Herc. 7, 6 sq, after the death of Speusippus. when Xenocrates was chosen head of the school (i.e. B C. 339), he returned home and established a school of his own (ἕτερον περίπατον καὶ διατριβὴν κατέστησατο). The stories about his death, apud Diog. 89–91, Suid. sub voce, Ind. Herc. 9, sq., which are in all other respects improbable, and remind us of the similar myths about Empedocles (see vol. i. 605 sq), say that it occurred there.

[13] His comprehensive knowledge is obvious not only from the width of his literary activity and the remnants of his works, extending as they do to all parts of science then known—metaphysics, physics, ethics, politics, music, rhetoric, history, and geography (see Diog. v. 86 sqq.; further information apud Roulez, 18 sqq.; 52 sqq.; Muller, loc. cit.), but from the frequent mention of him in the ancients. Cicero calls him (Tusc. v. 3, 8) *doctus imprimis*; (Divin. i. 23, 46) *doctus vir*, Plutarch borrows from him many pieces of information, and adv. Col. 14, 2; p. 1115 (cf. n p. suav. viv. 2, 2, p. 1086), represents him as one of the most important philosophers of the Academic and Peripatetic school. On the other hand, Plutarch also calls him, Camill. 22, μυθώδης καὶ πλασματίας, Timæus ap. Diog. viii. 72 παραδοξολόγος, the Epicurean in Cic N. D i. 13, 34 says: *puerilibus fabulis refersit libros*, and several instances of his uncritical credulity are also known to us; cf. Diog. viii. 67, 72; Io. Lydus, De Mens. iv. 29, p. 181; Cic. Divin. i 23, 46; Athen xii. 521 e. We shall find that his contributions to philosophy were unimportant; but as a physicist, owing

Philippus of Opus, a distinguished mathematician and astronomer, editor of the Laws, and probably author of the Epinomis;[15] and Hestiæus of Perinthus.[16] The

to his doctrine of the revolution of the earth round an axis, he takes no inconsiderable position; and if the quotation, p. 34, 73 ('Menedemus'), is correct, not only his fellow-pupils, but Plato himself must have made much of him. His writings, with regard to which Diog. v. 92, perhaps wrongly, charges him with plagiarism, were composed at least partly in the form of dialogues; cf. Diog. 86; Cic ad Att. xiii. 19; ad Quintum fr iii. 5; Procl in Parm. i. end; vol. iv. 54. His manner of exposition is rightly praised by Diogenes, 88 sq.

[14] Diogenes represents him among the Peripatetics, after having himself called him a Platonist, v. 86; Stobæus also treats him as a Peripatetic, Ecl i. 580; cf. 634; Cicero, however (Divin. i. 23, 46; N.D. 1. 13, 34; Tusc. v. 3, 8; Legg. iii. 6, 14); Strabo (xii. 3, 1, p. 541); and Suidas 'Ηρακλείδ. place him under the Platonic school. Proclus in Tim. 281 E, cannot intend to contradict what he himself said p. 28 C; either the words are to be understood differently or the text to be altered. That Heraclides was a pupil of Plato is indubitable, and is confirmed among other things by his editing the Platonic discourses on the Good (Simpl Phys. 104 b.; see p 362, 2), and by the fact (Procl. in Tim. 28 C), that Plato caused him to collect the poems of Antimachus in Colophon. (Cf. Krische, 325 sq.; Bockh d. Kosm. Syst. d. Plat. 129 sq.) That he subsequently went over to the Peripatetic school seems improbable from what we know of his philosophy; that he heard Aristotle (Sotion ap. Diog. 86) is unlikely, because of the relative ages of the two, and because he left Athens before Aristotle's return. His views confirm our opinion of a connection with the Pythagoreans (Diog. loc. cit). He himself, in the fragment ap. Porphyr. in Ptolem. Harm. p. 213 sqq. (apud Roulez, p. 101), quotes a passage from Archytas.

[15] Philippus of Opus was, according to Suid. Φιλόσοφος (before this word the lemma Φίλιππος 'Οπούντιος has undoubtedly fallen out; cf. Bernhardy ad loc., Suckow, Form d. plat. Schr. 149 f.), a pupil of Socrates and Plato. Really, however, he was only the pupil of the latter; as we see from the further statement ὃν δὲ κατὰ Φίλιππον τὸν Μακεδόνα. He divided Plato's Laws into twelve books; the thirteenth he seems to have added himself. In harmony with the latter statement Diog. iii. 37 says ἔνιοί τέ φασιν ὅτι Φίλιππος ὁ 'Οπούντιος τοὺς Νόμους αὐτοῦ μετέγραψεν ὄντας ἐν κηρῷ. τούτου δὲ καὶ τὴν 'Επινομίδα φασὶν εἶναι. Proclus follows the same supposition when (in the quotation of the Προλεγ τ. Πλάτ. φιλοσ. c. 25; Plat. Opp. ed. Herm. vi. 218) he proves the spuriousness of the Epinomis by showing that Plato could not possibly have had time for its composition, as death prevented him from τοὺς νόμους διορθώσασθαι. Philippus is not, however,

celebrated astronomer, Eudoxus of Cnidos,[17] had also

expressly mentioned. Among the twenty-three written treatises which Suidas cites as belonging to Philippus, there are six moral treatises, a work on the Gods in two books, treatises about the Opuntian Locrians, about Plato, &c., and eleven mathematical, astronomical, and meteorological works. As an astronomer (σχολάσας τοῖς μετεώροις) Philippus is mentioned not merely by Suidas, but had made himself an important reputation in this department; cf. Plut. n. p. suav. v. sec. Epic. ii. 2, p. 1093; Hipparch. in Arat. Phœn. i. 6; Geminus, Isag. in Ar. Phœn. c. 6, p. 47 Halma; Ptolem Φάσεις ἀπλανῶν, who often cites his ἐπισημάσια together with those of Calippus, Euctemon, &c.; Plin. H. nat. xviii. 31, 312; Vitruv. De Archit. ix. 7; Stob. Ekl. i. 558; Joh. Lyd. De mens. iv. 13; Alex. Aphr. in Meteorol. 118 a. (Arist. Meteorol. ed. Ideler, ii. 127), who tells us about his explanation of the rainbow. As Bockh has shown (Sonnenkreise d. Alten, 34 sqq.) by a comparison of all the statements about him and his writings, 'Philippus the Medmæan' (from Medama in Bruttium) is not distinct from him. This Philippus is mentioned by Steph. Byz (De Urb. Μέδμαι), and apud Procl. in Eucl. 19, and p. 67 fr. (where Μεδμαῖος is to be substituted for Μεταῖος or Μενδαῖος), in a catalogue of the mathematicians of the Platonic school who succeeded the Opuntian Philippus; it may be that Philippus was born at Opus, and afterwards lived in Medama, a Locrian colony, or *vice versâ*. We must suppose that there was only one well-known astronomer of this name, because most of the passages which mention the astronomer Philippus designate him simply by this name, without finding it necessary to add 'the Opuntian' in order to distinguish him from any other of the same name. When e. g. Alexander loc. cit. says simply Φίλιππος ὁ ἑταῖρος Πλάτωνος, there can be no doubt that he did not know two Platonic scholars of this name.

[16] Hestiæus is mentioned as a Platonist by Diogenes, iii. 46, as the editor of the Platonic discourses on the good by Simpl. Phys. 104 b. cf. supra, p. 26, 53; his own investigations are referred to by Theophrastus, Metaph. p. 313 (Fragm. 12, 13 Wimm.); Stob. Ecl. i. 250; Exc. e Floril. Jo. Damasc. 17, 12 (Stob. Floril. ed. Mein. iv. 174)

[17] Ideler on Eudoxus, Abhandl. d. Berl. Akad. v. J. 1828; Hist. phil Kl. p. 189 sqq. v. J. 1830, p. 49 sqq. Eudoxus' native town is unanimously called Cnidos, and his father, ap Diog. viii. 86, Æschines The year of his birth and death is not known; Eusebius' statement in the Chronicon, that he flourished Ol 89, 3, makes him much too old. It is true that he brought over letters of recommendation from Agesilaus to Nectanabis of Egypt (Diog. 87), and if Nectanabis II. is intended, this journey must have happened between Ol. 104, 3, and 107, 3 (362 and 350 B.C.); if Nectanabis I, not before Ol. 101, 2 (374 B.C.). Æl. V. H. vii. 17 represents him as visiting Sicily somewhat later than Plato, and consequently after 367

attended Plato's lectures,[18] and occupied himself, in addition to his own particular science, with enquiries of a more general kind.[19] Of these enquiries we know very

B.C. (see p. 32, 67). With this agrees the statement of Apollodorus ap. Diog. 90, who makes him flourish Ol. 103, 1 (367 B.C.). (The words must refer to him; the preceding clause εὑρίσκομεν— ὁμοίως is either spurious or more probably to be rejected altogether as a gloss.) His age is given in Diog. viii. 90, 91 as fifty-three years According to Arist. Eth. N. x. 2 beginn. i. 12, 1101 b 28; Metaph. xii. 8, 1073 b. 17 sqq, i. 9, 991 a. 17, xiii. 5, 1079 b. 21, he could not have been living at the time these treatises were composed. Poor as he was, he obtained, through his friends, the means for his educational travels (Diog. 86 sq.). Besides Plato (see following note), Archytas and the Sicilian physician Philistio are mentioned as his teachers (Diog. 86); in Egypt, the priest Chonuphis is said to have introduced him to the knowledge of his caste (Diog. 90, Plut. Is. et Os. c 10, p 354; Clemens Strom i. 303 D, Philostr. v. Soph i. 1, makes him extend his travels still farther). Strabo (see 22, 43) gives the duration of his residence there as thirteen years, which is just as incredible as Strabo's other statement that he was in company with Plato; Diog. 87 speaks only of one year and four months. The statements of Diodorus, i 98, Seneca, Qu Nat. vii 3, 2, as to the results of his Egyptian travels, are certainly much exaggerated (cf Ideler, 1828, 204 sq). Afterwards, he studied in Cyzicus (Diog. 87, who adds some improbable details, Philostr. loc. cit., cf. Ideler, 1830, 53); later on he lived in high honour in his native city, to which he gave laws (Diog. 88; Plut. adv. Col 32, 9, p. 1126; cf. Theod. cur. gr. aff. ix. 12, p. 124); his observatory was shown for a long time (Strabo, ii. 5, 14, p. 119, xvii. 1, 30, p. 807). His character is praised by Arist. Eth. N. x. 2 beginn. On his writings and discoveries as a mathematician and astronomer see Ideler loc. cit.

[18] According to Sotion apud Diog. 86, the fame of the Socratic schools brought him to Athens, where, however, he only stayed two months. Cicero, Divin. ii. 42, 87; Rep. i. 14, 22, calls him *Platonis auditor*, Strabo, xiv. 2, 15, p. 656, and Procl. in Eucl. i. 19 (67 Friedl), his ἑταῖρος; Plut. adv. Col. 32, 9, p. 1126, his συνήθης together with Aristotle; Philostr. v. Soph. i. 1, says. Εὔδ. τοὺς ἐν Ἀκαδημίᾳ λόγους ἱκανῶς ἐκφροντίσας, Alex. Aphrod. ad Metaph. i. 9, 991 a. 14 . Εὔδ. τῶν Πλάτωνος γνωρίμων, Asclep. ibid. Πλατωνικός, ἀκροατὴς Πλάτωνος. Cf. Sosigenes apud Schol. in Arist. 498 a 45, perhaps on the authority of Eudemus. The unhistorical statements in Plut.. gen. Socr. 7, p 579 (ep. Plat. xiii. 360 c.), and the more probable statements, v. Marc 14, qu. conviv. viii. 2, i. 7, p. 718, presuppose a close connection of the two. Diogenes counts Eudoxus among the Pythagoreans, so, too, Iambl. in Nicom. Arithm. p. 11.

[19] This is presupposed in the statement ap. Diog. that the physi-

little, and that little is directly opposed to genuine Platonism. Xenocrates was followed, as head of the Academy, by Polemo,[20] whom he had converted from a disorderly life to serious purpose and moral rectitude, by the influence of his personal character and discourses.[21] The successor of Polemo was his scholar and friend Crates,[22] whose eminent fellow-disciple Crantor [23]

cian Chrysippus heard from him τά τε περὶ θεῶν καὶ κόσμου καὶ τῶν μετεωρολογουμένων Eudocia, *sub voce*, makes of this treatises περὶ θεῶν, and the like.

[20] Polemo of Athens succeeded his teacher, Ol. 116, 3 (31¾ B C.), see 840, 1, and died, acc to Euseb. Chronicon, Ol. 127, 3 (270 B.C.), at a good old age, as Diog. says iv. 20. With this agrees the statement that Arcesilaus, who died at seventy-five, Ol 134, 4 (241 B.C.), Diog. 44, 71, and who was consequently born 316 B.C., lived in friendship with Crantor (who died before Polemo) and with Polemo himself (Diog iv. 22, 27, 29 sq). The statement that Arcesilaus flourished in Ol. 120, i e. 300 B C. (Diog. 45, following Apollodor.), cannot be brought into agreement with this, but is of no importance, standing as it does in such direct contradiction with the most certain fundamental points, that we must suppose that there is either a confusion or a mistake in writing.

[21] The event is well known and frequently mentioned; see Diog. iv. 16 sq.; Ind. Hercul. 13 (which follows the same source as Diogenes, viz. Antigonus the Carystian); Plut. de adulat. c. 32, p. 71; Lucian, Accus. c. 16 sq.; Epictet. Dissert. iii. 1, 14, iv. 11, 30; Origen c. Cels. i. 64, iii. 67, Themist. orat. xxvi. 303 D; Horace, Sat. ii. 3, 253 sqq.; Valer. Max. vi. 9, ext. 1; Augustine, epist. 154, 2 c., Julian, i. 12, 35. In Diog. iv. 17 sqq. (Ind. Herc. loc. cit.) we get instances of the grave dignity, the immovable firmness, and the noble tranquillity for which Polemo afterwards became distinguished. Otherwise we know nothing about his life.

[22] The Athenian Crates lived in the most intimate friendly relationship with Polemo, as did Crantor and Arcesilaus afterwards (Diog. iv. 17, 21 sqq.; Ind. Herc. 15, 16, v. in sqq). He seems not to have held the office of head of the school for long, as his predecessor died in the year 270 B C, and his successor, whose revolutionary activity must have lasted some time, died in 241 B.C, v. supra. According to Diog. 23, he left behind him not only philosophical writings and treatises on comedy, but popular and diplomatic orations. He cannot have remained aloof from politics.

[23] Kayser, De Crantore Academico, Heidelb. 1841. Crantor was born at Soli, in Sicily, where he is said to have soon attracted attention. Thence he came to Athens, where he frequented the school of Xenocrates, together with Polemo (Diog. iv. 24; Ind. Herc. 16, 1 sqq.); he cannot, therefore,

had previously died. Next to Crates came Arcesilaus; with him the Academy entered on a new phase of scientific development, which must be considered later on.

The members of the Older Academy professed to maintain Plato's doctrine generally unaltered;[24] but they chiefly adhered to its later form. In pursuing his enquiries into numbers and their elements, they approximated very closely to the Pythagoreans, so that their metaphysics became an abstruse dogmatism[25] with a large admixture of arithmetical and theological mysticism. At the period when Plato's metaphysics showed Pythagorean tendencies, we find that his Ethics were of the more popular kind described in the Laws; and this was also the

have been more than a year younger than Polemo. Nevertheless, after Xenocrates' death, he refused the invitation to establish a school of his own, and continued to listen to the discourses of his admired friend (Diog 24 sq. 17). With Arcesilaus, whom he won over for the Academy, he lived in the most confidential connection, and left him a considerable property (Diog. 28 sq. 24 sq.; Numen ap Enseb. præp Ev. xiv. 6, 3). He died before Polemo, apparently at a good old age (Diog. 27, 25), but the year of his death cannot be fixed more definitely. His writings, altogether of moderate extent (30,000 lines, says Diog. 24), are lost, except a few fragments (collected by Kayser, p. 12 sqq.), which, however, still enable us to recognise his choice diction (Diog. 27) and pleasing fullness of style. The most celebrated of them was his small treatise περὶ πένθους (Cic. Acad. ii. 44, 135; Diog. 27), which was copied by Cicero in his Consolatio, and, in some points, in the Tusculans, and by Plutarch in his Consolatio ad Apollonium: cf. Kayser, 34 sqq., who gives the views of Wyttenbach and others on this subject.

[24] That they actually did so is asserted by Cicero, following Antiochus (see Acad. i. 4, 14, cf. 12, 43; Fin. v. 3, 7, 8, 6, 16); Acad. i. 9, 34 (on Speusippus, Xenocrates, Polemo, Crates, Crantor): *diligenter ea, quæ a superioribus acceperant, tuebantur*; cf. Diog. iv. 1, of Speusippus On the contrary, Numen. ap. Euseb. præc. Ev. xiv. 5, 1 sqq., and Euseb. himself, ibid. 4, 14 · πολλαχῇ παραλύοντες τὰ δὲ στρεβλοῦντες, οὐκ ἐνέμειναν τῇ πρώτῃ διαδοχῇ, which Numenius strongly blames. Which was right will be seen immediately

[25] The Academician apud Cic. Acad. i. 4, 17, sq. designates the dogmatic formulation of the system as a departure from the Socratic manner common to Aristotle and the contemporary Platonists.

case with the philosophers of the Academy. Unlike their master, they seem to have neglected the severer enquiries of Dialectic; nor did they (except in the direction of astronomy and mathematics) pay much attention to the investigation of natural science, already discouraged by him. We know, however, so little about these men that it is often impossible to combine, even by probable conjecture, the scattered fragments of their doctrines that have come down to us into any connected whole.

Plato's nephew, Speusippus,[26] though greatly inferior to Aristotle in philosophic genius, seems to have resembled him in his desire for definiteness and experimental completeness of knowledge. Being convinced of the interdependence of all knowledge, he was of opinion that it is impossible to possess a satisfactory knowledge of anything without the knowledge of all things besides: for to know what a thing is, we must know wherein it is distinguished from other things; and to know this, we must know how these other things are constituted.[27] He therefore sought to gain a basis

---

[26] Cf. on his doctrine Brandis, Gr.-röm. Phil. ii. b. 1, p. 6 sqq. On the Pythagorean and Platonic doctrine of numbers, Rhein. Mus, v. Niebuhr and Brandis, ii 4; Ritter, ii. 524 sqq., Ravaisson, Speusippi de primis rerum principiis placita, Par 1838; Krische, Forschungen, i. 247 sqq.

[27] Arist. Anal. Post. ii. 13, 97 a. 6: οὐδὲν δὲ δεῖ τὸν ὁριζόμενον καὶ διαιρούμενον ἅπαντα εἰδέναι τὰ ὄντα. καίτοι ἀδύνατον φασί τινες εἶναι τὰς διαφορὰς εἰδέναι τὰς πρὸς ἕκαστον μὴ εἰδότα ἕκαστον. ἄνευ δὲ τῶν διαφορῶν οὐκ εἶναι ἕκαστον εἰδέναι. οὗ γὰρ μὴ διαφέρει, ταὐτὸν εἶναι τούτῳ, οὗ δὲ διαφέρει, ἕτερον τούτου. By τινὲς we are to understand Speusippus, according to the commentators in loc., Philoponus, Themistius, i 92, 15 sq., Sp, and an anonymous writer who appeals to Eudemus (Schol. in Arist. 298 a. 11–25). Whether Themistius has preserved Speusippus' own words is uncertain. Writers so little trustworthy as Philoponus and the later Eustratius in Post. Anal. 50 a. o. b. o., cannot be depended on for the statement that Speusippus used the dictum in order to invalidate conceptual definition and division. Such eristic views are ascribed to

THEORY OF KNOWLEDGE. 567

for enquiry by means of a comparative survey of the different spheres of the Actual.[28] And while thus attributing greater worth to experience than Plato had done, his theory of knowledge softened the abrupt opposition which Plato had assumed between the sen-

Speusippus by no ancient authority: ὅροι and διαιρέσεις are expressly attributed to him, rightly or wrongly. (Diog. iv. 5 : the διαιρέσεις may be those spoken of above, 46, 5, whereas our Pseudo-Platonic definitions are too poor, and contain too much that is Peripatetic, to suit Speusippus.) Such views, in fact, are utterly at variance with his whole scientific attitude: he is dogmatic, and even in the little we know of him, by no means deficient either in definitions or divisions. Of the latter we shall have instances presently, for the former, cf. Plut. plat. qu. viii. 4, 3, p. 1007, where a definition of Time is given.

[28] To this belongs that enquiry concerning names which Simplicius mentions in Categ. (Schol. in Arist. 43 b. 19 a. 31, 41 b. 30; and 7 β, 9 a, δ Basil). (Names are divided into ταὐτώνυμα and ἑτερώνυμα: on the one side, ὁμώνυμα and συνώνυμα; and on the other ἑτερώνυμα, πολυώνυμα, and παρώνυμα.) Cf. Diog. iv. 2 : οὗτος πρῶτος, καθά φησι Διόδωρος ...., ἐν τοῖς μαθήμασιν ἐθεάσατο τὸ κοινὸν καὶ συνῳκείωσε καθόσον ἦν δυνατὸν ἀλλήλοις. This can hardly refer to anything but a comparative survey; the essential connexion of the sciences had been already propounded by Plato, and with far greater completeness than by Speusippus, for Speusippus posited different principles for the different spheres of Being. A comparative survey of natural history was contained in the ten books of the Ὅμοια, or, according to the fuller title given in Diog. 5: τῶν περὶ τὴν πραγματείαν ὁμοίων (the preceding διάλογοι is justly questioned by Krische, Forsch. 253, for the reason that a work of this kind could hardly be written in the dialogic form · perhaps διαλογαί is the right reading. Diogenes connects with it one or two other similar works: διαιρέσεις καὶ πρὸς τὰ ὅμοια ὑποθέσεις). In this treatise, as we see from the fragments in Athenæus, Speusippus examined the various kinds of plants and animals, classing together those that are related, and separating the unlike. Cf. Athenæus iii 86 c.: Σπεύσιππος δ' ἐν δευτέρῳ Ὁμοίων παραπλήσια εἶναι κήρυκας, πορφύρας, στραβήλους, κόγχους ... ἔτι ὁ Σπεύσιππος ἐξῆς πάλιν ἰδίᾳ καταριθμεῖται κόγχους, κτένας, μῦς, πίννας, σωλῆνας, καὶ ἐν ἄλλῳ μέρει ὄστρεα, λεπάδας. Again, 105 b.. Σπεύσιππος δὲ ἐν δευτέρῳ Ὁμοίων παραπλήσιά φησιν εἶναι τῶν μαλακοστράκων κόρακον, κ.τ.λ. iv.133 b.. ἔστι δ' ἡ κερκώπη (ζῷον ὅμοιον τέττιγι καὶ τιγονίῳ, ὡς Σπεύσιππος παρίστησιν ἐν τετάρτῳ Ὁμοίων vii. 303 d.: Σπεύσιππος δ' ἐν δευτέρῳ Ὁμοίων διίστησιν αὐτὰς (the θυννίδες) τῶν θύννων. ix. 369 a : Σπεύσιππος δ' ἐν δευτέρῳ Ὁμοίων ῥαφανὶς, φησὶ, γογγυλὶς, ῥάφυς, ἀνάρρινον, ὅμοια. Similarly, vii. 300 c., 301 c., 327 c., 308 d., 313 a., 319 b., 323 a., 329 sq.

sible and rational perception, by interposing a Third between them. 'The Immaterial,' said Speusippus, 'is known by means of scientific thought—the Material, by scientific perception;' under this he included observation guided by understanding.[29] In proportion, however, as he directed his attention to the Particular of experience he departed from that Unity of the highest principles, which Plato had striven to obtain. Plato, according to the later view of his system, had shown the One and the Great-and-Small to be the most universal elements in all things; and at the same time had left the essential difference between the Sensible and the Ideal unexplained, and seemingly unregarded. Speusippus saw the necessity of more accurately determining and discriminating these two principles. Plato had identified the One with the Good and the divine Reason.[30] Speusippus distinguished the three concepts from one another.[31] The Good, he believed, could not stand as the ground of all Being, at the beginning of

[29] Sextus, Math. vii. 145 : Σπεύσιππος δὲ, ἐπεὶ τῶν πραγμάτων τὰ μὲν αἰσθητὰ, τὰ δὲ νοητὰ, τῶν μὲν νοητῶν κριτήριον ἔλεξεν εἶναι τὸν ἐπιστημονικὸν λόγον, τῶν δὲ αἰσθητῶν τὴν ἐπιστημονικὴν αἴσθησιν· ἐπιστημονικὴν δὲ αἴσθησιν ὑπείληφε καθεστάναι τὴν μεταλαμβάνουσαν τῆς κατὰ τὸν λόγον ἀληθείας. ὥσπερ γὰρ οἱ τοῦ αὐλητοῦ ἢ ψάλτου δάκτυλοι τεχνικὴν μὲν εἶχον ἐνέργειαν, οὐκ ἐν αὑτοῖς δὲ προηγουμένως τελειουμένην, ἀλλὰ τῆς (? διὰ τῆς) πρὸς τὸν λογισμὸν συνασκήσεως ἀπαρτιζομένην. καὶ ὡς ἡ τοῦ μουσικοῦ αἴσθησις ἐνάργειαν (ἐνέργειαν) μὲν εἶχεν ἀντιληπτικὴν τοῦ τε ἡρμοσμένου καὶ τοῦ ἀναρμόστου, ταύτην δὲ οὐκ αὐτοφυῆ, ἀλλ' ἐκ λογισμοῦ περιγεγονυῖαν. οὕτω καὶ ἡ ἐπιστημονικὴ αἴσθησις φυσικῶς παρὰ τοῦ λόγου τῆς ἐπιστημονικῆς μεταλαμβάνει τριβῆς πρὸς ἀπλανῆ τῶν ὑποκειμένων διάγνωσιν. We must not, however, infer from these passages that Speusippus understood by αἴσθησις ἐπιστημονικὴ an immediate, primarily aesthetic perception (Brandis, ii. b. 1, p 9), though, like Aristotle, he distinguished, in the sphere of thinking knowledge, between the immediate knowledge of principles and the mediate knowledge of that which is derived from them.

[30] Vide p. 321 sqq.
[31] Vide p. 280 sqq.

Being, but only as the goal and completion of Being, at the end of the chain, as we see in the case of individuals: they begin with imperfection and only attain to perfection[32] in the course of their development. And the One cannot coincide with the Good, otherwise the Many must coincide with the Evil; and according to this, Good and Evil must be first causes as well as the One and the Many.[33] Although, therefore, he admitted that the One was akin to the Good, and its most essential constituent,[34] yet he separated them so as to make the One a principle and the Good its result.[35] As a third element,

[32] Vide p. 286, 167.

[33] Metaphysics, xii. 7, 1072 b. 30. ὅσοι δὲ ὑπολαμβάνουσιν, ὥσπερ οἱ Πυθαγόρειοι καὶ Σπεύσιππος, τὸ κάλλιστον καὶ ἄριστον μὴ ἐν ἀρχῇ εἶναι, διὸ καὶ τῶν φυτῶν καὶ τῶν ζῴων τὰς ἀρχὰς αἴτια μὲν εἶναι, τὸ δὲ καλὸν καὶ τέλειον ἐν τοῖς ἐκ τούτων (an argument belonging, doubtless, to Speusippus only, and not to the Pythagoreans) οὐκ ὀρθῶς οἴονται. (The other reading adopted by Themistius and Philoponus, which substitutes Λεύκιππος for Σπεύσιππος, is rightly rejected by Krische, Forsch. 250, 1.) This theory of Speusippus is also referred to in Metaphysics xiv. 5 (at the beginning): οὐκ ὀρθῶς δ' ὑπολαμβάνει οὐδ' εἴ τις παρεικάζει τὰς τοῦ ὅλου ἀρχὰς τῇ τῶν ζῴων καὶ φυτῶν, ὅτι ἐξ ἀορίστων ἀτελῶν δὲ ἀεὶ τὰ τελειότερα, διὸ καὶ ἐπὶ τῶν πρώτων οὕτως ἔχειν φησὶν, ὥστε μηδὲ ὄν τι εἶναι τὸ ἓν αὐτό. Further, in chapter 4, 1091 a., 29 sqq., as to how the first Causes are related to the Good, πότερον ἐστί τι ἐκείνων . . . . αὐτὸ τὸ ἀγαθὸν καὶ τὸ ἄριστον, ἢ οὒ, ἀλλ' ὑστερογενῆ. παρὰ μὲν γὰρ τῶν θεολόγων (the ancient Cosmogonies) ἔοικεν ὁμολογεῖσθαι τῶν νῦν τισὶ (Speusippus) οἳ οὔ φασιν, ἀλλὰ προελθούσης τῆς τῶν ὄντων φύσεως καὶ τὸ ἀγαθὸν καὶ τὸ καλὸν ἐμφαίνεσθαι.

[34] Cf. Aristotle, Metaphysics, xiv. 4, 1091 b. 30 If the One is conceived as the Good, the second principle (Plurality or the Great-and-Small) must be identified with the Bad-in-itself. διόπερ ὁ μὲν (Pseudo-Alexander, following, no doubt, Alexander, here mentions Speusippus; and it is clear from what we have said above that no one else can be intended) ἔφευγε τὸ ἀγαθὸν προσάπτειν τῷ ἑνί, ὡς ἀναγκαῖον ὄν, ἐπειδὴ ἐξ ἐναντίων ἡ γένεσις, τὸ κακὸν τὴν τοῦ πλήθους φύσιν εἶναι. And in xii. 10, 1075 a 36, after the Platonic theory of the identity of the One and the Good has been opposed by the same arguments as in xiv. 4. οἱ δ' ἄλλοι οὐδ' ἀρχὰς τὸ ἀγαθὸν καὶ τὸ κακόν.

[35] Cf. Aristotle, Eth. N. i. 4, 1096 b. 5 πιθανώτερον δ' ἐοίκασιν οἱ Πυθαγόρειοι λέγειν περὶ αὐτοῦ (τοῦ ἀγαθοῦ), τιθέντες ἐν τῇ

distinct from the One and the Good, came the efficient cause or Reason;[36] but this he combined with the Platonic World-soul, and the Pythagorean central fire; for he supposed the world to be ruled by animate power, having its seat in the centre and in the circumference, and extending itself throughout the whole space of the universe.[37] Plato's Ideal principle is thus resolved by Speusippus into three principles, which are analogous to Aristotle's formal, efficient, and final causes, but are far from having the precise determination and the universal significance of these. The second

τῶν ἀγαθῶν συστοιχίᾳ τὸ ἕν (they did not hold the One to be the Good itself, but placed it, in the table of contraries (vide vol. i. 302), beside the Good and Perfect) οἷς δὴ καὶ Σπεύσιππος ἐπακολουθῆσαι δοκεῖ. In Metaphysics, xiv. 4, 1091 b. 14 (τῶν δὲ τὰς ἀκινήτους οὐσίας εἶναι λεγόντων οἱ μέν φασιν αὐτὸ τὸ ἓν τὸ ἀγαθὸν αὐτὸ εἶναι. οὐσίαν μέντοι τὸ ἓν αὐτοῦ ᾤοντο εἶναι μάλιστα), the words οὐσίαν, κ.τ.λ., are also to be taken in this connection. In spite of the arguments of Bonitz (see his remarks on this passage), I cannot give up the possibility (Plat. Stud. 277) that some words, such, perhaps, as οἱ δὲ τοῦτο μὲν ἔφευγον, have been lost from their immediate context.

[36] Cf. the passages already quoted. According to Metaphysics, xiv. 5 (vide supra, note 33), Speusippus would not even allow that the Original One was existent, for he supposed that its union with the Many was the cause that first produced a Being In support of this opinion he might have appealed to Plato, Parmen. 141 E.

[37] Vide p. 286, 167. Cf. Metaph. vii. 2, 1028 b. 19. Plato has three substances—the Idea, the Mathematical principle, and sensuous things: Σπεύσιππος δὲ καὶ πλείους οὐσίας, ἀπὸ τοῦ ἑνὸς ἀρξάμενος, καὶ ἀρχὰς ἑκάστης οὐσίας ἄλλην μὲν ἀριθμῶν, ἄλλην δὲ μεγεθῶν, ἔπειτα ψυχῆς. The commentators paraphrase this passage, as Brandis remarks, on no other authority than their own; and it is very improbable that the addition of Asclepius (Schol. in Arist. 740 a. 16, 741 a. o.) to the Aristotelian examples, καὶ πάλιν ἄλλην οὐσίαν νοῦ καὶ ἄλλην ψυχῆς, κ τ.λ., which is not to be found in Alexander (740 b. 18), rests on any historical tradition. The separation of divine Reason from the One is involved in the theorem mentioned above—the Best cannot be the First. Anaxagoras, who maintained that Reason is original, was contrasted by Aristotle with Speusippus, in regard to this doctrine (Metaph. xiv. 4, 1091 b. 8 sqq.; cf. a. 33 sqq.), as Ravaisson truly observes (p. 17).

principle, Plato's Great-and-Small, he described, in contrast to the One, as Plurality,[38] thus connecting it with the Pythagorean categories.[39] From Unity and Plurality, however, he derived numbers only; for the explanation of everything else, he set up several other principles,[40] related to the former, and yet distinct from

[38] Cf. Cicero, N. D. i. 13, 32 (according to Philodemus): *Speusippus Platonem avunculum subsequens et vim quandam dicens, qua omnia regantur, eamque animalem, evellere ex animis conatur cognitionem Deorum.* Minucius Felix repeats this; Octav. 19. Cf. Theophrastus, Metaph., 322 (Fr. 12, 32, Wimm.): Σπεύσιππος σπάνιόν τι τὸ τίμιον ποιεῖ τὸ περὶ τὴν τοῦ μέσου χώραν. τὰ δ' ἄκρα καὶ ἑκατέρωθεν (perhaps this ought to be read χώραν τά τ' ἄκρα ἑκατέρωθεν, the extreme ends on both sides, the circumference of the globe in its two halves). That this τίμιον, dwelling in the centre and in the circumference, is the Deity as World-soul, is clear from the analogy of the central fire, to which the same place was assigned as to the τίμιον (vide vol. i. 357 sq.); and from the Timæus, 36 E. This account of the soul Speusippus took literally, and combined it with the doctrine of the central fire. With this view of the World-soul (vide supra 355, 154) we should connect the statement of Iamblichus (Stob. Ecl. i. 862, cf. Diog. iii. 67), that he conceived the soul ἐν ἰδέᾳ τοῦ πάντη διαστατοῦ: to him, as to other philosophers, the soul is that which is everywhere present, and fills all space. Ravaisson's proposal (p. 40 sq.) to substitute ἀδιαστάτου for διαστατοῦ is, therefore, inadmissible. His conjecture (p. 18 sq.) that Aristotle is referring to Speusippus when he says that νοῦς cannot be merely δύναμις, but must be ἐνέργεια (Metaph. xii. 6, 9, 1071 b. 17 sqq. 1074 b. 19, 28), also appears quite unfounded; Speusippus certainly made a distinction between the first, imperfect Being and νοῦς. But for the same reason Krische is wrong in asserting (p. 256) that he regarded the divine Reason as the primal oppositionless cause. In that case the theory τὸ ἄριστον μὴ ἐν ἀρχῇ εἶναι (vide notes 33 and 37) could not be ascribed to him. Speusippus held that Reason, like the World-soul of the Timæus, was primarily derived or created. Lastly, I cannot agree with Ravaisson (p. 21) or Brandis, ii. b. 1, 14, in referring the passage in Cicero to the Original One, to which Speusippus would seem to have attributed a specific activity. This description appears far more applicable to the World-soul spoken of by Theophrastus, which cannot coincide with the One. The quotations in note 37 are sufficient to prove that the One was not conceived by Speusippus as an animate nature.

[39] Vide vol. i. 302.

[40] Cf. Aristotle, Metaph. xiv. 4, and Pseudo-Alexander on this passage (vide supra, note 34), and also in c. 5, 1092 a. 35 ἐπεὶ τοίνυν τὸ ἓν ὃ μὲν τῷ πλήθει ὡς

them,[41] just as he had supposed the Good as related to the One, but not identical with it. Thus he obtained a plurality of spheres, united not by the identity, but by the similarity of their ultimate causes.[42] That uni-

ἐναντίον τίθησιν; and C 1, 1037 b. (cf. Z 27, 30): οἱ δὲ τὸ ἕτερον τῶν ἐναντίων ὕλην ποιοῦσιν, οἱ μὲν τῷ ἑνὶ τῷ ἴσῳ τὸ ἄνισον, ὡς τοῦτο τὴν τοῦ πλήθους οὖσαν φύσιν, οἱ δὲ τῷ ἑνὶ τὸ πλῆθος. Here Pseudo-Alexander refers only to the Pythagoreans, but Aristotle evidently alludes to Speusippus, for he continues. γεννῶνται γὰρ οἱ ἀριθμοὶ τοῖς μὲν ἐκ τῆς τοῦ ἀνίσου δυάδος τοῦ μεγάλου καὶ μικροῦ, τῷ δ' ἐκ τοῦ πλήθους, ὑπὸ τῆς τοῦ ἑνὸς δὲ οὐσίας ἀμφοῖν. It is clear from what follows that he is concerned with the Platonists, for he expressly says that this determination was chosen because Plato's Great-and-Small relates too exclusively to that which is in Space. Cf. also Metaph. xii. 9, 1085 a. 31 (vide infra, note 42), 6, 4 sqq; xii 10, 1075 b. 32, and probably the beginning of x; xiv. 1, 1087 b. 30 sqq. According to Damascius, De Princip. p. 3 (οὐ γὰρ ἓν ὡς ἐλάχιστον, καθάπερ Σπεύσιππος ἔδοξε λέγειν), we might suppose that Speusippus had also denoted the One as the Least But from Aristotle, Metaph xiv. 1, 1087 b 30 sqq., we find that this cannot have been the case. Damascius, most likely, made a false deduction from that passage.

[41] Metaph. vii. 2; vide supra, note 37. Following this precedent, and in agreement with Ravaisson (p. 37), Brandis (p 10), Schwegler, and Bonitz (see their comments on the passage), we may consider Metaph. xii. 10, 1075 b. 37, as applying to Speusippus, and not, as Pseudo-Alexander thinks, to the Pythagoreans. The words are: οἱ δὲ λέγοντες τὸν ἀριθμὸν πρῶτον τὸν μαθηματικὸν καὶ οὕτως ἀεὶ ἄλλην ἐχομένην οὐσίαν καὶ ἀρχὰς ἑκάστης ἄλλας, ἐπεισοδιώδη τὴν τοῦ παντὸς οὐσίαν ποιοῦσιν (οὐθὲν γὰρ ἡ ἑτέρα τῇ ἑτέρᾳ συμβάλλεται οὖσα ἢ μὴ οὖσα) καὶ ἀρχὰς πολλάς. In that case we must also regard Metaph. xiv. 3, 1090 b. 13, as a reference to him: ἔτι δὲ ἐπιζητήσειεν ἄν τις μὴ λίαν εὐχερὴς ὢν περὶ μὲν τοῦ ἀριθμοῦ παντὸς καὶ τῶν μαθηματικῶν τὸ μηθὲν συμβάλλεσθαι ἀλλήλοις τὰ πρότερα τοῖς ὕστερον. μὴ ὄντος γὰρ τοῦ ἀριθμοῦ οὐθὲν ἧττον τὰ μεγέθη ἔσται τοῖς τὰ μαθηματικὰ μόνον εἶναι φαμένοις, καὶ τούτων μὴ ὄντων ἡ ψυχὴ καὶ τὰ σώματα τὰ αἰσθητά. οὐκ ἔοικε δ' ἡ φύσις ἐπεισοδιώδης οὖσα ἐκ τῶν φαινομένων, ὥσπερ μοχθηρὰ τραγῳδία. Cf. Schwegler in loc

[42] Metaph iii 9. Aristotle asks how spatial magnitudes are to be explained on the presupposition of Plato's theory of numbers; and having discussed the derivation of the line from the Long-and-Short (vide supra, p. 519, 8), and the like, he proceeds (1085 a. 31), οἱ μὲν οὖν τὰ μεγέθη γεννῶσιν ἐκ τοιαύτης ὕλης, ἕτεροι δὲ ἐκ τῆς στιγμῆς (ἡ δὲ στιγμὴ αὐτοῖς δοκεῖ εἶναι οὐχ ἕν, ἀλλ' οἷον τὸ ἕν) καὶ ἄλλης ὕλης οἵας τὸ πλῆθος, ἀλλ' οὐ πλήθους. The fundamental opposition of the One and Plurality, from which this derivation starts, shows that it belongs to Speusippus.

FIRST PRINCIPLES. NUMBERS. 573

form interdependence of the whole universe, which Plato and Aristotle so strongly maintained, was, as Aristotle says, broken up by Speusippus.

The highest sphere in this series is that of numbers. These, with Speusippus, occupy the place of Ideas, which he entirely abandons. Numbers are, according to him, the First of all that exists; and though he denies the distinction between mathematical and Ideal numbers, yet he separates them, in their existence, from sensible objects, as Plato separates his Ideas;[43] and he gives the same reason for this procedure that Plato gave for his: namely, that no knowledge would be possible if there were not a nature exalted above the sensible.[44] But

[43] Vide note 37.

[44] Aristotle often mentions the theory that mathematical numbers and magnitudes alone, with the exception of Ideas, exist apart from the Sensible. In Metaph. xiii. 1, he specifies three opinions on this point: 1) The philosophers who discriminated the Ideas from mathematical numbers; 2) those who declared them to be the same; and 3) those who only allowed the existence of mathematical numbers (ἕτεροι δέ τινες τὰς μαθηματικὰς μόνον οὐσίας εἶναί φασι), either as undivided from the Sensible, καθάπερ λέγουσί τινες (the Pythagoreans, not, as Susemihl thinks, Genet. Entw. ii. 520, 668, some Platonist unknown to us. The theory that mathematical number is the only number, and that it is not separated from the objects of sense, is adduced, c. 8, 1083 b. 8 sqq.; xiv. 3, 1090 a. 20 sqq., 30 sqq.; i 6, 987 b. 27 sqq.; Physics, iii. 4, 203 a. 6, as a distinctive doctrine of the Pythagoreans; Aristotle never attributes it to a Platonist), or κεχωρισμένα τῶν αἰσθητῶν (λέγουσι δὲ καὶ οὕτω τινές). He then combats the two latter theories (c. 2); the second at p. 1076 b. 11 sqq. Aristotle also distinguishes (Metaph. xiii. 6, 1080 b. 11) three different views among those who held numbers to be οὐσίαι χωρισταί; it is manifest, from the opening of the chapter, that he is speaking only of these. οἱ μὲν οὖν, he says, ἀμφοτέρους φασὶν εἶναι τοὺς ἀριθμούς, ... καὶ χωριστοὺς ἀμφοτέρους τῶν αἰσθητῶν. οἱ δὲ τὸν μαθηματικὸν μόνον ἀριθμὸν εἶναι τὸν πρῶτον τῶν ὄντων κεχωρισμένον τῶν αἰσθητῶν (cf. Z 25 sqq) καὶ οἱ Πυθαγόρειοι δ' ἕνα τὸν μαθηματικόν, πλὴν οὐ κεχωρισμένον, and so forth, ἄλλος δέ τις τὸν πρῶτον ἀριθμὸν τὸν τῶν εἰδῶν ἕνα εἶναι, ἔνιοι δὲ καὶ τὸν μαθηματικὸν τὸν αὐτὸν τοῦτον εἶναι. (Further details presently.) The doctrine mentioned in the second passage is referred to in xiv. 2, at the end, where Aristotle opposes two theories: τῷ ἰδέας τιθεμένῳ and

the relation of the One to numbers involved him in a

τῷ τοῦτον μὲν τὸν τρόπον οὐκ οἰομένῳ διὰ τὸ τὰς ἐνούσας δυσχερείας ὁρᾶν περὶ τὰς ἰδέας ... ποιοῦντι δὲ ἀριθμὸν τὸν μαθηματικόν. Of the latter he then says, οὐθενὸς γὰρ οὔτε φησὶν ὃ λέγων αὐτὸν εἶναι, ἀλλ' ὡς αὐτήν τινα λέγει καθ' αὐτὴν φύσιν οὖσαν, οὔτε φαίνεται ὢν αἴτιος (for neither does he who assumes this number maintain that it is the cause of anything, since he represents it as a self-subsistent essence; nor does it show itself to be so; the αὐτὸν εἶναι has to be completed by the αἴτιον that follows. See also xiv. 3, 1090 a. 20 sqq. The Pythagoreans held things to be themselves numbers, because they thought they discovered in them many numerical determinations: τοῖς δὲ τὸν μαθηματικὸν μόνον λέγουσιν εἶναι ἀριθμὸν οὐθὲν τοιοῦτον ἐνδέχεται λέγειν κατὰ τὰς ὑποθέσεις, ἀλλ' ὅτι οὐκ ἔσονται αὐτῶν αἱ ἐπιστῆμαι ἐλέγετο. Aristotle continues, in opposition to this view, δῆλον ὅτι οὐ κεχώρισται τὰ μαθηματικά, and he repeats, in regard to its basis, οἱ δὲ χωριστὸν ποιοῦντες (that is to say, τὸν μαθηματικὸν ἀριθμὸν), ὅτι ἐπὶ τῶν αἰσθητῶν οὐκ ἔσται τὰ ἀξιώματα, ἀληθῆ δὲ τὰ λεγόμενα καὶ σαίνει τὴν ψυχήν, εἶναί τε ὑπολαμβάνουσι, καὶ χωριστὰ εἶναι. ὁμοίως δὲ καὶ τὰ μεγέθη τὰ μαθηματικά. Cf. xiii. 9, 1086 a. 2: οἱ μὲν γὰρ τὰ μαθηματικὰ μόνον ποιοῦντες παρὰ τὰ αἰσθητά, ὁρῶντες τὴν περὶ τὰ εἴδη δυσχέρειαν καὶ πλάσιν, ἀπέστησαν ἀπὸ τοῦ εἰδητικοῦ ἀριθμοῦ καὶ τὸν μαθηματικὸν ἐποίησαν. From these he afterwards discriminates, οἱ τὰ εἴδη βουλόμενοι ἅμα καὶ ἀριθμοὺς ποιεῖν and ὁ πρῶτος θέμενος τά τε εἴδη εἶναι καὶ ἀριθμοὺς τὰ εἴδη καὶ τὰ μαθηματικὰ εἶναι. As to the philosophers who are to be credited with this doctrine, commentators are so undecided and contradictory (cf. Ravaisson, p. 29; Schwegler loc. cit.; Bonitz, Arist. Metaph. ii. 544 sq), that it is easy to see they are theorising on the basis of the passages in Aristotle, without any real knowledge of the matter. But we may, at any rate, gather from what has been quoted, that Aristotle is here concerned not with Pythagoreans (as Pseudo-Alexander believes, p. 1076 h. 19), but with Platonists. He describes the adherents of the doctrine in question clearly as such; for he says they were led to it by the difficulties of Plato's doctrine of Ideas He observes that they differ from the Pythagoreans in assuming numbers and magnitudes to exist apart from things (as Plato did with regard to his Ideas); and they make use of the same argument that Plato brought forward for the separation of Ideas from things (supra, p. 225 sq., p. 231 sq), namely, that there could be no knowledge if the object of knowledge were not exalted above the Sensible (ὅτι οὐκ ἔσονται αὐτῶν αἱ ἐπιστῆμαι ἐλέγετο, Metaph. xiv. 3; vide supra). What Platonist it was who thus departed from the Ideas, and assumed transcendental and hypostasized numbers in their place we may infer from Metaph. xii. 10, 1075 b. 37; xiv. 3, 1090 b 13. We found that (on account of the parallel passage quoted in note 41) this passage could only relate to Speusippus; so that the words οἱ δὲ λέγοντες τὸν ἀριθμὸν πρῶτον τὸν μαθηματικὸν, and τοῖς τὰ μαθηματικὰ μόνον εἶναι φαμένοις, must also point to him.

difficulty; for in order to separate the One, as first cause, from the Derived, he found himself obliged to distinguish it by the name of the 'First One' from the unities contained in numbers; so that, as Aristotle observes, at this point, at any rate, he reverted to the separation of Ideal and mathematical number.[45]

In the same way he assumed magnitudes to exist as specific substances, above and beyond sensible things; but the Platonic distinction of mathematical and Ideal magnitudes[46] was of course not allowed by Speusippus. Mathematical numbers are the First, mathematical magnitudes the Second.[47] Like the Pythagoreans, he attempted to prove various analogies between them;[48] and in the same Pythagorean strain,

We are reminded of him too in Metaph. xiii. 8, 1083 a. 21, where a distinction is drawn between those who held Ideas to be numbers and ὅσοι ἰδέας μὲν οὐκ οἴονται εἶναι οὔθ' ἁπλῶς οὔτε ὡς ἀριθμοὺς τινας οὔσας, τὰ δὲ μαθεματικὰ εἶναι καὶ τοὺς ἀριθμοὺς πρώτους τῶν ὄντων, καὶ ἀρχὴν αὐτῶν εἶναι αὐτὸ τὸ ἕν; and in xiv 4, 1091 b. 22, where it is said that the identification of the One with the Good is beset with difficulties· συμβαίνει γὰρ πολλὴ δυσχέρεια, ἣν ἔνιοι φεύγοντες ἀπειρήκασιν, οἱ τὸ ἓν μὲν ὁμολογοῦντες ἀρχὴν εἶναι πρώτην καὶ στοιχεῖον, τοῦ ἀριθμοῦ δὲ τοῦ μαθηματικοῦ. In this latter place especially (according to the proof given on p. 568) the reference to Speusippus is unmistakable. In the same manner the allusion to him in Z 32, διόπερ ὁ μὲν ἔφευγε τὸ ἀγαθὸν προσάπτειν τῷ ἑνί, clearly refers to Z 22 sqq. Ravaisson rightly appeals (p. 30) to Metaph. vii. 2, 1028 b. 21, 24, to show that Speusippus did not identify numbers with Ideas. Susemihl, loc. cit., agrees in this view of Speusippus' doctrine; but thinks that the reference to him in xiii. 5, 1076 b. 11 sq. extends to Plato and Xenocrates as well. From c. 1, 1076 a. 22, compared with Z 32, it is, however, clear that Aristotle is only dealing with those who τὰς μαθηματικὰς μόνον οὐσίας εἶναί φασιν.

[45] Vide the quotations from Metaph. xiv. 3, in the preceding note. Another argument, seemingly employed by Speusippus, is to be found in Metaph. xiv. 3, 1090 b. 5 sqq.: cf. vii. 2, 1028 b. 15; iii. 5.

[46] Metaph xiii 8, 1083 a. 20 sqq.

[47] Vide p. 518.

[48] Metaph. xiii 6, 1080 b. 23 (according to the quotation on p. 573): ὁμοίως δὲ καὶ περὶ τὰ μήκη καὶ περὶ τὰ ἐπίπεδα καὶ περὶ τὰ στερεά. xiv. 3, 1090 a 35: οἱ δὲ χωριστὸν ποιοῦντες (τὸν ἀριθμὸν)...

he praises the perfection of the number ten, as shown partly in its arithmetical properties, and partly, in that its elements, the first four numbers, underlie all geometrical proportions.[49] Plato, in his later period, certainly made greater concessions to the Pythagorean theory of numbers than was consistent with the spirit of his system; but in his successor this tendency preponderated to such an extent that in his metaphysics he would be altogether a Pythagorean, did not the separation of numbers from things (a remnant of the doctrine of Ideas) constitute a very essential difference between true Pythagoreism and his adaptation of it.

Speusippus seems to have paid little attention to natural science. Theophrastus censures him for neglecting, like most of the Platonists, to pursue his derivation of the Particular from Primary Causes far enough; and for the superficial and disjointed manner in which he brings his principles to bear on all things beyond the sphere of numbers and mathematical quantities.[50] His writings (as far as we can judge

εἶναί τε ὑπολαμβάνουσι καὶ χωριστὰ εἶναι· ὁμοίως δὲ καὶ τὰ μεγέθη τὰ μαθηματικά.

[49] In his work on the Pythagorean numbers according to Iamblichus, Theol. Arith. p. 62, he treats minutely περὶ τῶν ἐν αὐτοῖς γραμμικῶν (the numbers resulting from geometric proportions) πολυγωνίων τε καὶ παντοίων τῶν ἐν ἀριθμοῖς ἐπιπέδων ἅμα καὶ στερεῶν. We must here bear in mind that in the Greek mathematics of the Pythagoreans, arithmetic was wont to be expressed geometrically; we hear of plane and solid numbers, of quadratic, cubic, oblong, gnomonic, circular numbers, and so on. In the same treatise Speusippus (loc. cit. p. 63) attempts to prove that the number ten is contained in geometrical entities and figures: he finds, for example, one in the point; two in the line; three in the triangle, as the simplest plane; four in the pyramid, as the simplest cube: cf. vol. i. 349 sq. and supra, p. 331, 103, and p. 519, 8.

[50] Vide the fragment in the Theol. Arithm. loc. cit. and the extracts from it in the preceding note. Further details presently.

from their titles [51]) consist, in addition to those already mentioned, of descriptive rather than investigatory works: [52] they include books on Metaphysics, Theology, Mathematics, Ethics, Politics, and Rhetoric.[53] Of the Physics of Speusippus tradition has preserved very little. Aristotle may perhaps be alluding to him when he accuses the Platonists of making Space, as the sphere of mathematical and corporeal magnitudes, begin simultaneously with these.[54] We are told that he

[51] Metaph. p. 312 (Fr. 12, 11 Wimm.): νῦν δ' οἵ γε πολλοὶ (of the Pythagoreans) μέχρι τινὸς ἐλθόντες καταπαύονται καθάπερ καὶ οἱ τὸ ἓν καὶ τὴν ἀόριστον δυάδα ποιοῦντες the Platonists (and more particularly Plato, p. 519, 10) τοὺς γὰρ ἀριθμοὺς γεννήσαντες καὶ τὰ ἐπίπεδα καὶ τὰ σώματα, σχεδὸν τἆλλα παραλείπουσι, πλὴν ὅσον ἐφαπτόμενοι, καὶ τοσαῦτο μόνον δηλοῦντες, ὅτι τὰ μὲν ἀπὸ τῆς ἀορίστου δυάδος, οἷον τόπος καὶ κενὸν καὶ ἄπειρον, τὰ δ' ἀπὸ τῶν ἀριθμῶν καὶ τοῦ ἑνός, οἷον ψυχὴ καὶ ἄλλ' ἄττα, χρόνον δ' ἅμα καὶ τὸν οὐρανὸν καὶ ἕτερα δὴ πλείω· τοῦ δ' οὐρανοῦ πέρι καὶ τῶν λοιπῶν οὐδεμίαν ἔτι ποιοῦνται μνείαν· ὡσαύτως δ' οὐδὲ οἱ περὶ Σπεύσιππον, οὐδὲ τῶν οὐθεὶς, πλὴν Ξενοκράτης.

[52] Diog. iv 4 sq. In this catalogue several of his known works are missing. Whether they are altogether omitted, or are quoted under other titles, we do not know. Among these are: the treatise on Pythagorean numbers (vide note 49), unless this is included in the Μαθηματικὸς (Proclus says, Eucl. 22, vide 77 Fr, that Speusippus called all geometrical propositions θεωρήματα); the treatise πρὸς Κλεοφῶντα (vide note 66), which perhaps may be identical with the πρὸς νομοθεσίας of Diogenes; περὶ φιλοσόφων (Diog. ix 23; cf. the φιλόσοφος, iv. 4); and the Platonic discourses on the Good (Simplicius, Phys. 32 b. m These can hardly be the 'one book' περὶ φιλοσοφίας which Diogenes describes). With regard to the Πλάτωνος περίδειπνον (vide p. 1, 1) Fischer, in his life of Speusippus, 38, conjectures that it may be the same as the Eulogy of Plato (p. 1, 1), since this might have assumed the form of a discourse at Plato's funeral feast (or perhaps several such discourses), and the statements of Apuleius about Plato, which we derive from Speusippus, may have been taken from it. Among these, however, we can only reckon with certainty the quotations, p 6, 5, and p 44, 111. In Plutarch, Quæst. conv. Prœm. 3. p. 612, we perhaps have a reference to this work It is also possible that, as Hermann and Steinhart suppose (vide supra, p. 1, 1), the title περίδειπνον was incorrectly bestowed upon Speusippus's treatise.

[53] Vide note 28.

[54] I include the treatise περὶ ψυχῆς with the metaphysical works, as it seems to have been chiefly concerned with the World-soul (supra, note 38).

P P

defined Time as Quantity in motion;[55] that he adhered to the mathematical derivation of the elements; assuming, however, with Philolaus, five elements,[56] instead of Plato's four: that he declared not only the higher, but the irrational part also, of the soul to be immortal,[57]—a divergence from Plato,[58] which may have been occasioned by the difficulties resulting from the opposite theory, in regard to the doctrine of Metempsychosis; for it can scarcely be doubted that so great an admirer of Pythagoras was an upholder of that doctrine. These scanty notices contain all that we really know about the Physics of Speusippus, and

[55] Metaph. iv. 5, 1092 a. 17· ἄτοπον δὲ καὶ τὸ τόπον ἅμα τοῖς στερεοῖς καὶ τοῖς μαθηματικοῖς ποιῆσαι ... καὶ τὸ εἰπεῖν μὲν ὅτι ποῦ ἔσται, τί δέ ἐστιν ὁ τόπος, μή. As this observation is immediately preceded by a criticism on a doctrine of Speusippus, Ravaisson (44) and Brandis (ii. b. 1, 18) suppose that it refers to him. But there is no real connection between the two passages. Bonitz therefore thinks it may belong elsewhere—perhaps to Metaph. xiii. 8, 9.

[56] τὸ ἐν κινήσει ποσὸν (Plut. Plat. qu. viii 4, 3, s. 1007). This definition leaves it uncertain whether the quantity of motion (properly, in the sphere of motion) is meant, or quantity which is in a state of motion (the motion of something contained in space).

[57] In the treatise on Pythagorean numbers, according to Theol. Arithm. p. 62, he writes, περὶ τῶν πέντε σχημάτων, ἃ τοῖς κοσμικοῖς ἀποδίδοται στοιχείοις, ἰδιότητος αὐτῶν (this αὐτῶν should be omitted, or ἰδιότητός τε αὐτῶν substituted) πρὸς ἄλληλα καὶ κοινότητος ἀναλογίας τὲ καὶ ἀνακολουθίας (ἀκολουθίας or ἀντακολουθίας). Even were it possible, it is certainly not probable, that the words ἃ—στοιχείοις are merely a comment of Iamblichus. It appears, then, from this passage that Speusippus made the five regular figures correspond with the five elements, thus departing from the original doctrine of Plato, like Xenocrates and the author of the Epinomis; and that, in agreement with Philolaus and the later form of Platonism, he considered Ether to be a fifth element (supra, p. 372, 21; 521, 14; and vol. i. 350 sq).

[58] Olympiodorus in Phædon. p. 98, Finckh: ὅτι οἱ μὲν ἀπὸ τῆς λογικῆς ψυχῆς ἄχρι τῆς ἐμψύχου ἕξεως ἀπαθανατίζουσιν, ὡς Νουμήνιος. οἱ δὲ μέχρι τῆς φύσεως, ὡς Πλωτῖνος ἔνι ὅπου. οἱ δὲ μέχρι τῆς ἀλογίας, ὡς τῶν μὲν παλαιῶν Ξενοκράτης καὶ Σπεύσιππος, τῶν δὲ νεωτέρων Ἰάμβλιχος καὶ Πλούταρχος. οἱ δὲ μέχρι μόνης τῆς λογικῆς, ὡς Πρόκλος καὶ Πορφύριος. οἱ δὲ μέχρι μόνον τοῦ νοῦ φθείρουσι γὰρ τὴν δόξαν, ὡς πολλοὶ τῶν Περιπατητικῶν. οἱ δὲ μέχρι τῆς ὅλης ψυχῆς, φθείρουσι γὰρ τὰς μερικὰς εἰς τὴν ὅλην.

anything else that may here and there be gathered on this subject is far less interesting or important.

Our information is likewise very meagre concerning his Ethics, though Speusippus devoted many of his writings to the subject;[59] but we may take for granted that his principles were generally those of Plato.[60] No trace, however, is discernible of the peculiar theory of virtue, and the idealistic scheme of politics which we find in the Platonic state. It is said that he sought the Highest Good or Happiness in the perfection of natural activities and conditions: this perfection being chiefly effected by virtue, which was thus declared by Speusippus, as by Plato, to be the most essential condition of happiness.[61] He allowed, however, a certain value to health, freedom from troubles, and even to external goods:[62] but he would not admit Pleasure to be a good,[63] still less the inference that it

---

[59] Vide 417 sq.

[60] In Diogenes' catalogue the treatises περὶ πλούτον, περὶ ἡδονῆς, περὶ δικαιοσύνης, περὶ φιλίας, πολίτης, περὶ νομοθεσίας, the Ἀρίστιππος, and probably other dialogues, relate to this subject.

[61] Cicero's observation (vide note 24), which seems to refer chiefly to morality, is not binding upon us, as it originates with the Eclectic Antiochus, following whom Cicero maintained the perfect agreement of the older Peripatetics with Aristotle (De orat iii. 18, 67; Acad. i 4, 17 sq.; ii. 5, 15, Fin. iv. 2, 5, v 3, 7, 8, 21; Legg. i. 13, 38; Offic. iii. 4, 20: cf. Krische, Forsch 248 sq). Similarly. Diog iv. 1, ἔμεινε μὲν ἐπὶ τῶν αὐτῶν Πλάτωνι δογμάτων, taken literally, would prove too much.

[62] Vide Clem. Strom. 418 D Σπεύσιππος τὴν εὐδαιμονίαν φησὶν ἕξιν εἶναι τελείαν ἐν τοῖς κατὰ φύσιν ἔχουσιν· ἢ ἕξιν ἀγαθῶν· ἧς δὴ καταστάσεως ἅπαντας μὲν ἀνθρώπους ὄρεξιν ἔχειν. στοχάζεσθαι δὲ τοὺς ἀγαθοὺς τῆς ἀοχλησίας εἶεν δ' ἂν αἱ ἀρεταὶ τῆς εὐδαιμονίας ἀπεργαστικαί. Cf. Cicero, Tusc. v. 10, 30: he regarded poverty, disgrace, and the like as evils, but taught that the wise man was always happy.

[63] Vide preceding note, and Plut. Comm. not. 13, 1, p. 1065: οἱ τοῦ Ξενοκράτους καὶ Σπευσίππου κατηγοροῦντες ἐπὶ τῷ μὴ τὴν ὑγείαν ἀδιάφορον ἡγεῖσθαι μηδὲ τὸν πλοῦτον ἀνωφελές. Cicero, however, Legg. i. 13, 38, numbers them both among those who held that only the Laudable-in-itself was a *magnum bonum.* According to

must be so if Pain be an Evil. There is an opposition, he said, not only between the Evil and the Good, but between one evil thing and another; just as the Greater is opposed not only to the Equal, but also to the Less.[64] Another argument of his is mentioned, by which he sought to prove that law deserves respect, and that the wise man ought not to withdraw himself from its rule.[65] Though it is impossible to gain a connected idea of the Ethics of Speusippus from such fragments as these, we can at least perceive that they coincided in the main with the principles of the Older Academy.[66]

Cic. Tusc. v. 13, 39, and Seneca, Epist. 85, 18 sq. (vide infra, chap. xx n. 71), they both maintained that virtue is of itself sufficient to give happiness, but added that happiness, to be perfect, requires other goods

[64] Cf. Aristotle, Ethics, iv. vii. 14, beginning (Eustratius in Eth. Nic. 166 b. m. cannot be considered an original source); pain is an Evil, therefore pleasure must be a Good. ὡς γὰρ Σπεύσιππος ἔλυεν (that is to say, as follows) οὐ συμβαίνει ἡ λύσις, ὥσπερ τὸ μεῖζον τῷ ἐλάττονι καὶ τὸ ἴσῳ ἐναντίον· οὐ γὰρ ἂν φαίη ὅπερ κακόν τι εἶναι τὴν ἡδονήν. Cf x 2, 1173 a 5; vii. 12, 1152, b 8; Gellius, N. A. ix. 5, 4: *Speusippus vetusque omnis Academia* (this, doubtless, is an exaggeration) *voluptatem et dolorem duo mala esse dicunt opposita inter sese, bonum tamen esse, quod utriusque medium foret.* It does not appear a legitimate inference from Eth. N. x. 2 that Speusippus in this discussion of pleasure was opposing Eudoxus (Krische, 249, 1; Brandis, 14, 36). As he wrote upon Aristippus, it is much more likely that he had the Cynic philosopher in view.

[65] A similar distinction, not, however, entirely coincident with the above, is employed by Plato with regard to the same question; vide Rep. ix. 584 D sqq.

[66] Clemens Strom. ii. 367 A· Σπεύσιππος γὰρ ἐν τῷ πρὸς Κλεοφῶντα πρώτῳ τὰ ὅμοια τῷ Πλάτωνι ἔοικε διὰ τούτου γράφειν. εἰ γὰρ ἡ βασιλεία σπουδαῖον ὅ τε σοφὸς μόνος βασιλεὺς καὶ ἄρχων, ὁ νόμος, λόγος ἂν ὀρθὸς, σπουδαῖος. This argument, which was similarly employed by the Stoics (cf. Stobæus, Ecl. ii. 190, 208), is probably directed against the Cynic contempt for law (Pt. i. 277, 3), and Speusippus, in the words ὅ τε σοφὸς, κ.τ.λ., is indirectly referring to the opposite presupposition. The maxim that the wise man only is a ruler has not been handed down to us by express tradition as belonging to the Cynics, but it greatly resembles much that we do know of them, and it has an obvious connection with the Socratic doctrine. It is, therefore, very probable that the Stoics may have borrowed it from the Cynics (vide part i. p 276 and p. 141, 1).

CHAPTER XV.

THE OLDER ACADEMY CONTINUED.—XENOCRATES.

XENOCRATES resembled Speusippus in his strong predilection for Pythagoreanism [1] and his high estimation of mathematics,[2] and he developed the tendencies of Plato's later works to an even greater extent than his predecessor. While arriving at a higher degree of systematic completeness, he did not, however, venture to abandon the original ground-work of Platonism so entirely as Speusippus had done in regard to Ideas: he was therefore in many respects a more genuine Platonist. As he was much longer at the head of the Platonic school, and was besides a very prolific writer,[3]

---

[1] Cf. Iambl. Theol. Arithm. p. 61, g. E: παρὰ Ξενοκράτους ἐξαιρέτως σπουδασθεισῶν ἀεὶ Πυθαγορικῶν ἀκροασέων, μάλιστα δὲ τῶν Φιλολάου συγγραμμάτων.

[2] The importance he attached to this science is shown by his numerous and apparently comprehensive treatises on Mathematics and Astronomy. Cf. the titles ap. Diog. iv. 13 sq.: λογιστικὰ (9 books), τὰ περὶ τὰ μαθήματα (6 books), περὶ γεωμετρῶν, περὶ ἀριθμῶν θεωρία, περὶ διαστημάτων, τὰ περὶ ἀστρολογίαν, περὶ γεωμετρίας. The Πυθαγόρεια may have contained some mathematical elements. He is said to have dismissed a pupil, ignorant of mathematics, as wholly unprepared for philosophy (λαβὰς οὐκ ἔχεις φιλοσοφίας) Plut. Virt. Mor. C 12 end, p 542; Diog. 10, alibi; Krische, Forsch p. 317.

[3] V. Diog. iv. 11 sqq., and Wynpersse ad loc. 190 sq, 197 sqq. The life of Plato is not mentioned (cf. on it p. 337, 1), nor the treatise περὶ τῆς ἀπὸ τῶν ζῴων τροφῆς (Clemens, Strom. vii 717 D), unless contained in the Πυθαγόρεια. The satires mentioned in Apuleius, Floril. iv. 20, should perhaps be ascribed to Xenophanes (Diogenes ii. speaks of ἔπη), and the treatise

we may justly consider him as the principal representative of the Old Academy.[4] Unfortunately his doctrine is too imperfectly known to enable us to reproduce even its main characteristics with accuracy. We must therefore content ourselves with piecing together the traditions we possess, filling up the lacunæ by such probable conjectures as we may.

Of the three divisions of Philosophy, which had already been employed by Plato, but were first expressly recognised by Xenocrates,[5] Logic or Dialectic (the name is uncertain) must have included in the first place the theory of cognition, and the propædeutic part of reasoning, to which he devoted numerous writings;[6] secondarily, probably, discussions on genus and species, and the highest contradictories:[7] while enquiries concerning ultimate principles[8] might come under the head of Physics.[9] That which is most distinctive in Xenocrates is his Theory of Knowledge. Plato divided knowledge first of all into the knowledge of reason and the knowledge of sense, subdividing the former into the higher dialectical, and the lower

περὶ τῆς Πλάτωνος πολιτείας (Suidas Ξενοκρ.) may be identical with that περὶ πολιτείας in Diogenes. Whether the work περὶ τἀγαθοῦ (v. p. 26, 53) is the Platonic discourse edited by Xenophon (Simpl. Phys. 32 b. m.) cannot be decided.

[4] So in Simplicius loc cit. he is called ὁ γνησιώτατος τῶν Πλάτωνος ἀκροατῶν.

[5] V. supr. 165, 33.

[6] Cf. Cicero, Acad. ii. 46, 143; and the titles περὶ σοφίας, περὶ φιλοσοφίας, περὶ ἐπιστήμης, περὶ ἐπιστημοσύνης, περὶ τοῦ ψεύδους, τῶν περὶ τὴν διάνοιαν (twice), περὶ τοῦ ἐναντίου, λύσις τῶν περὶ τοὺς λόγους, λύσεις περὶ μαθημάτων, τῶν περὶ τὴν λέξιν, τῆς περὶ τὸ διαλέγεσθαι πραγματείας, and περὶ μαθητῶν, unless this is a mistake arising out of μαθημάτων.

[7] περὶ γενῶν καὶ εἰδῶν, περὶ εἰδῶν (unless this title is equivalent to that of περὶ ἰδεῶν) ἐναντίων α'.

[8] Writings περὶ τοῦ ἀορίστου, περὶ τοῦ ὄντος, περὶ τοῦ ἑνὸς, περὶ τἀγαθοῦ, περὶ ἰδεῶν, περὶ ἀριθμῶν.

[9] If (which is not certain) he carried out the division so strictly.

THEORY OF KNOWLEDGE. 583

mathematical cognition;[10] and the latter into notion or envisagement (Vorstellung) and perception (Wahrnehmung). Xenocrates reckoned only three stages: Thought, Perception, and Envisagement. Thought, he said, is concerned with all that is beyond the heavens; Perception with the things in the heavens; Envisagement with the heavens themselves; for though they are beheld with the bodily eye in astronomy, they become the object of thought. The thinking cognition guarantees knowledge; the sensible cognition is also true, but not to the same extent; in envisagement truth and falsehood are equally to be found.[11] Accordingly, while Plato separated philosophic from mathematical thought, even that of pure mathematics, Xenocrates included both in his notion of knowledge,

He may have enunciated it generally, without having assigned its place to each single investigation in one of the three parts.

[10] Cf. p. 218 sq.

[11] Sext. Math. vii 147; Ξενοκράτης δὲ τρεῖς φησιν οὐσίας εἶναι, τὴν μὲν αἰσθητήν, τὴν δὲ νοητήν, τὴν δὲ σύνθετον καὶ δοξαστήν. ὧν αἰσθητὴν μὲν εἶναι τὴν ἐντὸς οὐρανοῦ, νοητὴν δὲ πάντων τῶν ἐκτὸς οὐρανὸν, δοξαστὴν δὲ καὶ σύνθετον τὴν αὐτοῦ τοῦ οὐρανοῦ ὁρατὴ μὲν γάρ ἐστι τῇ αἰσθήσει, νοητὴ δὲ δι' ἀστρολογίας. τούτων μέντοι τοῦτον ἐχόντων τὸν τρόπον τῆς μὲν ἐκτὸς οὐρανοῦ καὶ νοητῆς οὐσίας κριτήριον ἀπεφαίνετο τὴν ἐπιστήμην, τῆς δὲ ἐντὸς οὐρανοῦ καὶ αἰσθητῆς αἴσθησιν, τῆς δὲ μικτῆς τὴν δόξαν, καὶ τούτων κοινῶς τὸ μὲν διὰ τοῦ ἐπιστημονικοῦ λόγου κριτήριον βέβαιόν τε ὑπάρχειν καὶ ἀληθὲς, τὸ δὲ διὰ τῆς αἰσθήσεως ἀληθὲς μὲν, οὐχ οὕτω δὲ ὡς τὸ διὰ τοῦ ἐπιστημονικοῦ λόγον, τὸ δὲ σύνθετον κοινὸν ἀληθοῦς τε καὶ ψευδοῦς ὑπάρχειν. τῆς γὰρ δόξης τὴν μέν τινα ἀληθῆ εἶναι, τὴν δὲ ψευδῆ· ὅθεν καὶ τρεῖς Μοίρας παραδεδόσθαι, Ἄτροπον μὲν τὴν τῶν νοητῶν, ἀμετάθετον οὖσαν, Κλωθὼ δὲ τὴν τῶν αἰσθητῶν, Λάχεσιν δὲ τῶν δοξαστῶν. This division of the Actual seems to be referred to by Theophrastus (Metaph. p 313; Fr. 12, 12, Wimm., after the words quoted p. 858, 2): οὗτος γὰρ ἅπαντά πως περιτίθησι περὶ τὸν κόσμον, ὁμοίως αἰσθητὰ καὶ νοητὰ καὶ μαθηματικὰ, καὶ ἔτι δὴ τὰ θεῖα. Μαθηματικὰ here must mean the οὐρανία or the object of astronomy. the θεῖα, only added incidentally by Theophrastus, form no separate class, but, as we shall see presently, are found in the three others, so far as they are treated from a theological point of view.

and the object of both in his notion of the supercelestial;[12] while Plato admitted no truth at all in the perception of sense, as distinct from thought, Xenocrates conceded to it a lesser amount of truth. According to Sextus, he treated this subject in a most confused manner, sometimes restricting envisagement to a definite sphere, sometimes speaking of it in an entirely general sense.[13] Of his Logic we only know that (perhaps in opposition to Aristotle) he endeavoured to reduce all other categories to the Platonic distinction[14] of the Absolute and the Relative.[15] In the conception of his highest metaphysical principles, Xenocrates followed Plato; except that he made more constant use of arithmetical designations, and at the same time connected them more closely with theology. He declared Unity and Duality—Duality meaning here indeterminate Duality—to be the primary Causes; the former he identified with the Straight, the latter with the Crooked. He also called Unity the first or male divinity, the Father, Zeus, and Reason; Duality the female divinity, and the mother of the gods.[16] Numbers, he said, resulted from the union of

[12] This expression resembles the ὑπερουράνιος τόπος, Phædr. 247 c., the comparison of pure mathematical knowledge with philosophical knowledge corresponds with the comparison of the mathematical numbers with the Ideas, &c.; see below.

[13] The former, when he assigned to it the heavenly element as its peculiar province; the latter, when he represented the opposition of truth and error in notions or envisagements as the combination of thought and perception, by an application of the Platonic principle (see 172, 6; 209, 102); that both spring from the combination of notions.

[14] On which cf p. 277 sq.

[15] Simpl. Categ. γ. b. 6, Schol. in Arist 47 b. 25: οἱ γὰρ περὶ Ξενοκράτην καὶ Ἀνδρόνικον πάντα τῷ καθ' αὑτὸ καὶ τῷ πρός τι περιλαμβάνειν δοκοῦσιν, ὥστε περιττὸν εἶναι κατ' αὐτοὺς τοσοῦτον τῶν γενῶν πλῆθος.

[16] Stob. Ecl. i. 62: Ξενοκρ. . . .

FIRST PRINCIPLES. NUMBERS. 585

these two;[17] and he seems to have defined the relation of numbers to Ideas in such a manner that he neither,

τὴν μονάδα καὶ τὴν δυάδα θεούς, τὴν μὲν ὡς ἄρρενα πατρὸς ἔχουσαν τάξιν, ἐν οὐρανῷ βασιλεύουσαν, ἥντινα προσαγορεύει καὶ Ζῆνα καὶ περιττὸν καὶ νοῦν, ὅστις ἐστὶν αὐτῷ πρῶτος θεός· τὴν δὲ ὡς θηλείαν, μητρὸς θεῶν δίκην, τῆς ὑπὸ τὸν οὐρανὸν λήξεως ἡγουμένην, ἥτις ἐστὶν αὐτῷ ψυχὴ τοῦ παντός. (The latter, if correct, shows great confusion; Xenocrates, as we shall find later on, considered the soul to be a number; and duality is the one element of every number and also of the soul-number; see below). It is possible that Xenocrates, like the Pythagoreans in their numerical analogies, did not avoid this confusion, at least in expression. Philolaus had already designated duality as Rhea, mother of the gods, the Pythagoreans gave the same name to the central fire: see vol. i. 337, 1; 356, 4. This evidence justifies us in ascribing to Xenocrates, out of the different determinations of the Platonists as to the first principles (see 322, 83), those which placed unity and the indefinite dyad at the head. Theophrastus says (see p. 576, 51 and 583, 11) that he went further than all others in the derivation of the individual from these two principles; and Plut. an. procr. 2, 1 (see note 26), says that he represented numbers and the soul, so far as it is a number, as springing from them. The opposite of unity and the indefinite dyad was understood in two ways. Some understood the principle opposed to unity as the Unlike or the Great-and-Small, interpreting in this way the

δυὰς ἀόριστος (Metaph. xiv. 1, 1088 a. 15: οἱ δὲ τὸ ἄνισον ὡς ἕν τι, τὴν δυάδα δὲ ἀόριστον ποιοῦντες μεγάλου καὶ μικροῦ, cf. p 1087a. 7 sqq.) Others spoke only of the unit and the indefinite dyad, without referring this concept to the Unlike (ibid. c. 2, 1088 b. 28: εἰσὶ δέ τινες οἱ δυάδα μὲν ἀόριστον ποιοῦσι τὸ μετὰ τοῦ ἑνὸς στοιχεῖον, τὸ δ' ἄνισον δυσχεραίνουσιν εὐλόγως διὰ τὰ συμβαίνοντα ἀδύνατα). Perhaps this was the doctrine of Xenocrates. He may have put the ἀόριστον for duality; a treatise of his περὶ τοῦ ἀορίστου is mentioned (Diog. 11): according to Plutarch loc. cit. he called it still more indefinitely plurality, if Plutarch gives his own words. In order to denote the flux of all corporeal things, he made use of the expression τὸ ἀέννοον, perhaps with reference to the well-known Pythagorean verse (see vol. i. 342 b.). Cf. Stob. Ecl. i. 294 Ξενοκράτης συνεστάναι τὸ πᾶν ἐκ τοῦ ἑνὸς καὶ τοῦ ἀεννάου, ἀέννοον τὴν ὕλην αἰνιττόμενος διὰ τοῦ πλήθους [τὸ πλῆθος]. Theodoret. cur. gr. aff. iv. 12, p. 57: Ξενοκράτης ἀέννοον τὴν ὕλην, ἐξ ἧς ἅπαντα γέγονε, προσηγόρευσεν.

[17] He expressly explained, however, that this process is not to be conceived as a temporal origin. Ps.-Alex. ad Metaph xiv. 4, 1091 a. 27 refers to him the remark of Aristotle in this passage, that the γένεσις τῶν ἀριθμῶν is clearly set forth not merely τοῦ θεωρῆσαι ἕνεκεν, and this is made still more credible by the fact that Xenocrates availed himself of the same expedient in his Psychogony; cf. p. 595.

like Plato, discriminated Ideas, as Ideal numbers, from mathematical numbers; nor, like Speusippus, abandoned the Ideas; but rather identified mathematical number itself with the Idea.[18] Similarly with regard

[18] Of the different developments of the doctrine of numbers in Aristotle (see p. 573, 44), that given above probably belongs to Xenocrates · cf Ravaisson (Speus. plac. p. 30) and Brandis (ii. b. 1, p. 16) with Metaph. xiii b. 1080 b. 23 sqq., where, after the quotation p. 573, Aristotle continues ὁμοίως δὲ καὶ περὶ τὰ μήκη καὶ περὶ τὰ ἐπίπεδα καὶ περὶ τὰ στερεά. οἱ μὲν γὰρ ἕτερα τὰ μαθηματικὰ (sc. μήκη, &c) καὶ τὰ μετὰ τὰς ἰδέας· (the Platonic view, that mathematical magnitudes are different from Ideal magnitudes, the consequents of the Ideas; see p. 519) τῶν δ' ἄλλως λεγόντων οἱ μὲν τὰ μαθηματικὰ καὶ μαθηματικῶς λέγουσιν, ὅσοι μὴ ποιοῦσι τὰς ἰδέας ἀριθμοὺς μηδὲ εἶναί φασιν ἰδέας. οἱ δὲ τὰ μαθηματικά, οὐ μαθηματικῶς δέ · οὐ γὰρ τέμνεσθαι οὔτε μέγεθος πᾶν εἰς μεγέθη, οὔθ' ὁποιασοῦν μονάδας δυάδα εἶναι (not all unities, when taken two together, produce dualities). In denying that all magnitudes can be resolved into other magnitudes, Xenocrates' doctrine of indivisible lines can scarcely be mistaken. This assertion is attributed to those who do not wish either to put aside Ideal magnitudes with Speusippus, or to distinguish them from mathematical magnitudes with Plato. These are clearly the persons who treat Ideal number in relation to mathematical in a similar way; and we have therefore every reason to refer both these views to Xenocrates. This supposition is substantiated by the quotation from Sextus, p. 538, 11. According to the fundamental principle that the degrees and forms of knowledge depend upon the object (see p. 225; p. 331, 103), Plato distinguished mathematical knowledge from philosophic knowledge, just as he distinguished mathematical numbers and magnitudes from Ideal. If Xenocrates yielded the first distinction he must be supposed to have done so with the second, making Ideas and mathematical things equal. Both in their coincidence form the supersensuous world, τὰ ἐκτὸς οὐρανοῦ; they comprehend that super-celestial place, in which Plato placed the Ideas only. The coincidence of the mathematical element with the Ideas is mentioned by Aristotle, Metaph. xiii. 8, 1083 b. 1; ibid. c. 9. 1086 a. 5; xiv. 3, 1090 b. 27; and vii. 2, 1028 b. 24, where Asclep Schol. in Ar. 741 a. 5, sees a reference to Xenocrates He remarks, xiii. 9, that this form of the doctrine virtually does away with mathematical numbers, even if they are recognised nominally. Ps.-Alex. ad Metaph. 1080 b. 11; 1083 b. 1; 1086 a 2, connects the view of Xenocrates about numbers with that of Speusippus, and attributes to the former the denial of Ideal numbers, and to the latter the identification of Ideal with mathematical numbers. Contradictory as this statement is, it cannot demand consideration as opposed to the statements of Aris-

INDIVISIBLE MAGNITUDES.

to magnitudes, he desired to do away with the distinction of Ideal and mathematical without really abolishing either the one or the other.[19] In the derivation of magnitudes he seems to have followed Plato:[20] while endeavouring to reduce them to their primary elements, he arrived at the theory—which Plato had already approached,[21]—that all figures ultimately originate out of the smallest, and consequently indivisible, lines.[22] Thus he appears to have assumed in each

totle. What were the views of the genuine Alexander it is hard to say. According to Syrianus ad Metaph. 1080 b. 14 (Schol. in Arist. Supplem. 902 a. 4), he had the following words relating to Speusippus (supra, p. 573): οἱ δὲ τὸν μαθηματικὸν μόνον ἀριθμὸν εἶναι, κ.τ.λ., referring to τοὺς περὶ Ξενοκράτην, οἳ χωρίζουσι μὲν τὸν μαθηματικὸν (sc. ἀριθμὸν) τῶν αἰσθητῶν, οὐ μέντοι μόνον εἶναι νομίζουσι. This, however, stands in such absolute contradiction with the statement of Aristotle which it is intended to explain, that it cannot be attributed to Alexander; it seems more likely that Syrianus made the addition, οἳ χωρίζουσι, κ.τ λ, in his own name, to correct Alexander.

[19] See previous note

[20] Metaph. xiv. 3. Aristotle, in the words quoted (p. 519, 8), seems to mean Xenocrates; in any case, the words must partly hold good of him, for (Z 31) he continues: οὗτοι μὲν οὖν ταύτῃ προσγλιχόμενοι ταῖς ἰδέαις τὰ μαθηματικὰ διαμαρτάνουσιν (the same objection which he elsewhere makes to Xenocrates, see previous note) οἱ δὲ πρῶτοι δύο τοὺς ἀριθμοὺς ποιήσαντες, τόν τε τῶν εἰδῶν καὶ τὸν μαθηματικὸν ἄλλον, &c. Themist. De an. i. 2 (ii. 21, 7 Sp.) concludes his elucidation of the passage quoted, 329, 98, in agreement with the statements of Aristotle, with the words. ταῦτα δὲ ἅπαντα λαβεῖν ἔστιν ἐκ τῶν περὶ φύσεως Ξενοκράτους.

[21] See p. 519, 8.

[22] This striking assertion is frequently ascribed to Xenocrates; see Procl. in Tim. 215 F; Alex. ad Metaph 992 a. 19, 1083 b. 8; Themist. Phys. f. 18, i. 122, 13 sqq. Sp., Simpl. Phys. 30 a. o. u. b. u 114 b ; De Cœlo, 252 a. 42 K (Schol. in Ar. 510 a. 35); ibid. 294 a. 22, Philop. Phys. B 16 u.; C 1 o.; M 8 m. (Schol. in Ar. 366 b. 17), who disputes that this was actually the doctrine of Xenocrates. Schol. in Arist. 323 b. 41; 384 a.: 36 b. 2; 469 b. 16, 25, 515 a. 13. Syrian Schol. in Ar. Suppl. 902 b. 21 sq. According to some of these evidences, the Aristotelian treatise (see vol. ii. b. 64, 1, 2nd edit.), attributed by others to Theophrastus, on the indivisible lines was directed against him, and to him it is conjectured belong the grounds for the supposition set forth in the beginning (968 b 21). One of these (968 a. 9, see following nt.), expressly depends on the doctrine of Ideas; a second (Z 14), perhaps,

species of magnitudes an indivisible element; otherwise, he thought, the Ideas of the line, the triangle, &c., would not be the first in their kind; their parts would precede themselves.[23]

is connected with the Platonic doctrine of the elements. However, it was not merely this doctrine of the elements which led Xenocrates to his theory, according to Arist. Metaph. i. 9, 992 a. 10-22; xiii. 6 (see p 586, 18), it seems, like the corresponding Platonic statements previously, to have been laid down first in the metaphysical construction of spatial magnitudes. In Phys vi. 2, 223 b. 15 sqq. Aristotle probably had Xenocrates in his mind, although he does not mention him, Themist. Philop. and Simpl. loc. cit. ad Phys. i 3, 187 a. 1, according to Alex. and Porphyry, refer partly to him and partly to Plato. These passages, however, seem to relate equally to the Atomists. From the passage De an. i. 4 end— where it is remarked against Xenocrates that if the soul were supposed to be a number, and the units contained in this number were identical with the points in the body, no separation of the soul from the body would be imaginable, εἴ γε μὴ διαιροῦνται αἱ γραμμαὶ εἰς στιγμάς — no conclusion can be arrived at with regard to the peculiar doctrines of Xenocrates the subject here under discussion is merely the generally acknowledged principle, that lines are not composed of points and are not to bo resolved into points. Of course it is in itself possible, although Aristotle loc. cit. 409 a. 3 rather seems to contradict it, that Xenocrates held the same views as Plato on this point (see p. 519, 8).

[23] Cf. two passages of Aristotle: De insec. lin. 968 a. 9, where one of the first reasons for the supposition of indivisible lines is: εἰ ἔστιν ἰδέα γραμμῆς, ἡ δ' ἰδέα πρώτη τῶν συνωνύμων, τὰ δὲ μέρη πρότερα τοῦ ὅλου τὴν φύσιν, διαιρετὴ ἂν εἴη αὐτὴ ἡ γραμμὴ, τὸν αὐτὸν δὲ τρόπον καὶ τὸ τετράγωνον καὶ τὸ τρίγωνον καὶ τὰ ἄλλα σχήματα, καὶ ὅλως ἐπίπεδον αὐτὸ καὶ σῶμα· συμβήσεται γὰρ [? perhaps ἄρα] πρότερ' ἄττα εἶναι τούτων. Gen. et corr. i. 2, 316 a 10: the atoms of Democritus are far more conceivable than the smallest triangles of the Timæus. ἴδοι δ' ἄν τις καὶ ἐκ τούτων, ὅσον διαφέρουσιν οἱ φυσικῶς καὶ λογικῶς σκοποῦντες· περὶ γὰρ τοῦ ἄτομα εἶναι μεγέθη οἱ μέν φασιν ὅτι τὸ αὐτοτρίγωνον πολλὰ ἔσται, Δημόκριτος δ' ἂν φανείη οἰκείοις καὶ φυσικοῖς λόγοις πεπεῖσθαι (which Philop. ad loc. 7 a. m. explains, without knowing whether it refers to Plato himself or to his scholars) The assertion, that without the supposition of indivisible magnitudes, the Ideas of the line, of the triangle, &c., must be divisible, is less suited to Plato himself than for Xenocrates The former had, in the separation of the Ideal and mathematical magnitudes, the means of avoiding this conclusion, he could conveniently distinguish Ideal magnitudes from mathematical by means of their indivisibility, just as he distinguished Ideal numbers from mathematical by means of their inconnectibility.

Xenocrates derived the soul also from the two first

Xenocrates, on the other hand, who identified the ideal and the mathematical, was debarred from this expedient. It is, however, expressly (Synanus, Schol. in Ar. Suppl. 902 b 22 sq.) said of him: τὴν αὐτογραμμὴν (cf. the αὐτὴ ἡ γραμμὴ of the treatise π. ἀτόμων γραμμ.) οὐκ ἠνείχετο τέμνεσθαι οὐδὲ τὰς κατὰ τοὺς μέσους λόγους τῆς ψυχῆς (see p. 348 sq.) δρωμένας γραμμάς. Now, the treatise on the indivisible lines supposes a special discussion on this subject, we can only ascribe it to Xenocrates and not to Plato, it therefore seems most probable that Xenocrates was the first to express and maintain the supposition of indivisible magnitudes Cf. Porphyr. ap Simpl Phys. 30 a. n.: οἱ δὲ περὶ Ξενοκράτην τὴν μὲν πρώτην ἀκολουθίαν (of the people of Elea) ὑπεῖναι συνεχώρουν, τουτέστιν ὅτι εἰ ἕν ἐστι τὸ ὂν καὶ ἀδιαίρετον ἔσται οὐ μὴν ἀδιαίρετον εἶναι τὸ ὄν. διὸ πάλιν μηδὲ ἓν μόνον τὸ ὂν ἀλλὰ πλείω. διαιρετὸν μέντοι μὴ ἐπ' ἄπειρον εἶναι, ἀλλ' εἰς ἀτόμά τινα καταλήγειν. ταῦτα μέντοι μὴ ἄτομα εἶναι ὡς ἀμερῆ καὶ ἐλάχιστα, ἀλλὰ κατὰ μὲν τὸ ποσὸν καὶ τὴν ὕλην τμητὰ καὶ μέρη ἔχοντα, τῷ δὲ 'εἴδει ἄτομα καὶ πρῶτα, πρώτας τινὰς ὑποτιθέμενος εἶναι γραμμὰς ἀτόμους καὶ τὰ ἐκ τούτων ἐπίπεδα καὶ στερεὰ πρῶτα. Here the assertion that the indivisible magnitudes of Xenocrates are not intended to be indivisible in space, is probably an explanation of Porphyry himself, with just as little historical value as the expedient which even Simplicius (30 a. below) availed himself of, in justifiable wonder at the unmathematical principle of so mathematical a man as Xenocrates. But Xenocrates did probably represent the first surfaces and bodies as indivisible (with the words at the end of the predicate ἄτομα is to be supplied from what precedes). Stobæus attributes to him the doctrine of indivisible bodies, when he compares him with Diodorus (see Pt. i. p. 228), who supposed only such, but not indivisible lines (Ecl. i. 350: Ξενοκράτης καὶ Διόδωρος ἀμερῆ τὰ ἐλάχιστα ὡρίζοντο), and i 368 (see 875, 4) says of him, that he forms the elements out of the smallest bodies. Finally, Aristotle, De cœlo, iii. 8, 307 a 20, seems to refer to Xenocrates where he objects to the Platonic doctrine of the elements that if the tetrahedron must become warm and burn because of its angles, the same must be the case with the mathematical bodies, ἔχει γὰρ κἀκεῖνα γωνίας καὶ ἔνεισιν ἐν αὐτοῖς ἄτομοι καὶ σφαῖραι καὶ πυραμίδες, ἄλλως τε καὶ εἰ ἔστιν ἄτομα μεγέθη, καθάπερ φασίν. By these ἄτομα μεγέθη he must mean not merely indivisible lines; or we get indivisible spheres and pyramids among mathematical figures, and have to understand not the Atomists, but the Platonists as intended; it is only they who attribute a self-subsisting existence to mathematical bodies. The point of Aristotle's objection is that mathematical atoms (the πρῶτα στερεὰ of Xenocrates) must have elementary qualities just as much as the physical atoms. As we may see in Heraclides and Eudoxus, it was only a short step from Plato's doctrine of the elements to Atomistic

causes.[24] In his appendix to the Timæus he calls it a self-moved number:[25] for the combination of unity with indefinite duality gives rise in the first place to number: when to this is added, in the Same and the Other, the first cause of permanence and of change,

[24] What follows, and the quotation pp. 348, 355; p. 365, 5 seem to have occurred in the treatise on the soul (Diog. iv. 13). Xenocrates did not write a regular commentary on the Timæus, as might be supposed from the quotations in Plutarch and Proclus; Procl. in Tim. 24 A expressly calls Crantor ὁ πρῶτος τοῦ Πλάτωνος ἐξηγητής. In the fifth book of his Physics, however, as Themist. De an. i. 4, 5, p. 56, 10 sqq., 59, 19 sqq., Speng. remarks, Xenocrates thoroughly explained his views on the soul.

[25] De an. i. 2, 404 b. 27: some lay stress upon the moving power in the concept of the soul, others, e.g. Plato, upon the capacity of knowledge, while they compose it out of the elements of things in order that it may be able to know everything: ἐπεὶ δὲ καὶ κινητικὸν ἐδόκει εἶναι καὶ γνωριστικόν, οὕτως ἔνιοι συνέπλεξαν ἐξ ἀμφοῖν, ἀποφηνάμενοι τὴν ψυχὴν ἀριθμὸν κινοῦνθ' ἑαυτόν. Aristotle then returns to this definition c. 4, 408 b. 32, in order to subject it to a searching criticism. He quotes the same definition Anal. post. ii. 4, 91 a 35 again, without mentioning its author. That it was not propounded by Plato is clear from the first of these passages; and that it belongs to no one else than Xenocrates is clear from Plut. ao. procr. c. 1. 5, p. 1012: Ξενοκρ. ... τῆς ψυχῆς τὴν οὐσίαν ἀριθμὸν αὐτὸν ὑφ' ἑαυτοῦ κινούμενον ἀποφηνάμενος. Procl. in Tim. 190 D (Ξενοκρ. . . . λέγων κατ' ἀριθμὸν εἶναι τὴν ψυχὴν οὐσίαν). Alex. in Topica, 87 m. 211 o. 238 m.; Simpl. De An. 7 a. n. 16, b. n.; Themist. loc. cit (cf. previous note) and Anal. post. i. 2, p. 68, 12; Sp. Philop. De An. A 15 o. B 4 o. 16 m. C 5 o., E 11 m.; Anal. post. 78 b. m.; Schol. in Arist. 232 b. 38; Macrob. Somn. 1. 14; Stob. Ecl. ii. 794, who represents the definition as originating with Pythagoras (so Nemes. nat. hom. p. 44), of course without justification. Iambl. apud Stob ii. 862: ὡς δ' αὐτοκινητικὸν [ψυχὴν] Ξενοκράτης. Cic. Tusc. 1. 10, 20: *Xenocrates animi figuram et quasi corpus negavit esse, verum numerum dixit esse, cujus vis, ut jam antea Pythagoræ visum erat, in natura maxima esset.* Andronicus apud Themist. De An. p. 59 Sp. understands Xenocrates' definition as expressing merely the fact that the soul by its own agency (κινῶν ἑαυτὸν) effects the combination of matter into the organic body, which results in definite numerical relations. He therefore identifies the definition with the denotation of the soul as harmony of its body. This meaning is improbable, and unsupported either by Aristotle's exposition and criticism of the definition, or the precedent of Plato's Timæus.

there is imparted to number the faculty of rest and of motion.[26] Whether the reason which Aristotle quotes [27] for this definition may really be ascribed to Xenocrates is somewhat doubtful; and it is equally uncertain how far, like Plato in the Laws, he expressly connected the belief in a Divine Providence [28] with the doctrine of the soul.

This doctrine Xenocrates seems to have applied in his Cosmology,[29] by seeking to prove [30] in the different parts of the world a graduated scale of animate life; and, in each individual soul, a specific combination of the highest principles of Unity and Duality.[31] Thus we are told that he not only attributed a Divine nature to the heavens and the stars, and in this sense spoke of eight Olympian gods,[32] but that he

---

[26] Plut. loc. cit. c. 2 : οἱ μὲν γὰρ οὐδὲν ἢ γένεσιν ἀριθμοῦ δηλοῦσθαι νομίζουσι τῇ μίξει τῆς ἀμερίστου καὶ μεριστῆς οὐσίας· ἀμέριστον μὲν γὰρ εἶναι τὸ ἕν, μεριστὸν δὲ τὸ πλῆθος, ἐκ δὲ τούτων γίνεσθαι τὸν ἀριθμὸν τοῦ ἑνὸς ὁρίζοντος τὸ πλῆθος καὶ τῇ ἀπειρίᾳ πέρας ἐντιθέντος, ἣν καὶ δυάδα καλοῦσιν ἀόριστον. ... τοῦτον δὲ μήπω ψυχὴν τὸν ἀριθμὸν εἶναι· τὸ γὰρ κινητικὸν καὶ τὸ κινητὸν ἐνδεῖν αὐτῷ· τοῦ δὲ ταυτοῦ καὶ τοῦ ἑτέρου συμμιγέντων, ὧν τὸ μέν ἐστι κινήσεως ἀρχὴ καὶ μεταβολῆς, τὸ δὲ μονῆς, ψυχὴν γεγονέναι, μηδὲν ἧττον τοῦ ἱστάναι καὶ ἵστασθαι δύναμιν ἢ τοῦ κινεῖσθαι καὶ κινεῖν οὖσαν.

[27] Anal. Post. loc. cit.: οἱ μὲν οὖν διὰ τοῦ ἀντιστρέφειν δεικνύντες τί ἐστι ψυχὴ ἢ τί ἐστιν ἄνθρωπος ἢ ἄλλο ὁτιοῦν τῶν ὄντων, τὸ ἐξ ἀρχῆς αἰτοῦνται, οἷον εἴ τις ἀξιώσειε ψυχὴν εἶναι τὸ αὐτὸ αὑτῷ αἴτιον τοῦ ζῆν, τοῦτο δ' ἀριθμὸν αὐτὸν αὑτὸν κινοῦντα.

[28] This we should attribute to him, even apart from Plut. Comm. not. 22, 3, p. 1069.

[29] It has been already remarked, p. 577, 51, and p. 583, 11, on the authority of Theophrastus, that he entered into more detail on this subject than any other Platonist. To this belong the treatises φυσικὴ ἀκρόασις (6 books), and τὰ περὶ ἀστρολογίαν (6 books), further π. θεῶν (see note 32).

[30] This latter point seems to come from the passage of Theophrastus, just mentioned; but how it was worked out we cannot say.

[31] Speusippus, as we have seen, on the contrary, represented the universe as developing itself from incompleteness to completeness.

[32] Stob. Ecl. i. 62, after the quotation in note 16: θεὸν (al. θεῖον) δὲ εἶναι καὶ τὸν οὐρανὸν καὶ τοὺς

acknowledged the Elements as Divine powers, and, like Prodicus,[33] gave them the names of gods.[34] This points to the notion that the soul permeates all parts of the cosmos and works in them all; a theory which is involved in his assertion [35] that even the beasts have in them some instinct of the Divine.[36] The part of the soul that rules in the heavens he seems to have denoted as the higher Zeus; [37] the part that is at work

ἀστέρας πυρώδεις ὀλυμπίους θεοὺς καὶ ἑτέρους ὑποσελήνους, δαίμονας ἀοράτους. ἀρέσκεται [-κει] δὲ καὶ αὐτὸς [-ῳ] (here follows a slight lacuna, which Krische, Forsch. 323 fills up with the words θεῶν δυνάμεις; better, perhaps, θείας εἶναι δυνάμεις) καὶ ἐνδιοικεῖν τοῖς ὑλικοῖς στοιχείοις. τούτων δὲ τὴν μὲν (lacuna: supply διὰ τοῦ ἀέρος "Ηραν) προσαγορεύει, τὴν δὲ διὰ τοῦ ὑγροῦ Ποσειδῶνα, τὴν δὲ διὰ τῆς γῆς φυτοσπόρον Δήμητραν. ταῦτα δὲ (adds the narrator) χορηγήσας τοῖς Στωικοῖς τὰ πρότερα παρὰ τοῦ Πλάτωνος μεταπέφρακεν. Cic. N.D. 1. 13, 34 (following Philodemus): *Xenocrates .. in cujus libris, qui sunt de natura Deorum* (π. θεῶν αʹ βʹ Diog 13), *nulla species divina deseribitur: Deos enim octo esse ducit; quinque eos, qui in stellis vagis nominantur; unum qui ex omnibus sideribus, quæ infixa cælo sunt, ex dispersis quasi membris simplex sit putandus Deus* (perhaps a reference to the Orphic mythus of Zagreus); *septimum solem adjungit, octavumque lunam.* Clemens, Protrept. 44 A: Ξενοκρ. ἑπτὰ μὲν θεοὺς τοὺς πλανήτας, ὄγδοον δὲ τὸν ἐκ πάντων αὐτῶν (read π. τῶν ἀπλανῶν) συνεστῶτα κόσμον αἰνίττεται. Xenocrates undoubtedly, like Plato (see p 385 sq.), imagined the stars to be animated.

[33] See vol. 1 928.
[34] Cf. nt. 2. These elementary gods are not to be confounded, as Krische, Forsch. p. 322 sq. shows, with the demons of the nether world. Xenocrates, with Plato and the Orphics, draws a definite distinction between demons and gods (see p. 593, 38), and would not have attributed to the former the names of the greater gods.
[35] Connected with the popular belief in the possibility of divination from many animals.
[36] Clemens, Strom. v. 590 c.: καθόλου γοῦν τὴν περὶ τοῦ θείου ἔννοιαν Ξενοκράτης .. οὐκ ἀπελπίζει καὶ ἐν τοῖς ἀλόγοις ζῴοις.
[37] Plut. Plat. qu ix. 1, 2. p. 1007: Ξενοκράτης Δία τὸν μὲν ἐν τοῖς κατὰ τὰ αὐτὰ καὶ ὡσαύτως ἔχουσιν ὕπατον καλεῖ, νέατον δὲ τὸν ὑπὸ σελήνην. Clemens, Strom. v. 604 C Ξεν . τὸν μὲν ὕπατον Δία τὸν δὲ νέατον καλῶν. This denotation refers partly to the ὑπάτη and νήτη, the highest and lowest string, with which the corresponding parts of the universe might be compared, according to the Pythagorean conception of the harmony of the spheres (Krische, 316, 324, whose further conjectures, attractive as they are, I cannot follow. The supposition

on the earth and in the terrestrial atmosphere, as the lower Zeus. But as in this inferior sphere evil is found side by side with good, and harm with beneficence, Xenocrates considers the world to be ruled not only by gods, but by dæmons, who are intermediate between the divine perfection and human imperfection.[38] In harmony with the popular faith, he makes two classes of dæmons (a materialising exaggeration of the double World-soul in the Laws), the good and the bad. The bad might be propitiated with certain religious services, which Xenocrates does not connect with the worship of the good.[39] He agrees, however, with some other

of a Ζεὺς μέσος corresponding to the μέση of the strings, which Ζεὺς, according to what will be cited note 46, could be placed only in the region of the moon, is forbidden by the position of the universe. This position is entirely distinct from that of the μέση. Again, to attribute to the elements a soul of the lowest kind, a mere ἕξις, is not conformable to their divine nature), partly to the Orphic designation of Pluto as Ζεὺς νέατος (Brandis, p. 24, with reference to Lobeck Aglaoph. 1098). The meaning of that expression can hardly be other than the one supposed in the text; by the soul of Zeus Plato meant the soul of the universe (see p. 266, 122, p. 187, 172); with him Xenocrates looks upon the collective divine souls as one soul Plato, Laws, x. 898 D, immediately concludes the animation and divinity of the stars from the rule of the soul in the universe.

[38] Plut. De Is. c. 25, p. 360: (δαιμόνων μεγάλων) οὓς καὶ Πλάτων καὶ Πυθαγόρας καὶ Ξενοκράτης καὶ Χρύσιππος, ἑπόμενοι τοῖς πάλαι θεολόγοις, ἐῤῥωμενεστέρους μὲν ἀνθρώπων γεγονέναι λέγουσι καὶ πολλῇ τῇ δυνάμει τὴν φύσιν ὑπερφέροντας ἡμῶν, τὸ δὲ θεῖον οὐκ ἀμιγὲς οὐδ' ἄκρατον ἔχοντας, κ.τ.λ. Ibid. def. orac c 13, p. 416: παράδειγμα δὲ τῷ λόγῳ Ξενοκράτης μὲν ... ἐποιήσατο τὸ τῶν τριγώνων, θείῳ μὲν ἀπεικάσας τὸ ἰσόπλευρον, θνητῷ δὲ τὸ σκαληνόν, τὸ δ' ἰσοσκελὲς δαιμονίῳ· τὸ μὲν γὰρ ἴσον πάντῃ · τὸ δ' ἄνισον πάντη τὸ δὲ πῇ μὲν ἴσον πῇ δ' ἄνισον, ὥσπερ ἡ δαιμόνων φύσις ἔχουσα καὶ πάθος θνητοῦ καὶ θεοῦ δύναμιν For the facts cf. Plato, Symp. 202 D, &c.

[39] Plut. def. orac. c. 17, p. 419: φαύλους δαίμονας .. ἀπέλιπεν ... καὶ Πλάτων καὶ Ξενοκράτης καὶ Χρύσιππος. De Is. c. 26 ὁ δὲ Ξενοκράτης καὶ τῶν ἡμερῶν τὰς ἀποφράδας καὶ τῶν ἑορτῶν ὅσαι πληγάς τινας ἢ κοπετοὺς ἢ νηστείας ἢ δυσφημίας ἢ αἰσχρολογίαν ἔχουσιν,

philosophers[40] in describing the soul of man as his dæmon.[41] How far he combined the rest of the Greek divinities with his system we do not know.[42]

In regard to the material constituents of the universe Xenocrates carried out the same theory of a graduated scale of perfection. This appears in his view of the elements, in the derivation of which he seems to have resembled Plato, except that he made them originate, not immediately from planes, but, primarily from atoms,[43] and, like Philolaus, reckoned

οὔτε θεῶν τιμαῖς οὔτε δαιμόνων οἴεται προσήκειν χρηστῶν, ἀλλὰ, εἶναι φύσεις ἐν τῷ περιέχοντι (the atmosphere around the earth) μεγάλας μὲν καὶ ἰσχυρὰς, δυστρόπους δὲ καὶ σκυθρωπὰς, αἳ χαίρουσι τοῖς τοιούτοις καὶ τυγχάνουσαι πρὸς οὐδὲν ἄλλο χεῖρον τρέπονται.

[40] E.g. Heraclitus and Democritus; see vol. i. 590, 5; 748, 1: Plato, see p. 501.

[41] Arist. Top. ii. 6, 112 a. 37: Ξενοκρ. φησὶν εὐδαίμονα εἶναι τὸν τὴν ψυχὴν ἔχοντα σπουδαίαν· ταύτην γὰρ ἑκάστου εἶναι δαίμονα, which Alex. Top. 94 m. repeats. Cf. Stob. Serm 104, 24· Ξενοκρ. ἔλεγεν, ὡς τὸ κακοπρόσωπον αἰσχει προσώπου . . οὕτω δαίμονος κακίᾳ τοὺς πονηροὺς κακοδαίμονας ὀνομάζομεν. Krische, p. 321, I think too artificially, brings these tenets into connection with the supposition that the souls freed from bodies are δαίμονες.

[42] From Iambl. V. Pyth. 7 we might conclude that in all points he followed the usual opinion. The passage runs thus: παραιτητέοι γὰρ Ἐπιμενίδης καὶ Εὔδοξος καὶ Ξενοκράτης, ὑπονοοῦντες, τῇ Παρθενίδι (the mother of Pythagoras) τότε μιγῆναι τὸν Ἀπόλλω καὶ κύουσαν αὐτὴν ἐκ μὴ οὕτως ἐχούσης καταστῆσαί τε καὶ προαγγεῖλαι διὰ τῆς προφήτιδος, which, however, is quite incredible. We must know more precisely what Xenocrates said, and whether or not he mentioned the Apolline origin of Pythagoras merely as a tradition. In Cic. (see note 32) the want of a *species divina* is made an objection to him, and, in general, it is scarcely credible that a pupil of Plato, even Xenocrates, would have approved of an anthropomorphism of this kind.

[43] Stob. Ecl. i. 368 : Ἐμπεδοκλῆς καὶ Ξενοκράτης ἐκ μικροτέρων ὄγκων τὰ στοιχεῖα συγκρίνει, ἅπερ ἐστὶν ἐλάχιστα καὶ οἱονεὶ στοιχεῖα στοιχείων, and the quotation in note 23. Stobæus expressly distinguishes his view from the Platonic view; the distinction, however, cannot have been very important, since Aristotle nowhere mentions it specially. Xenocrates must have enunciated it only after the completion of Aristotle's writings on natural science.

æther as a fifth primary Element.[44] He included the higher elements (which Plato had also connected[45]) under the name of the Rare or Subtle, as opposed to the lowest element, which he denominated the Dense. This latter, he said, is sometimes in greater proportion, sometimes in less, and unites itself variously with the other elements. The stars and the sun consist of fire and the first density; the moon of her own atmosphere and the second density; the earth, of fire, water, and the third density.[46] He guarded himself, however, against the assertion of a beginning of the world in time; and he viewed the Timæus, and its account of the creation of the soul and of the universe, not as giving a chronological statement, but as showing the different constituents of the universe and of the soul in their reciprocal relations.[47] A definition of Time which inclines to

[44] See note 23.
[45] See p. 374.
[46] Plut. fac. lun. 29, 3 sq., p. 94, 3: Xenocrates, following the precedent of Plato (Epin. 981 c. sq.), recognised that the stars must be composed out of all the elements: ὁ δὲ Ξενοκράτης τὰ μὲν ἄστρα καὶ τὸν ἥλιον ἐκ πυρός φησι καὶ τοῦ πρώτου πυκνοῦ συγκεῖσθαι, τὴν δὲ σελήνην ἐκ δευτέρου πυκνοῦ καὶ τοῦ ἰδίου ἀέρος, τὴν δὲ γῆν ἐξ ὕδατος καὶ πυρὸς καὶ τοῦ τρίτου τῶν πυκνῶν· ὅλως δὲ μήτε τὸ πυκνὸν αὐτὸ καθ' αὑτὸ μήτε τὸ μανὸν εἶναι ψυχῆς δεκτικόν
[47] Arist. De Cœlo, i 10, 279 b. 32: ἦν δέ τινες βοήθειαν ἐπιχειροῦσι φέρειν ἑαυτοῖς τῶν λεγόντων ἄφθαρτον μὲν εἶναι [sc. τὸν κόσμον] γενόμενον δὲ οὐκ ἔστιν ἀληθής· ὁμοίως γάρ φασι τοῖς τὰ διαγράμματα γράφουσι καὶ σφᾶς εἰρηκέναι περὶ τῆς γενέσεως, οὐχ ὡς γενομένου ποτὲ, ἀλλὰ διδασκαλίας χάριν ὡς μᾶλλον γνωριζόντων ὥσπερ τὸ διάγραμμα γιγνόμενον θρασαμένους. Simpl. ad loc. p. 136 b. 33 Karst. remarks that Xenocrates is here meant, Schol. 488 b. 15 (he is followed by two further scholia, ibid. 489 a. 4, 9, one of them extends the statement to Speusippus, apparently quite arbitrarily); and to put the fact beyond all doubt, Plut. an. procr. 3, p. 1013, says, after quoting the explanations of Xenocrates and Crantor· ὁμαλῶς δὲ πάντες οὗτοι χρόνῳ μὲν οἴονται τὴν ψυχὴν μὴ γεγονέναι, μηδ' εἶναι γενητὴν, πλείο-

the Platonic theory,[48] and a system of Astronomy not very well authenticated,[49] are all that remain to us of the Physics of Xenocrates, except the following psychological theorems:—that the soul is a purely spiritual essence[50] and can exist apart from the body;[51] that Reason originates from without (that is, from a previous state of existence[52]), and that even the irrational part of the soul is immortal.[53] Whether Xenocrates extended the privilege of immortality to the

νας δὲ δυνάμεις ἔχειν, εἰς ἃς ἀναλύοντα θεωρίας ἕνεκα τὴν οὐσίαν αὐτῆς λόγῳ τὸν Πλάτωνα γινομένην ὑποτίθεσθαι καὶ συγκεραννομένην· τὰ δ' αὐτὰ καὶ περὶ τοῦ κόσμου διανοούμενον ἐπίστασθαι μὲν ἀΐδιον ὄντα καὶ ἀγένητον· τὸ δὲ ᾧ τρόπῳ συντέτακται καὶ διοικεῖται καταμαθεῖν οὐ ῥᾴδιον δρῶντα τοῖς μήτε γένεσιν αὐτοῦ μήτε τῶν γενητικῶν σύνοδον ἐξ ἀρχῆς προϋποθεμένοις ταύτην τὴν ὁδὸν τραπέσθαι (cf note 17, on a similar expedient, made use of by Xenocrates on a like occasion). Hence Censorinus, di. nat. 4, 3, reckons Xenocrates and all the old Academy, together with Plato, amongst those who seem to have supposed that mankind was always in existence.

[48] Stob Ecl i 250 Ξενοκράτης [τὸν χρόνον φησὶ] μέτρον τῶν γεννητῶν καὶ κίνησιν ἀΐδιον. Both definitions are Platonic; see Tim. 38 A, 39 B sq., and supra, p. 383.

[49] Stob Ecl i. 514 (Plut. plac. ii. 15, 1): Ξενοκράτης κατὰ μιᾶς ἐπιφανείας οἴεται κεῖσθαι (Plut. κινεῖσθαι) τοὺς ἀστέρας, οἱ δ' ἄλλοι Στωικοὶ πρὸ τῶν ἑτέρων τοὺς ἑτέρους ἐν ὕψει καὶ βάθει. This statement can refer only to the planets, which Xenocrates with Plato would have placed in the plane of the ecliptic, whereas neither he nor anyone else could misplace the collective fixed stars in the same plane with the planets. The words, ἄλλοι Στωικοί, indicate that some other name than Xenocrates, perhaps Zeno or Cleanthes, preceded, which is, perhaps, to be substituted for Xenocrates, or, more probably, has fallen out of the text.

[50] Cic. Acad. ii. 39, 124: the soul, according to Xenocrates, is *mens nullo corpore*. Nemes. nat. hom. 31: he proves the incorporeality of the soul with the principle. εἰ δὲ μὴ τρέφεται, πᾶν δὲ σῶμα ζῴου τρέφεται, οὐ σῶμα ἡ ψυχή.

[51] Arist. De An i. 4, end (in the criticism of the Xenocratic definition): ἔτι δὲ πῶς οἷόν τε χωρίζεσθαι τὰς ψυχὰς καὶ ἀπολύεσθαι τῶν σωμάτων, κ.τ.λ. This definition is clear in reference to the disciple of Plato, but Philoponus, ad loc. e. 14, is not to be regarded as an authentic source.

[52] Stob. Ecl. i. 790: Pythagoras, Plato, Xenocrates, and others teach θύραθεν εἰσκρίνεσθαι τὸν νοῦν, where the Aristotelian expression is to be reduced to Platonic notions as above.

[53] See note 38.

souls of animals is not mentioned, but, as he ascribed to them a consciousness of God,[54] this is at least probable. He forbade the eating of flesh,—not because he saw in beasts something akin to man, but, for the opposite reason, lest the irrationality of animal souls might thereby gain an influence over us.[55] He seems to have considered the head to be the seat of reason, and the irrational part of the soul to be diffused throughout the whole body.[56]

Xenocrates, as may be imagined, bestowed special attention on ethics;[57] the importance of his personal instruction lay principally in this direction, and out of the whole number of his works more than half is devoted to ethical enquiries. We hear of writings on the Good, the Useful, the Pleasant, on Happiness, Wealth, Death, Freewill, the Affections, the nature and teachableness of Virtue, Justice, Equity, Wisdom, Truth, Holiness, Temperance, Courage, Liberality, Concord, Friendship, Domestic Economy, the

---

[54] See note 36.

[55] Clemens, Strom. vii. 717 D: δοκεῖ δὲ Ξενοκράτης ἰδίᾳ πραγματευόμενος περὶ τῆς ἀπὸ τῶν ζῴων τροφῆς καὶ Πολέμων ἐν τοῖς περὶ τοῦ κατὰ φύσιν βίου συντάγμασι σαφῶς λέγειν, ὡς ἀσύμφορόν ἐστιν ἡ διὰ τῶν σαρκῶν τροφή, εἰργασμένη ἤδη καὶ ἐξομοιουμένη ταῖς τῶν ἀλόγων ψυχαῖς. In the treatise of Xenocrates here mentioned the discussions on the three laws of Triptolemus were found, and on the prohibition against killing animals, which is attributed to him, and noticed by Porphyr. De Abstin. iv. 22.

[56] Cf Tertullian and Lactantius, the former says (De an. 15) that the *principale* has its seat, according to Xenocrates, in the crown of the head, the latter, Opif. D 16: *sive etiam mentis locus nullus est, sed per totum corpus sparsa discurrit, quod et fieri potest et a Xenocrate, Platonis discipulo, disputatum est.* Only in this case Lactantius must have put *mens,* where Xenocrates had spoken not of νοῦς but of the ψυχή.

[57] He would found the origin of philosophy in its moral influence; Galen, hist. phil. c. 3, end: αἰτία δὲ φιλοσοφίας εὑρέσεώς ἐστι κατὰ Ξενοκράτη, τὸ ταραχῶδες ἐν τῷ βίῳ καταπαῦσαι τῶν πραγμάτων.

State, Law, Kingship.[58] Thus there is scarcely any department of ethics of which he has not treated; yet, despite this extensive authorship, our knowledge even of his ethical doctrines is very small. We cannot, however, mistake the tendency of his morality, which, in all essential points, was in harmony with that of Plato and the rest of the Academy. All things, according to Xenocrates, are either goods or evils, or neither of the two.[59] Goods he divided, like the other Platonists, into those of the soul, the body, and the outer life;[60] but the highest and most important of goods he declared to be Virtue. Though, in agreement with the whole Academy,[61] he denied virtue to be the only good, he so distinctly gave it the preference[62] that Cicero says he despised

---

[58] Diog. mentions writings π. σοφίας, π. πλούτου, π. τοῦ παιδίου (? perhaps π παιδίων or π. παίδων ἀγωγῆς, or something of the sort, ought to be read, π αἰδοῦς is also a possible suggestion), π ἐγκρατείας, π. τοῦ ὠφελίμου, τοῦ ἐλευθέρου, θανάτου, ἑκουσίου, φιλίας, ἐπιεικείας, εὐδαιμονίας, π τοῦ ψεύδους, π. φρονήσεως, οἰκονομικὸς, π. σωφροσύνης, δυνάμεως νόμου, πολιτείας, ὁσιότητος, ὅτι παραδοτὴ ἡ ἀρετή, π. παθῶν, π. βίων (on the value of the different way of life, e g the theoretic, the political, and the life of pleasure), π. ὁμονοίας, δικαιοσύνης, ἀρετῆς, ἡδονῆς, βίου, ἀνδρείας, πολιτικὸς, τἀγαθοῦ, βασιλείας. (Cf. Plut adv. Col. 32, 9, p 1126.) Also the treatise on animal food; see supra, notes 3 and 55.

[59] Xenocr. apud Sext. Math. xi. 4: πᾶν τὸ ὂν ἢ ἀγαθόν ἐστιν ἢ κακόν ἐστιν, ἢ οὔτε ἀγαθόν ἐστιν οὔτε κακόν ἐστι, which is followed by an awkward argument in a circle.

[60] Cic. Acad. i. 5, 19 sq., on the authority of Antiochus, attributes this distinction to the Academy generally. and this statement, in itself not absolutely certain, is substantiated by the citation p. 520, 11.

[61] Cf. Cic. Legg. i. 21, 55; Tusc. v. 10, 30; Plut. com. not. 13, 1, p. 1065, and following note.

[62] Cic. Fin. iv. 18, 49: *Aristoteles, Xenocrates, tota illa familia non dabit* (the principle that only the Laudable is a good); *quippe qui valetudinem, vires, divitias, gloriam, multa alia bona esse dicant, laudabilia non dicant. Et hi quidem ita non sola virtute finem bonorum contineri putant, ut rebus tamen omnibus virtutem anteponant.* Cf. Legg. i. 13, 37 (supra, p. 579, 62).

everything else in comparison.[63] External and material goods,—health, honour, prosperity, and the like,—were placed by him in the second rank. He would have them, indeed, regarded as advantageous things, or goods, and their opposites as evils;[64] the Stoical view, which reckoned both as alike indifferent, being entirely alien to him.[65] It was only as compared with the higher goods and ills that these lesser seemed to him unworthy of consideration. In his conception of the highest good, Xenocrates was therefore forced to include all other goods together with Virtue. Happiness, according to his theory, consists in the perfection of all

---

[63] Tusc. v. 18, 51: *quid ergo aut hunc [Critolaum] prohibet, aut etiam Xenocratem illum gravissimum philosophorum, exaggerantem tantopere virtutem, extenuantem cetera et abjicientem, in virtute non beatam modo vitam sed etiam beatissimam ponere?* On account of the strictness of his morality Plut., Comp. Cim. c. Luc. c. 1, opposes the doctrines of Xenocrates to the Epicurean doctrines, just as he elsewhere opposes the Stoic to the Epicurean.

[64] Cic. Fin. iv. 18, see supra, note 62. Legg. i. 21, 35: if Zeno with Aristo explained virtue alone to be a good, and everything else quite indifferent, *valde a Xenocrate et Aristotele et ab illa Platonis familia discreparet. . . . Nunc vero cum decus . . . solum bonum dicat; item dedecus . . . malum . . . solum · divitias, valetudinem, pulchritudinem commodas res appellet, non bonas, paupertatem, debilitatem, dolorem in commodas, non malas: sentit idem quod Xenocrates, quod Aristoteles, loquitur alio modo.* Plut. c. notit. 13, see p. 579, 62. Ibid. 22, 3, p. 1069: Aristotle and Xenocrates did not, like the Stoics, deny, ὠφελεῖσθαι μὲν ἀνθρώπους ὑπὸ θεῶν, ὠφελεῖσθαι δὲ ὑπὸ γονέων, ὠφελεῖσθαι δὲ ὑπὸ καθηγητῶν. Also, Tusc. v. 10, 30, Cic. reckons Xenocrates amongst those who consider poverty, disgrace, loss of goods or fatherland, severe bodily pains, sickness, banishment, slavery, us indeed evils, but at the same time maintain *semper beatum esse sapientem.* From these passages it follows that Wynpersse is wrong (166 sq.) in believing that Xenocrates divided the things which are neither good nor bad into things useful (health, &c.) and things prejudicial (sickness, &c.) Good and useful, evil and prejudicial, are with him, as with Socrates and Plato, equivalent conceptions, but not all goods have the same value, nor are all evils equally bad.

[65] As Cicero says; see previous note.

natural activities and conditions;[66] in the possession of human virtue proper, and all the means conducing to it. Virtue alone produces happiness; noble activities and qualities alone constitute the essential nature of happiness, yet happiness cannot be complete without material and external goods,[67] which are thus, to use a Platonic expression,[68] to be considered not indeed as primary, but as concomitant causes of happiness. For this very reason, however, virtue stands alone as the proper and positive condition of happiness; the virtuous life must be identified with the happy life;[69] the wise man must under any circumstances be counted happy.[70] That he should not be perfectly happy,[71] in the absence

---

[66] Cicero attributes this tenet to the Academy generally, and refers to Polemo in support of it; Acad. ii. 42, 131. *honeste autem vivere fruentem rebus iis, quas primas homini natura conciliet, et vetus Academia censuit* (sc. *finem bonorum*), *ut indicant scripta Polemonis.* Cf. Fin. ii. 11, 34. He explains this determination with more detail, Fin. iv. 6 sq. (cf. v. 9 sqq.), with the remark that the Stoics themselves acknowledge in it the doctrines of Xenocrates and Aristotle, that it belongs not only to Polemo is clear from Plut. comm. not. c. 23, p. 1069: τίνας δὲ Ξενοκράτης καὶ Πολέμων λαμβάνουσιν ἀρχάς; οὐχὶ καὶ Ζήνων τούτοις ἠκολούθησεν, ὑποτιθέμενος στοιχεῖα τῆς εὐδαιμονίας τὴν φύσιν καὶ τὸ κατὰ φύσιν;

[67] Clemens, Strom. ii. 419 A: Ξενοκράτης τε ὁ Χαλκηδόνιος τὴν εὐδαιμονίαν ἀποδίδωσι κτήσιν τῆς οἰκείας ἀρετῆς καὶ τῆς ὑπηρετικῆς αὐτῇ δυνάμεως. εἶτα ὡς μὲν ἐν ᾧ γίνεται, φαίνεται λέγειν τὴν ψυχήν· ὡς δ' ὑφ' ὧν, τὰς ἀρετάς· ὡς δ' ἐξ ὧν, ἅς μερῶν, τὰς καλὰς πράξεις καὶ τὰς σπουδαίας ἕξεις τε καὶ διαθέσεις καὶ κινήσεις καὶ σχήσεις· ὡς τούτων οὐκ ἄνευ (read ὡς δ' ὧν οὐκ ἄνευ), τὰ σωματικὰ καὶ τὰ ἐκτός.

[68] See p. 339, 116.

[69] Arist. Top. vii. 1, 152 u. 7: Ξενοκράτης τὸν εὐδαίμονα βίον καὶ τὸν σπουδαῖον ἀποδείκνυσι τὸν αὐτὸν, ἐπειδὴ πάντων τῶν βίων αἱρετώτατος ὁ σπουδαῖος καὶ ὁ εὐδαίμων· ἐν γὰρ τὸ αἱρετώτατον καὶ μέγιστον. Cf. p. 875, 2.

[70] Cic. Tusc. v. 10; see notes 41 and 71.

[71] Cic Tusc. v. 13, 39 sq. (cf. 31, 87): *omnes virtutis compotes beati sunt*. on that point he agrees with Xenocrates, Speusippus, Polemo: *sed mihi videntur etiam beatissimi*: which is immediately supported by the remark that whoever (as they do) supposes three kinds of different goods can never attain to certainty as regards true

ETHICS.

of goods of the second order, would be incomprehensible from the Stoic point of view; but it entirely accords with the moderation of the Academy, and with the Xenocratic notion of Happiness. For if the possession of happiness is linked to the convergence of several conditions, it will be more or less perfect, according as these conditions are more or less completely present: happiness will be capable of increase and diminution; a distinction is at once allowed between the happy and the happiest life.

How strong was the conviction of Xenocrates that virtue alone could make men happy, may be seen from the stainlessness and austerity of his character,[72] and from the few further particulars that we possess with regard to his theory of morals. To free ourselves from the bondage of sensuous life, to conquer the Titanic element in human nature by means of the Divine, is our problem.[73] Purity not only in actions, but also in

happiness. Ibid. c. 18; see supra, note 62. Seneca, epist. 85, 18 sq.. *Xenocrates et Speusippus putant beatum vel sola virtute fieri posse, non tamen unum bonum esse, quod honestum est .. illud autem absurdum est, quod dicitur, beatum quidem futurum vel sola virtute, non futurum autem perfecte beatum.* Ep. 71, 18. *Academici veteres beatum quidem esse (scil. virum bonum) etiam inter hos cruciatus fatentur, sed non ad perfectum nec ad plenum.*

[72] Cf. p. 559.

[73] This appears to me the most probable meaning of two obscure passages. Tertull. ad nat. ii. 2 says: *Xenocrates Academicus bifariam facit (formam divinitatis), Olympios et Titanios qui de Cœlo et Terra.* If this division of the divinities in Xenocrates is intended for anything more than a historical notice, with reference to the old theogonies, it can only be understood by supposing that he interpreted the myth of the battle of the Olympians and the Titans with a moral purpose, and explained these two kinds of existences as being in mankind. In Xenocrates' own theology we look in vain for any point of connection; the dæmons perhaps, on account of their intermediate position between heaven and earth, may be denoted as the sons of these two kinds of deities; but they could scarcely be called Titans

the wishes of the heart, is our duty.[74] To this end Philosophy is our best help, for the philosopher has this advantage,[75] that he does voluntarily what others must be compelled to do by law.[76] Plato, however, had admitted an unphilosophical virtue, side by side with Philosophy, and Xenocrates still more distinctly emphasized the difference between the theoretic and practical spheres. Like Aristotle, he restricted Wisdom or Science to intellectual activity, and left practical conduct to prudence or discernment.[77] Of his numerous ethical treatises scarcely any fragments have been preserved;[78] but we cannot doubt his general

in opposition to the Olympians. Further, according to the Scholiast ap. Finckh, Olympiod. in Phædon. p. 66, nt. 2, he spoke of the Titanic prison in which we are banished; the scholiast remarks ad Phæd. 62 B · ἡ φρουρὰ . . . ὡς Ξενοκράτης, Τιτανική ἐστι καὶ εἰς Διόνυσον ἀποκορυφοῦται, where, however, it is not clear whether he compared men to the Dionysus of the Orphic hymns, in the power of the Titans, or to the imprisoned Titans whom Dionysus is to set free.

[74] Ælian, V. H. xiv 42: Ξενοκράτης . . . ἔλεγε, μηδὲν διαφέρειν ἢ τοὺς πόδας ἢ τοὺς ὀφθαλμοὺς εἰς ἀλλοτρίαν οἰκίαν τιθέναι· ἐν ταὐτῷ γὰρ ἁμαρτάνειν τόν τε εἰς ἃ μὴ δεῖ χωρία βλέποντα καὶ εἰς οὓς μὴ δεῖ τόπους παρίοντα. One cannot help thinking of Matth. 5, 28.

[75] Cf supra, note 57.

[76] Plut. virt. mor. c. 7, p. 446, adv. Col. c. 30, 2, p. 1124, Cic. Rep i. 2, 3, Serv. in Æn. vii. 204. The same statement is also attributed to Aristotle, who, indeed, Eth. N. iv. 14, 1128 a. 31, says of the χαρίεις καὶ ἐλευθέριος: οἷον νόμος ὢν ἑαυτῷ. The saying may have had several authors, and it may also have been wrongly transferred from one to another.

[77] Clemens, Strom. ii. 369 C: ἐπεὶ καὶ Ξενοκράτης ἐν τῷ περὶ φρονήσεως τὴν σοφίαν ἐπιστήμην τῶν πρώτων αἰτίων καὶ τῆς νοητῆς οὐσίας εἶναί φησιν, τὴν φρόνησιν ἡγούμενος διττήν, τὴν μὲν πρακτικὴν τὴν δὲ θεωρητικήν, ἣν δὴ σοφίαν ὑπάρχειν ἀνθρωπίνην. διόπερ ἡ μὲν σοφία φρόνησις, οὐ μὴν πᾶσα φρόνησις σοφία. Arist. Top vi. 3, 141 a. 6 · οἷον ὡς Ξενοκράτης τὴν φρόνησιν ὁριστικὴν καὶ θεωρητικὴν τῶν ὄντων φησὶν εἶναι, which Aristotle censures as superfluous; ὁριστικὴν alone would have been sufficient.

[78] There is only, perhaps, the saying ap. Plut. De audiendo, c. 2, p. 38, cf. qu. conv. vii. 5, 4, p. 706, that it is more necessary to guard the ears of children than of athletes.

ETHICS. 603.

agreement on these subjects with the Academy.[79] Of the contents of his political works, and of his discussions on Rhetoric and other kindred themes,[80] only a few unimportant [81] particulars are known.

---

[79] We may include Xenocrates in what Cicero says, Acad. ii. 44, 135 (specially of Crantor): that the apathy of the wise man was alien to the Older Academy.

[80] π. μαθημάτων τῶν περὶ τὴν λέξιν (31 books), π. τέχνης, π. τοῦ γράφειν.

[81] Plut. ap. Proclum in Hes. Ἔ. κ. Ἡμ. v. 374 (Plut. Fragm. ii. 20 Dübn.) remarks that he advises that only one heir should be appointed. Sext. Math. ii. 6 quotes from him the definition of Rhetoric as ἐπιστήμη τοῦ εὖ λέγειν, ibid 61, as πειθοῦς δημιουργός; Quintil. Instit. ii. 15, 4, 34, attributes both to Isocrates, i.e. to a writing bearing his name. The two names are often confused. The calculation mentioned by Plut. qu. conv. viii. 9, 3, 13, p. 733 of the number of syllables which could be formed out of the whole alphabet, might have occurred in one of the writings quoted.

CHAPTER XVI.

OTHER PHILOSOPHERS OF THE ACADEMY.

ENQUIRIES into primary causes, Ideas, and numbers were pursued by many other Platonists besides Xenocrates and Speusippus. We learn that the two principles of the later Platonic metaphysics were variously apprehended in the Academy, but that metaphysical science as a whole was neither advanced nor elucidated.[1] Besides the three principal theories of the relation of numbers to Ideas,—the Platonic, Speusippean, and Xenocratic,—Aristotle mentions a fourth, which assumed the absolute and independent existence of the Ideal numbers only,[2] and treated the mathematical sphere as a separate genus, without conceding to it an existence of its own above and beyond the things of sense.[3] Many different views were also taken of the origin of material things from numbers, and of numbers from first causes. This we

---

[1] Arist. Metaph. xiv. 1 sq. (see p. 332, 83; cf. p. 584, 16), c. 5, 1092 a. 35 sq.

[2] Metaph. xiii. 6, in the words quoted p. 573 · ἄλλος δέ τις, κ.τ.λ.

[3] Metaph. iii. 2, 998 a. 7: εἰσὶ δέ τινες οἵ φασιν εἶναι μὲν τὰ μεταξὺ ταῦτα λεγόμενα τῶν τε εἰδῶν καὶ τῶν αἰσθητῶν, οὐ μὴν χωρίς γε τῶν αἰσθητῶν ἀλλ' ἐν τούτοις. As this assertion immediately connects with and completes the one just mentioned, to the effect that only the Ideal numbers exist for themselves, both may probably be attributed to the same persons.

gather from the language of Aristotle, who censures the Platonists for describing numbers sometimes as unlimited, sometimes as limited by the number ten.[4] He says of the adherents of the latter view that they reduced the various derived concepts (for example, Emptiness, mathematical Proportion, Crookedness), some to numbers within the decad, others (for example, the contrasts of rest and motion, of good and evil[5]) to primary causes. With regard to the derivation of spatial magnitudes, there existed, as we have seen,[6] a variety of theories without much positive result. Most of these philosophers, however, did not attempt any explanation of the Derived from First Causes, but contented themselves, like the Pythagoreans, with indefinite and disconnected analogies.[7] Hestiæus alone is mentioned, with Xenocrates,[8] as having adopted a more satisfactory method; but our knowledge of him is pretty nearly comprised in that statement.[9]

---

[4] xii 8, 1073 a. 18; xiii. 8, 1084 a. 12, c. 9, 1085 b. 23, cf. xiv 4, beginn., Phys. iii. 8, 206 b. 30.

[5] Metaph. xiii 8, 1084 a 31: πειρῶνται δ' [γεννᾶν τὸν ἀριθμὸν] ὡς τοῦ μέχρι τῆς δεκάδος τελείου ὄντος ἀριθμοῦ· γεννῶσι γοῦν τὰ ἑπόμενα, οἷον τὸ κενὸν, ἀναλογίαν, τὸ περιττὸν, τὰ ἄλλα τὰ τοιαῦτα ἐντὸς τῆς δεκάδος· τὰ μὲν γὰρ ταῖς ἀρχαῖς ἀποδιδόασιν, οἷον κίνησιν, στάσιν, ἀγαθὸν, κακὸν, τὰ δ' ἄλλα τοῖς ἀριθμοῖς. Cf. Theophr. supra, 576, 51.

[6] See p. 519, 8, cf. 571, 40, and Metaph xiv. 2, 1089 b 11; vii. 11, 1036 b. 12: ἀνάγουσι πάντα εἰς τοὺς ἀριθμοὺς, καὶ γραμμῆς τὸν λόγον τὸν τῶν δύο εἶναί φασιν. καὶ τῶν τὰς ἰδέας λεγόντων οἱ μὲν αὐτογραμμὴν τὴν δυάδα, οἱ δὲ τὸ εἶδος τῆς γραμμῆς. ἔνια μὲν γὰρ εἶναι ταὐτὰ τὸ εἶδος καὶ οὗ τὸ εἶδος, οἷον δυάδα καὶ τὸ εἶδος δυάδος.

[7] Theophrast. see 576, 51; Arist. Metaph. xiii. 8 (see nt. 4). Still, however, from Metaph. 1. 9, 991 b 10; xiii. 8, 1084 a. 14; xiv. 5, 1092 b. 8 sqq., we cannot infer that many Platonists actually explained definite numbers as those of mankind, of beasts, &c.

[8] Theophrast after the quotation, p. 576, 51: πειρᾶται δὲ καὶ Ἑστιαῖος μέχρι τινὸς (to derive everything beside spatial magnitude) οὐχ ὥσπερ εἴρηται περὶ τῶν πρώτων μόνον.

[9] Besides the editing of the

PLATO AND THE OLDER ACADEMY.

Some noteworthy divergences from the doctrine of Plato were made by Heraclides of Pontus. With reference to his general point of view, he may certainly be considered a Platonist. The Epicurean in Cicero charges him with having sometimes treated spirit, sometimes the universe, as a Deity, and with having raised the stars, the earth, and the planets to the dignity of gods.[10] In this it is easy to recognise the Platonic view of the Divine Reason, the divine and animate nature of the world and of the heavenly bodies; for Heraclides would only have called these latter gods in the sense that Plato did, when he discriminated between the invisible God and the visible gods. His cosmology, however, differed from that of his master in several theories, chiefly the result of Pythagorean influences[11] to which he was very susceptible.[12] We learn that he assumed as the primary

---

Platonic discourses on the Good, we have (from Stob. Ecl. i. 250) the definition of time (φορὰ ἄστρων πρὸς ἄλληλα) as his, which does not deviate from the Platonic definition.

[10] N. De. i. 13, 34: *Heraelides .... modo mundum tum mentem divinam esse putat; errantibus etiam stellis divinitatem tribuit, sensuque Deum privat et ejus formam mutabilem esse vult, eodemque in libro rursus terram et coelum* (i.e. the ἀπλανὴς; the planets are already mentioned) *refert in Deos.* The words *sensuque . . vult* contain (as Krische, Forsch. p. 335 sq, correctly remarks) simply the conclusions of the Epicurean, and not historical statements as to Heraclides' views.

[11] Besides the doctrines to be quoted immediately, and the statement of Diog. v. 86, that he had been a pupil of the Pythagoreans, this is clear from his treatise on the Pythagoreans (ibid. 88), from his fictitious account of Abaris (see the two fragments which Müller, Fragm. Hist. gr. ii. 197, quotes out of Bekker's Anec. 145, 178, and Plut. Aud. po. c. i. p. 14) and from the accounts, probably borrowed from the former treatise, of the wonderful vanishing of Empedocles after the reanimation of an apparently dead man (Diog. viii. 67), and of the change of a bean into the form of a man after it has been buried in dung forty days (Joh Lyd de mens. iv. 29, p. 181).

[12] On account of these peculiar

constituents of all corporeal things minute bodies, not compounded of any ulterior parts. But, unlike the atoms of Democritus, these bodies are capable of affecting one another, and are therefore combined not by a merely mechanical union, but by actual interdependence.[13] What gave rise to this theory, which is carried out through various analogies [14] in his works, we do not know; but we can scarcely be wrong in

doctrines, Plut adv. Col. 14, 2, p. 1115, reckons Heraclides amongst the number of those who πρὸς τὰ κυριώτατα καὶ μέγιστα τῶν φυσικῶν ὑπεναντιούμενοι τῷ Πλάτωνι καὶ μαχόμενοι διατελοῦσι

[13] Dionys. ap. Euseb. præp. ev. xiv. 23, 3, after mentioning the Atomist theory: οἱ δὲ, τὰς ἀτόμους μὲν ὀνομάσαντες [read οὐκ ὄν.], ἀμερῆ φασιν εἶναι σώματα, τοῦ παντὸς μέρη, ἐξ ὧν ἀδιαιρέτων ὄντων συντίθεται τὰ πάντα καὶ εἰς ἃ διαλύεται. καὶ τούτων φασὶ τῶν ἀμερῶν ὀνοματοποιὸν Διόδωρον γεγονέναι, ὄνομα δέ, φασιν, αὐτοῖς ἄλλο Ἡρακλείδης θέμενος, ἐκάλεσεν ὄγκους. Sext. Pyrrh. iii. 32 : Heraclides and Asclepiades (on whom see vol. iii. a. 352, 2nd edit.) explain ἀνάρμους ὄγκους to be the causes of all things. Math. x. 318 on the same: (τὴν τῶν πραγμάτων γένεσιν ἐδόξασαν) ἐξ ἀνομοίων μὲν, παθητῶν δὲ (this is in opposition to the Atomists, whose atoms were equally unlike, but were ἀπαθῆ), καθάπερ τῶν ἀνάρμων ὄγκων (ἄναρμος means not compacted, not composed out of any parts). Stob. Ecl. i. 350: Ἡρακλείδης θραύσματα (sc. τὰ ἐλάχιστα ὡρίζετο). Galen, h. phil. c. 5, end (Opp. xix. 244): Ἡρακλείδης ... καὶ Ἀσκληπιάδης ... ἀναρμόστους (rd. ἀνάρμους) ὄγκους ἀρχὰς ὑποτιθέντες τῶν ὅρων [rd. ὅλων].

[14] In the fragment of a work on Music, which Porphyry quotes in Ptol. Harm pp. 213-216 Wall, and Roulez reprints, p. 99 sqq., Heraclides asserts that every note is properly an impact (πληγὴ) transmitted to the ear, and, as such, occupies no time but the moment between the act and the completion of the act of impact, but the dullness of our hearing makes several impacts following after one another appear as one; the quicker the impacts follow, the higher the note, and the slower, the lower the note. As he composed apparently continuous bodies out of Atoms, as discrete magnitudes, he imagined in notes discrete magnitudes as elements of the apparently continuous. —In the same fragment he also expresses the view, which we found in Plato, p. 428, 113, that the sight perceives objects by contact with them (ἐπιβάλλουσα αὐτοῖς), and from that he derives the conclusion that the perceptions of sight are quicker and more reliable than those of hearing. Of hearing he remarks: τὰς αἰσθήσεις μὴ ἑστώσας, ἀλλ' ἐν ταράχῳ οὔσας.

connecting it not only with the Platonic theory of the elements, but with the Pythagorean theory of atoms, of which Ecphantus is the well-known adherent.[15] Heraclides also agrees with Ecphantus in supposing the world to have been formed from the atoms by means of the Divine Reason.[16] He seems to have held the cosmos to be unlimited.[17] It is, however, of more importance to know that he taught, like Hicetas and Ecphantus,[18] the diurnal rotation of the earth and the immobility of the fixed stars: but the annual revolution of the earth around the sun, and the heliocentric system, were unknown to him.[19] He thought the sun

---

[15] See vol i. 426 sq.

[16] Cf. the passage quoted supra, note 10. On Ecphantus see loc. cit.

[17] Stob. Ecl. i. 440: Σέλευκος ὁ 'Ερυθραῖος (the well-known astronomer) καὶ 'Ηρακλείδης ὁ Ποντικὸς ἄπειρον τὸν κόσμον. The Placita mention only Seleucus, ii. 1, 5; but the account of Stobæus, who frequently has the more complete text, is not, therefore, to be rejected. The Placita even confirm that account, ii. 13, 8 (see vol. 1 366, 2); there only remains a doubt whether the concept of the unlimited is to be taken here quite strictly.

[18] The first who propounded this view was, according to Theophr. ap Cic Acad ii. 39, 123 (with which cf. Bockh d. Kosm Syst. Pl. 122 sqq.), the Syracusan Hicetas, and the fact that the Placita mention only Ecphantus with Heraclides seems the less important, if we suppose with Bockh that he was a pupil of his fellow-countryman Hicetas, and was the first who promulgated the theory in a written treatise. However this may be, in any case it seems that Heraclides is indebted for it to Ecphantus, with whom his atomic theory also is connected.

[19] Plut. plac. iii. ¶3, 3 : 'Ηρακλείδης ὁ Ποντικὸς καὶ "Εκφαντος ὁ Πυθαγόρειος κινοῦσι μὲν τὴν γῆν, οὐ μὴν γε μεταβατικῶς, τροχοῦ [δὲ] δίκην ἐνιζομένην ἀπὸ δυσμῶν ἐπ᾽ ἀνατολὰς περὶ τὸ ἴδιον αὐτῆς κέντρον. (The same, with some variations, is found apud Euseb. pr. evan. xv. 58; Galen, hist. phil. c. 21.) Simpl. De Cœlo Schol. in Arist. 495 a. 31. διὰ τὸ γεγονέναι τινὰς, ὧν 'Ηρακλείδης τε ὁ Ποντικὸς ἦν καὶ 'Αρίσταρχος, νομίζοντας σώζεσθαι τὰ φαινόμενα τοῦ μὲν οὐρανοῦ καὶ τῶν ἀστέρων ἠρεμούντων, τῆς δὲ γῆς περὶ τοὺς τοῦ ἰσημερινοῦ πόλους ἀπὸ δυσμῶν κινουμένης ἑκάστης ἡμέρας μίαν ἔγγιστα περιστροφήν. τὸ δὲ ἔγγιστα πρόσκειται διὰ τὴν τοῦ ἡλίου μιᾶς μοίρας ἐπικίνησιν. Ibid. Schol. 506 a. 1 (cf ibid. 505 b 46): ἐν τῷ κέντρῳ δὲ οὖσαν τὴν γῆν καὶ κύκλῳ κινουμένην, τὸν δὲ

had only two satellites, Mercury and Venus.[20] Like the Pythagoreans, he held that the heavenly bodies, especially the moon, were orbs similarly constituted to ours.[21] The globular shape of the earth, then generally believed by philosophers, he takes for granted.[22] Passing over some other physical theories[23] of Heraclides, and turning to his doctrine of the human soul, we find that here too he adopted the more ancient Pythagorean view rather than the Platonic. He declared the soul to be a luminous ethereal essence.[24] Before entering into bodies, souls were to abide in

οὐρανὸν ἠρεμεῖν Ἡρακλ. ὁ Ποντικὸς ὑποθέμενος σώζειν ᾤετο τὰ φαινόμενα. Schol. 508 a 12: εἰ δὲ κύκλῳ περὶ τὸ κέντρον [ἐποιεῖτο τὴν κίνησιν ἡ γῆ], ὡς Ἡρακλ. ὁ Ποντ. ὑπετίθετο. Geminus ap. Simpl. Phys. 65, loc cit. διὸ καὶ παρελθών τις. φησὶν Ἡρακλείδης ὁ Ποντ. ἔλεγεν, ὅτι καὶ κινουμένης πως τῆς γῆς, τοῦ δ' ἡλίου μένοντός πως, δύναται ἡ περὶ τὸν ἥλιον φαινομένη ἀνωμαλία σώζεσθαι. (Cf. on these passages, and in opposition to the perverse conclusions which Gruppe, Kosm., Syst. d Gr. 126 sqq., has drawn from them, Bockh, loc. cit., p. 127 sqq) Procl. in Tim 281 E: Ἡρακλείδης . . . κινῶν κύκλῳ τὴν γῆν

[20] Chalcid. in Tim. p. 200, Meurs. and Bockh, loc. cit, p. 138, 142 sq. Cf. also Ideler, Abh. d. Berl. Akad. 1830, Phil. hist. Kl. p. 72.

[21] Stob. Ecl. i. 514 (Plac. ii. 13, 8), see Pt i. 366, 2; cf. 561, 2; ibid. i. 552· Ἡρακλείδης καὶ Ὠκελλος [τὴν σελήνην] γῆν ὁμίχλῃ περιεχομένη. The comets, on the other hand, and some similar phænomena, Heracleitus considered to be luminous clouds: Stob. Ecl. i. 578 (Plac iii. 2, 6; Galen, h phil. c. 18, p. 288). The myth of Phaethon (who, as Jupiter, is transferred to the sky, Hyginus, poet. astron. ii. 42), he gives merely historically.

[22] To this supposition we may refer the narrative of a circumnavigation of the earth, ap. Strabo, 11. 2, 4, 5, p. 98, 100.

[23] On ebb and flow, Stob Ecl i. 634; on the shivering in ague, Galen, De tremore, c 6, vol. vii. 615 K; on the perceptions of sense, which he explained, according to Plutarch, plac. iv. 9, 3, with Empedocles, by the hypothesis of affluxes and pores; cf. also note 14.

[24] Stob Ecl. i. 796. Ἡρακλ. φωτοειδῆ τὴν ψυχὴν ὡρίσατο. Tertull. De an. c. 9. the soul is not *lumen, etsi hoc placuit Pontico Heraclidi.* Macrob. Somn i 14: he designated the soul as a light. Philip. De An. A 4 u · he considered the soul to be an οὐράνιον σῶμα, which is equivalent to αἰθέριον. In a treatise attributed to him, περὶ τῶν ἐν ᾅδου, the

the Milky Way,[25] the bright points in which were themselves such souls. There is no record to show how he brought his dæmonology[26] and belief in divination[27] into combination with this, or whether he even attempted to do so.

Although, however, there were many points on which Heraclides differed from Plato, he agreed with him at least in his moral principles. From his treatise on Justice we find instances quoted to show that wrong-doing is overtaken by punishment;[28] and in his work on Pleasure he cites, as against a Hedonic panegyric,[29] numerous cases in which want of temperance has led to ruin, arguing the question of the acutest pleasure being found in a madman.[30] This is quite as much Pythagorean as Platonic;[31] the two

genuineness of which might reasonably be doubted, the activities of the soul were explained as merely a product of the body· Plut. utr. an. an corp. &c.; Fragm. i. 5.

[25] Iambl. ap. Stob. Ecl. 1. 904, cf. supra, p. 28, 4.

[26] For the dæmons, a doctrine natural in such a Pythagorean, cf. Clemens, Protrept. 44 c : τί γὰρ 'Ηρακλείδης ὁ Ποντικὸς, οὐκ ἔσθ' ὅπῃ οὐκ ἐπὶ τὰ Δημοκρίτου καὶ αὐτὸς κατασύρεται εἴδωλα (i.e. in the description of the divine). The εἴδωλα of Democritus are, in fact, dæmons (see vol. i. 757), and to the dæmons airy or vaporous bodies are attributed; cf. Epinomis, 984 B sqq. (see below).

[27] Some instances of prophetic dreams are adduced by Cic. Divin. i. 23, 46; Tertull. De an. c. 46; Plut. Alex. 26, from Heraclides. His interest in oracles is proved by his treatise π. χρηστηρίων, of which fragments are given by Rouler, 67 sq; Muller, Fragm. hist. gr. ii. 197 sq.

[28] From Athen. xii. 521 c. sq.; 533 sq.

[29] The fragment apud Athen. xii. 512 a. sqq., in which it must remain undecided what adversary he had immediately in view, can only be considered in this way, not as the philosopher's own opinion.

[30] Cf. the fragments apud Athen. xii. 525 sq.; 533 c.; 536 sq.; 552 sq.; 554 c.

[31] The definition of happiness quoted vol. 1 398, 3, refers also to the Pythagorean Ethics. On the other hand, the quotation of Hermias in Phædr. p. 76 ed. Ast, is genuinely Platonic: φιλίαν [φιλίας] εἶναι τὸν ἔρωτα καὶ οὐκ ἄλλου τινὸς, κατὰ συμβεβηκὸς δέ (this Aristo-

schools coincide even more in their moral doctrines than in their philosophic theories.[32]

Eudoxus widely departed from Platonic precedents in Ethics as well as in his Physics. In the sphere of Physics, the theory of Ideas seems to have been too ideal for him, and the participation of things in Ideas too shadowy. In order to connect material things more closely with his philosophy of Nature, he assumed that they receive their qualities by means of the admixture of the substances to which these qualities originally belong; and he accordingly set in the place of the Ideas Anaxagorean homœomeries.[33] It is therefore of little consequence whether or not he retained the Ideas in name.[34] In his Ethics, he agreed with Aristippus in pronouncing Pleasure the highest good, appealing to the fact that all men desire pleasure and avoid pain; that all strive for pleasure for its

telian expression must belong to the narrator of the account) τινας ἐκπίπτειν εἰς ἀφροδίσια.

[32] This holds good only of the practical results, for the scientific substantiation and development of the Platonic Ethics were wanting in the Pythagoreans.

[33] Arist. Metaph. i. 9, 991 a. 14 the Ideas contribute nothing to the stability of things, μὴ ἐνυπάρχοντά γε τοῖς μετέχουσιν · οὕτω μὲν γὰρ ἂν ἴσως αἴτια δόξειεν εἶναι ὡς τὸ λευκὸν (the white colour) μεμιγμένον τῷ λευκῷ (the white object). ἀλλ' οὗτος μὲν ὁ λόγος λίαν εὐκίνητος, ὃν Ἀναξαγόρας μὲν πρῶτος Εὔδοξος δ' ὕστερον καὶ ἄλλοι τινὲς ἔλεγον. Ibid. xiii. 5, 1079 b. 18, almost the same, word for word. On the first passage, Alexander remarks, subsequently appealing (Schol. 573 a. 12) to the second book of the Aristotelian treatise π. ἰδεῶν: Εὔδοξος τῶν Πλάτωνος γνωρίμων μίξει τῶν ἰδεῶν ἐν τοῖς πρὸς αὐτὰς τὸ εἶναι ἔχουσιν ἡγεῖτο ἕκαστον εἶναι, καὶ ἄλλοι δέ τινες, ὡς ἔλεγε .... μίξει τῶν ἰδεῶν τὰ ἄλλα. The editor of Alexander ad Metaph. 1079 b. 15 classes Eudoxus with Anaxagoras: οὗτοι δ' οὐ συντάττουσι τὰς ἰδέας.

[34] This point cannot be made out, because Aristotle says nothing about it; as regards Alexander, again, we cannot be sure whether he kept strictly to the exposition of the Aristotelian treatise on the Ideas.

own sake, and that there is absolutely nothing to which Pleasure does not give additional value.[35] These divergences from Plato are so important that Eudoxus can scarcely be called a follower of his, however greatly the Academy may otherwise be indebted to him.

In the author of the Epinomis,[36] on the contrary, we recognise a true Platonist; but a Platonist who, like the Pythagoreans, made all science to consist in the knowledge of numbers and quantities, and the stars, and in a theology bound up with this. The Epinomis, intended as a supplement to the Laws, is an enquiry into the nature of that knowledge which we distinguish by the name of wisdom; the knowledge which alone can make happy men and good citizens, and give capacity for the administration of the highest offices; which is the final goal of the actions of the best educated, and insures a blessed existence after death.[37] This knowledge, we are told, does not lie in those mechanical skills which supply our common necessities, nor in the imitative arts, which have no serious purpose beyond mere amusement, nor in either of those activities which are without true intelligent discernment, and are regulated by uncertain opinion, such as the art of the physician, the pilot, or the lawyer; nor does it consist in merely natural docility

---

[35] Arist. Eth. N. i. 12, 1101 b. 27; x. 2 beginn. (cf. Diog. viii. 88) with the addition· ἐπιστεύοντο δ' οἱ λόγοι διὰ τὴν τοῦ ἤθους ἀρετὴν μᾶλλον ἢ δι' αὐτούς. διαφερόντως γὰρ ἐδόκει σώφρων εἶναι, &c. Alex. Top. 119 in following Arist.

[36] The Platonic origin of which, even apart from the unplatonic nature of the contents, and other proofs (see p. 561, 15), would be at once refuted by the dry and wearisome manner of its exposition.

[37]. 973 A sq; 976 D; 978 B, 979 B sq; 992 A sqq.

and acuteness.[38] The indispensable condition of true wisdom is the knowledge of number, and all connected with it,—that great science which has been given us by Uranos, highest of the gods, and author of all good things. He who is ignorant of number,[39] and cannot distinguish the straight from the crooked, may indeed possess courage and temperance, and every other virtue, but is destitute of wisdom, the greatest virtue of all.[40] It is number which not only is required by all arts, but always produces what is good and never what is evil; it follows that where number is lacking, and there alone, evil and disorder are present. Only the man conversant with number is capable of understanding and teaching what is right and beautiful and good.[41] Dialectic[42] is to be regarded as a help to this scientific education; but the culminating point is Astronomy, which is concerned with the fairest and divinest of all visible things;[43] and the chief reason of this pre-eminence is that Astronomy makes possible to us a true piety, which is the best virtue. Only by means of Astronomy are we delivered from that baneful ignorance which keeps us from the real knowledge and

---

[38] 974 D-976 C.

[39] Together with the pure doctrine of numbers, the author, 990 c. sqq., mentions, in agreement with Plato (Rep. vii. 524 D sqq; see p. 216), geometry, stereometry, and harmony.

[40] 976 C-977 D; cf. 978 B sqq.; 988 A sq.

[41] 977 D sqq.; 979 A sqq, with which cf. the quotation from Philolaus, vol. i 294, 1.

[42] 991 C: πρὸς τούτοις δὲ τὸ καθ' ἓν (the individual) τῷ κατ' εἴδη προσακτέον ἐν ἑκάσταις ταῖς συνουσίαις, ἐρωτῶντά τε καὶ ἐλέγχοντα τὰ μὴ καλῶς ῥηθέντα πάντως γὰρ καλλίστη καὶ πρώτη βάσανος ἀνθρώποις ὀρθῶς γίνεται, ὅσαι δὲ οὐκ οὖσαι προσποιοῦνται, ματαιότατος πόνος ἁπάντων. The latter words seem to apply to astronomers who would rely exclusively on observation, like Eudoxue.

[43] 991 B, 989 D sqq.

worship of the heavenly gods.[44] If we may believe that there are gods who care for all things and fill all things, if the soul be really prior to the body, and nobler,[45] if a Divine reason, a good soul,[46] have fashioned the Cosmos and directs its course, overcoming the working of the evil soul,[47] where can that reason be more active in operation than in the most glorious and best ordered parts of the Cosmos, the stars? Is it conceivable that such great masses could be moved by any other power than a soul, that the perfect regularity of their motions could proceed from any cause except their own inherent reason? Can we suppose that earthly creatures were endowed with souls, and the shining heavenly natures left destitute of them?[48] On the contrary, we should ascribe to them the most blessed and perfect souls; we should consider them either as gods or the images of gods, as bearers

[44] 989 A sqq; 985 D, 980 A sq; cf also 988 A (on the religious prejudice against meteorology).

[45] 980 C; 988 C sq.–991 D, with reference to the discussions of the Laws mentioned p. 344, 384 sq., 500, 32

[46] λόγος ὁ πάντων θειότατος (986 C). this reason coincides with the soul, to which, in 984 C alibi, the formation of the living being is ascribed, the ἀρίστη ψυχὴ, which effects the φορὰ καὶ κίνησις ἐπὶ τἀγαθόν (988 D).

[47] 988 D sq., with which cf. the remarks p. 544, sq.; 549, 129.

[48] 981 E–984 A. As regards the magnitude of the stars, it is remarked, 983 A sq., that we are to suppose the sun larger than the earth, and likewise all the planets of wonderful magnitude. With respect to the sequence and rotation of the stars, the Epinomis, 986 A–987 D, agrees with Plato· still there is one deviation from the Platonic exposition (according to the προλ. τ. Πλάτωνος φιλοσ. c. 25, already made use of by Proclus as an argument against its Platonic origin), in that, acc. to 987 B, the Planets are made to move towards the right, the firmament of the fixed stars towards the left; see p. 382, 40. The author remarks, 986 E, 987 D sqq., that Astronomy came to the Greeks, like everything else, from the barbarians; he hopes, however, that the Greeks will soon bring it to a higher state of perfection.

of powers divine, as absolutely immortal, or at any rate possessing all-sufficient length of life.[49] They are, in a word, the visible gods, and are all (not merely the sun and moon) entitled to equal veneration:[50] the popular mythical divinities, on the other hand, are treated in the same apologetic manner by this author as by Plato.[51] After these gods come the Dæmons. As there are five distinct elements,[52] so there are distinct genera of living beings, in each of which some one element preponderates.[53] In this order, the heavenly gods with their fiery nature occupy the highest place; mankind, animals and plants, as earthly creatures, the lowest;[54] midway between them are three classes of Dæmons. Of these, two are invisible, with bodies of æther or of air; the Dæmons of the third class, provided with watery or vapoury bodies, sometimes hide themselves and sometimes visibly appear. All intercourse between men and gods is by means of these dæmons: they reveal themselves in dreams and oracles, and in various ways: they know the thoughts of men: they love the good and hate the bad: they are susceptible of pleasure and the reverse; whereas the gods, exalted above these emotions, are in their nature only

---

[49] 981 E sq; 983 E sq.; 986 B, where undoubtedly the meaning is that the star-spirits ought to be considered as the true gods. The author leaves it undecided whether the visible body of the stars is connected with them in a loose or in a strict and inseparable union.

[50] 984 D; 985 D sq.

[51] 984 D (cf. supra, p. 500). Moreover, here also (985 C sq.) we find the principle that legislation ought not to interfere with the established worship, nor to introduce fresh objects of reverence without pressing reasons.

[52] Æther, besides the four Empedoclean elements. The author assigns to æther a place between fire and air: 891 C–984 B sqq.

[53] 981 C sq.; cf. supra, p. 521, 14 and p. 595, 46.

[54] 981 D sq.

capable of intelligence and thought.[55] Far beneath them is man: his life is full of trouble, disorder, unreason: and few of his race find true happiness in this world.[56] But whoever combines the above-mentioned knowledge of heavenly things with virtue and morality, shall be rewarded with happiness,[57] and look forward to an entrance after death, as elect and consecrate, into a blessed existence, where, freed from the multifariousness of his present nature, he shall live in the contemplation of the heavens.[58] We recognise the spirit of the Platonic School, not only in this expectation, but in the further contents of this work: in the propositions concerning the worth of knowledge, the passionlessness of the gods, the reason that governs the universe, the dependency of the corporeal upon the soul, the animate nature of the world, and the divinity of the stars. Yet, not to mention minor differences, how great is the distance between the astronomer, to whom astronomy is the acme of wisdom, and the starry heaven the highest object of contemplation, and the philosopher who would lead us from the visible to the Idea, from Mathematics and Astronomy to Dialectic! As, therefore, the Epinomis in all probability belongs to the first generation of Plato's disciples,[59] it serves to confirm

---

[55] 984 E–985 C; cf. supra, p. 593.
[56] 973 D sqq.; 982 A; 983 C; 985 D; 992 C
[57] 992 C sq.; cf. 973 C
[58] 973 C; 986 D; 992 B sq.
[59] This supposition is supported by 1) the tradition indicated p. 561, 15, which alone, of course, would be too weak to prove it completely. But 2) in support of the tradition we see that the contents of the treatise are very suitable to a man like Philippus, a mathematician and astronomer, no stranger to ethical, political, and theological enquiries. The magnitude of the stars, which is here (983 A sq.) so

the fact, sufficiently attested otherwise, that the Old Academy had even then, in many of its members, departed very far from genuine Platonism, and had sacrificed pure philosophic enquiry to a predilection for mathematics and mathematical theology.

After the death of Polemo, this mathematical speculation and, generally speaking, purely theoretic philosophy would seem to have receded more and more in favour of Ethics, if, indeed (as we see exemplified in Crantor), they did not entirely die out. Polemo had himself advanced a principle which reminds us of the Cynics,[60] but was probably intended by him in a sense less strict than theirs—viz. that man should exercise himself in actions, and not in dialectical theories.[61] And certainly this philosopher appears to have effected more by his own personal influence than in any other way.[62] In his theory of morals he faithfully follows his master. His maxim is, Life according to Nature.[63]

strongly emphasised, was discussed by Philippus in a special treatise (π. μεγέθους ἡλίου καὶ σελήνης καὶ γῆς) 3) The treatise before us, 986 A sqq., discovers no advance in astronomical knowledge beyond Plato; in 986 E, 987 D sq., it designates the science of astronomy as still young amongst the Greeks, and looks forward to a completion of what has been learnt from the barbarians as a thing of the future The tact that Aristotle does not mention the Epinomis, not even Polit. ii. 6, 1265 b. 18, seems unimportant, even apart from what is remarked p. 74 sqq. It may, of course, have been written by a contemporary of Aristotle, even if it is later than the Politics, or, at least, if it was not in circulation as Platonic at the time of the composition of the Politics.

[60] See Pt. i. 248, 3

[61] Diog. iv. 18. ἔφασκε δὲ ὁ Πολέμων δεῖν ἐν τοῖς πράγμασι γυμνάζεσθαι καὶ μὴ ἐν τοῖς διαλεκτικοῖς θεωρήμασι, καθάπερ ἁρμονικόν τι τεχνίον καταπιόντα καὶ μὴ μελετήσαντα, ὡς κατὰ μὲν τὴν ἐρώτησιν θαυμάζεσθαι κατὰ δὲ τὴν διάθεσιν ἑαυτοῖς μάχεσθαι.

[62] Diog. iv. 17, 24.

[63] Clemens (see p. 597, 55) mentions special συντάγματα περὶ τοῦ κατὰ φύσιν βίου belonging to him.

But this he makes to depend on two conditions,— Virtue, and the possession of those goods which Nature originally prompts us to desire—such as health and the like.[64] Although, however, the second condition is indispensable to perfect happiness,[65] it is of far less consequence than the first. Without virtue, says Polemo, no happiness is possible; without material and external goods, no complete happiness. In this, his teaching is in full agreement with that of Plato, Speusippus, and Xenocrates. In other respects we know little of him, except what may be gathered from some isolated definitions.[66]

Of his successor Crates we know still less; but as

---

[64] Plut. c. not. 23 (see p. 600, 66), Cic. Acad. ii. 42 (ibid.); Fin. ii. 11, 33 sq.: *omne animal, simul ut ortum est, et se ipsum et omnes partes suas diligit; duasque quæ maximæ sunt imprimis amplectitur, animum et corpus; deinde utriusque partes .... in his primis naturalibus voluptas insit, necne, magna quæstio est. Nihil vero putare esse præter voluptatem* (Cic. is engaged with an Epicurean), *non membra, non sensus, non ingenii motum, non integritatem corporis, non valetudinem summæ mihi videtur inscitiæ. Atque ab isto capite fluere neccsse est omnem rationem bonorum et malorum. Polemoni, etiam ante Aristoteli, ea prima visa sunt, quæ paulo ante dixi: ergo nata est sententia veterum Academicorum et Peripateticorum, ut finem bonorum dicerent secundum naturam vivere,* i.e. *virtute adhibita frui primis a natura datis.* Ibid. iv. 6, 14 sq.: *cum enim superiores, e quibus planissime Polemo, secundum naturam vivere summum bonum esse dixissent, his verbis tria significari Stoici dicunt .... tertium autem, omnibus aut maximus rebus iis, quæ secundum naturam sint, fruentem vivere,* which, according to the account of the Stoics, was adopted by Xenocrates and Aristotle in their determination of the highest good.

[65] Clemens, Strom. ii. 419 A: ὁ γὰρ Ξενοκράτους γνώριμος Πολέμων φαίνεται τὴν εὐδαιμονίαν αὐτάρκειαν εἶναι βουλόμενος ἀγαθῶν πάντων ἢ τῶν πλείστων καὶ μεγίστων. (Cf. Cic. Fin. iv 6; v. previous note.) δογματίζει γοῦν, χωρὶς μὲν ἀρετῆς μηδέποτε ἂν εὐδαιμονίαν ὑπάρχειν, δίχα δὲ καὶ τῶν σωματικῶν καὶ τῶν ἐκτὸς τὴν ἀρετὴν αὐτάρκη πρὸς εὐδαιμονίαν εἶναι. Cic. Tusc. v. 13; v. supr. 600, 71.

[66] E g. ap. Plut. Ad princ. inerud. iii. 3, p. 488: τὸν Ἔρωτα εἶναι θεῶν ὑπηρεσίαν εἰς νεῶν ἐπιμέλειαν, and the quotation from Clemens on p. 597, 55.

his name is invariably associated with the Academy,[67] and from his personal relations with Polemo and Crantor, we may conclude that he was a loyal adherent of the School. We possess a few more explicit details concerning Crantor, partly from his exposition of the Timæus,[68] partly from his Ethical writings, but chiefly from his book on Grief. From the first of these sources we learn that he disputed, like Xenocrates, the beginning of the soul in time; and regarded the account in the Timæus merely as an expository form:[69] that with a true comprehension of his author, he conceived of the soul as compounded out of the primary constituents of all things, and more particularly out of these four elements—the Sensible, the Intelligible, the Same, and the Other; so that it is in a position to know all things:[70] that he explained the harmonious numbers in the Timæus in a manner that modern writers have recognised as the true one:[71] and that he (certainly erroneously) held the mythus of Atlantis to be a real history.[72] If his views of Plato correspond, as can hardly be doubted, with his own views, his comments sufficiently prove that he held the Platonic doctrine of the soul in its original sense. How far such was the case with other parts of Metaphysics, we cannot be sure; but in his Ethics, Crantor appears as a true representative of the

[67] E.g. ap. Cic. Acad. i. 9, 34, where Crates is expressly classed with the true keepers of Platonic doctrine.

[68] The first commentary on that work; v. supr. 590, 24.

[69] Procl. in Tim. 85 A; Plut. an. procr. iii. 1, p. 1013.

[70] Plut. i. 5; ii. 4 sq.; v. supr.

[71] Plut. xvi. 5, 20; iii. 29, 4 Cf. supr. and Kayser, De Crantore, pp. 22–33.

[72] Procl. in Tim 24 A.

Academy. We find, from a fragment[73] of considerable length, and full of oratorical grace, that he accorded the first place among goods to virtue; the second to health; the third to pleasure; the fourth to riches; which can only be understood as agreeing with the generally received doctrine of the Academy. We further read that he denounced the Stoical indifference to pain as the murder of natural human feelings, and advocated moderation in grief,[74] which is also truly Platonic.[75] He was opposed, like the rest of the School, to the entire suppression of the affections, and required only their due limitation, appealing in defence of this view to the uses which Nature designed for these emotions.[76] We may judge of the reputation which he

---

[73] Ap. Sext. Math. xi 51–58.

[74] Plut Consol. ad Apoll i. 3, p. 102: μὴ γὰρ νοσοῖμεν, φησὶν ὁ 'Ακαδημαικὸς Κράντωρ, νοσήσασι δὲ παρείη τις αἴσθησις, εἴτ' οὖν τέμνοιτό τι τῶν ἡμετέρων, εἴτ' ἀποσπῷτο. τὸ γὰρ ἀνώδυνον τοῦτο οὐκ ἄνευ μεγάλων ἐγγίγνεται μισθῶν τῷ ἀνθρώπῳ· τεθηριῶσθαι γὰρ εἰκὸς ἐκεῖ μὲν σῶμα τοιοῦτον, ἐνταῦθα δὲ ψυχήν. Cic. Tusc. iii. 6, 12, translates this; and we may infer that the words at the beginning of the chapter—οὐ γὰρ ἔγωγε συμφέρομαι τοῖς τὴν ἄγριον ὑμνοῦσι καὶ σκληρὰν ἀπάθειαν ἔξω καὶ τοῦ δυνατοῦ καὶ τοῦ συμφέροντος οὖσαν—are also from Crantor. Of what follows, we can only conjecture that it belongs to him in substance, and that, accordingly, he regarded apathy as doing away with benevolence and friendship, and sought for 'metriopathy' instead (cf. note 76). Kayser rightly recognises traces of this passage in Seneca, Cons. ad. Helv. 16, 1; Cons. ad Polyb. 17, 2, cf. ibid. 18, 5 sq.

[75] Kayser (p. 6 sq.; 39 sq.) sees an innovation of Crantor's here, and seeks its explanation in the ill-health of the philosopher. Brandis, however (ii. b. 1, 40), rightly refers to Cic. Acad i. 9; ii. 44 (v. following note), and the agreement of his doctrine with the tenets of the other Academics on happiness. It has been pointed out, 444, 1, that Plato declared himself against apathy, and with special reference to the case contemplated by Plut. loc. cit. c. 3 beginning.

[76] Cic. Acad. ii. 44, 135. *Sed quæro, quando ista fuerint ab Academia vetere decreta ut animum sapientis commoveri et conturbari negarent? Mediocritates illi probabant, et in omni permotione naturalem volebant esse quendam modum* (which almost presupposes the term μετριοπάθεια). *Legimus*

enjoyed, and of the purity of his principles, from the fact that he was associated with Chrysippus as teacher of Ethics.[77] His various fragments contain evidence that he believed, like Plato, in souls being placed upon earth for their punishment and purification; and that, sensible of the evil inseparable from human life, he saw in death the transition to a better existence.[78] All this is in thorough accord with the thought of the Older Academy. When, therefore, Cicero mentions Crantor among those who remained faithful[79] to the doctrine of Plato, it is at least so far true, that he made no deviations from that form of it which prevailed after Speusippus and Xenocrates. Its original spirit and contents, however, were but very imperfectly reproduced in the Platonic School. Though the Ethics there taught may be the Ethics of Plato, even the earliest representatives of his philosophy had already departed from the speculative groundwork of pure Platonism. The next generation seems to have

omnes *Crantoris, veteris Academici, de luctu: est enim non magnus verum aureolus et, ut Tuberoni Panætius præcipit, ad verbum ediscendus libellus. Atque illi quidem etiam utiliter a natura dicebant permotiones istas animis nostris datas; metum cavendi causa misericordiam ægritudinemque clementiæ: ipsam iracundiam fortitudinis quasi cotem esse dicebant.*

[77] Horace, Epp. i 2, 4.

[78] Plut. loc. cit. c. 27: πολλοῖς γὰρ καὶ σοφοῖς ἀνδράσιν, ὥς φησι Κράντωρ, οὐ νῦν ἀλλὰ πάλαι κέκλαυσται τἀνθρώπινα, τιμωρίαν, ἡγουμένοις εἶναι τὸν βίον καὶ ἀρχὴν τὸ γενέσθαι ἄνθρωπον συμφορὰν τὴν μεγίστην, repeated, according to Lactantius, Inst ii. 18 fin., by Cicero in his work on Consolation (Kayser, p. 48). Crantor expresses himself on the miseries of life ap. Plut loc. cit. c. 6, 14; Kayser points out (p 45) from Tusc. i. 48, that in the latter place the story about Euthynous comes from Crantor (we get similar complaints of the evils of life in the Epinomis) In c. 25 Crantor observes how great a consolation it is not to suffer by one's own fault. On Cicero's use of Crantor, cf. Heine, De fonte Tuscul. Disp. 10 sqq.

[79] Acad. i. 9, 34.

confined its attention entirely to Morality; and when Arcesilaus inaugurated a new period in the history of the School, this led still farther away from the position of the founder. Only a portion of Plato's spiritual legacy descended with his garden to the Academy: the full inheritance passed over to Aristotle, who was thereby qualified to transcend his master.

INDEX.

N.B.—In the Index, as elsewhere in this book, when two numerals occur (e.g. 31, 64), the first refers to the page, the second to the note. When two or more pages are intended, it is expressly stated (e.g. pp. 25, 556).

ACADEMY, Plato's garden, pp. 25, 556; Older Academy, 553-618; character of its Philosophy, 565
Æschines, the orator, not Plato's pupil, 31, 64; the Socratic, 15, 26
Æsthetics, Plato's, 505 sqq.
Æther, Plato's conception of, 273, 21; Speusippus', 578, Xenocrates', 595; in the Epinomis, 615
Agriculture and trade in the Republic, 471; in the Laws, 531
Albinus, his arrangement of Plato's works, 99
Alexander the Great, respect for Xenocrates, 559, 10
Alexandrian Library 52
Amyclas, an Academic, 553, 1
Animals, Soul of, pp. 432, 433; human souls pass into, pp. 393, 406; consciousness of God ascribed to, 596
Anniceris, a Cyrenian, rescued Plato from slavery, 24; said to have purchased the Academy garden for him, 28, 61
Antisthenes, the Cynic, hostility to Plato, 36, 85
Apollo, myths connecting Plato with, pp. 9, 44
Archelaus of Macedonia, Plato's alleged friendship with, 35, 76
Aristander, defined the Soul as a self-moving Number, 355, 154
Aristides, the Locrian, disciple of Plato, 553, 1

Ariston, Plato's father, 3, 3
Aristonymus, disciple of Plato, 30, 64
Aristotle, references to Plato's works, pp. 26, 54-72; criticism of Plato's doctrine, pp. 232, 517
Art, subordinated to Ethics, 480; Plato's view of, pp. 505-514; Inspiration the source of, 508; Imitation the characteristic of, 509; supervision of, 511; particular arts, 513
Ast, his classification of the Dialogues, 101
Astronomy, pp. 216, 613
Atoms, Heraclides' theory of, 606-608
Authenticity, criterion of, in Platonic works, 77; the Laws', 548
Axiothea of Phlius, a woman who attended Plato's lectures, 554, 1

BEAUTIFUL, the, 192, 193, 506
Being and Non-being, 226 sq., 241, 304; and Becoming, 228 sq.
Body, the human, 388 sqq.; relation of the Soul to the, 219, 421
Bryso of Heraclea, 553, 1; the mathematician, 553, 1

CALIPPUS, murderer of Dion, 30, 64
Chabrias, a Platonist, 31, 64
Chemical theories, Plato's, 377

624   INDEX.

Children, community of, pp. 477, 481; weakly, exposed, 485; education of, 478
Chio, a Platonist, loc. cit
Christianity, relation of Platonism to, 505, 47
Classes, separation and relation of, in the State, 471
Classification, Plato's principle of, 204
Clearchus of Heraclea, 30, 64
Colours, theory of, 378, 35
Concepts, formation and determination of, 199; see Ideas
Consciousness, ordinary. pp. 170–175
Coriscus, a Platonist, 554, 1
Courage, as a division of the Soul, 413, 430; its depreciation in the Laws, 530
Crantor, 349, 150; 364, 5; 618 sq.
Crates, 618
Creator of the World, pp. 284, 363, 390

*D*ÆMONOLOGY of Plato, 501; of Xenocrates, 593, of the Epinomis, 615
Death, pp. 389, 399; Preferable to sickly life, 482
Decad, perfection of the, 576
Delian problem solved by Plato, 22, 42; Bryso failed to solve, 554, 1
Delius of Ephesus, disciple of Plato, 554, 1
Demetrius of Amphipolis, 554, 1
Democritus, on verbal expression, 211
Desire in the irrational Soul, 414 sq., 430
Dialectic, 150; Platonic contrasted with the Socratic, 151; constituents of, 196–204; Zeno's, 203, narrower sense of, 225
Dialogue, philosophic, why adopted by Plato, 153–159

Dialogues, Socratic, 119; Phædrus, 129; Lysis, Lesser Hippias, Charmides, Laches, Protagoras, Euthyphro, Apology, Crito, 120; Dialectical; Gorgias, Meno, Theætetus, Euthydemus, 125–127; Sophist, Politicus, Parmenides, Philebus, Euthydemus, Cratylus, Symposium, Phædo, 136–140; Republic, Timæus, Critias, Laws, 140–143; Spuriousness of lost, 46
διάνοια and νοῦς, 218, 147
Dion, Plato's intimacy with, 24; hostile aggression on Dionysius, 34
Dionysius the Elder, 24; the younger, 32
Diseases, 433
Divination, 431
Duality, indefinite, 322, 89; Xenocrates' doctrine of, 590

*E*CPHANTUS, held the Pythagorean theory of atoms and the diurnal rotation of the Earth, 608
Education in the Republic, 215, 478; in the Laws, 541
Elements, Plato's theory of the, 368–378; Xenocrates', 594
Enemies, Love of, pp 182, 454
Epinomis, the, 612; probably written by Philippus of Opus, 561, its point of view, 312; Number, 613; Astronomy, 614; Dæmons, 615, Future Existence, 616
Erastus, a Platonist, 554, 1
Eros, 191 sqq, 455, 618, 66
Ethics, of Plato, 435 sqq, 529; of Speusippus, 579; of Xenocrates, 597; of Heraclides, 610; of Polemo, 617; of Crantor, 619
Euclides of Megara, 14
Eudemus of Cyprus, a Platonist, 554, 1
Eudoxus of Cnidos, pp. 562, 611

INDEX.

Euphæus, a Platonist, 30, 64
Evil, Cause of, 340, evil-doing proceeds from ignorance, 420

FOOD, animal, forbidden by Xenocrates, 597
Freewill, 419, 503
Friendship, 196, 69, 455

GOD, Plato's concept of, 281 sqq.; 438, 495 sqq.; Speusippus', 569; Xenocrates', 584; Heraclides', 606
Gods of Polytheism, 500, 591, 606
Good, highest, Plato's, 436 eqq.; Speusippus', 479; Xenocrates', 599; Polemo's, 618; Crantor's, 620; The, 280 sqq.
Goods, Community of, in the Republic, 481; abandoned in the Laws, 540
Grammatical discussions in Plato, 214, 130
Great and Small, 299 sqq., 322
Guardians or warriors, in the Republic, 470 sqq.; in the Laws, 531
Gymnastic and music in Education, 479, 542

HAPPINESS and Virtue, 445; see The Good
Harmony in the Universe, 347 sqq.
Heaviness and lightness, 376
Helicon of Cyzicus, the astronomer, 554, 1
Heraclides of Pontus, 606; His theory of atoms, 607; of the Universe, the Soul, Ethics, 608-610
Heraclides the Thracian, 30, 64
Heraclitus of Ephesus, refutation of his doctrine, 184; on names and things, 211; Plato's relation to, 233

Herbart on the gradual transformation of the Doctrine of Ideas in the Dialogues, 102
Hermann's arrangement of the Dialogues, 102
Hermodorus, the Platonist, 554, 1
Hestiæus of Perinthus, disciple of Plato, pp. 561, 605

IDEAS, doctrine of, founded on that of Knowledge and Being, 225, 228; proofs as given by Aristotle, 232; historic origin of, 233; concept of, 237; as universals, 238; as substances, 240; as concrete entities, 240; as numbers, 254; as living powers, 261; world of, 271; highest, 276; relation of sensible objects to, 315, immanence of things in, 317; participation of things in, 335; theories of, in the Academy, 604
Imitation, distinctive of art, 509
Immortality, 379 sq., 404, 616, of the irrational part of the soul, held by Speusippus and Xenocrates, pp. 578, 596
Induction, Socratic and Platonic, 199 sqq.

JUSTICE, 182–187, 452, relation to happiness, 445 sq.; in the State, 465; in the laws, 530

KNOWLEDGE, Plato's theory of, pp. 170 sqq., 183, 218 sq., 395 sq.; Speusippus, 566; Xenocrates, 582

LANGUAGE, relation to Philosophy, 210
Lasthenia, a woman who attended Plato's lectures, 554, 1
Law, martial, 482, based on Phi-

S S

losophy, 466; substituted for the ruler, 532
Laws, the, Latin form of Platonism in, 517; point of view, 522; philosophy less prominent in, 523; religious character of, 525; mathematics in, 527; ethics of, 529; particular legislation of, 531; politics and social regulations of, 523, 540, divergences from Plato's original point of view in, 543; authenticity of, 548
Leo, of Byzantium, the elder, a Platonist, 554, 1
Leonides, a Platonist, 30, 64
Letters, Plato's, spuriousness of, 87
Limited and unlimited, pp. 264, 352
Logic, no Platonic theory of, 208
Lycurgus, the orator, a Platonist, 30, 64
Lying, when permissible, 454

MAGNET, the, 378, 35
Magnitudes, Plato's derivation of, 331, 103, p. 579; Speusippus', 575; Xenocrates', 587, various theories about, 605
Man, 388 sqq.
Marriage, Platonic view of, 456, 541
Mathematical principle, 352
Mathematics, relation to Philosophy, 216 sq.; in the Laws, 526; in the Academy, pp. 555, 556
Matter, Platonic, 293 sqq.; difficulties of this theory, 312, the cause of Evil, 323 sq. 340
Megara, Plato's sojourn at, 14
Menedemus, 30, 60
Meno, 125
Metaphysics of the Academy, 604
Meteorological theories of Plato, 378, 35
Method, scientific, 150 sqq., 196 sqq.

Miltas, Platonist and soothsayer, 554, 1
Morality, 454 sqq
Munk, his arrangement of Plato's Works, 106
Music, in education, pp. 214, 479, 542; art of, 572 sq.; in the universe, 348, 140
Myths, 160–163, 194, note 66; 396, 502

NATURE, explanation of, 338; life according to, 600 (Xenocrates'), 617 (Polemo)
Necessity and Reason both causes of the world, pp. 295, 337
Notion, ordinary, or envisagement, 170, 583
νοῦς, pp. 262, 337 sq.; and διάνοια, 218, 147
Numbers, Platonic theory of, 254, sqq., 517; Speusippus', 572; Xenocrates', 586; The Epinomis, 613

ONE, The, and The Good, pp. 285, 569; and The Many, 231, 252
ὄνομα and ῥῆμα, 214, 130
Opinion, and Knowledge, 171 sqq., 416
Oral teaching compared with written, 26
Order of Plato's writings, 93 sqq.
Other, The, and The Same, 278, 342, 347, 357

PAMPHILUS, a Platonist, 554, 1
Parentage, influence of, 422; supervision of, pp 477, 541
Perception, relation of, to knowledge, pp. 170, 171, 218, 428, 583
Perictione, Plato's mother, 4, 3
Personality, seat of, 417; of God, pp. 286, 289; of the created, gods, 385

Phenomena, relation of, to ideas, 314 sqq.
Philip of Macedon, relation to Plato, 35, 76
Philippus of Opus, 50, 13; 552, 561. See *Epinomis*
Philolaus, the Pythagorean, works purchased by Plato in Italy, 20, 34
Philosophy, Platonic, relation to the Socratic, 144 ; to the Pre-Socratic, 147; method, 150; dialogic form, 153, myths, 160; division of the system, 164, Propædeutic, 170-214; dialectic, or doctrine of ideas, 225-277; physics, 293, 386, Man, 388-433, ethics, 435-492; relation to religion, 494-503; to art, 505-514; later form of, 517-548; of the Academy, 565-622
Phocion, a Platonist, 30, 64
Phormio, ibid.
Physics, Plato's, 293-433, Speusippus', 576, Xenocrates', 594
Physiological theories of Plato, 421 sqq.
Plants, soul of, 416, 83, 432
Plato, authorities for his biography, 1, 1; birth, 2, 2; family, 3; wealth, 4; childhood and youth, 5-9; relation to Socrates, 9; sojourn at Megara, 14; travels, 15, first visit to Sicily, 23; teaching in the Academy, 25; attitude to politics, 29, second and third Silician journeys, 32; death, 35; character, 36; relations with other Socratics, 36, 85; alleged plagiarism, 38; Apolline myths, 44
Plutarch of Chæronea, 348, 140; 364, 5
Poetry, cultivated by Plato in his youth, 8; his estimation of, pp. 572, 578
Polemo, 617
Posidonius of Apamea, relation to Plato, 355, 154

Prayer, pp. 497, 499
Pre-existence, 389 sq., 404, 407
Priests, in the Laws, 502
Providence, Divine, 498
Prudence, meaning of, in the Laws, 524, 529
Punishment, end of, 447, 36
Pythagoreans, Plato's first acquaintance with, 20; relation of Plato's philosophy to, pp. 233, 527, 555, 556
Pytho, a Platonist, 30, 64

QUANTITY, Plato's category of, 277; in Motion, Speusippus' definition of Time, 578

REASON, see νοῦς, connected with sphere of fixed stars, 359; and Necessity, see Necessity; Relation to Courage and Desire, 414
Recollection, 406-410
Religion, Plato's views on, 494 sq.; in the Laws, 525; popular, 500, 591, 613
Republic, see State, when composed, 141
Retribution, future, 391 sq., 407 sq.
Rhetoric, 190, 514; Plato's opinion of
Rulers in the Republic must be Philosophers, 466; class of, omitted in the Laws, 531

SCHLEIERMACHER'S classification of the Dialogues, 99
Sense, relation to Reason, 436 sqq.
Sensuous Perception, pp 170, 428, 609, 23
Sex, Difference of, 433
Sicily, Plato's journeys to, pp. 15, 29

628　　　　　　　　INDEX.

Smell, Plato's theory of, 428, 113
Socher and Stallbaum, their chronological arrangement of Plato's works, 101
Socrates, Plato's relation to, 9; manner of life different from Plato's, 41; personality in the Dialogues, 159; connection of his philosophy with Plato's, see Platonic Philosophy
Sophistic, 183-189
Sophron, writer of Mimes before Plato's time, 155, 12
Soul, of the Universe, see World-soul; human, 389 sqq.; relation to the body, 421; in the Laws, 527; Theory of Xenocrates, 591; of Heraclides, 609; of the Epinomis, 614; Plato's tripartite division of the, 413
Space, 305, 312
Speech, see Language
Speusippus, 553-578; theory of knowledge, 566; first principles, the Good and the Soul, 568; Numbers and Magnitudes, 572-575, Physics, 576; Ethics, 578
Spheres, heavenly, 379 sqq.
Stars, Theories of Plato on the, 357, 379-382, 499, Xenocrates, 591, Heraclides, 608-610; The Epinomis, 614
State, end and problem of, 461; Philosophy the condition of the true, 466; Aristocratic character of Plato's, 869; based on his whole system, 473; Social regulations of the, 477-481, whence Plato derived his ideal, 482; affinity with modern, 490; defective States, 492; of the Republic and the Laws compared, 533
Steeds of the soul, in the Phædrus, 392, 12
Suicide disallowed by Plato, 459

TELEOLOGICAL view of Nature, 338
Temperance, 452, 529
θεία μοῖρα, 176, 20
Theætetus of Heraclea, ⎫
Timolaus, ⎬ Platonists, 554, 1
Timonides, ⎭
Timotheus, ibid. 30, 64
Theodorus instructed Plato in Mathematics, 21
Thought, all stages of, included in Philosophy, 220 sq.
Thrasyllus' arrangement of the Dialogues, 98, 15; 99
Time, Plato's theory of, 366, 382; Speusippus', 578; Xenocrates', 595
Tones, musical, in the Timæus, 348, 140; Heraclides' theory of, 607, 14
Transmigration, 391, 406 sqq.

UNITY and Duality, how regarded by Plato, 279, 146, 518; by Xenocrates, 584, by the Platonic Schools, 322, 83
Universal, Nature of, and relation to the Particular, 240, 337 sq; Law as a, 468
Universe, see World
Unlimited, not identified with Matter by Plato, 521

VIRTUE, 444; Socratic and Platonic doctrine of, 448, Natural disposition to, 449; Customary and philosophic, 450; Plurality of, 451, Primary, 451; consists in harmony, 474
Void, the, Space, 305

WEISSE'S arrangement of the Dialogues, 107
Wisdom, Plato's definition of, in

the Republic, 452; in the Laws, 529
Wives, Community of, 481, 485
Women, Plato's opinions about, 456, 487, 542
World, Origin of the, 363 sqq.; according to Plato, 363 sqq.; Xenocrates, 595; Crantor, 619; periodical changes in the, 382, 383; shape of the, 376, perfection of the, 387; system, 379 sqq., 608, 609
World-soul, Plato's theory of the, 341 sqq.; Speusippus', 570; Xenocrates', 592; Crantor's, 619; Evil, in the Laws, 543

XENOCRATES, 581; his explanation of the Timæus, 355, 154, 364, 5; character, 588; Triple division of Philosophy, 582; the theory of Knowledge, 583; of Unity and Duality, 584; of Numbers, 584 sq.; Magnitudes, indivisible lines, 587, the Soul, 589; Cosmology, 591; Dæmons, 593, Elements, formation of the world, 595; Psychology, 596; Ethics, 597
Xenophon, his alleged enmity with Plato, 37, 85; conjectured authorship of the Second Alcibiades, 50, 13

YEAR, the Cosmical, 382

ZENO, his writings, 155, 12; relation of Plato's method to that of, 203
Zeus, 287, 172; 387, 500, 592

⁂ This Index has been compiled (with some additions) from Dr. Zeller's Register to the 'Philosophie der Griechen.'

LONDON : PRINTED BY
SPOTTISWOODE AND CO, NEW-STREET SQUARE
AND PARLIAMENT STREET

WORKS IN GREEK LITERATURE.

THE STOICS, EPICUREANS, and SCEPTICS. Translated from the German of Dr. E. ZELLER, Professor in the University of Heidelberg, with the Author's approval, by the Rev. OSWALD J. REICHEL, B.C.L. and M.A. Vice-Principal of Cuddesden College. 8vo. 14s.

SOCRATES and the SOCRATIC SCHOOLS. Translated from the German of Dr. E. ZELLER, with the Author's approval, by the Rev. OSWALD J. REICHEL, B.C.L. and M.A. Vice-Principal of Cuddesden College. 8vo. 8s. 6d.

ARISTOTLE'S POLITICS; the Greek Text of Books I. III. and VII. With a Translation by W. E. BOLLAND, M.A. late Post Master of Merton College, Oxford; and with Introductory Essays by A. LANG, B.A. late Fellow of Merton College, Oxford. [*In the press.*

ARISTOTLE'S POLITICS; Greek Text, with English Notes. By RICHARD CONGREVE, M.A. formerly Fellow and Tutor of Wadham College, Oxford. New Edition, revised, 8vo. 18s.

ARISTOTLE'S ETHICS; Greek Text, illustrated with Essays and Notes. By Sir ALEXANDER GRANT, Bart. M.A. LL.D. Principal of the Edinburgh University. Third Edition, revised and in great part rewritten. 2 vols. 8vo. 32s.

ARISTOTLE'S NICHOMACHEAN ETHICS. Newly Translated into English. By ROBERT WILLIAMS, B.A. Fellow and late Lecturer of Merton College, Oxford. 8vo. 12s.

Greek Literature.

PINDAR'S EPINICIAN or TRIUMPHAL ODES. In Four Books; together with the Fragments of his Lost Compositions. Revised and Explained by J. W. DONALDSON, M.A. 8vo. 16s.

XENOPHON'S EXPEDITION of CYRUS into UPPER ASIA; principally from the Text of SCHNEIDER. with English Notes by JOHN T. WHITE, D.D. Oxon Latest Edition. 12mo. price 7s. 6d.

NOTES on THUCYDIDES, Books I. II and III. Original and Compiled. By J. G. SHEPPARD, M.A. and L. EVANS, M.A. Second Edition. Crown 8vo. 10s. 6d.

THUCYDIDES' HISTORY of the PELOPONNESIAN WAR. Translated into English by RICHARD CRAWLEY, Fellow (non-Resident) of Worcester College, Oxford; and formerly Scholar of University College, Oxford. 8vo. 10s. 6d.

A SHORT HISTORY of GREEK CLASSICAL LITERATURE. By the Rev. J. P. MAHAFFY, M A Trin. Coll. Dublin, Author of 'Social Life in Greece,' &c. 1 vol. crown 8vo.
[*In preparation*

SPEECHES of THUCYDIDES, translated into English for the use of Students; with an Introduction and Notes. By HENRY MUSGRAVE WILKINS, M.A. 8vo. 6s.

SCRIPTORES ATTICI; a Collection of Excerpts from *Xenophon, Thucydides, Plato, Aristotle,* and *Lucian,* with English Notes, adapted for the Use of Middle Forms. By HENRY MUSGRAVE WILKINS, M.A. Crown 8vo. 7s. 6d.

A PROGRESSIVE GREEK ANTHOLOGY, containing the First Four Books of the Odyssey; Extracts from Anacreon, Simonides, Tyrtæus, Sappho, Erinna, Mimnermus, Solon, Theognis, Plato, Theocritus, Callimachus, Moschus, Meleager, Euripides, &c. with English Notes. By HENRY MUSGRAVE WILKINS, M.A. 12mo. 5s.

London, LONGMANS & CO.

MARCH 1886.

GENERAL LISTS OF WORKS
PUBLISHED BY
Messrs. LONGMANS, GREEN, & CO.
PATERNOSTER ROW, LONDON.

HISTORY, POLITICS, HISTORICAL MEMOIRS, &c.

Arnold's Lectures on Modern History. 8vo. 7s. 6d.
Bagwell's Ireland under the Tudors. Vols. 1 and 2. 2 vols. 8vo. 32s.
Beaconsfield's (Lord) Speeches, edited by Kebbel. 2 vols. 8vo 32s.
Boultbee's History of the Church of England, Pre-Reformation Period. 8vo. 15s.
Bramston & Leroy's Historic Winchester. Crown 8vo. 6s.
Buckle's History of Civilisation. 3 vols. crown 8vo. 24s.
Chesney's Waterloo Lectures. 8vo. 10s. 6d.
Cox's (Sir G. W.) General History of Greece. Crown 8vo. Maps, 7s. 6d.
— — Lives of Greek Statesmen. Two Series. Fcp. 8vo. 2s. 6d. each.
Creighton's History of the Papacy during the Reformation. 2 vols. 8vo. 32s.
De Tocqueville's Democracy in America, translated by Reeve. 2 vols. crown 8vo. 16s.
Doyle's English in America. 8vo. 18s.
Epochs of Ancient History :—
    Beesly's Gracchi, Marius, and Sulla, 2s. 6d.
    Capes's Age of the Antonines, 2s. 6d.
    — Early Roman Empire, 2s. 6d.
    Cox's Athenian Empire, 2s. 6d.
    — Greeks and Persians, 2s. 6d.
    Curteis's Rise of the Macedonian Empire, 2s. 6d.
    Ihne's Rome to its Capture by the Gauls, 2s. 6d.
    Merivale's Roman Triumvirates, 2s. 6d.
    Sankey's Spartan and Theban Supremacies, 2s. 6d.
    Smith's Rome and Carthage, the Punic Wars, 2s. 6d.
Epochs of Modern History —
    Church's Beginning of the Middle Ages, 2s. 6d.
    Cox's Crusades, 2s. 6d.
    Creighton's Age of Elizabeth, 2s. 6d.
    Gairdner's Houses of Lancaster and York, 2s. 6d.
    Gardiner's Puritan Revolution, 2s 6d.
    — Thirty Years' War, 2s. 6d.
    — (Mrs.) French Revolution, 1789-1795, 2s. 6d.
    Hale's Fall of the Stuarts, 2s. 6d.
    Johnson's Normans in Europe, 2s. 6d.
    Longman's Frederick the Great and the Seven Years' War, 2s. 6d.
    Ludlow's War of American Independence, 2s 6d.
    M'Carthy's Epoch of Reform, 1830-1850, 2s. 6d.
    Morris's Age of Queen Anne, 2s. 6d.
    — The Early Hanoverians, 2s. 6d.
    Seebohm's Protestant Revolution, 2s. 6d.
    Stubbs's Early Plantagenets, 2s. 6d.
    Warburton's Edward III , 2s. 6d.
Freeman's Historical Geography of Europe. 2 vols. 8vo. 31s. 6d.

London : LONGMANS, GREEN, & CO.

Froude's English in Ireland in the 18th Century. 3 vols. crown 8vo. 18s.
— History of England. Popular Edition. 12 vols. crown 8vo 3s. 6d. each.
Gardiner's History of England from the Accession of James I. to the Outbreak of the Civil War. 10 vols. crown 8vo 60s.
— Outline of English History, B.C. 55–A.D. 1880. Fcp. 8vo. 2s. 6d.
Grant's (Sir Alex.) The Story of the University of Edinburgh. 2 vols. 8vo. 38s.
Greville's Journal of the Reigns of George IV. & William IV. 3 vols. 8vo. 36s.
— — — Reign of Queen Victoria, 1837-1852. 3 vols. 8vo. 36s.
Hickson's Ireland in the Seventeenth Century. 2 vols. 8vo. 28s.
Lecky's History of England in the Eighteenth Century. Vols. 1 & 2, 1700-1760, 8vo. 36s. Vols. 3 & 4, 1760-1784, 8vo 36s.
— History of European Morals. 2 vols. crown 8vo. 16s.
— — Rationalism in Europe. 2 vols. crown 8vo. 16s.
— Leaders of Public Opinion in Ireland. Crown 8vo. 7s. 6d.
Longman's Lectures on the History of England. 8vo. 15s.
— Life and Times of Edward III. 2 vols. 8vo. 28s.
Macaulay's Complete Works. Library Edition. 8 vols. 8vo. £5. 5s.
— — Cabinet Edition. 16 vols. crown 8vo. £4. 16s.
— History of England :—
Student's Edition. 2 vols. cr. 8vo. 12s. | Cabinet Edition. 8 vols. post 8vo. 48s.
People's Edition. 4 vols. cr 8vo. 16s. | Library Edition. 5 vols. 8vo. £4.
Macaulay's Critical and Historical Essays, with Lays of Ancient Rome In One Volume :—
Authorised Edition. Cr. 8vo. 2s. 6d. | Popular Edition. Cr. 8vo. 2s. 8d.
or 3s. 6d. gilt edges.
Macaulay's Critical and Historical Essays :—
Student's Edition. 1 vol. cr. 8vo. 6s. | Cabinet Edition. 4 vols. post 8vo. 24s.
People's Edition. 2 vols. cr. 8vo. 8s. | Library Edition. 3 vols. 8vo. 36s.
Macaulay's Speeches corrected by Himself. Crown 8vo. 3s. 8d.
Malmesbury's (Earl of) Memoirs of an Ex-Minister. Crown 8vo. 7s. 6d.
Maxwell's (Sir W. S.) Don John of Austria. Library Edition, with numerous Illustrations. 2 vols. royal 8vo. 42s.
May's Constitutional History of England, 1760-1870. 3 vols. crown 8vo. 18s.
— Democracy in Europe. 2 vols. 8vo. 32s.
Merivale's Fall of the Roman Republic. 12mo. 7s. 6d.
— General History of Rome, B.C. 753-A.D. 476. Crown 8vo. 7s. 6d.
— History of the Romans under the Empire. 8 vols post 8vo. 48s.
Noble's The Russian Revolt Fcp. 8vo. 5s.
Pears' The Fall of Constantinople. 8vo. 16s.
Seebohm's Oxford Reformers—Colet, Erasmus, & More. 8vo. 14s.
Short's History of the Church of England. Crown 8vo. 7s. 6d.
Smith's Carthage and the Carthaginians. Crown 8vo. 10s. 6d.
Taylor's Manual of the History of India. Crown 8vo 7s. 8d.
Walpole's History of England, 1815-1841. 3 vols. 8vo. £2. 14s.
Wylie's History of England under Henry IV. Vol. 1, crown 8vo. 10s. 6d.

BIOGRAPHICAL WORKS.

Bacon's Life and Letters, by Spedding. 7 vols. 8vo. £4. 4s.
Bagehot's Biographical Studies. 1 vol. 8vo. 12s.

London: LONGMANS, GREEN, & CO.

Carlyle's Life, by Froude. Vols. 1 & 2, 1795-1835, 8vo. 32s. Vols. 3 & 4, 1834-1881, 8vo. 32s.
— (Mrs.) Letters and Memorials 3 vols. 8vo. 36s.
De Witt (John), Life of, by A. C. Pontalis. Translated. 2 vols. 8vo. 36s.
English Worthies Edited by Andrew Lang. Crown 8vo. 2s. 6d. each.
    Charles Darwin, by Grant Allen. | Marlborough, by George Saintsbury.
Grimston's (Hon. R.) Life, by F. Gale. Crown 8vo. 10s. 6d.
Hamilton's (Sir W. R.) Life, by Graves. Vols. 1 and 2, 8vo. 15s. each.
Havelock's Life, by Marshman. Crown 8vo. 3s. 6d.
Hullah's (John) Life. By his Wife. Crown 8vo. 8s.
Macaulay's (Lord) Life and Letters. By his Nephew, G. Otto Trevelyan, M.P. Popular Edition, 1 vol. crown 8vo. 6s. Cabinet Edition, 2 vols. post 8vo. 12s Library Edition, 2 vols. 8vo. 36s.
Mendelssohn's Letters. Translated by Lady Wallace. 2 vols. cr. 8vo. 5s. each.
Mill (James) Biography of, by Prof. Bain. Crown 8vo. 5s.
— (John Stuart) Recollections of, by Prof. Bain. Crown 8vo. 2s. 6d.
— — Autobiography. 8vo. 7s. 6d.
Mozley's Reminiscences of Oriel College. 2 vols. crown 8vo. 18s.
— — Towns, Villages, and Schools. 2 vols. cr. 8vo. 18s.
Müller's (Max) Biographical Essays. Crown 8vo 7s. 6d.
Newman's Apologia pro Vitâ Suâ. Crown 8vo. 6s.
Pasolini's (Count) Memoir, by his Son. 8vo. 16s.
Pasteur (Louis) His Life and Labours. Crown 8vo. 7s. 6d.
Shakespeare's Life (Outlines of), by Halliwell-Phillipps. Royal 8vo. 7s 6d.
Southey's Correspondence with Caroline Bowles. 8vo. 14s.
Stephen's Essays in Ecclesiastical Biography. Crown 8vo. 7s. 6d.
Taylor's (Sir Henry) Autobiography. 2 vols. 8vo. 32s.
Telfer's The Strange Career of the Chevalier D'Eon de Beaumont 8vo. 12s.
Trevelyan's Early History of Charles James Fox. Crown 8vo. 6s.
Wellington's Life, by Gleig. Crown 8vo. 6s.

MENTAL AND POLITICAL PHILOSOPHY, FINANCE, &c.

Amos's View of the Science of Jurisprudence. 8vo. 18s.
— Primer of the English Constitution. Crown 8vo. 6s.
Bacon's Essays, with Annotations by Whately. 8vo. 10s. 6d.
— Works, edited by Spedding. 7 vols. 8vo. 73s. 6d.
Bagehot's Economic Studies, edited by Hutton. 8vo. 10s. 6d.
— The Postulates of English Political Economy. Crown 8vo. 2s. 6d.
Bain's Logic, Deductive and Inductive. Crown 8vo. 10s. 6d.
    PART I. Deduction, 4s. | PART II. Induction, 6s. 6d.
— Mental and Moral Science. Crown 8vo. 10s. 6d.
— The Senses and the Intellect 8vo. 15s.
— The Emotions and the Will. 8vo. 15s.
— Practical Essays. Crown 8vo. 4s. 6d.
Buckle's (H. T.) Miscellaneous and Posthumous Works 2 vols. crown 8vo 21s.
Crozier's Civilization and Progress. 8vo. 14s.
Crump's A Short Enquiry into the Formation of English Political Opinion. 8vo. 7s 6d.
Dowell's A History of Taxation and Taxes in England. 4 vols. 8vo. 48s.
Green's (Thomas Hill) Works. (3 vols.) Vol. 1, Philosophical Works. 8vo 16s.

London: LONGMANS, GREEN, & CO

Hume's Essays, edited by Green & Grose. 2 vols. 8vo. 28s.
— Treatise of Human Nature, edited by Green & Grose. 2 vols. 8vo. 28s.
Lang's Custom and Myth : Studies of Early Usage and Belief. Crown 8vo. 7s. 6d.
Leslie's Essays in Political and Moral Philosophy. 8vo. 10s. 6d.
Lewes's History of Philosophy. 2 vols. 8vo. 32s.
List's Natural System of Political Economy, translated by S. Lloyd, M.P. 8vo. 10s. 6d.
Lubbock's Origin of Civilisation. 8vo. 18s.
Macleod's Principles of Economical Philosophy. In 2 vols. Vol. 1, 8vo. 15s. Vol. 2, Part I. 12s.
— The Elements of Economics. (2 vols.) Vol. 1, cr. 8vo. 7s. 6d. Vol 2, Part I. cr. 8vo. 7s. 6d.
— The Elements of Banking. Crown 8vo. 5s.
— The Theory and Practice of Banking. Vol. 1, 8vo. 12s.
— Elements of Political Economy. 8vo. 16s.
— Economics for Beginners. 8vo. 2s. 6d.
— Lectures on Credit and Banking. 8vo. 5s.
Mill's (James) Analysis of the Phenomena of the Human Mind. 2 vols. 8vo. 28s.
Mill (John Stuart) on Representative Government. Crown 8vo. 2s.
— — on Liberty. Crown 8vo. 1s. 4d.
— — Essays on Unsettled Questions of Political Economy. 8vo. 6s. 6d.
— — Examination of Hamilton's Philosophy. 8vo. 16s.
— — Logic. 2 vols. 8vo. 25s. People's Edition, 1 vol. cr. 8vo. 5s.
— — Principles of Political Economy. 2 vols. 8vo. 30s. People's Edition, 1 vol. crown 8vo. 5s.
— — Subjection of Women. Crown 8vo. 6s.
— — Utilitarianism. 8vo. 5s.
— — Three Essays on Religion, &c. 8vo. 5s.
Miller's (Mrs. Fenwick) Readings in Social Economy. Crown 8vo. 2s.
Mulhall's History of Prices since 1850. Crown 8vo. 6s.
Sandars's Institutes of Justinian. with English Notes. 8vo. 18s.
Seebohm's English Village Community. 8vo. 16s.
Sully's Outlines of Psychology. 8vo. 12s. 6d.
Swinburne's Picture Logic. Post 8vo. 5s.
Thompson's A System of Psychology. 2 vols. 8vo. 36s.
Thomson's Outline of Necessary Laws of Thought. Crown 8vo. 6s.
Twiss's Law of Nations in Time of War. 8vo. 21s.
— — in Time of Peace. 8vo. 15s.
Webb's The Veil of Isis. 8vo. 10s. 6d.
Whately's Elements of Logic. Crown 8vo. 4s. 6d.
— — Rhetoric. Crown 8vo. 4s. 6d.
Wylie's Labour, Leisure, and Luxury. Crown 8vo. 6s.
Zeller's History of Eclecticism in Greek Philosophy. Crown 8vo. 10s. 6d.
— Plato and the Older Academy. Crown 8vo. 18s.
— Pre-Socratic Schools. 2 vols. crown 8vo. 30s.
— Socrates and the Socratic Schools. Crown 8vo. 10s. 6d.
— Stoics, Epicureans, and Sceptics. Crown 8vo. 15s.
— Outlines of the History of Greek Philosophy Crown 8vo. 10s. 6d.

London : LONGMANS, GREEN, & CO.

MISCELLANEOUS WORKS.

A. K. H. B., The Essays and Contributions of. Crown 8vo.
    Autumn Holidays of a Country Parson. 3s. 6d.
    Changed Aspects of Unchanged Truths. 2s. 6d.
    Common-Place Philosopher in Town and Country. 3s. 6d.
    Critical Essays of a Country Parson. 3s. 6d.
    Counsel and Comfort spoken from a City Pulpit. 3s. 6d.
    Graver Thoughts of a Country Parson. Three Series. 3s. 6d. each
    Landscapes, Churches, and Moralities. 3s. 6d.
    Leisure Hours in Town. 3s. 6d. Lessons of Middle Age. 3s. 6d.
    Our Little Life. Essays Consolatory and Domestic. Two Series 3s. 6d.
    Present-day Thoughts 3s. 6d. [each.
    Recreations of a Country Parson. Three Series. 3s. 6d. each.
    Seaside Musings on Sundays and Week-Days. 3s. 6d.
    Sunday Afternoons in the Parish Church of a University City. 3s. 6d.
Arnold's (Dr. Thomas) Miscellaneous Works. 8vo. 7s. 6d.
Bagehot's Literary Studies, edited by Hutton. 2 vols. 8vo. 28s.
Beaconsfield (Lord), The Wit and Wisdom of Crown 8vo. 3s. 6d.
   — (The) Birthday Book. 18mo. 2s. 6d. cloth ; 4s. 6d. bound.
Evans's Bronze Implements of Great Britain. 8vo. 25s.
Farrar's Language and Languages. Crown 8vo. 6s.
French's Nineteen Centuries of Drink in England. Crown 8vo. 10s. 6d.
Froude's Short Studies on Great Subjects. 4 vols. crown 8vo. 24s.
Lang's Letters to Dead Authors. Fcp. 8vo. 6s. 6d.
Macaulay's Miscellaneous Writings. 2 vols. 8vo. 21s. 1 vol. crown 8vo. 4s. 6d.
   — Miscellaneous Writings and Speeches. Crown 8vo. 6s.
   — Miscellaneous Writings, Speeches, Lays of Ancient Rome, &c. Cabinet Edition. 4 vols. crown 8vo. 24s.
   — Writings, Selections from. Crown 8vo. 6s.
Müller's (Max) Lectures on the Science of Language. 2 vols. crown 8vo. 16s.
   — Lectures on India. 8vo 12s. 6d.
Smith (Sydney) The Wit and Wisdom of. Crown 8vo. 3s. 6d.

ASTRONOMY.

Herschal's Outlines of Astronomy. Square crown 8vo. 12s.
Nelson's Work on the Moon. Medium 8vo. 31s. 6d.
Proctor's Larger Star Atlas Folio. 15s or Maps only, 12s 6d.
   — New Star Atlas. Crown 8vo. 5s Orbs Around Us. Crown 8vo. 5s.
   — Light Science for Leisure Hours. 3 Series. Crown 8vo. 5s. each.
   — Moon. Crown 8vo. 10s. 6d.
   — Myths and Marvels of Astronomy. Crown 8vo. 6s.
   — Other Worlds than Ours. Crown 8vo. 5s.
   — Sun. Crown 8vo 14s. Universe of Stars. 8vo. 10s. 6d.
   — Pleasant Ways in Science. Crown 8vo. 6s.
   — Studies of Venus-Transits. 8vo. 5s.
Webb's Celestial Objects for Common Telescopes. Crown 8vo. 9s.
   — The Sun and his Phenomena. Fcp. 8vo. 1s.

THE 'KNOWLEDGE' LIBRARY.
Edited by RICHARD A. PROCTOR.

How to Play Whist. Crown 8vo. 5s.	Star Primer. Crown 4to. 2s. 6d.
The Borderland of Science. Cr. 8vo. 6s.	The Seasons Pictured. Demy 4to. 5s.
Nature Studies. Crown 8vo 6s.	Strength and Happiness. Cr. 8vo. 5s.
Leisure Readings. Crown 8vo. 6s.	Rough Ways made Smooth. Cr. 8vo. 6s.
The Stars in their Seasons. Imp. 8vo 5s.	The Expanse of Heaven Cr. 8vo. 5s.
Home Whist. 16mo. 1s.	Our Place among Infinities. Cr. 8vo. 5s.

London : LONGMANS, GREEN, & CO.

CLASSICAL LANGUAGES AND LITERATURE.

Æschylus, The Eumenides of. Text, with Metrical English Translation, by J. F. Davies. 8vo. 7s.
Aristophanes' The Acharnians, translated by R. Y. Tyrrell. Crown 8vo. 2s. 6d.
Aristotle's The Ethics, Text and Notes, by Sir Alex. Grant, Bart. 2 vols. 8vo. 32s.
— The Nicomachean Ethics, translated by Williams, crown 8vo. 7s. 6d.
— The Politics, Books I. III. IV. (VII.) with Translation, &c. by Bolland and Lang. Crown 8vo. 7s. 6d.
Becker's *Charicles* and *Gallus*, by Metcalfe. Post 8vo. 7s. 6d. each.
Cicero's Correspondence, Text and Notes, by R. Y. Tyrrell. Vol. 1, 8vo. 12s.
Homer's Iliad, Homometrically translated by Cayley. 8vo. 12s. 6d.
— Greek Text, with Verse Translation, by W. C. Green. Vol. 1, Books I.–XII. Crown 8vo. 6s.
Mahaffy's Classical Greek Literature. Crown 8vo. Vol. 1, The Poets, 7s. 6d. Vol. 2, The Prose Writers, 7s. 6d.
Plato's Parmenides, with Notes, &c. by J. Maguire. 8vo. 7s. 6d.
Sophocles' Tragœdiæ Superstites, by Linwood. 8vo. 16s.
Virgil's Works, Latin Text, with Commentary, by Kennedy. Crown 8vo. 10s. 8d.
— Æneid, translated into English Verse, by Conington. Crown 8vo. 9s.
— Poems, — Prose, — Crown 8vo. 9s.
Witt's Myths of Hellas, translated by F. M. Younghusband. Crown 8vo. 3s. 6d.
— The Trojan War, — — Fcp. 8vo. 2s.
— The Wanderings of Ulysses, — Crown 8vo. 3s. 6d.

NATURAL HISTORY, BOTANY, & GARDENING.

Allen's Flowers and their Pedigrees. Crown 8vo. Woodcuts, 5s.
Decaisne and Le Maout's General System of Botany. Imperial 8vo. 31s. 8d.
Dixon's Rural Bird Life. Crown 8vo. Illustrations, 5s.
Hartwig's Aerial World, 8vo. 10s. 6d.
— Polar World, 8vo. 10s. 6d.
— Sea and its Living Wonders. 8vo. 10s. 6d.
— Subterranean World, 8vo. 10s. 6d.
— Tropical World, 8vo. 10s. 6d.
Lindley's Treasury of Botany. Fcp. 8vo. 6s.
London's Encyclopædia of Gardening. 8vo. 21s.
— — Plants. 8vo. 42s.
Rivers's Orchard House. Crown 8vo. 5s.
— Rose Amateur's Guide. Fcp. 8vo. 4s. 6d.
— Miniature Fruit Garden. Fcp. 8vo. 4s.
Stanley's Familiar History of British Birds. Crown 8vo. 6s.
Wood's Bible Animals. With 112 Vignettes. 8vo. 10s. 6d.
— Common British Insects. Crown 8vo. 3s. 6d.
— Homes Without Hands, 8vo. 10s. 6d.
— Insects Abroad, 8vo. 10s. 6d.
— Horse and Man. 8vo. 14s.
— Insects at Home. With 700 Illustrations. 8vo. 10s. 6d.
— Out of Doors. Crown 8vo. 5s.
— Petland Revisited. Crown 8vo. 7s. 6d.
— Strange Dwellings. Crown 8vo. 5s. Popular Edition, 4to. 6d.

London: LONGMANS, GREEN, & CO.

THE FINE ARTS AND ILLUSTRATED EDITIONS.

Dresser's Arts and Art Manufactures of Japan Square crown 8vo. 31s. 6d.
Eastlake's Household Taste in Furniture, &c. Square crown 8vo. 14s.
Jameson's Sacred and Legendary Art. 6 vols. square 8vo.
    Legends of the Madonna 1 vol. 21s.
    — — — Monastic Orders 1 vol. 21s.
    — — — Saints and Martyrs. 2 vols. 31s. 6d.
    — — — Saviour. Completed by Lady Eastlake. 2 vols. 42s.
Macaulay's Lays of Ancient Rome, illustrated by Scharf. Fcp. 4to. 10s. 6d.
The same, with *Ivry* and the *Armada*, illustrated by Weguelin. Crown 8vo. 3s. 6d.
Moore's Lalla Rookh, illustrated by Tenniel. Square crown 8vo. 10s. 6d.
New Testament (The) illustrated with Woodcuts after Paintings by the Early Masters. 4to. 21s. cloth, or 42s morocco
Perry on Greek and Roman Sculpture. With 280 Illustrations engraved on Wood. Square crown 8vo. 31s 6d.

CHEMISTRY, ENGINEERING, & GENERAL SCIENCE.

Arnott's Elements of Physics or Natural Philosophy. Crown 8vo. 12s. 6d.
Bourne's Catechism of the Steam Engine. Crown 8vo. 7s. 6d.
    — Examples of Steam, Air, and Gas Engines. 4to. 70s.
    — Handbook of the Steam Engine. Fcp. 8vo. 9s.
    — Recent Improvements in the Steam Engine. Fcp. 8vo. 6s.
    — Treatise on the Steam Engine. 4to. 42s.
Buckton's Our Dwellings, Healthy and Unhealthy. Crown 8vo. 3s. 6d.
Crookes's Select Methods in Chemical Analysis. 8vo 24s.
Culley's Handbook of Practical Telegraphy. 8vo. 16s.
Fairbairn's Useful Information for Engineers. 3 vols. crown 8vo. 31s. 6d.
    — Mills and Millwork. 1 vol. 8vo 25s.
Ganot's Elementary Treatise on Physics, by Atkinson. Large crown 8vo. 15s.
    — Natural Philosophy, by Atkinson. Crown 8vo. 7s. 6d.
Grove's Correlation of Physical Forces. 8vo. 15s.
Haughton's Six Lectures on Physical Geography. 8vo. 15s.
Heer's Primæval World of Switzerland. 2 vols. 8vo. 12s.
Helmholtz on the Sensations of Tone Royal 8vo. 28s.
Helmholtz's Lectures on Scientific Subjects. 2 vols. crown 8vo. 7s. 6d. each.
Hudson and Gosse's The Rotifera, or 'Wheel Animalcules.' With 30 Coloured Plates. 6 parts. 4to 10s. 6d. each.
Hullah's Lectures on the History of Modern Music. 8vo. 8s. 6d.
    — Transition Period of Musical History. 8vo. 10s. 6d.
Jackson's Aid to Engineering Solution. Royal 8vo. 21s.
Jago's Inorganic Chemistry, Theoretical and Practical. Fcp. 8vo. 2s.
Kerl's Metallurgy, adapted by Crookes and Rohrig. 3 vols. 8vo. £4. 19s.
Kolbe's Short Text-Book of Inorganic Chemistry. Crown 8vo. 7s. 6d.
Lloyd's Treatise on Magnetism. 8vo. 10s. 6d.
Macalister's Zoology and Morphology of Vertebrate Animals. 8vo. 10s. 6d.
Macfarren's Lectures on Harmony. 8vo. 12s.

London: LONGMANS, GREEN, & CO.

Miller's Elements of Chemistry, Theoretical and Practical. 3 vols. 8vo. Part I. Chemical Physics, 16s. Part II. Inorganic Chemistry, 24s. Part III. Organic Chemistry, price 31s. 6d.
Mitchell's Manual of Practical Assaying. 8vo. 31s. 6d.
Northcott's Lathes and Turning. 8vo. 18s.
Owen's Comparative Anatomy and Physiology of the Vertebrate Animals. 3 vols. 8vo. 73s. 6d.
Payen's Industrial Chemistry. Edited by B. H. Paul, Ph.D. 8vo. 42s.
Piesse's Art of Perfumery. Square crown 8vo. 21s.
Reynolds's Experimental Chemistry. Fcp. 8vo. Part I. 1s. 6d. Part II. 2s. 6d. Part III. 3s. 6d.
Schellen's Spectrum Analysis. 8vo. 31s. 6d.
Sennett's Treatise on the Marine Steam Engine. 8vo 21s.
Smith's Air and Rain. 8vo. 24s.
Stoney's The Theory of the Stresses on Girders, &c. Royal 8vo. 36s.
Swinton's Electric Lighting: Its Principles and Practice. Crown 8vo. 5s.
Tilden's Practical Chemistry. Fcp. 8vo. 1s. 6d.
Tyndall's Faraday as a Discoverer. Crown 8vo. 3s. 6d.
— Floating Matter of the Air. Crown 8vo. 7s. 6d.
— Fragments of Science. 2 vols. post 8vo. 16s.
— Heat a Mode of Motion. Crown 8vo. 12s.
— Lectures on Light delivered in America. Crown 8vo. 5s.
— Lessons on Electricity. Crown 8vo. 2s. 6d.
— Notes on Electrical Phenomena. Crown 8vo. 1s. sewed, 1s. 6d. cloth.
— Notes of Lectures on Light. Crown 8vo. 1s. sewed, 1s. 6d. cloth.
— Sound, with Frontispiece and 203 Woodcuts. Crown 8vo. 10s. 6d.
Watts's Dictionary of Chemistry. 9 vols. medium 8vo. £15. 2s. 6d.
Wilson's Manual of Health-Science. Crown 8vo. 2s. 6d.

THEOLOGICAL AND RELIGIOUS WORKS.

Arnold's (Rev. Dr. Thomas) Sermons. 6 vols. crown 8vo 5s. each.
Boultbee's Commentary on the 39 Articles. Crown 8vo. 6s.
Browne's (Bishop) Exposition of the 39 Articles. 8vo. 16s.
Colenso on the Pentateuch and Book of Joshua. Crown 8vo. 6s.
Conder's Handbook of the Bible. Post 8vo. 7s. 6d.
Conybeare & Howson's Life and Letters of St. Paul:—
 Library Edition, with Maps, Plates, and Woodcuts. 2 vols. square crown 8vo. 21s.
 Student's Edition, revised and condensed, with 46 Illustrations and Maps. 1 vol. crown 8vo. 7s. 6d.
Cox's (Homersham) The First Century of Christianity. 8vo. 12s.
Davidson's Introduction to the Study of the New Testament. 2 vols. 8vo. 30s.
Edersheim's Life and Times of Jesus the Messiah. 2 vols. 8vo. 42s.
— Prophecy and History in relation to the Messiah. 8vo. 12s.
Ellicott's (Bishop) Commentary on St. Paul's Epistles. 8vo. Galatians, 8s. 6d. Ephesians, 8s. 6d. Pastoral Epistles, 10s. 6d. Philippians, Colossians and Philemon, 10s. 6d. Thessalonians, 7s. 6d.
— Lectures on the Life of our Lord. 8vo. 12s.
Ewald's Antiquities of Israel, translated by Solly. 8vo. 12s. 6d.
— History of Israel, translated by Carpenter & Smith. Vols. 1-7, 8vo. £5.

London: LONGMANS, GREEN, & CO.

Hobart's Medical Language of St. Luke. 8vo. 16s.
Hopkins's Christ the Consoler. Fcp. 8vo. 2s. 6d.
Jukes's New Man and the Eternal Life. Crown 8vo. 6s.
— Second Death and the Restitution of all Things. Crown 8vo. 3s. 6d.
— Types of Genesis Crown 8vo. 7s. 6d.
— The Mystery of the Kingdom. Crown 8vo. 3s. 6d.
Lenormant's New Translation of the Book of Genesis. Translated into English. 8vo. 10s. 6d.
Lyra Germanica: Hymns translated by Miss Winkworth. Fcp 8vo. 5s.
Macdonald's (G.) Unspoken Sermons. Second Series. Crown 8vo. 7s. 6d.
Manning's Temporal Mission of the Holy Ghost. Crown 8vo. 8s. 6d.
Martineau's Endeavours after the Christian Life. Crown 8vo. 7s. 6d.
— Hymns of Praise and Prayer Crown 8vo. 4s. 6d. 32mo. 1s. 6d.
— Sermons, Hours of Thought on Sacred Things. 2 vols. 7s. 6d. each.
Monsell's Spiritual Songs for Sundays and Holidays. Fcp. 8vo. 5s 18mo. 2s.
Müller's (Max) Origin and Growth of Religion. Crown 8vo. 7s. 6d.
— — Science of Religion. Crown 8vo. 7s. 6d.
Newman's Apologia pro Vitâ Suâ. Crown 8vo. 6s.
— The Idea of a University Defined and Illustrated. Crown 8vo. 7s.
— Historical Sketches. 3 vols. crown 8vo. 6s. each.
— Discussions and Arguments on Various Subjects. Crown 8vo. 6s.
— An Essay on the Development of Christian Doctrine. Crown 8vo. 6s.
— Certain Difficulties Felt by Anglicans in Catholic Teaching Considered. Vol. 1, crown 8vo. 7s. 6d. Vol. 2, crown 8vo. 5s. 6d.
— The Via Media of the Anglican Church, Illustrated in Lectures, &c. 2 vols. crown 8vo 6s. each
— Essays, Critical and Historical. 2 vols. crown 8vo. 12s.
— Essays on Biblical and on Ecclesiastical Miracles. Crown 8vo. 6s.
— An Essay in Aid of a Grammar of Assent. 7s. 6d.
Overton's Life in the English Church (1660-1714). 8vo. 14s.
Rogers's Eclipse of Faith. Fcp. 8vo. 5s.
— Defence of the Eclipse of Faith. Fcp. 8vo. 3s. 6d.
Sewell's (Miss) Night Lessons from Scripture. 32mo. 3s. 6d.
— — Passing Thoughts on Religion. Fcp. 8vo. 3s. 6d.
— — Preparation for the Holy Communion. 32mo 3s.
Smith's Voyage and Shipwreck of St. Paul. Crown 8vo. 7s. 6d.
Supernatural Religion. Complete Edition. 3 vols. 8vo. 36s.
Taylor's (Jeremy) Entire Works. With Life by Bishop Heber. Edited by the Rev. C. P. Eden. 10 vols. 8vo. £5. 5s.
Tulloch's Movements of Religious Thought in Britain during the Nineteenth Century. Crown 8vo. 10s. 6d.

TRAVELS, ADVENTURES, &c.

Aldridge's Ranch Notes in Kansas, Colorado, &c. Crown 8vo. 5s.
Alpine Club (The) Map of Switzerland. In Four Sheets. 42s.
Baker's Eight Years in Ceylon. Crown 8vo. 5s.
— Rifle and Hound in Ceylon. Crown 8vo. 5s.
Ball's Alpine Guide. 3 vols. post 8vo. with Maps and Illustrations:—I. Western Alps, 6s. 6d. II. Central Alps, 7s 6d. III. Eastern Alps, 10s. 6d.
Ball on Alpine Travelling, and on the Geology of the Alps, 1s.

London: LONGMANS, GREEN, & CO.

Bent's The Cyclades, or Life among the Insular Greeks. Crown 8vo. 12s. 6d.
Brassey's Sunshine and Storm in the East. Crown 8vo. 7s. 6d.
— Voyage in the Yacht 'Sunbeam.' Crown 8vo. 7s. 6d. School Edition, fcp. 8vo 2s. Popular Edition, 4to. 6d.
— In the Trades, the Tropics, and the 'Roaring Forties.' Édition de Luxe, 8vo. £3. 13s. 6d. Library Edition, 8vo. 21s.
Crawford's Across the Pampas and the Andes. Crown 8vo. 7s. 6d.
Dent's Above the Snow Line. Crown 8vo. 7s. 6d.
Froude's Oceana; or, England and her Colonies 8vo. 18s.
Hassall's San Remo Climatically considered. Crown 8vo. 5s.
Howitt's Visits to Remarkable Places. Crown 8vo. 7s. 6d.
Maritime Alps (The) and their Seaboard. By the Author of 'Véra.' 8vo. 21s.
Three in Norway. By Two of Them. Crown 8vo. Illustrations, 6s.

WORKS OF FICTION.

Beaconsfield's (The Earl of) Novels and Tales. Hughenden Edition, with 2 Portraits on Steel and 11 Vignettes on Wood. 11 vols crown 8vo. £2. 2s. Cheap Edition, 11 vols. fcp. 8vo. 1s. each, sewed; 1s. 6d. each, cloth.
Black Poodle (The) and other Tales. By the Author of 'Vice Versâ.' Cr. 8vo. 6s.
Brabourne's (Lord) Friends and Foes from Fairyland. Crown 8vo. 6s.
Harte (Bret) On the Frontier. Three Stories. 16mo. 1s.
— — By Shore and Sedge. Three Stories. 16mo. 1s.
In the Olden Time. By the Author of 'Mademoiselle Mori.' Crown 8vo. 6s.
Melville's (Whyte) Novels. Cheap Edition. 8 vols. fcp. 8vo 1s. each, sewed; 1s. 6d. each, cloth.
The Modern Novelist's Library. Crown 8vo. price 2s. each, boards, or 2s. 6d. each, cloth :—

By the Earl of Beaconsfield, K G
  Lothair.
  Sybil.
  Coningsby.
  Tancred.
  Venetia.
  Henrietta Temple.
  Contarini Fleming.
  Alroy, Ixion, &c.
  The Young Duke, &c.
  Vivian Grey.
  Endymion.
By Bret Harte.
  In the Carquinez Woods.
By Mrs Oliphant.
  In Trust, the Story of a Lady and her Lover.
By James Payn.
  Thicker than Water.

By Anthony Trollope.
  Barchester Towers.
  The Warden.
By Major Whyte Melville.
  Digby Grand.
  General Bounce.
  Kate Coventry.
  The Gladiators.
  Good for Nothing.
  Holmby House.
  The Interpreter.
  The Queen's Maries.
By Various Writers.
  The Atelier du Lys.
  Atherstone Priory.
  The Burgomaster's Family.
  Elsa and her Vulture.
  Mademoiselle Mori.
  The Six Sisters of the Valleys.
  Unawares.

Oliphant's (Mrs.) Madam. Crown 8vo. 3s. 6d.
Payn's (James) The Luck of the Darrells. Crown 8vo. 3s. 6d.
Reader's Fairy Prince Follow-my-Lead Crown 8vo. 5s.
Sewell's (Miss) Stories and Tales. Cabinet Edition. Crown 8vo. cloth extra, gilt edges, price 3s. 6d. each :—
  Amy Herbert. Cleve Hall.
  The Earl's Daughter.
  Experience of Life.
  Gertrude. Ivors.
  A Glimpse of the World.
  Katharine Ashton.
  Laneton Parsonage.
  Margaret Percival. Ursula.

London: LONGMANS, GREEN, & CO.

General Lists of Works. 11

Stevenson's (R. L.) The Dynamiter. Fcp 8vo. 1s. sewed; 1s. 6d. cloth.
— — Strange Case of Dr. Jekyll and Mr. Hyde. Fcp. 8vo. 1s. sewed; 1s 6d. cloth.
Sturgis' My Friend and I. Crown 8vo. 5s.

POETRY AND THE DRAMA.

Bailey's Festus, a Poem. Crown 8vo. 12s. 6d.
Bowdler's Family Shakespeare. Medium 8vo. 14s. 6 vols. fcp. 8vo 21s.
Dante's Divine Comedy, translated by James Innes Minchin. Crown 8vo 15s.
Goethe's Faust, translated by Birds. Large crown 8vo. 12s. 6d.
— — translated by Webb. 8vo. 12s. 6d.
— — edited by Selss. Crown 8vo 5s.
Ingelow's Poems. Vols. 1 and 2, fcp. 8vo. 12s. Vol. 3 fcp. 8vo 5s.
Macaulay's Lays of Ancient Rome, with Ivry and the Armada. Illustrated by Weguelin. Crown 8vo. 3s. 6d. gilt edges.
The same, Annotated Edition, fcp 8vo. 1s. sewed, 1s. 6d. cloth, 2s. 6d. cloth extra.
The same, Popular Edition. Illustrated by Scharf. Fcp. 4to. 6d. swd, 1s. cloth.
Macdonald's (G.) A Book of Strife. in the Form of the Diary of an Old Soul: Poems. 12mo. 6s.
Pennell's (Cholmondeley) 'From Grave to Gay.' A Volume of Selections. Fcp 8vo. 8s.
Reader's Voices from Flowerland, a Birthday Book, 2s. 6d. cloth, 3s. 6d. roan.
Robinson's The New Arcadia, and other Poems Crown 8vo 6s
Shakespeare's Hamlet, annotated by George Macdonald, LL.D. 8vo. 12s.
Southey's Poetical Works. Medium 8vo. 14s.
Stevenson's A Child's Garden of Verses. Fcp. 8vo. 5s.
Virgil's Æneid, translated by Conington. Crown 8vo. 9s.
— Poems, translated into English Prose. Crown 8vo. 9s.

AGRICULTURE, HORSES, DOGS, AND CATTLE.

Dunster's How to Make the Land Pay. Crown 8vo. 5s.
Fitzwygram's Horses and Stables. 8vo. 10s. 6d.
Horses and Roads By Free-Lance. Crown 8vo. 6s.
Lloyd, The Science of Agriculture. 8vo. 12s.
London's Encyclopædia of Agriculture. 21s.
Miles's Horse's Foot, and How to Keep it Sound. Imperial 8vo. 12s. 6d.
— Plain Treatise on Horse-Shoeing. Post 8vo. 2s. 6d.
— Remarks on Horses' Teeth. Post 8vo. 1s. 6d.
— Stables and Stable-Fittings. Imperial 8vo. 15s.
Nevile's Farms and Farming. Crown 8vo. 6s.
— Horses and Riding. Crown 8vo. 6s.
Steel's Diseases of the Ox, a Manual of Bovine Pathology. 8vo. 15s.
Stonehenge's Dog in Health and Disease. Square crown 8vo. 7s. 6d.
— Greyhound. Square crown 8vo. 15s.
Taylor's Agricultural Note Book. Fcp. 8vo. 2s 6d.
Ville on Artificial Manures, by Crookes. 8vo. 21s.
Youatt's Work on the Dog. 8vo. 6s.
— — — — Horse. 8vo. 7s. 6d.

London: LONGMANS, GREEN, & CO.

SPORTS AND PASTIMES.

The Badminton Library of Sports and Pastimes. Edited by the Duke of Beaufort and A. E. T. Watson. With numerous Illustrations. Crown 8vo. 10s. 6d. each.

    Hunting, by the Duke of Beaufort, &c.
    Fishing, by H. Cholmondeley-Pennell, &c. 2 vols.
    Racing, by the Earl of Suffolk, &c.

Campbell-Walker's Correct Card, or How to Play at Whist. Fcp. 8vo. 2s. 6d.
Dead Shot (The) by Marksman. Crown 8vo. 10s. 6d.
Francis's Treatise on Fishing in all its Branches. Post 8vo. 15s.
Jefferies' The Red Deer. Crown 8vo. 4s. 6d.
Longman's Chess Openings. Fcp. 8vo. 2s. 6d.
Peel's A Highland Gathering. Illustrated. Crown 8vo. 10s. 6d.
Pole's Theory of the Modern Scientific Game of Whist. Fcp. 8vo. 2s. 6d.
Proctor's How to Play Whist. Crown 8vo. 5s.
Ronalds's Fly-Fisher's Entomology. 8vo. 14s.
Verney's Chess Eccentricities. Crown 8vo. 10s. 6d.
Wilcocks's Sea-Fisherman. Post 8vo. 6s.
Year's Sport (The) for 1885. 8vo. 21s.

ENCYCLOPÆDIAS, DICTIONARIES, AND BOOKS OF REFERENCE.

Acton's Modern Cookery for Private Families. Fcp. 8vo. 4s. 6d.
Ayre's Treasury of Bible Knowledge. Fcp. 8vo. 6s.
Brande's Dictionary of Science, Literature, and Art. 3 vols. medium 8vo. 63s.
Cabinet Lawyer (The), a Popular Digest of the Laws of England. Fcp. 8vo. 9s.
Cates's Dictionary of General Biography. Medium 8vo. 28s.
Doyle's The Official Baronage of England. Vols. I.–III. 3 vols. 4to. £5. 5s.; Large Paper Edition, £15. 15s.
Gwilt's Encyclopædia of Architecture. 8vo. 52s. 6d.
Keith Johnston's Dictionary of Geography, or General Gazetteer. 8vo. 42s.
Latham's (Dr.) Edition of Johnson's Dictionary. 4 vols. 4to. £7.
—   —   —   —   —   Abridged. Royal 8vo. 14s.
M'Culloch's Dictionary of Commerce and Commercial Navigation. 8vo. 63s.
Maunder's Biographical Treasury. Fcp. 8vo. 6s.
—   Historical Treasury. Fcp. 8vo. 6s.
—   Scientific and Literary Treasury. Fcp. 8vo. 6s.
—   Treasury of Bible Knowledge, edited by Ayre. Fcp. 8vo. 6s.
—   Treasury of Botany, edited by Lindley & Moore. Two Parts, 12s.
—   Treasury of Geography. Fcp. 8vo. 6s.
—   Treasury of Knowledge and Library of Reference. Fcp. 8vo. 6s.
—   Treasury of Natural History. Fcp. 8vo. 6s.
Quain's Dictionary of Medicine. Medium 8vo. 31s. 6d., or in 2 vols. 34s.
Reeve's Cookery and Housekeeping. Crown 8vo. 7s. 6d.
Rich's Dictionary of Roman and Greek Antiquities. Crown 8vo. 7s. 6d.
Roget's Thesaurus of English Words and Phrases. Crown 8vo. 10s. 6d.
Ure's Dictionary of Arts, Manufactures, and Mines. 4 vols. medium 8vo. £7. 7s.
Willich's Popular Tables, by Marriott. Crown 8vo. 10s.

London: LONGMANS, GREEN, & CO.

A SELECTION
OF
EDUCATIONAL WORKS.

TEXT-BOOKS OF SCIENCE, MECHANICAL AND PHYSICAL.

Abney's Treatise on Photography. Fcp. 8vo. 3s. 6d.
Anderson's Strength of Materials. 3s. 6d.
Armstrong's Organic Chemistry. 3s. 6d.
Ball's Elements of Astronomy. 6s.
Barry's Railway Appliances. 3s. 6d.
Bauerman's Systematic Mineralogy. 6s.
— Descriptive Mineralogy. 6s.
Bloxam and Huntington's Metals. 5s.
Glazebrook's Physical Optics. 6s.
Glazebrook and Shaw's Practical Physics. 6s.
Gore's Art of Electro-Metallurgy. 6s.
Griffin's Algebra and Trigonometry. 3s. 6d. Notes and Solutions, 3s. 6d.
Jenkin's Electricity and Magnetism. 3s. 6d.
Maxwell's Theory of Heat. 3s. 6d.
Merrifield's Technical Arithmetic and Mensuration. 3s. 6d. Key, 3s. 6d.
Miller's Inorganic Chemistry. 3s. 6d.
Preece and Sivewright's Telegraphy. 5s.
Rutley's Study of Rocks, a Text-Book of Petrology. 4s. 6d.
Shelley's Workshop Appliances. 4s. 6d.
Thomé's Structural and Physiological Botany. 6s.
Thorpe's Quantitative Chemical Analysis. 4s. 6d.
Thorpe and Muir's Qualitative Analysis. 3s. 6d.
Tilden's Chemical Philosophy. 3s. 6d. With Answers to Problems. 4s. 6d.
Unwin's Elements of Machine Design. 6s.
Watson's Plane and Solid Geometry. 3s. 6d.

THE GREEK LANGUAGE

Bloomfield's College and School Greek Testament. Fcp. 8vo 5s.
Bolland & Lang's Politics of Aristotle. Post 8vo. 7s. 6d.
Collis's Chief Tenses of the Greek Irregular Verbs. 8vo. 1s.
— Pontes Graeci, Stepping-Stone to Greek Grammar. 12mo. 3s. 6d.
— Praxis Graeca, Etymology. 12mo. 2s. 6d.
— Greek Verse-Book, Praxis Iambica. 12mo. 4s. 6d.
Farrar's Brief Greek Syntax and Accidence. 12mo. 4s. 6d.
— Greek Grammar Rules for Harrow School. 12mo. 1s. 6d.
Hewitt's Greek Examination-Papers. 12mo. 1s. 6d.
Isbister's Xenophon's Anabasis, Books I. to III. with Notes. 12mo. 3s. 6d.
Jerram's Graecè Reddenda. Crown 8vo. 1s. 6d.

London: LONGMANS, GREEN, & CO.

Kennedy's Greek Grammar. 12mo. 4s. 6d
Liddell & Scott's English-Greek Lexicon. 4to. 36s.; Square 12mo. 7s. 6d.
Linwood's Sophocles, Greek Text, Latin Notes 4th Edition. 8vo. 16s.
Mahaffy's Classical Greek Literature. Crown 8vo. Poets, 7s. 6d. Prose Writers, 7s. 6d.
Morris's Greek Lessons. Square 18mo. Part I. 2s. 6d.; Part II 1s.
Parry's Elementary Greek Grammar. 12mo. 3s. 6d.
Plato's Republic, Book I. Greek Text, English Notes by Hardy. Crown 8vo. 3s.
Sheppard and Evans's Notes on Thucydides. Crown 8vo 7s. 6d.
Thucydides, Book IV. with Notes by Barton and Chavasse. Crown 8vo. 5s.
Valpy's Greek Delectus, improved by White. 12mo. 2s. 6d. Key, 2s. 6d.
White's Xenophon's Expedition of Cyrus, with English Notes 12mo. 7s. 6d.
Wilkins's Manual of Greek Prose Composition. Crown 8vo. 5s. Key, 5s.
— Exercises in Greek Prose Composition. Crown 8vo. 4s. 6d. Key, 2s 6d.
— New Greek Delectus. Crown 8vo. 3s. 6d. Key, 2s 6d.
— Progressive Greek Delectus. 12mo. 4s. Key, 2s. 6d.
— Progressive Greek Anthology. 12mo. 5s.
— Scriptores Attici, Excerpts with English Notes. Crown 8vo. 7s. 6d.
— Speeches from Thucydides translated Post 8vo. 6s.
Yonge's English-Greek Lexicon. 4to. 21s.; Square 12mo. 8s. 6d.

THE LATIN LANGUAGE.

Bradley's Latin Prose Exercises. 12mo. 3s. 6d. Key, 5s.
— Continuous Lessons in Latin Prose. 12mo 5s. Key, 5s 6d.
— Cornelius Nepos, improved by White. 12mo. 3s. 6d.
— Eutropius, improved by White. 12mo. 2s. 6d.
— Ovid's Metamorphoses, improved by White. 12mo. 4s. 6d.
— Select Fables of Phædrus, improved by White. 12mo. 2s. 6d.
Collis's Chief Tenses of Latin Irregular Verbs. 8vo. 1s.
— Pontes Latini, Stepping-Stone to Latin Grammar 12mo. 3s. 6d.
Hewitt's Latin Examination-Papers. 12mo. 1s 6d.
Isbister's Cæsar, Books I.-VII. 12mo. 4s.; or with Reading Lessons, 4s. 6d.
— Cæsar's Commentaries, Books I.-V. 12mo. 3s. 6d.
— First Book of Cæsar's Gallic War 12mo. 1s. 6d.
Jeffcott & Tossell's Helps for Latin Students. Fcp. 8vo. 2s.
Jerram's Latinè Reddenda. Crown 8vo. 1s. 6d.
Kennedy's Child's Latin Primer, or First Latin Lessons. 12mo. 2s.
— Child's Latin Accidence. 12mo. 1s.
— Elementary Latin Grammar. 12mo. 3s. 6d.
— Elementary Latin Reading Book, or Tirocinium Latinum. 12mo. 2s.
— Latin Prose, Palæstra Stili Latini. 12mo. 6s.
— Subsidia Primaria, Exercise Books to the Public School Latin Primer. I. Accidence and Simple Construction, 2s. 6d. II. Syntax, 3s. 6d.
— Key to the Exercises in Subsidia Primaria, Parts I. and II. price 5s.
— Subsidia Primaria, III. the Latin Compound Sentence. 12mo. 1s.
— Curriculum Stili Latini. 12mo. 4s. 6d. Key, 7s. 6d.
— Palæstra Latina, or Second Latin Reading Book. 12mo. 5s.

London: LONGMANS, GREEN, & CO.

A Selection of Educational Works.

Millington's Latin Prose Composition. Crown 8vo. 3s. 6d.
— Selections from Latin Prose. Crown 8vo. 2s. 6d.
Moody's Eton Latin Grammar. 12mo. 2s. 6d. The Accidence separately, 1s.
Morris's Elementa Latina Fcp. 8vo. 1s. 6d. Key, 2s. 6d.
Parry's Origines Romanæ, from Livy, with English Notes. Crown 8vo. 4s.
The Public School Latin Primer. 12mo. 2s. 6d.
— — — Grammar, by Rev Dr. Kennedy. Post 8vo. 7s. 6d.
Prendergast's Mastery Series, Manual of Latin. 12mo. 2s. 6d.
Rapier's Introduction to Composition of Latin Verse. 12mo. 3s. 6d. Key, 2s. 6d.
Sheppard and Turner's Aids to Classical Study 12mo. 5s. Key, 6s.
Valpy's Latin Delectus, improved by White. 12mo. 2s. 6d. Key, 3s. 6d.
Virgil's Æneid, translated into English Verse by Conington. Crown 8vo. 9s.
— Works, edited by Kennedy. Crown 8vo. 10s. 6d.
— — translated into English Prose by Conington. Crown 8vo. 9s.
Walford's Progressive Exercises in Latin Elegiac Verse. 12mo. 2s. 6d. Key, 5s.
White and Riddle's Large Latin-English Dictionary. 1 vol. 4to. 21s.
White's Concise Latin-Eng. Dictionary for University Students. Royal 8vo. 12s.
— Junior Students' Eng.-Lat. & Lat.-Eng. Dictionary. Square 12mo. 5s.
Separately { The Latin-English Dictionary, price 3s.
{ The English-Latin Dictionary, price 3s.
Yonge's Latin Gradus. Post 8vo. 9s.; or with Appendix, 12s.

WHITE'S GRAMMAR-SCHOOL GREEK TEXTS.

Æsop (Fables) & Palæphatus (Myths). 32mo. 1s.
Homer, Iliad, Book I. 1s
— Odyssey, Book I. 1s.
Lucian, Select Dialogues. 1s.
Xenophon, Anabasis, Books I. III. IV. V. & VI. 1s. 6d. each ; Book II. 1s.; Book VII. 2s.

Xenophon, Book I. without Vocabulary. 3d.
St. Matthew's and St. Luke's Gospels. 2s. 6d. each.
St. Mark's and St. John's Gospels. 1s 6d. each.
The Acts of the Apostles. 2s 6d
St. Paul's Epistle to the Romans. 1s 6d.

The Four Gospels in Greek, with Greek English Lexicon Edited by John T. White, D.D. Oxon. Square 32mo price 5s.

WHITE'S GRAMMAR-SCHOOL LATIN TEXTS

Cæsar Gallic War, Books I. & II V. & VI. 1s. each. Book I. without Vocabulary, 3d.
Cæsar, Gallic War, Books III. & IV. 9d. each.
Cæsar, Gallic War, Book VII. 1s. 6d.
Cicero, Cato Major (Old Age). 1s. 6d.
Cicero, Lælius (Friendship). 1s. 6d.
Eutropius, Roman History, Books I & II. 1s. Books III. & IV. 1s each.
Horace, Odes, Books I. II. & IV. 1s each.
Horace, Odes, Book III. 1s. 6d.
Horace, Epodes and Carmen Seculare. 1s.

Nepos, Miltiades, Simon, Pausanias, Aristides. 9d.
Ovid. Selections from Epistles and Fasti. 1s.
Ovid, Select Myths from Metamorphoses. 9d.
Phædrus, Select Easy Fables, 9d.
Phædrus, Fables, Books I. & II. 1s.
Sallust, Bellum Catilinarium. 1s. 6d.
Virgil, Georgics, Book IV. 1s.
Virgil, Æneid, Books I. to VI. 1s. each. Book I. without Vocabulary, 3d.
Virgil, Æneid, Books VII. VIII. X. XI XII. 1s 6d. each.

London: LONGMANS, GREEN, & CO.

THE FRENCH LANGUAGE.

Albités's How to Speak French. Fcp. 8vo. 5s. 6d.
— Instantaneous French Exercises. Fcp. 2s. Key, 2s.
Cassal's French Genders. Crown 8vo. 3s. 6d.
Cassal & Karcher's Graduated French Translation Book. Part I. 3s. 6d.
    Part II. 5s. Key to Part I. by Professor Cassal, price 5s.
Contanseau's Practical French and English Dictionary. Post 8vo. 3s. 6d.
    — Pocket French and English Dictionary. Square 18mo. 1s 6d.
    — Premières Lectures. 12mo. 2s 6d.
    — First Step in French. 12mo. 2s. 6d. Key, 3s.
    — French Accidence. 12mo. 2s. 6d.
    — — Grammar. 12mo 4s Key, 3s.
Contanseau's Middle-Class French Course. Fcp. 8vo.:—

Accidence, 8d.	French Translation-Book, 8d.
Syntax, 8d.	Easy French Delectus, 8d.
French Conversation-Book, 8d.	First French Reader, 8d.
First French Exercise-Book, 8d.	Second French Reader, 8d.
Second French Exercise-Book, 8d.	French and English Dialogues, 8d.

Contanseau's Guide to French Translation. 12mo. 3s. 6d. Key, 3s. 6d.
    — Prosateurs et Poètes Français. 12mo. 5s.
    — Précis de la Littérature Française. 12mo. 3s 6d.
    — Abrégé de l'Histoire de France. 12mo. 2s. 6d.
Féval's Chouans et Bleus, with Notes by C. Sankey, M.A. Fcp. 8vo. 2s. 6d.
Jerram's Sentences for Translation into French. Cr 8vo 1s Key, 2s. 6d.
Prendergast's Mastery Series, French. 12mo. 2s 6d.
Souvestre's Philosophe sous les Toits, by Stièvenard. Square 18mo. 1s. 6d.
Stepping-Stone to French Pronunciation. 18mo. 1s.
Stièvenard's Lectures Françaises from Modern Authors. 12mo 4s 6d.
    — Rules and Exercises on the French Language. 12mo. 3s. 6d.
Tarver's Eton French Grammar. 12mo. 6s 6d.

THE GERMAN LANGUAGE.

Blackley's Practical German and English Dictionary. Post 8vo. 3s. 6d.
Buchheim's German Poetry, for Repetition. 18mo. 1s. 6d.
Collis's Card of German Irregular Verbs. 8vo. 2s.
Fischer-Fischart's Elementary German Grammar. Fcp. 8vo. 2s. 6d.
Just's German Grammar. 12mo 1s. 6d.
    — German Reading Book. 12mo. 3s. 6d.
Longman's Pocket German and English Dictionary. Square 18mo. 2s. 6d.
Naftel's Elementary German Course for Public Schools. Fcp. 8vo.

German Accidence. 9d.	German Prose Composition Book. 9d.
German Syntax. 9d.	First German Reader. 9d.
First German Exercise-Book. 9d.	Second German Reader. 9d.
Second German Exercise-Book. 9d.	

Prendergast's Mastery Series, German. 12mo. 2s. 6d.
Quick's Essentials of German. Crown 8vo. 3s. 6d.
Selss's School Edition of Goethe's Faust. Crown 8vo 5s.
    — Outline of German Literature. Crown 8vo. 4s. 6d.
Wirth's German Chit-Chat. Crown 8vo. 2s. 6d.

London: LONGMANS, GREEN, & CO.

CPSIA information can be obtained
at www.ICGtesting.com
Printed in the USA
LVHW081334070121
675984LV00005B/16

9 781344 895347